the natural guide to

Bali

Enjoy Nature, Meet the People, Make a Difference

Yayasan Bumi Kita
Equinox Publishing

Menjangan
Island

West Bali
National Park

Gilimanuk

Pemuteran

Gerokgak

Seririt

Singara

Lovina

Buleleng

Busungbiu

Melaya

Jembrana

Pupuan

Negara

Mt. Batuka
2276

Bali Strait

Pekutatan

Medewi

Tabanan

Antosari

Yeh Gangg

Indonesia

Equator

Bali

Indian Ocean

N

Bali

Scale 1:600 000

0 km   10 km   20 km

Legend

District (Kabupaten**)**

District Limit
Surfing Site
Diving Site

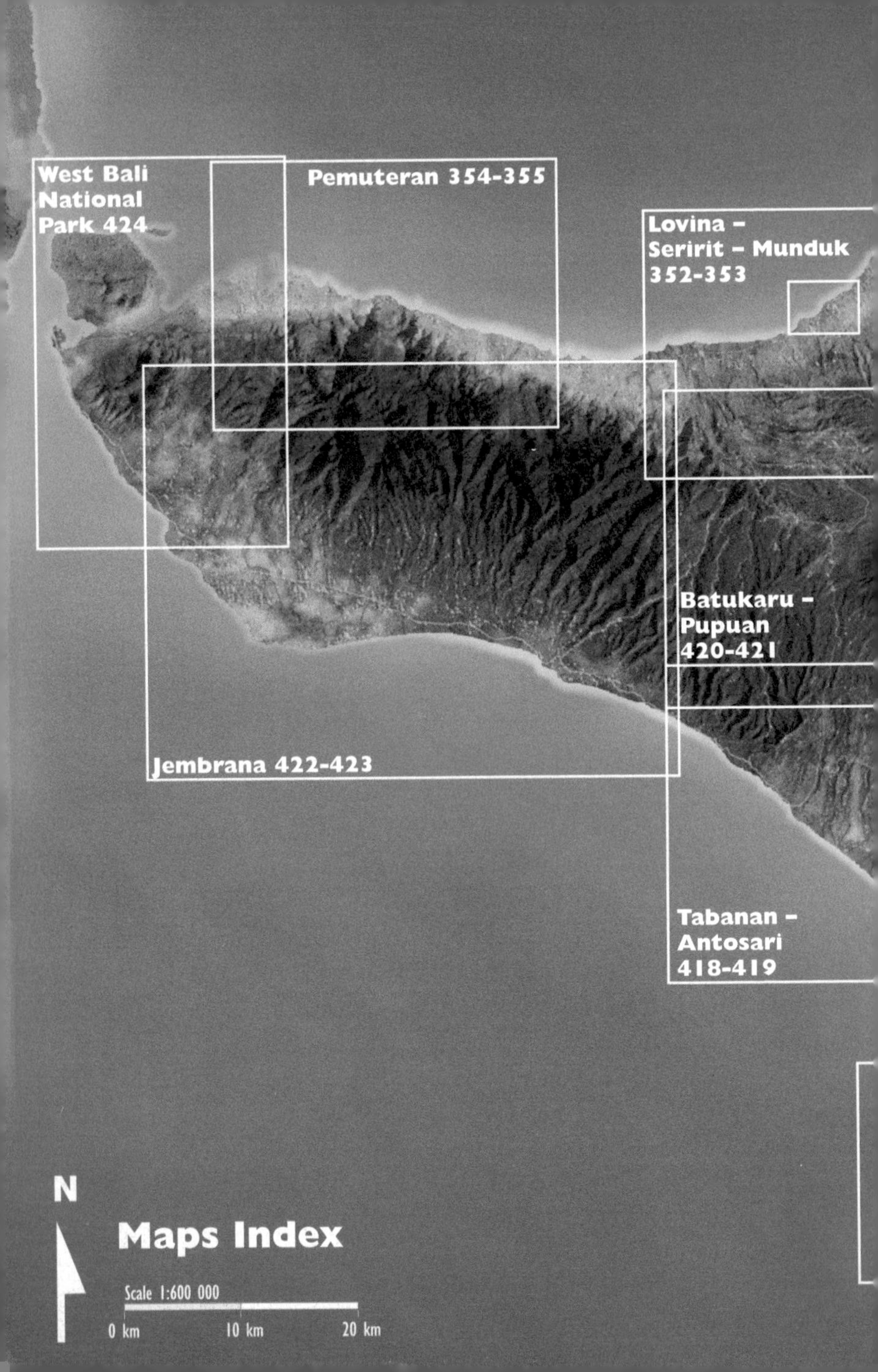

West Bali
National
Park 424

Pemuteran 354-355

Lovina –
Seririt – Munduk
352-353

Batukaru –
Pupuan
420-421

Jembrana 422-423

Tabanan –
Antosari
418-419

N

Maps Index

Scale 1:600 000

0 km   10 km   20 km

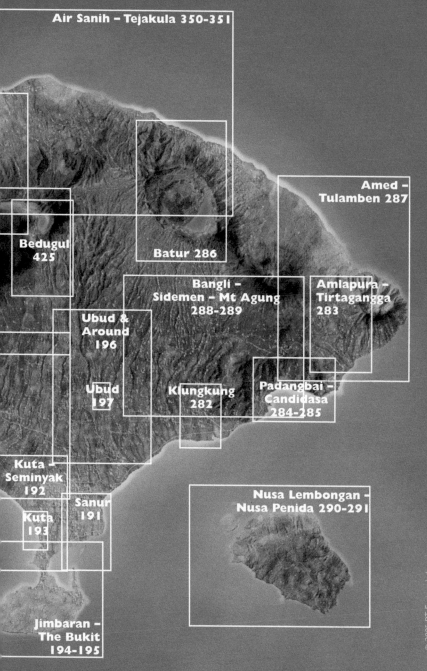

Air Sanih – Tejakula 350-351

Amed – Tulamben 287

Bedugul 425

Batur 286

Bangli – Sidemen – Mt Agung 288-289

Amlapura – Tirtagangga 283

Ubud & Around 196

Ubud 197

Klungkung 282

Padangbai – Candidasa 284-285

Kuta – Seminyak 192

Sanur 191

Kuta 193

Nusa Lembongan – Nusa Penida 290-291

Jimbaran – The Bukit 194-195

© 2005 PT Enrique Indonesia

EQUINOX PUBLISHING
PO Box 6719 JKSGN
Jakarta 12062
Indonesia

www.equinoxpublishing.com

The Natural Guide to Bali
edited by Anne Gouyon
First Edition, 2005
Printed in Indonesia

The Natural Guide to Bali is the first of a series of guide books dedicated to the appreciation and respect of nature and people, brought to you by the Bumi Kita Foundation (www.naturalguide.org). The book is written by a team of ecologists and anthropologists with contributions by Balinese journalists, sociologists and artists who cast a loving but critical eye over their island.

Introduction

South Bali – *Beyond Kuta and Ubud*

The Hidden Life of South Bali

East Bali – *Below the Volcanoes*

North Bali – The Other Side of Bali

West Bali – *A Vision of Abundance*

Jakarta, November 2004

Ecotourism in Indonesia can become a key tool to improve the
people's welfare and contribute to ecological protection. In fact,
ecotourism has already succeeded in turning communities away
from destructive environmental practices and moving them towards
conservation in several places in Indonesia.

The Indonesian Ecotourism Network (Indecon) welcomes the
publication of *The Natural Guide to Bali*. We believe that this book
will benefit tourists and local communities alike – as well as the
various groups that are involved in ecotourism and community-
based tourism.

The Natural Guide to Bali is contributing to an important aspect of
the development of ecotourism. Our experience at Indecon has
taught us that marketing and promotion are among the biggest
obstacles to the development of community-based tourism. For this
reason, the publication of *The Natural Guide to Bali* is in line with our
vision of ecotourism development in Indonesia. Besides helping the
people by increasing the inflow of visitors, this book also provides
education both for the tourists and the local people while
supporting environmental conservation efforts.

I wish you the best of success.

Ary Suhandi
Executive Director
The Indonesian Ecotourism Network

© Djuna Ivereigh

Farmer and water buffalo near Jatiluwih

A Natural Way of Travelling

Bali Travel Tips

- *Follow a duck between two rice fields and see where it leads you.*
- *Talk about life with the young villagers who speak a bit of English.*
- *Do like the Balinese: wake up early to catch the glorious mornings; nap during the afternoon heat.*
- *Follow one of our trekking roads, and try to turn left when advised to turn right.*
- *Prefer little side roads to main roads.*
- *Don't feel obliged to visit all the recommended temples, lakes and volcanoes.*
- *Try to do and see as little as possible in as much time as possible.*

Once upon a time, the earth was walked by hearty travellers. With endless time on their hands, they set out into the unknown, enjoying the journey more than the destination. Some never came back, those who did were changed forever.

Travel has changed. As 21st century tourists, we choose our two-week holidays from a catalogue. A click on a website, a renewal of a passport, and off we are to the other end of the planet. Once there, we demand the best: good food, safe transportation, fabulous landscapes, bright smiles – and no other tourists. We take guide books to feel safe, save time, and plan the adventure.

Yet the best part of travelling often takes place when things do not go as planned – when we take a wrong turn and discover a fabulous landscape – when our vehicle breaks down in the mountains and we spend a great week with the villagers who rescued us. These are the stories that stay, the ones we tell back home.

This sort of travel is still possible in Bali, as soon as you escape the major tourist haunts of Kuta, Ubud, Tanah Lot, Besakih, or Lake Batur. These places are all very attractive – if you don't mind sharing them with hundreds of visitors and eager vendors. Don't regret missing any of these famed spots, or not making a "complete tour" of the island. Bali has more friendly villages, stunning rice fields, luxuriant forests, majestic mountains, and fascinating temples than you could ever dream of. Keep your itinerary flexible with room for the unplanned, the unchartered, the unknown.

Opening the Gates

As you start your personal journey to Bali, this guide is meant as a door opener. We provide you with the main directions you need to orient yourself in this maze of gorgeous landscapes and cultural subtleties. Here and there, we offer a few glimpses into its hidden life and propose a few keys to understanding its complexities and contradictions. We give tips about great places to stay and things to do to approach the nature and culture of Bali. We take you to winding country roads and side-walks, rural markets, and secretive temples – away from the crowded spots to lesser known places where intimacy and smiles have been preserved. Use these tips to get started, then close our book and discover by yourself a new magic corner.

The Life Behind the Landscape

Have you ever wondered, in front of a staircase of rice paddies, how every tiny terrace gets its share of water? Did you ever want to ask why mighty banyan trees wear chequered aprons around their trunks?

In Bali, like in many places with living traditions, land and people work hand in hand. Every hill and tree belong to a community or a farmer, every slope has been sculpted by generations. Everything is there, and not anywhere else, for a purpose. Even the wild forests on the highest mountains are homes to scores of gods and spirits. We hope to tell you their stories, so that you'll look at a landscape and see trees grow, harvests ripen, farmers struggle, communities prosper, and deities smile their inscrutable smiles.

Our stories are told by insiders – people who were born on Bali or call it home. Local authors, journalists, illustrators, and photographers have seized the

About this Book

*Read our introduction, **"The Hidden Life of Bali,"** and discover how the environment, history, religion, and culture of the island are interwoven. Then read **"Traveller in Bali"** to get started on your practical journey. From there on, enter Bali through our **four main chapters**, arranged following the compass – starting from the **south**, where most travellers arrive, to the **east** and its natural wonders, then the **north**, the unknown side of Bali, and ending in the wild, beautiful **west**. Each chapter is divided into smaller sections where you'll find tips about **Where to Stay** and **What to Do**. Here and there, special 'Hidden Life" features take you one step beyond the tourist landscape.*

© Ujung Wicaksono

Banyan tree with poleng cloth

© Eliric Penot

Mother and child at an otonan (birthday) ceremony

🐾 *Bali is not a museum kept intact for tourists, a frozen place where we enter "just for looking." It is alive and changing. We have asked local authors to write intriguing or thought-provoking stories in the "**Hidden Life**" sections of each chapter. Read about beach gigolos and the reviving of old dances in south Bali. Find out how palm trees help to tackle poverty and child labour in the east. See how bombed out corals are being grown again by nature lovers in north Bali, and learn about endangered birds and the fight for democracy in west Bali.*

opportunity to tell you about the Bali they love. Each of their viewpoints is different and each holds a part of the truth: their part, heartfelt and alive.

A Living World, a Changing World

Next time your car is stuck behind a religious procession, you'll have ample time to ponder what goes in the mind of the young lady with offerings towering above her head. When she dreams of Nirvana, does she mean eternal paradise or a rock band on TV? The island is changing fast, modernity is welcome, yet people keep traditions alive. Every night, in the raunchiest discotheques in Kuta, employees arrange offerings to deities on the dance floor before guests arrive. Bali has a unique way of adapting to changes without losing its core, much like a person passing through various stages of life while retaining the same soul. To make your journey more lively, we show you some of the changes taking place in Bali.

Some of these changes bring new worries. Pollution is taking its toll everywhere, especially in the busy south. Rather than toiling in the rice fields, many farmers sell their land to outsiders building tourist resorts and shopping malls, and end up empty-handed. Yet many Balinese are responding to the challenges of modern times with the support of some of the many visitors who have fallen in love with Bali. We are happy to tell you their stories, those of the many people and organisations who are struggling to preserve – or, in some cases, restore – the spirit and beauty of Bali.

Make a Difference

If Bali is changing, both for better and for worse, what may be our influence on this process? As we frolic in unspoiled countryside, we leave more than footprints. Have we ever wondered what happens to that plastic bottle after we discard it? What is our impact on people's minds when we push a camera in their face, and spend in one day what they earn in one month?

In Bali, like elsewhere, mass tourism has encouraged disruption: prostitution in Kuta, drugs in Seminyak, vanished beaches in Candidasa, aggressive vendors in Batur, and the expropriation of Balinese from their own land throughout the island.

Yet, like a beautifying mirror, the admiring look of foreigners has fuelled Balinese self-pride and the desire to preserve the attributes of their culture – sometimes as a defence against the onslaught of external influences. Striking features like *kecak* dances, lively paintings, and the picturesque architecture of some hotels, have been moulded out of traditional substance by foreigners and Balinese blending their creative streaks. Colourful cere-monies, elaborate temples, and traditional *alang-alang* thatch roofs that take days of work to assemble are all made possible by the inflow of funds brought by tourism. And many of the initiatives to work on more grass-roots issues – keeping Bali clean from pollution, or helping its poorer children to access education – have been started by locals and outsiders working together.

Nature-Friendly, Community-Friendly

Very often, just the choice of where you stay, and whom you travel with, means a lot. Having travelled around Bali, we have discovered great little hotels off the main tourist roads. We also met dedicated people who struggle for their corner of earth: architects who respect traditions, hotel owners who work with locals to clean the beaches, village leaders who train youngsters to become inspiring guides for visitors, dive masters who protect and reha-bilitate the coral. We are happy to introduce these peo-ple to you. Moreover, we hope to bring conscious, responsible travellers to them so they can enjoy the suc-cess they deserve – in the hope that this will inspire more people to follow in their path.

For each regional section of our book, we propose a selection of places to stay in all price ranges, from inexpensive homestays to luxury boutique resorts.

Dos and Don'ts

As travellers, we can bring change, both positive and negative. The way we address people and the way we bargain make a difference. Where we buy our handicrafts, whether we throw litter on the roadside or refuse plastic bags when shopping, whether we ask permission before taking the photograph of an old lady – everything counts. We have asked local people what makes a difference, and we tell you about it. Here and there, we give you tips on how to respect and support the people and nature of Bali.

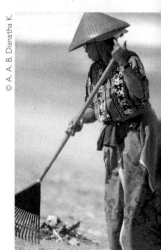

© A. A. B. Dianatha K.

Keeping Kuta Beach clean

Selling banana leaves on the way to school

www.naturalguide.org
The Natural Guide lives from the participation of many helpers. Join the club! Our website is there for you. If you make great discoveries, please share them with us. We will encourage responsible travellers to give them the encouragement they need. Tell us also about the places that have changed – hotels do close down or change management and quiet areas do get built up. Help us to find out and inform other travellers. Log on to our website to know about the latest changes, and tell uss about your trip.

We also give ideas of places to eat and things to do: where to trek, dive, bike, and shop, or learn about history, religion, cooking, rice growing, and painting. All these places have been selected based on a unique rating system, taking into account how they care about their natural environment and the local communities around them (read the next page).

How to Help, Beyond Travelling

Travellers who survey Bali with open eyes and an open heart often fall in love with the place. Many are also disheartened by some aspects of what they see: rivers filled with plastic, people in deep poverty begging for a better life, children painting cute toys to sell abroad. As you develop a bond with Bali, you may want to do more than just being respectful and staying in the "good" hotels. There are many ways to help out. Throughout the book, we give tips on great community organisations struggling to preserve Bali's natural environment and helping its people to feed themselves, stay healthy, and send their children to school.

Everything you do can help. Contact these people and get interested in their work. Visit them and observe what they do; you'll learn much more than in any museum. Volunteer to help them, make a donation, or raise funds for them. You'll bring back home the best holiday souvenir: the satisfaction of having changed someone's life for the better.

Lose Yourself and Tell Us About It

In the end, we'd be more than happy if at some point you forget our book and do it your way. Read other books about Bali, make friends with its people and learn from them. Follow the butterfly or the old man with a smile. Open your eyes and hearts to make new encounters and unearth hidden treasures.

There, at a corner of a country road, lurks the spirit of travel and the magic of Bali, still alive for wandering souls.

Keys to our Rating System

The method used to rate each hotel and activity proposed in our guidebook has been defined based on international standards for sustainable tourism and eco-tourism – big words which mean that a tourism operation should protect its environment and strive to benefit local communities. We consulted with local people, especially social and environmental organisations based in Bali, to adapt these standards to their realities, and incorporate local standards like the Tri Hita Karana. The places we recommend are all first assessed by trained members of our team.

First, we check that our selection is "*traveller-friendly*." We choose hotels and tours set amidst beautiful natural or traditional settings where you'll get great service in safe, comfortable, and clean surroundings, with occasions to discover local nature and culture.

We strive to recommend businesses that are helping to conserve and enhance their environments. Hence we check whether each hotel, dive shop, or guided tour is "*nature-friendly*" – whether they preserve the landscapes around them; give preference to local, renewable resources; make efforts to save water, chemicals, and energy; dispose of waste in a responsible manner; and contribute to environmental education and conservation efforts.

Last but not least, we give preference to businesses that are "*community-friendly*" – those who treat their staff above local standards; keep harmonious relations with neighbouring communities and participate in their social development; provide economic opportunities to local people; and support local culture, arts, and crafts. In each place, we give a ♥ rating to hotels, restaurants, or tours which make significant efforts to offer a great experience to travellers, while supporting nature conservation and local communities. The most dedicated get an outstanding ♥ ♥ rating. By choosing them, you'll support their efforts and make your stay all the more enjoyable and worthwhile.

Tourism with a Heart

Each of the recommended hotels or activities in our book has been selected based on a unique rating system indicating how well they take care of travellers, nature and local communities. Look for our ♥ and ♥ ♥ rated places to find the most traveller-friendly, nature-friendly, and community-friendly places. Don't hesitate to write to us at ***www.naturalguide.org*** *to give feedback and suggest more places worth our heartfelt attention.*

© D. & W. Postlethwaite

Diver meets turtle near Menjangan Island

The deadly crater of Mt Agung, 3142m

© Leonard Lueras

Of Fire and Water

By Jim Jarvie and Anne Gouyon

The Gods' Stone

Ash and rock fragments hurled from volcanoes end up compacted as volcanic sandstone or tuff, called paras in Bali. This grey material, which looks like cement, is nearly as soft as wood. It provides the basis for the infinite variety of sculptures on temples. Easily carved, it is also quickly eroded by rainfall. With their creations being constantly washed away, sculptors in Bali are always offered more work. The short-lived paras has kept the art of Balinese sculpture alive.

© Elizabeth E. Listyowati

Buddha statue made of paras stone

The serene landscapes of "the Island of the Gods" can be as deceptive as the peaceful demeanour of its people. Bali's majestic mountains, serrated coastal edges, and long gorges carved by rushing water are all the product of geological violence that always threatens.

Bali is thought to have arisen from the sea about three million years ago. A geological daughter of Java, it is separated from its mother by a shallow strait only 2km wide. With Sumatra, Borneo, and Java, Bali sits on the Sunda plate, one of many similar tectonic plates that make up the earth's surface in a moving jigsaw puzzle. Like rafts floating on the earth's magma, these blundering bullies push and shove each other into the underlying molten layer.

Some 250km south of Java and Bali, the rigid Sunda plate, moving southward at the speed of 6cm a year, squares off with the Indo-Australian plate, forcing it underneath. Even at this gentle speed, the momentum generated by these huge masses of rock creates enormous tension, which is released in sporadic earthquakes. Molten magma from deep below rushes to the surface, giving birth to a long arc of volcanoes along the divide. Further south, where the Indo-Australian plate plunges downward, the Java Trench runs more than 4,000km parallel to the coast, reaching a depth of 7,725m south of Java.

The tiny island of Bali – 5,561sq.km, 140km east-west and 70km north-south – has inherited six major volcanoes from all this energy. Their cones pierced the limestone that probably once covered most of the island. Two of them, Agung and Batur, are still active, erupting after dormant periods that lull people into a false sense of security. The tallest, Mt. Agung, soars to 3,142m. Its latest major blast, in 1963, killed over a thousand people. The devastation is still visible on its lava-covered slopes.

River near Singaraja

Yet the Balinese keep rebuilding their houses near the volcanoes, attracted by the bounty they generate. The deadly peaks are also the main source of wealth on the island. Eruptions over the centuries have laid blankets of nutrient-rich ash. Carried to fields by the many rivers flowing from the mountains, they provide a natural fertiliser. Perhaps this is why the Balinese don't believe that anything is inherently good or bad – in their world, good can be borne of evil and vice versa, and man must strive to keep both in balance.

Living Out of Water

Providers of life and death, the volcanoes are the abode of Balinese gods – but water is the source of life and its purifying element. In fact, the Balinese brand of Hinduism is sometimes called *Agama Tirta*, the Religion of the Holy Waters. Yet the gift of water is not distributed evenly throughout the island of the gods.

Bali's monsoonal climate has two alternating wind patterns. From April to September, winds dried by Australia's barren interior blow from the southeast. With relatively dry air, this is a pleasant season of bright sunny days and cool nights. From November to March, during the wet season, winds from the southwest blow over Bali, laden with moisture after a long marathon run over the Indian Ocean. They pass over the southern plains and are soon blocked by the chain of volcanoes running parallel with the north coast. As the wet air ascends the mountain slopes, it cools, condenses, and unleashes its water in heavy storms.

Bali is located about 600 miles south of the equator. The island is warm year-round with an average temperature of 27°C. Being in the south, December is the summer month – yet it is only slightly warmer than the coolest period of the year. As with temperature, humidity varies little and sits at around 80%. The only significant climatic variation on Bali is in the colder mountains. The elevation cools temperatures by 5 to 10°C and provides abundant humidity; mountain areas are refreshing but rainy.

A Balinese Bounty

Graced by the southwest monsoons, the south of Bali receives two metres of rainfall per year, distributed over 200 rainy days. The rain falls in brisk storms, quickly followed by blue skies. Natural and man-made waterways carry nutrient-rich water from the mountains down the gentle slopes of Tabanan, Badung, Gianyar, Klungkung, and Amlapura. Carved into terraces by generations of farmers, these hills nourish thirsty rice fields – one hectare of rice needs one million litres of water per year.

Managing the flow of water and its fair distribution to thousands of villages and individual farms requires more than technical skill. It demands a well-organised society, with a strong set of rules, to share water and coordinate rice planting over entire valleys. These complex institutions and the wealth generated by farmers have given birth to a rich culture, seen at its best in the densely populated rice bowls of the south.

A Water Geography
From the chain of volcanoes that runs east-west, water scours channels to the sea, carving steep ravines and gorges along north-south axes. Look at any map to see the result. Most roads and communication routes follow the watersheds up and down the island. East-west travel has always been difficult. To escape floods, villages sit on ridges over the valleys. In the past, this led to isolation and protection of human communities. The rich southern kingdoms were long separated from each other by these same river-carved walls and slopes.

Further up the slopes, where the land is slightly less wet and not worth terracing, the landscape is filled with a glorious mix of coffee, cocoa, clove, palm, banana, and fruit trees, fed from the rich volcanic soils. This is the realm of the pungent durian; the sweet *rambutan*, a hairy cousin of the lychee; the snake-skinned *salak*, and the mangosteen – a fruit so delicate that Queen Victoria offered huge rewards for one to be brought to England fresh. To the Balinese these are traditional gardens; to Western scientists, "agroforestry", a unique man-made forest with a complex structure supporting an incredible diversity of plants and animals. Crops grown amidst such semi-natural conditions in a fertile environment need few pesticides and no chemical fertilisers. This is a perfect place to look for tasty organic coffee and fruits.

On the upper slopes, rainfall reaches three metres a year and the weather is cooler. These are good conditions for vegetable growing, as illustrated by the farms found around Lake Beratan and Lake Batur. Higher still, where agriculture is impossible, natural montane forest dominates

Mangosteen

with lush ferns, broad-leaf trees, and cone-bearing trees. Likewise, in the northwest of the island, where the soils are drier and poorer than in the centre, lies an expanse where people are rare and forests can still be found. This is where the West Bali National Park is located.

The Other Side of Paradise

The environment changes dramatically over the volcanic ridge. The steep slopes and narrow coastal areas in the north and east of Bali are in a rain shadow. With only 50-80 rainy days a year, a dry, scrubby terrain dominates a parched landscape. With too little water to grow rice, communities in the north and east survive on tough, dry crops like maize, peanuts, and tobacco, grown during part of the year only.

© Dwi Rahmad Muhtaman

Tobacco farmer near Amed

Like the Bukit Peninsula in the south and near the isles of Nusa Penida and Nusa Lembongan, these barren areas stand on the periphery of Balinese society. Travellers who drive through Seraya around the eastern tip of Karangasem – whose name means "coral and salt" – come back haunted by scenes of misery, unexpected on this rich island. Further north, on the dry slopes of Mt Agung, lie some of the poorest villages in Bali. Balinese kings would banish enemies into exile in these arid areas.

Away from the Sea

The Balinese fear the ocean as much as they revere their mountains. Most of Bali's southern coast is battered by fierce waves. These swells can be attributed to the island's proximity to the edge of the Sunda shelf, which drops deeply into the Indian Ocean a few kilometres offshore. Seasonal upwellings create unpredictable currents. Running normally at 1-2km per hour, they can increase 2-3 fold in seasonal transitions. It is impossible to swim against these currrents, which also make boat navigation hazardous. Maritime access is better on the eastern and northern coasts, which are largely surrounded by a shallow ocean. Yet with a coast rich in coral reefs, shipwrecks have been numerous on these shores throughout history.

Bali has very few naturally-protected harbours. The main one is found in Buleleng, in north Bali, which for centuries was the gateway for trade and external influences on the island. It was the administrative capital of Bali in the Dutch colonial period. Today, the only commercial harbour for big ships is found at Padangbai, while smaller boats use the port of Tanjung Benoa south of Sanur. Only very small fishing boats access the rivers and coast through treacherous waters.

The Deep Blue Gold
Tourism and the modern market economy are giving a new value to the Balinese seas. Land in barren coastal areas is reaching sky-high prices. The demand for sea products has soared, bringing modern, powerful fishing boats belonging mostly to outsiders who compete with local fishermen. The coral reefs of Bali and the deep waters south of the island support rich marine fauna that attracts divers. Even the dry coasts of the Bukit Peninsula, Nusa Penida, and Lembongan have found new riches. Their waves delight surfers, while their shallow western coasts are perfect for growing seaweed, a valuable crop exported to Japan for food and cosmetics.

This pattern has supported an inland-looking culture, where all things upstream (*kaja*) are pure, while those downstream (*kelod*) are impure – until they reach the ocean, where everything is purified, enabling the start of a new cycle. Living on the coasts, risking their lives on dangerous seas, fishermen are the outcasts of society. Balinese find the fascination of western tourists for beaches extremely odd.

Threatened Wonders

These riches are now threatened by pollution, destructive fishing methods, and aggressive tourism ventures that anchor boats and pontoons into fragile coral. The inland environment is also being damaged by erosion, pollution, and deforestation. Its flagship bird itself, the Bali starling, is on the verge of extinction. Even more worrying are the threats to the island's most precious thread of life: water.

Yet everywhere, Balinese and outsiders are reacting and committing themselves to defending their paradise. Here lies the last hope for Bali's environment. From its natural bounty – slopes, rivers, a generous climate, and a great diversity of flora and fauna – an incredible diversity of human-influenced landscapes has emerged. This flowering beauty and diversity has in turn attracted many outsiders who revere Bali, ready to defend its qualities. Let's hope this book will make you one of them.

Land use map of Bali

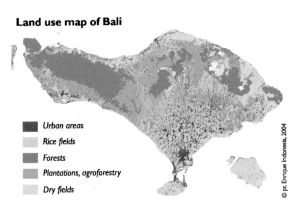

- ■ Urban areas
- Rice fields
- ■ Forests
- ■ Plantations, agroforestry
- Dry fields

© pt. Enrique Indonesia, 2004

Gardens of Eden

By Jim Jarvie and Jean-Marie Bompard

Clove plantations
around Munduk

Bali is so densely populated that there is very little natural forest left, especially at low altitudes. Small remnants of the original lowland forest can still be found in deep and isolated gorges, or in the West Bali National Park. Like elsewhere in Indonesia, it exhibits a bewildering mix of species, dominated by the massive trees of the Dipterocarp family.

Above 1,200m, montane forests, with thick leaves and bold flushes of young red vegetation, present a different experience. Ferns become more common, as do epiphytes, including orchids, which grow on the branches of trees. As altitude increases, trees become smaller. Higher still is the sub-alpine domain, densely coated with mosses and lichens. In the drier areas, deciduous forests, losing their leaves in dry season, offer an austere landscape reminiscent of Mediterranean areas – this is the monsoon forest, found especially in the National Park.

On the coastal areas, a few patches of mangrove forest can still be admired, especially in west Bali, near Tanjung Benoa in the south, or on the small island of Nusa Lembongan off the east coast. Yet the main riches of the coastal areas, in terms of flora and fauna, are the coral reefs. Nicknamed "the rainforest of the sea" for their incredible diversity, they are threatened today (read "Endangered Seas" in the east Bali chapter).

Trees Needed

The use of trees is well regulated by traditional rules of Balinese society. Apart from individual gardens and fields, useful trees are often found in community-owned "agro-forests" mixing natural species and planted trees. However, pressed by urgent economic needs, farmers find it difficult to maintain trees, especially slow-growing, hardwood species. In many areas, forested hills are becoming bald. A few organisations are struggling to help farmers plant trees.
Contacts:
Bhakti Wahana Bali
M 0818 344 654
Yayasan Wisnu
T 0361-735 320
greenbali@denpasar.
wasantara.net.id

© Djuna Ivereigh

© Ulung Wicaksono

Lotus

A Wealth of Fruits

A market tour is ideal to sample the local fruits. Besides the variety of bananas (biu), the hairy rambutan, the snake-skinned salak, the sweet mangosteen (manggis), and the stinking durian, hailed as queen and king of fruits, our eyes are caught by the chubby jack-fruit (nangka) or the big pomelo (juruk bali). Try less well-known species such as the ceroring, a sweet-and-sour variety of langsat, the small berries of bignay (buni), or the white wani mango. Along the dry northern coast, mango and tamarind trees provide fruit, but are also a highly appreciated source of shade.

Trees for the Gods

Visitors don't need to look into the wild to admire the Balinese flora – the whole island is a garden of plants used for rituals and daily life. Here and there, towering trees found near cemeteries or temples are remnants of the original forest. Balinese believe these majestic trees are inhabited by spirits and demons. They preserve and worship them, dress their trunks with sacred, symbolic clothes, and place shrines at their feet or in their branches. The most ubiquitous are the relatives of the fig tree, especially the massive banyans (*beringin*), a symbol of immortality, towering above almost every village. Another sacred species is the milk wood tree or *pule* (Alstonia). It is believed to bear the spirit of Durga, the goddess of death. Its soft wood, easy to carve, is used to make dance masks, in particular the fearsome masks of the Witch-Queen Rangda used in ritual dance shows. Witches are believed to congregate around a relative of the silk-cotton tree, the *kepuh* (Bombax).

Bali's floral emblem is an unremarkable tree, akin to mahogany, with plain flowers, the *majegau* tree (Dysoxylum densiflorum). Its sweet-smelling wood, known for its strength and beauty, can only be used in sacred buildings or to construct royal cremation towers. Once found in every village, it is now becoming rare. All around the island other flower species such as the champak, frangipani, hydrangea, cananga, boungainvillea, and hibiscus, found in all compounds, are used for offerings. The lotus that is important in Buddhism has been carried through into Balinese Hinduism. Its delicate silhouette graces gardens as well as natural wetlands.

Trees for the People

Trees and palms seen along roadsides reflect Bali's long agricultural traditions and contact with the outside world. These are the plants of daily life, such as the coconut, bamboo, banana, sugar cane, betel leaf, and areca nut. They are used as food or medicine, or as materials for ustensils, ritual offerings, or construction. Bamboos and palms, like the coconut and *lontar*, are grown for almost every possible use, from food to water carriers, parchment to clothing.

Originally from India, the **neem** tree (*Azadirachta indica*), well adapted to semi-dry areas, is known in Bali as *intaran*. Its fruit, seeds, oil, leaves, roots, and bark have many uses in traditional Indian medicine. Brought to Bali hundreds of years ago, probably by Indian traders, it is now common in the driest areas, where nothing else will thrive. Neem oil is also a natural way to protect crops, animals, and people from insects. It contains a substance which affects the insects' behaviour by mimicking a hormone. Instead of killing the pests, it prevents them from attacking plants and reduces their growth and reproduction without all the harmful effects associated with insecticides.

Wood is mostly imported from neighbouring islands, such as teak from East Java or ironwood and *meranti* from Kalimantan. With only a few thousand hectares of forest, local timber production can't meet the demand, even taking account of some illegally logged timber. Local wood represents only a small part of the 50,000 cubic metres annually needed by the woodcarving industry, and mostly originates from small plantings of fast growing leguminous trees on private lands.

Perhaps more surprising, Bali is becoming more and more dependent on its neighbours for supplying some basic but very important *agricultural products* that are needed in large quantities for daily life and religious ceremonies. Bamboos, coconuts, and young coconut leaves for making offerings are imported from Java. Jackfruit wood for building shrines comes from East Java and Sulawesi, and *ijuk*, the black fibre of sugar palm used for thatching temples, from Java and Lombok. In fact, many of the 335 or so native and introduced plants used in rituals are becoming hard to find. Even the gardens of Eden are starting to suffer from ecological erosion.

The Magic Oil

In the highlands of west Bali, PT Intaran has created a small unit producing crude neem oil, which can then be further processed into a wide range of products – pet shampoos, insect repellents, and eco-friendly pesticides. Enquire at **PT Intaran** *or* **Yayasan MACK**, *a foundation dedicated to the development of neem:*
T 0361-735 822
www.indoneem.com

Neem products can also be bought at the **Sunrise Organic Market** *in Kerobokan (north of Kuta):*
T 0361-735 823/824.

The **GUS Foundation** *provides eco-friendly pest control services using neem products:*
T 0361-752 046.

Passion fruit and sugar apples in Seririt's market

A Living World

A weaving bird

Wallacea

*Bali sits on a geological edge at the end of Asia; a point not lost on biologist **Alfred Russell Wallace**. Inspired by the observtions of Sclater, a bird zoologist, he drew what is now called the "Wallace line" between Bali and neighbouring Lombok. On Bali and westward are a flora and fauna borne from mainland Asia. To Bali's east, across the deep ocean separating it from Lombok, are animals and plants from the different raft on which Australia and New Guinea sail. The transition zone around this line is now called Wallacea and is considered a biodiversity "hot spot".*

The animals of Bali are represented by a mix of indigenous and introduced species, most of them also found on Java. A few species are unavoidable when travelling. Macaque monkeys are found around temples and in the wild. They are inquisitive and sometimes aggressive. The ones who see many visitors are used to stealing anything hanging, from cameras to glasses or earrings, so be careful around the tourist-trodden "monkey forests" or near famous temples like Uluwatu.

Geckos, small lizards, are ubiquitous in human habitations. Watch them at night gathering around lights and eating bugs; they are harmless and a useful, natural method of pest control. The biggest ones, the tokay gecko, can reach 14 inches. Their "gek-kaw" or "tok-kay" call is a feature of Balinese nights that you may remember for a long time. The infinite variety of calls from the many frogs and toads thriving in Balinese rice fields are also likely to stay as a vivid musical memory.

Bat species are numerous in Bali. Always an impressive sight is seeing the huge fruit bats, or flying foxes, leaving their roosts in vast numbers to seek food from the fruit trees in the surrounding forests and farms. Smaller bats inhabit caves (*goa* in Balinese), special sites which are always sacred. Bali has also no less than 320 bird species, 204 of which are full-time residents – including the almost-extinct Bali starling (read feature in the west Bali chapter). Less charismatic but mostly harmless, snakes, lizards, and amphibians add to the mix.

Other species are more elusive, such as the *cerdik* – smart and savvy – mouse deer (*Tragulus javanicus*). Weighing in at 1-2kg, and being sensibly shy, seeing one in the wild is a rare and rewarding experience. A more well-known deer, also difficult to see, is the larger *menjangan* (*Cervus timorensis*). At the other end of the weight scale, look for the 900 kg *banteng* cattle (*Bos javanicus*) with its elegant white legs. Only a few are still living wild in the West Bali National Park.

Domesticated species that are common in Bali include the water buffalo or the more common small ox (*sapi*), a tamed version of the wild *banteng*. Pigs are ubiquitous, although the local varieties, with their black skin, sagging back, and pot belly dragging to the ground, are being replaced by less remarkable pink-skinned, larger European breeds. Ducks are a feature of the rice fields, especially around Ubud. Marching in flocks behind their duck-keeper, they feed happily on freshwater snails, relieving rice fields of this harmful pest.

Fighting cocks are kept in most villages and given great care in order to participate in ritual fights where fortunes can be made – and lost – in one day. To the misery of tourists, street dogs are the animals most frequently encountered. Although they rarely bite, they enjoy barking at newcomers. Held in low esteem by the Balinese, they are not well cared for and often exhibit salient ribs and mangy skin full of parasites.

Meeting Beauties and Beasts

Most of Bali's wild animals are shy. To see them, get good local guidance and be careful not to cause a disturbance. A good way to start is the **West Bali National Park**, or any of the recommended trekking routes in the forested areas of the north (around Munduk), east (around Mt Abang, Mt Agung, or Mt Seraya) or west (around Mt Batukaru).

Bird-watchers can have fun in Bali. An easy place to begin with is the beautiful **Bali Bird Park** near Ubud (see Ubud section p.179). To see birds in the wild, get a pair of binoculars, a good bird field guide, and take early morning walks around rice fields or forests.

Bird-watching trips are organised in the National Park, in the Puri Lumbung eco-tourism centre of Munduk, and in the Sarinbuana eco-lodge below Mt Batukaru. Let's hope that with more visitors interested in Balinese fauna, more tour operators will think of adding such trips to the standard menu of temples and ceremonies.

Island Life

The number of species found on an island is related to its size. Bali's flora and fauna is based on Java's, but with fewer plants and animals represented. Java has 137 species of mammals, Bali probably somewhat fewer. There is still work to be done in listing what species are distributed where. Even the possibility of new mammal discovery remains in Bali, particularly among the rodents and bats.

© Djuna Ivereigh

Mouse deer in the National Park

© Elizabeth E. Listyowati

Painting of the Klungkung puputan battle in the Semarapura Museum

Better to Die than Surrender – A Balinese History

Based on writings by Jean Couteau, Anda Djoehana, and Bill Dalton

Balinese history is based on a few archaeological remains and old chronicles. Some of them, written long after the events, relate mythical versions rather than facts. Key aspects are interpreted differently by various scholars – even history is a living matter in Bali, always subject to change as power shifts. The main source for the early history section is "The Peoples of Bali" by Angela Hobart, Urs Ramseyer, and Albert Leemann. For subsequent sections, we made extensive use of the provocative book by Adrian Vickers, "Bali, a Paradise Created." The more recent influence of tourism has been analyzed by Michel Picard in "Bali, Cultural Tourism and Touristic Culture."

Bali has a long history of ambivalent relations with the outside. Traders and invaders took turns in bringing direct or indirect influences from India, China, the Middle East, and Europe. Always ready to fight to the end rather than surrender, the Balinese nevertheless took in these influences and blended them into a unique culture that seems both alien and welcoming to newcomers – to the extent that many contemporary artefacts of Balinese culture have been shaped by the fascination of foreigners with Bali-the-Paradise.

Today, lovers of Bali worry that the island may be up for sale. What the spear has not conquered can be acquired by bank notes as more and more rice fields get turned into tourism resorts. Yet since the end of the authoritarian regime of President Soeharto in 1998, regional autonomy has increased. For better or for worse, local and traditional authorities are seizing power back. At the root of this endless story of flirting with outsiders while struggling for self rule lies a complex story of kingdoms battling with each other to control the island's riches and the symbolic power bestowed by religious rituals.

The Origins

Very little is known about the prehistoric stages of Balinese history. The Balinese themselves trace their origins to India and the Indianised courts of Java. According to their own myth, the first person to set foot on Bali was **Rsi Markandeya**, a Hindu saint coming from East Java with a group of followers to turn the forests into cultivated land. These original Balinese, or *Bali Mula*, are said to have settled first around Besakih, on the slopes of Mt Agung – the site of Bali's Mother Temple.

With no archaeological remains older than 2000 years, very little is known about the first dwellers of Bali. It is likely that for tens of thousands of years during the Stone Age, small bands of hunter-gatherers foraged on the island. They were probably related to the *Homo erectus* whose remains have been found on Java, and to the ancestral New Guineans and Aborigines of Australia.

Around 2000 BC, Austronesian migrants, originally from southern China, reached the Indonesian archipelago. In a succession of migratory waves, they expanded into the Pacific and Indian oceans, uniting most of Southeast Asia, part of Melanesia, and Madagascar in a family of related Malayo-Polynesian languages and cultures. This Austronesian component may account for some of the Balinese food habits such as pork and betel, as well as the mountain and ancestors' cult, and open-air temples. Although these people were rice farmers, it seems that rice cultivation was adopted in Bali only around 600 BC, with the arrival of the Vietnamese **Dong Son** bronze culture in Bali. The 180cm-tall, hourglass-shaped kettle gong found in **Pejeng** near Ubud, known as the "Moon Drum", dates from this period.

India reaches Bali

The Hindu religion and culture was brought to Indonesia about 2,000 years ago, seemingly by Indian traders who were attracted to these waters by gold, spices, and sandalwood. Bali, however, was a rather peripheral post on these routes. It became really "Indianised" only in the

First Encounters with the Past

*The oldest archaeological sites found in Bali date 2,000 years ago. One is located in Pacung, on the northeast coast; the most famous is in **Gilimanuk**. These finds point to a culture of fishermen, hunters, and farmers using tools made of stone, bronze, and iron. They buried their dead along with tools, weapons, and objects indicating status, such as decorated pots, spearheads, daggers, as well as bronze and pearl jewellery – enabling the dead to continue their life in the nether world.*

© The Natural Guide

Ancient sarcophagus excavated in Pacung

8th century, during the golden age of the Sumatra-based, Hindu-Buddhist kingdom of **Sriwijaya**, which exerted its influence over large parts of Southeast Asia. Alongside Javanese traders, Buddhist missionaries participated in this process, without any direct colonisation – Balinese rulers adopted Indian political and religious systems out of their own will, as a means to strengthen their power.

The Chinese Lion
China exerted a subtle influence on Bali. Chinese coins were the only currency used for many years, and villages still keep some as sacred. The Barong, one of the main figures of the Balinese pantheon, bears the influence of animist cults, Indo-Javanese mythology, and Chinese symbolism. A lion-like character, he represents the spirit of the forest. Originally fearsome, he can be tamed and turned into a protective deity. The Balinese Barong dance, during which he fights the witch-queen Rangda, may have its origins in the lion dance performed during the Chinese New Year to ward off bad spirits.

Early Kingdoms and Javanese Influences

Bronze edicts dating from AD 882-914 provide glimpses into this period. Bali had a wealthy economy. The surplus generated by diversified agriculture enabled the growth of specialised craftsmen clans – dyers, weavers, gold- and blacksmiths, builders of irrigation channels, musicians, dancers, etc. In this hierarchised society, kings ruled hand in hand with priests, under the central authority of Sri Kesari **Warmadewa**, the first Balinese king known to us. Hindu cults, Vishnuite and Shivaite, were practiced side by side with Buddhism – with a strong Tantric element. Village communities took part in masked dances, metallophone music shows, and puppet dramas staged by the royal courts, inspired from Indian epics like the Ramayana and Mahabharata. The main centres of political and religious activity were in the centre of the island around **Pejeng** and **Goa Gajah**.

At the end of the 10th century, the influence of Java increased as Balinese King **Udayana** married a Javanese princess. Their son, King **Airlangga**, reigned over Bali from East Java (1019-49). The three-tiered temple system of Bali was probably commenced then by the legendary priest **Empu Kuturan**. The cliff temple of **Gunung Kawi**, in Gianyar, was also built during this period.

The Majapahit Era

Over the next centuries, the prosperous rice-growing kingdom of **Majapahit** in East Java grew in power until it controlled most of the sea trade in the archipelago and came to dominate its neighbours. In 1343, the

© Djuna Ivereigh

A Barong mask

troops of Majapahit, headed by its vizier **Gajah Mada**, are said to have invaded Bali, crushing a fierce local resistance and finally establishing court in **Gelgel**, near Klungkung. Some mountain villages, however, retained more independence: they are today's *Bali Aga*, or "original Balinese" villages.

During this period, Bali inherited many cultural features from Java, and in particular its syncretic Buddhist Shivaist religion. Classical literature forms and architectural concepts were derived from Majapahit, as well as the caste system. Dance and theatre evolved from Javanese models and narratives, as well as painting and sculpture, strongly influenced by puppet-show theater (*wayang*). This supposedly turned the ancient, "barbarian" Bali into "the renascent Bali of aesthetic elegance and liturgical splendour," as noted by Geertz in *The Interpretation of Culture*. In fact, some scholars, like Geertz, view the Majapahit invasion as a myth needed to justify the position of the Balinese upper castes, who regard themselves as descendents of the Majapahit and their refined civilisation.

Yet by the end of the 14th century, Bali was already recovering its independence. Weakened by internal feuds, Majapahit was losing its grip. On the northeast coast of Java, small Muslim trading communities were mutating into powerful states, including the sultanate of **Demak**, which eclipsed the floundering Majapahit.

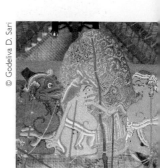

© Godeliva D. Sari

Shadow puppet or wayang

The Golden Age

As the role of Muslim traders grew in importance, people in Sumatra and Java were converting to Islam. The aristocracy, artists, and scholars of Majapahit who refused the new religion moved to Bali, inaugurating an era of splendour that would later be seen as the island's golden age (Michel Picard, *Bali, Cultural Tourism and Touristic Culture*). This vision of Bali as the refuge of enlightened Hinduism against Islam is now controversial — yet it remains a founding theme of Balinese identity.

Peasants and Artists
Beyond the myth of a urbane Majapahit bringing civilisation to Bali, the exchange between the two cultures can be viewed as a two-way process: "Little by little, as secondary courts were set up inland, the imported culture took on Balinese-cum-peasant features. The unique reality of Balinese culture is that it combines the sophistication of a cosmopolitan culture to the raw vitality of a peasant one" (Jean Couteau).

© Djuna Ivereigh

*Hindu priest leading
a ceremony*

The Birth of Paradise
*When the first Dutch
expedition reached Bali in
1597, Europeans were
caught in religious wars.
They were wary of the
progress of Islam, always
portrayed as the enemy of
Christianity. Landing on an
opulent Bali, the Dutch
were fascinated by its
royal courts and garish
Hindu culture, which they
viewed as the counter to a
scary Islam. Bali became a
paradise refuge headed by
a friendly "Heathen."
To add to the nascent
myth, three of the
exhausted sailors of the
expedition jumped ship
and refused to go home.
Bali-the-Paradise was born.*

In the 16th century, King **Baturenggong** was able to expand Bali's suzerainty from Gelgel over parts of East Java, Lombok, and Sumbawa. His reign witnessed a renaissance of Hindu arts, letters and religion, fostered by the great reformer priest **Danghyang Nirartha**, who had settled in Bali in the 1540s from East Java.

Having been in contact with Islam, Nirartha decided to strengthen Balinese Hinduism by emphasising the idea of the Oneness of God. He is considered the ancestor of the Brahmana Siwa, the main priestly kinship group of Bali. A great architect, he surrounded the island by a series of guardian temples, such as Tanah Lot and Uluwatu.

The Slave Traders

By the 16th century, Europeans were starting to dominate Southeast Asia. The "paradise" island was becoming the centre of slave trade in the archipelago. Balinese princes sold debtors, political opponents, and prisoners of war, men and women alike, as soldiers and manpower to the Dutch. This trade changed the political balance of the island. Located in the southeast, far from the main maritime trade routes location, Gelgel lost of its might. It broke into pieces after a coup in 1560, and Bali became an unstable maze of warring kingdoms.

Benefiting from its harbour on the north coast, Buleleng rose to power. Enriched by the slave trade, its king occupied Blambangan in East Java in 1691. Later on, Karangasem came to prominence by occupying Lombok in 1740, while Blambangan passed under the control of Mengwi, which retained it for most of the 18th century.

In the 1840s, after their victory during the Java war, the Dutch were obtaining submission of one Indonesian potentate after the other. The Balinese kings, however, were resisting. They would verbally recognise Dutch suzerainty, but never signed formal arrangements.

An important point of discord between Dutch and Balinese was the law of the sea. "International law" denied the right of salvagers to retrieve shipwrecked cargoes: it was piracy. To the Balinese, it was a just reward for saving the ship and crew. In 1846, a dispute over such a case in Buleleng gave the Dutch a pretext to land troops in north Bali. It took three years to the Dutch to defeat the Balinese soldiers, who fought fiercely to the end. In 1849, the Dutch finally gained control over Buleleng, followed by Jembrana in west Bali.

Fighting Till the End

Over time, the Dutch defeated the Balinese kingdoms one by one, a task eased by the internal feuds that weakened them. Using the pretext of a revolt in Lombok in 1894, the invaders attacked and subdued the island – thereby gaining control of Karangasem, then its vassalage. Feeling threatened by its neighbours, Gianyar put itself under Dutch protection in 1900. Bangli hesitated. Only the rich courts of Badung and Tabanan and the prestigious kingdom of Klungkung, heir to the rulers of Gelgel, remained independent.

In 1906, the Dutch used the pretext of a new shipwreck "pillage" to land in Sanur and attack Badung. Armed with shields and spears, the Balinese had no hope to win the battle against Dutch guns – and surrender was out of question. As the Dutch were advancing toward Denpasar, they were surprised to see a procession of white-dressed men, women, and priests, all running silently toward them. Ordered to stop, they accelerated instead, to be mowed down a few metres from the stunned soldiers. The survivors turned their weapons against themselves in an orgy of suicidal killing: men and women stabbing each other, finishing off the injured while a priest were reciting mantras, ushering these noble souls to Wisnu's heaven.

What had started like a military promenade for the Dutch ended up a river of blood. Three thousand Balinese died during these *puputan* (literally, "terminations") at the Kesiman, Satria, and Pemecutan palaces. Two years later, a similar *puputan* decimated the House of Klungkung. Arrested by the Dutch, the raja of Tabanan committed suicide rather than facing exile.

The Adventurers

*After the dramatic explosion of **Mt Tambora** in 1815, Bali went through a period of exceptional wealth – perhaps partly due to the fertile ashes left by the eruption. The island became an exporter of rice, coffee, and pork, especially to the new British colony of Singapore. European presence was that of traders and adventurers. One of these was Mads Lange, a Danish trader who set up business in Kuta in the 1830s, living in splendour with his two wives, one Chinese, one Balinese. Dealing in weapons, Chinese coins, and opium, and having a good knowledge of the island's trade network, he was the intermediary between the Dutch and the local kings and traders – much like the foreign trade agents dealing furniture in Bali today.*

© Djuna Ivereigh

Roasting a pig; Kamasan painting from Klungkung

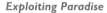

Sawing the Branch

As the Dutch attempted to "modernise" Bali, they bred future enemies. They threw a network of roads over the island, achieving economic unity. A modern bureaucracy was set up, which soon constituted, with the Chinese, Arab, and Muslim traders, the core of a new elite. The use of Malay, so far limited to minorities, quickly expanded with the opening of schools which used this language, creating a bridge with the other islands of the archipelago. Meanwhile, sons of the aristocracy sent to Java for studying were becoming part of a pan-Indonesian network of educated youth, who were to give rise to the independence movement.

© Iskandar

Exploiting Paradise

Bali was now part of the Dutch East Indies, a small island in an archipelago as large as the United States. The main royal houses were decimated, bereft of their power and, soon, impoverished: the sponsorship of the arts shifted to the village communities.

Hoping to make up for the emotion stirred at home by the *puputan*, the Dutch embarked on a policy of preserving and exploiting Balinese culture. They opened shipping routes to bring in wealthy travellers, many of them famous artists or scholars, like Charlie Chaplin or Margaret Mead, attracted by garish images of "the island of the gods." Coming on the KPM (Dutch Royal Lines) the tourists would land in Buleleng, drive to Denpasar in a limousine and be welcomed with dances at the Bali Hotel. Later came the trip to Ubud, a small principality that had escaped the Dutch destruction since its mother kingdom, Gianyar, had voluntarily rejoined the colony. Some of these visitors stayed on the island, mostly in Ubud and Sanur. Paramount among these were painters Walter Spies and Rudolf Bonnet, who contributed to the renaissance of Balinese dance and fine arts.

Towards Independence

In 1942, the Japanese invaded the Dutch East Indies, submitting the Balinese to a harsh rule of crop requisitions and brutality. Foreign artists landed in camps, like Bonnet, or were deported, like Spies, who died at sea. The Japanese occupation spurred the nationalist movement. When the Dutch came back to recover their colony after the war, they were welcomed by cries of "*Merdeka*" ("Freedom") and "Revolution". On 17 August 1945, in Jakarta, Soekarno read the proclamation of independence of the new Republic of Indonesia. While the Dutch were trying to get the Balinese kings on their side, Balinese youths resisted. A guerilla war ensued, mainly in the central mountains, while in the lowlands, the Dutch and their partisans were arresting and torturing the pro-Republican youths.

In May 1946, a small body of independence fighters, led by Ngurah Rai, was surrounded by Dutch troops in **Margarana**, to the north of Mengwi. In a repeat of the Badung slaughter, they all disappeared in a *puputan* "fight to the last." But the Dutch were facing increasing opposition. In 1949, **Anak Agung Gede Agung**, the king of Gianyar, joined the independence movement. As resistance mounted all over the archipelago, the invaders chose to withdraw. At the end of 1949, Indonesia was independent, with **Soekarno** as its first president.

© Iskandar

Modern irrigation works. Left: celebrating Independance Day

Enter the New Order

Once rid of its invaders, Bali was again facing its own internal divisions. Conflict ripened between reformist groups, challenging the old caste system and advocating land reforms, and those who defended traditional aristocratic rule. Peasants seized land from rich landowners, who retaliated by burning the sharecroppers' huts and crops. The landlords sided with the Indonesian Nationalist Party (PNI), and the reformists with the Communist Party (PKI). On 30 September 1965, the contradictions blew up nationwide: a military coup resulted in Soekarno's ouster, and a previously unknown general, **Soeharto**, rose to power.

The "New Order" government, as President Soeharto labelled its authoritarian rule, sought to uplift the Indonesian economy, which was in dire straits. Using foreign investment, international aid, and oil revenues, a team of young technocrats educated abroad shaped the modernisation of Indonesia. From 1965 to 1985, the country moved from the brink of famine to rice self-sufficiency under the so-called "green revolution".

This newfound prosperity came at the cost of freedom. Leaving behind the turmoil of the Soekarno years, political stability was a prerequisite for foreign investment. The "Father of Development," as Soeharto called himself, exerted a tight control on its people, with the excuse of protecting the country from the "lurking threat" of communism.

Killings in Paradise
The circumstances of the 1965 coup that ended the rule of Soekarno are still debated, including the possible involvement of the CIA. Until 1998, official history attributed the coup to the communist party, justifying the mass killings that followed – between 500,000 and 1,000,000 people suspected of communist ties were massacred. The killings were especially ferocious in Bali, and encompassed clan rivalries and conflicts between land holders and land reformers. Between 50,000 and 100,000 people died in Bali, with the victims often throwing themselves on the knives of their murderers, puputan-style. Although rarely talked about, this massacre overshadows Bali's collective memory.

The New Order also sought to unite the country, a challenge in an archipelago of 13,000 islands, with over 100 million people (220 million today) spread over 4,000km, and speaking different languages. Unity came with strong control over local riches – from mining to forestry and plantations – by the central government and its business friends. Regional cultures and local institutions were stripped of their power.

Cultural Tourism and the Balinese Exception

Bali, ever the exception, occupied a special place in this scheme. In the 1970s, a study conducted for the World Bank recommended that Bali be the main focus of Indonesian tourism development. The aim was to bring in foreign currency and restore the country's degraded image. The proponents realised that beyond palm-fringed beaches, tourists came to Bali for its vibrant culture. Hence, like the Dutch before, the Indonesian government sought to preserve and exploit Balinese culture – often in a sanitised form easier to digest by the visitors, from shortened ceremonies to specially staged dances. "Cultural tourism" was born. With all its ambiguities, it still remains at the core of Balinese development.

The pull of their culture and the resilience of their multiple communal organisations enabled the Balinese to shelter themselves partly from the New Order centralisation. The dual administration created by the Dutch, was maintained. The *desa dinas*, or official village, serves the needs of the central administration: issuing identity cards, counting voters, collecting land taxes. The *desa adat*, or customary village, partitioned in *banjar* or hamlets, is the true authority at the grass root level, along with the irrigation groups (*subak*). Most Balinese also belong to one of the many associations (*sekehe*) arranged by occupation, such as fishermen's groups, dancers' groups, etc. On top of this, all pay allegiance to their extended family network and, above all, to their village religious authorities.

The Drug Dealers

A Balinese social worker, Sugi Lanus, noted once that "the minute Bali declared itself a tourism destination, it automatically declared itself ready for drugs and prostitution – for tourism, quietly, requires them."*
Yet these are hardly new items in Bali. Opium smoking and prostitutes, many of them slaves, were part of the leisurely life of the island's rajas. The Dutch quickly established a monopoly on opium trade, which accounted for 75% of the island's administrative budget by the end of 1908. It took the combined clamour of local organisations and "ethicists" in Holland to end the legal drug trade in the 1930s.

*In Bali, Living in Two Worlds, Urs Ramseyer, Ed.

© Dedok

Cultural Tourism.
Right: PDI-P supporters.

While the Balinese retained their customary institutions, it does not mean they controlled tourism money. Most investment and profits were in non-Balinese hands – foreigners, Jakarta-based businesses, and Soeharto cronies. Mega-projects like the golf resort near Tanah Lot, or the Pecatu resort above Jimbaran, were imposed on the Balinese through armed land expropriation. The new ventures employed many migrants from Java, Lombok, or other parts of Indonesia. A few Balinese – and foreigners in love with Bali – came to question a model in which culture became a commodity, sold by outsiders to other outsiders.

© Djuna Ivereigh

Zaman Edan, the Time of Madness

The mid-1980s saw a shift in national economic policies. After two decades of protectionism and wise investment in agriculture, the new motto became "export-led growth." Strongly advocated by the World Bank, this new orientation meant financial deregulation and devaluation of the national currency. More tourists visited Bali – and other parts of Indonesia – to take advantage of new infrastructures, relaxed visa policies and a cheap rupiah.

As foreign investment poured in, an ageing President Soeharto failed to control the appetites of his children and cronies. The country was marred by corruption scandals. Referring to an old Javanese chronicle, people started to talk about *zaman edan* – the time of madness. In 1997, the Asian financial crisis brought an end to the artificial prosperity of the 1990s – foreign loans invested by complacent banks in scam projects that would never be profitable, but lined the pockets of their proponents. As the value of their money crumbled, poverty struck Indonesians. The people took to the streets, looting businesses owned by Chinese-Indonesians, the group seen as holding the country's wealth.

Soeharto finally stepped down in 1998. Two years later, democratic elections – the first in more than 30 years – gave the presidency to **Gus Dur**, later replaced by **Megawati Soekarnoputri**, daughter of Soekarno.

A Modern Puputan

In 2000, the first Indonesian elections since the fall of Soeharto were eagerly followed in Bali. The PDI-P party of Megawati, favoured by the Balinese, had won the majority nationwide. Yet before the reform of the election code, the president was still chosen by the parliament, who elected Muslim leader Gus Dur. Fearing that their favourite candidate would not even become vice president, the Balinese rioted, cutting telephone poles to make barricades and burning government offices. As told by a smiling hotel worker: "If Megawati had not became vice president, we would have burnt Bali to the ground, even if it meant no more tourism income for a decade." As always, better to die than surrender.

Sowing Democracy

Freedom by Internet
Like all around the world,
civil society organisations
in Bali have been prompt
to use the Internet to
defend their causes. A
good example is the SOS
Bali In Danger forum.
Started as a small discus-
sion group centred around
the controversial construc-
tion of a power plant in
Lovina (read north Bali
chapter p. 318) it has
quickly grown to encom-
pass other issues linked
with environmental gover-
nance, from geothermal
energy in Central Bali to
drainage issues in Kuta.
Another lively forum, cen-
tred on culture in contem-
porary Bali, is the Bali Arts
and Culture Newsletter.

The period since 1998 has often been labelled as the era of *Reformasi*. New leaders started to restore the freedom of the press, trade unions, and civil society. Reforms curtailed the power of the army – a permanent threat to Indonesia's nascent democracy. In 2002, a drastic decentralisation law returned most control over local resources to district-level governments (there are nine districts in Bali, and about 350 in Indonesia).

While freeing local forces, this fast shift of power came with some downsides. Corruption has often simply moved from the central to the local government. Foreign investors are kept away by legal confusion, multiple taxation levels, and conflicts with local communities trying to retrieve ancestral land given away to mining or plantation companies. Inequalities deepen between poor provinces – such as the ones to the east of Bali – and richer ones – those with oil, coal, or forests in Borneo and Sumatra. With reduced control, forests are destroyed at an increased speed.

In Bali, the fall of the New Order curbed controversial projects of the Soeharto family. Balinese regained authority of their island. Beer outlets were banned on the beach, as it is considered sacred. Then again, excesses lurk. Not all Balinese appreciate the growing zeal of village militia enforcing Hindu traditions and chasing *pendatang* (immigrants from other parts of Indonesia). Like elsewhere in Indonesia, Balinese face the task of balancing autonomy claims with national coherence, tolerance, and the rule of law.

Another consequence of the new era of freedom is the rise of civil society. Non-governmental organisations have been mushrooming, defending causes ranging from women's rights to the environment, workers or the rights of local communities – while some are merely vehicles for disguised private interests. With all their excesses and shortcomings, local institutions and civil society groups are the much-needed seeds of democracy, and the place where tomorrow's Indonesia is being shaped.

© Iskandar

Pecalang in uniform, wearing a swastika – the Hindu symbol of the sun and good fortune

© Leonard Lueras

Plastic used to scare birds away from rice fields

By Yuyun Ismawati

Rising civil society organisations and the increasingly strong regional government of Bali need to tackle the so-called "paradise paradox" – economic development, fuelled by tourism, threatens to destroy the very marvels tourists have come to admire.

The Plastic Nightmare

Anyone who stays in Bali will eventually find a temple, forest path, river, or beach polluted by plastic waste, such as empty water bottles, bags, snack wrappings, etc. Tourists are often dismayed to see elegant Balinese in ceremonial attire discarding litter around sacred temple grounds. Before harvest time, thousands of plastic strips flutter above rice fields, modern scarecrows meant to keep birds away from the ripening grains. And many municipalities and hotels send their sewage into the ocean, off the very beaches where their guests play.

While tourists turn their noses while swimming among plastic bags, perhaps planning their next holiday elsewhere, Balinese are the first to suffer. Discarded rubbish clogs drains and irrigation channels, which become a breeding ground for rats, mosquitoes, and other disease-carrying animals. Fishermen search desperately for vanishing eels and fish in polluted rice fields, rivers, and oceans. And thousands of Balinese risk losing their jobs when disgruntled tourists shun their dirty shores.

You Can Help

Tourists have more influence than they may realise on environmental behaviour in Bali – as paying consumers and models for many young Balinese. Tips:

- *Avoid buying plastic bottles.*
- *Ask your hotel to refill your bottle from its drinking water dispenser.*
- *Carry a cloth bag with you and refuse plastic bags.*
- *Give your empty plastic bottles to scavengers.*
- *Carry a bag with you to collect waste from soiled natural sites.*
- *Give preference to eco-friendly businesses.*

© Dedok

In Love with Plastic

© Ulung Wicaksono

Yet Balinese don't seem to mind the plastic. Local tradition believes that nature can manage itself. This was realistic when populations and their consumption were low, food was wrapped in banana leaves and water carried in earthware jars. But recently, plastic has invaded every aspect of life – and many Balinese, without an environmental education, have yet to realise that it takes years to degrade.

Most Balinese feed their organic waste to pigs, and burn the rest at the back of their garden, or throw it into rivers. Part of the waste – cans, plastic bottles, paper – is collected by scavengers, who sell it for recycling. These poor folks, however, are eyed with suspicion by the communities, and villages are guarded by signs warning *Pemulung Dilarang Masuk* (Scavengers Stay Out).

River in the Bestala valley

Water, Water Everywhere...Until When?

Just as challenging as solid waste is the water issue. This may seem hard to believe after seeing so many lush rice fields and waterfalls. Yet experts and NGOs, like the Wisnu Foundation, are warning against pollution and upcoming water shortages, which could strike the urban areas of southern Bali before 2010.

Traditional institutions managing water, like the *subak* irrigation groups, have been weakened by modernisation. The government has put restrictions on the use of water by hotels and industries, but they are rarely enforced. With everyone pumping deeper and deeper, groundwater reserves are depleted. The government often just pipes water from springs to meet the needs of urban areas, leaving farmers without water for their rice fields.

Another issue is electricity. Bali imports most of its power from nearby Java. Staunch defenders of their autonomy, Balinese would prefer to set up their own sources of electricity. Some of the upcoming projects are based on renewable energies, like a proposed geothermal plant in the central mountains. Others continue to rely on unsustainable fossil fuels, with outdated technologies threatening the environment, like the new thermal plant being constructed near Lovina.

Fighting for Generation Next

The government regularly comes up with its own solutions to these issues, sometimes creating new problems of its own. A big project has been designed to manage the rubbish of Tabanan and south Bali, which concentrate 50% of the island's population and 85% of its tourism. The objective is to process the waste of a landfill located in Suwung, near Sanur. The only proposal so far is to build a huge incinerator at high cost. Besides the pollution, this project would put hundreds of people out of job – the scavengers who edge out a meagre living by collecting recyclable items from the landfill, and the 200 pig herders who feed their animals from the organic waste.

In Gianyar, the local government has agreed to a cheaper solution, advocated by local environmental groups like Bali Fokus, and partially-funded by international aid. A small facility has been built to sort the waste manually – thereby creating employment – and send it for recycling.

Across Bali, community groups coordinated under the Bali Clean-Up campaign put waste bins in strategic spots and organise "beach clean-up" days which gather hundreds of adults and schoolkids. Organisations like Bali Fokus lobby hotels and the government to promote better environmental management. Others, like the GUS Foundation and PPLH, design environmental awareness campaigns and education kits. Around Kuta, Legian, and Seminyak, the Parum Samigita mobilises hotels, government, and citizens to set up a sensible waste management system for this tourist-crowded area.

It will take years to make changes in the behaviour of people, the island's infrastructure, and the laws and their enforcement. In the meantime, travellers can set an example and demand responsible behaviour from the hotels they patronise.

The Green Fighters

Bali Fokus
T 0361-743 57 96
F 0361-270 737
www.balifokus.or.id

Bhakti Wahana Bali
(Bali Clean-Up)
T/F 0361-464 429
M 081 83 44 654
ybwbali@yahoo.com
nimadewidiasari@yahoo.com

GUS Foundation
T 0361-759 323
gusinbali@yahoo.com

Yayasan Idep
T/F 0361-974 152
idep@dps.centrin.net.id

**PPLH (Environmental
Education Centre)**
T/F 0361-287 314
www.pplhbali.or.od

Parum Samigita
T/F 0361-761 65 76
samigita@dps.centrin.net

Wisnu Foundation
T/F 0361-735 320
wisnu@wisnu.or.id

© Erdi Lazuardi

Collecting plastic garbage in the mangrove

© Iskandar

Back from a temple anniversary ceremony (odalan)

An Introduction to Balinese Religion

By Jean Couteau

Balinese Hinduism, the religion of most of the population of Bali, has a following of 3.1 million people – along with 160,000 Balinese Muslims, 45,000 Christians, and 21,000 Buddhists. It is the unique product of a historical process mixing ancient local cults with Hindu and Buddhist influences, and preserving strong ties to nature.

Animist Roots

Ubiquitous in Bali, nature manifests itself in gigantic trees, dark gorges, surf-beaten beaches, and ominous volcanoes. Nature also pervades human creation: rice terraces moulded into the hillsides, family compounds immersed in greenness, temples open to vast landscapes. Natural forces are thus inseparable from human life. Nature is viewed as power, and each of its components – trees, forests, valleys, rice fields – is subjected to a spirit or deity which "owns" it (duwe), and has to be provided with a shrine (pelinggih) and fed with offerings (sajen) made of local agricultural products. These deities may visit the humans during temple festivals.

Sacred Trees, Revered Ancestors

The popular face of Balinese religion is dominant in the mountainous areas of the island, around the *Bali Aga* villages. It also persists elsewhere as the deepest aspects of beliefs and rituals, blending indigenous Austronesian components with ancient Hindu-Buddhist elements which reached Bali 2000 years ago. The roots of this tradition are animist, and combine cults of natural elements and fertility with ancestral worship.

This primordial essence shows in the cult of phallic and vaginal objects, usually megalithic, as well as large trees. Each revered tree is "dressed up" as a sign that it is "alive", and harbours a shrine where people present their offerings. One of the key characters of Balinese lore, the *Barong* (dragon-lion), is lord of the forest, and its mask is cut "live" from the swath of a sacred *pule* tree. Every village is protected by a sacred banyan (*waringin*), the leaves of which are used to make effigies of the dead. Linked to life by its protective side, the banyan is thus also linked to death and the ancestors on the other side – for maintaining a balanced link between the living and the deceased is key to Balinese harmony.

Mountains occupy a key position as the ancestors' abode. When a Balinese dies, he is said to "go back home," returning to the "old country" above the mountains where departed souls dwell. Always present, the ancestors' souls may return during temple festivals – dances and offerings are prepared to welcome them. Dead souls may also reincarnate into newly born children of the family, or be called upon by a medium (*balian*) to give advice to the living.

Shiva-Buddha, the Indo-Javanese Streak

Bali was part of an Indian-based trade network as early as the first century AD. Indian religious influences, however, remained minor until the ninth century, when Sanskrit inscriptions appear. Buddhism was the first dominant creed, but various Hindu sects soon took root and eventually outgrew it. Java was the filter of much of these alien influences, and by the 13th century, the local religion was already a syncretism of Indian, Javanese and indigenous Balinese elements. In the next century, the domination of Majapahit brought the Javanese version of Hinduism – a syncretism of Shivaite and Buddhist elements – which dominated hitherto.

Far from replacing local lore, Indian cosmology, mythology, and philosophy have been grafted onto it, and given a new life in the Balinese world. While retaining their indigenous structure, architectural principles took Indian names. Similarly, the Shivaite *linggam* cult, of Indian origin, is often no more than a cover for an older megalithic, phallic fertility cult.

The blend took different flavours depending on the areas and strata of Balinese society. The further away from the royal centres of power, the more "indigenous" the tradition. Far from the courts, the Bali Aga villages

Cosmic Rituals

For Balinese Hindus, the material world and man itself are both an element and a structural duplicate – a mirror – of the cosmos. What happens in this world is an echo of similar processes in the invisible world. Hence the importance of rituals designed to maintain or restore harmony of both the material and the spiritual realm. Every unfortunate event – from road accidents to floods or terrorist attacks – is thought to be a manifestation of an imbalance and leaves behind unwanted, negative spirits that are dealt with through purification rituals.

© Jean-Marie Bompard

A dragon figure at a ceremony in Ubud

have only been indirectly touched by the Shiva-Buddha streak. All around the island, the peasantry has stuck to its local customs to a larger extent than the *brahmana* priests, who had direct access to Sanskrit-derived texts.

© Iskandar

Poleng penjor *cloths at a temple ceremony*

It's not all Black and White

Unlike other religions seeking the victory of Good over Evil, Balinese Hinduism sees the world as the field of encounter between demonic and divine forces which must be kept in balance. This is symbolised in the poleng, *a sacred cloth placed where strong, potentially negative forces need to be placated. The* poleng *is a chequered, black-and-white pattern, creating grey squares where black and white treads cross each other. It illustrates the balance between demonic and godly forces, and the permanent process of transformation of good-into-bad and bad-into-good, which is at the root of life.*

Man and the Cosmos

The Shiva-Buddha tradition brought the Hindu cosmic framework, in which the world is a living totality uniting spiritual and material elements in an unending process of transformation. Beyond its many manifestations, the Oneness of God is the merging of spirit/masculine and matter/feminine principles, uniting the three forces of creation (Brahma), balance (Wisnu) and destruction (Shiva). Man is subjected to a similar process of integration and transformation: the *samsara* or transmigration of the soul. Incarnation binds the soul to a body, and is seen as a hellish condition, which one should strive to overcome by achieving *moksa* or ultimate enlightenment – then the soul and body may rejoin their cosmic equivalent.

Another Indian influence is the imposition of a caste system over the Balinese social structure. The four castes of Hindu theory: *brahmana* (priests), *satria* (warriors), *wesia* (traders), and *sudra* (commoners), already Javanised, were added to an indigenous system of rank opposing "aristocrats" to "commoners." Added to a kinship system of *warga* (family clan), this makes for the complex divisions of Balinese society. The Shiva-Buddha facet of Balinese religion revolved around the *puri* (palace) and the *gria* (priestly households). The kings or rajas kept the agrarian system in place and united it. The high priests of Brahmana descent, while providing the king's power with its ideological foundation, consecrated the system with their mantras and holy water. This hierarchy is challenged today.

Modern Hinduism

As the new Republic of Indonesia took shape after WWII, the quirks of Balinese values ran counter to the demands of a nation-state thriving towards modernity. To gain recognition by its Muslim and Christian partners,

Balinese Hinduism needed to modernise. Initiated in the 1920s, a reform movement brought Hindu universalism, in a deep departure from the localised nature of Balinese faith. In 1961, Hinduism became a nation wide religion under the official name of Hindu Dharma – gathering six to seven million followers claiming a common Hindu heritage in Java, but also in the north of Sumatra or in the heart of Borneo forests.

Returning to old Indian scriptures such as the Veda or the Bhagavadgita, the Council of Hindu Affairs (*Parisadha Hindu Dharma*) promoted a "rationalisation" of Balinese faith – eliminating "polytheistic" ambiguities which tarnished its image in the eyes of Muslims or Christians. Belief in God was emphasised over formal rituals of animistic colours. The many gods of the Hindu Balinese pantheon are now defined as mere manifestations of this one powerful principle. The ancestor's cult has been redefined: one does not automatically reincarnate among his kin, as the local tradition has it, but in a condition dependent on the quality of one's deeds (*karmapala*) in one's past life.

In parallel, a revision of the caste divisions was advocated. The traditional caste system based on descent (*wangsa*) is now said to be a misinterpretation of the Vedas, according to which one's real caste (*warna*) is based on merit. Although the debate is ongoing, this has eliminated legal and formal status differences between the existing descent groups.

Yet as the Hindu authorities attempted to adapt Balinese values to the modern world, considerable leeway was allowed in the interpretation of the faith and in the implementation of rites, in accordance with the Balinese tradition of tolerance or "*desa, kala, patra*" (adaptation to place, time, and circumstances). Hindu Dharma could thus evolve as a single trunk with an indefinite number of branches and twigs – illustrating the Indonesian national motto: *Bhinneka Tunggal Ika* or "Different but One" derived from the Sutasoma, an Old Javanese poem still held sacred in Bali.

The Blind and the Elephant

Balinese tolerance is based on a relative perception of truth. The truth, although it may exist, is not knowable. An old Indian scripture illustrates this through the story of a group of blind men asked to describe an elephant. As each of them was allowed to touch a different part, they came with their own views, both correct and yet false: "it's a snake," said the one feeling the trunk, "it's a drum," said the one, touching the foot, "no, it's a mountain," laughed the last one, touching the beast's belly. This classic parable, found also in Buddhism, teaches an open brand of scepticism and an acceptance of multiple forms of faith.

© Djuna Ivereigh

Holy water, the modern version

© Iskandar

Burning a bull-shaped sarcophagus

A Short History of Balinese Cremation

By Degung Santikarma

Dead, not Leaving

Although in theory someone who has behaved badly during their lifetime can come back as a worm or a scraggly street dog, Balinese Hindus believe they mostly reincarnate back into their own families. Many Balinese parents will visit a traditional psychic after a birth to discover which relative was reborn in their child. Since one may be meeting their loved one again soon, first in the family temple where the ancestors reside and later in the spirit of a newborn, no Balinese would want to mar this relationship with a cheap ceremony. Cremation is a debt owed by the living to the dead, and the spirits of those who lie uncremated may haunt their families until the proper rite is performed.

The cremation ceremony is one of the most popular tourist attractions in Bali – a spectacular rite involving the labour of hundreds of people, thousands of ritual offerings, and expenses worth several years of a Balinese's salary. But while cremations are part of a long-standing tradition, they also reflect the social shifts and changes taking place in contemporary Bali.

For Balinese Hindus, the burning of the body is one step in a ritual process meant to free the soul or *atman* from its worldly ties, and return the body to the five elements – earth, fire, water, wind, and space. It enables the soul to join the ranks of the deified ancestors who watch over the living, and to reincarnate in the body of a child.

While tourists sometimes express discomfort at the thought of attending the last rites of someone unknown, for Balinese, death is a public affair. When a Balinese dies, the news is broadcast to the village by pounding on a *kulkul* split gong. The extended family and members of the *banjar* (village) rush to help with the preparations. Packed on ice, the body lies in state, with food and drink laid out for it and for the stream of guests. As the body must not be alone, a group of men keep a 24-hour guard, fuelled by coffee, cigarettes, and palm liquor and entertained by all-night gambling sessions.

Fighting after the End

Yet as communal and welcoming as a cremation may seem, there are sometimes real tensions taking place behind the scenes. In pre-colonial days, powerful kings would be cremated along with their wives and key servants who were expected (willing or not) to glorify the king by their suicides on the funeral pyre. But cremations also provide an arena for resistance to excessive power. As communal affairs, these ceremonies offer the opportunity not only to strengthen community ties but to convey conflicts and resentment.

The worst punishment for an unruly Balinese is not to be imprisoned or killed, but a kind of "social death": being refused the right to be cremated by the community on the village grounds. Such traditional sanctions, known as *kesepekan*, are so feared that in 1997, the village of Kesiman was able to stop the then-governor of Bali, Ida Bagus Oka, from claiming the village's coastline for a multi-million dollar beach resort project. A member of the village, Governor Oka was defeated not by the threat of legal action, but by the fear that when he died, his body would be left unburned and his family humiliated.

As recently as twenty years ago, cremation ceremonies could also become occasions for staging violent protests. During the procession, those carrying the sarcophagus and the cremation tower spin them around at the village crossroads, in order to confuse the spirit of the dead so that he or she cannot find the way back home to haunt relatives. But if the deceased was someone not very well liked in the village – an arrogant official or a stingy noble – boisterous horseplay could grow more serious. Spinning the tower with a vengeance, villagers could topple the body out onto the street. In extreme cases, Balinese would *ngarap* – tear the body to bits with their hands or even their teeth. Of course, such outbursts fit poorly with tourism images of Balinese as gentle, peaceful, spiritual people. And so as tourists started watching cremations, the government banned the practice of *ngarap*.

A Public Affair

Although Balinese are, of course, sad when loved ones die, strong emotions are believed to bind the departed soul to the family, preventing it from moving on to the afterlife – so people try to keep the mood light. The ritual washing of the body by kin and villagers is often a rather raucous occasion. Jokes fly about the body of the deceased, with pointed comments about the sexual equipment – or inadequacy thereof – the most common. Since Balinese attend such occasions all year long, even children grow intimate with matters of life and death at a young age.

© Leonard Lueras

A sarcophagus ready to be burned

So Much Money, so Little Time

Besides cleaning up cremations, tourism has affected their scale. New wealth flowing into the island meant that middle-class Balinese could afford to stage more expensive ceremonies. Balinese who lacked the cash for spectacular send-offs began selling land so as not to be outdone by the neighbours. If today the average cost of a simple cremation ceremony in south Bali or Ubud ranges from Rp15 to 20 million and a medium-sized ceremony from Rp40 to 200 million, a cremation for a king can cost as much as 500,000 dollars – needed to fund processions of thousands of retainers, vats of holy water, months of preparation, engraved invitations, media advertisements, press passes, and a public relations officer. Meanwhile, Balinese from poorer regions like east Bali may cremate their dead for as little as two million rupiah.

But as tourism and the new competitions for status created by wealth encouraged cremations to grow flashier, it also led them to become more efficient. Cremation ceremonies that used to take at least five or six hours were cut down to a mere hour or two, letting busy Balinese hurry back to tend their hotels or handicraft shops. Short cremation ceremonies also were more appealing to the tourists themselves. Lengthy debates took place within Hindu authorities to decide whether propane blowtorches could be used to speed up cremation (the answer was yes, as long as the initial flame comes from a priest).

Despite the demands of modernity, cremations remain genuine, colourful events at the heart of communal life – don't miss a chance to witness one. Local travel agents, tour guides, and hotel staff will tell you where to see a cremation. While Balinese families do not charge fees to tourist guests, travel agents may offer packages including transportation, explanation of the rituals, and appropriate Balinese clothing. While it's not necessary to offer a monetary donation, it is important to behave respectfully – read our tips in the side column, and don't forget your camera.

❈ Visitors should be dressed in a sarong and a temple sash, and avoid grubby T-shirts or singlets. Don't get in front of the procession with your camera, or position yourself higher than the priest. While tourists are welcome to watch and photograph the proceedings, don't try to enter the home of the bereaved family unless you are invited or know them personally. Be careful not to get trampled by the men carrying the cremation tower and sarcophagus – stay back from the side of the road, especially near crossroads where they are most likely to spin the body in circles.

© Leonard Lueras

Carrying the coffin up the cremation tower.

Animal Sacrifices

By Diana Darling

Many visitors to Bali are taken aback by the use of animals in religious ceremonies. Rituals have a sliding scale of size, which is partly defined by the number and type of animals to be sacrificed. For small purification ceremonies, the size goes from "one chicken" to "five chickens plus so-many ducks." A small village wedding might be "two pigs." The immense purification ceremonies conducted in 2002 after the bombing of a night-club in Kuta required the sacrifice of 79 animals, some of them rare. But perhaps the most appalling to outsiders is the ritual drowning (*makelem*) of live animals to honour the deity of a lake or sea – or their throwing into a volcano to appease the mountain's deities.

Drowning ducks at a purification ritual after the Bali bomb blast in 2002

The Balinese universe is populated by a variety of invisible energies, each of which must be acknowledged in a precisely-defined manner through offerings. These ambivalent energies mutate between positive and negative in a way that is often translated as "gods" and "demons." Gods are pleased by flowers, pretty dances, and sweet things like cakes and fruit, while demons prefer raw meat, strong drink, and noisy music. Any Balinese rite will comprise offerings to both polarities.

Sharing with the Community

Animal sacrifices are also an occasion of sharing meat – still a luxury for poor Balinese families – among the community. The animals are acquired by designated village members and brought to the temple. They are given offerings, with a mantra wishing them a human reincarnation, before their throats are cut. Then men sort themselves into different work groups to prepare the carcasses for cooking. Some of the meat is set aside for offerings. This may be cooked or raw, but much of it becomes various forms of satay or kebabs, arranged in bundles and brought by the men into the temple. The rest of the meat is cooked and shared by the community.

Holy Kebab

Most temples have a simple kitchen outside the temple walls, where dozens of men and women prepare the rice, meat, spices, and other things that go into both offerings and lunch. Although most offerings are made by women, the most visually striking may be that which is constructed by men: the Christmas-tree-like gayah or satay gede (giant kebab) built of pork fat that has been carved into decorative shape, and ornamented with a gazillion satay sticks and small red chillies. This vegetarian's nightmare must be a delight to the most hard-to-please demon.

From Illegal to Compulsory Cockfights

Another form of animal sacrifice is the cockfight, which takes place in the temple's outer courtyard, or in a special cockfighting pit. Like other pleasures in life (such as music, theatre, and lively ceremonies), this supremely male sport has long been part of religious ritual. The spilling of blood is considered necessary to appease the disruptive energies or "demons". But beyond the ritual, millions of rupiah are won and lost in the amazingly quick gambling that takes place during the fights.

During the New Order, from 1966 to 1998, all forms of gambling were forbidden and most cockfighting was illegal. Only a few fights were allowed for ritual purposes. They took place in the outer courtyard of the temple or in family courtyards, with the men in temple dress. A police permit was required and no gambling was allowed.

In the new era of decentralisation, gambling is back with a fury. Village communities organise cockfights to raise money for the village coffers. Since the income is used to restore temples or other public buildings – including cockfighting pavilions – the gambling is justified in the name of local traditions. Some villages even make it a duty for all men to participate in these "cultural" cockfights. Those who don't attend, or don't bring a well-groomed, duly aggressive cock, are subject to embarrassingly large fines.

Obviously, the revival of this tradition was not good news for the cocks – not to mention the thousands of Balinese families who, every year, lose their life savings around the gambling pit. Besides foreigners, a number of Balinese, especially intellectuals and modern Hindu reformists, object to compulsory cockfighting and animal sacrifices. Yet most scholars agree that these rituals are deeply rooted in Bali's view of the world. Hence if any changes take place, they may need to come from within, at a pace acceptable by the many Balinese who hold that animal sacrifices are needed for rituals to be effective – and can't imagine life without a good cockfight.

Cocks fighting

© Ulung Wicaksono

What's in a Name

By Degung Santikarma

On first look, the process of naming in Bali seems a rather simple business. The first child in a family is called Wayan, or Putu if the family is of high caste. The second is called Made, the third Ketut, the fourth Nyoman, and then the cycle repeats. Commoners are given the prefix "I" for males and "Ni" for females, while those of the upper castes are given aristocratic titles: Ida Bagus or Ida Ayu, Cokorda, or Gusti. A personal name such as Rai or Glebet or Sadra may also be added at the end. It seems all very rational – until you meet people called I Made Radio or Anak Agung Putu Carlos Santana.

According to Balinese tradition, it made little sense to spend hours finding the perfect name for your child since most people switched names several times over a lifetime. Birth-order names and caste titles required little thought, and even so-called personal names were rather impersonal and easy. If a mother went into labour in the marketplace, her baby might be called I Made Peken (market). A child with a dented head could be called Ni Wayan Belek (squishy), and I Nyoman Cengkeh (clove) was perfect for a boy born during the clove harvest. A mother who craved leafy vegetables during pregnancy might call her child I Ketut Kelor (spinach), or Ni Nyoman Suba (enough) if she was fed up with childbearing.

As babies matured into children, their names would be often modified to reflect their characteristics – like Kembung (blister) for a child who would get burned playing with fire, Krebek (thunder) for a child afraid of storms, or Glebet (crash) for a boy who would often fall down. A child plagued by frequent illnesses would be taken to a traditional healer, who would advise the parents to change the name to confuse evil spirits. And when children grew up to have their own children, they would then be known as "father of X" or "mother of X" and later "grandfather or grandmother of X," giving up their own names for the next generation.

IDs and Jails

When the Dutch took control of Bali in the early 20th century, names took on a new meaning – people should have one and only one name. Not only did this reflect western conviction that humans were unique individuals before being members of a community, it made it easier to spread modern notions of ownership and social control. Schools, population records, land certificates, and jails needed something permanent in black and white. After independence, the new Indonesian state happily embraced modern marvels like birth certificates and identity cards. The name game became a serious one.

© Dedok

From Spinach to Neon

After Indonesian independence, Balinese began to see the name as an opportunity to express one's cultural identity. Modern parents stopped naming their children for their misshapen heads and lack of hair, and started giving them glorious-sounding Sanskrit names like Ananda or Astakarma, or modern monikers like Susi or Viki. Some people got even more creative. In my neighbourhood, there are the young cousins Anak Agung Ngurah Hendrix and Anak Agung Putu Carlos Santana. And next door to them are a whole family named I Wayan Neon, I Made Radio, Ni Ketut Kopling (car transmission), Ni Nyoman Lampu (lamp), and I Gede Telpon (telephone).

But even the modern pressure to stick to one name couldn't stifle the Balinese conviction that a name is meant to be modified. I Wayan Dempul, whose father worked at a repair shop, was named after a brand of car wax, but had his name changed to I Wayan Suprapta (good behaviour) after he kept getting into trouble. I Made Dwiputra became I Made Bodrex after a brand of medicine that cured him of his frequent childhood fevers. I Made Darga had his name changed to I Made Deger (weird thoughts) when, as a child, he'd sit in corners talking to himself. But after he grew up, he renamed himself I Made Jagger – a better branding strategy towards the opposite sex.

From Lenin to Lennon

Balinese names are a good indicators of shifts in social winds. I Ketut Lenin, born in the 1960s when the Indonesian Communist Party was popular, became I Ketut Lennon after the party fell from power and The Beatles rose to prominence. Today, hundreds of Balinese babies bear names like Ni Made Megawati, after their parents' favourite presidential candidate, or I Ketut Dollar, after their parents' currency of choice – or even Anak Agung Made Turis (tourist), probably hoping they will become tour guides.

© Dedok

Casting a Name

Names also reflect one's positioning in the complex and ever-moving maze of the Balinese social hierarchy. Almost any tour guide can tell you a bit about Balinese history – chronicles of priests reaching enlightenment at faraway temples and glorious kings conquering each other's land, wives, and slaves. The deeds of these legendary ancestors, contained in the historical texts known as *babad* and performed in traditional Balinese dramas, form the basis of the Balinese "caste system" inherited from Indo-Javanese influences (read the section on religion). Priests (*brahmana*) can be identified by the titles "Ida Bagus" for males and "Ida Ayu" or "Dayu" for females. Princes (*ksatria*) use the titles Cokorda, Anak Agung, or I Gusti. Members of the merchant caste (*wesia*) use the title Gusti. Women of lower caste who marry into the nobility are called "Jero", meaning "insider".

From Caste to Class

Caste first came under attack in the 1920s as a movement of educated Balinese commoners, called the *Surya Kanta*, argued that the caste system did not fit with modern times. They claimed that social status should be based on a person's qualities and accomplishments, not on their birthright. They also disagreed with traditional practices surrounding caste, such as the prohibition of upper-caste women marrying lower-caste men, and the custom of commoners speaking respectful high Balinese to the priests and nobles while these upper castes spoke back in coarse low Balinese. Modern Hindu reformist trends also tried to depart from traditional caste divisions based on inherited status.

Economic changes, however, dealt a more powerful blow to caste-based hierarchies. In feudal times, caste used to be linked with military power, enabling its bearers to control significant wealth, such as slaves and land. A whole century of colonisation and market economy has reshuffled the cards of wealth. Slaves are banned, and land ownership does not mean much without the capital to turn it into a high-profile resort.

Hence, being born to a high caste doesn't guarantee the good life anymore. A *brahmana* might work as a bartender, a *ksatria* as a bricklayer, a *wesia* as a tour guide and a *jaba* as corporate CEO. Just like everyone else, princes must pay for their coffee at the neighbourhood *warung* — even if they still get a few extra satay sticks at the village temple festival. Those who still live in royal courts have to live by a tradition which expects them to hold expensive, prestigious rituals from birth to marriage to death. Often strapped for cash, they try to use their heritage as a source of wealth. Some turn their palaces

Caste and You

Travellers don't need to worry excessively about the subtleties of caste in Bali. If your bellboy is a brahmana, he'll still be happy to carry your bags, and you don't need to defer if your cokorda driver looks like he's about to go off the road. Naming can be sensitive, but while those of high caste may take offense at being called Bapak or Ibu — the Indonesian words for "Mr" or "Mrs" — most Balinese will forgive foreigners who don't know local etiquette. Ask your Balinese friends how they would prefer to be called. And if you hear a bit of Balinese history, remember that it's not just a story of the past, it's also part of an ever-changing present.

© Leonard Lueras

A modern Ubud princess

into tourist guesthouses. Others develop arts foundations with the help of moneyed patrons, many of them
foreigners, attracted by the prestige that nobility continues to carry.

Not without my Caste

Although caste no longer indicates material wealth or
occupation, this doesn't mean that status has lost its
shine. People of a higher caste are still treated with deference by most Balinese, and they are often called upon
to arbitrate a conflict, for their opinion carries more
authority than that of a commoner.

Hence even in this era where Indonesia searches for
democracy, many Balinese seem to have adopted the old
motto of the U.S. Army: "Be all that you can be." Not
only are Balinese going out and getting MBAs and PhDs,
they're embracing new caste titles with enthusiasm.
Indeed to understand just how important caste is to
today's Balinese, all one needs to do is open up the Bali
Post, the island's daily newspaper. There you'll not only
find ads for motorbikes, rice cookers, slimming powders,
and English classes, but Bali's most popular column:
"*Asal-Usul*" or "Origins". Readers who have forgotten
their families' glorious pasts – or who are troubled by
the notion that they might not have one – can write in
and request a retelling of their history that leaves out all
the embarrassing bits.

Even property is often royalised, especially in the
tourism industry. Now anyone with enough money can
live in a housing complex called Taman Griya (the
Brahmana Garden). Most tourists will at least sleep or
dine once in a hotel or restaurant which name starts with
Puri or Palace. This is only fitting since in many ways, foreigners have become the new lords, staying in the kind of
luxury Bali once reserved to the island's rulers, their
every whim catered to by a corps of willing tour guides,
deferential waiters and smiling masseuses, some of which
might be the descendants of princely families.

Ups and Downs

*Caste has always been fairly
flexible in Bali, leaving room
for endless reshuffling. Even
in the old days, a talented
commoner who attracted
the interest of a prince
could be awarded a noble
title. A high-ranking* ksatria
*who moved from his palace
to a faraway village might
go down a notch, while a
minor noble who built a
palace in some isolated hills
could call himself a king.
Princely heirs marrying
lower-caste women would
slip down a rung. A com-
moner could elevate his
family status after hearing a
whisper in the night saying
that he was the descendant
of the mythical head of a
powerful clan – while
someone ill could visit a
traditional psychic and find
out that the problem was
not worms, but some long-
ago royal forebearer who
had been forgotten.*

© Iskandar

Young pecalang (village militia) on watch

Sixteen-Year Old in Bali

By Degung Santikarma

As night falls on a village temple near Denpasar, a crowd begins to gather. But the tourists ready to take shots become confused when instead of Balinese worshippers dressed in sarongs and temple sashes, their cameras frame a group of Balinese teens in Mohawk hairdos, worn jeans, nail-studded bracelets, and army boots.

As the loudspeakers crackle to life, a figure steps to the microphone. Dressed in traditional Balinese clothing, he welcomes the audience to the anniversary of the village youth organisation. Over the excited shouts of the crowd, he announces the groups on tonight's bill. They're not the traditional *gamelan* orchestras or temple dancing troupes, but a line-up of local bands: Djihad, Small Dictator, Commercial Suicide, Recidivist, and The Three Little Pigs. The first band's lead vocalist, a skinny teenager with long, red-streaked hair, takes the stage, shouting out "*Pree...dom!*" in local English – most Balinese find it hard to pronounce the letter "f". Then he launches into a song by British punk band The Sex Pistols. As a horde of black-clothed boys – and a few black-clothed girls – thrash and clash in the temple courtyard, one elderly villager looks on in confusion. "Where's the art in it?" he asks. "Maybe those children need to be bathed in holy water so they'll stop acting like demons."

From the Vedas to MTV

Despite repeated calls to conserve Balinese culture, many of the island's young people have found that tradition can no longer contain their imaginations. New media, from the Internet to MTV to glossy magazines, have invaded the island. Thirty years ago, most Balinese teenagers followed in their parents' footsteps, becoming farmers or fishermen. For many young Balinese today, culture has become less about how things used to be than a way of expressing their identities.

©Iskandar

A punk monster statue at a Balinese New Year festival

© Iskandar

*A modern Balinese
making offerings*

Punk Tourism?
*Despite their T-shirts
proclaiming anti-capitalism,
young Balinese punks don't
mind to see their island
turned into a marketplace
for tourism. They love to
ask foreigners for help
decoding the English lyrics
of their favourite songs.
"I just wish the tourists
weren't all so interested
in gamelan music and
Balinese dances," says
18-year-old Wayan Karda.
"If the tourists were all
punks, then Bali would
really be the island of
paradise!" Don't miss a
chance to chat with young
Balinese and learn what
they think of Nirvana (the
rock band) and Nirvana
(the afterlife).*

Spiritual Punks

After the show, the teenagers gather to chat at the small
food stall next door. "We're bored with Balinese culture,"
says 16-year-old Agus. "We want to live lives that aren't
stuck in tradition." This means hitting up their mothers
for funds to rent a neighbourhood music studio, complete
with tinny drum kit and dubious electric guitars. There's
no money for drugs, even if they were interested, but
sometimes they can scrape together enough for some
arak palm liquor. Hairdos are done with glue and iodine
instead of expensive salon dyes. Motorbikes are creatively
redesigned, removing any accessory that signals safety or
comfort. Helmets are covered with slogans like "anti-mili-
tarism," "subversive underground," and "the government
lies," along with names of favourite bands.

Yet the rebellious youths never miss a religious ritual. Sixteen-year-old Gus Nik warns, "If you're not dili-
gent in your duties at the temple, or you forget to ask
God to protect you, you might get attacked by demons."
He says that he needs to make ritual offerings, because
demons are extra-threatening to teenagers who stay out
late at night. Gus Nik also believes in the Hindu concept
of reincarnation. He hopes to live his next life in London,
where he can meet the punk rock stars he idolises. He
sees no contradiction between his firm faith and his liking
of an American group called Bad Religion.

His friend Putra, 17-years-old, has turned his bed-
room into a gathering place for Denpasar's disaffected
youth, covering his walls with posters proclaiming
"Anarchy!" and "Destroy the System!" At night, Putra
sleeps with his body wrapped in chains, a practice
admired by his friends. Yet when his father wakes him
up early in the morning, asking him for a ride to the
hotel where he works as a tour guide, Putra switches
into the polite language and demeanour Balinese culture
demands of its sons. Pulling on a large helmet so no
prospective girlfriend can recognise him, Putra carries
his father on the back of his bike, driving carefully so the
old man will not be bothered by the bumpy road.

The Mall Gang

Not all Balinese youth choose punk, however, as their means of establishing an alternative identity. For middle-class kids, popular gathering places are the more upscale haunts like the island's malls.

As elsewhere, Saturday night at a Balinese mall offers a swarming mass of teenage fun, fashion, and hormones. Dressed in the latest trendy Western-style clothes, boys and girls make eyes at each other as they ride up and down the escalators or congregate in the food court. Most of them have little money to spend. They are just there to look – and to be seen. Loudspeakers blare pop music and the kids flirt using a blend of coarse Balinese, Jakarta youth slang, and choice English words picked up from the television. Like teens all over the world, they use this code to look cool and make plans for parties without being understood by their parents.

Back in the village

Of course, not all Balinese youth have equal access to modern pop culture. In Banyuning, a small fishing hamlet on the dry coast of east Bali, teenage girls spend their days collecting water from the communal pump, cutting grass to feed their families' pigs, and working in the corn fields. Teenage boys go out with their fathers to fish, or when the waves are too strong, lounge around drinking palm liquor and telling tall tales. Few children go to school past elementary level, and some girls have never seen the inside of a classroom at all – their parents believe it makes little sense to invest in educating daughters, who will only leave home to marry. But even in such isolated villages, young people still create their own contemporary cultures.

At night when the work is done, teenagers gather at the house of one of the few village residents who owns a television to watch the latest soap operas and celebrity gossip. The television's owner opens a refreshment stand, and the kids buy bottles of Fanta and packets of homemade popcorn. On Saturday

Net Culture

Like their counterparts on the other side of the world, Balinese youth love modern means of communication. The wealthiest ones spend hours typing short messages on their mobile phones. More affordable, Internet cafés are within the reach of everyone. All around the island, Bali's warnet – short for warung, or shop, and Internet – hold rows of computers separated by partitions. There, for Rp5,000 an hour, young Balinese can explore worlds far from home, or chat safely with friends as close as the other side of town.

© Dedok

Environmental School

Balinese youth know very little about the ecological problems plaguing their island, and have more pressing issues in mind. Most have no idea that plastic doesn't degrade like a banana leaf wrap. Yet because clean air, water and beaches are the assets of their future, a few organisations are educating kids on green issues. One of them, Yayasan GUS, has released a video for teens, showing two young couples out for a day of flirting. As they find out that every quiet little corner is filled with waste, their fun is quickly spoiled. At the end, local pop stars state their aversion to using plastic, in the hope that these role models will influence young Balinese.

© Iskandar

After a ceremony in Besakih

nights, a travelling outdoor cinema showing Hindi films and bloody action B-movies comes to town. Girls seize this chance to dress up like the kids on TV, curling their hair, putting on cheap perfume, and painting their faces from a shared cache of makeup. On the walk back and forth with no streetlamps to expose them, boys and girls can flirt and tease and – if they dare – sneak off for a few moments of private time. After a large catch of fish, village youth may also gather to perform *joged*, a sexy folk dance, or to sing the rowdy traditional songs of *gegenjekan*.

Many Banyuning kids also get a first-hand experience of modernity through labour migration. Around half of the village's young women are off working as housemaids in urban areas, where they learn to speak Indonesian, wear trendy clothes, and value watches, wallets, and radios. Young men, whose labour is needed on the fishing boats, stay home. Eighteen-year-old Suryani, who has worked in Denpasar for two years, admits this creates a gap between genders: "Men only know about fish, but I know all the words to the songs on television." Yet the number of young women who fail to return home after their sojourns in the city can be counted on one hand. Suryani explains that not only would she miss her family if she married a man from Denpasar, but that life in the village, despite its difficulties, is free of the regulations of modern bureaucracy. "If I marry a fisherman and I decide I don't like him, I can just leave him. If I married in the city, there's all these new things like courts and divorce certificates."

In Banyuning, kids know there's only a few years left before they'll become adults. Most girls are married by 16 or 17, and become mothers soon after. A young woman who's turned 20 is already an "old virgin" and has little chance of marriage, unless she's willing to accept a widower or a place as a second wife. But even in the restricted village environment they yearn to explore, like kids everywhere across the world, the joy of creating their own youth culture.

© Leonard Lueras

Behind the Smile: the Lives of Balinese Women

By Cok Sawitri and Leslie Dwyer

Balinese women have become a trademark of the tourism industry. Glorious images of their strength, sensuality, and elegance ornament every hotel brochure, coffee table book, and postcard. Women participate in the gorgeous pageantry of Balinese ritual, gracefully balancing towers of handcrafted offerings on their heads. They dance for the gods at temple festivals, dressed in glorious costumes that show off their legendary beauty. Far from being secluded by tradition, women can be seen working in the fields or at construction sites, buying and selling in the marketplace, and driving motorbikes all around the island.

These images hide the complex reality of Balinese women's lives. The strong Balinese women who work alongside men make up less than 40% of the paid workforce. Women occupy lower status jobs, whether in agriculture, tourism, or trade. In the fields, men perform the better-paid tasks like ploughing or planting, while women undertake the domestic unpaid tasks of weeding, threshing, and drying rice. In tourism, men act as drivers and tour guides, positions that get them a chance to collect fat commissions from restaurants and craft shops, while women work low-paying jobs like waitresses or

Ritual Duty

Women are responsible for maintaining much of the Balinese ritual glory immortalised in tourist snapshots. While men prepare certain ceremonial foods, build cremation towers, and march in ritual processions, women are in charge of everything else. They direct family ceremonies, and spend on average five hours a day crafting the offerings to the gods needed for everyday devotions, holidays, and life cycle rituals. The praise women receive as "guardians of Balinese tradition" often comes at the cost of aching backs and sore fingers.

hotel receptionists. In the market, women vastly out-number men, but they trade lower-priced goods while men sell livestock, motorbikes, and land. And women who work, no matter how prestigious their degrees or how high their wages, are still expected to be responsible for all that goes on in the household.

Decision-making in Bali is also dominated by men. Politics is a majority-male domain. Women are considered to be executants, and rarely participate in *banjar* hamlet councils or *subak* agricultural societies.

Balinese wives handle daily money matters, paying food or school fees, and doling out cigarette money or cockfighting funds to their husband. This, however, is hardly experienced as a privilege. Men reserve the right to approve major expenses – or to put the family motorbike at stake at the cockfights. Moreover, money is traditionally seen as coarse matter, to be handled by women, who are less refined. Few Balinese men would compromise their pride by bargaining down to the last rupiah at the market. This allows women a certain freedom. Unhampered by the need to be always polite, women – especially older ones – can be more open with each other, exchanging jokes and sexual gossip.

For Better and for Worse

The sensuous Balinese woman who bewitches men with her beauty and serves her husband with gentle grace may also hide more than a conflict. In contemporary Bali, the official divorce rate is below 5%. Some Balinese attribute it to a traditional harmony between Balinese men and women. The reality may be starker.

In Balinese society, descent, status, and inheritance are traced through the male line. While a high caste man can marry anyone he pleases (even a Western tourist), a woman may only marry someone of at least the same standing or risk becoming a social outcast. A Balinese woman "marries out," leaving her home to become a member of her new husband's community. Before her

A Legacy of Equity
Rather than an indigenous trait, the domination of men over the community is a recent introduction – probably from the Javanese Majapahit culture which dominated Bali in the 14th century. In the Bali Aga ("mountain Balinese") villages, where ancient social structures are still present, male/female pairs of elders sit on the village council (read feature on Tenganan in the east Bali chapter p. 220).

© Ulung Wicaksono

Daily duties

marriage, she takes ceremonial leave of her father's temple and ancestors. Her children will be members of her husband's family, and all property will be passed to the sons.

While arranged marriages are no longer common, a woman had better choose wisely, for once she marries, there's usually no turning back. Should she divorce, her husband's family keeps her children and the property acquired during the marriage. Unlike customary law, national law gives women a right to a share of marital property – hence most Balinese men make sure their divorce is handled by the village authorities rather than in a civil court. A divorced woman might be accepted back into her parents' or brother's house, but may be treated as little more than a boarder, with no rights and no voice. A widow will usually stay with the family of one of her sons. With children – especially sons – to support and protect her, she may even grow into a position of relative power and influence in the home, served by her daughters-in-law. But with no husband or nearby children, a woman is out of place.

Hence Balinese women will go to extraordinary lengths to avoid divorce and the related shame – turning a blind eye to a husband's infidelities, laziness, drunkenness, or even violence. Besides divorce, rebellious women, or those who can't give birth to a son, are threatened to become a co-wife, for Balinese husbands can take as many wives as they please – in rural areas, around 10% of men have more than one wife. While it's quite possible, just like anywhere in the world, for Balinese husbands and wives to have loving, happy, fair relationships, this is a matter of luck and personality rather than a value supported by custom and law.

Modern Hopes, Modern Challenges

Things are now changing a bit for women, especially in urban areas. Many families are more aware of the need to educate and respect their daughters, and there are Balinese women doctors, lawyers, and professors.

Witchcraft and Money

Balinese widows are not expected anymore to throw themselves on their husband's pyre. But divorcées and widows – both called balu in Balinese – may still be accused of black magic. Left alone while no longer virgins, it is feared that they will seduce other women's husbands with their tricks. Widows are often at the centre of inheritance conflicts. They are entitled by customary law to hold their husbands' property for their sons. But in tourist areas where land prices are rapidly rising, her husband's family may be eager to sell – and tempted to label a witch the woman who stands in the way of a quick fortune.

© Iskandar

All Balinese children are now required by law to attend elementary school, and the numbers of girls going on to junior high and high school are rising. The number of men with more than one wife has fallen dramatically, and polygamy, once glorious, is now often judged backward – in fact, national law bans a government employee from taking a second wife without the permission of the first. Contraception is easily available to married women (unmarried women cannot participate in the national family planning programme), although the pressure to have sons remains as strong as ever. Women with wealth can open bank accounts in their own names to save against the possibility of divorce, and several local organisations, including the Legal Aid Foundation, offer support for women seeking divorce in civil courts.

But women also face new trials. For every woman who works, another woman must take on extra responsibilities for making ritual offerings. Modernity has created a widening gap between the "career woman" who can afford to hire a maid, and the traditional woman who devotes her life to her family and the gods. Even tourism has sometimes helped make women's lives more stressful. The pressure many Balinese feel to conserve tradition in the face of foreign influence means that the ritual calendar has become even more busy, requiring additional labour from women.

The recent decentralisation movement is strengthening Balinese customary law against national law and Westernisation – making it more difficult for women to advocate rights to inheritance, political participation, and the custody of their children. Even national law is no guarantee of equality: women must have their husbands' permission to obtain passports or take out bank loans. If a woman marries a foreigner, her children not only have no rights according to Balinese customary law, but no right to Indonesian citizenship. Behind the postcard images, the reality of the world of Balinese women remains a challenging one.

Helping Hands
You can help these organisations which provide support to women:

Mitrakasih
Women's Communication Forum
T 0361-223 010
rajswari2003@yahoo.com

LBH Bali
(Legal Aid Organisation)
T 0361-223 010
lbhbali@indo.net.id
www bali.lbh.or.id

Bali Sruti
T/F 0361-222 464
(Studies and campaigns on women's rights)

PKBI Bali
T/F 0361-430 214
(Specialises on teenagers' and women's health issues, with an attached clinic)

Making offerings

Women's Secrets

By Cok Sawitri

Before Bali became a tourist destination, Balinese women's bodies were no big secret. For the sensual way of the day was to wrap oneself tightly in a sarong, leaving one's breasts bare. This risqué style of women's dress lured colonial-era visitors to Bali. But in the 1930s, Balinese students on a moral mission, in the name of modernity, requested women to cover their breasts from the pornographic focus of foreign cameras. Yet sexuality remained firmly anchored in Balinese life, expressed in popular folktales, art, mythology, medicine, and mystical rites – sometimes clothed in seductive symbolism and coy innuendo, and sometimes spoken of in terms as refreshing and realistic as they seem vulgar.

© Iskandar

Woman in traditional clothes

Bath Talk

Nowadays, many western visitors assume – just as many Balinese wish them to – that local women are shy, repressed creatures bound by traditional society.

Yet behind this proper façade, Balinese women have their own ideas about sex. Just go one morning with women as they bathe in the river. As a woman washes her hair, her friends will tease her, asking, "Did you till the fields last night?" – for a married woman, a morning shampoo often means that she had sex the night before. Women will measure their beauty in frank terms, comparing the sizes of their breasts, the curves of their hips, the thickness of their pubic hair, or the shapes of their waists and behinds – attributes usually linked to a woman's fecundity. They will often end up talking about men's bodies, speculating about the size of their privates in a straightforward style that invites jokes, laughter, and blushing. Expect them to remark on how a man's appearance is no warrant of his abilities: "One doesn't judge a winning cock by just its crow or its fine feathers. It's the wave of its 'spur' in the fighting pit that determines its value."

Young Coconuts

Popular sex imagery puts its environment to full use. Women may evoke nyuh gading *(yellow coconuts) to describe round breasts,* acengkel gonda layu *(a bundle of wilted greens) for the size of their waist, or will mock one's ugly buttocks by calling it a monkey's behind (*jit bojog*). When youngsters are taught the varieties of edible plants, they learn a rhyme for* kecicang, *a green vegetable, which compares it to a long penis reaching up to the sky. Even children learn verses with double entendres, like* "Capung gadang, capung gadang kuk-kuk-kang! Anak bajang, anak bajang, ankuk-angkuk-kang!" – "Green cricket, green cricket, goes kuk-kuk-kang! Young maidens, young maidens go angkuk-angkuk-kang (the sound of thrusting hips)!"*

Fertility Rites

In Selat, near Amed (east Bali), a fertility ritual called "Usaba Dong-Ding" is held the day before Nyepi, the Balinese New Year. At the peak of the ritual, the temple priests take two wooden statues, one male and the other female, and press them together in simulated sexual intercourse, to the enthusiastic cheers of the watching crowd. In another ritual in Sesetan, Denpasar, the village youth hold a yearly mass kissing ceremony that is believed to ward off illness. Even in quite sacred settings, there is an incredible honesty to Balinese conceptions of sexuality that has yet to be repressed.

© Djuna Ivereigh

Love scene in a Kamasan painting, Klungkung

For those Balinese women who are not yet married, sexual topics are still rather taboo, as young girls are not supposed to have the knowledge that comes with having a husband. But this doesn't mean that unmarried women are ignorant; they often consult their older sisters and married friends. This may lead to more concrete explorations with one's unmarried peers – which are not considered as shameful homosexual encounters, but as an acceptable relief before marriage, and a way to prepare for the wedding night.

Princesses and Working Women

There are, of course, differences in the ways in which women of various generations, social statuses, and economic situations talk about sex. Sex is discussed quite openly among labourers and farmers. Working men and women like to talk about traditional herbal medicines, exchanging recipes for remedies reputed to enhance attractiveness or increase stamina.

The Balinese nobility, by contrast, has traditionally expressed sexuality in more refined and indirect terms. Yet court women could draw upon a whole cannon of mystical science, and the experience of commoner nannies and servants. To win the favour of men, women would draw *rajah*, supernaturally powerful tattoos, on their vaginas. Even in the isolation of the royal palaces, noble women developed their own strategies to give expression to desires.

In contemporary Bali, however, certain cultural and political forces have conspired to keep sex under wraps. The modern state has tried to project an image of Indonesia as developed and refined, and considers sexual frankness to be the mark of the primitive. In the contemporary school system, "sexual education" focuses on dry matters of reproduction, family planning, and, more recently, the dangers of AIDS and sexually-transmitted diseases. Yet sexual knowledge continues to be related orally and informally, through innuendo or humour, always accompanied by a ticklish curiosity.

© Dedok

Getting There and Around

Preparing your Trip

Filling your brains, filling your heart

Passing rice fields to visit an old temple in the forest is always fun. It becomes a riveting experience as you unmask the life behind the view: the convolutions of water from terrace to terrace, the intricacies of Hindu epics, the profusion of orchids under the trees. Before leaving, pick up some of the many books written about the island – luscious novels and candid travelogues, bird-watching and diving guides, scholarly essays, and lively debates about where Bali comes from and where it heads to. And as you learn about Bali's nature and culture, you'll be less likely to offend people with a wrong gesture or unwittingly destroy a rare coral species. For trying to understand people and natural life is the first step towards respecting them.

Filling your suitcase

Light packing makes travel easier, especially in Bali, this shopper's dream come true. Why bring piles of shorts and T-shirts when you can buy them cheaply on the spot? And at the end of your trip, you'll be desperate for space in your luggage to fill with souvenirs.

Bali has a warm climate all year long, so light cotton clothes are ideal. One thing that you may not readily find

When to Travel

Bali has a tropical, humid climate with an average temperature of 27°C year-round. It rains often, sometimes for a few days in a row, during the wet monsoon (Nov-Mar). The most pleasant weather is during the dry monsoon (May-Sep), when the days are less wet and the nights cooler. The peak tourist season is in August and around Christmas; it is better to travel off-season to get better deals and smaller crowds. However, even during the peak season, tourists remain concentrated around a few popular spots, and lesser-known rural areas remain rather quiet.

Take your Time

Air travel is a major source of greenhouse gases responsible for global warming. Jumping in an airplane to spend one week at the other end of the planet is not very eco-friendly. Leave home less frequently, staying longer in your final destination. This is the best way to experience the real joy of travelling, slowly falling in love with a country, its nature and people.

© Gilles Guerad

Fighting cock in a cage

in Bali are good hiking shoes, and any kind of shoes in large sizes. To roam around the countryside, bring a pair of strong hiking sandals, a light sweater for mountain travelling, and a light rain jacket. You won't have many occasions for camping in Bali, except in the National Park, but the guards can supply you the needed gear. Bring one clean, modern outfit – long-sleeve shirt, a good pair of trousers, or a decent skirt for women. They will be needed if you are invited to a formal occasion or ceremony by new Balinese friends.

Before leaving, ask your doctor for a tropical travel prescription: mosquito repellent, sun-block, a soothing cream for rashes and burns, hydrating cream, an antiseptic kit for small cuts, pain killers, and all you need to treat heartburn and light diarrhea – the standard reaction to new, spicy food. If you follow a medical treatment, bring enough for your stay and write down both the commercial and scientific name of your medicine in case you lose it (it may be available in Bali, but under a different brand). Other useful accessories include a pair of prescription sunglasses if needed, and small foam earplugs if your sleep is light – cocks seem to never sleep in Bali, and village life starts at 5am.

If you have a choice, it is better to use several small bags, so you can leave some of your gear at a hotel or a friend's place when taking a side trip. It is also worthwhile to purchase a smart travellers' belt or pouch in which you can safeguard your money and travel documents.

Planning for the Worst

Travelling in Bali is rather safe, but theft can always occur. Having a copy of your plane ticket, credit card, and passport (or a record of their numbers) will make it easier to process their replacements. Keep a copy with you, and leave another one with somebody at home.

Most credit cards supply you with travel and health insurance when you purchase your ticket. If not, travel agents will be able to sell you insurance policies. Before leaving, inquire about the exact nature of the coverage, and the procedure to follow if needed. Ask for the number to call in case of emergency, and always have it with you. Write down the local numbers of your country's embassy in Jakarta and their consulate in Bali.

Getting There

Bali has an *international airport* (Ngurah Rai, also known as the Denpasar airport) which is well served by most airlines. You'll find a wide range of flights going to Bali from Europe, North America, Australia, and most places in Asia. Most travel agents and on-line ticketing services offer excellent fares to Bali. Book early if you intend to spend time in Bali around July-August, Easter, or Christmas.

You can also fly to Bali *from other places in Indonesia*. The most reputable domestic airline is the national carrier Garuda. Over the last few years, however, many new airlines have been set up, linking various places in Indonesia at competitive prices. Call a travel agent to find about the latest specials, which vary constantly. Beware that planes are often overbooked between Denpasar and Jakarta around weekends and national holidays.

Once in Indonesia, you can also reach Bali *by sea*. Ferries link Ketapang, in East Java, to Gilimanuk, in west Bali, all day long. The trip lasts about 30 minutes, to which you must add the time needed to buy your ticket, wait around, load, and unload. You can take a car, a bicycle, or a motorcycle with you on the ferry, but check first if your vehicle rental company allows it. You can also easily travel by ferry between Bali and Lombok. Passenger boats departing from Benoa harbour link Bali to other islands in Indonesia. The major operator is Pelni, the national shipping company. Inquire directly at their office or at a travel agent for the latest routes and tariffs.

Public buses are the cheapest way to travel from Bali (Ubung Terminal, Denpasar) to Java. You can get a bus to Surabaya (about Rp80,000; 10h), Yogyakarta (Rp150,000; 16h), or Jakarta (Rp200,000; 24h). Tourist shuttles, like Perama, are a bit more expensive, but go all

Organised Tours
When planning your trip, beware standard package tours with low-price, all-inclusive deals – you may well end up at a bland hotel in a tourist ghetto. However, you can get good packages from small operators dealing in eco-tourism or cultural tourism. Some of them can even plan tailored trips for small groups. Before choosing a tour operator, enquire about their ethical chart, or their social and environmental policy. Their response will give you a good idea of their commitment to nature and culture, and is a good indicator of the quality of their services. Check our web list on p. 430 to get some ideas.

the way to Kuta or Ubud. In all cases, it is better to buy your ticket ahead of time at the terminal, or from a travel agent. There are various level of comforts, the most expensive buses have air-conditioning and are quite comfortable. Don't necessarily expect a tranquil journey though. Most buses play very loud music or videos. Anxious passengers will be kept awake by the hair-raising speeds at which the drivers cut through the dense traffic.

Visas

New visa requirements were introduced by the Indonesian government in February 2004. Travellers from some countries (including France, the UK, and Germany) get a 30-day tourist visa on arrival for US$25, while others have to request it at an Indonesian embassy or consulate. If you request your visa at the embassy prior to departure, you can obtain a 60-day permit. None of these tourist visas can be extended locally. If you plan to stay more than 60 days, you'll have to leave the country to get a new visa (many tourists do so by going to Singapore). You can also request a business visa or a socio-cultural visa, which can be extended locally until a maximum of six months. For both you'll need a "sponsor" letter from a person or organisation in Indonesia.

There has been a lot of uproar in Indonesia over the new visa policy. Many travel agents feared that it would reduce arrivals. Some people pointed out that the reduced length of the visa-on-arrival will limit the length of stay of travellers. Although this has no impact on star-rated hotels catering to package tours, it may reduce the number of backpackers on extended trips – those who bring income to faraway places, and patron the small hotels and restaurants owned by local people.

There may still be changes in the visa policy, so you should inquire at the nearest Indonesian consulate at least two weeks before departure. In all cases, you'll need a passport with at least a six-month validity. Keep safely

Useful Numbers

Ngurah Rai Airport:
0361-751 011

Garuda Airlines Office:
0361-227 824;
0361-234 916
24h, all-Indonesia
booking service:
080 714 278 32

Perama buses:
0361-751 875

Pelni ships:
0361-723 689;
0361-763 963

Travel Agencies:
Sanur:
Anta: 0361-234 116
Vaya: 0361-285 555
Kuta-Seminyak:
KCB: 0361-751 517
Bayu Buana: 0361-755 788

Denpasar Tourism Office:
0361-234 569
Mon-Thu 8am-3pm,
Fri 8am-1pm.

the card handed to you by immigration officers on arrival, you have to produce it when departing. When leaving the country, bring enough money to pay for your departure tax at the airport (Rp100,000 at the time of writing).

Customs

Indonesia prohibits the import of arms, drugs, and pornographic material. Each adult passenger is allowed to bring one litre of alcohol and 200 cigarettes. There are restrictions on the import of videos. Computers, cameras, and tape recorders are supposed to be declared and re-exported. In practice, this probably won't be necessary, unless you bring unusual quantities of material of professional quality.

Indonesia is a signatory of the **CITES Convention** regulating the trade of endangered species. This prohibits the import and export of any object made from turtle shells, ivory, rare species of snakes, and endangered shell or coral species. In any case, you should not support the trade of anything made out of living creatures removed from the wild and the ocean: just don't buy any of these products, and don't patron the shops that sell them.

Arriving in Bali

Most travellers reach Bali by plane, landing at the Ngurah Rai International Airport just south of Kuta. Once there, the safest thing to do is hop in a taxi to reach your preferred place to stay. Look for the official taxi counter and buy your ticket there – around Rp30-50,000 to most nearby tourist destinations.

It can be a hassle to find a good hotel on your first night, after 15 hours in a bus or plane. Good-value places are often full during the peak season. The best strategy is to book a hotel by fax or Internet for your first night on the island. Most hotels, even those in faraway areas, will be able to send a car to fetch you at the airport. Make sure, however, to reconfirm your booking, exact time of arrival, and pick-up arrangements before leaving.

The Corruption Plague
Bred by poverty and the small wages of civil servants, corruption is particularly rife in poor countries. Indonesia has one of the world's worst records. In this very young nation-state with a weak rule of law, many people feel that their allegiance goes first to their own community. When in a position of power, they may then use it to serve their own interests and their family network. This means that visitors can get away with minor offences, from traffic violations to overstaying their visa, by discreetly negotiating a payment with the officer in charge. This only feeds the corruption beast, and can also lead to trouble. To avoid such unpleasant situations, inquire into the rules of the country, and try to abide to them.

© Djuna Ivereigh

Statue of a policeman in Klungkung

Money

As soon as you arrive, you're going to need some Indonesian rupiah. You can change some at the airport or at your hotel, but the rates are not very good. It is better to withdraw cash from one of the airport's ATMs.

Money changers are found all around the tourist areas of Kuta and Ubud. They usually offer better rates than banks. To avoid being cheated, follow the tips in the side column. It is normally easy to change banknotes in US dollars, Euros, and Australian dollars. However, you'll get a much better rate for higher denominations ($50 or 100 rather than 10 or 20). Any note which has been folded, tainted, written on it, or torn up may be rejected. US dollar notes from 1996 or with a serial number starting with CB are often hard to change, so avoid them.

It may be difficult to change *traveller's checks*, depending on which bank issued them. They always carry a lower rate than cash. To avoid carrying too much cash, bring an international *credit card*. You'll find ATMs accepting Visa and Mastercard in any town – look for the logos of Bank BCA, BNI, Lippo, or any other bank's ATMs. You pay a 2 to 3% commission on these withdrawals, but the rate is good, so it's worth it.

Always try to *pay cash* when shopping, withdrawing money first from an ATM. There have been many cases of credit card fraud in Indonesia. Crooks obtain credit card numbers when you shop and use them months later for huge transactions, usually in other parts of Asia. If you do use your card, inform your bank at home and keep an eye on your account for unexpected debits. Your bank's insurance should cover the loss if you react quickly.

Getting Around

Public transport is a rather slow, but fun way to go around Bali, allowing you to meet Balinese people and share a bit of their lives. It is definitely more friendly – not to mention eco-friendly – than to travel in a rental car, especially if you're on your own.

Safe Money Changing

• *Only choose money changers with an established shop, avoid shabby back-alley counters or deals made in the street.*

• *Beware of anyone offering rates much above the average – you may soon find that yes, it was too good to be true.*

• *Always check the conversion on your own pocket calculator or a piece of paper.*

• *Recount the notes yourself, separating them one by one – some money changers fold the banknotes in two, so you may count twice the same note if you count from one side of the bundle.*

• *Don't let anyone distract you and don't lose sight or hold of the money after counting it.*

The most ubiquitous vehicle in Bali is the *bemo*, a small mini-bus fitting 10 to 20 people, or even more depending on its size and the degree of squeezing of the passengers. Bemos are easy to spot by their yellow plates, which in Indonesia indicate public transport or a taxi (black plates are private vehicles and red ones, government). You'll find bemos on all the main roads. They can be rare on smaller roads, especially in the afternoon after markets are closed.

Bemos take fixed routes, sometimes indicated on their fronts, and stop wherever a passenger wants to hop on or leave. To get on one, look at the driver and wave your hand towards the side of the road. Upon reaching your destination, ask the driver to stop and pay your fare. Bemo fares are usually very cheap, from a few hundred to a few thousand rupiah. Before planning a bemo trip, it is a good idea to ask at your hotel about the routes, times of travel, and fares. If you are not too sure where you should get off, indicate your destination to the driver and to the other passengers, they will tell you when to stop. You can also ask them what is the proper fare. Always carry small change with you – you can't expect a bemo driver to give you change for a Rp50,000 or even 10,000 bank note. Some bemos can be chartered for the day, with a driver. There is no fixed rate, but it should not cost you more than a rental car.

Taxis can easily be found around Denpasar and the nearby tourist spots (Kuta-Seminyak and Sanur). The best ones belong to the Blue Bird company and are of blue colour. You can call one from your hotel (T *0361-701 111*) or flag one down at almost any place along the road. Apart from special spots like the end of Double Six Road in Seminyak, the driver should always put the meter on, if not, threaten to get out of the car and take another one. Fares are very moderate – it costs about Rp10,000 to go around Kuta or Sanur, Rp30,000 to go to the airport, and Rp50,000 to go from Sanur to Kuta. Round the fare to the next thousand rupiah and consider leaving a tip.

Public buses travel between the district capitals of Bali. Each main town has one or several bus and bemo terminals serving different destinations. Denpasar's Ubung terminal serves the northwest and west of Bali, Batubulan the north, east and centre (including Ubud), while Tegal serves the south. Buses don't stop as often as bemos, so they are much faster (frighteningly so in some cases). Count about Rp10,000 for each 50km. Perama shuttles are more comfortable and serve the main tourist areas directly, saving you the need to get to the bus terminal. Count about Rp30,000 per 50km.

© Dedok

© Dedok

Car rental is a good option if you travel with a group of friends or family. Avoid large vehicles for Bali's narrow and crowded roads. Instead, choose a small Suzuki Jimny (around Rp80,000 per day), a slightly larger Daihatsu Feroza (around Rp100-120,000), or a more comfortable Toyota Taruna (Rp200,000). Car rental agencies are everywhere in tourist areas. Negotiate the rate and take the time to test drive the car first, especially before embarking on a journey around the island. Don't hesitate to pay a bit more for a car in a better condition. It is worthwhile to purchase insurance (all car rentals propose it) but make sure you understand exactly what it covers.

An international driver's license is required to drive on Bali. You'll also need confidence, patience, and a degree of luck to negotiate your way around Bali's crowded roads, at least in urban areas. Things are easier once in the countryside, but you can never predict when a child or a chicken will try to cross the road. Driving is on the left-hand side.

If you lack confidence, think twice before taking the wheel. Major accidents are rare since chances are few to drive over 60km/h. However, you may bump into a motorcycle or a pedestrian. If that happens in the middle of a village, things can get nasty – Balinese are prone to taking justice in their hands, and get very emotional when they or a loved one is hurt. Regardless of whose fault the accident is, you'll be expected to cover hospital bills and car repairs (practically no one is insured in Bali, and most rental car insurance doesn't cover third-party liability). In such cases, avoid the police but consider asking advice from your hotel manager, or, better, a Balinese friend.

For an additional Rp50,000 a day, most car rental companies will supply you with a *driver*. Test his driving abilities first and check whether you get along well. Inform the driver of how many days you plan to travel. If more than a day, you're going to have to pay for his accommodation and food on top of his fee. Clarify how

Motorcycle Taxis

*You can find an **ojek**, or motorcycle taxi, in most places in Bali. They wait for passengers around main tourist spots, or in special places called pangkalan ojek. They usually carry a spare helmet for the passenger. Negotiate your fare before you hop on – a few thousand rupiah in most cases. Ojeks are good fun and often the only available option in remote areas. You can even charter one for a whole day. Make sure you feel confident in the way the person is driving.*

many hours the driver works (normally not more than eight), and how much is the charge for any overtime.

Don't expect your driver to know all the roads of the island. Most drivers are not too adventurous, and they prefer to stick to the most frequented tourist circuits only. If you want to explore lesser-known areas, get a good map and plan on being the co-pilot.

Drivers will try to make you stop at their favourite shops, hotels, and restaurants. Be aware that this is no sign of their quality but rather an indicator of how fat the drivers' commission when they bring guests in – the commission can range between 10 and 30%; drivers and guides make more money this way than from their wages. In some cases, a driver may try to deter you from going to other places, especially to remote areas far from business opportunities. Remain nice and friendly, but make it clear that you are the one who decides where you want to go.

Motorbike rental is also easily available in tourist areas, and extremely cheap (around Rp25,000 to Rp50,000 per day, depending on the model and the duration). Insurance is not available. A good helmet is required, covering the ears. The rental company should supply it. Make sure it fits and is in good condition; if not, buy one along the road. You can find good ones for around Rp100-150,000, a worthy investment. The company will not require your international driver's license, but cops will if you're arrested. Make sure it covers small motorbikes (most rental motorbikes are 125cc or smaller).

Although a great way to enjoy the island, motorbike driving is extremely dangerous in Bali's traffic. With a lack of good medical care, a small accident can easily turn into a very nasty experience, especially if you lose consciousness and are being taken to a local hospital. Keep it in mind and drive very, very cautiously. Buy a large waterproof poncho, available in any roadside shop, and keep it under the seat for flash rains.

Bicycles are available for rent in the main tourist areas of Bali such as Kuta-Seminyak, Ubud, Lovina, and Amed. Prices vary from Rp10,000 to 25,000 per day. Bring your own helmet and safety gear if you intend to do a lot of biking. Main roads and urban areas are not bicycle-friendly. It is better and safer to keep biking for quiet rural roads. Avoid the hot midday hours, use a hat, and drink a lot. Apply sunblock on arms and neck when driving a motorbike or a bicycle in the sun.

© Dedok

Where to Stay

Homestays are found all around Bali in the low and middle price range. While some are just plain hotels, a real homestay means that you share the compound of a local family. Many homestays are run by mixed Balinese-Western couples, offering the best of both worlds. They may not have a restaurant, but most can serve a table d'hôte – set menu – or order food from a nearby warung. The owners and staff will usually be delighted to take you out for walks and tours, drag you in full Balinese gear to the next temple ceremony, or teach you Balinese cooking. If you know a bit of Indonesian, you can also negotiate to sleep at local people's homes in villages.

Beyond the large, star-rated hotels lining up the beach-fronts of Sanur, Nusa Dua, and Kuta, Bali has an amazing – overabundant in some places – choice of accommodations. Tight competition means that the price-to-quality ratio is good for travellers, especially outside the peak season. Whether you spend US$2000 per night in a Hollywood star haven, or US$5 in a bamboo-walled homestay, you're guaranteed to have a great time.

Balinese people have a well-deserved reputation for graciousness. Even in the smallest hotels, the staff compensate in friendliness what they may lack in Western-style hotel training – especially if you are patient and smiling. This makes a holiday in Bali unforgettable.

From Cultural Tourism to Sustainable Tourism

Aware of the fact that foreigners come to the island for its rich culture, most hotel architects have been careful to keep some original Balinese traits such as *alang-alang* thatch roofs, Balinese *bale* (open-air pavilions perfect for lazing), or *candi bentar* (split gates decorated with carvings). With the exception of huge modern hotels built from the 1950s to 1970s, no building is allowed to be taller than a coconut tree. All hotels incorporate Hindu symbols in their decoration, and keep at least one shrine for offerings to the gods.

Until recently, however, most hotels in Bali were unaware of the need to have a social and environmental policy – especially in small hotels, which tend to make little use of natural resources and employ family as staff. In recent years, with more organisations campaigning about green issues, a number of hotels have taken measures to reduce their ecological footprint, and share more benefits with the local people. Encourage them by staying with them (look for our one-heart or two-heart rated hotels). They are also the ones which usually offer the best service in great surroundings, with plenty of occasions to enjoy the local nature and culture.

© Dedok

Eco-friendly hotels

The first step starts with building and landscaping: eco-friendly hotels blend their buildings into the environment, and maximise the use of local, renewable materials such as coconut timber or recycled wood. More and more hotels and restaurants are reducing their use of plastic such as packaging and bottles. It is also becoming more common for hotels to sort their garbage for recycling. A few have even started to build smart wastewater gardens which filter grey water.

More and more hotels are also taking steps to reduce their use of electricity by using low-consumption bulbs, using natural ventilation instead of air-conditioning, or using solar heating. Water-saving measures include using wastewater for gardening, designing shady gardens with low evaporation, and asking guests to reuse their towels instead of washing them everyday. These little steps reduce the negative impact of tourism on the environment – but even more important are the steps taken to educate travellers, staff, and local communities (especially schoolkids) about ecological issues.

As far as *social impact* is concerned, most hotels in Bali are now committed to employing local people, which often means providing them with additional training. Concerned hotels make contributions to local communities and social organisations – for example, by funding schools or health services – and offer their guests a chance to participate through donations. More importantly, they try to provide economic opportunities to local people, by chartering fishermen's boats, sponsoring local dance groups, or selling locally-made crafts.

Eco-Simplicity

Do you really need air-conditioning on a holiday? For a real exotic trip, learn to enjoy simple settings close to Bali's natural and traditional environment. Choose hotels that minimise their use of natural resources. Fall in love with fans, mosquito nets, and the night breeze rather than power-hungry air conditioning that shuts you off from the outside. You'll soon learn to appreciate the cool air and the frog serenades that are a hallmark of Balinese nights.

© Dedok

Hotel Categories

At the *lower end* of the price-range (**category 1, below Rp 150,000**), travellers will find a large choice of **losmens** (guesthouses), homestays, or inexpensive hotels – especially in popular backpacker areas like Kuta, Ubud, Candidasa, Lovina, Amed, Lake Batur, and Nusa

Lembongan. From Rp40,000 and up (breakfast not included), you can get plain rooms with a small fan and a simple bathroom with cold water, in varying states of freshness and cleanliness. For a little bit more – between Rp80,000 and 150,000 – you can get surprisingly good accommodations, with pleasant rooms in nice settings, sometimes with a small pool, hot water bathrooms and air-conditioning. However, such inexpensive, good value accommodations are more difficult to find outside the main tourist areas. Most small hotels expect their guests to pay cash.

In the **middle range**, Bali offers an impressive choice of charming small hotels and homestays. **From Rp150,000 to Rp 300,000 (category 2)**, or **Rp300,000 to Rp 600,000 (category 3)**, you can get a comfortable, nicely decorated room with a hot water bathroom. Those in category 3 often have a small pool and air-conditioning. Most of these hotels have vehicles and tour guides ready to pick you at the airport and take you around the island. They usually have restaurants (count Rp30-60,000 per meal), and good breakfasts included in the room fare. Most accept credit cards, especially in category 3, but it is better to inquire first. It is easier to get a discounted price by paying cash.

In the **upper range**, travellers in search of luxury will find a good choice of **boutique hotels** in beautiful settings. Prices vary tremendously, **between $60 to 120 a night (category 4)** or **above $120 (category 5)**. In these price ranges you can expect air-conditioning (except in cool mountain areas), hot water bathrooms, a good restaurant (Rp50-100,000 per meal), a pool, and excellent service.

As you travel around Bali, you'll soon find out that it is not just the price but the quality of the setting and service that makes a difference. Good value places fill up quickly around July-August, Easter, and Christmas. There are always enough fall-back plans so you don't need to book all your trip in advance. However, once you have decided on a location, it is worth calling to make a booking.

House Rentals

If you intend to stay more than two weeks in Bali, especially as a family, and don't want to travel around too much, it can be worthwhile to rent a house. Prices may vary from US$50 to 500 per night for a two to three bedroom house, depending on the location, facilities, season, and length of stay. There are many websites offering house rentals in Bali, most of them quite expensive. Another alternative is to book a hotel first, and find a house after you're in Bali, by looking at advertisments (expect that this will be difficult in peak season).

Most houses come fully equipped with linens, towels, kitchen implements, and are staffed with at least a maid and a security guard. It is worth inquiring about the exact equipment you're getting: are there a swimming-pool, air-conditioning, fans, and mosquito nets? A worn-out kitchen stove or a modern kitchen? Ask also about the exact coverage of the price – does it include electricity, laundry, and maid service? Will the maid cook for you? Is there babysitting available? All these little details make a great difference in the price.

Ad Boards
If you stay long in Bali or come regularly, it is worth knowing where to look for a house, a great nanny, an Indonesian language class, or a shipping service. In most cafés you'll find the Bali Advertiser, a free publication loaded with small ads for expatriates and visitors. In Seminyak, look for the ad boards of Krakatoa, opposite the start of Jl. Dyana Pura, Café Moka, on the main road (Jl. Seminyak), or Rudy's Wartel at the start of Jl. Double-Six. In Ubud, look in Bali Buddha, Casa Luna, or Café Pujer.

Where to Eat

As noted by famous Chef Heinz van Holzen in his great book, *The Food of Bali*: "most tourists leave Bali without having eaten one single, genuine Balinese meal."

Most restaurants in tourist areas serve a universal mix of plain Western food and Indonesian dishes, most of them originating from outside Bali. Only a few of them make the effort to serve authentic Balinese recipes. They are usually the ones that propose fun cooking classes, a great way to experience the joy of local markets and taste the infinite variety of spices – shallots, garlic, turmeric, galingale, lemongrass, coriander, kaffir lime, nutmeg, cinnamon, cardamom, or tamarind – that are the hallmarks of Balinese cuisine.

© Bali-Photo

Traditional Balinese kitchen

Daily Food, Festive Food

Apart from ritual festivities, eating in Bali is a casual affair, not a social occasion. Women get up early to go to the market, and prepare stacks of rice, vegetables and soy cakes, which stay in the kitchen for everyone to help themselves when they desire. People eat quickly with their hands, often alone, squatting in a corner or sitting on the edge of the family pavilion (bale). This is why visitors are seldom invited to eat with a Balinese family, unless there is a ceremony. Then, lavish assortments of food are prepared by men and women, partly as offerings for the gods, partly to be shared by the community. And everyday, deities receive their food offerings before the family is allowed to eat.

© Bali-Photo

Nasi campur *side dishes*

Warung Food

Everywhere along the streets you'll find the ubiquitous *warung*, a generic name for local restaurants or food stalls — sometimes nothing more than a trestle table with a wooden bench, protected by a plastic canopy. They usually serve popular Balinese and Indonesian dishes, some of them of Chinese or Indian origin. This may include a variety of soups (*sop* and *soto*), the ubiquitous *nasi goreng* (fried rice), *mie goreng* (fried noodles), *cap cai* (stir-fried vegetables, often mixed with seafood, fish balls, or chicken), *ayam goreng*, *panggang* or *bakar* (fried, roasted, or grilled chicken). Don't miss the ever-popular satay (small kebabs served with a rich peanut sauce), and particularly the Balinese version, the delicate and spicy *sate lilit* (brochettes of minced fish and seafood). Here and there, you may find small outlets serving the most popular Balinese delicacy, roasted pork or *babi guling* served with *lawar*, a Balinese dish mixing finely chopped vegetables, meat, and spices. Everywhere in tourist spots you'll find a great choice of fresh grilled fish and seafood.

To get a taste of a variety of local specialities, ask for *nasi campur* (mixed rice): a different experience each time, it usually combines a bowl of rice with shredded chicken, vegetables, fried peanuts, soybean cake, and a rich seasoning of spices and hot chilli sauce. Everywhere on the roads you'll find **kaki lima** (literally: five feet), a mini-kitchen on wheels pushed by a vendor and selling one variety of food, such as satay, *bakso* (meatball or fish ball soup), or *martabak* (pancakes).

Many travellers are wary of eating in warungs, and blame poor hygiene for any stomachache. In truth, the risk of being poisoned in local warungs is minimal. Having no or very little food storage capacity, the cooks get their ingredients fresh from the market everyday. With a regular clientele of locals, they cannot take the risk of serving stale dishes. Hence the best way to choose a warung is simply to look at the number of clients, especially of the non-tourist type.

However, Western stomachs do require a bit of adjustment time to the spicy, often fried dishes served in warungs. Most travellers suffer from the aptly-named *turista* during the first few days. To prevent it, eat a lot of white rice and steamed vegetables, and ask for your food to be served *tidak pedas* (not spicy). If you are hit by *turista*, drink enough fluids to keep hydrated.

Effigies of Dewi Sri on a lamak *(hanging offerings made of palm leaves)*

Vegetarian in Bali *(by Diana Darling)*

In Bali, eating vegetarian is hardly new: meat was considered a luxury long before it became bad for you. In the days before the tourism boom, people ate meat only on ceremonial occasions when animals were sacrificed. Poor people were forced to look to other sources of protein, such as eggs, nuts, legumes, and the processed soybean products from Java, *tempe* – a tasty cake made of fermented beans – and *tahu* (the local tofu). Hence Balinese have developed a vegetarian cuisine of great variety and savour.

Popular with visitors, *gado-gado* is a plate of steamed vegetables (usually pale in colour, such as bean sprouts or cabbage) served with slices of steamed rice cake (*lontong*), and covered with a tasty peanut sauce. It is normally augmented by *sambal* (a hot chilli paste sometimes containing shrimp paste), as well as boiled eggs or *tahu*. When this peanut sauce is enhanced with *kencur* (galingale root), chillies, and savoury leaves, it becomes the *pecel* sauce for green vegetables in *nasi pecel*.

Lightly steamed vegetables can also be mixed with freshly grated coconut and spices in *urab*. The Indonesian version of crudités is *sayur lalapan* – big wedges of raw cabbage, cucumber, and other fresh vegetables such as tiny round eggplant, served with a hot chilli and tomato *sambal*. If you have a chance, try purely exotic vegetables like *pakis* (fern tips) or *nangka* (young jackfruit, usually cooked in a rich coconut milk and spice sauce). For a refreshing snack, taste the sweet-and-sour *rujak*, a plate of sliced fruits with a thick and pungent sauce.

The Rice Goddess

Rice is the staple food of Bali. Balinese consider that they have not eaten if they don't get a plate of rice. Dewi Sri, the Rice Goddess, is perhaps the most revered deity in the island, personifying the very forces of life. You'll see her symbol, a hour-glass figure usually made of coconut leaves or rice stalks, around fields, and hanging from the beautiful penjor (richly decorated bamboo poles) lining Balinese roads during ceremonies.

What to Do at Sea

All year long, monsoon winds push waters from the deep Indian Ocean onto the southern and western shores of Bali. Reaching the coast, these masses of water turn into waves as they bounce onto the island's drop-off and reefs. The nascent waves are further swollen by the gentle trade winds blowing from the land, which prevent them from breaking too quickly. The result are endless barrels, pounding from the sea in a machine-like rhythm that has struck awe in generations of surfers.

The monsoon winds blow from the southeast during the dry season (May-Oct) and from the southwest in the wet season (Nov-Mar). Combined with land-borne winds, they yield strong, shifting currents, especially during intermediate seasons. Currents and waves make swimming perilous on most of the southwestern coast of Bali. Swimmers looking for quiet spots, especially with children, will prefer the northern and eastern coasts.

Water Sports

Surrounded by coral, reefs, and waves, Bali offers limited opportunities for water sports other than diving and surfing. However, you can find a choice of *windsurfing*, *canoeing*, and *parasailing* in Sanur, close to the harbour of Tanjung Benoa in south Bali, and in Lovina (north Bali).

Dolphin-watching tours are on offer in the south of Bali or around Lovina in the north. Unfortunately, they often turn into dolphin chases. Before embarking on such a trip, ask if the operators follow internationally-accepted guidelines to respect dolphins and whales (read more in the Lovina section, north Bali).

When staying on the quiet coasts of east and north Bali, hop on a local fisherman's boat for a sunrise *fishing trip* (usually around Rp50,000). You can thus experience the joys of fishing without adding to the existing destruction of marine life – a better idea than sponsoring one of the fishing tours organised for tourists.

No Plastic

If you ask for drinking water in a restaurant, chances are you'll get bottled water, or a glass of boiled tap water. Ice is also normally made with boiled water. It is better to avoid buying water in plastic bottles, which end up lining the beach. Ask for water in glass bottles, or carry your own water bottle and ask if you can refill it. Most hotels and restaurants have a mineral water dispenser for their staff and clients, and will be glad to let you use it (offer to pay). Instead of imported cola, enjoy the exquisite fresh fruit juices found in every single warung.

© Iskandar

Surfers on Geger Beach

Bali Underwater

A paradise for snorkellers and scuba divers, Bali is lined with splendid coral reefs sheltering some of the earth's most diverse marine life – struggling to survive pollution, careless tourism, destructive fishing, and global warming (read more in the north Bali chapter).

The east coast of Bali has some of the best dive sites around. Besides the famous shipwreck of **Tulamben**, great coral reefs dot the shores of **Amed**, **Padangbai**, and **Tejakula**. For skilled divers, the islands of **Nusa Penida** and **Lembongan** offer great sites, often with strong currents and many pelagic species, including the mythical mola-mola. On the northwest coast of Bali, **Pemuteran** and the nearby **Menjangan Island** have quiet waters and great coral.

Snorkelling equipment is available for rent in most hotels (around Rp20,000 per two-hour session). If you want to explore deeper, even with your own equipment, it is safer to go with a local dive shop which knows the sites and currents. The typical cost for one dive, including equipment rental, is usually around US$30, depending on the distance, duration, and total number of dives.

Most of Bali's famed dive sites can be can accessed on a daylong tour from any tourist spot, including Kuta or Sanur. However, each of these locations also has excellent hotels and dive shops. By staying at the spot, you'll get into the water before the swarms of day-trippers, and will have more time to discover lesser-known, less crowded reefs. And by spending your money locally, you'll give incentive to the local communities to preserving the coral reefs.

Sailing Trips

Most hotels on the coast can arrange sailing trips along the shores of Bali. Several companies arrange tours to the nearby islands of Nusa Lembongan and Penida. A day trip to the islands with lunch and a number of activities costs around US$85-100 per person.

© D & W Postlethwaite

Purple tube anemone in Gilimanuk Bay

Tell me whom you Dive with...

Not all the dive shops offer the same level of service, safety, and concern for marine life. The best ones, indicated by our 🩶 and 🩶 🩶 icons are struggling to defend Bali's marine life. They take care of preserving the coral during dives, clean the beaches, and support reef rehabilitation projects or the installation of mooring buoys. The success of such projects usually depends on their capacity to enlist the support of the local population. This is always a challenge in a country where poor communities have more pressing needs than environmental care – even if they need the marine life to survive as fishermen or hotel workers.

T 0361-720 331
F 0361-720 334
www.balihaicruise.com
> Go to Benoa Harbour
and turn left at the first
T-junction. Bali Hai is on
the left side of the street.

T 0361-725 864
F 0361-725 866
www.bali-sensations.com

T 0361-723 629
F 0361-722 077
www.wakaadventure.com

♥ Ombak Putih
T 0361-766 269
F 0361-766 546
www.indonesiacruises.com
> In Kuta, Simpang Siur.

♥ Queen of the Sea
T 0361-742 56 04
www.queenofthesea.info

♥ Sea Trek
T 0361-283 192
F 0361-285 440
ww.anasia-cruise.com
> In Sanur, Jl. Danau
Tamblingan.

Bali Hai offers a wide range of marine-based activities, including sailing aboard its luxurious catamaran and water activities for children. Other choices include water sliding and snorkelling from their pontoon, which has been erected without destroying coral reefs. Bali Hai keeps a few comfortable huts in their resort for those who want to explore the island at will.

Another alternative is to sail to Nusa Lembongan with Sail Sensation, a catamaran owned by the Lembongan resort. The trip includes cycling around the island, exploring the mangrove on a traditional boat, and touring seaweed farms. The beautiful, eco-friendly Waka Nusa resort also offers day trips to Nusa Lembongan on the 23m Waka Louka catamaran.

Live-Aboard Cruises

The islands east of Bali offer an incredible diversity of landscapes and traditions and a stunningly rich marine life. Travelling by boat gives you the opportunity to reach places off the beaten track; from the Jurassic dragons and coral reefs of Komodo to traditional cultures and historical heritage of the Lesser Sunda islands.

Several companies offer discovery trips to the eastern islands, from a few days to two weeks or more, aboard luxury boats. The boats are derived from traditional Bugis schooners, called *phinisi*, and equipped with top-notch navigation equipment and luxury facilities, such as individual air-conditioned cabins, showers, and modern kitchens. Compressors and other dive equipment are also available on board.

All the companies listed in the side column make efforts to preserve the marine environment, using mooring whenever possible, and bring their waste back to Bali for proper disposal. They also provide benefits to local communities by encouraging guests to purchase goods from local people, using local tour guides, and funding schooling or other community programmes.

Surfing: A Love Story with Waves

With great waves and a relaxed, inexpensive beach life, Bali is a surfer's dream come true. It is also a good entry point to explore other surfing paradises in Indonesia, whether on the southern coast of Java, on the western coast of Sumatra or in the Lesser Sunda islands (Nusa Tenggara). The best surfing season in Bali is May to October. The only exception is Sanur, which faces the east and can be surfed between November and April.

Beginners will be happy to start in the **Kuta-Seminyak** area, where gentle swells break on safe sand. These beaches, however, are also crowded and polluted. Quieter waves suited for all surfers are found in **Medewi** on the west coast, or on **Playground** in the isle of Nusa Lembongan. Most surfers, however, come to Bali to ride the world class dream barrels found on the **Bukit Peninsula**, with a beautiful background of white sand beaches and limestone cliffs, crowned by the Uluwatu temple. Experienced surfers will have a go at **Uluwatu**, **Padang-Padang**, **Dreamland**, **Bingin** and the aptly-named **Impossibles**. Less-skilled ones can practice their skills in easier spots like **Geger** or **Blabangan**. All are dotted with spiky reefs that have claimed much surfer's flesh. Booties are a must. **Nusa Dua**, **Sanur**, and **Nusa Lembongan** also have strong, challenging waves for those ready to leave their surfing Mecca on the Bukit.

♥ ♥ *Eco-Surfers*

Surfing is a nature-friendly sport, relying only on the energy of the waves and man – or, more and more, woman. Most aficionados are happy with bamboo huts and warung food, providing income to local people, and consuming few natural resources. Concerned with Bali's degraded air and waters, several surf shops have gathered to sponsor GUS, a dynamic nonprofit organisation. Since its creation, GUS has built public toilets with recycled wastewater facilities on Uluwatu, conducted regular beach clean-ups and provided environmental education for youth. Contact:
T 0361-759 323
gusinbali@yahoo.com

What to Do Inland

While most tourists think of Bali as a beach destination, Balinese see the mountains as the abode of the gods and are wary of the ocean. As you'll leave the shores for the beautiful villages of inland Bali, you'll discover an enchanting realm where nature and culture mix endlessly.

© Dedok

Trekking and Hiking

Walking is the best way to enjoy rural Bali. Equip yourself with a good map (the Bali Street Atlas, edited by

Dealing with Dogs

As you walk around Bali, you'll have to deal with the many stray dogs on beaches and along village roads. Looked down upon by Balinese, they are chronically underfed and suffer from horrendous skin diseases. They display a lot of aggressiveness towards anyone stepping in their territory. Most of the dogs are more unpleasant than dangerous, and they bark much more than they bite. Most of them will run away if you pretend to pick up some small stones and throw them in their direction. If you feel threatened by a dog in a village, ask help from local passersby, who will happily chase the dogs away for you. If you feel pity for those wretched animals, contact the **Street Dog Foundation (Yayasan Yudisthira)** *T 0361-286 226 balidogs@ix.netcom.com www.yamp.com/balidogs*

Periplus, is the most complete to date) and start exploring the island on any of its many small roads. In each chapter, we have selected a few **trekking routes** leading to fascinating landmarks or beautiful landscapes. Most of them are on small asphalt roads, on which you'll encounter few vehicles apart from motorcycles. If you wish to get inside the rice fields and forests on non-asphalt tracks, you're going to need a local guide.

Many hotels or tour operators are proposing good **guided walks**, for example, rice field or mountain walks. Most of them are rather easy and can be completed by any traveller in reasonable physical condition, with no equipment other than a good pair of hiking sandals or sport shoes. **Hiking** on Bali's main mountains, such as Mt Agung (3142m), Mt Abang (2152m), Mt Lesong (1860m), and Mt Batukaru (2276m) is a bit more demanding. Make sure you wear comfortable hiking shoes or sport shoes before starting the ascent. In all cases, bring plenty of water, a good hat, and a light jacket for the chilly conditions at the summit. Don't attempt to climb these mountains without a good professional guide. Bring a flashlight if the ascent starts at night, as is usually the case on Mt Agung.

Rafting

There are quite a few good rivers for rafting in Bali, especially at the end of the rainy season (Nov-March) when the streams are full. The most well-known is the Ayung River, surrounded by stunning landscapes with monkeys cheering in the morning breeze. You'll find many companies advertising rafting tours, of uneven quality. The two operators below combine fun, sporty trips with care for the beautiful nature in which they operate.

Sobek is the oldest rafting operator in Bali, offering fun and safe trips on the Ayung and Telaga Waja rivers, passing natural stone carvings and waterfalls (US$50 for 1.5 hours, with lunch). Clear briefings are provided in English, French, German, or Chinese.

Sobek provides mineral water in banana-leaf glasses to avoid the use of plastic, and conducts regular river-cleaning programmes. Don't expect to stay dry during your rafting fun. You'll get totally soaked after engaging in a water fight with another team, or passing under one of the waterfalls. At the end of the trip, you can get off the rubber boat and swim to the ending point. Sobek also offers **jungle trekking** in the West Bali National Park, and **cycling tours** in Batukaru and the Batur area.

Bali Adventure Rafting is another well-established company offering fun trips on the Ayung River (US$66 for 1.5 hours, with lunch). The trips give you time to take pictures of pretty natural sights. Don't be surprised if you come across local people taking their daily bath in the river. Avoid staring at them or taking a photograph – after all, you're in their bathroom. Bali Adventure Rafting has trained its staff to respect the environment and participates in river-cleaning activities.

T 0361-287 059
F 0361-289 448
sales@sobek.co.id
www.sobekbali.com

T 0361-721 480
F 0361-721 481
www.baliadventuretours.com

Cultural Discoveries

Bali offers endless occasions to get acquainted with its vibrant culture. Colourful *religious ceremonies* will probably be held near your hotel during your stay, just ask the staff for such occasions. In most cases, they'll be glad to take you as guests. Ask them for the proper attire (normally a sarong, a sash, clean sandals, and a decent shirt) and know the code of behaviour. Many hotels also organise regular *dance or music shows*. Lovers of *painting* will be at home in the beautiful museums, galleries, and art shops of **Ubud**.

Temples

Large or small, simple or elaborately carved, temples are everywhere in Bali. According to I Gde Pitana (in *Bali: Living in two Worlds*, ed. by Urs Ramseyer), this maze of temples can be divided into four main categories.

Public temples are open to everyone. At the peak of the hierarchy is **Pura Besakih** on the slopes of Mt Agung, which is part of a group of nine directional temples:

Do It Yourself
If you wish to be more than a spectator, many hotels or galleries propose classes in which you can get initiated to one of the many arts of Bali, from painting to carving, dancing, playing gamelan, weaving, or even cooking. The best places for such discoveries are in Ubud, or in less well-known cultural and ecotourism centres such as Klungkung, Sidemen, or Munduk.

Besakih (northeast), Lempuyang (east), Goalawah (southeast), Andakasa (south), Uluwatu (southwest), Batukaru (west), Pucakmangu (northwest), Batur (north), and Pusering Jagat in the centre. Communities around the island have erected – and continue to erect – dozens of smaller public temples.

More private are the *pura warga* (ancestral temples). They belong to groups claiming the same ancestors, which are worshipped in these temples. The next category includes the village temples, and the last one groups occupational temples such as the *subak* (irrigation) temples, market temples, and sea temples for fishermen.

Temples and Nature

The architecture of Balinese temples reflects the connection of mankind to God, but also to nature, as reflected in the Tri Hita Karana philosophy. The Balinese temple is open to its environment, with three open courtyards in ascending levels of sanctity, replicating the tripartite structure of the cosmos. More than in the actual architecture, the genius of the temples' builders are found in exquisite carvings inspired by the Ramayana and Mahabharata epics, and sometimes from more modern events, like the sculptures from Dutch colonisation in the temples near Sangsit in north Bali.

Temples are often located on impressive hills, mountain flanks, seashores, or even caves, with a felt energy from their surroundings. In most cases, the structures and sculptures date from the 20th century, but have been appropriated from old sites of worship, usually animist, that may date centuries back. Hence old remains can often be seen in the form of rough stones, often oddly shaped, which attract particular veneration from local communities as the legacy of ancestral worship. Travellers who visit temples for the architecture may sometimes be disappointed. Those in search of great natural sites will always be rewarded, for each temple is the pretext for a fabulous excursion, where the journey is as important than the destination.

Temples made Easy
Travellers will often encounter mountain temples (pura bukit), sea temples (pura segara), lake temples (pura danau) temples for market deities (pura pasar), and seeds (pura melanting), and royal or state temples (pura penataran). Each village also harbours its own trilogy of temples. The pura puseh, *or temple of the origins, is located in the most uphill (kaja) end of the village, to honour the ancestors of the community. The* pura desa, *at the heart of the village, is its ritual and social centre. At the downhill or kelod end, the* pura dalem, *or death temple, guards the cemetery, and is often adorned with grotesque carvings, sometimes very graphic, illustrating the punishments awaiting sinners in the afterlife.*

Body and Soul

Meditation is an integral part of Hinduism, and Balinese mythology is full of stories of priests having attained enlightenment, or *moksa*, after spending time in prayer and contemplation at a sacred site – usually on top of a mountain or on some rocks beaten by the waves. Balinese are strong believers in occult psychic forces. In bad times, most villagers will ask advice from a priest or a *balian* – spiritual healer – rather than calling a doctor or a lawyer. In short, they believe that most problems in this world (*sekala*) reflect some imbalance in the netherworld (*niskala*), and can be redressed by appropriate rituals and behaviour. Balinese have also long been experts in health and well-being. Traditional treatments to heal and beautify, including massage, scrubs, lotions, and herbal medication (*jamu*) are part of daily life.

Massages: Beach, Salon, or Spa?

Hence it should be no surprise that New Age adepts feel at home in Bali. A growing number of hotels, spas, health centres, and yoga teachers cater to the crowd of travellers in need of care for their body and soul. But how is a first-time traveller to sort between this swarm of massages, *cakra* healing, and zen resorts?

The first rule is to look for simplicity. In most places on Bali, you can get a good, healthy massage for Rp50,000 per hour, whether on the beach or in the comfort of your hotel room – just ask the receptionist. Most family salons can pamper you like a king for a reasonable price, from manicure to foot or head massage. Your back may not be scrubbed better in an exclusive spa, but you'll get more ornate architecture, soft *gamelan* music and gaudy tropical flowers than in many temple ceremonies.

Yoga and meditation adepts will find a few classes in this book, especially in Ubud and Seminyak. Other reputable places offering such practices are the Gandhian Ashram in Candidasa, the Nirarta Centre in Sidemen, Gaia-Oasis in Tejakula, Zen in Seririt, and Prana Dewi in Batukaru.

The World of **Balian**
When it comes to **traditional healers** *(*balian*), no guidebook can help you. This is where travellers can start their own journey in the endless realm of Balinese spirituality. If you feel tempted, read as much as you can on Balinese religion and culture to understand where your gurus come from. Beware instant fixers who pretend to have a magic cure for an aching back or a lost soul. Remember that real traditional guides and healers don't ask for money upfront – they leave it up to you to make a donation.*
In all cases, take the time to know the people, follow the advice of local friends, and, in the end, listen to your intuition.

© Dedok

Shopping

Whether you're after cheap trinkets or silk sarongs, you will quickly fill your suitcases in Bali, especially in Kuta and Seminyak (for clothes and furniture) and in Ubud (for arts and crafts). As you travel around the island, don't hesitate to buy handicrafts locally, either from a manufacturer or in a market. You'll get cheaper prices and most of the money will stay with the locals.

Textiles often come from the Lesser Sunda islands. Furniture is made in Java, using timber from Java and Borneo, and finished in Bali. Most handicrafts are produced in family homes in Bali (read more in the Ubud section, p.150 and in the east Bali chapter, p. 189). To contribute to a good cause while buying great souvenirs, you'll find fair trade addresses in the Ubud section.

If you need to shop for food or any kind of modern-life item, there are well-stocked shopping centres in Denpasar (Tiara Dewata, Matahari, Ramayana), in Kuta (Bali Galleria, Kuta Galleria), in Seminyak (Bintang Supermarket), and in Sanur (Hardy's, Makro).

The End of Forests?

Furniture making comes at a cost for Indonesian forests. Suppliers are required to source their wood from legal sources, but false certificates abound as 75% of the timber is logged illegally. Even "legal" sources of wood may not be sustainable. Teak is sourced from over-exploited plantations in Java, where tree sizes are declining. Hardwood, such as merbau, balau, nyatoh, or bengkirai mostly comes from plundered rainforests. To err on the safe side, buy furniture from more renewable sources like coconut, fibre, or bamboo. The WWF, with support from the World Bank, is trying to establish sustainable wood supply chains. Read more at www.forestandtradeasia.org

More Tips for the Traveller

Opening hours

Government offices, airlines, and banks are normally open from 8am to 3pm on Monday to Friday. Most shops and travel agents are open at least from 9am to 5pm Monday to Saturday, and some also on Sunday. In most areas, you'll find either supermarkets or small shops (warung) selling a bit of everything from 8am to 8pm, 7 days a week. In urban areas, Circle K shops operate on a 24/7 basis, selling all things needed for various emergencies, from snack food to beer, aspirin, raincoats, and condoms.

Public Holidays

With five official religions, Indonesia is blessed with an impressive choice of public holidays. The most important nationwide is *Lebaran* (the end of the Muslim fasting month or Ramadan), during which most people take a one-week break and travel back home, congesting buses, airplanes, and trains. Bali fills up with local tourists, many of them ethnic Chinese, during Lebaran and Christmas.

Balinese, however, put more emphasis on the endless string of Hindu festivals. The most important are *Galungan* and *Kuningan*, celebrated over a 10-day period every 210 days (the length of the main Balinese calendar). Many shops are closed for a few days, but hotels keep normal hours. On the days before Galungan, the island fills up with red-coloured *penjor*, the arc-shaped coconut-leaf and bamboo decorations that signal a ceremony. Flapping banners wish everyone a "Happy Galungan and Kuningan." With thousands of temples dressed up in new yellow clothes, small rural roads become incredibly pretty.

Equally of importance is *Nyepi*, the Balinese New Year, which takes place near the first day of April. It is a day of silence, a time to pause and free one's mind from negative emotions. During these 24 hours, everyone on the island, be they Balinese, tourist, or military commander, is forbidden to go out in the street or to light lamps. Rather lax a few decades ago, these rules are now strictly enforced by village militia (*pecalang*). The only Hindu festival turned into a national holiday, Nyepi has become an opportunity to assert Balinese ethnic pride towards modern Indonesia. Even the airport is shuttered, except for emergency evacuations.

Spend Nyepi in a small hotel or in the countryside to enjoy the atmosphere – all of Bali falls dark, and the moonless sky, unclouded by the exhaust of cars and motorbikes, is patterned with the bright shine of stars. In sharp contrast, the day before Nyepi is marked by loud and bright purification rituals and popular parades, especially around the main streets of Kuta, Sanur, Ubud, and Denpasar.

New Year Monsters

If you face a 3m-high green-fanged version of Alien sprouting from its giant egg in the street of Kuta, next to a pink-and-purple dancing elephant and the giant statue of a terrorist with a bomb in hand, don't blame the mushroom in your omelette. These are harmless **ogoh-ogoh***, huge replicas of demons that will be paraded through the streets on the night before Nyepi. Crafted from wooden frames, paper, and paint, they symbolise the disruptive forces of the invisible world that must be brought into balance before the New Year. The parade is accompanied by the raucous noise of gongs, shouts, and firecrackers meant to scare the demons away. The night ends with the ogoh-ogoh set on fire.*

© The Natural Guide

Ogoh-ogoh

Electricity

You'll find a 220-240V AC power supply in most of Bali. Plugs follow the common two-pin European model. Power is unstable, but total blackouts are infrequent. Bring or buy a flashlight for going around in poorly-lit villages or small guesthouses. It can be difficult to find batteries in remote villages. Bring rechargeable batteries: they are cheaper and less polluting.

Photography and Video

You'll find good quality film in most places in Bali (except in remote areas, where it may have been stored for too long). Film can usually be developed and printed in less than an hour, but the quality is uneven. If you're after good pictures, especially slides, process the film back home, and avoid keeping it too long in extreme heat.

If you bring a digital camera, buy some extra memory cards before leaving home so you can store all those great shots. Bring your own tapes if you have a non-digital video camera. Make sure they are sealed and obviously unused, since there are import restrictions on filmed material in Indonesia.

Communications: Post, Telephone, Internet

There are *postal offices* (*kantor pos*) and postal agencies all around Bali. Expect your letters to take at least 5 to 15 days to arrive back home. Important documents should be sent by certified mail or, better, by international courier, such as FedEx (Jimbaran T 0361-701 727) or DHL (Legian T 0361-762 138; Sanur T 0361-283 823).

Most hotels will let you use their *phone* for local calls. For long-distance, it is cheaper to use a wartel – *warung telekomunikasi*. These small, private-run facilities offer good phone and sometimes even fax service. You can also use public phones, found in blue booths in public areas, but not always in good shape. Rather than using coins, buy a phone card first (*kartu telpon*), available at money changers, wartel, and many shops. In tourist

Photo-Ethics

Most Balinese love to be photographed, but only when they look their best – not when toiling in dirty rags. Old villagers may believe that you take a piece of their soul with their image. Younger ones will freeze, stone-faced, as soon as you try to take a "natural" snapshot. Here are a few tricks to take lively pictures while making friends:

Don't:

• *photograph people by surprise or without their consent;*

• *insist to take pictures of people in dirty clothes or embarrassing situations.*

Do:

• *get to know people before starting to photograph them;*

• *if you promise to send a picture, write the address correctly and keep your word.*

areas, you can also purchase a pre-paid phone card allowing you to call abroad at a discount price – a good idea since the normal rate of an international call is around Rp10,000 per minute. To dial a number abroad, add 008 or 001 in front of the country code.

Bali has a good *GSM* network, except in some rural areas. Bring your mobile phone, and check with your phone operator if your roaming options allow you to make and receive calls in Indonesia. You will then be able to make local calls at a moderate price, but anyone calling you from within Indonesia will have to dial your home number at a huge cost. A better option is to buy a pre-paid *SIM card* from one of the local GSM operators such as Telkomsel, ProXL, or Satelindo. Insert the chip in your cell phone, and you'll get a temporary, local mobile number. Call your GSM company at home before departure to check whether your cell phone can be used with other operators, and have it unlocked if necessary.

Young Indonesians love the *Internet*, and you'll find friendly, inexpensive Internet cafés and *warnet* (*warung Internet*) in most towns and tourist centres. A few ones around Kuta and Ubud have good broadband access. Otherwise, expect slow and erratic connections.

Travelling with Children in Bali

By Leslie Dwyer

Travelling with children can be work or fun, especially in a tropical country. Balinese are so helpful and love children so much that they will lessen the work and increase the fun. Learn a few tips, relax, and enjoy being on the island that reveres children.

Balinese Hindus believe that their ancestors have reincarnated in their offspring, and these newly-returned spirits are treated with affection and respect, and spoken to in the polite form of the Balinese language (except when they're teething at 2am). Small children sleep securely between their parents – also a good method of

Phone Numbers
Phone numbers in this book are indicated in the way you must dial them from within Indonesia. When we write T 0361-234 567, the first four digits (0361) are the area code. Bali area codes are: 0361 (south, Tabanan and Gianyar); 0362 (north); 0365 (west); and 0363 and 0366 (east). When you dial locally, drop the area code (dial 234 567 directly). If you dial from abroad, drop the initial 0 and add 62, the country code for Indonesia: (dial : + 62 361 234 567). Numbers starting with 08 are mobile phones (indicated by M), they change often and can be hard to reach. They stay the same wherever you call from Bali. To dial them from abroad, drop the initial 0 and add 62. Numbers change often in Indonesia; when in doubt, call 108 for directory assistance.

Learning the gamelan

Revered, not Spoiled
The anthropologist Margaret Mead observed in the 1930s that the ideal Balinese child is polos – obedient and polite, with an emphasis on harmony with society over individual expression. Her observations still ring true. Rather than spanking their children, Balinese encourage them to follow the crowd by frightening them with everything from demons to doctors, and gently correct their mistakes in etiquette and language. This combination of strategically-induced fear and utter security in their family's love produces the miraculous result of a well-behaved, tantrum-free child.

birth control. Babies are not supposed to touch the earth until they are six Balinese months old, at which time an *otonan* or "descent to the earth" ceremony is held. Balinese kids start their life cuddled in slings wrapped across their mothers' bodies, nursed on demand, their every cry addressed by a crowd of aunties and grandmas offering advice and distraction.

Hotel Facilities and Babysitting

Make sure you ask about children's facilities and extra costs before you book a hotel. Some go all out, offering children's activities, special menus, kiddie pools, roll-away beds, or cribs in the rooms. Other hotels, especially in steep mountainous areas, are ill-fitted for small children. The Balinese patience with children is a big help to parents of difficult kids. Few restaurants will bat an eye at being asked to concoct something special for the less-than-adventurous child. At most casual restaurants and hotels, a nice member of the staff may even walk around with your impatient baby while you finish your meal.

Most fancy hotels offer **babysitting services** and some even have kids' camps that offer day programmes where you can drop off your children. Even if you're not a guest, you can usually call them up and book a spot for your child. Almost any hotel can find a local young woman to babysit your kid – although she may not speak English. Make sure that she knows how to contact you in case of emergency, and that she understands what kind of childcare you expect. Unless she's worked for Westerners before, she might not know how to put on a diaper or how to sanitise feeding equipment. Be clear about foods that are not allowed and what's off-limits – the deep end of the pool or the street, for example. Hotels that offer babysitting services may have set rates (usually far more than the babysitter gets). If you're hiring someone on your own, around Rp100,000 per day would be a reasonable rate.

Things to Bring for your Kids

Most things you could imagine your children needing are available in modern supermarkets in Bali, including toys. Beware, however, the toy-like handicrafts sold in tourist shops, from colourful mobiles to wooden cats. They are decorative items, and may not be safe toys for young kids. One item that you need to bring with you is a basic medical kit (ask your family doctor), including a portable mosquito net. If you plan to do a lot of travelling around Bali, you may want to bring a light car seat. In most parts of Bali, where sidewalks are broken or nonexistent, a stroller is more of a bother than a blessing. If you bring one, choose a lightweight umbrella stroller that can be folded up.

The same *health and safety* precautions that apply to adults are valid for children. Remind your kids that tap water is not to be ingested; inexperienced toothbrushers should use bottled water. Use a lot of sunblock and make your kids wear sunglasses, hats, and loose cotton clothing to avoid heat rashes. Travel with your own toilet paper and hand wipes, and be prepared to explain the mysteries of the squat toilet.

Safe Travel

Bali is a very safe and tolerant place to travel for all kinds of travellers – including women, gay and lesbian people, and senior citizens. The main dangers come from road traffic (read more on p. 74). Even outdoor sports are usually quite benign in Bali. Beware strong waves and nasty currents when swimming on the south and west coasts. Only go diving, rafting, or sailing with reputable operators and inquire about their insurance.

Theft and aggression are remarkably low. Be extra cautious, however, in tourist areas, and around Batur (read p. 266). Stick to basic rules of safety: avoid flaunting cash or expensive equipment; don't carry too much cash; keep your money in separate, safe pockets; and store valuable items in hotel safes.

Kids' Fun

There's no shortage of fun and educational things to do with children in Bali. For active kids, there's swimming, surfing, windsurfing, white water rafting, mountain climbing, rice field trekking, bicycling, horseback riding, and plenty more.

For the artistically inclined, there are lively, colourful performances galore (stick to the abbreviated tourist versions if your kids have short attention spans). Many hotels offer dance or music activities for children. Favourites with kids are the **Pondok Pekak** library in Ubud, with its great range of children's activities, the **Jenggala Ceramics factory** in Jimbaran, where kids can learn pottery, and the enchanting **Bali Bird Park** to the south of Ubud.

© Dedok

© Dedok

Mosquitoes *transmit many of the diseases that threaten travellers. There is no malaria in the main resort areas of Bali; however, dengue fever is prevalent during the wet season. You should contact a doctor if you have persistent fever and symptoms of a viral illness. The best advice is to reduce the risk of being bitten. Wear light-colored clothing that covers most of the body (long sleeves and long pants), especially at dusk. Use an insect repellent; make sure that there is mosquito netting on all windows and a bed net sprayed with Permethrin. If there is no mosquito net, use insect spray or mosquito coils and note that air-conditioning also repels mosquitoes. Don't camp or stay near breeding grounds, such as stagnant water or drains.*

In most places, you'll find that many people will try to start a conversation, especially in remote areas where foreigners are few. Remain friendly and apply common sense rules when dealing with strangers. If you find yourself in conflict with a local, try to stay calm. Perhaps because Balinese are highly emotional, they value self-control and despise displays of anger. Being firm and poised will work wonders. Losing your temper can lead to a dangerous escalation of wrath, and going to the police may further complicate things. Try to ask for help from a Balinese friend or your hotel manager.

Health and Emergencies
By International SOS

The risks of living in and traveling through the tropics are often underestimated, but also at times exaggerated. As a traveller, you need to look at the risks, and then have a contingency plan for unexpected events during your stay.

Reducing Health Risks

The first rule is to *reduce risks*. Before leaving, obtain any necessary routine medical/dental care. Carry a copy of your health record and include an ample supply of prescription and routine medications in your carry-on luggage. Carry copies of the actual prescriptions.

All routine *vaccinations* should be current; these include tetanus, diphtheria, polio, measles-mumps-rubella, varicella, and influenza. Vaccinations recommended for Indonesia are hepatitis A, hepatitis B, Japanese encephalitis, rabies, and typhoid.

Tap *water* is unsafe throughout Indonesia. Stick to bottled or boiled water, or bottled beverages. Avoid ice in budget hotels/restaurants and remote parts. Food served in well-patronised restaurants is considered safe, but always choose fresh food that has been thoroughly cooked and is served hot. Prefer fruit that you wash and peel yourself. Always wash your hands before eating.

Diarrhea is the most common travel-related illness. Choosing safe food and water will reduce the risk of developing diarrhea. The main treatment of travellers' diarrhea is to replace lost fluids. Continuously sip clear fluids such as water, soft drinks, or weak tea. Avoid dairy drinks, alcohol, and coffee. Most cases of travellers' diarrhea will resolve in one or two days. Occasionally, intravenous rehydration is required, especially if there has been significant vomiting or diarrhea. Children are very susceptible to dehydration – seek medical advice or attention early. Obtain medical advice if there is no improvement after 24-36 hours or if you develop fever, bloody stools, or become light headed or dizzy.

*Remember that you can not be transferred out of a country unless you have valid travel documents. Do not leave your **passport** overnight in a place where it cannot be accessed in an emergency.*

Emergency Solutions & Plans

Having a contingency plan will help you get the best management in the event of injury or illness. Make sure you have a good comprehensive *travel insurance*. Check that your travel insurance covers hospitalisation and medical evacuation, which can be very expensive.

Carry a *first aid kit* in your luggage, with dressings and antiseptics as well as basic medications. Know how to administer basic first aid until appropriate help can be obtained.

Most local medical facilities have an *ambulance*; however, they may not be staffed with trained teams and the response time is often long. It is safer to call an *international medical assistance* facility. The approach to the provision of medical care as a service to both the population and the individual is quite different to what you may be used to. So it is important that you contact your insurance as soon as possible if you are sick or injured. In the event that your medical condition can not be treated in a safe way locally, it will be necessary that you be evacuated to a nearby centre of medical excellence or back to your home country. Your insurance carrier should arrange all of this for you.

This section has been prepared by the medical experts of **International SOS** *– The World's Largest Medical Assistance Company. Jl. Bypass Ngurah Rai 505 X, Kuta. T 0361-710 505 (24 hours) F 361-710 515 sos.bali@internationalsos.com www.internationalsos.com*

An AEA Company

Planning your Trip: The Best of Bali

If you plan on exploring Bali, a comprehensive map is needed. The Bali Street Atlas, easily found in book corners in tourist areas, is the most complete to date.

When planning your trip, look at the map for distances and count about one hour for 40km in your own vehicle, and twice that time in public transportation (to allow for multiples stops and waits). Move during the quieter, cooler hours of the morning, remembering that it rains more often in the afternoon and that public transportation becomes scarce in many areas after 2pm. Prefer the little side roads, always charming and less crowded.

Quiet Beach Resorts:

East	Amed (pebbles and black sand), p. 231
North	Pemuteran (grey sand), p. 342
East	Nusa Lembongan (white sand), p. 271
South	Sanur (grey sand, reclaimed), p. 133

Snorkelling and Diving:

East	Amed, p. 236; Tulamben (Liberty shipwreck), p. 243
East	Nusa Lembongan and Penida (pelagic species), p. 276
North	Pemuteran and Menjangan Island, p. 345
East	Padangbai and Candidasa, p. 217

Surfing:

South	The Bukit Peninsula (experienced surfers), p. 143
East	Nusa Lembongan (experienced), p. 276
South	Kuta – Seminyak (beginners), p. 126
West	Medewi (intermediate), p. 403

Stunning Ocean Views:

East	The Southwestern coast of Nusa Penida, p. 279
South	The Bukit Peninsula, p. 143; Uluwatu, p. 149
West	Lalanglinggah, p. 397
North	The Hinterland of Tejakula, p. 314

Mountain Hideouts:

East	Sidemen, p. 250
North	Munduk, p. 333
West	Batukaru – Jatiluwih, p. 374; Pupuan, p. 394

Awesome Rice Field Vistas:

Jatiluwih, p. 374; Pupuan, p. 394	*West*
Sidemen, p. 250; Amlapura – Tirtagangga, p. 228	*East*
Mayong and Bestala near Munduk, p. 331	*North*
The surroundings of Ubud, p. 175	*South*

Mountain Hiking:

Mt Agung, 3142m, p. 256; Mt Abang, 2152m, p. 270	*East*
Mt Batur, 1717m (beware unfriendly guides), p. 265	*East*
Mt Batukaru, 2276m, p. 379	*West*
Mt Lesong, 1860m, pp. 338 and 384	*North*

Walks and Treks, Bird Watching:

Munduk, p. 333; Mayong, p. 331	*North*
Amlapura – Tirtagangga, p. 228; Sidemen, p. 250	*East*
The West Bali National Park, p. 409	*West*
Batukaru – Jatiluwih, p. 374	*West*
Ubud and around, p. 175	*South*

History, Culture and Temples:

Klungkung, p. 207; Sidemen, p. 250;	*East*
Tirtagangga, p. 223; Bangli, p. 260	*East*
Ubud and the Petanu River Valley, pp. 153 and 184	*South*
Air Sanih – Tejakula, p. 310	*North*
Batukaru – Jatiluwih, p. 374; Jembrana, p. 401	*West*

Shopping and Going Out:

Ubud (arts and handicrafts, restaurants), p. 153	*South*
Kuta – Seminyak (clothes, handicrafts, furniture,	*South*
restaurants, nightlife), p. 127	*South*

New Age: Yoga, Meditation, Spas, Well-Being:

Ubud, p. 188; Seminyak, p. 128	*South*
Sidemen, p. 250	*East*
Batukaru, p. 376	*West*
Tejakula, p. 308; Seririt, p. 332	*North*

JAVA

Menjangan
Island

Pemuteran

West Bali
National Park

Bali Strait

Negara

Lovi

Mt Batukaru
2276m

Tabanan

DENPASAR

Giany

Ubud

Ngurah Rai
International Airport

Kuta

Bukit
Peninsula

Badung Stra

Indian Ocean

3D View of Bali 100-101

Bali Sea

Singaraja

Mt Batur
1717m

Mt Agung
3142 m

Bangli

Klungkung

Amed

Mt Seraya
1175m

Candidasa

Amlapura

Nusa
Lembongan

Lombok Strait

Nusa Penida

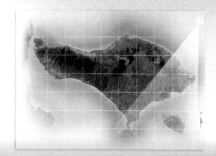

Indian Ocean

Nusa Penida

Nusa Lembonga

Mt Seraya
1238 m   Ujung

AMLAPURA

Lombok Strait

Pura
Lempuyang   **Abang**

Bangle   *Trek Pura
Lempuyang*

*Trek Bunutan -
Uyang Bangle*

Aas

Cape
Ibus   Leyan Lipah   Bunutan   Jemeluk   Amed

Bali Sea

Ngurah Rai
International Airport

DENPASAR

Nusa Dua

Mt Agung
3142 m

Badung Strait

Rendang

Candidasa

Tanah
Aron

Laga

Trek
Tanah Aron

Datah

Muntig

Culik

Butadawa
Kelod

Batuniti

Tutung

Tulamben

Lombok

Mt Agung
3142 m

Nusa Peni

Lake Batur

Mt Penggilingan
2153 m

Mt Pol
2063

Mt Catur
1865 m

Bedugul

Lake Bratan   *Lake Buyan*   *L*

Wanagiri   As
                        Gob

Sawan

*Trek Selat -
Asah Gobleg*

Jagaraga

Selat

SINGARAJA   Pemaron   Tukadmungga   Anturan   Kalibukbuk
                                                            Kalia:

Lovina

Bali Sea

N

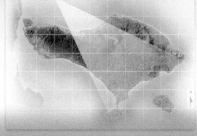

3D View of North Bali 104-105

Indian Ocean
Ngurah Rai
International Airport
DENPASAR
Badung Strait
Mt Batukaru
2276 m
Mt Lesong
1860 m
Tabanan
nblingan
Munduk
Pupuan
Banyuseri
Bestala
Pedawa
Mayong
Trek Bestala -
Banjar
Buddhist
temple
Hot Springs
Temukus
Banjar
Seririt

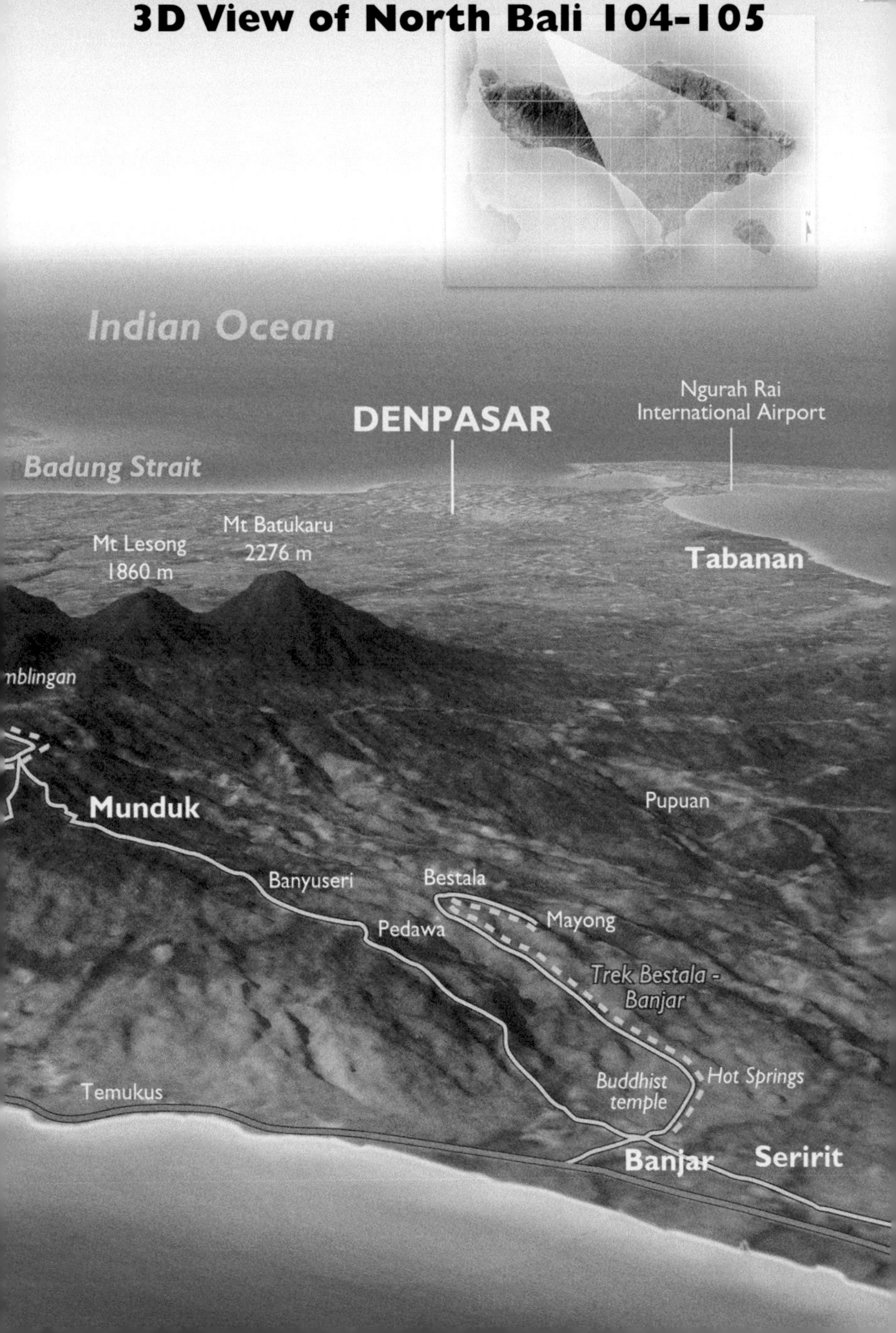

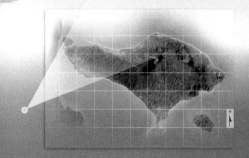

Bali Sea

Pemutera

Menjangan Island

Pejarakan

Mt Mel
340 r

Mt Prapat Agung
322 m

Labuhanlalang

Sumberkelampok

*Palasari
Reservoir*

**West Bali
National Park**

Blimbingsari

Palas

Gilimanuk

Cekik

Klatakan

Melaya

Candikesu

Bali Strait

3D View of West Bali 106-107

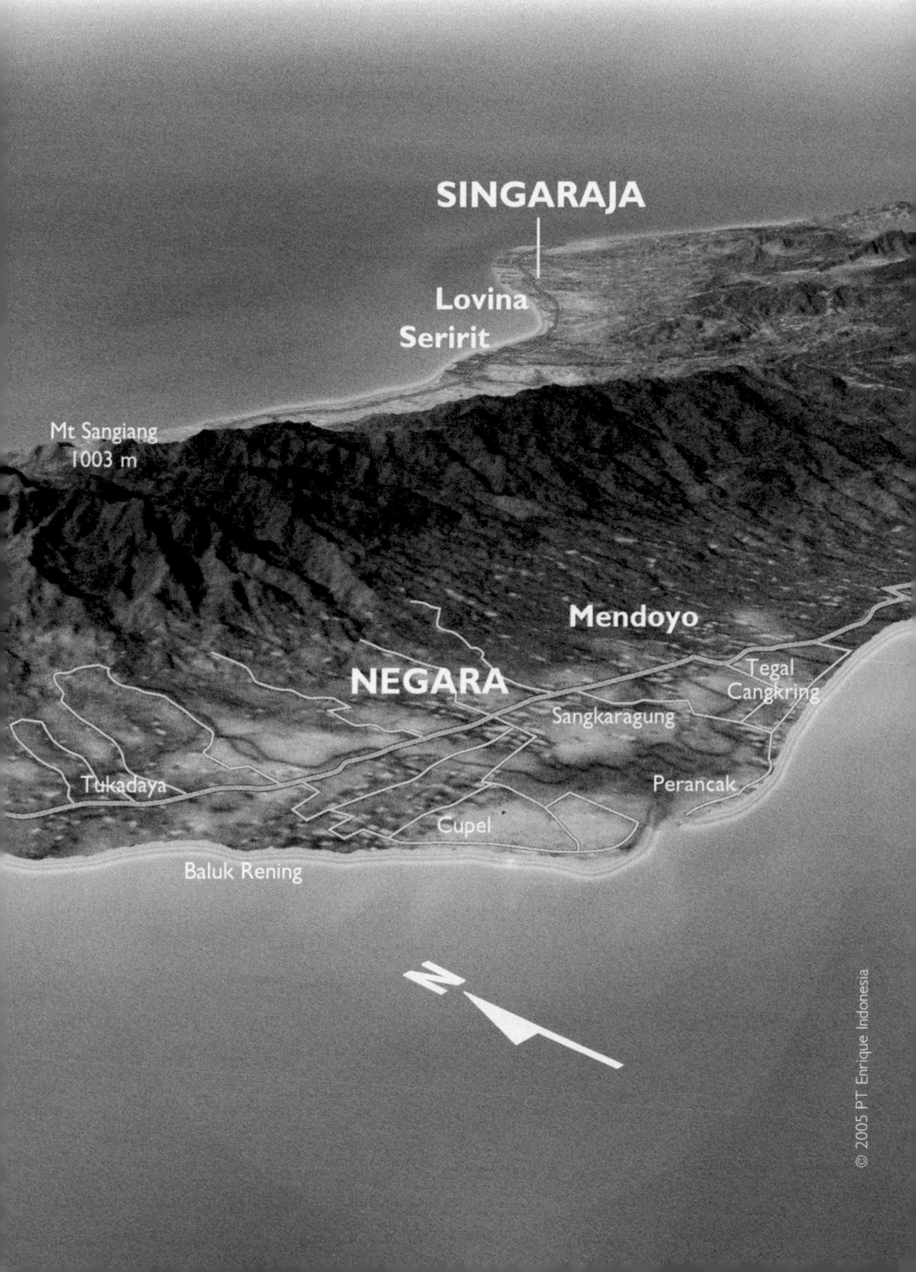
SINGARAJA
Lovina
Seririt
Mt Sangiang
1003 m
Mendoyo
NEGARA
Tegal
Cangkring
Sangkaragung
Tukadaya
Perancak
Cupel
Baluk Rening
N

© A.A.B. Dianatha K.

South Bali
in a **Nutshell**

Surfing the day away

A History of Tourism

Lured by the waves of Kuta and Uluwatu, the beach resorts of Sanur and Nusa Dua, or perhaps Seminyak's nightclubs and Ubud's boutiques, many visitors to Bali never make it past the southern districts of Gianyar and Badung. Most of them reach the island through the Ngurah Rai International Airport near Kuta.

Yet until World War II, travellers reached Bali through the northern harbour of Buleleng. After the end of the Dutch conquest in 1908, Westerners became fascinated with the flamboyant culture of south Bali, and the colonial government decided to promote tourism in this part of the island. From Buleleng, the first tourists were brought via limousine to Denpasar, where the Dutch opened the first official hotel in 1928 – the Bali Hotel, which still stands today.

Soon afterward, a wave of foreign artists discovered Bali. Shunning the bland Bali Hotel, they found their way to **Ubud**, in the heart of the culturally-rich kingdom of **Gianyar**. There, Prince Tjokorde Gede Agung Sukawati had engineered a movement of renewal in the fine arts, with the help of foreign painters Walter Spies and Rudolf Bonnet. A travellers' hostel opened in Campuhan in 1937, on the site of the present-day Hotel Tjamphuan. Cultural tourism was born.

Hard Facts

- *900 sq.km – 15 percent of Bali's area*
- *1,150,000 people – 37 percent of Bali's population*
- *Capitals: Denpasar (capital of the Province of Bali, officially 500,000 inhabitants) and Gianyar*
- *1250 people per sq.km.*
- *31,000 hotel rooms (85 percent of Bali's hotel capacity)*
- *28,000 hectares of rice fields – one-third of Bali's rice-growing area*

In the meantime, the first generation of beach-combers discovered with awe the endless waves of **Kuta Beach**. In 1936, an American couple built the Kuta Beach Hotel, a few bamboo and thatch bungalows between the palm grove and the beach. Surfing and backpacking tourism was born.

In the 1960s, after the turmoil of World War II and Indonesian independence, **Sanur Beach**, with its quiet waters protected by reefs, became the focus of tourism development. Soekarno, the flamboyant president of the newly independent republic, inspired by Soviet-style modernism, built the bland high-rise Bali Beach Hotel on the north end of Sanur. Five-star tourism was born. It later found its best expression in the tourism complex of **Nusa Dua** (read side column).

Tourist arrivals increased with the official inaugura-tion of the international airport in 1969. After 1985, a wave of airline deregulation and devaluation of the national currency made Indonesia a cheaper destination. Kuta extended to the north, merging with **Legian** and **Seminyak**, and turned into a carnival of branded surf wear shops and fake Rolex vendors, backpackers' home-stays and deluxe hotels, along with a mind-blowing quan-tity of restaurants, pubs, and nightclubs.

The most dedicated surfers left Kuta's crowded beach for the challenging waves of the arid **Bukit Peninsula** to the south. Meanwhile, tourists in search of culture and authenticity flocked to **Ubud**, turning this peaceful village into a buzzing hub of handicraft markets, painting galleries, organic restaurants, rice field home-stays, and boutique hotels.

The Proud Kingdoms

The Kingdom of Gianyar is home to some of Bali's most ancient and holiest sites, including the "Moon of Pejeng", a 2,000-year-old bronze drum, the Goa Gajah hermitage at Bedulu, and the royal tombs at Gunung Kawi. Its his-tory reflects the complex struggles between lineages that have shaped Bali's history over the centuries.

Protecting Bali from Tourists

In the 1970s, with the advice of the World Bank and a group of French experts, President Soeharto launched a grand scheme of planned tourism development for Bali. Efforts concentrated on a 425-hectare resort in **Nusa Dua**. *This enclave of five-star hotels was built with foreign capital. With its wide, paved lanes and manicured gardens, it does not appeal much to travellers in search of authenticity. Yet it sheltered the rest of Bali from the damages of mass tourism. It also provided well-planned infrastructure, avoiding the waste prob-lems that plague areas with unplanned tourism development like Kuta.*

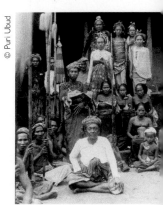

© Puri Ubud

The Ubud Royal Family

*From Mass Killing
to Mass Tourism*
*In 1906, the Dutch used
the pretext of a dispute
over a shipwreck to land on
the beach in Sanur.
The raja of Badung and his
court, women and children
included, dressed in their
best ceremonial clothing and
marched into the Dutch
gunfire. This was the most
striking of the puputan, or
die-rather-than-surrender
fights, that accompanied the
takeover of Bali by the colonial forces. To bury this
memory and the outcries it
drew in Europe, the Dutch
authorities launched a policy
of tourism-development-
cum-cultural-conservation,
hoping to turn Bali into a
showcase of "enlightened
colonialism".*

The village of Bedulu in Gianyar had been the site of a capital of Bali since before the 14th century. It seems that the Majapahit warriors who allegedly conquered Bali in 1343 established their first capital at Samprangan, near today's Gianyar. In the 18th century, two rival princely courts rose in the region – one in Gianyar and the other in Sukawati. The latter moved to Peliatan and Ubud, and has ever since contested Gianyar's suzerainty.

In the 19th century, Gianyar was caught in the battles which pitted the kingdoms of south Bali against each other, much to the advantage of the Dutch. In 1885, the king of Gianyar sought help from the Dutch army against his neighbours, and Gianyar became a Dutch regency in 1900. This status enabled his successors, Agung Ngurah Agung and his son Anak Agung, to become prominent figures of Balinese diplomacy.

Badung, for its part, was a relatively secondary kingdom until the 18th century. But as sea trade grew in importance, its position near the shore became an asset – besides Buleleng, Badung has the only safe harbour on the island, sheltered from the rough Indian Ocean by the Benoa Cape. In 1891, the Pemecutan clan from Badung defeated the great kingdom of Mengwi.

Meanwhile, the Dutch were tightening their grip on Bali. In the name of "ethical policies", they tried to end ancient Balinese practices such as slavery and widow-burning – while trying to control the profitable opium trade. Badung became one of their fiercest opponents, until it was defeated in the bloodiest of the *puputan* wars (read side column).

Beyond Tourism

More than half the population of south Bali is involved in tourism, while the rest, outside Denpasar, are chiefly farmers. Besides giving rise to hotels and restaurants, tourism has enabled the local arts to flourish, for better and for worse. Everywhere, especially around Ubud, villagers turn out all sorts of handicrafts for the export

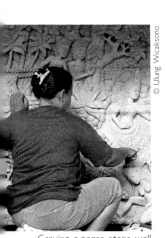

© Ulung Wicaksono

Carving a paras stone wall

market – silver jewellery, elaborate statues of Hindu gods, bright-coloured mobiles, penis-shaped wood carvings, bushy-haired figures serving as CD-holders – the list is endless.

This buoyant industry, mostly home-based, swallows a lot of manual labour. With so many people absorbed in tourism and trade, the famed rice fields of south Bali are often cultivated by families coming from economically-depressed areas of Bali, Java, and Lombok. They can be seen camping in makeshift huts along the fields during harvest season. Tourism also absorbs a lot of workers from outside. And many of the hands carving crafts around Ubud – often belonging to children – come from the poorest villages of Karangasem (read feature on p. 203).

The drop in tourist arrivals following the Kuta bombing in 2002, reinforced by the SARS epidemic and a general climate of insecurity, has deeply affected the island, especially in the south. Many Balinese think that this should be an occasion to work on the problems that plague the tourist areas – overpopulation, landscapes degraded by the anarchic construction of shopping malls, and growing water shortages. One of the most pressing issues is the lack of waste management, sending tons of plastic garbage onto the beaches during the rainy season.

But investing in environmental management when income has dropped proves difficult. Meanwhile, the government and the tourism industry try to replace missing Europeans with tourists from closer destinations in Asia – although they tend to stay for shorter periods and spend less money. If the tourism pie fails to grow back, many fear reprisals of Balinese against migrants in a general context of increasing ethnic conflicts in Indonesia. As they have done before, the Balinese will have to draw on the strength of their culture and their sense of pride and independence to find ways out of these challenges.

Beyond the Bomb
On the night of 12 October 2002, a bomb exploded in one of Kuta's most popular discotheques, killing more than 200 people, most of them foreigners. The bombing was perpetrated by terrorists from so-called "Islamist" groups in Java. Faithful to the best of Bali's spirit, community leaders were able to avoid violence between the various communities of Bali. Representatives of all religions preached peace and attended purification ceremonies side-by-side. Crowds of volunteers, many of them foreigners, provided help to the victims. NGOs are still collecting donations for the local victims' families. Contact: www.balirecoverygroup.org

At a ceremony after the 2002 bombing

*Getting There and
Around*

*Travellers landing at the
airport will find a taxi
counter offering fixed
fares to most destinations
in south Bali – about
Rp25,000 for Kuta,
50,000 for Canggu,
Jimbaran, or Sanur, and
100,000 for Ubud. This is
safer and cheaper than
following anyone proposing
"transport." Kuta-
Seminyak, Sanur, and
Ubud are the easiest
places to find car rentals,
motorbike rentals,
and taxis. Everywhere,
people passing by with
cars and motorbikes offer
you "transport" – make
sure you know the rates
and negotiate well. To get
to Ubud and around, you
can also use the many
bemos serving the interior
routes, or a more comfortable **Perama** bus servic-
ing tourist destinations
(T 0361-751 551).*

© Ulung Wicaksono

A masked dancer

Traveller in South Bali

Travelling in south Bali is easy – the only challenge is to
find peace and quiet. Everywhere, everything and everyone seem devoted to offering tourists an endless choice
of accommodations, "transport", food, and various legal
or illegal ways to have fun. Yet it is still possible to find
quiet places with a natural feeling in south Bali.

Most travellers spend their first night around *Kuta*
and *Seminyak*, close to the airport, with an infinite choice
of good accommodations at all prices. Travellers in search
of nature and peace will quickly leave the crowded beaches of Kuta and Seminyak – although they may like to
come back later for a bit of shopping or partying.

A few kilometres away, the older resort of *Sanur*
offers a peaceful alternative with a good choice of
accommodations along tree-lined streets, and a quiet
beach with easy swimming – well suited for children.

For small white sand beaches and mythical surf
waves, spend a bit of time around the *Bukit Peninsula*
to the south of Kuta, enjoying great hotels above stunning views of the cliffs and the blue ocean.

A stay in Bali would feel incomplete without a stop
in *Ubud*, the gateway to the "true Bali" – although Ubud
seems to have turned painting, dancing, and rice field
views into commodities just as Kuta did with sunsets and
magic mushrooms. Beyond the busy streets and art markets, you will still find family homestays and wonderful
little hotels hidden in the rice fields. This is also a great
place to get introduced to Balinese nature and culture
through rice field walks, herb walks, bird-watching tours,
and an endless array of dancing, painting, cooking, or
music classes – not to mention great museums, painting
galleries, and ubiquitous dance performances.

Around Ubud, touring the old kingdom of Gianyar,
travellers in search of culture and history will find great
archeological sites such as Tirta Empul or Gunung Kawi.
Everywhere in the countryside, in the surrounds of
Ubud, you will find a great choice of accomodations in
all price ranges.

Selling Lust and Love in Bali

By Degung Santikarma and Leslie Dwyer

Five years ago, 23-year-old Slamet hopped on a bus from East Java to Bali, carrying a canvas bag filled with his capital: some tight-fitting jeans and T-shirts, an intermediate-school diploma, and a well-thumbed English dictionary. Hours later, he emerged in the bright lights of Kuta Beach, where he changed his name. From then on, he would be known as Surya, a Sanskrit word for the sun.

The Surya of today is a far cry from the Slamet of the past. His light brown skin has been baked dark and his wiry body has filled out with muscles. His everyday language is no longer Javanese, but a confident – if still a bit confused – English. What he learned in school has been forgotten for what he's learned on the beach: everything from astrology and meditation to surfing the waves and cyberspace. He can say "I love you" in seven languages, and he has cultivated the manners of a gentleman, opening doors, lighting cigarettes, and pulling out chairs for his lady friends. He also gives a mean massage. Slamet/Surya is no longer a Javanese rice farmer's son, but a self-described Balinese gigolo.

The Making of Balinese Men

Bali is one of the few places where romance tourism thrives by offering female travellers the companionship of young men. Unlike elsewhere in Asia, where foreigners are lured by stereotypes of docile Eastern femininity, in Bali, it is male sexuality that is bought and sold.

This informal industry of sex/love/companionship for hire rests upon a thick layer of erotic images which have built up over decades of Western encounters with Bali. Stereotypes of the island stress the sensual – a tropical temple of worldly pleasures. Dark-skinned and different, the gigolos provide an exotic escape and a transgression from Western norms. They offer an invitation to cross lines of culture and colour, but also the reassurance that with their soft, spiritual ways, they won't lead women into any real trouble.

Ambiguous Images

Since the early 20th century, the Western images of Balinese males played into visitors' fears and fantasies. The Balinese, said to be gifted with a natural grace, were also rumoured to possess guna-guna – a magical method of capturing the hearts and wallets of prospective lovers. Armed with daggers and dancing in trance, they seemed to possess a primitive virility. Yet their flowing hair, long fingernails, elegantly-draped sarongs, and gentle manners sent an ambiguous message – at once dangerous and docile, fierce and feminine.

© Dedok

Trading Dreams

For many men who work the beaches and bars of Bali, the motivation for becoming a gigolo is simple – a ticket out of poverty and some fun along the way. Searching for the big score, they use a street-honed psychology to target older or wealthier women inclined toward "meaningful relationships" and spending money, rather than younger girls out for a good time. They ferret out women's insecurities and fill up the gaps in their confidence with flowery words and rapt attention. "I offer five star service," says Surya. "I'll be a tour guide, a friend, a lover. I'll give women more attention than they've ever had before. The key is to make women believe you really care."

These relationships involve economic transactions, but payments are not straightforward. One man might get a new motorbike, the other merely a cold bottle of beer and a hot shower in the morning. "Being a successful gigolo is not so much about how you look but about whether your brain is sharp," says 34-year-old Gede, who prowls the Legian strip. He explains that the most important thing is that what one receives – whether it's cash, a plane ticket to Australia, an expensive meal, or a set of clothes – be seen as a "gift" given freely by the "girlfriend." Surya agrees: "Women don't want to think they're paying for sex or for love. If I'm trying to get a woman to give me money, I'll say that my parents are sick and can't afford the doctor. The woman has to think she's giving it to you because she wants to."

For Western women, on the other hand, a relationship with a Balinese man offers a step out of the gender, class, and racial politics of their homelands. They can escape cultural ideals that confine women to a subordinate role. With a week's wages in their wallets, they can live in luxury, dispensing gifts to those who attract their favours. They can even escape the dreariness of democracy and become the consort of a priest or a prince. Or they can simply have a good time, doing things they might never have dreamed of, knowing that no one at home ever need find out.

Just Married

Mixed Balinese-Western couples find it hard to have relationships that go past the gigolo stereotypes. "You fall into this trap of trying to prove that your relationship is different, that it's not just about sex and money," says Cindy, *a 35-year-old Canadian woman who has been married to Ngurah, a 42-year-old Balinese, for five years. "You make sure that people know that you didn't meet on the beach and that your husband has his own money. But people make assumptions anyway."*

© Dedok

Many of their boyfriends also see their relationships with Western women as an escape from the class and caste politics of their own society. 56-year-old Made Karya of Ubud claims to have had relationships with 75 Western women for the experience. "I never thought about money. If I had, I could have had my own hotel by now," he says, laughing. Wayan, a 26-year-old who took a job at a Kuta hotel hoping to marry with a Western woman, explains why he prefers foreign girlfriends: "Balinese women just look at how much money you have. If you don't have a car, a mobile phone, a good job, or a good family, they'll leave you for someone who does. Western women don't care about all that. They believe in love." Even Surya agrees somewhat: "Of course, most of the appeal of Western women is that they're rich. But the other part is that they don't care about your background. They just care about how you treat them."

The Perils of Playing Casanova

Hidden behind the excitement and adventure, however, lurks heartbreak. Those who fall victim to the gigolo phenomenon are not only those women who find themselves ripped off by lies and lavish requests. The men also run the risk of getting hurt. "Rule number one is don't fall in love," says Surya. Stories are common of promises broken, with return visits cancelled and plane tickets that never arrive. Made Karya recounts how it was a broken heart that finally caused him to swear off Western women. Karya recounts the ancient Balinese tale of Rajapala to explain his feelings (read sidebar).

"The tourists are like angels," he says. "They fly down to Bali on their airplanes. There are thousands of them, and we watch them in their bikinis on the beach. We steal from them, maybe, but we want them to stay. And sometimes we fall in love. But they come from another world, and so they leave. And sometimes it hurts your heart." Karya seems to hover briefly on an edge between tears and laughter. But then he smiles. "That's the price you pay for experience."

© Dedok

The Tale of Rajapala

"A king named Rajapala once saw a group of angels bathing in the river. The gods had allowed them to come down from the heavens to see the earth's beauty. Rajapala stole the scarf of an angel, so when it was time for them to fly back to heaven, she was left behind. Rajapala begged her to stay. After a while, they fell in love. The gods allowed her to stay on earth, on the condition that when they called her back she had to go. Rajapala and the angel were married and they had a son. But when the child was five years old, the gods called the angel, and she had to leave her husband and child behind, flying to heaven on her beautiful wings."

Kuta – Seminyak

Selling kites on Kuta beach

Kuta Survival Kit

- Sleep in Kuta (best-value accommodations).
- Comb the beach in Legian or Seminyak (if you like people) or in Kerobokan and Canggu (if you don't).
- Shop in Kuta for surf wear, in Seminyak and Kerobokan for furniture, everywhere for handicrafts and clothes.
- Dine in Kerobokan, party in Seminyak.
- Get a beach massage, never miss a sunset.
- Ignore the pushy vendors or say "Tidak, terima kasih" ("No, thanks") with poise.
- Be firm and bargain hard, but remain nice with everyone.
- Beware of drugs unless you like jail.
- Stop minding the crowds, the shops, and the pollution. Relax and enjoy, or hit the road.

Kilometres of sand beaten by the surf, a mythic sunset, a "laissez-faire, laissez-aller" ambiance, good value accommodations, and a funky nightlife draw crowds to the strip of beach stretching from Kuta to Seminyak. True, many visitors are also repelled by the pushy vendors, the prostitution, and the crowded beaches. Hate it or love it, Kuta is just one face of Bali – not the most pristine, but one that sells. After a sharp drop following the terrorist attack on a nightclub in 2002, tourist numbers have been growing. Other issues, like increasing pollution, prevent some travellers from returning. Many Balinese are aware that they need to do some serious homework to revamp the image of their most famed beach.

In the meantime, Kuta and surrounds still have a lot to offer if you like a bit of relaxed beach life. Starting from the south, the first village near the airport is **Tuban**, which has some good accommodations, although a bit far from the action. North of Jalan Bakung Sari starts **Kuta** proper – a maze of lanes packed with shops, restaurants, and hotels. Many of them are excellent values, offering surprising peace in lush gardens.

North of Jl. Melasti, Kuta gives way to **Legian**, which is now as dense as Kuta. Further north, after Jl. Pura Bagus Taruna (more commonly known as Jl. Rum Jungle), Legian merges with **Seminyak** – a slightly more upmarket resort, with chic boutiques, a few good hotels, and the best nightlife around.

At Jl. Laksmana (known as Jl. Oberoi for its flagship hotel), Seminyak becomes **Kerobokan**. This is where the newest crowd of expatriates live, many of them French and Italian, and a whole range of good bars and restaurants have opened to satisfy this food-loving clientele. The quiet beaches along Jl.Oberoi and Petitenget have a few very good, upmarket hotels. Further north, the quieter villages of **Umalas** and **Canggu** offer a haven of peace among rice fields, a few minutes away from the fun of Kuta and Seminyak.

Where to Stay – Kuta Proper

This mythical village is confined within a square formed by the beach and Jl. Pantai Kuta (Kuta Beach Street) on the west, Jl. Melasti on the north, Jl. Tanjung Mekar on the east, and Jl. Bakung Sari on the south. The area is halved by Jl. Legian, which runs north-south and is fringed with shops. The best places to stay are between Jl. Legian and Jl. Pantai Kuta. Within walking distance of the beach and the pubs, you will find amazingly quiet and green hotels in the maze of lanes (or "gangs") that run around Poppies' Lane and Jl. Benesari. Most hotels can arrange transportation and tours, but beware that your guides will tend to take you to the places where they get the highest commissions when you shop or eat.

In the low price range, *Kedin's II* is good value. It has simple, clean rooms with tiny terraces, arranged around a small, well-tended garden and pool. It is located on Gang Sorga, which runs between Poppies' Lanes I and II.

Another good value, although less well-tended, is *Ayu Beach Inn*. Located on Poppies' Lane I, it has a pool and a choice of plain, terraced rooms, with or without A/C and hot water, and is surrounded by lush plants.

With a lush garden and a large pool, *Hotel Sorga* ("Paradise Hotel") is one of the best deals around. It has clean, nice rooms with simple and pleasant decorations in a Balinese-style terraced brick building along Gang Sorga. You can choose rooms with or without A/C and hot water at varying prices.

> *Many travellers spend their first night in Kuta. It is easily accessed by taxi from the airport or by bemo from Denpasar. When going around, beware that each street (Jalan or Jl.) has two names: the official name (seen on street signs and official plans) and the colloquial name. The latter usually derives from the first hotel, bar, or restaurant that was built on the road. Hence Jl. Laksmana is generally known as Jl. Oberoi, Jl. Abimanyu as Jl. Dyana Pura or Jl. Gado-Gado, Jl. Arjuna as Jl. Double Six, Jl. Werkudara as Jl. Puri Bagus Taruna or Jl. Rum Jungle, Jl. Yudistra as Jl. Padma, and Jl. Dewi Sartika as Jl. Kartika Plaza.*

❶ 15 Rm – Swp
T 0361-763 554

❶❷ 30 Rm – Htw
A/C Rst Swp
T 0361-752 091;
0361-753 314
F 0361-752 948
ayubeach@mail.com

❶❷ 45 Rm – Htw
A/C Rst Swp
T 0361-751 897
F 0361-752 417
sorga@idola.net.id

❷ 45 Rm – Htw
A/C Rst Swp
T 0361-765 804
T 0361-752 483
www.sujibglw.com

♥**❷ ❸**   31 Rm –
Htw A/C Rst Swp
T 0361-757 409
F 0361-758 414
unshotel@denpasar.
wasantara.net.id
www.unshotel.com

❹ 20 Rm
Htw A/C Rst Swp
T 0361-751 059
F 0361-752 364
www.poppiesbali.com
> On Poppies' Lane I

© Ulung Wicaksono

Learning to surf

Also on Gang Sorga, *Suji Bungalow* is set in an amazingly wide, open garden with a good-sized pool. All the rooms, set in terraced white buildings, are simple and clean, some with hot water and A/C. At the back of the garden, a few suites occupy the two storeys of pleasant *lumbung*-shaped bungalows. This is a perfect place for families, with a children's pool and playground.

Further north, on Jl. Benesari, a quiet street running between Jl. Legian and Jl. Pantai Kuta, *Un's Hotel* is an exceptionally good value. It features large rooms decorated with antiques, as well as bamboo furniture on the terraces and pleasant bathrooms. They are set in a building around a large pool in lush gardens enlivened by bird songs. Some rooms have A/C, and all have solar-heated hot water. The Balcony Restaurant serves Mediterranean food and fish.

In a different price range, *Poppies' Cottages*, an extension of the old Poppies, has the reputation of being "an institution in Kuta." It offers comfortable cottages, decorated with style, with good privacy and a well-tended garden. The hotel has a small, pleasantly-landscaped pool and a comfortable Internet office and library. The nearby Poppies' Restaurant is an old classic in Kuta, providing international food in a romantic garden atmosphere.

Where to Stay – Tuban (south of Kuta)

South of Jl. Bakung Sari is where the actual village of Tuban begins. It has a good surfing beach, although it tends to be more dirty than in Kuta. From Tuban Beach you can take boats to **Airport's**, a quieter beach appreciated by surfers. Two busy, parallel roads run north-south through Tuban: Jl. Tuban, which goes towards the airport, and Jl. Kartika Plaza (or Dewa Sartika), which runs behind a row of large, star-rated hotels set along the beach. Between those two streets, starting in front of the Musro discotheque, a quiet lane called **Gang Puspa Ayu** shelters a few inexpensive hotels with green gardens. This is a good alternative to Poppies' Lane, but is further away from the beach, restaurants, and shops.

In the low price range, *Bunut Gardens* has clean rooms with bamboo beds in a terraced building around a tiny, but lush, garden with tall trees.

❶ ❷ 13 Rm
T/F 0361-752 971

Dayu Beach Inn has slightly more comfortable rooms around a small pool in a green but rather unkempt garden. The rooms are clean but a bit bland, and the surroundings are a bit run-down, but it is good value if you want air-conditioning and a pool.

❶ 16 Rm – Htw A/C Swp
T/F 0361-752 263

Slightly more upmarket, *Hotel Pendawa* is an excellent value choice, one of the best in this price range around Kuta. It features nicely decorated rooms set around a vast garden filled with palm trees and frangipani, with a good-sized pool around which you can lounge at ease – a haven of peace a few minutes away from Kuta.

❷ ❸ 44 Rm – Htw A/C Swp Rst
T 0361-752 387
T/F 0361-757 777
pendawa_hotel@hotmail.com

Nearby, *Hotel Flamboyan* has nice, plain rooms with small terraces, some with A/C. Hidden in a dense garden, they offer good privacy. At the back of the garden, you can take a dip in a very small pool.

❷ ❸ 15 Rm – Htw A/C Swp
T 0361-752 610
F 0361-759 527
flambinn@indo.net.id

Where to Stay – Legian and Seminyak

A bit less dense than Kuta, this area has good accommodations on the roads than run between Jl. Seminyak (the main north-south axis) and the beach, most of them in the middle to high-end price range.

One of the oldest hotels around, *Three Brothers Bungalows*, on Jl. Padma, has maintained a relaxed atmosphere. Its pleasant cottages, with various levels of price and comfort, with or without A/C, are spread in a large and green garden around a good-sized pool. This is a good place for families.

❷ ❸ 50 Rm – Htw A/C Rst Swp
T 0361-751 566;
0361-757 224
F 0361-756 082

Ramah Village Bungalows is another good value, a surprising green oasis in the heart of Seminyak. It features very simple cottages with one or two bedrooms, with spacious individual terraces downstairs, and open rooms under *alang-alang* thatch roofs upstairs. Some are a bit run-down. The whole charm of this place is that it is set amidst exuberant vegetation, giving it a natural feeling. No restaurant, but breakfast can be ordered.

❶ ❷ 18 Rm – Htw Swp
T 0361-754 852
T 0361-730 793
www.balirama.com
> In a little gang off Jl. Seminyak near the Bintang supermarket.

❷ ❸ 23 Rm – Htw
A/C Swp
T 0361-733 525;
0361-733 525 / 526
F 0361-732 526
pondoksara@hotmail.com
www.pondosarah.com

❸ ❹ 41 Rm – Htw
A/C Rst Swp
T 0361-730 768;
0361-730 367;
0361-733 914 / 915
F 0361-730 469
baliagung@denpasar.
wasantara.net.id
www.bali-agung.com

❹ 16 Rm – Htw
A/C Rst Swp
T 0361-734 793
F 0361-736 111
amartabali@
dps.centrin.net.id
www.amartabali.com

♥♥ **❺** 75 Rm – Htw
A/C Rst Bch Swp
Gvw Shw Spa
T 0361-730 361
F 0361-730 791
reservation@
theoberoi-bali.com
www.oberoihotels.com

If you want to feel that you have your own house in Bali, *Pondok Sarah Bungalows* is an excellent value. It is often full, so book in advance. The stylish thatch-roofed villas have one to three bedrooms in tiny walled gardens, some with A/C, 500m from the beach at the end of Jl. Double Six. No restaurant and breakfast served, so you'll have to cook for yourself or walk to the many warungs on the main street.

Further north, at the end of Jl. Abimanyu, *Bali Agung Village* is probably the only resort with a rice view within walking distance of the trendy bars of Seminyak. The main building offers comfortable rooms with pleasant terraces, some overlooking the rice paddies to the back of the compound. A few elegant, individual thatch-roofed bungalows are also available. The hotel is at the beginning of Jl. Sarinande, 200m from the beach.

Also close to the beach, at the end of Jl. Abimanyu, is *Amarta Villas*. This small boutique resort offers stylish villas where you can hide in total privacy, enjoying individual teak terraces and semi-open bathrooms. The cottages are set in a small, green compound with a cute pool and a romantic atmosphere. This is a good place for families as you can rent the entire villa with two bedrooms.

Where to Stay – Kerobokan

A recent extension of Seminyak towards the north, Kerobokan has some good, middle-to-upmarket accommodations. Its long, grey-sand beaches are rather quiet, but the strong surf makes swimming perilous.

A Beachfront Garden at The Oberoi

A majestic banyan tree marks the entrance to this five-star boutique hotel on Jl. Laksmana. Everything around induces peace: the 15-hectare beach front garden, filled with colourful frangipani and elegant palms, the murmur of many lotus ponds, or the magnificent pool surrounded by teak decks. The rooms are set in discrete stone and thatched-roof cottages, some of them with their own walled garden and private pool, with elegant Balinese-style split gates. The hotel staff and management participate in the cleaning of the local beach in cooperation with local village authorities, keeping this long, large stretch of sand spotless.

Set in a lush two-hectare garden at the back of the road to Petitenget, *Vila Lumbung* offers stylish cottages and villas shaped like traditional rice ganaries or *lumbung*, and covered with wooden tiles or *alang-alang* grass. A large, landscaped pool is a perfect place to relax. The peacefulness of this green hideaway is wonderful, given that it is only a few minutes away from the beach and the night life of Seminyak.

Where to Stay – Canggu

Perfect to escape the crowds amidst lush rice fields and near quiet surf beaches, Canggu is a good place to stay if you have your own vehicle. If you don't, you can still reach most hotels in Canggu by taxi (about Rp 20,000 and 30 minutes from Kuta).

Live in a Museum at the Tugu

This boutique hotel houses luxury suites full of antiques and cultural artefacts, some dating from the 16th century. The lobby is covered with a high *alang-alang* roof supported by wooden pillars and shelters a century-old *gamelan* set. One of the dining rooms displays rare photos from the period of the *puputan* wars. Two pavilions are named after famous painters, Le Mayeur and Walter Spies. Both are adorned with furniture and artwork from the artists' original homes, and have their own pool and dining lobby. In the front, facing a lotus pond, an elegant Chinese-style dining room is decorated with silk in yellow and crimson. To experience the ambiance of an old Javanese kitchen, enjoy your Indonesian dinner at Waroeng Tugu, a dining room decorated with bricks, clay pottery and traditional earthenware. Ask for Balinese cooking, dancing, and music classes, or bicycle rental.

④ *32 Rm – Htw A/C Rst Swp*
T 0361-730 204
T 0361-731 106
www.hotellumbung.com
> *On Jl. Petitenget, 800m away from the beach.*

> *To access Canggu from Kuta, head north to Jl. Raya Kerobokan and follow it until the junction of Jl. Raya Canggu (follow the signs to Hotel Tugu).*

⑤ *26 Rm – Htw A/C Rst Swp Shw Cls Spa*
T 0361-731 701
F 0361-731 704
www.tuguhotels.com
> *From the Canggu-Kerobokan intersection, head west on Jl. Raya Canggu for 3.5km, following the hotel's signs until you reach the end of the road.*

south

❷ ❸ *20 Rm – Htw
A/C Rst Swp Bcy
T 0361-730 258
F 0361-731 663
bolare@indosat.net.id
> Follow the road to
Canggu for 2km, then turn
towards Berawah Beach
after the Canggu Clinic,
and turn left at the
next junction.*

❹ ❺ *10 Rm – Htw
A/C Swp Bch
T/F 0361-736 433
M 081 238 254 73
www.nirampevillage.com
> Follow the sign of
Hotel Tugu, then turn left
to Jl. Nelayan on the
intersection of Pantai
Batu Mejan-Batu Bolong.*

♥ *On the west side of
Jl. Legian, not far from
Matahari.
T 0361-751 003;
0361-761 113*

♥ *On the southern part
of Jl. Pantai Kuta.*

In the more affordable category, just a few steps from Berawah Beach, *Bolare* has comfortable red brick bungalows in tranquil surroundings. The standard rooms are simple, with bamboo furniture facing a lush palm grove. The suites, with pretty terra-cotta tiles and ceramic objects are hidden in a peaceful corner facing the beach. Strong currents make swimming dangerous, but the serene coast is perfect for a relaxing stroll or sunbathing. The pleasant pool is available for a few laps. Check for guided tours or go bike touring for Rp30,000 per day. Free transport is provided to Kuta or Denpasar.

Set in the middle of rice fields, facing the quiet Batu Bolong Beach, *Ni Rampe Village* offers comfy bungalows, each equipped with a pleasant swimming pool. The thatch-roofed bungalows are furnished with smart wooden furniture and spread in a well-tended garden. There is no restaurant, but the staff will gladly help you prepare your own meal in the small kitchen, unless you prefer to dine at nearby Eco Beach. Ask the friendly manager for tour programmes or to arrange your transportation. Reservations are required.

Where to Eat – Kuta Proper

Organic Bliss at Aromas Café

This vegetarian place extends to the back of Jl. Legian on a large, breezy terrace under a high *alang-alang* roof, surrounded by green lotus ponds. The friendly staff is ready to explain with pride how the vegetables are grown organically (or at least with very few chemicals) in the mountains. The menu offers a fantastic choice of juices, salads, sandwiches, and Indonesian or Balinese dishes (Rp 25-35,000 per dish).

The Old Kuta at Made's Warung

This tiny roadside restaurant can get a bit noisy and hot during daytime, but it is a perfect place for a relaxed dinner. It can be difficult to get a table and you have to share it with other people. Made's Warung opened 30 years ago when a young woman called Made realised her

family could no longer afford to send her to school. She opened a small bamboo-walled warung, which became popular with surfers. She owns two bustling restaurants, smartly decorated with teak furniture and old pictures of Bali. The menu has a great choice of international dishes as well as local specialties – the *nasi campur* (mixed rice) is an all-time favourite. Made's Warung participated actively in collecting donations after the Kuta bomb blast.

Mexican Festival at TJ's

One of the oldest places around, TJ's has a relaxed atmosphere in quiet, spacious grounds in the heart of Poppies' Lane I. The menu features Californian-Mexican dishes (Rp25-40,000 per dish). TJ's collects donations for a Kuta-based charity which funds schooling for poor children.

T 0361-751 093
> On Poppies' Lane I, a few metres after Poppies' Cottages.

Another favourite with travellers is the *Kopi Pot*, serving Indonesian dishes, salads, steaks, and mouth-watering desserts on a pleasant terrace above Jl. Legian.

Where to Eat – Seminyak

Made's Warung has opened a larger branch of its famous Kuta restaurant in Seminyak. The menu is the same as in Kuta, but the setting is more sophisticated, set around a large, quiet terrace where you can dine under frangipani trees, surrounded by a gallery of fine boutiques, including a well-stocked bookshop.

T 0361-732 130
> Along the main road (Jl. Seminyak).

JP's offers simple, yet original and tasty Western and local food in a friendly atmosphere. The main attraction is the excellent choice of live music, starting at around 9pm, featuring good local bands playing world music.

> At the beginning of Jl. Abimanyu (or Jl. Dyana Pura).

Just opposite JP's, *Zula* is a great little outlet serving vegetarian, organic,and health food either to take away or to eat there on small tables.For quality, authentic Indonesian food at reasonable prices, stop by at any time at the small and friendly *Warung Baku Dupa*. This relaxed, unpretentious place is open 24 hours and is perfect to quiet a sudden hunger pang at the end of a night of partying.

On Jl. Abimanyu.

> On Jl. Abimanyu (or Jl. Dyana Pura), just after the famous Santa Fe bar.

The beachfront at the end of Jl. Arjuna (Jl. Double-Six) is lined up with laid-back cafés offering the standard choice of salads, sandwiches, plain Western dishes, and local food. *Tekor Bali* is an all-time favourite, featuring a varied menu on a pleasant terrace.

Where to Eat – Kerobokan

Fine Dining at Kafé Warisan

T 0361-731 175;
0361-732 762
www.kafewarisan.com
> On Jl. Raya Kerobokan. The Warisan sponsors the cleaning of the beach in Kerobokan.

During your stay in Bali, make sure you treat yourself at this elegant restaurant, serving French and Mediterranean food in a terrace surrounded by frangipani trees and facing the rice fields – an exceptional fine dining experience in a dim-light setting, perfect for a romantic outing (main courses Rp50-100,000).

A Garden Night at Loloan

On Jl. Kayu Jati, off Jl. Petitenget (opposite the Body Works). Owned by the leader of a local environmental organisation, Loloan is committed to eco-friendly waste management.

Hidden along a quiet street, Loloan serves an innovative, refined cuisine based on Balinese and other Asian specialties, mixed with more exotic ingredients (most dishes Rp50-100,000). The vast setting, green garden, and quiet pool are perfect for a relaxing evening.

Where to Eat – Canggu

Facing the surfing spot in Canggu Beach, also known as **Eco Beach**, the cosy *Beach House* serves simple meals in an airy wooden *bale* with a thatch roof (about Rp30-60,000; add another Rp20-30,000 for a fresh seafood course). The location is especially enjoyable, and the terrace facing the beach is a classic for sundowners. Check the programme of live music.

A simpler option is to sit in one of warungs lining up along the beach, offering the standard *nasi campur*, noodles, and sandwiches.

What to Do – Kuta and Seminyak

A Time for Remembering

© Ulung Wicaksono

Praying at sunset

Bali, "the Morning of the World," lost its innocence on 12 October 2002. A group of terrorists detonated two bombs in front of the Sari Club – the only discotheque in Bali which was patronised exclusively by foreigners, most of them young Australians. The bomb killed more than 200 people and overwhelmed the capacity of the local hospitals. An exemplary mobilisation of donors and volunteers, many of them belonging to the expatriate community of Bali, helped to provide care for the victims – especially the Indonesian people who could not afford expensive treatment.

After the tragedy, many feared reprisals against the Muslim and Javanese migrants working in Bali (the crime was perpetrated by a Java-based group acting in the name of Islam). Yet the Balinese showed how a community with a strong sense of self and spirituality can respond to violence peacefully. Leaders of various faiths prayed side-by-side during purification ceremonies, sending messages of hope to their members.

As you pass along Jl. Legian, not far from the 14 Roses Hotel, take time to stop at the little memorial erected at the bomb site. Plain and dark, it has the list of the victims and a small altar where people deposit flowers, pictures, and cards. Anyone who loves Bali and peace will find it hard not to shed a tear.

Bali Recovery

Two web sites have been set up after the Kuta bombing, acting as a hub for sharing information and gathering funds to help the victims and their families. Check www.balisos.com or www.balirecoverygroup.org, which lists local organisations helping Balinese families and children, such as Bali Hati, Yayasan Ibu Peduli, Crisis Care, and the KIDS Foundation.

A Sunset Ritual on Seminyak Beach

Everyday between 5:30 and 7pm, the sun at Kuta Beach gets ready for its compulsory ritual of painting the sky in bright yellows, reds, and purples. And because every sunset is different and free, the legendary beach gathers dozens of admirers every evening. With a drink in hand or just a relaxed smile, strangers sit on the sand and become friends for a while. With fewer pushy vendors than Kuta, no noisy road, and a good frontline of relaxed cafés, the beach at Seminyak, at the end of Jl. Double Six, is perfect for a friendly sunset. For a more trendy, upmarket experience, get a cocktail and try to grab a lounge chair in the beautiful setting of Kudeta Bar, on Jl. Laksmana – the perfect place to see and to be seen. To escape the crowds, go further north to Canggu and have a sunset drink at the Beach House on Eco Beach.

© Rama Surya

A ceremony in Kuta after the bomb

T 0361-731 402
F 0361-731 403
umalas@idola.net.id
Jl. Lestari 9X,
Bjr. Umalas Kauh,
Kerobokan.

Another great way to enjoy the beach, whether at sunset or early in the morning, is to hop on the back of a horse at *Umalas Stables*. Rice field tours are also on offer. Committed riders can get excellent, professional riding lessons, with great horses and ponies for children. Horse lovers can stay in one of the stylish rooms or studios above the stables, with good rice field views and free use of the swimming pool.

"Osama Don't Surf"

Surfing used to be learned the hard way. You had to paddle your board past the waves, watch the aficionados in awe, try to imitate them, and get knocked down over and again. Today you don't need to swallow tons of water to learn those fancy tricks seen in photographs – or at least stand long enough to catch the eye of an admirer. If you've never surfed, Kuta Beach is your chance. The waves are gentle, the landing is on soft sand, and half of the crowd look like they don't know what they're doing either. The water, however, is polluted, especially during the rainy season (November-February, which is not surf season anyway). Health-conscious surfers wear ear plugs to prevent infections.

 Several surf schools offer beginner courses; they can fetch you at your hotel. All promise that you'll learn to stand on your first lesson; some offer a refund if you don't. Prices vary between US$25 and 39 per lesson. All provide protective shirts and helmets.

Cheyne Horan Surf School
T/F 0361-735 858
www.schoolofsurf.com
> In front of Zanzibar in Seminyak.

Bali Learn to Surf
T 0361-761 869
www.balilearntosurf.com
> At the Hard Rock Hotel in Kuta.

Pro Surf School
M 081 23 675 141
www.prosurfschool.com
> At the northern end of Jl. Pantai Kuta.

Surfboards are available for rent all around the beach, as well as bodyboards for the less adventurous. Most surf shops, as well as free tabloids distributed in bars, display surf tide charts. Before starting, learn a bit of surf ethics – like waiting in line for the wave and not cutting in front of other surfers, which may be dangerous. Get the surf attitude: cool, relaxed, and tolerant. As they print on T-shirts in Kuta: "Osama don't surf!"

Although a bit crowded, the beaches of Kuta, Legian, and Seminyak are the best for beginners. There is a bit less of a crowd – but stronger, more dangerous waves – on **Petitenget Beach**. Only a short ride from the crowded Kuta, **Canggu Beach**, also known as **Eco Beach**, offers soft left and right rolls, occasionally peeling into "just-a-perfect-tube-to-ride" – as told by Kiki, a local surfer. A few hundred metres west of Canggu Beach, **Pererenan** offers a good right-hander, sometimes tunnelling, as well as a left-hander.

Learn to Dive with Eco-Friendly Aquamarine

Although not a dive destination per se, Seminyak is the perfect place to learn diving, starting in the safety of a pool. It is also a good base to access more pristine parts of the island. To book a course or a dive trip, contact **Aquamarine**, a professional organisation that takes a great care for safety and puts divers of all levels in a trusting environment. This eco-friendly dive shop will teach you how to protect marine life while diving. It has initiated several programmes to conserve Bali's endangered coral, such as the setting of mooring buoys around the island in cooperation with other dive shops and local partners.

T 0361-730 107;
M 081 236 588 29
F 0361-735 368
www.aquamarinediving.com
> On Jl. Raya Seminyak 2A.

A government sign warning against drugs

Dance the Night Away in Seminyak

Rather than Kuta itself, Seminyak is the place to go out at night. This is a scene of open bars and night clubs, where a relaxed, unassuming crowd moves from one place to the other as the night passes. Beware, however, that some of the friendly girls (and boys) may be prostitutes. The bars get frenetic in summer, when European tourists pack as much fun as they can in this inexpensive, tropical alternative to Ibiza. Popular places go out of fashion as quickly as the monsoons change, so better ask around for the best bar of the moment, or look out for **The Beat**, a free publication devoted to the local party scene. Keep your ears opened for special occasions, like full-moon beach parties.

A typical night out in Seminyak would probably start with a sunset drink at *Kudeta*, a luxurious bar and restaurant set around a large garden opening to the beach – kept clean by the efforts of Kudeta and neighbouring hotels. This is also a perfect place for a drink after dinner, or for a superb brunch guaranteed to cure all hangovers.

Drugs are on offer everywhere around Kuta and Seminyak. Don't be lulled by the easy availability. Several foreigners caught with drugs are rotting in the prison at Kerobokan. The police may raid night clubs, parties, tourist houses, cars, and taxis, even checking the pockets of passersby on their way to a party.

Party Gods

In the Island of the Gods,
even shops and nightclubs
have their share of rituals
and offerings. Before every
raunchy night of techno
music, the dance floor of
the Double Six is carefully
adorned with little
palm-leaf cups filled with
flowers, cakes, and rice,
and marinated with arak
liquor (albeit much less
than late night patrons).
For the Balinese, spirits and
gods are alive everywhere,
and offerings are always
needed to keep the
balance between
good and bad.

The Kuta Karnival, a peace
festival held every September.

© A.A.B. Dianatha K.

Local party animals usually dine around Jl. Laksmana, which packs a mind-blowing choice of good-value restaurants, from fish specialties to Italian, Greek, and Japanese – nothing typically Balinese here. If you plan to go out, dine late, as most bars don't fill up before 12pm or 1am. Dinner is usually followed by a drink in Kudeta, or at the sophisticated *Hu'u Bar* (Jl. Petitenget), above a green garden and a pool.

Jl. Abimanyu (known as Jl. Dyana Pura) has a more relaxed scene with a lot of live music joints. You can start with a good dinner at *JP's* restaurant, which features local bands playing world music from 9pm to 12am. A bit further on, the *Santa Fe* keeps the spirit of the old Seminyak alive, with a dense crowd shaking at the sound of loud, enthusiastic local rock bands. Around 1am, the street starts to get really packed, as Jl. Dyana Pura has turned into an endless row of bars opened to the road, including the gay-friendly Q-Bar and Kudos.

A typical night out may end up at the beach at the end of Jl. Double Six, where party goers can choose between the trendy Déjà Vu or the most popular nightclub around, the famous *Double Six*, which starts to come alive around 3am. Besides its colourful crowd of all sorts in various states of intoxication, the attraction of Double Six is its large terrace opening to a vast pool crowned by a bungee-jumping tower, occasionally used by a daring (or very drunk) party animal.

Massage: The Dancing Hands

To soothe tired muscles after an exhausting programme of surfing, shopping and partying, you can avail yourself of an infinite number of massage and spa possibilities. The simplest and cheapest are the *beach massages*. They are administered on the spot by dedicated ladies registered with the local village association. They all wear clothes labeled "*Desa Adat Kuta*" (for "Traditional Village of Kuta"). A reasonable price is around Rp50,000 for a one-hour massage, which you can request more or less strong (*keras*) depending on your taste. You can also get spoiled with a pedicure, manicure, or foot massage.

These ladies, coming from farming families, may not always have very smooth hands, so it may feel like you're getting a scrub at the same time – but they are very friendly and, unlike in posh outlets, they keep most of the money (minus a small fee for the village association). Get pampered on a rented mattress in the shadow of an umbrella, so your masseuse doesn't have to sweat under the hot sun. Also along the beach, in Petitenget, to the right of La Luciola Restaurant, there are a few huts where you can get good massages while looking at the waves.

If you want to be treated in an indoor setting, most hotels should be able to call a masseuse for you. Alternatively, you can get a great service at any small neighbourhood salon. Ask for a shoulder massage while having a haircut, and don't miss the opportunity to try a **"cream bath"** – an hedonistic, two-hour-long massage of the scalp and neck under a thick layer of cream that foams above your hair. A good place for such treatment is the friendly *New Planet Beauty Salon* on Jl. Seminyak (opposite Café Moka, *T 0361-731 880*), or *Body and Hair Solutions* on Jl. Kerobokan in Banjar Taman, near Lola Restaurant.

For something a bit more sophisticated with essential oils, flower petals, and sweet music, you can try any of the spas that have mushroomed, especially in posh hotels. Beware that in many cases, you're going to pay more than Rp200,000 for a massage which may not be better than on the beach – you pay for the environment. Below is a small selection of excellent spa treatments and massages at a reasonable price in a great atmosphere. Better call to make a booking.

Body Works in Kerobokan, is an all-time favourite offering good spa-and-body treatments and excellent massages in a peaceful setting.

Farm Yoga

For a great experience of yoga, perfect for shy beginners as well as advanced headstand practitioners, check out Olop's place on Jl. Drupadi I, #7. Yoga sessions are performed in the morning (8am) or afternoon (4pm) in a relaxed atmosphere in a wide, open-air wooden hall or bale, *facing a wide garden where farm animals wander peacefully.*

© Dedok

T 0361-733 317
> Jl. Kayu Jati (off Jl. Laksmana).

T 0361-730 828
espace_bali@yahoo.com

T 0361-736 740
www.jarimenari.com

For aromatherapy (massage with essential oils), scrub treatments, and energising reflexology (healing foot massage), try *Espace* on Jl. Seminyak, opposite Café Moka. They also sell massage oils and spa products. A newer outlet, *Jari Menari* ("dancing fingers"), also on Jl. Seminyak, offers professional massages performed by an amazingly well-trained team of masseurs. Their offerings include a unique four-hand relaxation session performed by two practitioners working in harmony.

Shopping for Fun and Souvenirs

Kuta, Legian, and Seminyak are a paradise for shoppers. Cheap souvenirs can be found in the street markets, where most of the profits go to local vendors. Clothes are on offer all around, with a strong bias towards surf gear and hippie wear. Great silver jewellery is another specialty of Bali. You can find it in posh shops or in little displays opened under your eyes at any minute by any of the countless street vendors selling rings, sunglasses and fake watches.

© Elizabeth E. Listyowati

Bamboo windchimes waiting for tourists

Handicrafts, home decor, and furniture are especially good in the shops of Seminyak and Kerobokan. If you stay long enough, you can even get items made precisely to your design and measurements. You can even get your order of a table and chairs shipped to your home. Be aware that most of the wood furniture is made of teak which comes from the over-harvested, illegally-logged teak forests of Java and Vietnam.

As much as possible, purchase items made of fibre, coconut, and bamboo, which are beautiful and made of readily available materials that don't deplete natural forests. Avoid purchasing items made of tortoise or seashells.

> *Near the Sunrise School on Jl. Mertasari, Kerobokan.*
T 0361-735 824;
0361-735 823
Open 8am-5pm except Sundays.

For organic products, check out the *Sunrise Organic Market* in Kerobokan. You can get fresh fruits and vegetables, but also great gift ideas – from organic coffee to herbal teas, sea salts, and even body care products, including neem-oil products from pet shampoo to healthy massage oils. Ask for the schedule of yoga classes.

Buying "Okeley" eyewear

Copyright or Right to Copy?
By Degung Santikarma

Travellers wandering along the streets of Kuta may wonder what happened to copyright. Fancy malls boast "Polo" and "Prada" products at prices too low to be true. There are "Guci" handbags, "Relex" watches, and "Nilkon" cameras, all at a fraction of the price of their genuine counterparts. Even pharmacies sell – often unknowingly – fake medicine. Pirated music CDs abound, selling from Rp10-15,000 each, and computer software that would cost hundreds of dollars in their licensed versions can be found for Rp25-75,000. DVDs of the latest films range from Rp20-60,000, depending on the quality of the reproduction and your bargaining skills. It's even possible to find blockbusters within days of the Hollywood premiere – recorded from the back of a movie theatre with a handycam. Even money may be faked; Indonesia has one of the highest rates of counterfeit bills in the world.

While the Indonesian government, under pressure from international agencies, regularly promises to crack down on copyright infringement, conducting highly-publicised "sweeps" of counterfeit sellers, enforcement never lasts long. Part of the reason is, of course, economic and political. A licensed piece of software is worth several months of an employee's salary. Most Balinese can't

Buyers should, of course, beware of counterfeits – the quality of fake branded goods is usually far from the original. While most computer software seems indistinguishable from the real thing, they may sometimes develop nasty bugs. Some bootleg DVDs are close kin to their copyrighted cousins, but poorly recorded VCDs tend to cut out just when the action gets tense – and when captured from the back of a theatre, may be enriched with the silhouettes of people getting up to buy popcorn. Music CDs are a bargain, but the sound quality is often low.

imagine why Bill Gates would begrudge them a bit of rice for promoting his software. A lack of law enforcement in general, and a sense of more pressing issues to worry about, leave the police with a lack of commitment to enforcing the law (and besides, they're not paid enough to buy the licensed version of Police Academy XIV, either).

Artists or Community Workers?

The booming business for *bajakan* – Indonesian for counterfeits – also has a lot to do with Balinese notions of creativity and ownership. Traditional society had sculptors and dancers, painters and musicians, but no "artists". Those who made things – whether they were elaborate carvings, religious offerings, plain furniture, or shoes – were called *tukang*, or "workers". A farmer might also work as a *tukang gambar* or picture maker, and a pig herder might double as a dancer. There was no scale of hierarchy that set "artists" above "craftspeople", no sense that someone who knew how to draw pictures was more special than someone who knew how to make really tasty eel fritters. "Art" was one way among many others of serving one's society and one's gods. Most creations were community property, made for temples or villages, and there was no sense that works should be preserved – statues were left to be worn down by the rains, and cremation towers were elaborately carved and painted only to be set afire.

Without the stress on individual creativity found in the West, the idea of "intellectual property" is alien to many Balinese. Traditional painters learn their craft like children learn to cook or make offerings: by copying the works of the more experienced. Copying is not considered lazy or corrupt, but is rather seen as a homage to the expertise of the masters. Furniture and handicraft makers in Bali know that they stand no chance to sue a competitor who has copied their design. Likewise, don't expect your money to be refunded if Mariah Carey's voice sounds hoarse on your counterfeited CD, or if fake aspirin leaves you with an intact headache.

Poor-quality products can be recognised by their photocopied and misspelled covers, but better-quality pirated CDs, DVDs and software usually look real with professional-quality covers, fake security stickers and copyright infringement warnings. While it's highly unlikely you'll get into trouble with the law in Indonesia, if you're thinking of importing such goods back to your home country, you may have a bit of explaining to do should your customs department open your bags.

© Iskandar

A "SQNNY" music player

Sanur Beach

Kids playing football on Sanur beach

The Sleeping Beauty

With its serene streets lined with majestic trees, Sanur is a peaceful alternative to Kuta, especially for families. The lovely white-sand beach started to suffer from erosion after reclamation projects on nearby Serangan Island. Since 2002, however, a Japanese-funded project has restored the beach, bringing light-brown sand from Nusa Dua. Piers have been erected to protect the coast. Despite initial concerns about the impact of this project, local communities appreciate the efforts to restore the original landscape, which brings visitors back.

The salvaged beach, with its calm waters, provides a pleasant playground for kids. Sanur is also a good place to try out sea-based activities like **snorkelling**, **windsurfing**, or **canoeing**. Although its coastline is protected from the waves by reefs, Sanur has a few good **surfing** spots. If you want to embark to the wilder islands of Nusa Penida and Lembongan (see p. 271), you'll find boats ready to take you in front of the Sanur Beach Hotel. Tired of the ocean? Opt for **mangrove trekking** and **bird-watching**, or discover rare orchids and other unusual tropical flowers at the **Bali Orchid Garden**. Besides bland international hotels, Sanur has a good choice of accommodations, especially along the peaceful Jl. Danau Tamblingan.

Serangan Island
This island off Sanur is known for its temple, **Pura Sakenan**, *which attracts many Balinese worshippers, especially during the Kuningan festival. Its name means* **Turtle Island**, *but most turtles have disappeared, hunted for their meat and eggs, or chased away by reclamation projects. In the 1990s, the family of President Soeharto planned a huge tourism resort on the island, evicting locals from their land. The project has now been stopped, but a bridge has been constructed between Serangan and the mainland. Controversial turtle farms are still active on the island. The local community is fighting to restore the battled sea life, with the help of the* **Bahtera Nusantara Foundation**:
T/F 0361-242 405
bahteranusantara@indo. net.id

Where to Stay – Northern Sanur

❶ *20 Rm – A/C Rst Shw*
T/F 0361-288 289
wateringhole_sanurbali
@yahoo.com

Located next to the beach on Jl. Hang Tuah, *Watering Hole I* offers simple, comfortable, and affordable rooms. The rooms are spread in a two-storey building, Balinese-style, with bamboo ceilings. There are three large family rooms facing the street. The owner is a relative of *Puri Satria*, an old royal family in Denpasar, and the staff will take you for a short tour to the palace on request. Every Thursday, a *legong* dance performance enlivens the dining atmosphere.

Where to Stay – Central Sanur

Support Nature at Hotel Santai

♥ ♥ **❶ ❷** *16 Rm –*
Htw A/C Rst Swp
T/F 0361-287 314
santai@indosat.net.id
www.pplhbali.or.id
> Indicated by the PPLH sign board on the inland side of Jl. Danau Tamblingan.

As hinted in its name, which means "loosen up," this friendly hotel offers simple rooms in a relaxed and warm atmosphere. The hotel is managed by an environmental organisation, the PPLH (*Pusat Pendidikan Lingkungan Hidup* – Environmental Education Centre). You'll find a small library inside the lobby with a collection of books about environmental issues. The simple, pleasant rooms are in a two-storey building, facing a small pool. The upstairs multifunction room is used for trainings or yoga sessions. In front, Santai Café greets you under a lush shade of old trees and a traditional *lumbung*. Opt for the special seafood fried rice or the tasty vegetarian dishes.

Experience Balinese Art in Griya Santrian

♥ **❸ ❹** *94 Rm –*
Htw A/C Rst Bch Swp
Shw Bcy Spa
T 0361-288 181
F 0361-288 185
www.santrian.com
> On the beach side of Jl. Danau Tamblingan.

In a more upmarket category, Griya Santrian, hidden in a lush garden with bird songs and a cool breeze from the beach, is ideal for travellers with kids. A verdant garden encircles every room. The highlight is a gallery in the middle of the compound, where young local artists hold painting exhibitions. Egg painting and wood carving exhibitions are also held regularly, as well as demonstrations of offerings, every morning at the *bale kembar*. During the high season, Griya Santrian conducts dance lessons for local children every Saturday afternoon. Cycling around Sanur can be arranged at Rp35,000/person/day.

A Walk in the Park at the Bali Hyatt

The only large hotel in our selection, the Bali Hyatt is set in an eight-hectare garden bursting with orchids, frangipani, and lily ponds, and sheltering 600 species of animals and plants. Next to the wide, white-sand beach, the pool is adorned with a waterfall and a stone-carved replica of the ancient cave of Goa Gajah. A child activity centre offers outdoor programmes to keep the little ones busy while their parents are relaxing.

In a lower price range, set in a family compound a five-minute walk away from the beach, *Yulia Homestay II* is good value. Some of the rooms have beautiful woodcarving ornaments. Choose the wooden upstairs room to catch the fresh breeze from the sea. The friendly owner can arrange tours or provide information on cultural events in the area.

Located on the beach side of Jl. Danau Tamblingan, *Laghawa Beach Inn* is ideally located in a two-hectare garden, perfect for families. The highlights of this hotel are beautifully hand-carved doors and windows, and sculptures spread out in the garden creating an elegant and intimate ambience. Lounge at ease in a big *lumbung* while watching wild birds flying around freely.

Located at the end of Jl. Bumi Ayu, *Bumi Ayu Bungalows* offers simple and beautiful rooms with bamboo-woven walls and wooden furniture. Some rooms are shaded by a grove of palm trees facing the garden. The beach is only a few minutes away. Ask the staff to arrange a traditional massage.

Set in an opulent garden, *Tandjung Sari Hotel* offers a perfect hideaway. This gorgeous compound full of Balinese and Dutch colonial antiques has an intimate, yet convivial, feeling. Each comfortable, red brick bungalow with a thatched roof has a private garden and an open-air shower. Enjoy a luxurious view of Sanur Beach with Mt Agung in the background at the beachfront restaurant. The adjacent *bale* is used for dance practice by local children on Saturday afternoons.

♥ ➎ *390 Rm – Htw*
A/C Rst Bch Swp
Div Shw Bcy Spa
T 0361-281 234
F 0361-287 693
balihyatt.inquiries@
hyattintl.com
www.bali.hyatt.com
> On the beach side of
Jl. Danau Tamblingan.

➊ ➋ *7 Rm – A/C Rst*
T 0361-287 495
kf_billy@indo.net.id
> Next to Laghawa
Beach Inn on Jl. Danau
Tamblingan.

➌ *28 Rm – Htw*
A/C Rst Bch Swp
T 0361-288 494
F 0361-282 533
www.laghawahotel.com

➋ ➌ *58 Rm – Htw*
A/C Rst Swp
T 0361-289101;
0361-286 051
F 0361-287 517
bumi_ayu@hotmail.com

➎ *26 Rm – Htw A/C*
Rst Bch Swp Shw
T 0361-288 441
F 0361-287 930
tansri@dps.centrin.net.id
www.tandjungsari.com
> On the beach side of
Jl. Danau Tamblingan.

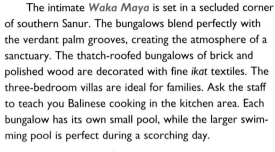

4 5 14 Rm – Htw
A/C Rst Swp Bcy Spa
T 0361-289 912
F 0361-270 761
www.wakaexperience.com

The intimate *Waka Maya* is set in a secluded corner of southern Sanur. The bungalows blend perfectly with the verdant palm grooves, creating the atmosphere of a sanctuary. The thatch-roofed bungalows of brick and polished wood are decorated with fine *ikat* textiles. The three-bedroom villas are ideal for families. Ask the staff to teach you Balinese cooking in the kitchen area. Each bungalow has its own small pool, while the larger swimming pool is perfect during a scorching day.

Sanur – Where to Eat

Sanur has a good choice of relaxed cafés and restaurants, mostly along Jl. Danau Tamblingan or on the beachfront.

♥ ♥ T 0361-287 374
> Near Hotel Santai on
Jl. Danau Tamblingan.

Our preference goes to *Café Batujimbar*, which has an excellent vegetarian selection as well as health food and organic vegetables for Rp25-50,000. The founder promotes organic food growing in the highlands of Bali. A counter sells Jenggala ceramics from Jimbaran.

The nearby *Hotel Santai* has a plain café (previously named Tali Jiwa Café) serving inexpensive local dishes and vegetarian specialties, in a tiny verdant garden with a friendly atmosphere.

♥ T 0361-289 398
> Jl. DanauTamblingan.

In a quiet corner of Jl. Danau Tamblingan, the *Lotus Pond* offers seafood, Italian cuisine, and local specialties. The dining space is in a spacious open *bale* with carved wooden doors and panels; traditional dance shows are staged regularly. This is a good place to taste the Balinese smoked duck, *bebek betutu*, for Rp50-65,000.

Another delightful experience is to have a simple dinner at one of the many restaurants set up along the beach, where you can enjoy seafood and simple local dishes. Our favourite is *Café Kesuma*, which serves good, fresh grilled fish and is the most quiet on the beachfront, at the end of Kesumasari Street on Semawang Beach.

A lobster shrine in Sanur

© Elizabeth E. Listyowati

Also along the beach, *Bonsai Café* is a perfect place for a relaxing snack, a drink, or an inexpensive dinner, with a good selection of seafood and Indonesian dishes. Set on the breezy seafront and displaying a collection of bonsai, it is favoured by the locals, especially for its bar open until 2am. Find it just north of La Taverna Hotel, at the end of a small lane going towards the beach from Jl. Danau Tamblingan, behind Mykonos Restaurant.

For a relaxing experience of local cuisine, try *Warung Mak Beng*, one of the best Balinese warungs according to *Latitudes* magazine. It serves Balinese fish specialities, including a tasty fish soup. Located opposite the Grand Bali Beach Hotel, the warung is very popular with local people at lunchtime. It closes around 4pm.

For a more sophisticated setting, at the busy intersection of the Ngurah Rai bypass and Jl. Hang Tuah, *Café Wayang* boasts an elegant dining room enlivened by smooth jazz music. Choose between Indonesian food and Western dishes for Rp45-65,000. Come on Friday or Saturday evenings to enjoy live performances of Latin and jazz bands starting at 9pm.

Sanur – What to Do at Sea

Sanur is known as a relaxed beach resort and the locals love to stroll along the beach during public holidays and weekends. It is also a centre for watersports such as *canoeing*, *windsurfing*, and *parasailing*. Try these exciting sports at the *Blue Oasis Beach Club*. They will indicate you the best spots for surfing and windsurfing, depending on the season. There you can rent equipment at reasonable prices (US$4 per hour for an ocean kayak, US$20 per half-day for a sailboard) or take classes from beginner to advanced levels.

Surfing is also possible in Sanur, especially during the off-season in other sites (December to March), when Sanur gets an offshore west wind. Waves break about 500m from the shore, with occasional long barrels. The best waves, at *Hyatt Reef* (in front of the Bali Hyatt Hotel) and *Blue Reef* (in front of the Sanur Beach Hotel), break on sharp corals and are not recommended for beginners – better bring your booties. *Baby Reef*, slightly south of the Blue Reef, a smaller wave breaking on sand-covered coral, is more suited for the less adventurous. Get information and surf boards at the Blue Oasis Beach Club.

A Night Market
The name of Sanur's night market, *"Pasar Senggol,"* means "to bump lightly into someone." This lively market is so packed with bits and pieces on sale that one can hardly move around without shoving into other visitors. The market lets you "bump" into all kind of counters selling satay (kebabs), local sweets, music CDs, underwear, kitchenware, and toiletries. Alive from 5-10pm at the corner of Jl. Danau Tamblingan and Jl. Sindhu, this is the best place to enjoy night and food like the locals do, amidst smoke swirling over cooking stoves.

On Jl. Danau Tamblingan, at the Sanur Beach Hotel. T 0361-288 011, ext. Blue Oasis. bluebc@geocity.com

© Iskandar

Pasar Senggol *in Sanur*

♥♥ ⚕

T 0361-287 945;
288 829; 281 751
F 0361-287 945
enadive@denpasar.
wasantara.net.id
www.indo.com/diving/ena
> Jl. Tirta Ening #1.

Pro and Eco at Ena Dive

One of the most professional dive shops around Bali, Ena is also dedicated to nature conservation – they participate in reef check programmes with the WWF as well as coral rehabilitation, and organise monthly beach-cleaning with local villagers. The well-trained dive masters have an excellent knowledge of the marine life of Bali, and they make sure that guests respect the coral.

♥ ⚕

T 0361-270 791;
0361-270 792
F 0361-287 065
info@airbalidiving.com
www.balidiving.com
> On the beach side of
the Ngurah Rai Bypass,
3km south of McDonald's.

In Love with the Reefs at Air Diving Academy

This dive shop, previously known as **Aqua Pro**, was among the initiators of "Friends of the Reef" in early 2000, along with the WWF, The Nature Conservancy, Reef Check International, and local NGOs. The programme carries out surveys and ecological rehabilitation around Bali. The dive shop supports coral protection and rehabilitation undertaken by the Bahtera Foundation with local fishermen in Les village, near Tejakula (see p. 315). Take an "eco-dive" trip to Tejakula to learn directly about this fascinating project.

♥ ⚕

T 0361-270 759;
0361-285 065
F 0361-270 760;
0361-271 138
info@bidp-balidiving.com
www.bidp-balidiving.com
> Jl. Danau Poso #26.

A Dive for Everyone at BIDP

Bali International Diving Professionals has selected great dive sites suitable for divers of all levels – they offer courses for 8-12-year-old children, disabled divers, and technical diving using nitrogen. The truly romantic will be thrilled by the underwater wedding package.

What to Do – Mangroves and Orchids

Mangrove Trekking and Bird Watching

The coast around Sanur used to be lined with mangrove, a special type of tree that thrives on salty grounds. Mangrove trees can grow where nothing else will. They protect the coasts from erosion and salinity, and shelter an endless variety of birds, mammals, crustacea, and fish. A trek or boat tour along this strange ecosystem, where tree roots grow above the mud and where the frontier between land and water is forever changing, is a unique experience. Thanks to the **Mangrove Information**

© Erdi Lazuardi

Mangrove seeds

Centre (MIC) created near Sanur with the help of the Japanese government, travellers can enjoy the beauty of the mangrove and learn about efforts set up to conserve this endangered ecosystem – more than 15 kinds of mangrove have been planted in this area. The MIC offers short walks in the mangrove or a full 1.5-hour trekking tour as requested. Bird lovers may spot some of the 70 kinds of birds in the area, such as the osprey (*Pandion haliateus*) or the cute, small blue kingfisher (*Alcedo coerulescents*). Binoculars are provided. Enjoy the walk in the early morning when wild birds are most active. Canoeing is also possible.

Open: 8am-5pm
T/F: 0361-726 969
micjica@indosat.net.id
A small fee for the
guide is requested.

Beauties and the Beast at the Bali Orchid Garden

Have you ever dreamed of seeing the most delicate white orchid and the rarest of black orchids? Have you ever been visited, in your nightmares, by a six-foot-high flower that smells like a decaying corpse, or by flowers armed with tentacles like those of mygale spiders? All these fantasies will come true at the Bali Orchid Garden.

Jl. Bypass Tohpati
T 0361-466 010
F 0361-466 011
www.baliorchidgarden.org
www.junglegeeks.com
Entrance fee: Rp50,000
Open everyday,
8am-6pm.

Hidden along the busy Sanur Bypass, this oasis of calm and beauty displays samples of common and rare orchid species from throughout Indonesia – as well as many other colourful tropical plants, such as aroids and heliconias, in a nicely-landscaped setting. The collection is beautifully tended by the owner, an orchid lover who has instilled his passion to his enthusiastic staff. A key attraction is the giant *Amorphophallus titanum* from Sumatra, which can grow to 1.80m with its single leaf and deadly smell. Its flowering takes a few years, but overshadows all the orchid beauties.

Orchid flower boxes, with a quarantine inspection certificate, can be ordered two days prior to your departure from Bali for an original gift (US$10-25).

The owner of Bali Orchid Garden, Troy Davis, also manages *Jungle Geeks*, which offers **jungle tours** into the deepest forests of southeast Asia – from simple rainforest walks to more involved tours where visitors get a chance to learn about ecology, flora, and fauna.

© Troy Davis

Secundum *orchid*

The Struggle to Save Bali's Turtles

By Degung Santikarma and Andre Syahreza

A giant turtle laying eggs

At a *banjar* (village) meeting hall in Kesiman, south Bali, a group of men are whiling away the cool evening hours in front of a tiny black and white TV set. As the programming shifts from national news and celebrity gossip to a local talk show, the men grow more interested. Tonight's subject is turtles and how Balinese can help stop the slaughter of their dwindling population. The environmental activists appearing on the show explain that the six sea turtle species found in Indonesian waters are now endangered, and that if killing and consumption of turtles continue at the present pace, in a few years there will be none left at all.

But the men in the *banjar* aren't buying it. "Come on, don't tell me you don't like turtle satay with a little chilli and salt?" one man taunts the television guests. "Why should we let those foreigners from those environmental organisations tell us what we can and can't eat?" grumbles another man.

Turtle Rituals

In precolonial times, turtles were brought as royal gifts for the Balinese kings by seafaring Bugis traders. In beachfront communities like Sanur, Jimbaran, Tanjung Benoa, Kuta, and Kesiman, the trapping of a turtle in a fisherman's net was cause for celebration. Turtles were eaten and their shells carved into ornaments like bracelets and hair combs. Turtles were even used as a kind of traditional mediator of social relationships. The practice of ngejod, *still alive in south Bali, entails distributing hundreds of sticks of turtle satay for a wedding or other family ceremony.*

Rituals and Tourists

Attempts to stop the slaughter and sale of the green sea turtle (*Chelonia mydas*) have led to perhaps the most intense debates over the relationship between human interests and ecological concerns in Bali. Especially in south Bali, where economic and ritual life revolve around the sea, green turtle meat has been used for centuries as part of religious and community events. Turtles – along with a host of other land and sea life – have also been used for sacrifices to the gods in Balinese Hindu rituals.

But in the 1970s, with the rise of mass tourism, Bali's turtle population began to shrink drastically. Not only were turtle shells sold as souvenirs, turtle soup became a highlight of many hotel menus. Beaches that had been the turtles' nesting grounds were occupied by tourist facilities. Turtles are extremely sensitive to changes in their habitat, with noise and lights dissuading them from leaving the water to lay their eggs. Their slow movements and clumsy, paddle-like legs make them easy prey for predators. Scientists estimate that only two to ten percent of turtle eggs survive to maturity in the wild. In a Bali booming from the tourism business, the turtles' chances were growing even slimmer.

Activists and the Government

In 1990, under pressure from local conservation organisations, the governor of Bali banned the sale of turtle meat in Bali's restaurants and limited the turtle trade to the port of Tanjung Benoa. In deference to communities who argued that turtle was a necessary part of Balinese religious ritual, the decree set a quota of 5,000 turtles per year which could be killed for traditional ceremonies. But the Balinese government had neither the facilities – nor, many environmental activists claimed, the inclination – to monitor the slaughterings. Ketut Sarjana Putra from the WWF claims that under the quota system, turtle killings in Bali reached a high of 27,000 per year. In fact, the quota system lured traders from other parts of Indonesia to Bali, making Tanjung Benoa the centre for an estimated 80% of the national turtle trade.

After concluding that the quotas were ineffective in protecting the turtles, environmental organisations recommended a total ban on turtle trading in Bali. Yet after a new decree banned turtle trade in 1999, the activities continued, shifting underground after a few police raids. The large-scale traders – most of whom, Ketut Sarjana Putra claims, come from other islands – process hundreds of turtles a month through their heavily-guarded turtle pens. They coordinate their businesses with mobile phones, travelling in luxury sedans. They can use their wealth to make strategic payments to the authorities. They can also mobilise the inhabitants of places like Tanjung Benoa, where locals and migrants live from turtle trade, pushing them to resort to violence when necessary.

© Iskandar

Back from turtle slaughtering

Turtle Money

Today in Tanjung Benoa, a turtle with a 80 to 90cm diameter shell can fetch from Rp400,000 to Rp500,000. Before a major religious ceremony, it can reach up to Rp1,000,000 once killed and parcelled into satay sticks. At such prices, a dead turtle can feed an entire family for a month. Small-scale turtle traders in Tanjung Benoa claim their incomes average between Rp500,000 and Rp700,000 a month – about as much as the wage of a government civil servant, and not far from those of environmental activitists.

Selling turtle satay

© Iskandar

In 2003, a young member of the Indonesian NGO, ProFauna, was attacked by villagers as she came to monitor the turtle population with Forest Department staff. Local officials are not immune from the lure of wealth, either, and some turtle trading takes place under the guise of official conservation and tourism facilities. As noted by Robin Marinos of Earth Advocates, an organisation that lobbies the authorities to pass and enforce conservation laws, "Today, Balinese turtles are growing so rare that fishermen have to go as far as Kalimantan to find some."

Conservation and Culture

Besides economic motives, some Balinese have difficulties understanding why they should stop their consumption of turtle. The concept of "endangered species" is new to Bali. It challenges local belief that everything in the sea is created by powerful gods who will protect this bounty for the use of humans. This traditional thought worked well for centuries, when a sparse population used small boats to feed their community. But this kind of thought may be ill-suited to the modern world, where the technologies for destroying the environment have reached unprecedented levels, feeding a growing population and the insatiable greed of a few merchants.

Ketut Sarjana Putra acknowledges that the ban on turtle consumption has left some Balinese confused. But he believes that if Balinese understood the reasons behind it, they would come to agree. He lays partial blame on Bali's governor, who prohibited the turtle trade without proper communication to the people. "They should have thought about setting up programmes to explain the ban to the people and to provide economic assistance to those who were going to lose money," he says.

The controversy over turtle conservation continues to rage, with the turtles, unable to speak for themselves, at the centre of the debate. Hopefully by the time all the arguing among humans is over, there will still be turtles left to benefit from the verdict.

Turtles and Priests

Ida Pedanda Gede Ngurah Kaleran, a Hindu high priest from Sanur who has become active in ecological issues, believes religion is no excuse for the slaughter of turtles. "This may be Balinese custom, but it's not part of the Hindu religion. The true Hindu religion teaches us ahimsa, the principle of non-violence." Ida Pedanda Kaleran suggests that the emotionally-laden concept of Balinese tradition has in fact been manipulated by some people seeking profits – and by those Balinese who simply like the taste of turtle. "If I count up how many turtles are really needed for religious ceremonies, the total each year is 300 to 500 at most," he claims.

© A. A. B. Dianatha K.

Jimbaran – The Bukit

Surfing the Bukit's waves

The Morning of the Earth

In 1970, Albert Falzon, a young Australian filmmaker, came to Bali to make "a really beautiful, positive film about the world." His movie, **The Morning of the Earth**, made history, using infrared camera and slow-motion to film impossible surf tricks with "songs of freedom and peace and waves" as the sole commentary. Besides documenting the relation between surfers and nature, the film revealed the 10-foot-high barrels lining up along the Bukit Peninsula against a dramatic background of cliffs and caves. Soon, surfers started to leave the gentle waves of Kuta for the challenging breaks of the Bukit.

Even if you're not a seasoned surfer, you'll enjoy this dry land outcrop, raised 200m above the ocean. Guarding the top end of the peninsula, the temple of **Uluwatu** adds an aura of spirituality to the heart-stopping cliffs. Covered with a meagre vegetation of bush, cacti, cassava, and kapok trees, the Bukit becomes verdant only from December to March. It is lined with white-sand beaches, although it is difficult to swim at most of them. Quiet waters can be found in the bay of Jimbaran or on Geger Beach. The peninsula harbours the tourist enclave of Nusa Dua and its flock of five-star hotels. Nature lovers will prefer one of the few hidden gems presented below, with fantastic ocean views where you may spot a dolphin or a whale.

For a Drop of Water

Like nearby Nusa Penida and for the same reasons, the Bukit Peninsula suffers from a chronic water shortage. The limestone ground dissolves the rainwater, which disappears deep underground. Hence until recently, Balinese avoided this area, which had the reputation of a refuge for the destitute and a home for black magic. Hotels set on the Bukit are dependent on rain catchments or on water piped in from the mountains. This may become a problem as water shortages are predicted for Bali in the coming years. In the meantime, choose eco-friendly hotels which recycle and save this precious resource, and remember to use it sparingly.

Where to Stay – Jimbaran

An Eco-Lodge at Udayana

♥ ♥ ❸ 16 Rm –
Htw A/C Rst Swp Trk
T 0361-261 204;
0361-742 86 75
F 0361-701 098
iniradef@indo.net.id
www.ecolodgesindonesia.com

> From Denpasar or Kuta,
head on the Ngurah Rai
Bypass towards Nusa Dua,
then enter the Udayana
Campus (Kampus Udayana).
Turn right at the first turn
and head straight to the end
of this road or until you see
the lodge's sign.

Tucked away inside the complex of Bali's oldest university, the lodge is set high up in the Jimbaran hills. It has wonderful views of the Benoa harbour, with Mt Rinjani and Mt Agung in the back. The rooms are in a two-storey building set in a garden full of bougainvilleas, sheltering many species of birds and butterflies. The eco-friendly construction uses solar power and two extensive rainwater tanks. The lodge is surrounded by 32 hectares of bush land, providing guests with an ample choice of treks for walking or bird-watching. In the afternoon, try the cricket net or tennis court and dip into the fresh, spotless pool to cool down your aching muscles.

Where to Stay – Bingin and Balangan

Dream in the Breeze at Mick's Place

♥ ❸ 5 Rm –
Swp Gvw Rst Bcy
M 081 239 133 37
micksplacebali@
yahoo.com.au

> Head on the Ngurah
Rai Bypass towards Nusa
Dua. Then turn right at
Uluwatu. Follow the road
until Pecatu (around
10km) and turn right
towards Bingin beach.

Hidden in a green garden facing the ocean, these relaxing bungalows have half-walls with wooden shields, letting the sea breeze cool down your nights. A small pool sits at the edge of the cliff, next to a *bale bengong*, perfect for day-dreaming. Guests can walk down to Dreamland or Bingin Beach, tour the area on a mountain bike, or join yoga classes. Mick has built rainwater catchments and uses wastewater in the garden. Ask to see the saplings of *Morinda citrifolia* (*noni*), an Asian medicinal plant. Mick helps the villagers plant *noni* as a source of income.

A Cliff Haven at Mu

♥ ❹ 5 Rm –
Htw A/C Rst Bch
Swp Gvw Bcy
T 0361-742 82 49
M 081 239 039 24
jbataillardbali@hotmail.com
www.mu-bali.com

> Turn left after Mick's.

Not far from Mick's, but a bit more upmarket and comfortable, Mu offers open thatch-roofed bungalows with hammocks in a peaceful atmosphere. Perched on the top of the cliff, the garden offers superb views over Dreamland. Besides swimming, surfing or biking, you can join a yoga session or exercise on the spacious wooden deck. End your day with a seafood dinner facing the sunset over the bay. Mu and Mick's participate in a beach cleaning and recycling programme.

At the far end of Balangan Beach, *La Joya* welcomes guests in a spacious villa and a set of bungalows, smartly decorated with fine textiles and wooden furniture in a pleasant garden. The large pool has a special children's area, while the villa sleeps six people and has its own small pool. An open *bale* dining room serves snacks and sandwiches. For lunch or dinner, check the set menu and place your request in the morning.

❸ ❺ 11 Rm – Htw
A/C Rst Bch Swp Gvw
M 081 856 58 39
www.la-joya.com
> From Jimbaran, go to Dreamland through the deserted complex of Pecatu. Just before the beach, a board indicates the bumpy road to La Joya.

Where to Stay – Tanjung Benoa

Turtles and Peace at Rumah Bali

Built like a miniature Balinese village, each of these thatch-roofed bungalows is furnished with elegant wooden furniture and equipped with an outdoor bathroom. Join the exciting cooking classes in the *paon* (traditional Balinese kitchen), try the jogging track around the vast garden, then plunge into the spacious and spotless pool. Private butler service is offered for parents who want a night out.

The owner, Heinz, who also owns the great Bumbu Bali Restaurant, likes to spread his concern for environmental issues among his staff, well-trained in proper waste management. Wastewater is recycled and reused to tend the spacious garden. But his main dedication is towards saving the turtles – hence you may spot a few of them swimming in the garden ponds. Inquire at the front desk about helping the turtle programme.

🤍🤍 **❹ ❺** 26 Rm –
Htw A/C Rst Swp Cls
T 0361-771 256
F 0361-771 728
hvhfood@indosat.net.id
www.balifoods.com
www.indochef.biz
> On the inland side of Jl. Pratama, 200m from Bumbu Bali.

✳ Leave a donation to Turtles Unlimited, the turtle conservation programme coordinated by the owner of Rumah Bali and Bumbu Bali.

On the inland side of the road, *Taman Sari* provides peaceful accommodations in a friendly ambiance. The thatch-roofed bungalows are set in a spacious garden, with a wooden bridge over the curved pool. The bright-coloured marble rooms are decorated with smart wooden furniture and Balinese carvings. It is only a ten-minute walk to the beach for a morning stroll or snorkelling – after which you may want a massage for US$20 at the spa, fully equipped with a Jacuzzi and sauna. The poolside restaurant serves Thai and Balinese specialities and appetising seafood for Rp60-85,000.

❹ ❺ 10 Rm – Htw
A/C Rst Swp Spa
T 0361-773 953
F 0361-773 954
tarisuit@indosat.net.id
www.tamansarisuite-bali.com
> 2km from the Nusa Dua-Tanjung Benoa junction.

Where to Eat – Jimbaran Beach

A fish dinner on the quiet beach of Jimbaran is a must-do in Bali. Lined up in the soft white sand, dozens of warungs tempt guests with fresh fish grilled over coconut-husk fires. Guests choose from ice boxes – red snapper is a favourite, as well as squid, lobsters, clams, and prawns. The price is set per 100g and includes rice, vegetables, sauces, and fruits. Come around 6pm to enjoy the sunset.

There are two strings of seafood warungs. The stalls in **Jl. Pemelisan Agung**, popular with locals, have simple plastic chairs and canvas tents (count about Rp50,000 for a full meal). Head for *Roman Café*, *Lia*, or *Jimbaran Beach Café*. Less crowded, **Muaya Beach** has more refined warungs with wooden tables, guest toilets, and tiled kitchens. Prices are twice as expensive. *Café Menega* and *Kalang Anyar* receive good reviews.

Where to Eat – Tanjung Benoa

Delectable Balinese food at Bumbu Bali

Food-lovers will savour this authentic Balinese cuisine by former Ritz-Carlton Chef Heinz Van Holzen. Choose among the duck in banana leaf, the vegetable chicken salad, or roast pork, unless you prefer fresh squid, seafood kebab, or grilled fish. Firm appetites will head for the set menu (Rp145,000), with its complete sample of Balinese treats. Dance performances are held during the tourist season, but the real fun is to observe the cook perform in the open traditional kitchen. **Cooking lessons** let you start at 6am with a visit to the Jimbaran market. The chef will then guide you through 25 Balinese recipes – showing you the use of a stone mortar and uncovering the secrets of ginger, galingale, or lemongrass.

In the centre of Tanjung Benoa, *Warung Nyoman* offers tasty Balinese dishes and grilled seafood for Rp65-85,000. The airy restaurant has a relaxed ambiance with a small flowery garden and a fishpond. During high season, children perform traditional dances in the evening. Call for a free transfer from Nusa Dua or Tanjung Benoa.

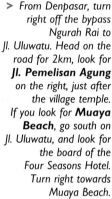

> From Denpasar, turn right off the bypass Ngurah Rai to Jl. Uluwatu. Head on the road for 2km, look for **Jl. Pemelisan Agung** on the right, just after the village temple. If you look for **Muaya Beach**, go south on Jl. Uluwatu, and look for the board of the Four Seasons Hotel. Turn right towards Muaya Beach.

♥ ♥ (∈) 🐚
T 0361-774 502
F 0361-771 728
hvhfood@indosat.net.id
www.balifoods.com
www.indochef.biz
> On the beach side of Jl. Pratama.

(∈) T/F 0361-778 677
warung_nyoman@telkom.net
> On the beach side of Jl. Pratama.

What to Do – Impossible Surf at the Bukit

Turning off the Ungasan-Uluwatu road, a battered road passes through the deserted complex of Pecatu Indah towards the coast, finally splitting into two small paths leading to idyllic white-sand beaches. The right turn leads to **Balangan**, known for its serene surroundings and perfect soft lefthanders. It's possible to swim in the cove, but watch out for big surfs. A few small warungs trim the shore. The left road turn leads to the aptly named **Dreamland**. The surfs along this shore provide short right handers, longer lefts, and occasional barrels to any surfer's delight. Once in the water, you may be surprised by the rare company of a *dugong dugong* (sea cow).

Just a stroll down from Dreamland, **Bingin** is known for its consistent and finely tunnelled barrels. The beach is named after a large banyan tree, or *beringin*, which once grew on the cliff – an unlikely spot for this species, which is not fond of ocean winds. Owing to its perfect waves and short lefthanders, Bingin is more crowded than other areas. Non-surfers can swim in the crook of a small lagoon. Meanwhile, **Impossibles**, down the coast from Bingin, churns longer and speedier peaks for right-handers. The swelling surf, however, makes it hard to swim. Climb up to the cliff just after the parking lot, where you'll be greeted by an awesome ocean vista, stretching from Impossibles to Padang-Padang.

Padang-Padang is often referred to as "the pipeline", owing to its great left-hander. Its peaks are reserved to the best wave riders. Another famous break for skilled surfers is **Uluwatu**, accessed through Suluban beach, 2km away from the Uluwatu temple. This is where Albert Falzon filmed "an ocean stacked with barrelling lefthanders to peel forever and ever." A relaxed walk on the beach is possible by climbing down the cliff via a small pathway from the temple, though swimming is unquestionably dangerous. As dusk starts to fall, you may find yourself surrounded by troops of persistent monkeys which can make your climb back unpleasant.

The Ghost Resort

After two decades of agricultural and economic progress, the last decade of President Soeharto's reign was marked by delirious projects fomented by his children, with very little concern for local people. One of them was the Pecatu resort, which was meant to cover a whole hill in the Bukit Peninsula, over Dreamland Beach. Villagers were intimidated until they were compelled to sell their land to the project. The whole hill was bull-dozed and a wide asphalt road was built. The whole area is now abandoned and has a ghost feeling as you drive through it to reach the beaches.

© A. A. B. Dianatha K.

A perfect tunnel at Padang–Padang

© Ulung Wicaksono

Bingin beach

What to Do – Dream Beaches

If you don't dare to surf, beaches around the Bukit are perfect for a lazy afternoon. They are set against beautiful landscapes and offer a bit of white sand, a rarity in Bali. Don't expect peaceful swimming among the rough waves and coral breaks. Enjoy the sight of surfers, both in and out of the water. Bringing booties may protect your feet, but avoid stepping on coral.

For peaceful swimming, head for the lagoon-like waters of *Geger Beach*, just south of Nusa Dua. It also has a good surf wave, but it breaks far away from the coast. This long stretch of white sand extends between two temples and is considered sacred by the Balinese, who conduct ceremonies there. The rest of the time, it is worshipped by local expatriates, who come here with their families to enjoy the quiet turquoise waters and the great simple food served on the relaxed terrace of the **restaurant** above the sand. Balinese also love to come here to fish. Here and there, you may notice a few poles used to delineate seaweed farms.

> To reach Geger Beach, drive south on the Ngurah Rai Bypass to Nusa Dua. Follow the sign to Nikko Bali. Around 300m from Amanusa resort, turn right on a small asphalt road towards the beach. Park your vehicle on the small parking lot near the beach.

What to Do – Under and Above Water

Dive and More at Yos Marine Adventure

Yos offers PADI dive courses in English, Japanese, German, and Indonesian, and a wide range of water sports – choose the eco-friendly ones like windsurfing, canoeing, or sailing and stay away from noisy jet skiing. If you are just too tired to dive, try snorkelling tours in Nusa Dua, or hop on their glass-bottomed boat to discover the marine life without getting wet. Yos organises beach cleaning programmes and has started a coral rehabilitation programmes in Pemuteran (see p. 348).

T 0361-773 774;
0361-775 438;
0361-775 440
F 0361-775 439
yosbali@indosat.net.id
www.yosdive.com
> In Tanjung Benoa, on Jl. Pratama #106x.

T 0361-772 726
F 0361-753 809
www.baruna.com
www.komodo-divecruise.com
> On Jl. Pratama, next to Grand Mirage Hotel.

Another dive shop worth a mention is *Baruna*, one of the oldest operators in Bali, also offering PADI courses in English, Japanese, German, and Indonesian, and participating in beach cleaning programmes. Baruna offers sailing trip packages of four to eight nights to the lesser Sunda islands of Komodo, Sumba, and Flores.

What to Do – Uluwatu, the Cliff Temple

Sanctified as one of the six main directional temples of Bali, or *sad kahyangan*, **Pura Luhur Uluwatu** hovers on a stunning spot above the Indian Ocean, at the tip of the Bukit Peninsula. Mpu Kuturan, a Javanese priest who came to Bali in the beginning of 11th century, is believed to have founded the temple. The temple is also associated with the legendary 16th century priest, Danghyang Nirartha, who built several famed sanctuaries around Bali, until he achieved *moksa* at Uluwatu – the liberation from the endless cycle of rebirth, to become one with the infinite.

The building of Uluwatu, made of dark grey coral, is rather simple – letting the magnificent natural setting absorb the humbled visitor. Beware the resident troupe of monkeys, quick at snatching sunglasses, earrings, and cameras. The three *candi bentar* (split gateways) are adorned with wing-shaped carvings representing the phoenix. The gateway into the inner sanctuary, which is closed to non-worshippers, bears an arch sculpted with a sneering *bhoma*, guarding the sanctuary from evil intruders. From the terrace, visitors can peer inside the sanctuary, housing a three-tiered *meru*. The scene over the southern coastline from the terrace is superb. From the temple, follow the pathway on your left along the cliff's edge, admiring the vistas over the ocean and the temple's *meru* perched on the cliff.

© Ulung Wicaksono

Sunset at Uluwatu temple

Make your Own Pot at *Jenggala Ceramics*

Jenggala Ceramics is a perfect place to hunt for an earthenware gift. It has a two-hour introductory course for adults and children, where you'll have the fun of handling muddy clay and create your own piece for US$10, including materials. Though some useful ceramics terms – such as slab work, pinch, and hand throwing – will be used during the course, don't become too serious. As an apprentice said, the course can be as rewarding as it is fun.

T 0361-703 311
F 0361-703 312
www.jenggala-bali.com
➤*Take the Ngurah Rai Bypass towards Nusa Dua. Turn right at the intersection with the sign of McDonald's Jimbaran to Jl. Uluwatu. Look for Jenggala Ceramics' sign on the main road.*

Fair Trade in Bali

By Degung Santikarma, with the contribution of John MacDougall (Primitive in Bali).

Farmers and Termites

Once a poor farming village in the hills north of Ubud, Tegallalang is now a row of "art shops" selling brightly-painted carved cats. Farmers who could barely eke a living out of their rice terraces drive around in BMWs, renovate their houses and family temples, and hold grandiose cremation ceremonies for their ancestors. Residents joke that they have changed from *petani*, or farmers, into *tetani*, or termites, living off the wood from which they carve their crafts. Hired hands from east Bali farm their ancestral lands – that is, what lands haven't been sold to finance the building of art shops.

With exports officially valued at US$1.5 billion a year, handicrafts are big business in Bali, giving birth to new social classes. At the top of the scale are the foreigners – from the beachcombers who finance their holiday by selling cheap sarongs in flea markets, to the seasoned agents of large retail firms. Balinese make up the middle and lower rungs. The local elites are the intermediaries – drivers, guides, and "quality control" specialists – who negotiate between Western buyers and local producers. Then there are the Balinese middlemen who buy crafts cheaply in villages and sell them to art shop owners. At the bottom of the scale are the masses of Balinese producers.

Carved cat CD holders

© Ulung Wicaksono

Climbing up the Ladder

Success in the handicraft industry depends less on one's artistic skill than on a combination of market access and capital. Those producers lucky enough to have inherited land in prime tourist areas have direct access to buyers. Being able to afford an education also helps; producers who cannot speak English are at a severe disadvantage. It also hard for small-scale artisans to amass the capital needed to accept large orders, as many buyers expect the producer to front the costs of raw materials and labour.

The image of Balinese craftspeople as soulful artists engaged in a traditional way of life hides stark realities. While some handicraft makers from artistic centres around Ubud may have learned painting or stone carving from their parents, many choose this sector as the only way to work out of poverty. Their works make it to market because they are cheaply produced with poorly paid labour and inexpensive raw materials. In fact, many crafts made in Bali have no relationship with the local culture.

Carved giraffes and panda bears, Christmas tree ornaments, Native American dream catchers, Australian didgeridoos, and Inuit carvings are all made in Bali to be sold as "authentic" elsewhere. The success of their producers is their ability to copy a sample brought by a foreign buyer. Indeed creativity is risky, especially for Balinese who have little understanding of the cultural context that makes Westerners want to own carved cats holding fishing poles in the first place.

A Balinese Version of Fair Trade

Agung Alit, a Balinese social welfare activist, founded the Mitra Bali Foundation, Bali's first "fair trade" organisation, in 1993, to address these concerns. The buyers who work with Mitra Bali must pay provide craftspeople a 50% deposit on orders, allowing small-scale producers to participate without going into debt or selling the family land. Producers are taught to calculate their material and labour costs instead of accepting out of desperation whatever a buyer offers. Mitra Bali also organises a producers' mutual aid society lending money or labour to members in need.

Mitra Bali also tries to raise awareness of safe working conditions. There is a long way to go since most craft makers consider safety masks and gloves as expensive and cumbersome, shunning them even when breathing toxic varnishes or using sharp tools. The foundation also encourages producers to use materials that do not contribute to environmental devastation, like easily-grown coconut and *albasia* woods, and they sponsor the replanting of trees felled for craft production.

Primitive in Bali

After a century of international fascination with the complex figures of Balinese artistry, minimalism is in favour – strong lines, abstract contours, raw, "natural" materials. Shunning elaborate carvings of the Hindu pantheon, collectors crave the "primitive" art of Papua or Sumatra. But labour and fax machines are rare in the rainforest, making it difficult for tribes people to supply foreign buyers. Filling the gap, some Balinese craft makers are emulating the "crude" designs of Papuan art. As noted by one of them: "Carving primitive figures is so much easier. We use rough tools, simple coloration, and cheap wood, instead of the quality materials and long polishing required for traditional Balinese statues."

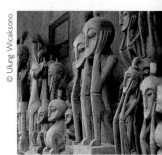

Bali-made "primitive" art

© Ulung Wicaksono

Workshop in Tegallang

♥ ♥ *A member of the International Fair Trade Association, Mitra Bali operates as a cooperative federating over 100 handi-craft producer groups, comprising over 1,000 Balinese crafts-people. This number is expanding as Fair Trade products leave specialty shops for the shelves of large retailers.*

Mitra Bali Foundation:
*Jl. Gunung Abang
Banjar Lodsema,
Lodtunduh, Ubud.
T 0361-295 010
F 0361-295 616
www.mitrabali.com*

Retail Shop in Ubud:
*Jl. Raya Andong.
T 0361-744 00 04*

Cultural Traps along the Way

Most importantly for the farmers-turned-craftsmen, Mitra Bali acts as a cultural translator. The organisation helps Balinese to produce work to international standards and decipher odd market trends – like the shift from carved bananas to giraffe CD-holders – rather than merely copying samples. For craftspeople who wish to explore new forms, Mitra Bali operates a design centre that has a library of references and holds workshops where foreign buyers can explain their needs.

Yet no matter how fair one tries to make it, trade is still trade. Once Balinese enter the global arena, they are expected to become modern market players, often at the expense of tradition. Overseas buyers expect products on time. They can't afford to care about the proper days to cut wood according to the Balinese calendar, or to wait while a producer is off at a cremation ceremony. In practice, this means that buyers often choose to work with the larger, more experienced producer groups who can guarantee delivery of large Christmas or peak season orders, rather than the smaller groups just getting off the ground.

International alternative trade organisations that order from Mitra Bali also expect a certain number of social changes to come from participating in fair trade, some of which make little sense to Balinese producers. Western concerns about child labour, for example, are often difficult for Balinese to accept (read the feature on p. 203). Gender inequality is also hard to address, for no matter how many Balinese women are taught to carve cats, they still, according to Balinese customary law, are unable to take part in village decision-making processes, or to inherit their parents' land. Even with the rapid influx of wealth, social change comes slowly in Bali. Organisations like Mitra Bali still have a long way to go to find acceptable solutions, and need the help of concerned buyers from overseas who give the preference to Fair Trade products.

Ubud

By the lotus pond

Where Two Rivers Meet

Throughout the centuries, the emerald beauty and fertility of the surrounding hills drew congregations of princes and artists to Ubud. But the destiny of Ubud as a point of confluence may have been sealed in the 8th century by Rsi Markendya, a wandering priest from Java. According to legend, he found his perfect meditation site in **Campuhan**, where the eastern and western branches of the Wos River meet. Today, travellers can admire the peaceful **Gunung Lebah** temple near this holy site, below the suspension bridge at the western edge of Ubud.

In the 1930s, east and west met again around Ubud's vibrant arts scene. The local prince, **Tjokorda Gede Agung Sukawati**, opened his palace to foreign travellers and artists. Among them were painters **Walter Spies** (1880-1942) and **Rudolph Bonnet** (1895-1978). Inspired by the lush tropical dreams of painter Henri Rousseau, they settled in Campuhan, on the site of the **Tjampuhan Hotel**, which still belongs to the court of Ubud.

As more foreigners joined them, crossing their visions and techniques with the century-old themes and mastery of the Balinese, Ubud became a world-known centre for the arts. Spies' fellows such as Kobot, Gusti Made Barat, and I Dewa Ketut Rungun gave birth to the Pengosekan and Padangtegal schools in their respective villages. Later, Dutch fauvist painter Arie Smit and

> *Of the three roads leading from Denpasar to Ubud, the western one is the most scenic and the least heavily used. Drive first to Batubulan, and turn left at the Barong statue. You will then pass the pleasant **Bali Bird Park** and the stone-carving village of **Tegaltamu**, both worth a stop on the way. Further up the road, you will drive through the village of **Sayan**, above the stunning Ayung River valley. Shortly after the Amandari hotel, turn right to reach western Ubud via **Penestanan** and **Campuhan**.
Another pleasant road takes you from Denpasar to southern Ubud through the peaceful villages and rice fields of **Lodtunduh** and **Pengosekan**.*

Tjokorda Gede Agung Sukawati.

© Ulung Wicaksono

A barong dancer at rest

Money Temples

The busy main road going to Ubud through Celuk Batuan, and Mas is lined with "art shops", handicraft markets and galleries. Celuk specialises in silverwork, Mas in carving, and Ubud sells pretty much anything that can be painted, carved, or crafted. Local tour guides dub Celuk, Mas, and Ubud "the three temples" ("Kahyangan Tiga"), in a cynical reference to Bali's three holiest temples. Taking tourists through these three villages yield them fat commissions — from 20% up to 50% — on any purchase made by their clients.

Balinese painter Cakra founded the Young Painters School in Penestanan, while I.B. Made Widja created the miniaturist Batuan School. Besides painters, Ubud attracted scores of writers, musicians, dancers, and anthropologists, and, as summed up by writer Made Wijaya, became a meeting place for "glamorous globe-trotters", from Margaret Mead to Charlie Chaplin.

Ubud remained a quaint painters' village after the war and throughout the 1950s and 1960s. Agung Rai, a local collector, still remembers how he cycled down to Sanur to sell a few paintings to the first tourists. Ubud had to wait until the 1970s to see the flow of visitors increase in the wake of the most prestigious of them all: Queen Elizabeth II.

Eyebrows were raised around Bali as Her Majesty insisted on visiting **Pengosekan**, a low-caste, isolated artists' village. Pak Mokoh, a local painter, is still grateful for Her Majesty's visit. "It was in 1974, we had no road, but we still organised an exhibition for the Queen. I don't remember if she bought any paintings, but the government built a road to Pengosekan for her, and we still get to use it." Soon after, in 1979, the villagers created the Pengosekan community of farmers and artists, paying a tribute to the Balinese way of life through their art.

In the following years, with more travellers shunning commercial beachfronts for artsy hill spots, Ubud grew into a vast art-and-tourist market, absorbing Pengosekan and other villages such as **Penestanan**, **Peliatan**, **Petulu**, and **Tegallantang**. Rice paddies were drained to build guest houses and restaurants, most of them catering to budget travellers in search of authenticity. Since the late 1980s, trendy restaurants and exclusive resorts started to mushroom, such as the exquisite Amandari, built above the Ayung River ridge. Yet despite the growing crowds, Ubud remains a great gateway to the best of Bali, especially if you choose to stay in the outskirts, where village life is intact.

The Many Faces of Ubud

There is an endless choice of accommodations in Ubud, most of it very good value. You can start with simple, US$5-a-night bungalows at the back of family compounds, and climb up the price range to hedonistic hotels and spas at US$100-a-night – or much more.

Many families offer a few rooms in their compounds in *Central and Northern Ubud*, along the streets branching out south of the main road (Jl. Gotama, Hanoman, and Jembawa), or north of the main road (on Jl. Kajeng, Sriwedari, and surrounds). Here, budget travellers may find a vivid community life hidden behind a maze of shops and restaurants where health food competes with Balinese warungs and trendy cafés.

There is a high density of guest houses and resorts in *Southern Ubud*, especially along *Monkey Forest Road*. This once-quiet lane leading through rice paddies to a tiny sacred forest has turned into a tourist bazaar, where "zen" shops can be found side-by-side with more terrestrial outlets. Travellers looking for peace and good views will have to push to the southeast end of Monkey Forest Road, or to the end of Hanoman Street in Pengosekan, a 20-minute walk from Central Ubud. Also in Southern Ubud, but with no direct road access to the centre of town, the lovely hamlet of *Nyuhkuning* is a perfect haven of peace.

At the *western end of Ubud*, along the quiet *Bisma Lane* on the way to *Campuhan*, it is still possible to flavour the original atmosphere of Ubud, amidst dense groves, vibrant streams, and dream-like rice fields. Travellers who want to escape the crowds will push even further to the hills *around Ubud*.

While Ubud is the perfect place to relax and watch the rice grow, active types will find many opportunities for fun discoveries. Nature lovers may spend hours trekking, biking, or bird-watching. Art fans will get a unique chance to enjoy and even learn the many arts of Ubud before filling their bags in craft shops and galleries.

Getting Around

It is easy to get to Ubud and the nearby villages with one of the many bemos travelling the busy roads around this area. Red bemos to Campuhan, Kedewetan, and Payangan start from the market. They wait for passengers in front of the Tourism Information Centre, across from the Pura Desa Adat temple on the main road. For more comfort, **Perama** *buses operate from the southern end of Jl. Hanoman, a 15-minute walk from Ubud's main road. They link Ubud with Kuta, Sanur, Lovina, Padangbai, and Candidasa, and can pick up passengers at their hotel (T 0361-973 316; 0361-974 722).* **Mountain bikes** *can be rented from many shops or guest houses (Rp15-20,000 per day).*

© Iskandar

At a ceremony

Where to Stay – Central Ubud

Staying between the closed walls of a Balinese family compound is a rewarding, once-in-a-lifetime experience. Ubud offers many opportunities for guests and hosts to discover each other, provided they are ready to bridge their cultural differences. Don't hesitate to look for the right homestay until you feel at home – you may end up leaving a piece of your heart in Ubud, like many Westerners before you.

A Homey Nirvana

❤ ❶ ❷ 6 Rm – Htw Cls
T/F 0361-975 415
rodanet@denpasar.
wasantara.net.id
➤ *In Padangtegal Kaja,*
Jl. Gotama – between
Ubud's main road and
Dewi Sita Street.

Guests feel at home in the compound of Pak Nyoman and his wife Ni Wayan at Nirvana Homestay. Both are charismatic characters, ready to introduce you to Ubud with intelligence and passion. Nyoman is an artist and an activist, teaching *batik* painting and watercolour drawing. Yet for him, life is the ultimate art and he finds as much culture in a kitchen as in a museum. Should you need a more secluded place for a longer stay, ask for **Nirvana Kubu di Sakti**, their second residence in the rice fields.

Into the Past at Matahari Cottages

❤ ❸ 7 Rm – Htw
Rst Swp
T 0361-975 459
seanseantw@yahoo.com
www.matahariubud.com
➤ *On Jl. Jembawan.*

These quaint cottages, in the heart of Ubud, are also run by a Balinese family. Each cottage has its own personality and decoration. Victorian afternoon tea is served on antique china and silver between 2 and 5pm (Rp55,000 per person). Guests can also enjoy the small pool which overlooks the river. The managers take care of the environment by recycling paper and glass; they run the cottages and restaurant primarily on solar power.

❹ ❺ 16 Rm – Htw A/C
Rst Swp Gvw Shw
T 0361-973 178
F 0361-973 179
www.wakaexperience.com
➤ *Follow Jl. Sueta towards*
Sambahan for about 2km, a
5-minute drive north from
the centre of Ubud.

In the upmarket category, *Waka di Ume* is set along a gentle hillside on Jl. Sueta in Sambahan, in the northern part of Ubud. Open to the surrounding paddies, this resort is an invitation to absorb the stunning vista extending to the sea. It makes use of the textures and colours of local materials to secure a natural, yet refined atmosphere. Every Tuesday and Thursday, guests are freely invited to join a 90-minute walk in the rice fields. Yoga sessions are also planned.

Where to Eat – Central Ubud

The centre of Ubud is brimming with restaurants; new eating places open every day. New Age eaters will be happy to sample a wide choice of organic, vegetarian, and health food. There are also many great Balinese warungs and a few posh restaurants.

A Health Food Smorgasbord

The *Bali Buddha Café* lets hungry guests enjoy a rich variety of fresh fruit juices and tonics, as well as fresh salads, or home-made pasta and pizzas with delicious toppings. Most ingredients are organic. A variety of sweet treats, such as wheat-free butterscotch brownies, is also available. If you would like to enjoy this wonderful food in the comfort of your own hotel, Bali Buddha is more than happy to deliver for a small fee.

© Jean-Marie Bompard

Ritual fruit offerings

Just below, the *Andalan Health Food Store*, striving to support the development of organic farming in Bali, offers a great variety of organic fruits and vegetables, rice and grains, as well as herbs, teas, and coffee. Guests can also purchase fresh organic soymilk, preservative-free tofu, and *tempe* (soy cake), homemade yoghurt, soups, dressings, jams, cakes, and snacks. Andalan Health Food Store offers home delivery of its organic produce, baked goods, and healthy meals around Ubud.

Health food fans will also enjoy the *Hanoman Juice Bar* (Jl. Hanoman #12), which serves a variety of pure fruit juices and health cocktails, including extract of wheatgrass shoots, using organic fruits and vegetables. Light meals are also available, and guaranteed MSG-free.

Facing the soccer field in a little foot gang off Jl. Dewi Sita, the recently opened *Deli Cat* (T/F 0361-971 284) serves good value healthy food with a Scandinavian touch.

Further north on Jl. Kajeng #35, the small vegetarian restaurant of the **Ubud Sari Health Centre** serves organic soups, salads, and sandwiches and a variety of juices in a simple and relaxing atmosphere, which you can combine with a trip to their spa.

♥♥
T 0361-976 324;
T/F 0361-978 963
andalan@indo.net.id
> On Jl. Jembawan 1, in front of the Post Office.

The owners of Bali Buddha Café have created **ABC Solutions**, which offers waste management services to households and small tourist operations in the Ubud area. Recyclable waste is collected on a weekly basis, sorted, and transported to Java for recycling (Bali still lacks adequate recycling facilities).

T 0361-974 393

A Sample of Balinese Food

T 0361-978 249
M 081 64 70 19 62
> Jl. Gotama #13
Padangtegal Kaja.

The owners
are ready to teach you
their best recipes for
Rp100,000 per person,
lunch included.

If you've ever dreamed of eating bamboo shoots (*rebung*) or banana stems (*ares*), check out **Biah-Biah**. This small restaurant offers an original selection of Balinese dishes in a rustic and pleasant atmosphere. The nicely-prepared portions are small and inexpensive. The unique Biah-Biah soup is available when this weed (*Monochoria vaginalis*) is growing in the rice paddies.

T/F 0361-975 447
> Jl. Monkey Forest.

The old Ubud is still alive at *Café Wayan*. It all started as a bamboo hut, where Ibu Wayan and her husband sold coffee to rice farmers back from the fields or on their way to the temple. They have created a network employing over 130 staff from the local communities. Don't miss the traditional Balinese buffet served on Sunday evenings or the famous cakes.

T 0361-975 487
> On Jl. Kajeng #24
(next to Threads of Life
Textile Art Centre).

On the north end of the main road, you can also sample good Balinese food at **Rumah Roda** Restaurant. On Sunday evenings, Pak Darta and his wife offer an excellent buffet dinner at a reasonable Rp30,000 – perfect to quiet your hungry stomach after one of their **rice field walks**. Another good classic, on Jl. Monkey Forest, is *Ibu Rai*, serving simple, popular Indonesian and Western food of good quality.

A Chic Evening

T 0361-975 660
> Jl. Raya Ubud.

Among the well-established restaurants along the main street, *Café Lotus* is famous for its beautiful setting facing a lotus pond in front of the royal family temple.

T 0361-978 305
> Jl. Raya Ubud #1,
opposite the Pura Desa
(Village temple).

To spot the intelligentsia of Ubud, have a drink or a gourmet meal at *Ary's Warung*. Once a small stall catering for backpackers, occasionally serving "magic mushrooms", it has evolved into a posh outlet with a stylish, although a bit chilly décor, which would fit in Manhattan just as well as in Ubud. The owner, Odeck Ariawan, supports the social and environmental activities of the local community, and strives to promote Ubud. Despite a very modern kitchen, you can still enjoy the famous duck *à la betutu*, a Balinese dish requiring seven hours of preparation.

Where to Stay – Monkey Forest

A King's Life at Tegal Sari

Well-located, tasteful, and friendly, this exquisite accommodation has gained the reputation of being the best hotel in its price range in Bali. It offers a wide range of facilities and services, including an outdoor gym, a library, massage and baby-sitting at moderate prices, and free transport within Ubud. Trekking in the rice fields, cycling, cooking and batik classes, dancing classes, and kite-flying for children of all ages are also on offer. Booking several months in advance is highly advisable.

The nearby *Greenfields Bungalows*, on Pengosekan Street, may appear ordinary and a bit run down in comparison to Tegal Sari. However, nature lovers will appreciate the quiet setting of the simple bungalows facing extensive rice fields with the Monkey Forest in the background and the salt water pool.

♥ ❷ ❸ 14 Rm – Htw A/C Rst Swp Gvw Trk Cls Bcy
T 0361-973 318
F 0361-970 701
www.tegalsari-ubud.com
> Indicated by modest signs on the south of Hanoman Street across the Perama bus depot.

❷ ❸ 15 Rm – Htw A/C Swp Gvw
T 0361-975 798;
0361-977 100
F 0361-977 200
greenfieldbali@hotmail.com

Arts and Luxury at the Arma Resort

Lovers of tranquillity will appreciate the luxury rooms and villas of this four-hectare property (formerly the Kokokan Hotel), overlooking the rice fields and crossed by the river Tirta Tawar. Art lovers will appreciate the proximity and free access to the Agung Rai Museum of Arts (ARMA). The resort features an open stage and an outdoor theatre where Balinese classical dance and music are performed frequently. Guests can also observe the classes provided for free to young local students in Balinese dance, music, and drawing by the ARMA Foundation.

♥ ❹ ❺ 25 Rm – Htw A/C Rst Swp Gvw Shw Cls
T 0361-976 659
F 0361-975 332
www.armaresort.com
> On Jl. Bima, Pengosekan.

Where to Stay – Nyuhkuning

It is worth the effort to find this secluded hamlet. You can access it from **Singakerta**, turning right after the petrol station on the way to Sayan, or from **Pengosekan**, south of the ARMA Museum. From Ubud, walk to the Monkey Forest and follow a small path starting behind the ticket counter at the eastern corner of the Monkey Forest.

A coconut–leaf and bamboo penjor

© Djuna Ivereigh

Beautiful Nature at Alam Indah and Alam Jiwa

10 Rm –
Htw A/C Rst Swp
Gvw Trk
T/F 0361-974 629
www.alamindahbali.com

At Alam Indah (Beautiful Nature), the owners of Café Wayan, Ibu Wayan and Pak Ketut, have created an ambience reflecting the serenity of Bali's rural areas. The skilled and smiling staff make the guests feel at home in the spacious and comfortable rooms set amidst a green, Balinese-style compound. Alam Indah offers opportunity to discover the heart of Balinese culture – try the great rice field walks guided by Pak Darma.

10 Rm –
Htw A/C Swp Gvw Cls
T/F 0361-977 463

A 15-minute walk from sister hotel Alam Indah, *Alam Jiwa* (the Soul of Nature) is a bit more luxurious retreat set amidst rice fields. Woodcarving classes can be arranged with nearby workshops. Both Alam Indah and Alam Jiwa are committed to reducing their environmental impact and are affiliated with the ABC recycling programme.

A Bamboo World at Linda Garland's

7 Rm –
Htw A/C Swp Gvw
T 0361-974 028
F 0361-974 029
lindag@indosat.net.id
www.lindagarland.com

Sheltered on ten hectares of riverside land in the rolling hills of Nyuhkuning, Linda Garland's estate offers a unique balance between man-made structures and natural integrity. It comprises four rental houses (the River House, Waterfall House, Bamboo Garden House, and Coconut House), a 30-metre-long swimming pool, and extensive space to meditate about the simplicity and usefulness of bamboo.

Buy Bamboo
The EBF promotes furniture, housewares, and jewellery made of bamboo sourced from sustainably managed plantations, and created by renowned designers. The packaging explains the environmental value of bamboo and the work of the EBF. Contact Linda Garland's estate or www.bamboocentral.org

Guests can visit the adjacent **Environmental Bamboo Foundation** (EBF), founded by designer Linda Garland in 1993 to protect tropical forests by promoting and demonstrating the many conservation and development opportunities offered by bamboo. The foundation has propagated more than 35,000 seedlings for agroforestry and watershed reclamation projects initiated in Bali. A training centre, surrounded by bamboo gardens and nurseries, was also created in1994 in **Penglipuran**, near Bangli in east Bali. The EBF trains community groups and entrepreneurs interested in establishing their own facilities for bamboo preservation. To support the development of bamboo, buy some of the foundation's well-designed bamboo products.

Where to Eat – Southern Ubud

At the southeastern end of Monkey Forest Road, towards
Jl. Hanoman, *Kubuku Café* (*T 0361-974 742*) is a simple
place to relax in a natural environment. Enjoy the view
over rice fields, or pop up at dusk to be lulled by a chorus
of frogs. Kubuku serves a selection of vegetarian dishes
and delicious fruit juices, especially jackfruit juice. Those
looking for a secluded retreat far away from Ubud may
ask Pak Wayan, the owner of Kubuku, for information
about the **Ayun Sari Indah Bungalows** located in
Singaperang, about 20km north of Ubud.

Food offering for a ceremony

   Bebek Bengil (the Dirty Duck) is a classic in Ubud.
It owes its name to its first guests, a flock of ducks that
left a web of muddy footprints all over the place, just
before the soft opening in 1990. Since then, the lovely
setting on a terrace has made the restaurant famous, as
well as its flagship dish, "the Bebek Bengil crispy duck" –
half a duck steamed and deep fried (about Rp60,000).

T 0361-975 489
> On Jl. Hanoman in
Padangtegal.
cafepujer@hotmail.com

   For more spicy food and a simple, authentic experience, try the gorgeous *nasi campur* at *Warung Teges* (Jl.
Raya Peliatan, *T 0361-975 251*), a favourite with locals.

A World of Peace at Café Pujer

Walking from Monkey Forest Road to Nyuhkuning, stop
at this tiny and peaceful café for a natural refreshment
or an inexpensive light lunch (soups, salad, and bread for
Rp20,000). A favorite among young Japanese travellers,
Café Pujer is dedicated to building world peace through
non violence and understanding other cultures.

T 0361-974 062
> Jl. Nyuh Bulan #5,
Nyuhkuning.
cafepujer@hotmail.com

  *Casual, free Indonesian
language classes held on
Monday, Wednesday, and
Friday at 11am.*

Where to Stay – Bisma Lane

The western edge of Ubud retains a bit of its rural
atmosphere, with virtually no shops and few buildings.
The quiet Jl. Bisma is a perfect hideaway with good
accommodations; the mud road keeps many travellers
away.

  *Refill your water
bottle at the friendly
Roda Mas Internet Café
(T 0361-973 325).*

   In the low price range, *Vera* offers five spotlessly
clean rooms with mosquito nets facing a lotus pond and
surrounded by rice fields 500m from Ubud's main road.

❶ 5 Rm – Htw
T 0361-975 960

① ② 7 Rm –
Htw Swp Gvw
T 0361-975 976
F 0361-972 513

② 14 Rm –
Htw A/C Swp
T 0361-970 760;
0361-972 484
F 0361-970 516
www.nicks_club.com

② ③ 16 Rm –
Htw Swp Gvw Cls
T 0361-973 282
www.casalunabali.com

♥ ④ ⑤ 2 Rm – Htw Swp
www.teras-sungai.com
> Off Jl. Bisma – Follow the
cement lane on the left just
after the Tri Nadi Health
Centre, before the
Honeymoon Guesthouse.
Ask the manager,
a member of the Palace
dance group, about shows
and ceremonies.

① ② 5 Rm – Htw
T 0361-979 103
> On the way to
Campuhan, follow a little
path on the right, before
the Melati Hotel.

For total peace amidst the shade of dense gardens around a lovely pool, try *Bucu View Bungalows* – *bucu* means "end corner", and you'll have to look for this well-hidden place on the right side of Jl. Bisma, at the end of a small cement road going down towards the river.

Just after the cross to Bucu, follow a narrow cement path through the rice fields to *Nick's Hidden Cottage* – you will easily spot this Balinese-style, two-storey building with its pagoda-like tower at the entrance. The spacious rooms and small terraces over-look the pool and the jungle-covered river valley.

Honeymooners or plain lovers of Ubud will enjoy the *Honeymoon Guesthouse*. The nice Balinese-style rooms are set in the garden of the family compound of Ketut Suardana and Janet De Neefe, owners of the **Casa Luna** and **Indus** restaurants. The hosts have chosen to provide simple fans instead of air-conditioning to enjoy the cool Ubud nights. Meals can be ordered from Casa Luna.

In the Trees at Teras Sungai

This luxury hideaway is hidden in dream-like vegetation rolling down to the Mumbul River. The two-room villa accommodates four people, and offers an open-air dining room and *bale* near the small pool. The environmentally-friendly construction is cool all year long, without air conditioning. The friendly staff will cook wonderful food upon request.

Where to Stay – Campuhan

If you haven't found your perfect nest in Jl. Bisma, go a bit further west on the way to Campuhan where a few great hotels, faithful to the spirit of Ubud, provide a perfect haven.

In the low price range, *Jagi Bungalows* welcomes guests in the quiet environment of Penestanan, in the western outskirts of Ubud. The simple, clean bungalows are located near rice fields in the back of the house of Ibu Nyoman and Pak Ketut Jana. Guests can use the swimming pool of the Melati Hotel, within walking dis-tance, for a fee of Rp10,000.

Live with a Balinese Painter at Made Punia's

This great homestay is the perfect place to get immersed
into Ubud's artistic life. Made Punia and his wife rent a
beautiful, comfortable two-storey house, with fantastic
views of the forests and rice fields. Spend time in Made's
studio, below the house, to discover his intricate paintings. Made and his wife keep a complete *gamelan* set,
which local villagers play once a week; guests may join in
for a practice, or wait for Made's daughter to start
undulating to the music. Ask Made to show you the
steep path down to a cool bath in the river, and you'll
feel like a character in a Balinese painting. Made can also
escort you on walks in the surrounding area – start early
on the morning to experience the magic light and flocks
of birds.

> ♥ ❷ 2 Rm – Htw
> Gvw Trk Cls
> M 081 23 97 73 05
> > On the Campuhan
> ridge path, about 500m
> north of Klub Kokos.
> Call in advance to check
> for room availability and
> get picked up. You can
> enjoy good Western and
> Indonesian cuisine at the
> Klub Kokos restaurant
> down the road.

　　Off the main road of Ubud, before the Campuhan
Ridge, *Abangan Bungalows* is a peaceful, good value
refuge short walk from Central Ubud. Hidden behind
the office, a row of simple, two-storey bungalows in
shape of traditional barns faces the ridge above a deep,
forested gorge. Fireflies and frogs entertain the guests at
night. The little path behind the bungalows is a good
starting point for rice field walks.

> ❷ 16 Rm – Htw A/C
> Swp Gvw
> T 0361-975 977
> F 0361-975 082
> > Up the steep cement
> ridge, on the left just after
> passing under the aqueduct
> on the way to Ubud from
> Campuhan.

A Family Life at Klub Kokos

Nestled in landscaped gardens near the Campuhan
Ridge, Klub Kokos is a family hotel. The clean and comfortable bungalows have equipped kitchens; the hotel
also features a play-room with lots of colourful toys, an
extensive library, an Internet room, and a large salt
water pool.

　　Klub Kokos was established by a local artist and his
Australian wife. Devoted to the local communities, they
support health and education programmes, such as a
library for schoolchildren. Donations are welcome.
Guests can become part of the local cultural life – this is
your chance to reveal your hidden talents in Balinese
dances; basket or kite making, painting, woodcarving, and

> ♥ ❷ ❸ 7 Rm – Htw
> Swp Trk Cls
> T/F 0361-978 270
> cathy@klubkokos.com
> www.klubkokos.com
> > Located on the quiet
> Campuhan Ridge path,
> the hotel can be accessed
> by car from the north, or
> by cycle or walk via the
> Campuhan Ridge walk.

gamelan percussions, taught by local artists from the nearby villages of Bangkiang Sidem and Sebali. Scenic walks around the area can also be arranged.

❸ ❹ *5 Rm – Htw*
T 0361-975 165
F 0361-975 282
murnishouses@yahoo.com
> *From Campuhan to Ubud, take the steep lane going up on the right after the aqueduct, and look for the last compound on the right towards the paddies.*

Lovers of the old Ubud will relish the four guest-houses of **Murni's**, hidden in the nice garden of a cosy Balinese compound on the edge of rice fields – there is no signboard, so you may need to ask for directions. Everything is made to make guests feel at home in peaceful seclusion, yet it is within walking distance from Ubud's main street. Gourmets will appreciate the great breakfasts, with Murni's famous home-made yoghurt.

Royal Hospitality at Ibah Luxury Villas

In faithful respect of the sacred Campuhan site, Ibah has been crafted with passionate skill by Tjokorda Raka Kerthyasa, a gifted mask carver and a member of the Ubud Royal Family. "Don't make Bali more Balinese than it is. Balinese architecture is very simple," he likes to point out. Nestled in the shade of a dense, two-hectare garden on the banks of the Campuhan River, this unique gem exudes a diffuse, mysterious atmosphere. Ibah participates in the local recycling programme and promotes walks around Ubud. Its owner strives to preserve the environment and culture of Ubud through local community bodies and foundations.

♥ ♥ ❺ *15 Rm – Htw*
A/C Rst Swp Gvw Spa
T 0361-974 466
F 0361-974 467
ibah@dps.centrin.net.id
www.ibahbali.com
> *In Campuhan, after the suspension bridge on the left when going up to Ubud.*

Where to Eat – Western Ubud

Eat in the Gorge at Murni's

In 1974, Ni Wayan Murni opened Ubud's first restaurant, where she served a mix of Western and Balinese food. Since then, generations of travellers have enjoyed the quality of her cuisine. Despite increasing road traffic, the four open-air levels facing the splendid river gorge offer absolute tranquillity in a totally out-of-this-world atmosphere. It's a most pleasant place for a great healthy breakfast (Rp45,000) or dinner (about Rp75,000). Vegetarian meals, home-made yoghurts, fantastic fruit juices, cakes, and pies are also on the MSG-free menu.

♥ *T 0361-975 233*
F 0361-972 146
www.murnis.com
(a great site about Balinese culture)
> *On the Ubud side of the Campuhan bridge. Pick-up and return to your hotel from 7pm.*

For another choice of excellent, healthy food with an awesome view, relax in the tasteful setting of the *Indus Café*. The two-storey restaurant overlooks the Campuhan valley. On a bright morning, Mt Agung can be seen in its glory, rising over the eastern horizon – the perfect company for a vitamin-packed breakfast. Great Mediterranean food is available for lunch and dinner, including a good choice of tasty vegetarian dishes, as well as a wider range of Western, Indian, and Indonesian food. Yoga classes are offered on the lower level (see What to Do p. 189).

T 0361-977 684
F 0361-973 282
> Jl. Raya Sanggingan.

Frangipani (jepun)

Diners in search of a romantic candlelight experience will enjoy climbing up the stone steps, delicately orna-mented with frangipani flowers, leading to *Miro's Garden*. This reasonably-priced outlet (about Rp35,000 per meal) is set on a lovely open-air terrace and offers a wide range of Indonesian, Asian, and international dishes, with a good choice of soups, salads, rice, and noodle specialties, as well as vegetarian recipes.

T 0361-973 314
> Jl. Raya Ubud.

For a great gastronomic experience in a lovely gar-den setting, indulge yourself at *Mozaic Restaurant*, whose opening in 2001 was celebrated as the birth of modern international Balinese cuisine – find out with your own taste buds what that means. The fancy menu changes daily; the complete menu to taste the best spe-cialties is offered for US$25.

T 0361-975 768;
0361-976 755
www.mozaic-bali.com
> Jl. Raya Sanggingan
www.mozaic-bali.com

Where to Stay – Around Ubud

West of Ubud and to the north, exclusive resorts sell the stunning views of the Ayung River, treasured by movie stars and tycoons – as attested by the helipad waiting for the rich and powerful amidst the paddies. Winding towards Payangan and Kintamani, the road goes through a peaceful countryside. The air gets a bit cooler as you get further into the hills and gorges, and the rural landscape is a relief after the hustle and bustle of Ubud. Faraway from the crowds, nature lovers will find quality hideaways and exclusive resorts hidden in the hills.

Rice terraces around Ubud

A Green Retreat at Alam Sari

♥ ❸ ❹ ❺ *13 Rm –*
Htw A/C Rst Swp
Gvw Bcy Spa
T 0361-240 308
alamsari@indo.net.id
www.alamsari.com
➤ *Located in Keliki*
10km away from Ubud,
on the road to Taro.

These comfortable, modern bungalows are set nicely in a garden above the peaceful surroundings – although some noise may be heard from the road. This is a good place to learn about the Balinese way of life and start long walks in the rice fields. Alam Sari is one of the few hotels in the Ubud area that have established a waste-water treatment plant, which recycles water in the beautiful garden. A daily free shuttle is offered to Ubud, unless your prefer to walk, finding your way through the rice fields with directions from the friendly staff.

A Faraway Home at Taman Bebek

♥ ❺ *8 Rm –*
Htw Swp Gvw
T 0361-975 385
F 0361-976 532
tbvbali@indo.net.id
➤ *In Sayan.*

This charming little resort, which name means "the Duck Garden", was originally the mountain home of Australian designer and writer Made Wijaya, one of the most devoted admirers and defenders of Bali. It was built on the site of the 1930s home of composer Colin McPhee. Made Wijaya stresses that "the tiered roofs, inspired by the *bale gede* ceremonial pavilions of Bali's mountain settlements, act as passive cooling systems" – in other words, air-conditioning is not needed. True to the Balinese spirit, the simple architecture and wide verandas leave the final word to nature. Soon enough, standing above the Ayung valley without knowing if you are outside or inside, lost in a lush garden or a domesticated jungle, you'll feel both at home and at the edge of the world.

Arts and Luxury at Alila Ubud

♥ ❺ *64 Rm – Htw Rst*
Swp Gvw Trk Bcy Spa
T 0361-975 963
www.alilahotels.com
➤ *Desa Melinggih Kelod,*
Payangan.

Hidden in the hills of Payangan over the Ayung River, Alila Ubud is another luxury retreat which you may never want to leave. Standing on stilts over the ravine, the villas mix traditional and modern building materials in a peace-inspiring design with heart-stopping views from the individual wooden terraces. The stunning pool seems to flow endlessly towards the valley. Faithful to their dedication to entertain guests and promote the local culture, Alila Ubud offers a choice of tours, trekking, biking, and exhibitions by young local artists.

A Hill Retreat at Bagus Jati

In search of a jungle retreat near Ubud? Then hide in these luxurious bungalows, nestled around the contour of a verdant hill. Follow the jungle trek in the morning to be greeted by birds and lizards, then follow the spinning path down the valley towards an isolated waterfall sprouting from a rocky wall. Bagus Jati offers yoga, spa treatment, massages, and scrubs, all using natural herbs and oils. The open restaurant, overlooking the valley, offers cooking classes in a traditional Balinese kitchen. Bagus Jati plans to build a hydro-power station and share the output with nearby villages.

Built on the edge of the Campuhan valley in Bunutan, *Hotel Bunga Permai* offers simple, yet comfortable rooms in Balinese-style brick-and-cement bungalows, with splendid views of the valley. The friendly staff will guide you for walks through rice fields, coffee planta-tions, and isolated villages (count Rp125-225,000 per group of 2 or 3 persons for 3-hour or full-day guided walks, inclusive of transport and tip for the guide).

For more luxury, hide yourself in *Villa Kunang-Kunang*, set in three hectares of beautifully landscaped tropical gardens above the valley. The elegantly-furnished villas are divided into two independent storeys, with a jacuzzi upstairs. The saltwater pool merges with breath-taking views of rice terraces. Walk around the peaceful surroundings and ask the owners for an introduction to Ubud and its culture. Transportation is available at rea-sonable cost; food can be delivered from Murni's Warung.

In the middle of coconut groves and greenery, *Kampung Cottage* is a cosy retreat, next to the crafts market of Tegallalang. All cottages have light stone walls with thatched roofs and large windowpanes made of coconut wood. For total peace, choose the rooms locat-ed in the lower part of the garden, next to a small creek. The *lumbung*-style *bale* is pleasant for reading and dozing off a little during a blazing afternoon.

♥ ❺ 26 Rm – Htw Rst Swp Gvw Cls Spa
T 0361-978 885
F 0361-974 666
www.bagusjati.com
> Drive north from Ubud towards Tegallalang for 15km. Then, 3.5km after the Pujung junction, turn left to Banjar Jati. After 2km, find the hotel's sign on your right.

❸ 11 Rm –
Htw Rst Swp Gvw Trk
T/F 0361-977 551
permai@indo.net.id
> Just north of Kedewatan, a 15-min drive from Ubud's centre. Turn right after Kupu-Kupu Barong in Payangan.

❺ 3 Rm –
Htw A/C Gvw Swp
T 0361-972 146
F 0361-975 282
www.murnis.com
> In Ponggang, Payangan, 20min outside Ubud, on the road up to Kintamani.

❹ 12 Rm –
Htw A/C Rst
T 0361-901 201
F 0361-901 202
kampcafe@indo.net.id
www.kampungcafe.com
> Ceking, Tegallalang.

♥♥❷❸ 🦅 ⛛

T 0361-941 050
F 0361-941 035
suabali@indosat.net.id
www.suabali.co.id
> *From Ubud, drive*
towards Gianyar, then
turn left to Kemenuh
just before Goa Gajah.

🍀   *In recognition*
of its efforts to motivate
the Balinese to react to
the challenges of mass
tourism, Sua Bali has
earned an award for
socially responsible tourism
in Berlin.

> *On the right side of the*
road to Payangan, before
Cahaya Dewata Hotel,
indicated by a red
Djarum sign.

Rice terraces in Tegallalang

© Ulung Wicaksono

An Ecotourism Village at Sua Bali

"I wanted to create a place where visitors could really get to know Bali," explains Ida Ayu Agung Mas, "whereby tourists and hosts can meet on a equal footing." Sua Bali – literally, "Meet Bali" – is located near the small, traditional village of Kemenuh, 7km from Ubud and Gianyar. Everything is simple here, in a relaxed and personal atmosphere. Guests awaken and sleep to the songs of cicadas.

Sua Bali offers a deep introduction to the local culture. Guests can learn cooking, woodcarving or painting, or engage in discussions with experts on architecture, medicine, or rice cultivation. Upon arrival, guests learn about the everyday village life, its living and working rhythms, and the proper way to interact with villagers – from the behaviour expected during a temple ceremony, or more mundane considerations on how to bargain properly at a village shop.

Where to Eat – Around Ubud

Tired of fusion cuisine and New Age health food? Then get a taste of real local food at *Nasi Ayam Ibu Mangku*, or, a few shops away, try *Warung Makan Mardika*. This village near Ubud has the reputation to have the best *nasi ayam campur* (mixed rice with chicken) around. Watch the luxury Volvos and BMWs packed along the road – although the local warungs serve meals for Rp5-8,000, they are popular with many a Ubud businessman. Janet de Neefe, owner of Casa Luna and Indus restaurants, confesses in her recent cookbook, *Fragrant Rice*, that she loves to start the day with a plate of rice in one of these little outlets, where you can taste chicken fingers on request.

Further north, along the main road to Tegallalang, you can stop at the *Kampung Café* (near Kampung Cottage), or enjoy the peaceful *Biru Café* (formerly Blue Yogi Café), 3km north of the crafts market, which serves good Indonesian meals and excellent desserts.

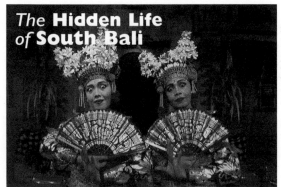

© Leonaard Lueras

The **Hidden Life** *of* **South Bali**

Legong dancers

A Dance for Every Day

By Ni Wayan Murni

It is almost impossible to spend even a few days in Bali, especially around Ubud, without witnessing a dance performance. Dances are offerings to gods and ancestors – staged to please the deities at religious ceremonies, to which they are invited by the priests. The most common are temple anniversaries (*odalan*), which take place once every Balinese year of 210 days. With tens of thousands of temples throughout the island, there is a very good chance of seeing one somewhere.

Dances also accompany rites of passage – from the many ceremonies accompanying the growth of Balinese babies to coming-of-age rituals like tooth-filing, followed by weddings and cremations. There are dances at exorcisms, held to rid the place of disruptive forces. Sensational dances are performed at times of crisis, such as epidemics, famines, and plagues. At these events, dancers, and sometimes even spectators, fall into trances.

Balinese dances – and the other performing arts – have a religious background. Many are ancient. Old stone statues, watching over proceedings in temples throughout Bali and Java, strike dance attitudes and wear dance costumes. The dances are Balinese but have been influenced by outside forces, including India, China, and Europe.

The best place to see dances and listen to the gamelan percussion is in their proper setting – in a temple, packed with people in splendid Balinese attire. Watch the women carrying offerings of fruit and flowers on their heads and placing them on special pavilions, and the white-clad priests intoning mantras, ringing bells, and muttering prayers with the moon and stars as the only lighting.

Applying make-up before a performance

© Leonaard Lueras

The First Eco-Epic?

Written in Sanskrit, the Indian Mahabharata (from Maha, greatness, and Bharata, victory). relates the rivalry between two groups of cousins, the Pandawas and the Korawas. No less than 88,000 verses are needed to tell their fights, in which good and evil come to life through intricate plots, until the heroes are liberated from these illusions in heaven. Nature is always present and powerful, with most of the stories taking place in deep forests and featuring a whole world of animal deities, from snakes to elephants and monkeys with whom the heroes must learn to ally.

© Djuna Ivereigh

A scene from the Ramayana in a Kamasan painting

Beyond the Story

Some dances have a story, often based on the old Indian epics, the *Ramayana* and the *Mahabharata*. It is almost impossible for the new spectator to follow the plot. Boys dance girls' parts, girls dance boys' parts. You cannot tell which are which; both wear heavy make-up. The same person may dance several roles, and scenes change with the barest of announcements. It's best just to sit back and enjoy the extreme beauty of the movements, the expressions, and the dazzling costumes. Lose yourself in the subtle, intricate, percussive sounds of the *gamelan* orchestra. Admire how the dancers and *gamelan* play as one: the dancers lead the drums, and the drums lead the *gamelan* without a conductor.

Many dances do not have a story, or at the most a very subliminal one. The most famous Balinese dance, the *legong*, is a good example – others are the *pendet* and *gabor*, which are dances to welcome the deities to a ceremony. More than the story, it's the rhythm, the atmosphere, and the feeling for space that bring the magic. In such dances, faces are like masks, emotion is underplayed, and even the gestures are abstract, although a few have dramatic meanings – shading the eyes with the hand indicates weeping; first and second fingers pointing at the end of a stiffly-extended arm is a gesture of anger or denunciation. Eyes move quickly from side to side to stress the rhythms and accents.

Because the epics on which the dances are based have a deep symbolic meaning, the characters exist in their own formal, spiritual world. There are stock characters who represent respected or not so respected qualities. The king and queen are refined or *halus*. The witches and monsters are coarse or *kasar*. They all have their own stylised movements and dress, and they speak in Kawi, an old language that few understand. The only real individuals are the clowns, who improvise, joke, and explain to the audience, in Balinese, what is happening onstage.

south

Dances for the Gods, Dances for the People

Dances are classified into the sacred – for the gods – and the secular – for humans. The most sacred dances (*wali*), like the *pendet*, *gabor*, *baris gede* and the masked dance, *topeng pejegan*, take place in the holiest, inner court of the temple (*jeroan*). The ceremonial dances (*bebali*), like the *ramayana* and *gambuh*, take place in the middle court-yard (*jaba tengah*). All these sacred dances are held when the priest is conducting the rituals and the temple is filled with people. At the same time, a shadow puppet per-formance (*wayang kulit*) may also be occurring.

Secular dances take place in the outer part of the temple or outside. Popular examples are the *legong*, the *kebyar*, and the lively solo *baris tungal*. New dances tend to fall into this category – dance is alive and well in Bali, and new choregraphies are created all the time. There are dance competitions throughout the island and nightly performances on Bali TV, the local television channel.

Although many new dances were created for Western consumption, the Balinese have been quick to adopt them. The most famous example is the *kecak* (mon-key dance). Initially choreographed by Walter Spies and Katharine Mershon in 1931 for a German movie, "Island of the Demons", it has become a favourite with Balinese and tourists alike. Similarly, the *oleg tumulilingan* (bumble-bee dance), was created by local choreographer, Mario of Tabanan, for the Peliatan dance troupe's tour of Europe and America in 1952. The *genggong* (frog dance), a favourite among children, is another example.

Some of the most classical dances of Bali have caught the heart of foreigners. An example is found in Batuan, near Ubud, famous for its *gambuh* – about which Beryl de Zoete and Walter Spies wrote in 1938: "Every dance-form… is ultimately derived from *gamboeh*; all dance technique originates in its movements, all scales and melodies from its peculiar *gamelan*." Today, foreign-ers and Balinese are allying in the "*Gambuh* Project" to save this enthralling mother of all Balinese dances.

© Bali-Photo

Dancer at rest

♥ **A Dance Rescue**
*At the end of the 1980s, the beautiful gambuh was dying amidst financial diffi-culties – it requires large sets of dancers, instruments and costumes – and disinterest among the Balinese. The rescue started when an Italian Dancer, Cristina Formaggia, felt in love with gambuh. She took ten years to study the old dance, becoming a recog-nised master of one of the main roles. Working with the Batuan temple troupe and nearby communities, she started the **Gambuh Preservation Project**, with the help of the Ford Foundation. Inquire at **Pura Desa Batuan** temple to witness their stunning performances, or buy the great CD, "Music of the Gambuh Theater", to sup-port the project.*

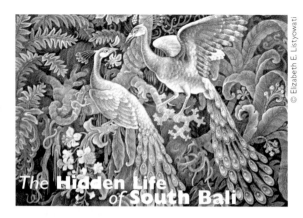

© Elizabeth E. Listyowati

Peacocks by Biang Raka,
Seniwati Gallery collection

Balinese painters: where art thou, art?

By Diana Darling

Religion and the Market

It used to be perfectly OK to say that "every Balinese is an artist," and for decades many people did so – in their letters home, in tourist brochures, and to the Balinese themselves – to the extent that this fabulous notion has become part of the island's official tourism profile. Perhaps this sounded less outlandish in the 1930s, when Miguel Covarrubias wrote in his instant classic, *Island of Bali*, that "everybody in Bali seems to be an artist." In those days, there were fewer opportunities to make souvenir trinkets or public statues of concrete.

Before the advent of tourism, painters and sculptors were mostly anonymous craftsmen who created works upon request for temples and palaces according to established conventions. The iconography was religious; the function was ceremonial or even magical; and the act of making these works was considered a devotional labour. Paintings depicted scenes from local myths or the great Hindu epics, the *Mahabharata* and the *Ramayana*. Sculpture was mainly guardian statuary – nearly always demonic and closely incorporated into the

Colours of Nature

Early Balinese painters had a limited range of colour to work with: they mainly used China ink and a few dyes derived from roots. Thus it is in terms of their composition and draughtsmanship, rather than colour, that Balinese paintings are to be appreciated. The initial drawing was laid down in great detail with charcoal, followed by outlines in ink, then colour, and finally highlighting with a wash of ground limestone. Today's traditional painters follow the same procedure with pencil, ink, and acrylics.

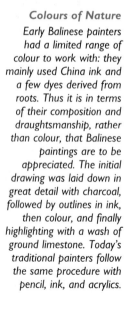

architecture of a temple or palace – or the very sacred effigies called *arca*, which function as vessels for deities.

These days, anyone visiting the Ubud area would be tempted to say that every Balinese owns an art shop. Ubud became known as a centre for the arts in the 1930s, thanks to the **Pita Maha** association – a group of painters and sculptors under the leadership of members of the Ubud palace family and the European artists Walter Spies and Rudolph Bonnet. The objective was to help local artists find a market for their work and to exert standards of quality control. The influence of these foreign artists is still debated among scholars – did they introduce perspective and realism in anatomy; was it they who introduced the idea of representing scenes from everyday life? Yet there is no question that they helped spawn the cottage industry of painting and sculpture that continues to dominate this part of Bali, from Tegallalang in the north, to Mas and Batuan in the south.

The Good, the Cute, and the Ugly

Most of the work found around Ubud shops and galleries is inexpensive, much of it is charming, some of it is good, and laced through it are pieces of real art, both traditional and modern. But how is a new visitor to sort through this immense quantity of stuff?

The first step is to educate one's eye by visiting the best collections. These are chiefly found in the several museums in and around Ubud: **Museum Puri Lukisan**, **Agung Rai Museum of Art (ARMA)**, and **Neka Museum** (see p. 180). All have important works in their permanent collections, representative of the main streams of Balinese painting.

Traditional and Contemporary Painters

Today's painters fall into two broad and occasionally overlapping categories: "artisanal" painters, working in established styles for the tourism market, and "contemporary" painters, striving for recognition on the international art scene.

An Eye for Details

Looking at traditional Balinese painting takes patience and entails some eye strain. In most styles, especially that of Batuan, canvases are filled with minute detail. Vegetation is stylised, but each leaf is painted and shaded. The patterns in the batik sarongs of even minor figures are carefully drawn. Even the air is populated with fine vibratory marks, as one might expect of this psychically-sensitive people. Part of the adventure for the viewer is discovering figures that emerge and retreat from the vegetation, or entire scenes – a dog fight, a love affair, a group of gamblers – taking place in a corner of the canvas.

Batuan style painting

© Djuna Ivereigh

Their work is found in profusion in the art shops lining the streets of Central Ubud, as well as in the large village of **Batuan** near Sukawati, and smaller villages around Ubud, such as **Penestanan** to the west and **Keliki** to the north, which specialises in very small paintings. Artisanal painters often work collectively under a master, whose studio is usually open to visitors. An example is Ngurah K.K., one of the original practitioners of the "Young Artist" school founded by the Dutch painter Arie Smit. His studio is in **Campuhan**, just uphill from the Tjampuhan Hotel on the other side of the road. Others are Dewa Batuan in **Pengosekan** and Ketut Budiana in **Padangtegal**. In these two painters' villages, one has only to wander through the gate of any house compound with a sign in front of it to make great discoveries.

Contemporary Balinese art may be found in several galleries around Ubud. They show works by artists from all over Southeast and East Asia, and by Westerners living in the region. The most prominent are **Komaneka** on Monkey Forest Road; **Sika Gallery** in Sanggingan; **Pranoto's Gallery** on Jl. Raya Ubud, Taman Kelod; **Seniwati** (devoted to art by women, especially Balinese) on Jl. Sriwedari 2B, Taman Kelod; **Galeri Sembilan** in Pengosekan; and the conspicuous-looking **Gaya Fusion of the Senses** in Sayan, with its huge double staircase leading to a smart restaurant. The Fine Art Gallery at the **Alila Ubud Hotel** in Kedewatan also holds regular exhibitions of regional artists.

Paying the Price

When buying art in Bali, prices can almost always be negotiated. Pricing systems vary among the dealers. Generally, they are not very advantageous to the artist. Many craft galleries buy paintings from the artist very cheaply, with the gallery keeping the profit, although some contemporary galleries are introducing commissions for the artists. Buyers should examine the stretcher carefully. Artisanal paintings may require some treatment to seal the surface.

© Leonard Lueras

I Wayan Putu Mokoh of Pengosekan

Ubud – What to Do

Ubud is the perfect place to get acquainted with the Balinese way of life. **Nature** lovers can start with a walk or biking tour to admire the lush vegetation and birds. Start on your own near Ubud, or hop on a **guided tour** to learn more about nature and culture. Museums are a great introduction to Balinese **arts and crafts**, which you may take further through a course in painting, dancing, or cooking. Make your visit complete by watching a **dance performance**, then explore the Petanu River valley to discover **ancient sanctuaries**. New Age adepts and hedonists will purify their **body and soul** in spas, health centres, or yoga and meditation classes. **Shoppers** will find endless occasions to satisfy their cravings, contributing to good causes at the same time.

A barong mask made of fibres

Walking, Biking and Birding around Ubud

The best way to discover Ubud is free: walk in any direction through the rice fields and watch the rice grow, the ducks waddle, and the children play.

One of Ubud's famous attractions is the *Monkey Forest Sanctuary*, located around a number of temple grounds at the southern end of Monkey Forest Road. The tiny sacred forest is home to hundreds of mischievous long-tailed macaques. You will become an object of their attention if you take any food with you. Better also to hide cameras, glasses, and jewellery – including earrings – which may be snatched away in a minute.

For a great introduction to the Ubud surrounds, try the mythical 90-minute circular walk around the *Campuhan Ridge*, also suitable for **mountain bikes**. The tour can begin from the Ibah Hotel or the Neka Art Museum. From Ibah, take the path on your left as you enter the road leading up to the hotel. The path takes you down some steps past **Pura Gunung Lebah**. It is paved for about 1km, then takes you along the ridge top through tall *alang-alang* grass. Stunning views of coconut groves, rivers, and rice fields are on either side.

Pura Gunung Lebah in Campuhan

Take the Campuhan Ridge walk in the early morning or late afternoon to avoid the heat as there are few trees on the ridge top. For a longer tour, you can continue along the ridge towards Keliki (app. 7km away), Taro (13km), and Kintamani (32km).

> North of the Ubud main road, take Jl. Tirta Tawar and head to Jungjungan, then to the right to Petulu, passing first Pura Desa Petulu. From Petulu, it is about 2.5km to the main road to catch a bemo to Andong and Ubud.

The plain terrace in front of the art shop of painter I Wayan Sogsag, amidst the rice fields, is a convenient place to get a drink and look at the amazing spectacle of birds. Look for its modest sign: "Warung - Resting place for see the birds."

At the end of the ridge top path, you will pass by a number of villas and restaurants, including Klub Kokos and Made Punia's Homestay, where you may drop by to have a drink or admire the paintings. Around 500m on, you will pass through the quaint village of Bangkian Sidem. At the end of the village, you will come to a fork in the road. The left route takes you on an asphalt road up a steep hill past the traditional villages of Payogan and Lungsiakan, ending up at the **Neka Art Museum**.

The *bird colony of Petulu*, a mere 3km to the north of Ubud, is home to no less than 6,000 cattle egrets, or *bangau* (Bulbulcus ibis). Together with other egret species such as the *kokok* (Egretta spp.), or herons such as the *blekok* (Ardeola speciosa) and *kowak* (Nycticorax nycticorax), they roost and nest in the trees along the village's main road.

The birds first appeared in Petulu in 1966 and are believed to be the souls of the thousands of victims killed in the anti-communist slaughter in 1965. It is prohibited to bother, capture, or shoot them, and the villagers protect them from snakes and civet cats. In the Pura Desa (village temple), an altar is dedicated to the spirits of the sacred birds, which are honoured during Tumpek Kandang – a ritual thanksgiving held every six months to honour domestic animals. These conservation efforts come with a price tag. As the gluttonous birds prey on any fish in the area, the Petulu farmers are the only ones in Bali who can't keep fish ponds or catch eels and frogs in the rice fields. They can only busy themselves cleaning the surroundings of the daily load of bird droppings.

From April to October, arrive late in the afternoon to watch the spectacle of thousands of egrets flying back at sunset to roost for the night in the village, turning the roadside trees white. During the breeding season, from November to March, most of the birds stay close to their nests and chicks. Cattle egrets are then easily recognised as they acquire brown, buff plumes on the head, back, and chest.

To the south of Ubud, near Kemenuh, 7km west of Gianyar, you may enjoy the refreshing view of the *Tegenungan waterfall*, dropping as high as 20m. The water flows into the Petanu River with a strong current, so swimming is unlikely.

> 1km west of the Blahbatuh market, take a side road heading south, and follow the road sign indicating the Waterfall Restaurant towards Tegenungan. A small path winds down to the base of the waterfall.

Guided Discoveries of Nature and Culture

Walking around Ubud will bring many questions, as every turn reveals a complex world of plants, animals, and human life. Take a tour with one of the great guides below and let them reveal a whole world of life, traditions, and secret stories hidden in the enchanting landscape.

The Magical World of Pak Darma

A banana leaf, a butterfly, and a bright flower creeping along the path will lead to fascinating stories as you walk around with Pak Darma, the owner of Rumah Roda restaurant. Under his expert eyes, every detail of the landscape finds its place as yet another colourful element of the Balinese art of living. Just tell him your interests, and benefit from his knowledge and friendship.

 Rumah Roda, Jl. Kajeng #24
T 0361-975 487
> The 2-3h walk starts behind Abangan Bungalows (US$10 per person, up to 4 persons, including transport and lunch).

Healing Herbs under your Feet

Watch your step as you walk around Ubud, for you may accidentally step on a timeless cure for hepatitis or diabetes – unless you are guided by Wayan Lilir and her husband Made Westi. Active environmentalists from a family of traditional healers, they feel they are in charge of a vanishing treasure: the local science of herbal remedies.

As they write: "We love to share our knowledge with those who want to learn about plant healing. Many people are missing so much, looking at landscapes from their car window…We offer a healthy walking experience where visitors will learn to spot invaluable herbs creeping in front of the beautiful vistas. We teach people how to identify each species with their eyes, nose, and tongue, before learning how to use each plant to remain healthy, in harmony with Mother nature."

Bali Herb Walks
T 0361-975 051
(call one day in advance).
supadupa@dps.centrin.net.id

The herb walks are arranged for 1 to 5 persons max, Mon through Thurs; 8:30am-12pm. They start in front of the Puri Lukisan Museum, on Ubud's main road (US$18 per person, including herbal drinks, cake, or fruits).

Bali Bird Walks
M 081 239 138 01
Tue, Fri, Sat, Sun 8:45am-
1:30pm, start at Mykonos
(formerly Beggar's Bush),
just after the Campuhan
bridge (US$33, including
shared binocular use,
water for the walks, and
lunch at Murni's Warung
or Mykonos).

c/o Tegun gallery
Jl. Hanoman 44.
T 0361-970 581
T/F 0361-973 361

♥ Casa Luna
8am-3:30pm
4-15 people, Rp200,000
per person including lunch.
T 0361-977 409
www.casalunabali.com
> On Jl. Raya Ubud,
between Jl. Bisma and
Monkey Forest Rd.

Bali Budaya Tours
Jl. Raya Pengosekan
(across from Pengosekan
Community of Artists)
T 0361-975 557
M 081 833 65 80
The tours can be booked
at many shops and hotels.
Groups up to a max. of 6,
Rp360,000 per person.

Singing Birds above your Eyes

As you join Bali Bird Walks, you'll suddenly understand why birds are hidden behind every tree leaf on Balinese paintings. Without being an expert ornithologist, you'll soon learn to spot some 30 out of over 100 bird species nestled in the rice fields and ravine forests around Ubud. Victor Mason, a long-standing ornithologist and author of *Birds of Bali*, created these walks, and still occasionnally leads them. Ten percent of the proceeds obtained from the walks are placed in the Bali Bird Park conservation fund.

Keep Walking Tours also offers great walks led by specially trained eco-cultural guides, covering a wide range of choices – from a one-hour visit of the Monkey Forest to a half-day itinerary through the surrounding villages, unless you prefer an enchanting late afternoon walk to the Petulu heronry, or a full day visit to archeological sites near Ubud.

Sugar and Salt

To escape from Ubud and get a glimpse of the life of traditional communities, hop in with the staff of the famous **Casa Luna Restaurant**. Every Sunday, they organise a whole-day tour to the hills and beaches of east Bali, where you will learn the timeless secrets of palm sugar making and sea salt extraction.

A Volcanic Breakfast

Ever dreamed of breakfast above a volcano? Then hook-up with Bali Budaya Tours. Guests are picked up at their hotel between 7:30 and 8am, and driven to the rim of **Mt Batur**, where breakfast is served. After a visit into the caldera, it is time to start cycling downhill, in order to arrive in Pejeng just in time for a great Balinese lunch. The tour ends at 4:30pm and involves less than two hours of cycling, with steps to visit coffee and fruit plantations or learn about bamboo weaving, Balinese architecture, and rice irrigation.

Another way to enjoy Mt Batur's crater while avoiding the throngs of guides in Toyabungkah is to start with I Gede Mangun, an experienced and friendly guide to the area. He manages *Bali Sunrise Trekking* from a small artshop near Batang Waru Restaurant, on Jl. Dewi Sita. The trek along the ridge of the vast crater, above Songan and Trunyan, is awesome. Book directly to get better prices.

Bali Sunrise Trekking
Jl. Dewi Sita.
T 0361-980 470
M 081 855 26 69
www.balisunrise2001.com

A Swarm of Wings at the Bali Bird Park

Walking amidst trees surrounded by rare birds from Bali, Java, and Papua is an unforgettable experience, especially for kids. The Bali Bird Park (*Taman Burung*) shelters a rich collection of feathered species, many of them endangered in their natural habitat. While the rarest birds are kept in cages, many others fly around in large enclosures reaching up to the treetops. One of them is equipped with a boardwalk leading you high into the trees' canopies.

In addition to a vast collection of Indonesian birds, primarily from the province of Papua, the Bali Bird Park hosts an impressive array of colourful species from Latin America, China, Africa, and Australia. Spectacular Indonesian birds include the rare Palm Cockatoo (the largest Cockatoo species); the Golden Neck Cassowary (one of the largest birds in the world); the Malayan Great Rhinoceros Hornbill, the King Bird of Paradise; and the highly threatened, endemic Bali Starling. Wild species, such as the iridescent blue Javanese Kingfisher are also known to visit the park.

The Park has informative labels about the birds; important information about current populations of endangered species is also provided. To preserve some of this wonderful diversity for future generations, the Bali Bird Park has set up a foundation dedicated to the preservation of the Bali Starling, Bali's only endemic bird. The foundation breeds the birds in captivity before releasing them into the wild (read more in the west Bali chapter, p. 411).

The Bali Bird Park is located 10km south of Ubud, on the road leading from Denpasar to Ubud via Sayan, next door to the Bali Reptile Park. Open daily, 8am-6pm. Entrance fee US$7.50 (adults) and US$3.80 (children).
T 0361-299 352;
0361-299 612
F 0361-299 614
balibirdpr@denpasar.
wasantara.net.id

© Djuna Ivereigh

A kingfisher rests on a banana leaf

An Introduction to Arts and Crafts

The rich natural wonders of Bali's central hills have inspired generations of artists. Starting from classical museums displaying amazing paintings filled with intricate renderings of Balinese life, visitors will have the chance to develop new skills through a rich diversity of classes from weaving to cooking, painting to flute playing.

Museum Puri Lukisan, the Painting Palace

*T/F 0361-971 159;
0361-975 136
www.mpl-ubud.com
>Jl. Raya Ubud.*

The Museum teaches Balinese dance, bamboo gamelan or flute playing (Rp125,000 for 90mn), woodcarving or batik (Rp375-475,000 per day, lunch included) with experienced teachers from the Ubud School of Art. Book at the Museum one day ahead to get a 20% discount.

Officially opened in 1956, Museum Puri Lukisan was the great enterprise of Tjokorda Gede Agung Sukawati, the prince of Ubud, and Dutch artist Rudolf Bonnet. It was built to preserve the heritage of their foundation, the Pita Maha association. The landscaping makes for a smooth transition into the world of painting – the visit starts by going up and down flights of stairs and crossing a bridge amidst the greenery. The central building houses treasures of both painting and sculpture from the pre-WWII period. The westernmost building holds works representing the principal movements in post-war, such as the "Young Artists" style in fauvist colours; the rather romantic "Ubud School" depicting scenes of the market place and fields; and the Pengosekan school with its Escher-like treatment of natural forms.

Treasures of the Neka Art Museum

*T 0361-975 974;
0361-975 034
F 0361-975 639;
0361-974 275
www.museumneka.com
> Jl. Raya Sanggingan, about two kilometres northwest of the centre of town.*

No one should miss this well-maintained museum. Founded in 1976 by Ubud-born Pande Wayan Suteja Neka, it has one of the most comprehensive public collections of Balinese and Indonesian art, including work by foreign artists such as Arie Smit and Walter Spies. The museum is laid out in seven pavilions housing seven principal collections. Of particular interest are the exemplary Kamasan works in the first pavilion, and the Lempad Collection, with a number of superb ink drawings of I Gusti Nyoman Lempad (1864-1978), perhaps Bali's most famous artist.

ARMA: The Agung Rai Museum of Art

ARMA was created in the 1980s by the young collector Agung Rai of Peliatan. Its grand scale reflects the style in fashion during the economic boom of Soeharto's late New Order. The four large galleries, connected by gardens with ornamental ponds, are the venue of both permanent and temporary exhibitions, as well as a book shop and a reference library.

The museum features a quality collection of classical and modern Balinese paintings, including notably the famous Calonarang, painted by Walter Spies during his first visit to Ubud. Visit the upper floor of the northern pavilion for a fine collection of classic Balinese paintings on permanent display.

Meet the Pengosekan Community of Artists

Painter Dewa Nyoman Batuan and his friends have been committed to Balinese Culture since the 1970s. The peculiar style known as "Fauna and Flora" evolved there at the end of the 1980s.

Applied to carved decorative items such as mirror and picture frames, the Pengosekan style had a worldwide commercial success – yet Pak Nyoman Batuan has not turned into a businessman. As an artist and philosopher, he goes on with the work of his life, painting cosmological mandalas, and is always happy to show the galleries to visitors. Together with friends, he offers lessons in painting, woodcarving, Balinese music, and dance.

Smart Fun for all Ages at Pondok Pekak

This great library boasts a collection of over 10,000 books in more than 10 languages, with a wide variety of reference material on Bali, Indonesia, and Asia, including non-fiction such as travelogues, anthropology, or philosophy, but also contemporary and classic literature. Books from the adult collection can be read at the library, rented, purchased, or traded.

T 0361-974 228;
0361-976 659
F 0361-974 229
www.armamuseum.com.
> In Pengosekan.

 ARMA houses an outdoor theatre where dance performances are held and Balinese children learn traditional dance and music. Check the programme of cultural workshops or just pop up to eat or drink at the pleasant ARMA café.

T 0361-975 321;
0361-977 329
F 0361-075 205
galpenos@baliclick.com

© Elizabeth E. Listyowati

Pengosekan–style painting, Seniwati Gallery collection

T 0361-976 194
pondok@indo.net.id
> On the east side of the football field on Monkey Forest Road.

Pondok Pekak offers to refill your mineral water bottle, enabling you to save money and reduce plastic waste. Ask for the custom driving, walking, or biking tours around Ubud, and other information services to make your stay in Ubud richer and easier. You can also enjoy juices, and Indonesian and vegetarian specialities at Warung Pondok Dadong.

Jl. Kajeng #24.
T 0361-972 187
F 0361-976 582
www.threadsoflife.com
> All classes must be booked in advance. "Textile tours" can be arranged for one day to two weeks. The two-week tours cover Bali and key locations in Indonesia.

Jl. Raya Ubud.
Rp20,000 per session.
T 0361-970 827

The **Pondok Anak-Anak Children's Library** is open three afternoons a week. The **Sanggar Pondok Pekak** boasts an open dance studio and a performance stage with *gamelan* gong and *joged* instruments. Check the programme for children's *legong*, *genggong* and **frog dance** performances, *gamelan*, poetry reading, lectures, and workshops. Multicultural programmes for children include Balinese dance, *gamelan*, a multi-language singing hour, story time and English classes. Adults can learn Indonesian, practice a cappella singing, and discover the arts of Bali through classes in dance, music, painting, and carving.

Threads of Life – the Indonesian Textile Arts Centre

Join this great 2-hour class to find out about the breadth and depth of textile traditions across Indonesia (Tuesdays, 10:30am, Rp50,000/person). Another 2-hour lecture examines the history and traditional uses of textiles in Indonesia (Thursdays, 10am, Rp70,000), unravelling the influence of the spice trade on indigenous peoples throughout the archipelago. The class includes an exploration of the use of natural dyes in the *ikat,* or tie-dye process, used to produce the finest textiles of Indonesia. Full-day workshops offer hands-on experience of the subtle art of drawn batik and *ikat*.

Seeing is Drawing at Pranoto's Gallery

Ever wanted to learn drawing? Then register at Pranoto's Gallery where budding artists can sweat, charcoal pencil in hand, in front of a nude model. Since the human body is the most challenging of all subjects, these drawing sessions are the best way to train the hand, eye, and mind. Besides, as explained by your hosts Kerry Pedergrast and Pranoto Raji, "life drawing will teach you to disengage the conceptual left brain that brings judgement, letting the perceptual right brain free to replicate shapes, textures, and colours – learning, at last, to see what is there and not what is in our minds." Local artists appreciate the gallery as a place to exchange techniques and support.

© Dominique Clarrisse

Learning how to play the gamelan

To practice *batik and watercolour*, join the painting lessons of Nirvana gallery pension, with I Nyoman Suradnya, an accomplished watercolorist and batik master who taught painting at the Darwin University.

Jl. Gotama.
T/F 0361-975 415
rodanet@denpasar.
wasantara.net.id

Spicy Hands at Casa Luna Cooking Classes

Learning about Balinese food and cooking is a great entry into the culture – and, as any participant can testify, it is plain fun. Classes start with a tour of the Ubud market. Don't miss this chance to spend a whole day wading through colours, smells, and exotic tastes, and impress your friends back home as you recreate the spicy joy of a Balinese meal.

Jl. Raya Ubud.
T 0361-973 283
F 0361-973 282
www.casalunabali.com
Friday classes are
specially-designed
for beginners.

A World of Dances

Ubud is the perfect place to discover the endless realm of Balinese music and dances. Some of the places mentioned above, like **ARMA** or **Pondok Pekak**, organise dance practices and shows. Most hotels stage performances – enjoyable, but lacking the magical, natural beauty of temple dances. Many tourist villages hold their own shows. The easiest way to see authentic dances is to ask your hotel's staff for the next ceremony in the nearby temples. Also ask them about proper attire and behaviour.

The dance troupes in Ubud Palace and Pura Dalem are of an international standard and frequently go abroad. There is a policy of rotating them as much as possible to prevent them from getting stale. Every evening, a different performance is held at 7 or 7:30pm in *Ubud Palace*. Down the road, next to Kunang-Kunang II shop, the beautiful *Pura Dalem* temple, softly lit by traditional coconut oil lamps, holds performances four times a week. There is a great *kecak*, fire and trance dance, on Mondays and Fridays at 7:30pm, a *barong* and *keris* dance on Thursdays at 7:30pm, and a dramatic *jegog* bamboo orchestra with dances on Wednesdays at 7pm. Pura Dalem is a key village temple, so performances can't take place if there is a ceremony. Ask at Murni's Kunang-Kunang II shop for more precise information.

*The **Ubud Tourist Information Office** on the main road has a list of performances*
T 0361-973 285.
A list of upcoming events is available on the website of the Ubud Community:
www.ubud.com

Prices at Ubud Palace and Pura Dalem are about Rp50,000. Most of the dancers and musicians are local villagers, who donate their services to the temple; funds go to the buildings' maintenance. Seating is outside and unreserved – arrive a bit early, equipped with mosquito repellent. Dress modestly since you are in a temple. Performances end around 9pm.

© Ulung Wicaksono

*Goa Gajah and Yeh Pulu are a short bemo ride from Ubud on the way to **Gianyar**. The area can also be explored on bicycle. Start early in the morning to avoid the crowd of tourist buses and the hassling vendors at the entrance of Goa Gajah. The visit to Yeh Puluh is quieter, and can be prolonged by a walk in the surrounding rice fields: start at Yeh Pulu, then find Puri Yeh Pulu Cottages, and from there follow the path to Goa Gajah, enjoying great views above the Petanu River. It is only a 1 km walk, but the path is not clear and you may need assistance to find your way.*

The *Ubud Water Palace* on the main road stages a *legong* dance on Saturdays at 7:30pm and a children's dance, accompanied by a women's *gamelan* group, on Tuesdays at 7:30pm (Rp 50,000).

Check the dance shows at *Pondok Pekak* – they also present a Frog Dance on Wednesdays and Saturdays at 8pm in the *Pura Padang Kerta* on Jl. Hanoman (Rp50,000, funds go to the library). For performances of classical *gambuh*, inquire in Batuan at *Pura Desa Batuan*.

Old Mysteries along the Petanu River

The ridges and valley between the Pakrisan and the Petanu rivers, flowing north-south from Mt Batur, were home to some of the earliest settlements and kingdoms of Bali. No less than 40 ancient temples are found in this narrow strip of land, which harbours the richest collection of antiquities on the island – from the earliest known kettledrum and clay stupa to more recent Shivaite sculptures, rock-cut sanctuaries, and sacred baths. Some of the architecture and inscriptions, written in Old Javanese, display the deep influence of East Java on the culture of Bali.

Goa Gajah: the Mystery of the Elephant Cave

One of the oldest sanctuaries in Bali, this mysterious complex was possibly a Buddhist meditation place in the 11th century. Its name itself, the "Elephant Cave" is a mystery – there were no elephants in Bali until tourist theme parks imported them from Sumatra. The elephant motifs found in Balinese art originate from India. The cave may derive its name from Old Javanese Chronicles, which mention a Buddhist hermitage at Lwa Gajah, the "Elephant River," which may refer to the Petanu. Other theories say that the site got its name from a statue of the elephant-headed god Ganesha found inside, or from the first Dutch colonial who found the place in 1923, and mistook the demon carved above the entrance for an elephant head.

Take time to walk around the site towards the Petanu and feel its energy, before entering the cave through the gaping, bulging-eyed face of the demon safe-guarding the sanctuary – its origin has puzzled genera-tions of scholars.

On a pavilion on the left side, the statue of a female deity surrounded by children evokes the story of Hariti, a devourer of children, who became the protector of children after converting to Buddhism. Two bathing pools occupy the centre of the courtyard. The layout of the cave is very similar to hermit cells found in East Java, and harbours both Hindu and Buddhist sculptures, attest-ing to the long cohabitation and mutual influences of these religions in Bali.

Lively Rock Carvings at Yeh Pulu

Two kilometres further, the 25m-long, life-size frieze of Yeh Pulu is carved into a cliff near a sacred well. Its name derives from "Yeh" (water) and "Pulu" (stone water container). Its origins are no less mysterious than Goa Gajah. Thought to date back to the 14th century, the huge, plain carving depicts scenes from everyday life, the significance of which remains unknown – although some hunting scenes may have been inspired by the Hindu legends of Krisna. Buried under thick vegetation, they were uncovered in 1925 by painter Nieuwenkamp, and since then have suffered from erosion.

The pleasant site of Yeh Pulu, among the rice fields, is much quieter than Goa Gajah. An old priest and his wife, guarding the site, are ready to provide explanations and make your visit a memorable one.

Pura Penataran Sasih, Temple of the Moon Drum

Pura Penataran Sasih ("the Moon Governance Temple") was the state shrine of the 10th century Pejeng kingdom. It has links with the Bali Aga mountain sanctuaries in Penulisan, on the rim of the Batur crater. Some fine sculptures of the pavilions in the temple courtyard date

© Ulung Wicaksono

Bathing pool in Goa Gajah. Previous page: dancers waiting for a performance

> *Shortly after Yeh Pulu, the road branches to the left towards Gunung Kawi and Kintamani, passing the Archeological Museum in Intaran. After about 1km, the road enters Pejeng, where Pura Penataran Sasih (the temple of the Moon Drum) is located on the right side of the road.*

The Fallen Moon

Pak Ketut Manta, a local guide, tells the legend of the Pejeng Drum: "In the old times, there were seven moons in the firmament. One fell down and landed on a coconut tree in Pejeng. The celestial object illuminated the village nights, leaving burglars jobless – until one of them climbed the tree, urinating on the moon to extinguish its light. The brave man did not survive the resulting explosion, but his mission was successful. The moon fell to ground, the light was extinct and night life could resume. Still today, you can see the breaks on the gong and the greenish patina from the burglar's urine."

back to the 10-12th centuries. Yet, all visitors flock around a simple pavilion, the shrine of the revered "Fallen Moon of Pejeng," a 186cm-high Bronze Age gong that may be the world's largest cast in a single piece, and the oldest archaeological artefact in Bali. Touching the sacred drum is strictly taboo. According to a local story told by painter Nieuwenkamp, a Dutch official struck the drum in 1875 to hear its tone, and fell ill the next day.

The intricate meandering patterns on the tympanum are typical motives of the Dong Son bronze-working tradition, which evolved in the Red River Delta in North Vietnam in the first millennium BC. It may have been cast locally as late as the first century AD. Clay moulds found near Denpasar and Sembiran attest that bronze drums were cast in Bali. Yet neither copper nor tin, the raw materials for bronze making, are found on the island. Hence I Wayan Ardika, a Balinese archaeologist, stresses that these huge bronze artefacts – also called rain drums, frog drums, or moko drums – bear witness to the intensive trade between Bali and other islands of the Indonesian archipelago (In: J. Miksic, ed.: *Ancient History. Indonesian Heritage*). Similar drums, of lesser size, have been found elsewhere in Indonesia. They still play a role in the culture of the island of Alor, in the Lesser Sundas.

Pura Kebo Edan, the Mad Buffalo Temple

This less well-known temple is found just south of Pejeng, on the left side of the road after the archaeological museum. It features the 3.6m-statue of a horned god, said to be Bhairawa, or Shiva in his "Terrible" manifestation. Endowed with a glorious penis pierced with pins – a custom supposed to enhance a woman's pleasure – the deity dances on the bodies of a copulating couple. Legend says that he wanted to have sex with the woman, but could not penetrate her with his giant member. When he found her with a mortal, he crushed them beneath his feet.

© Dedok

The temple is thought to be a legacy of the East Javanese Singasari kingdom, which ruled over Bali in the 13th century under King Kertanegara – an adept of Tantric, magic cults featuring frightening divinities such as Bhairawa (A. Hobart, U. Ramseyer and A. Leemann, *The Peoples of Bali*).

Gunung Kawi, the Poet's Mountain

Approximately 20km north of Ubud, near Tampaksiring, Gunung Kawi is a perfect excuse for a bike tour or a walk in the cool hours of the day. From Ubud, take the road or a bemo heading to Tampaksiring. Then veer east off the main road at a signpost located a few hundred metres after the Tampaksiring bemo station.

The spectacular site hides two rows of ancient tombs hewn out of the rock in a green watery canyon. From the main road, the walk down to the caves offers awesome views of terraced rice fields and coconut groves. Once you get to the valley bottom, take a sharp left before crossing the Pakrisan River to see the tombs of Anak Wungsu, an 11th century king, and his wives. Continue on the path leading left from the five royal tombs, passing through beautiful scenery to reach a small waterfall where you can enjoy a dip in the clean water.

About 500m north of Gunung Kawi, the springs of *Tirta Empul* are the holiest springs in Bali and a crowded tourist stop. Visit as early as 8am for a bit of serenity. Pass the small shops and the outer courtyard to a big banyan tree and a large *wantilan* (open pavilion for religious and cultural ceremonies). Behind a carved gate, 15 spouts pour spring water into two shallow, rectangular pools, with stony stools on which to sit and relax. Small boards explain in Balinese the properties of each shower, such as curing illnesses, blessing newly-built houses, or improving one's luck. Though you may not notice any changes in your luck, the fresh bath will enliven your mood. People bathe here for religious purposes, so wear a sarong rather than a swimsuit.

© Dominique Clarisse

Wall carving in Gunung Kawi Temple

Beyond the much trodden sites of Goa Gajah and Gunung Kawi, the Petanu and Pakrisan valleys keep many surprises. Here you can find a dolmen in the rice fields, or visit the **Goa Garba** cave hermitage, hidden below the 12th century **Pura Pengukur Ukuran** – the Temple where All Things are Measured (literally: "the Measurer of Measures"). Pak Ketut Manta, a young guide based near Pejeng, is ready to take you on a 2-hour walk around these hidden wonders (T 0361-982 149).

Body and Soul

A New Age paradise, Bali (and Ubud, in particular) hosts an ever-growing business of catering for the body and soul of the traveller, from hedonistic spas in five-star hotels to faith healers hidden in the back of a family compound. This is a unique chance to let West meet East and discover yoga, meditation, or the art of Balinese massage.

A Spa with a Heart at Spa Hati

Pamper yourself and support a good cause at Spa Hati. Treat yourself to a lavish massage, pedicure, or manicure and tone up your body with the "Looking Good" programme which allows you to use the gym, salt water Jacuzzi, and steam room for only Rp45,000 – all this in a relaxing setting.

Spa Hati was set up to raise fund for the activities of the **Bali Hati Foundation**, located in the same complex. Proceeds from your pleasure time will support the Bali Hati Resource Centre and the Taman Hati Elementary School located in Mas. They provide education, medical services, and free legal consultations for poor people. Donations are welcome.

Ubud Sari – The House of Beauty

Built on a waste lot turned into a green Eden in the heart of Ubud, this health resort welcomes hedonists in Balinese-style open pavilions, with a modern spa and beauty salon hidden amidst dense gardens. Ubud Sari offers a wide choice of beauty and revitalising programmes, such as a three-hour herbal treatment (US$50), a four-hour spa package (US$70), or a full week to restore your physical and spiritual health. Traditional Balinese and Javanese ingredients are combined with high-quality imported products.

Massage and More at the Body Works Centre

An institution in Ubud, Body Works was founded by Ketut Arsana, who learned spiritual healing from his grandfather, and later combined Balinese wisdom with

> *Log on to*
> ***www.balispirit.com***
> *to find more on yoga, meditation, well-being, and New Age resources in Bali*

> Jl. Raya Andong #14, Peliatan.
> T 0361-977 578
> F 0361-974 672
> spahati@dps.centrin.net.id

> To support the Bali Hati Foundation, contact:
> T 0361-977 576;
> 0361-979 056
> F 0361-974 672
> balihati@indo.net.id
> www.balihati.org

> Ubud Sari Health Resort Jl. Kajeng #35.
> T 0361-974 393
> F 0361-976 305
> www.ubudsari.com

> Jl. Hanoman #25, Padangtegal.
> T 0361-971 393
> T/F 0361-975 720
> www.ubudbody workscentre.com

massage techniques taught by Western friends. A great masseur and healer with an international reputation, he often gets called to soothe the muscles and minds of the many stars visiting Bali. He has trained more than thirty staff in his Body Works Centre, which provides a variety of health cures such as milk, seaweed, salt or spice baths, and massage using traditional Balinese oils.

For a bit of spiritual practice, meditation sessions and Ashtanga Vinyasa yoga classes are regularly held at *Tegun Gallery/Balispirit*.

Morning wake-up strengthening and relaxation yoga classes are available at *Indus Café* (see Where to Eat p. 165) – a great way to relax and appreciate the natural splendour of the Campuhan valley and ridge.

Hatha yoga can be practiced every morning at *Ubud Sari*; classes start at Rp50,000 per class (90min).

In **Nyuhkuning**, in the surroundings of the Alam Jiwa Hotel, I Ketut Bandiastra, the son of a Balinese priest, introduces visitors to Asanas yoga in his family compound at *Taman Hati Yoga and Meditation Centre* (Rp50,000, 90min-session).

A Heart for Shopping

Ubud and the surrounding villages offer endless opportunities to dedicated shoppers, with an amazing supply of handicrafts (or "handy crap", as the letters *f* and *p* are often mixed up in Indonesia). Coming from Denpasar in the south, the villages on the way to Ubud specialise in different kinds of crafts – stone carving in **Batubulan**, gold and silverworks in **Celuk**, painting and panel carving in **Batuan**, woodcarving in **Mas**, and painted wood objects in **Peliatan**. The **Sukawati Art Market** sells every kind of souvenir. This is an occasion to practice your bargaining skills, with poise and courtesy, always remembering that the prices are low and that real people live from making this stuff. To add the feel-good effect of supporting a good cause to the fun of shopping, try **Mitra Bali** (p. 152) or the other worthy places below.

For those who want to get more than muscle relief, Ketut Arsana is available for spiritual consultation.

> Jl. Hanoman #44.
T 0361-970 992
T/F 0361-973 361

> Jl. Raya Sanggingan.
T 0361-977 684
F 0361-973 282

> Jl. Kajeng #35.
T 0361-972 272

> T 0361-974 058;
0361-974 739
pondokfrog43@
hotmail.com

© Djuna Ivereigh

The Ayung River

Fair and Fine Textiles at Threads of Life

♥ ♥ Jl. Kajeng #24.
T 0361-972 187
F 0361-976 582
www.threadsoflife.com
> Located north of the
main Ubud road,
(open Mon-Sat
10am-6pm).

Besides its excellent textile classes, Threads of Life sources exquisite woven pieces from Bali, Sumba, Flores, Lembata, and Sulawesi. Threads of Life sponsors traditional textiles purchased directly from weavers, most of them women, arranging advance payments for pieces that often take years to complete. The aim is to restore pride in their culture and promote the aesthetic value of traditional textiles. By supporting hand spinning and the use of natural dyes, they also support local organic farming of cotton and indigo.

Herbs and Scrubs at Utama Spice

♥ Jl. Raya Kauh #8,
Pengosekan.
T 0361-975 051
M 081 238 160 20
supadupa@
dps.centrin.net.id

Ni Wayan Lilir and her husband I Made Westi of Bali Herb Walks work with village women to make natural products for home and spas – body scrubs (lulur), massage oils, relaxing bath salts coloured with natural dyes, perfumed candles, and a tasty herb tea. The ingredients are locally produced under the most demanding standards of quality and freshness. For a bit of do-it-yourself Balinese medicine, buy a pack of boreh, a time-tested ointment used by farmers to relieve muscle pains. Made of powdered rice, pounded rhizomes of galingale (kencur), and ginger, mixed with hot water, clove, and coriander, the paste is applied and left until it dries, enabling the soothing heat to penetrate the skin.

Eco-Friendly Gifts at Kertas Gingsir

♥ Retail shop: **Lingsir**
Jl. Dewi Sita, just beside
the football field
T 0361-977 984
www.kertasgingsir.com

Opened in1992, Kertas Gingsir sells a wide range of paper products – books, journals, stationery, cards, albums, photo frames, incense, and spa products. All are locally made from recycled materials with inclusion of agricultural by-products such as fibres of pineapple leaves.

> Jl. Raya Ubud, (near the
Post Office).
T 0361-970 320
T/F 0361-973 359
www.ganeshabooksbali.com

Ubud also has a few great **bookshops** with good titles about Bali and Indonesia, such as the *Ganesha Bookshop*, which also sells rare CDs of traditional and contemporary Indonesian music. Another good address is *Ary's Bookshop*, also on Jl. Raya Ubud.

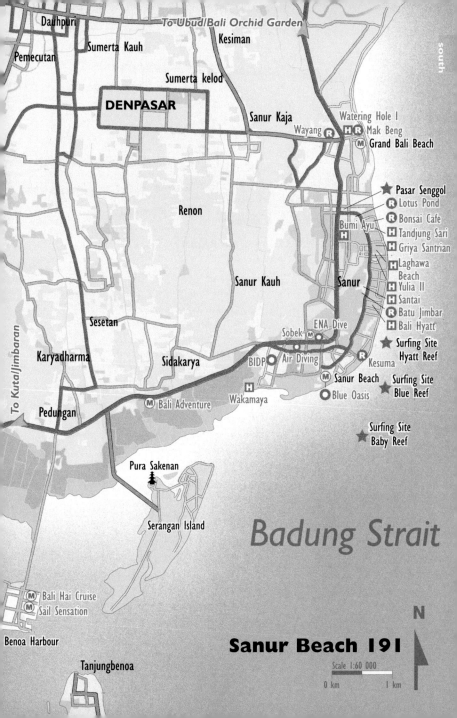

Dauhpuri

Pemecutan

Sumerta Kauh

Kesiman

Sumerta kelod

To Ubud/Bali Orchid Garden

south

DENPASAR

Sanur Kaja

Wayang Ⓡ Ⓗ Ⓡ Mak Beng

Watering Hole I

Ⓜ Grand Bali Beach

Renon

★ Pasar Senggol

Ⓡ Lotus Pond

Ⓡ Bonsai Cafe

Bumi Ayu

Ⓗ Ⓡ Ⓗ Tandjung Sari

Ⓗ Griya Santrian

Sanur Kauh

Sanur

Ⓗ Laghawa Beach

Ⓗ Yulia II

Ⓗ Santai

Ⓡ Batu Jimbar

Ⓗ Bali Hyatt

Sesetan

Ⓜ Sobek Ⓜ ENA Dive

★ Surfing Site Hyatt Reef

Karyadharma

Sidakarya

BIDP Ⓓ Ⓓ Air Diving

Ⓡ Kesuma

Ⓜ Sanur Beach

★ Surfing Site Blue Reef

Pedungan

Ⓜ Bali Adventure

Ⓗ Wakamaya

Ⓓ Blue Oasis

To Kuta/Jimbaran

★ Surfing Site Baby Reef

Pura Sakenan

Badung Strait

Serangan Island

Ⓜ Bali Hai Cruise

Ⓜ Sail Sensation

Benoa Harbour

N

Tanjungbenoa

Sanur Beach 191

Scale 1:60 000

0 km — 1 km

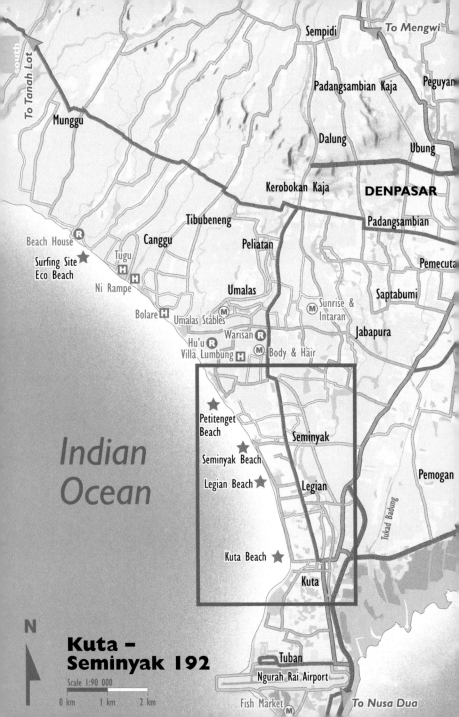

To Mengwi

Sempidi

Padangsambian Kaja

Peguyan

To Tanah Lot

South

Munggu

Dalung

Ubung

Kerobokan Kaja

DENPASAR

Padangsambian

Tibubeneng

Beach House ®

Canggu

Peliatan

Pemecuta

Surfing Site
Eco Beach ★

Tugu
Ⓗ

Ni Rampe

Ⓗ

Umalas

Saptabumi

Bolare Ⓗ

Umalas Stables

Ⓜ Sunrise &
Intaran

Warisan ®

Jabapura

Hu'u ®
Villa Lumbung Ⓗ

Ⓜ

Ⓜ Body & Hair

Petitenget
Beach ★

Seminyak

Indian
Ocean

Seminyak Beach ★

Legian Beach ★

Legian

Pemogan

Kuta Beach ★

Tukad Badung

Kuta

N

**Kuta –
Seminyak 192**

Tuban

Ngurah Rai Airport

Scale 1:90 000

0 km   1 km   2 km

Fish Market Ⓜ

To Nusa Dua

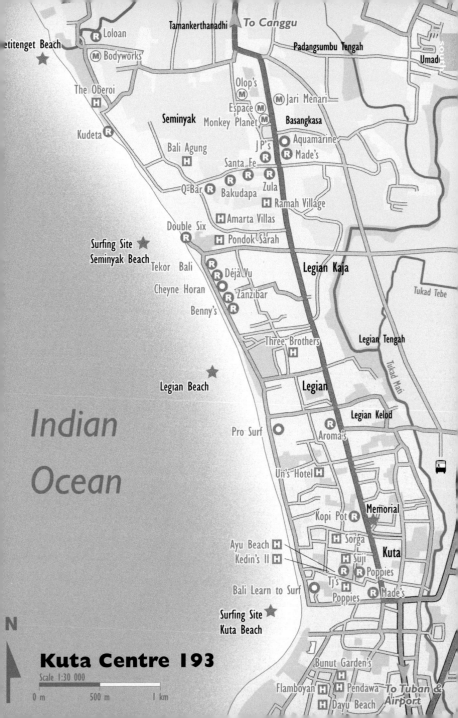

Tamankerthanadhi *To Canggu*

Petitenget Beach

R Loloan
M Bodyworks
Padangsumbu Tengah
Umadi

The Oberoi
H
Olop's
M
Espace M
Monkey Planet M
M Jari Menari
Basangkasa

Kudeta R
Seminyak

Bali Agung
H
JP's O Aquamarine
R Made's

Santa Fe
R R R Zula
Q-Bar R Bakudapa
H Ramah Village

H Amarta Villas
Double Six R
H Pondok Sarah

Surfing Site
Seminyak Beach
Tekor Bali
R Déjà Vu
Cheyne Horan
R Zanzibar
Benny's
Legian Kaja

Tukad Tebe

Three Brothers
H
Legian Tengah

Tukad Mati

Legian Beach
Legian

Pro Surf O
Legian Kelod
R Aroma's

Un's Hotel H

Indian

Ocean

Kopi Pot R
Memorial

H Sorga
Ayu Beach H
Kedin's II H
H Suji
R
R Poppies
Kuta

Bali Learn to Surf
O Tj's
H
Poppies
R Made's

N

Surfing Site
Kuta Beach

Kuta Centre 193

Scale 1:30 000

0 m   500 m   1 km

Bunut Garden's

Flamboyan H H Pendawa *To Tuban &*
H Dayu Beach   *Airport*

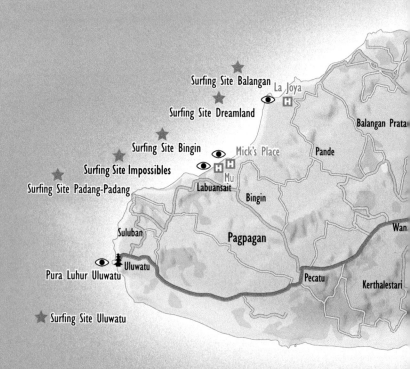

Indian Ocean

Surfing Site Balangan

La Joya

Surfing Site Dreamland

Balangan Prata

Surfing Site Bingin

Mick's Place

Pande

Surfing Site Impossibles

Mu

Surfing Site Padang-Padang

Labuansait

Bingin

Suluban

Pagpagan

Wan

Pura Luhur Uluwatu

Uluwatu

Pecatu

Kerthalestari

Surfing Site Uluwatu

To Denpasar

Kuta

Serangan Island

south

Tuban

Ngurah Rai Airport

Benoa Harbour

Ⓜ Fish Market

Tanjungbenoa

Kedonganan

Ⓡ Yos Dive
Ⓡ Baruna

baran Beach

Rumah Bali Ⓗ

Roman Ⓡ
Lia Ⓡ
baran Ⓡ

Ⓡ Bumbu Bali (Turtle Hatchery)

Jimbaran

ega Ⓡ Ⓡ Kalang Anyar

Ⓡ Warung Nyoman

Ⓜ
ur Seasons   Jenggala

Taman Sari Ⓗ

Ⓗ

Udayana Lodge

Mumbul

ukit Jimbaran

Bualu

☆ Nusa Dua Beach

Udayana University

Nusa Dua

Pande

Kajajati

Benoa

ngasansimpang

Sawangan Kaja

☆ Geger Beach

Ungasan   Petangan

Sawangan Kelod

Gerontang

Jimbaran – The Bukit 194-195

N

Scale 1:90 000

0 km   1 km   2 km

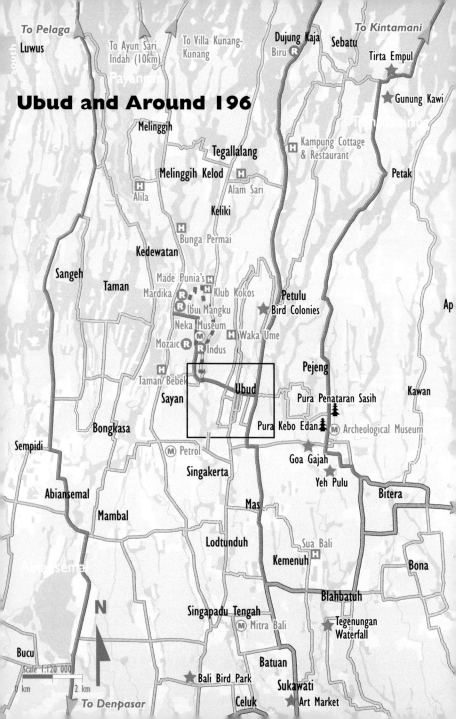

Ubud and Around 196

To Pelaga
Luwus

To Ayun Sari Indah (10km)
To Villa Kunang-Kunang

Dujung Kaja
Biru R

Sebatu

To Kintamani

Tirta Empul

Gunung Kawi

Payangan

Melinggih

Tegallalang

Kampung Cottage & Restaurant

Petak

Melinggih Kelod
Alila

Alam Sari

Keliki

Kedewatan

Bunga Permai

Made Punia's
Mardika R
Klub Kokos
Ibu Mangku
Neka Museum
Mozaic R
Indus
Waka Ume

Petulu
Bird Colonies

Ap

Taman Bebek

Sayan

Taman

Sangeh

Ubud

Pejeng

Pura Penataran Sasih

Kawan

Pura Kebo Edan

Archeological Museum

Bongkasa

Sempidi

Petrol

Singakerta

Goa Gajah

Yeh Pulu

Bitera

Abiansemal

Mambal

Mas

Lodtunduh

Sua Bali

Kemenuh

Bona

Blahbatuh

Abiansema

Singapadu Tengah
Mitra Bali

Tegenungan
Waterfall

Bucu

N

Scale 1:120 000
0 km   2 km

Bali Bird Park

Batuan

Sukawati

Celuk

Art Market

To Denpasar

Neka Museum

Sembahan

Lap Lapan

Taman Kaja

Nagi

Sika Gallery

Mitra Bali

Ubud Sari

Ubud Kaja

Campuhan

Spa Hati & Bali
Hati Fondation

Ibah

Threads Of Life

Andong

Abangan

Pura Gunung Lebah

Taman Kaja

Kutuh Kelod

Pura Dalem

Rumah Roda

Jagi

Puri Lukisan

Lotus

Seniwati

Murni's

Ambengan

Miro's Garden

Casa Luna

Ubud Palace

Pura Desa Adat

Internet Cafe

Ary's

Market

Pranoto's
Gallery

Penestanan Kaja

Teras Sungai

Nirvana

Honeymoon

Ibu Rai

Biah

Ganesha Bookshop

Bali Sunrise

Andalan Health Food

Ubud

Bucu View

Vera

Pondok
Pekak

Hanoman
Juice

Bali Budha Cafe

Nick's

Matahari

Padangtegal Kaja

Pura Padang Kerta

Pande

Wayan

Body Works

Komaneka

Padangtegal Kelod

Bebek Bengil

Tengah Kangin

Monkey Forest

Kubuku

Pujer

Peliatan

Tegal Sari

Alam Indah

Greenfields

Perama

Tengah Kauh

Pengosekan Kaja

Arma

Bali Budaya

Bamboo Foundation

Linda Garland's

Arma Resort

Alam Jiwa

Teges

Nyuh Kuning

Pengosekan
Community

Taman Hati
(Yoga)

N

Utama Spice

Ubud Centre 197

Scale 1:20 000

0 m   500 m   1 km

Teges Kawan

south

© Ulung Wicaksono

East Bali *in a* **Nutshell**

Mt Agung rising over the ocean

Hard Facts

- *1675 sq.km – a third of the area of Bali*
- *Three district capitals: Bangli, Klungkung (or Semarapura), and Amlapura*
- *750,000 inhabitants – a quarter of Bali's population*
- *450 people per sq.km*
- *95km of main coast, over 500km of rivers*
- *Highest peak of Bali, Mt Agung, 3142m*
- *Largest lake of Bali, Danau Batur, 17 sq.km*
- *Three off-shore islands: Nusa Penida, Lembongan, and Ceningan (200 sq.km)*

Below the Volcanoes

Captured by the spell of two generous monsters, the people of east Bali live in danger. Mt Batur and Mt Agung, the island's most active volcanoes, provide water and fertile ashes to the bountiful rice fields and Eden-like orchards of **Klungkung**, **Bangli**, and **Karangasem**.

Once in a while, the volcanoes take back the life they give. The last large eruption of Mt Batur, in 1917, destroyed 65,000 homes. In 1963, Mt Agung, the island's summit, erupted for the first time in human history, killing over 1000 people and displacing thousands of others. The surroundings were suddenly covered in ashes and lava, leaving behind moon-like landscapes from Tulamben to Ngis. This catastrophe took place during an important purification ceremony, at a time of political instability in Indonesia, and created a sense of dread and impeding chaos for a population attentive to signs sent by nature and the gods. Two years later, a failed coup d'état ended in the slaughter of approximately a million people throughout the country – more than the volcanoes of Bali ever achieved.

Overwhelmed by History

East Bali is rich in the historical and cultural legacy of the three kingdoms of **Klungkung**, **Bangli**, and **Karangasem**. Founded around 1700, *Klungkung* was the heir to the prestigious court of **Gelgel**, which once extended its power over parts of Java, Lombok, and Sumbawa. Although Gelgel lost its dominant position in 1651 due to palace intrigues, the royal court of Klungkung still holds a preeminent place among the Balinese aristocracy. The town of Klungkung harbours a wonderful cultural legacy visible in the Kerta Gosa court hall, with its painted ceilings in the classic style from the nearby artistic community of Kamasan.

The small kingdom of *Bangli*, located to the northwest of Klungkung, has also inherited ancient traditions. On the dark upper slopes of its volcanoes one can find villages populated by "mountain people". They have retained forms of social organization that predate Majapahit, much like the Bali Aga villages found in Bali's north and east. Today, Bangli has also the reputation of being home to more *balian*, or spiritual healers, than most other areas of the island; it is renowned for its black magic.

Extending over a vast area, with most of its population concentrated in the fertile rice-growing areas around Amlapura, *Karangasem* is the arch rival of Klungkung. Between the 17th and 19th centuries, it was able to dethrone its neighbour, extending its power over north Bali and Lombok. In the 19th century, Karangasem was ruled by a parent dynasty from the nearby isle of Lombok, until they were both defeated by the Dutch.

After Buleleng in the north and Jembrana in the west, in 1896, Karangasem became the third Balinese kingdom to be conquered by the Dutch. Rather than fall to its neighbours or the colonial power, Bangli chose to become a Dutch protectorate in 1909. Klungkung, however, refused to surrender. Like the king of Badung before him, the king of Klungkung marched into Dutch cannon fire with his wives and his court in 1908. This was the last of the *puputan* or fights to the death. Faithful to his legacy and adding to its prestige, Klungkung was thus the last court of Bali to fall to the invader.

Sacred Forces

In spite of – or perhaps because of – the threat they pose to human life, the volcanoes of Bali are revered as the abode of the gods. The highest one, Mt Agung, is the sacred centre of the island, and the home of **Pura Besakih**, *the Mother Temple of Bali. The nearby Lake Batur, the largest on the island, is considered to be the sacred source of the island's irrigation waters. The male deity of Agung and the female deity of Batur are said to have united to fertilize the island – a perfect metaphor for the combination of volcanic soils and countless streams that provide the foundation for Balinese rice cultivation.*

Ceremony in Besakih temple on Mt Agung

© Iskandar

With or without Water

As its volcanoes cast life and death, east Bali is an area of contrasts. Fed by ashes and rivers, the hills to the south of Mt Batur and Mt Agung harbour endless green terraces. This is a densely populated area rich in culture, museums, and temples, which has supported the growth of the cities of Bangli, Klungkung, and Amlapura. The upper slopes are covered with orchards, forests, bamboo groves, and spiky plantations of *salak* – a fig-shaped fruit, covered with brown scales, which hide a sweet and astringent flesh craved by Indonesians.

Rice fields near Amlapura

© Titiek Pratiwi

East Bali is also endowed with a quiet coastline, which lacks the strong surf that makes navigation – and swimming – so difficult in the southwest of the island. Like elsewhere on the island, the coastal areas are the poorest. This is especially true to the north and east of the main mountains: Mt Batur, Mt Abang, Mt Agung, and Mt Seraya at the easternmost tip of Bali. Rain clouds brought by the southwest monsoon are stopped by these peaks, leaving the eastern slopes surprisingly arid. There the volcanoes have cast death, and the burnt lava, black rocks and yellowish vegetation – except during the wet months of December to February – echo the landscapes of the rugged Sunda islands east of Bali. On the upper slopes live some of the poorest people of the island, surviving on a diet of cassava and suffering from multiple ailments due to insulation and malnutrition (read story in Tulamben section p. 243).

A Pinch of Salt

Fishing is the main resource of coastal communities. But the coast of east Bali, with its lack of rain and abundant sunshine, is also home to traditional salt panning, which can be seen on the coast in Kusamba, Ujung, Amed, Kubu, and Tianyar (read story in Amed section p. 239).

Besides boasting the most prominent volcanoes on Bali and its largest lake, the east harbours Bali's biggest offshore island, **Nusa Penida**, flanked by the islets of **Lembongan** and **Ceningan**. The few people living on these arid limestone plateaus, beaten by dangerous waves, would be the poorest of Bali if it was not for the income brought by seaweed farming since the 1980s. A former penal colony of Klungkung, Nusa Penida is also the feared abode of **Gede Macaling**, the fanged deity who is the reputed source of illness and evil in Bali.

Harvesting algae in Ceningan

© The Natural Guide

A World of Wonders

Travellers in search of nature wonders and living culture
will fall in love with east Bali. Following the coastal road
from the south, start first with a visit to *Klungkung*, the
historical capital of Bali, to get acquainted with its
vibrant artistic legacy – you may even spend one or
several nights in the heart of the Kamasan arts centre.

The next stop may be in one of the villages stretching
from *Padangbai* to *Candidasa*. Despite a bit of tourism
development, this coastline retains a relaxed atmosphere,
and is a good base to explore the charming countryside.
Padangbai, a quiet harbour with inexpensive accommodation, is the departure point of the ferries to Lombok
and Nusa Penida. Like Lovina in the north, Candidasa has
suffered from unplanned tourism development in the
1980s, and lost most of its beach when its coral reef was
mined to build hotels. It is now a quiet resort with good
accommodation in all price ranges, plenty of restaurants
and tourist facilities. Just before Candidasa, travellers
may stay in one of the homestyle accommodations in
isolated beachside villages between Manggis and Buitan.

Further east of Candidasa, the road roams back into
a hinterland of rice terraces. Become immersed in rural
life by staying in a friendly homestay or guesthouse near
Tirtagangga, where you can take a dip in the royal
baths, discover the local crafts, or trek endlessly around
the eastern reaches of Bali with local guides.

Less than one hour to the northeast of Tirtagangga
lies the enthralling coastline of *Amed* – a succession of
black sand and pebble beaches stretching from the actual
village of Amed to Selang, at the easternmost tip of Bali.
Wedged against steep mountains, this coast offers spectacular ocean views, total peace, and fantastic snorkelling
or diving. Amed is also a perfect base to explore the
nearby dive sites of *Tulamben* and its exceptional shipwreck. Under the burnt slopes of Mt Agung, the village of
Tulamben itself has few attractions other than its ocean
depths, so only dedicated divers will overnight there.

Hiking the Four Volcanoes
*Hikers in good physical
condition can try all
3142m of **Mt Agung** –
the steep descent is known
to be the toughest part.
Mt Abang (2152m) is an
enjoyable climb through
thick forest with very few
tourists. **Mt Batur**
(1717m) is much easier
with great views of the volcano's caldera, but is
crowded with visitors and
overzealous guides. An
easy yet lovely ascent with
dramatic views is the one
to Pura Lempuyang on
Mt Seraya (1175m).*

© Eric Penot

Mt Agung

The Southern Isles
*Off the southeastern coast, **Nusa Lembongan** is a small island with a wide choice of accomodations and white-sand beaches, which at times can get a bit crowded with tourists. Nearby, the islet of **Ceningan** and larger **Nusa Penida** are perfect places to escape the crowd, with amazing landscapes of arid hills and vertiginous cliffs. Great surfing and diving are also found here.*

Practicalities
The towns of Klungkung (also called Semarapura) and Amlapura (previously called Karangasem) have post offices and banks with ATMs as well as wartel phones. Money changers can be found in Candidasa and Amed. There are good Internet cafés in Candidasa, one in Amlapura and one in Amed – with capricious connections. For medical services, it is advisable to head back to the Denpasar-Kuta area.

Mountain lovers will head for the stunning slopes of Mt Agung. Lovely homestays and hidden resorts are found around *Sidemen*, which has kept intact the enchantment of Bali as it first enraptured travellers more than 50 years ago. Amidst its intricate rice fields and forested slopes, you'll find thousands of routes for trekking and a chance to glimpse inner peace along a mountain stream.

Heading west, the region of *Bangli* attracts few tourists, with the exception of its lovely **Pura Kehen** temple; it offers great excursions in traditional villages and bamboo forests. Climbing above Bangli, travellers can then reach *Kintamani* and *Batur*, which hold the best and the worst of Bali. The best is the breathtaking caldera of the Batur volcano and its lake, the worst is a swarm of aggressive guides and tourists' rip-offs, bred by mass tourism in this previously poor and insulated area.

Getting There and Around

From Denpasar or Kuta, the main road to east Bali goes through Batuan in the south of Ubud, and from then on to **Gianyar** (30km from Denpasar). From Gianyar, you can push towards **Klungkung**, **Candidasa** (40km from Gianyar), **Amlapura**, and **Amed** (30km from Candidasa), or head north towards **Bangli** and **Kintamani** (40km from Gianyar). This hinterland road is very crowded; you'll need at least one hour by car for every 30-40 km, and double as much by bemo.

A new coastal "bypass" road is being built, which should eventually link Sanur to **Kusamba** and Candidasa. It offers fast driving through a dull coastal area, linking Sanur to Amed in 2h to 2h30min. In 2004, the new road had already linked Sanur to **Lebih**. From Lebih, a charming country road heads up to Gianyar.

The main towns of east Bali – Bangli, Klungkung, and Amlapura and tourist spots like Kintamani, Padangbai, Candidasa, or Amed can be reached by **Perama** buses, or public transport from the **Batubulan** terminal in Denpasar. Other areas can be reached by bemo, but it is easier to have your own vehicle.

© Ulung Wicaksono

The **Hidden Life** *of* **East Bali**

A Child's Life of Labour

By Degung Santikarma

Mardu and Kacrut grew up together in a small village on the east coast of Bali, one of the poorest areas of the island. As children, Mardu and Kacrut were inseparable. The two boys went to primary school in the mornings, and played together in the afternoons while looking after their families' cows. They were something of an odd couple. Kacrut was known for his mischievous cunning, while Mardu was a quiet boy who liked to read and study. But if the villagers didn't expect to see Kacrut and Mardu become friends, few were surprised when both boys dropped out of school after the third grade. Indeed, few children in the area continue their education past primary school. Kacrut's parents, poor farmers with six children to support, and Mardu's mother, a widow with four children, could hardly afford the money for books, mandatory uniforms, shoes, and "teacher's gifts" that providing an education required.

Kacrut didn't mind much being forced out of school. He had never liked the lessons, oriented towards discipline and memorizing at the expense of creative thinking. Besides, he had heard from his older brother that he could earn some money by making handicrafts to sell to foreigners. And so, at the age of eight, Kacrut left his village for Tegallalang, a centre of handicraft production to

Beyond the Law
According to Indonesian law, children under 14 are prohibited from working, and children under 18 may not work in hazardous occupations. Yet a recent official report estimates that some 6.5 million Indonesian children are employed in factories, plantations, homes, on the streets, and in brothels. This number does not include many children working for their families. But as labour activists have found, eradicating child labour in Indonesia is more than just a matter of laws. For child labour is part of a complex that includes economic hardship, corrupt politics, and deeply embedded cultural notions of the meaning of both "childhood" and "labour".

Toys R' Them
Working every day from morning through afternoon, the small labourers of Bali turn out thousands of toys for kids in rich countries: smiling frogs, wooden puzzles, blocks painted with letters, and hanging mobiles whose bright colours and soft motion are meant to stimulate the intellectual development of their lucky owners.

© Ulung Wicaksono

At work near Tegallalang

the north of Ubud. There, Kacrut met hundreds of children like him, working in home-based workshops.

In the handicraft industry, children are assigned tasks according to their ages. The older children construct the wooden objects using saws, axes, and chisels. The younger children are responsible for sanding and painting. Competition among handicraft producers and slim profit margins mean that children working with harmful paints, varnishes, and sawdust are almost never provided with safety equipment like masks or gloves. At Kacrut's place of employment, many of the children had breathing difficulties, and one boy suffered burns from working with a blowtorch to make an object look "antique".

Although many employers in Bali are aware of laws that ban child labour, they also know that the regulations are rarely enforced. Employers skirt the law by claiming that the children are their own nephews or nieces who are being trained in useful skills. In fact, most employers seem convinced that they aren't doing anything wrong. "I don't just hire children to help make handicrafts," explains one of them. "My own two sons work, too. Why should I waste money sending them to school? They won't be able to get jobs when they graduate anyway. At least by working, they can make some money and learn a skill."

Defining Childhood and Labour

Whenever one talks about child labour in Indonesia, there is always the risk of playing into stereotypes. Some blame the lack of education of the parents, who breed unthinkingly with no thought for the future, sliding into poverty until their children are forced to labour. Others blame multinational capitalism and try to defend the rights of the poor peasants who, having lost their land to development, must now send their children to labour in the same factories and plantations that disenfranchised them in the first place. Yet despite international agreements, education programmes, labour rights movements, and other efforts to "empower" poor people, no one has found a definitive solution to the problem of kids like Mardu and Kacrut. Indeed, a closer look is needed to understand the ties of culture, politics, history, and economics that bind parents, children, and employers in a system of child labour.

In the modern West, children are considered to be fundamentally different from adults, with special rights of their own. As beings who are not yet fully formed, they must be protected until they reach adulthood. In Bali, however, children live in closer contact with the world of adults. If the West has over-18 movies and casinos, Bali has all-night, all-ages performances, rituals, and cockfights at which entire villages gather. While most parents will not make love in front of their children, the practicalities of parents and children sharing sleeping quarters mean that children grow up quickly understanding the facts of life. Youth become full members of the village *banjar* organization upon marriage, whether this happens at 14 or 40.

Likewise, most Balinese don't draw a rigid line around "labour" as a category. Children fly kites while watching the cows, hunt for frogs while helping to plant the rice, or sing while searching for firewood, just as adults gather to gossip and joke while harvesting or making offerings. There are no set "working hours" and the daily load is dependent on the vagaries of the weather and the harvest.

Finding the Way Back to school

Back in east Bali, Mardu, the quiet boy, missed his friend Kacrut. He also missed school. "I liked it," he says, "but there was no money to pay for it. What else could I do?" To help his mother, he began working in the village, sometimes as a construction coolie, or taking care of his neighbours' cows and chickens. At the age of ten, Mardu followed his older sister to the city of Denpasar, and began working in the market as a carrier, hauling loads of rice and other goods. Working ten hours a day, he could make around Rp200,000 a month, sharing a room

A Life of Dharma
Like in most traditional agrarian communities, Balinese find it natural that children should participate in the everyday world of work, from tending farm animals to preparing family meals, or participating in the endless round of ritual preparation. And up until recently, few Balinese – even adults – were paid for their time with wages. Work was for survival, but work was also dharma – a Hindu duty which is at once a responsibility, a service, a prayer, a sacrifice, and a call to life.

© Djuna Ivereigh

Carrying water to the salt fields

© Ulung Wicaksono

At work near Tegallalang

"Helping them to help themselves"

This is the motto of the **East Bali Poverty Project**, an NGO that implements community development programmes – from agriculture to health and schooling – to lighten the plight of poor children. Help them by sponsoring a child's education (US$300 for one year including school meals) or make donations to their health care and organic farming programs.
Contact: **www.eastbalipoverty project.org**

with his sister and other working children. "I liked it in the city," Mardu recalls. "There was electricity, television, lots of motorbikes, and smart people. But I missed my mother."

A few months after Mardu arrived in the city, his sister started working as a housemaid for a middle class family, who offered Mardu a light job, as well as a chance for both of them to continue their education. At first, Mardu was ecstatic. He was paid Rp100,000 a month for small domestic chores, plus free food, school fees, and books. But he still felt lonely. Soon he left for Tegallalang, looking for his old friend Kacrut. After two years of work, Kacrut, now 12 years old, was making Rp250,000 a month, nearly as much a school teacher. He enjoyed his job, for although the hours were long and the work repetitive and tiring, he laboured with a group of other children from his village. After trying to go back to school with Mardu for a while, he quickly lost interest, and started skipping school to hang out on the streets. At 14 years old, he felt ready to be independent, and went to live with his older brother, a street vendor and petty criminal, in Kuta Beach. "I heard that he can already drive a motorbike and that he's dyed his hair red," says Mardu. "Sometimes I get sad looking at the school books he left behind. I'm still saving them for him."

Mardu is now in his first year of high school in Denpasar. He reads voraciously and he says he wants to be a writer when he grows up. He hopes that when the time comes, he'll have enough money saved to go on to university. He has already saved up enough money to buy a small piece of land in his village for his mother and sister. Does he regret his experiences as a child labourer? Mardu says that he is happy about the way his life has turned out, for working kept him from becoming spoiled. "Of course, I wouldn't be happy if I hadn't been able to go back to school," he adds. He says that he has a message for Indonesian children: "If you just go to school it's not good. If you just work, it's also not good. For life, you need both."

Klungkung

© Leonard Lueras

The busy streets of Klungkung and the nearby villages of craftsmen and painters are perfect for an immersion in the best of Bali's arts and history.

Where to Stay

Most travellers pass quickly through Klungkung, and the town has only a couple of places to stay. Culture lovers will feel at home in the family compound of the *Kamasan Art Center*, amidst a community of painters and craftsmen (see below, What to Do). The owner, Ida Bagus Wijana, can guide visitors around the artists' studios. Ask to follow the family to the night market, or to the temple to experience Balinese rituals.

Where to Eat

Several small stalls are located in the centre of the town near the Kerta Gosa, serving local food for Rp10-20,000. Taste the spicy food of the warungs at the night market, mingling with local eaters in a friendly atmosphere.

What to Do – Arts and History at Taman Gili

Built in 1710, the Taman Gili (Island Garden) complex is the last remnant of the splendour of the old kingdom of Klungkung. Located in the heart of town, it houses the splendid painted ceilings of the Kerta Gosa, the Bale Kambang (floating pavilion) and the Semarapura Museum. The rest of the complex was destroyed during the *puputan* sacrificial war against the Dutch in 1908.

↖ *The floating pavilion*

> *Klungkung is easily reached by bus or bemo from Denpasar (Batubulan terminal), Ubud, Gianyar, Candidasa, or Amlapura. Once you have arrived at the bus terminal, go around the city by bemo or ojek.*

♥ ② 5 Rm
Trk Shw Cls Bcy
T/F 0361-462 611
g_legong@hotmail.com
> *In Kamasan village.*

© Godeliva D. Sari

Hell on the painted ceilings of the Bale Kambang

Fighting Pollution
The superb, unique paintings of **Kerta Gosa** *have been restored several times. The last restoration in 1989 was performed using acrylic colours. The natural dyes used previously have been muted considerably by the effects of the tropical climate, and also by the pollution of the busy Klungkung streets.*
T 0366-21 448
open 8am-4pm.

Men Brayut and her many children (detail)

Trk Bcy
T 0361-462 611
> *1km southeast of the centre of Klungkung.*

Located on the corner next to Jl. Puputan, **Kerta Gosa** is an open *bale* on a stage, with amazing painted ceilings. Before the Dutch invasion, the king and his priests would meet there to discuss important matters. It was later used as a court, and it is said that the six chairs in the hall symbolize the positions of a Brahmana priest, the king, two court clerks, a judge, and a Dutch representative. Inspired from the Mahabharata, the paintings were supposed to stir the accused by illustrating the horrifying punishments awaiting wrongdoers in hell, and the rewards awaiting the good in heaven. The technique follows the unique and elaborate style of Kamasan *wayang* paintings (see below).

Built in the middle of the complex, the **Bale Kambang** also features painted ceilings from Kamasan artists, inspired by Balinese folklore. The most picturesque illustrate the folk tale of Pan and Men Brayut, a hopelessly poor couple who spent their time fighting and reconciling with passion, and thus ended up with 18 children. This popular story has often been used by local family-planning programmes.

For amateur historians, the **Semarajaya Museum**, at the back of the spacious grounds, displays photographs of the Klungkung royal family, old newspapers relating to the *puputan* wars, and other remnants of Dutch colonization.

Paintings and Crafts around Klungkung

Kamasan Village and the Art Centre

Kamasan is the centre of the classical *wayang* painting style, which depicts scenes inspired from traditional shadow-puppet shows, or *wayang*, based on the Mahabharata or Ramayana epics. Like their model puppets, the characters are painted in three-quarter profiles and angular poses, and originally used natural dyes in nuances of red, ochre, blue, green, and black. As is often the case in Bali, they are collective rather than individual creations: the main artist does the sketch, another does the painting, and others finish the fine details.

Opened in 2001, the *Kamasan Art Centre* offers several cultural programs lasting one to several days, giving visitors a chance to practice the arts. Every afternoon, adults and children come to the centre for regular practice of *gamelan*, dance, silver craft, or painting. Although Kamasan painting tends to be dominated by men, the art centre also supports women artists. Besides painting, it is also possible to visit the silver craft studio (*bokor*), and see bullet-carving artists.

Gunarsa Museum of Classical and Modern Art

This museum, also known by its former name, **Museum Seni Lukis Klasik Bali**, was founded by Dr. Nyoman Gunarsa, a well-known Balinese painter. His paintings in brisk, lively lines and bright colours, inspired by Balinese dance, theatre, and daily life are displayed in the western building, with works by other contemporary artists. Gunarsa has also gathered an impressive collection of classical pieces salvaged from temples being renovated, or purchased abroad to be brought back to Bali – all this, according to the painter, as part of his *bhaktiyoga*, or service, to the world of art. The main building displays stone and wood statues, as well as magnificent classical paintings, mostly from the 17th to 19th centuries. The museum also harbours a collection of *gamelan* instruments, and finances a music and dance school for about a hundred local children. The shrill sound of their practice fills the air of the roomy buildings during the afternoons.

Gongs at Tihingan

From the Gunarsa Museum, follow the lovely country road for 3km to the quiet village of Tihingan, where craftsmen make traditional gong instruments. Small shops packed along the road display gongs in various sizes, as well as other crafts. Ask for a quick glance at the workshops, hidden behind the shops, to see traditional stoves and other manual tools used to produce the instruments.

*Work by local artists can be purchased in the Kamasan **showroom**; as well as good commercial reproductions on small cloths. Buy directly in Kamasan to support the artists.*

T 0362-22 255; 0362-22 256
F 0362-22 257
www.gunarsa.com
> *The museum is at the western entrance of Klungkung, behind the Trimurti statue surrounded by policemen statues.*

© The Natura Guide

Gamelan practice at the Gunarsa Museum

Situated on the interisland trade route, Klungkung is great for shopping. In the centre of town is a huge, covered, old-style marketplace, the largest in Bali – a real people's market. There you'll find basketry, and songket or ikat textiles. Along the main street (Jl. Diponegoro), a row of souvenir shops sells textiles, paintings, and carvings.

Gili Tepekong

© Leonard Lueras

From **Padangbai** to **Candidasa**

> Candidasa and Padangbai can be reached by shuttle bus from the main cities and tourist areas of the island, or by bemo from Klungkung or Amlapura. At the western end of Candidasa, **Perama** offers bus services to various destinations on the island (T 0363-41 114; 41 115; Kuta office: 0361-751 875; fare about Rp35,000 from Kuta). Candidasa has postal services, money changers, an ATM, wartel phones, Internet cafés, motorbike and car rentals. Travellers staying outside Candidasa will have to wait for a bemo on the main road, or ask their hotel staff for transportation.

After Klungkung, the eastbound road joins the coast near Kusamba, a long beach covered with salt farms, and alas rather dirty. The next stop is **Padangbai**, a lively harbour used as the starting point for **ferries** bound for Lombok, Nusa Lembongan, or Nusa Penida. This is a good base for **diving**, with an ample choice of hotels, at least in the low price categories. Travellers opting for a wider choice of accommodation and activities will prefer to stay a few kilometres further along the coast in the quiet villages of **Buitan**, **Manggis,** or **Sengkidu**, or in the once-popular beach resort of **Candidasa**.

Where to Stay – Padangbai

A long-standing favourite known for its friendly service, *Pantai Ayu Homestay* is located up on the hill, facing the hectic bay. The bungalows are basic and clean, with the best rooms on the second floor, offering good views and fresh breezes. On the third floor is a small restaurant with a view of the bay, serving inexpensive local food. Try the tasty "fish saos rajang" or the famous *bebek betutu* (duck cooked with herbs and spices).

❶ 10 Rm – Rst
T 0363-41 396

Topi Inn is situated at the quiet end of Jalan Silayukti in front of the beach. The simple rooms are in a two-storey thatch-roofed building made of wood and bamboo. On the second floor is a spacious breakfast area with two hammocks hanging in the corner. It has no restaurant, but there is a café across the road.

❶ 6 Rm –
T 0363-41 424
topiinn@hotmail.com
> At the eastern end of Jl. Silayukti.

A bit closer to the beach on a busy street, *Kembar Inn* offers clean rooms in a two-storey building. The rooms upstairs have better views of the bay, with a small breakfast area tucked in a corner to catch the morning breezes. The owner arranges guided tours and trekking, and a masseur is available next door.

❶ ❷ *11 Rm –*
Htw A/C Trk
T 0363-41 364
kembarinn@hotmail.com
> On Jl. Segara.

Where to Eat – Padangbai

There are many inexpensive restaurants and cafés in Padangbai. *Warung Pantai Ayu* on Silayukti Beach offers a good Balinese menu for Rp15-25,000. The small *Dewi Café* in front of Topi Inn provides a quiet place for a fresh drink and quick snacks for Rp10-15,000.

Where to Stay – Manggis and Buitan

Hollywood stars like to patron the Amankila, an exclusive, US$1000-a-night resort located above the ocean before Manggis. The rest of us can choose to spend between US$20 and 100 in one of the charming boutique hotels or homestays of Manggis and Buitan, outside the main tourist area of Candidasa. There is still a beach on this part of the coast, although it is mostly grey sand and pebbles, and is sometimes polluted by the tankers serving the oil storage station in the bay.

© Gilles Guérard

Fishing boats on the beach near Candidasa

Lumbung Damuh: from Trash to Paradise

This romantic gem features bungalows in form of *lumbung* or granaries, nestled in a dense grove of coconut and banana trees. Tastefully decorated bathrooms make you want to spend the morning under the shower. Yet this would be a waste of your time, for Tania and Lempot, your hosts, are always ready to take you around to discover the hills, waterfalls, and rural culture of east Bali.

The homestay is named after Lempot's grandfather. A trader of all sorts, he acquired the land from a Chinese merchant, who bartered it for a load of opium. Don't fantasize about the content of your breakfast, though. All you're going to get is a very legal, yet wonderful choice of homemade pancakes, fried rice, toast, or fruit salad.

♥ ♥ ❷ ❸ *4 Rm –*
Htw Bch Div Trk Bcy
T/F 0363-41 553;
M 081 236 899 44
www.damuhbali.com
> On the beach behind the Balina Beach Hotel, 5km before Candidasa.

Since she met Lempot and settled on this corner of beach, Tania embarked on a struggle to preserve the environment – an uphill battle for which she fights relentlessly by recycling the hotel's waste, teaching local children to keep the beach clean, and avoiding the use of plastic bottles and containers.

Style and Luxury at Alila Manggis

This environmentally-friendly boutique hotel, with a cold but elegant design, caters to the higher end of the market, with special price offers for Indonesians and local residents. Spacious rooms in tones of white, the upper ones with a balcony, surround a large garden of coconut and pandanus trees facing the Amuk Bay.

The restaurant is one of the best in Bali, and makes special efforts to use local ingredients, some of them grown organically. It features a cooking class which emphasizes east Bali recipes – with plenty of seafood, and red chilies that are particularly hot due to the dry weather. The class starts with a fun shopping tour of the Klungkung market, the largest in Bali.

Alila Manggis promotes the culture of east Bali, and offers opportunities to discover the area through guided tours, biking, and trekking. Water sports, diving and snorkelling can be arranged from the hotel. Yoga and tai-chi-chuan classes are featured on a regular basis.

Get Balinese at Villa Gading

This pretty compound opened to the sea has two villas that sleep four people each, an open-air dining room and a small swimming pool. A library and kitchen are available for the guests, and the staff, who are part of the family, will cook excellent local dishes or western food for you. The owners clean the beach every day and participate in waste collection programs for recycling.

Villa Gading is a good base to explore the neighbourhood – your hosts will take you for walks or tours, including a two-hour trek to Bukit Gumang. Water sports equipment is available, including **surfboards** and **windsurfers**. This is a perfect place for experiencing

Sidebar

55 Rm – Htw A/C Rst Bch Swp Div Trk Cls Bcy Ckr Spa
T 0363-41 011
F 0363-41 015
manggis@alilahotels.com
www.alilahotels.com

Alila Manggis supports Sensatia Botanicals, a cooperative from the village of Jasri, which makes coconut soap with scents like tropical seaweed or cinnamon swirl. Try them in your room and buy them to support the project.

4 Rm – Htw Bch Swp Div Trk Bcy Ckr
T/F 0363-41 729
www.villagading.com
> Hidden at the end of a small road leading to the beach, 100m after Alila Manggis.

Balinese rituals – ask your hosts to take you to a ceremony, and you'll find yourself dressed up in a Balinese sarong, kneeling amidst incense sticks and chanting priests.

Hidden in the hills of Manggis, *Puri Bagus Manggis* is a perfect hideaway if you don't need a beach. Its swimming pool is nicely built amongst rice fields and adorned with blooming orchids. Have a short morning stroll passing gardens and rice fields, or ask the staff to guide you for a longer trek to Tenganan or other neighbouring villages. Diving, cycling, tours, and cooking classes are organized with Puri Bagus Candidasa.

❹ 7 Rm – Htw A/C Rst Swp Div Trk Bcy Cls
T 0363-41 304; 41 131
F 0363-41 305
www.bagus-discovery.com
> Follow the sign at the entrance of Manggis, and drive 1km until the end of the village.

Where to Stay – Sengkidu

Just before Candidasa and close to its facilities, the village of Sengkidu has a good choice of accommodation in a quiet atmosphere.

Nirwana Cottages is hidden in a fertile garden dominated by coconut groves. Its contemporary Balinese-style bungalows are stretched over the garden and are set well apart. Relax in peace on the beach or on the spotless poolside, or eat healthy, MSG-free meals with homemade bread. Organic vegetables and spices are grown in the garden using the hotel's compost. Ask Ibu Handayani, the owner, for treks or tours with local guides.

♥ ❸ 12 Rm – Htw A/C Rst Bch Swp Div Trk Bcy Ckr
T 0363-41 136
F 0363-41 543
nirwana-cottages@telkom.net

A truly different place, *Pondok Pisang* features six thatched roof bungalows, each with a different shape and decor, in a spacious garden hidden at the end of a small road. An open *bale* is occasionally used by groups practicing yoga who appreciate the quiet environment and the energy coming from the ocean. There is no restaurant, but you can order snacks from the friendly staff.

❷ ❸ 8 Rm – Htw Bch
T 0363-41 065
T/F 0361-730 938
bananasbatik@yahoo.com
> Follow the signs to Candi Beach Hotel, then continue to the right until the road ends.

In the budget price bracket, *Flamboyant Beach Bungalows* offer simple, yet clean and comfortable rooms with attached cold water bathrooms in a quiet area near the beach. The thatch-roofed bamboo rooms are scattered among the lush gardens. Trekking to Tenganan and massage can be arranged through the front office.

❶ 11 Rm – Rst Bch Trk Bcy
T 0363-41 886

Where to Stay – Candidasa

With few tourists and a pleasant lotus-filled lagoon, Candidasa is a peaceful stop on the way to the east. It has good snorkelling, diving, and a wide choice of hotels, restaurants, and services. It is a good base for tours and walks in the countryside, especially to the old Bali Aga villages (read story on p. 220).

Once a romantic beach destination, Candidasa is a case in point of the impact of unplanned tourism. When this fishing village became popular in the mid-80s, local entrepreneurs started building dozens of hotels along the coast. For the construction, they needed lime, available in the coral beds that made up the reef. Wading out day and night into the shallow water, farmers and fishermen competed to collect coral for US$2 per day – enough to live comfortably by local standards.

Soon enough, without the protection of the coral reef, the waves ate away at the shore, and the beach disappeared underwater. To prevent further erosion, the reef was replaced with a concrete wall and a set of piers. Yet some locals say it was a blessing that the beach vanished – it prevented the installation of big chain hotels. Most hotels in Candidasa are now directly above the water. A bit of sand is accumulating along the piers, creating mini-beaches full of colourful *jukung* boats. This is still a far cry from the original lure of Candidasa, and after having lost the very reason why they were built, many of the hotels are often empty.

© Gilles Guérard

The sea wall in Candidasa

A Lush Dream at the Water Garden

With its dedalus of water ponds adorned with lilies and blossoming garden plants, this luxurious place has a unique and exquisite feel. The atmosphere is soothed by the murmur of flowing water, with the occasional splash of a red fish in front of the wooden decks of the well-decorated villas. The Water Garden promotes environmental cleaning activities in the area, and provides help to local orphanages as well as the East Bali Poverty Project. A donation box is available for contributions.

❹ 13 Rm – Htw
A/C Rst Swp
Div Trk Shw Ckr
T 0363-41 540
F 0363-41 164
waterg@dps.centrin.net.id
www.watergardenhotel.com
> *Located in the middle of Candidasa, on the mountain side of the road.*

A Green Stay at Asmara Dive Resort and Spa

This new romantic dive resort has been built by Yos, the founder of Yos Diving and a dedicated environmentalist. It features stone bungalows, each with its own fish pond, in a small garden filled with water plants. A special sys-

❸ 12 Rm – Htw
A/C Rst Bch Swp Div Trk
Cls Bcy Ckr Spa
T 0363-41 929
F 0361-775 439
www.asmarabali.com

tem of bio-filtering enables to clean and recycle waste water, and a coral rehabilitation program is planned in front of the beach. Check out the aromatherapy programme and the "fast-cooking" classes.

An Artist's Holiday at Dasawana

A good value in its price range, Dasawana is a peaceful place where guests are welcomed as friends; its owners also run the **Kamasan Arts Centre** in Klungkung. The bungalows are built over a verdant coconut grove near the pool; the ones with two beds and a small kitchen are suitable for families. Besides trekking to Sidemen or Tenganan, guests can join painting courses or cultural classes like *gamelan*, dance, or craftmaking in Kamasan. Paintings and crafts from Kamasan village are for sale. At the back of the hotel is a composting burrow to minimise the use of chemical fertilizers.

In the Coconuts at Ida's Homestay

This cozy, simple place is a reminder of what Candidasa looked like before the tourist boom. Its wood-and-bamboo bungalows, neatly furnished with antiques, are aligned in front of a coconut grove that spreads all the way to the shore. While other places have tried to cram as many rooms as possible onto their land, Ida's has chosen to keep a lot of open space. The little *bale* pavilions next to the shore are the perfect place to enjoy the cool breeze. Treks up to Mt Agung or Tenganan can be arranged by the staff. Ask about any upcoming *upacara* (ceremonies) and they'll be glad to take you there.

If you can't get a room at Ida's or are looking for something more comfortable, *Kelapa Mas*, the place next door, is a good alternative. It doesn't have the same natural feeling, but has still managed to keep a large garden. Its white brick cottages, facing the sea or the garden, are in reasonable condition. Kelapa Mas has an Internet café (Rp20,000/h), a library of books left by travellers, and a restaurant which features Balinese dance performances.

> *Near the beach at the eastern end of Candidasa, close to the Sindhu Brata Hotel.*

♥ ❷ ❸ 11 Rm – Htw A/C Rst Swp Div Trk Shw Cls Bcy Ckr
T/F 0361-462 611
> *Located just after the T-junction to Tenganan, on the hill side of the main road.*

♥ ❶ 6 Rm – Bch Trk
T 0363-41 096
jsidas1@aol.com
> *Located on the sea side of the road, into Candidasa, just before Kelapa Mas Homestay and the lagoon.*

❶ ❷ 22 Rm – Htw A/C Rst Bch Div Shw
T 0363-41 369
F 0363-41 947
kelapamas@hotmail.com
www.welcome.to/kelapamas

A Non-Violent Hope at Gedong Gandhi Ashram

❷ ❸ 10 Rm –
Bch Trk Shw Cls
T 0363-41 108
gandhiashram@telkom.net
> Find the blue gate of the
ashram on the sea side of
the road, at the eastern
end of Candidasa, near the
lagoon.

The creation of this special place in 1970 was the long-held dream of its founder, the late Ibu Gedong Bagus Oka, a remarkable woman well-known internationally for her work on interfaith and women's issues. Neatly described as "an on-going experiment in simple, non-violent living" the community embodies the ideals of Mahatma Gandhi. There are about 30 members of various faiths and origins, although most are young people from poor families of rural Bali.

Visitors sympathetic to the ashram's aims are welcome in the guest accommodations, a few simple, run-down bungalows in a wide coconut grove stretching out to the sea. Excellent vegetarian meals can be shared with members and other guests. **Volunteers** are welcome, living the life of the ashram, participating in prayers, yoga, or meditation, or lending a hand to daily chores ranging from peanut harvesting to maintaining the facilities. Guests have to follow a few rules: no smoking or alcoholic drinks within the ashram, and unmarried couples can't share a room. The **library** has an exceptional collection of volumes on non-violence. Temple visits, trekking, sailing, and snorkelling can always be arranged. Otherwise, take time out, absorb the ashram's routine, and just "be" without expectations.

♡ ♡ After the death of
its founder in 2002, there
was fear for the future of
the ashram and its young
members, many of them
come from poor families.
A group of international
friends of the ashram have
set up an educational fund,
collecting donations to
support the education of
young ashramites. Contact:
terrycox@globe.net.nz

❹ 48 Rm – Htw
A/C Rst Bch Swp Div Trk
Bcy Shw Cls Bcy Ckr Spa
T 0363-41 131
F 0363-41 290
www.bagus-discovery.com

At the eastern end of Candidasa, the clear marble and thatch-roofed bungalows of *Puri Bagus Candidasa* offer a casual and relaxing atmosphere. The lodgings are spread through the lush grounds around a pleasant pool. The spacious restaurant (US$15-20) has a great view of the sea and the nearby islands. Many activities can be arranged, including sailing with fishermen, or trekking to nearby villages. Cycling and cooking classes can be arranged with Puri Bagus Manggis.

❶ ❷ 8 Rm – Htw Bch
T 0363-41 086
F 0363-41 164
>On Jl. Pantai Indah

Next to Puri Bagus Candidasa, *Sekar Orchid* has quiet bungalows with simple bamboo furniture in a garden shielded from the noise of the road. No restaurant, but breakfast is served in a small *bale* facing the sea.

Where to Eat – Candidasa

While in Candidasa, don't miss a chance to eat at the *Water Garden Café*, featuring a refined and varied menu of Thai and local specialties, on a well decorated deck near the ponds (Rp40-60,000; *T 0363-41 540*).

At the western entrance to the village, *Lotus Seaview* offers good seafood and Balinese dishes for Rp55-70,000, with a great sea view (*T 0363-41 257*).

In the centre of Candidasa, the glossy, upmarket *Kedai Warung* offers Balinese and international dishes for Rp40-80,000. The restaurant is built as an open *bale* with a thatched roof on spacious grounds. Don't miss the delicious seafood soup (*T 0363-42 019; 42 020*).

Next door is the relaxed *Toke Café*, serving local and international food for Rp45-60,000, with a small *lesehan* (traditional seating on the floor) in the corner facing the bar. A small court with a pretty fountain is set in the back for occasional dance performances (*T 0363-41 991*).

Along the main road, the large *Kubu* restaurant, below the hotel of the same name, offers delicious grilled fish for Rp25-45,000 (*T 0363-41 532; 41 256*).

At the eastern end of Candidasa is the good value *Warung Astawa*, well-decorated in the local style with bamboo and a thatched roof. Balinese dances are performed every Saturday (*T 0363-41 363*).

Fishing boats near Candidasa

What to Do at Sea

The **Amuk Bay** (or Labuanamuk), stretching from Padangbai to Candidasa, has good diving sites where you may spot mantas, molas, sharks, and other pelagics. Padangbai has two main dive sites, called **Blue Lagoon** and **Citizen Point** (near Tanjung Sari), which are perfect for beginners and snorkellers. The tiny islands off Candidasa, **Gili Mimpang**, **Tepekong**, and **Biaha** can have strong currents and are for more experienced divers. Gili Mimpang is also good for snorkelling. Sea trips and snorkelling can be arranged with local fishermen on the beach or from your hotel (about Rp50,000 per hour).

♥ ⚲

T 0363-41 516
F 0363- 41955
gekodive@indosat.net.id
www.gekodive.com
> Located close to the
beach on Jl. Silayukti.

© Tonozuka Dive & Dives

Padangbai underwater

♥♥ ⚲

T 0363-41 929
> Near the beach
at the eastern end of
Candidasa, close to the
Sindhu Brata hotel.

> From the intersection
near the Padangbai port
entrance, go west towards
the post office, then take
a small path to the left
after the post office.

A Diving "Geko" in Padangbai

Ever heard of a gecko that dives, establishes funds for local villages, is concerned about plastic rubbish and spells its name in the Indonesian way as "geko"? If not, then come to Padangbai. With its 10.5m boat, Geko will take you to all the diving sites in east Bali (US$50-60 for two dive trips to Amed, Tulamben, or Nusa Penida). Ask for Geko's drift dive specialty and mingle with marine life like the Napoleon wrasse, sea turtles, and even occasional mantas and molas (sunfish). Glass-bottom boat tours are also available to check the underwater world without getting wet.

Geko is as busy out of water as it is in the water, initiating tree-planting programs, organizing beach cleaning and waste collection for recycling, and supporting the local school and clinic.

Growing Corals with Yos Diving Candidasa

This well-established dive shop, based in Sanur and Pemuteran, now has a branch in Candidasa at the new Asmara Dive Resort, offering courses and dive trips around the island (about US$60 for two dives). Like in its operation of Pemuteran, Yos plans to promote coral rehabilitation to replace the lost reefs in front of the beach, inviting divers to participate in the operation and to come back after a few years to monitor the growth of their coral.

In Search of "The Beach"

While the beaches of Padangbai and Candidasa have lost their splendor, the area harbours two quiet, unspoiled beaches. *Biastugal Beach* is nestled in the small and calm white sand bay of Pantai Biastugal (or Pantai Kecil), within walking distance to the western end of the main bay of Padangbai. Sun worshippers can laze undisturbed in the sole company of a few food stalls.

A mere 6km after Candidasa, *Pasir Putih* is a stretch of white sand beach hidden behind a rocky hill.

The small road leading to Pasir Putih beach offers a few good views of rice fields. After passing the rice fields and a small temple, a dirt road bends down through coconut groves to the beach. Apart from a few small food stalls, the beach is calm without any tourist facilities. The road was under repair at the time of writing, so it may be better to park just before the small bridge, or walk 1.5km from the main road.

Temples with a View

Around 200m east of the main bay near **Padangbai**, a complex of three temples sits on the top of the hill, with a good view of the bay. The biggest is **Pura Silayukti**, that has a side door with peculiar carvings of monkeys on guard. It is said that in the 11th century, Empu Kuturan, who introduced the three-temple system to Balinese villages, lived and meditated in this temple. At the back is Pura Telaga Mas, with a small basin filled by a holy water spring. Fifty metres to the south is Pura Tunjung Sari with its three-roofed *meru* and three smaller shrines.

At the top of Gumang Hill, the view from the **Pura Gumang** temple over **Candidasa** beach is worth a visit. Take the main road to Amlapura for 3km until you arrive at a shrine on the hillside of the road with a set of steep stairs opposite. Walk up the paved stairs to the top. It is one-hour steep walk with no shade. Once you are at the top, the view is great, with a cool breeze and uninterrupted stillness. Better to go in the morning with your most comfortable shoes and a sarong and sash.

What to Do – Bali Aga villages

Four kilometres after Candidasa, a small road leads to the left and passes the Bali Aga villages of **Bugbug**, **Timbrah**, **Asak**, **Bungaya**, and **Bebandem**. Although not as markedly different as Tenganan (see below), they make for a pleasant excursion on the way to Amlapura. Stop in each village and take time to explore the peaceful streets aligned around the *bale agung*, or village hall, that is the centre of life of the community.

> *From Candidasa to Pasir Putih, follow the main road towards Amlapura for 6km, then look for Jl. Segara Madu or Jl. Bias Putih and a sign reading "Virgin Club of Bias Putih" on the beachside. Follow the side road until a fork near a temple, and take the downhill path.*

© Eric Penot

Sunset in Amuk Bay

© Iskandar

The Highlanders

The Bali Aga, or mountain Balinese, trace their origins to the first settlers of Bali. There are about a hundred Bali Aga communities, mostly in the moutains of north and east Bali – although some, like Bugbug, are on the coast. They have retained customs and rites predating the influence of the Javanese kingdom of Majapahit in the 14th century. They don't burn their dead, and their hierarchical system is based on seniority and not on caste. They are viewed by lowland Balinese with a certain condescension but also with respect: they are the original Balinese and dwell in the mountains, the abode of the gods.

The **Hidden Life** *of* **East Bali**

Ritual pandanus battle in Tenganan

First and Third World in Tenganan

Of the Bali Aga communities in east Bali, Tenganan, a five-minute drive or one-hour walk from Candidasa, is the one which has kept the strongest hold on its traditions – and has been the most successful in marketing them.

As soon as we step out of our car in the parking lot outside the village, a tiny gray-haired lady greets us with a stern look. She makes sure that we park our car where we are supposed to, and hands out our parking ticket. In this remnant of a feudal, military culture aimed at protecting land and people from the outside, nothing is left to the hazard, and everyone has their place.

The map of Tenganan would make a New Yorker feel at home. Three parallel main streets run from the south to the north, connected by narrow east-west alleys. The minuscule village is carefully walled; impressive gates open to dense vegetation in each cardinal point. Every morning, the drum beats up 21 times to awaken the inhabitants and send them to their daily work. Every night at 9:30, after the village council meeting, the four lowest ranking members of the council, who are also the youngest, walk around the village to announce the curfew.

During the night, council members watch the *bale agung*, where the village keeps its heritage: old coins, and scriptures bearing the *awig-awig* customary laws bestowed upon their ancestors by the god Indra. In this imposing structure, which runs parallel to the main street in its middle, routine aspects of village life are discussed each night, and decisions are made for its development.

A bale and the drum that awakens every villager

To be a member of the village council, one has to be born in the right place. Tenganan is divided between dwellers of the first and second street, who form its ruling elite, and those living in the third street, who cannot become council members – although they are associated to the village's decision-making through their own "parliament", the *gumi pulangan*, consulted for major decisions. A man who marries an outsider is relegated to the third street; a woman has to leave the village – a permanent move, since she can't come back if widowed or divorced.

Land or Freedom

With so many marriage prohibitions in a village of about 300 families, the choice of a suitable partner is limited. Some children are born with inherited defects, and female fertility is low. Most young people look for Mr or Mrs Right outside, especially during junior high school, at the risk of losing their status. Nyoman, a young local guide, explains these harsh rules by the need to keep control of the land: "If a woman marries an outsider, she follows him and the village loses the land."

For in Tenganan, status means land control. About half of the village lives in the third street, but most of the land belongs to the aristocracy. Its members don't cultivate their land themselves, concentrating on more noble activities like making palm wine, the favourite drink of the god Indra.

Yet young people of Tenganan do not feel like leaving. "We always come back to Tenganan" explains Nyoman, "there are so many job opportunities because of tourism."

The Three Streets

The first main street is where the bale agung, *or main village hall, is located; it is also where the most lucrative tourist shops are found.*
The second street, parallel to the first one, is slightly less wide but still pleasant. The third street, on the eastern side of the village, is narrow and lower. This is where the village council relegates its members who have violated the law, contracted some infectious disease, or married an outsider.

Building Village Ecotourism

Colours and Trees
In the 1980s, Pak Sadra and the villagers of Tenganan started to plant 17,000 trees on the denuded hills behind Candi Dasa, with the help of the Gandhian Ashram and Quakers' donations. Their dream is to be able to grow the mengkudu tree again, (Morinda citrifolia or noni), whose roots give the red colour of the geringsing textiles. Used for ceremonies, these long scarves hold intricate patterns with symbolic meanings, and are believed to have healing and protective powers.

© Wisnu Foundation

A Geringsing *design*

💜 *To visit Tenganan with the* **Village Ecotourism Network,** *contact the Wisnu Foundation:*
T 0361-735 320
jed@denpasar.
wisantara.net.id

A curse and a blessing, tourism has glued the people of Tenganan together and encouraged them to revive their traditions. When Candidasa boomed as a tourist destination in the 1980s, Tenganan reoriented its economy towards the sale of handicrafts, such as textiles, and baskets made of *ata* grass. But as traditions had been lost, Tenganan was easily exploited by outsiders.

"With the boom of travelling to Candidasa, our people started to become tourism objects," explains Pak Sadra, a community leader. Tour operators charging their clients hundreds of dollars would leave less than US\$20 to the village. Knowing nothing about Tenganan, guides from outside fabricated stories. "They would tell tourists that *geringsing,* our sacred cloth, used to be dyed with human blood, or similar lies."

"In 1977," explains Sadra, "only five women of the village could still weave the *geringsing,* or double *ikat* cloth, which is unique to Tenganan." When people started to sell their old pieces to tourists, Sadra encouraged more women to make *geringsing*. "The main difficulty was finding the red dye. We had no more trees producing this ingredient, so we had to bring tons of dye by boat from Nusa Penida before starting to plant the trees again."

The next step was to motivate the young generation to revive traditions and be able to explain them to visitors. Pak Sadra started to challenge the village youth to continue local traditions by talking to the elders. With support from the **Village Ecotourism Network** of the Wisnu Foundation, he started to train young guides, establishing trekking trips during which hikers can discover Tenganan from the viewpoint of its people. This new generation of local guides, like Nyoman, is able to paint an honest portrait of their village. In many cases, he candidly admits that not everything can be explained, and has to follow the advice of Pak Sadra: "The meaning of old traditions is partially lost. It is for us to find our own interpretations to keep them alive."

© Leonard Lueras

Amlapura – Tirtagangga

Rice fields in Tirtagangga

A mere 6km from Candidasa, the road leaves the coast and heads towards *Amlapura*, also called Karangasem, after the name of the district of which it is the capital. A few kilometres to the north of town, *Tirtagangga*, with its exquisite royal **water gardens**, is a great area to relax. It has a wide choice of places to stay that are easy to access but, being close to the road, can be noisy during the day. The nearby villages of *Ababi* and, a bit further away, *Temega*, offer more tranquillity and a good choice of friendly homestays amidst vast rice fields. The surrounding verdant hills and the nearby Mt Seraya (1175m) are perfect for **trekking**, with good local guides available in Tirtagangga.

Where to Stay – Amlapura and Around

Travellers obliged to spend the night in town may stay at *Villa Amlapura*, which offers a row of clean rooms in a narrow yard with an attached café. Expect noise from the road heading to the bemo terminal and the market.

Outside Amlapura, travellers who want to be near the coast will enjoy *Irene's Villa*, with two spacious bamboo and thatch-roofed villas which can host four persons each in front of a charming garden. You can order meals from the friendly staff, or eat in the neighbouring restaurants. Weaving or cooking classes can be arranged.

> *Daily buses head to Amlapura from the Batubulan Terminal, just northeast of Denpasar (Rp8,000 one way, about 3h). To reach Tirtagangga, get off at the main intersection just before Amlapura, and hop on a red bemo going towards Culik (fare: Rp2,000 to Tirtagangga; the bemos operate from 4am to 6pm).*

❶ ❷ 4 Rm –
Htw Rst Trk
T 0363-23 246
> *On the right side of Jl. Gajah Mada.*

❷ 4 Rm –
Swp Trk Cls Bcy
M 081 23 641 364
irenehekking@hotmail.com
dongkik@hotmail.com
> *Near Jasri Beach. Call to be picked up.*

Where to Stay – Tirtagangga

❷ ❹ 10 Rm – Htw
Rst Swp Gvw Trk Bcy Shw
T 0363-21 697
❀ Dance performances
are held in the
garden during the peak
season.

❶ 8 Rm –
Htw Rst Gvw Trk Shw
T 0363-21 873
> Opposite of
Tirtagangga's entrance.

❶ 4 Rm –
Rst Gvw Trk Cls Bcy
T 0363-22 445
M 081 338 770 894
www.goodkarmatirtagangga.com

❶ ❷ 4 Rm –
Htw Rst Trk
T 0363-21 847
> Look for their sign on
the Amlapura-Culik road,
after the bridge beside the
Tirtagangga entrance.

> Take a small road to
the left at the fork,
1 km after Tirtagangga.
Along the road, signs
indicate each homestay.
Bemos do not serve Ababi,
so take an ojek at
the junction.

♥ ❸ 2 Rm –
Htw Gvw Trk Bcy Shw
T 081 236 252 71

Starting from the royal baths, the first place to stay is *Tirta Ayu Villa*. Tucked into the trees inside the water palace, it provides a unique opportunity to stay on the grounds of the last raja of Karangasem. Overlooking the pools, the largest bungalows are adorned with refined furniture and *ikat*, and have open-air bathrooms. The cheapest ones are in the back in a small white building.

A few steps away from the water gardens, *Rijasa Homestay* has clean rooms with simple bamboo furniture in a flowery garden. Expect some street noise during the day. The restaurant puts on dance shows every Wednesday and Saturday during the peak season.

A bit further away from the road, *Good Karma I* has small rooms with basic wooden furniture in duplex-style bungalows. Enter through the restaurant at the corner of the parking lot. Cooking classes are planned for the future.

A bit more comfortable, *Puri Sawah* ("the Rice Fields Palace") is located at the top of a steep lane near the water gardens' entrance. The pleasant rooms are set up in two-storey thatch-roofed bungalows; the priciest rooms upstairs have a nice view of the rice fields. The Rice Terrace Café sits in a peaceful corner at the back.

Where to Stay – Ababi

At the end of a hidden, bumpy road, this cool village is a perfect base from which to enjoy the region, facing superb rice field terraces on the western side. Accommodations are in homestays, each with its own small path to the water palace, a 15 to 30-minute walk through the rice fields. The homestays have no restaurants; meals can prepared on demand. They can arrange walks in the area, and sometimes dance shows.

A Family Stay at Villa Gangga

This tasteful place, run by a welcoming French-Balinese couple, offers comfortable bungalows in a spacious compound above the water gardens. The bungalows with thatched roofs and high ceilings are smartly decorated with fine textiles and have pretty, open bathrooms. The biggest bungalow with kitchenette can accommodate a family of four. Delicious Balinese and French food are available, including vegetarian dishes. The owners provide medical help for local children.

> Around 1km from the fork at the northern end of Ababi, just before Tanah Lengis. Call ahead to be picked up.

In the Rice Fields at Pondok Lembah Dukuh

Further south, this simple homestay has clean bungalows with bamboo furniture overlooking wonderful views of paddies. A bamboo *bale* is tucked in a quiet corner, inviting guests to lie down and doze off. Adding to the charm of the place, the owner has erected a small house, *Rumah Anak* (Kids' House), where village children can learn traditional dances and practice *gamelan* twice a week.

Just 50m away, *Pondok Batur Indah* offers clean rooms with basic furniture and bamboo-woven walls; the most expensive ones are bigger and placed in a quiet corner of the property.

❤ ❶ 4 Rm –
Htw Gvw Trk Bcy
M 081 236 182 53

❶ 4 Rm –
Htw Gvw Trk
T 0363-22 342
M 081 239 890 60

Where to Stay – Temega

A Mountain View at Cabe Bali

At the end of a 500m-long bumpy road through rice fields, Cabe Bali welcomes guests in a flower-filled garden, with a charming, spotless pool facing unending rice fields, and a fantastic view of Mt Seraya. The bungalows are airy with verandas and comfortable chairs to laze on. The restaurant serves meals for guests only, plus free coffee during the day. The shower is warmed with a solar heater.

Fifty metres further, *Pondok Wisata Pandan* has a few rooms in a bland two-storey building amidst rice fields, and in a small bungalow with kitchen. Trekking is arranged with Nyoman Budiarsa (see What to Do p. 228).

❤ ❸ 4 Rm – Htw Gvw
Swp Trk Bcy
T/F 0363-220 45
info@cabebali.com
www.cabebali.com
> Located 1.5km south of Tirtagangga, just follow the signs to the hotels.

❷ 4 Rm – Htw Gvw Trk
T/F 0363-22 883
pandanhouse@telkom.net
www.pandanhouse.nl

Where to Eat – Tirtagangga

There are warungs near the entrance of Tirtagangga, offering *nasi campur* (mixed rice), sandwiches, and soups for Rp15-25,000. Restaurants include *Rijasa*, in front of the hotel by the same name, *Good Karma*, and *Genta Bali*

A Feminist New Year
Nyepi, *the Balinese New Year, is a day of silence and prayer during which it is forbidden to leave the house, work, or make a fire. The village of Ababi has its own version of this event. Two months before Nyepi, Ababi celebrates a Women's Still Day (Nyepi Wanita) in Pura Kedaton – a temple devoted to Dewi Sri, the rice goddess. Women are not allowed to work on that day, but stroll down the streets in their best dress, while their husbands or brothers take care of the household. "Actually, the women prepare all the food the day before, so we only have to heat it," admits a local man. A month later, the village celebrates the Men's Still Day (Nyepi Pria), during which the men take a rest.*

> *The small northbound road to the Kebon Bukit temple is on the left side of the main road going from Amlapura to Taman Ujung, less than 1km before Taman Ujung.*

on opposite sides of the parking lot. The *Rice Terrace Café* of Puri Sawah serves excellent local food in peaceful surroundings. *Tirta Ayu Restaurant* is well located above the water garden, with a set menu for Rp50,000 and a great view of the pools.

What to Do – Amlapura and Around

Travellers interested in history can pay a brief visit to *Puri Agung*, the residence of the last raja of Karangasem. It has two attractive entries, with carved pagoda-like gates. At the Maskerdam building (a corruption of Amsterdam), two large photos of the last raja are on display beside other worn and weathered portraits of the past. Most of the rooms are empty, and the discoloured building echoes the faded grandeur of the old kingdom.

Around 5km south the town near the coast is **Taman Ujung**, the remnants of the first water palace built by the last raja. The site would be pleasant if it was not ruined by a flock of decaying bungalows built above it, and by ongoing heavy-handed renovation which have added a bulky fence around the whole area. On the road towards Taman Ujung, not far after Amlapura, there is a small **Buddhist monastery** or *viahara*.

The road towards *Pura Kebon Bukit* ("temple on the garden hill") is a pleasant drive or walk. After 5km, the road reaches Bukit Kelod where a smaller side road to the right leads to the temple. As is often the case in Bali, the temple is built around a particularly impressive tree, said to have grown from the walking staff of a princess of Karangasem. According to the legend, she planted it in the ground during a ceremony and then ascended up to heaven with her child, who was believed to be the son of the god of Mt Agung himself.

A Fragrant Tour of the Amlapura Market

For a bit of fun, lose yourself in *Pasar Amlapura – pasar* being the Indonesian rendering of the Arabic word *bazaar*. The main building, *Pasar Timur* (east market), occupies an entire block opposite the bemo station; it looks like a row of brick shops decorated with Hindu symbols. As is the tradition in Asia, the shopkeepers' tightly-packed homes rise above the narrow shops, the potted plants on their balconies dropping cascades of foliage over the street. The whole area resonates with a busy, yet timeless air.

Enter inside the market through narrow alleyways, passing by frail old ladies selling ready-made flower offerings. The northern (*utara*) section of the market displays row upon row of T-shirts and pants hanging over neat arrangements of underwear, sewing kits, and flip-flops in all colours and styles – though sizes larger than 9 may be in short supply.

For a feast of the senses, head towards the wet section in the south (*selatan*) amidst a bounty of grains, fruits, tobacco, bizarrely-shaped vegetables, and cakes in every conceivable – or inconceivable – shade of pink and green. This is the realm of local women who sit perched behind their scales or crouched on the floor amongst baskets of lime. Travellers with sensitive stomachs may want to avoid the lower or outside sections where meat and fish are sold. No one, however, will escape the pungent assault of the durian, the king of Asian fruits.

Between the market's dry and wet sections, men sit in a little alley selling gold rings set with polished stones the size of pigeons' eggs, as well as all kinds of sickles and knives, including the dreaded *keris* – the snake-shaped traditional weapon of the archipelago. Stone rings and *keris* can be taken to a *dukun*, or shaman, who, in exchange for an offering, will charge them with positive energy, protecting their owners against all evil.

The best *keris* are potent bearers of magic, an effective weapon in a country where nearly everyone believes in occult powers. Check on the condition of the blade and the ornamentation on the handle before buying, and bargain hard. Beware, it is impossible to know who the previous owner of a *keris* may have been, and what sort of spirits you may be bringing home...

✶ *Handicrafts used by the Balinese in their homes – woven baskets and mats, clay pots – make attractive, authentic, and inexpensive souvenirs. Find them on the western side of the market, behind the bemo station. Your money will directly benefit the local women.*

©The Natural Guide

Selling clay pottery in the market

Keris and Computers
What do a keris knife and a computer have in common, besides their potentially erratic behaviour? They are both made of metal, and hence receive offerings, along with all other metal tools and vehicles, during the yearly festival of Tumpak Landep.

What to Do – Tirtagangga and Around

A Royal Bath in the Water Palace

The grandson of the last raja of Karangasem runs a foundation dedicated to the maintenance of the water palace. Information and donations: www.tirtagangga.nl

Built in 1946 by the last raja of Karangasem – an architect, philosopher and poet – the complex was totally destroyed by the eruption of Mt Agung in 1963, followed by looting and abandonment. Today, after several renovations, the baths offer a wonderful fresh dip amid enveloping greenery. The pools are holy (Tirtagangga means "The Waters of the Ganges"), as their waters irrigate the rice fields of the whole region.

To enter the complex, you'll have to walk pass a crowd of persistent guides and cramped food stalls. Once in the gardens, the sight of the pools, the eleven-tiered fountain, the beautiful carvings, and the majestic banyan tree towering in the back is reviving. There are two pools open for swimming. While the smaller one is shallow, the bigger pool in the middle, with its clear and cool water, is worth a few strokes. It is particularly inviting under the early morning light and mist.

© Gilles Guerard

Bringing holy water from Tirtagangga

Trekking around Tirtagangga

The fertile land and hilly villages around Tirtagangga offer an endless choice of walks, from one-hour walks in the rice fields to one-day treks into highland villages and forests. **Good Karma** restaurant and **Genta Bali** sell a hand-drawn map for trekking, useful in exploring nearby rice fields. For longer walks, go with a local guide, who can be hired through your hotel. The normal fee is Rp15-25,000/hour for one or two persons; add around Rp10,000 for any additional participant. The ascent of Mt Agung can also be arranged from Tirtagangga.

For guided treks around Tirtagangga, contact Nyoman Budiarsa near the Genta Bali Warung (T 0363-22 436). We recommend the 6 to 7-hour trek from Dausa to Tanah Aron to enjoy the awesome views over terraced hills, Mt Agung, and south Karangasem.

A Guided Tour of Budakeling

On the hills between Tirtagangga and Bebandem, Budakeling is a community of farmers, artists and craftsmen – from dancers and painters to stone sculptors and engravers of Sanskrit *lontar* manuscripts. In its hamlets or *banjar*, silversmiths, goldsmiths (*pande mas*), and blacksmiths (*pande besi*) carry on their ancient trades.

The village is also home to a few families and priests known as *Brahmana Buddha*. These are followers of a Hindu cult, the *Budha Kasogatan*, which differs slightly from the Shiva rite dominant in Bali. Their presence in the village is said to date back to the 16th century when Danghyang Nirartha, a revered Hindu leader, invited a young Javanese priest of the *Budha Kasogatan* cult to attend a ceremony in Bali. To test his capacities, the local villagers buried a noisy goose under the ground and asked the visitor to guess the source of the clamour. The legend says that the priest identified the noisy beast as a dragon, making everyone laugh at his expense until a fuming dragon jumped out of the cage. The young priest tamed the dragon, which in *Budha Kasogatan* cult is the vehicle of holy men to the afterlife, and thus gained acceptance in the local community. The village was renamed Budakeling, from Buddha and Keling, the priest's village in East Java (*story by Ida Wayan Oka Plating*).

From the eastern end of Budakeling, a small road climbs up for about 8km towards **Tanah Aron**. Located at an altitude of 900m on the slope of Mt. Agung, the site offers a sweeping view to the south and, on a clear day, to Lombok. It hosts a monument to Bali's independence fighters and their leader, Ngurah Rai. You can also reach it by driving 3km northwards from Tirtagangga to Abang, where a small road on the left leads to Pidpid, 3km up in the mountains, and then finish on foot for another 3km.

The Amlapura-Muncan Road

The road heading west out of Amlapura offers pleasant views and several interesting stops. Five kilometres after Amlapura, before the Bali Aga village of **Bebandem** and its famous livestock market, you can find the road leading to Budakeling and Tirtagangga on your left. About 3km further, a small road on the right leads to Jungutan. Follow it to the temple of *Tirta Telaga Tista*, about 2km from the main road – a scenic walk through lovely countryside. More modest than the water palace,

♥ ☁☁ At the western entrance of Budakeling, coming from Bebandem, you'll notice a sign proudly indicating "Place for Asking-Café". This little warung is run by Ida Wayan Oka Plating, a young member of the community. He is eager to take visitors on a well-informed tour of Budakeling and its craftsmen or treks through nearby villages and rice fields, and loves to explain the local history in hesitant English.

© The Natural Guide

Plating's place at the entrance of Budakeling

> Just before Sibetan, follow the sign indicating "Kawasan Wisata Tirta". Walk north from this junction for about 2km. At the fork leading to Abian Tihing Kelod, turn left and continue for about 100m to reach this remote and lovely pond.

this site is also devoted to the cult of water, the foundation of Balinese prosperity. Surrounded by rice fields, the temple is set in the middle of a small pond ornamented with frangipani trees, with the hills of Jungutan beyond.

About 5km further, the road passes the village of **Sibetan**, well-known for its *salak plantations*. This small brown fruit, the size and shape of a fig, grows on spiky palms all over the Sibetan hills; it is sought after throughout Indonesia for its firm, sweet, and slightly astringent flesh, protected by a brown, snake-like skin.

A few kilometres further, just before the village of Duda, a small road on the left takes you to Putung. Stop at *Putung Restaurant* to enjoy a simple Indonesian meal with a unique view of Candidasa, Padangbai, and sometimes Nusa Penida. Choose a table next to the terrace's railing to catch the fresh mountain breezes amidst the song of crickets.

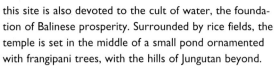

♥ 🍃🍂 *For a trek in the salak plantations of Sibetan, contact the* **Village Ecotourism Network** *(Jaringan Ekowisata Desa) of the Wisnu Foundation, which has trained some local guides. T 0361-735 320 jed@denpasar. wisantara.net.id*

Climbing in the Clouds at Pura Lempuyang

To the northeast of Tirtagangga, this temple is the pretext for a pleasant hike on **Mt Seraya**. First, drive or take a bemo to Ngis – follow the main road from Tirtagangga towards the north, then turn right after 2km. A steep road winds up first to **Pura Luhur**. This lower temple, which is visible from the whole area, offers a stunning view of Mt Agung through a split gate facing west, making for a perfect sunset vista. Cars have to stop there, but it is possible to go by motorbike, ojek, or on foot to the end of the road, 1km further, taking in breathtaking views over the forested slopes. From this point on, a stairway climbs up through the forest, often amidst dense clouds, for about an hour and a half. The steps end on the small, eerie site of the modest temple. If you have a guide, ask to go down through the forest on the west side of the temple to Basangalas village from where a bemo will take you back to the main road.

© The Natural Guide

Pura Lempuyang's entrance

Amed Beach

Sunset in Amed Beach

Living on Dry Land

After passing the verdant rice terraces of Tirtagangga, the landscape changes dramatically as one reaches the northeast coast. Hidden behind Mt Agung and the smaller Mt Seraya on the easternmost tip of Bali, the east coast receives little rainfall, and bears a lot of resemblance to Lombok, visible across the strait. Clinging to austere slopes, small communities carve a tough living from peanuts, cassava and fishing. Tourism is sparse and provides only a small additional income. It feels like another world as you drive along winding roads leading to black-sand beaches full of colourful *jukung* boats.

The area referred to by tourists as **Amed Beach** is a string of villages stretching to the east of the village of Amed. Tourism development started in this area only in the mid-90s, and in 1997, the Asian financial crisis put a halt to the building frenzy before it had a chance to ruin Amed like it did Candidasa and Lovina. Today, Amed has a good choice of hotels and dive shops pleasantly scattered along the coast. Several hotel owners are taking steps to preserve their environment, working with fishermen to clean the beach or organizing waste recycling. This is an area to relax, walk in the nearby hills, swim, explore great coral, and perhaps spot a dolphin.

> The northbound road from Amlapura to Singaraja passes awesome rice fields before reaching **Culik**. There, the main road continues straight to Tulamben while a smaller one leads east towards Amed. To reach Amed, stop in Culik and catch a bemo or an ojek to your final destination. Indicate clearly to which village or hotel you're going – the area called Amed by tourists stretches along 10km on the coast through the villages of Jemeluk, Bunutan, Lipah, Selang, and Aas, while for the locals, Amed refers to the first village to the west.

From Amlapura, an alternative road goes eastward through Ujung and Seraya, passing poor, arid areas. As it circles around Mt Seraya, it reveals dramatic views of the coast. Do it only with a good vehicle fit for steep and sharp curves.

Getting Around
Motorbikes can be rented at the Amed Café in Bunutan; check their condition first. Serious nature lovers can rent a pushbike – perfect between Amed and Bunutan, a bit challenging on steep curves after. You can also walk and go by bemo, but beware that they become rare after 4pm. If you are walking or biking, do like the locals: save your energy for the cooler hours in the morning, before 9, or in the late afternoon, after 4, when you also get the best light. The rest of the day is perfect for laying on the beach or snorkelling.

♥ ♥ ❷ ❸ *8 Rm –*
Htw Rst Bch Swp
Div Trk Shw Bcy
T/F 0363-23 462
hoteluyah@naturebali.com

> *Coming from Culik, the first hotel on the beach side after the left turn to Amed.*

Most hotels are concentrated along the coast in a few villages, the first one of importance being **Amed** proper, followed by smaller **Jemeluk**. This part of the coast is relatively flat, and the beach, more than a hundred metres wide in some places, is used for traditional salt panning. With the mighty cone of Mt Agung always in sight, the landscape has an eerie quality, especially when the late afternoon sun lends a golden shine to the square piles of coconut trunks and the conic baskets used for salt water collection (see p. 239).

After Jemeluk, the coast gets narrower and the road winds through **Bunutan** and **Lipah**, where quite a few small hotels have developed over the last ten years. Travellers who prefer total isolation can push on towards **Selang** and **Aas**, enjoying the views of *jukung* boats lined up along every bay as the road climbs above the sea amidst scant grasses, bushes, and rocks.

Where to Stay – Amed and Jemeluk

Taste the Salt of the Earth at Hotel Uyah

This charming place has spacious, well-decorated rooms lined around a small pool, each with its own terrace offering a moon-like view of the salt panning beach, stretching for a good hundred metres towards the sea. Great food is served at the Café Garam.

Hotel Uyah strives to be an "eco-hotel", preserving the environment while making guests happy. The facilities are built to save energy with a natural ventilation system and warm water supplied from a locally-made solar heater. The hotel's staff clean the beach regularly, and limit plastic waste by offering to refill your bottles from their containers of mineral water. Hotel Uyah ("The Salt Hotel" in Balinese) supports the local salt farmers, helping them to sell their produce to tourists, restaurants, and exporters at a higher price than what they get normally on the market. The friendly staff have been trained to guide tourists around the salt fields, and explain everything you ever wanted to know about traditional salt making.

About 1km further into Jemeluk, *Pondok Kebun Wayan* and its *Amed Café* are among the oldest establishments in the area. They have a wide choice of rooms offering different levels of comfort, packed against each other on a small garden along the road. It is not the most charming hotel in Amed, but is a convenient place to stay with many services, and a good choice of tours and guided treks to discover the region.

Where to Stay – Bunutan and Lipah

Relax at Santai Hotel

Santai is Indonesian for playing it cool, and this great place, although a bit pricey, is perfect for relaxation. The spacious bamboo and thatch-roofed cottages can sleep two to four persons; this is a good place for families with kids. A pool behind the small beach lets you lounge with an ocean view amidst a profusion of bougainvillea and frangipani. When tired of relaxing in the sun, ask to see dance shows performed by children from Jemeluk supported by Santai.

Santai participates in waste recycling; the beach is cleaned everyday by the hotel staff. The owners help fund the costs of schooling for local kids.

Get artsy at Prema Liong

This unique establishment is perched high on a hill with a lush garden, offering an exquisite view of the ocean. Designed by a young local architect, the spacious bamboo and grass bungalows are cooled by the sea breeze. The extra bed in the mezzanine enables sleeping for four persons if necessary.

The veranda of your bungalow or the hotel's *bale* are perfect places to enjoy a healing massage, after a healthy walk to the Uyang Bangle springs. Prema Liong strives to support the local arts, offering a large selection of dancing, cooking, painting, or wood and stone carving classes, and has organised a foundation to sponsor children's education.

❶ ❷ ❹ 18 Rm – Htw A/C Rst Bch Swp Trk Shw Bcy
T 0363-23 473
www.amedcafe.com

Near or at the Amed Café, you'll find a mini-market, postal service, money changer, motorbike rental (Rp50,000/day), a phone, and Internet café.

❹ 6 Rm – Htw A/C Rst Bch Swp Trk Byc
T/F 0363-23 487
santaibali@hotmail.com
www.santaibali.com
> Indicated by a sign on the beach side of the road after Kusumajaya Indah Bungalows.

❷ 4 Rm – Rst Gvw Trk Cls
T 0363-23 486
premaliong@hotmail.com
www.bali-amed.com
> On the hillside of the road just after a curve to the right, opposite the Bali Sunshine Hotel. Climb a few stairs to reach the reception.

A Garden Home at Le Jardin

♥ ❶ ❷ 4 Rm –
Htw A/C Rst Trk
T 0363-23 507
lejardin@indo.net.id
limamarie@yahoo.fr
*Tours and treks can be
arranged with the nearby
Vienna Beach Hotel.*
> *In Lipah Bay, on the
hill side of the road,
opposite Coral View Villas
and before Vienna
Beach Hotel.*

This little gem, which name is French for "the garden", is designed around hospitality and friendliness. Simple bungalows are set well apart in a colourful garden against an arid hill. Guests are offered a lower price if they choose to use the fans instead of air conditioners. Hot water comes from a simple, locally-made solar heater. The founder, a French-speaking nurse, provides health care to the neighbouring villagers and participates in local waste recycling initiatives. She serves excellent food in the cozy restaurant in front of the bungalows. Don't miss the fresh fruit pies and sorbets.

Just after Le Jardin, on the beach side of the road, *Vienna Beach* was the first hotel built on Amed Beach. Once a simple row of huts in which chickens roamed free, it has kept a simple, relaxed atmosphere with plain bamboo bungalows in a garden, each with its small veranda facing the ocean. Ask at the reception for tours and walks in the area, or for a relaxing massage.

❷ ❸ 13 Rm – Htw
A/C Rst Bch Trk Bcy
T 0363-21 883
viennabeach@hotmail.com
www.bali-amed.com

Where to Stay – Selang and Aas

Driving east past Lipah, the road climbs above the sea in sharp turns, revealing fantastic views of the ocean. On clear days, it is possible to spot the island of Lombok, about 35km away from Cape Ibus – an adventurer once swam the distance, followed by a boat for security. There are only a few hotels in Selang and Aas, which makes it an ideal location if you are after peace and quiet.

Under the Banyan Trees at Good Karma

♥ ♥ ❶ ❷ 17 Rm –
Rst Bch Trk Shw
M 081 747 133 52
> *At the entrance of
Selang, on a curve
after a steep descent*

"Talking and joking with Baba" says the name card of this little hotel, one of the first established in Amed Beach. The owner is a well-known figure engaged in defending rights of local communities, providing social care, and looking after the environment. Over the years, he has transformed the barren coast around his hotel into a dark, shading jungle of banyan trees under which plain wooden bungalows are nestled, each with its own little veranda facing the beach. This is a place to relax in simplicity, echoing the backpacker atmosphere of earlier days.

A Deluxe View at Blue Moon Villas

This good-value boutique hotel, set above the road in Selang, offers a few spacious, comfortable rooms elegantly decorated in shades of white. Lounge on the romantic balconies, around the attractive pool, or by the terrace of the small restaurant with a stunning view of the ocean. *Legong* dance and live acoustic guitar shows are held regularly during the high season. The owners participate in local waste recycling initiatives.

♥ ❹ *5 Rm – Htw A/C*
Rst Swp Gvw Trk Shw Bcy
M 081 236 225 97;
081 747 381 00
F 0363-23 520
info@bluemoonvilla.com
www.bluemoonvilla.com

Perched on the Hill at Eka Purnama

Hanging onto mountain slopes above the ocean, this charming spot offers another great view towards Lombok from the restaurant and the terrace of each room. The bamboo bungalows are simple yet comfortable and clean. The atmosphere is relaxed and friendly. The owners, Georges and Made, are nature lovers; ask them to point out treks to Pura Lempuyang or other destinations in the area. Eka Purnama participates in local waste recycling initiatives, and provides medical and educational assistance to local schoolchildren.

♥ ❶ ❷ *4 Rm –*
Rst Gvw Trk Shw Bcy
M 086 812 121 685
F 0363-23 520
geocowan@yahoo.com
www.eka-purnama.com

At the End of the World at Meditasi

Further down the road, in the village of Aas, Meditasi is for lovers of peace and simplicity. It has three plain, romantic all-bamboo cottages, with sliding doors opening to the sea. You'll feel as if you are at the end of the Earth. The small café is just a simple, long bamboo table facing the ocean.

❶ ❷ *3 Rm – Rst Trk*
F 0363-22 166

Amed Beach – Where to Eat

At the entrance of Amed, *Café Garam* ("The Salt Café", at Hotel Uyah) offers a great choice of local food, Thai specialties, and international cuisine on a wide terrace facing the beach, and is equipped with a billiard table. Don't miss the Caïpi-Arak, an improvisation on a caïpirinha using local *arak*, or palm liquor.

♥♥ *T/F 0363-23 462*

Genjek *performance*

⚜ *Salt is a great gift from Amed, available in small wooden or basketry boxes at Café Garam, or in plain bags along the road. The grey crystals are made of sea salt, which lends a subtle flavour to salads and fish. It can also be mixed with essential oils or dried flowers for a relaxing bath. Rather than giving money to people begging on the beach, buying their salt is the best way to help the local communities (read more on p. 239).*

Diving in Amed

On Wednesdays and Saturdays, a band supported by Café Garam performs *genjek*, a lively percussion and dance form popular in the villages of east Bali.

Other good places to eat near the beach include the *Amed Café* and the restaurant of *Hotel Santai*. Pushing towards Lipah, make sure you stop for a sunset drink or a light meal at *Waeni's Warung* for the most breathtaking view around Amed Beach. Further to the east, the tiny, friendly *Restaurant Gede*, huddled against the mountain after a steep descent from the Indra Udhyana Hotel, serves good fresh fish and seafood. Its terrace offers a view of rocky mountain slopes.

Amed Beach – What to Do at Sea

Amed Beach has some of the best coral of Bali, and is a possible entry point to the dive sites of **Tulamben**. Excellent sites for snorkelling and diving are found at the entrance of **Amed** village, which has good shallow corals suited for beginners and some steep walls for more advanced divers. In the bay of **Lipah**, a shallow shipwreck provides for easy diving and good snorkelling.

At the southern end of Amed Beach, the little rock outcrop of **Gili Selang** has excellent coral. The currents around the islet are extremely strong; make sure you go there with a guide and only if you are a good diver. Less daring sea lovers will enjoy snorkelling or diving around the bay before Selang.

Most hotels in Amed provide snorkelling equipment and can indicate good spots accessible from the beach. To really enjoy the sea and the best coral, hop on a boat and go around fishing, swimming, or snorkelling for about Rp60,000/h. Below is a selection of professional dive shops in the area. All offer great trips and PADI courses for beginners or experienced divers. Costs are around US$50 to 70 for dive trips in the area, which typically include two dives and lunch. Excursions to other sites around Bali can also be arranged.

Eco-Bubbles at the Amed Dive Centre

The recently-opened Amed Dive Center is attached to Hotel Uyah, found at the entrance to Amed. The motto of the dive shop is "Make Bubbles, No Troubles". Despite this relaxed self-definition, it is professionally-run and offers a large range of daily dive trips around Amed and Tulamben, or to other destinations such as Tepekong, Menjangan, or Nusa Penida Islands. PADI open water, advanced, and rescue diver courses can be arranged, as well as first aid courses or special environmental courses to learn about coral reefs. This eco-friendly dive shop has started a project to foster coral reef regeneration, sinking barrels that serve as a starting point for coral growth. For sea lovers, the Amed dive centre also offers day trips or live-board diving and **sailing** safaris, on its 18m traditional vessel – no luxury facilities, this is for real sea lovers.

T/F 0363-23 462
www.ameddivecenter.com
info@ameddivecenter.com
> Behind Hotel Uyah at the entrance of Amed

Amed Dive Center's motto

Take an Eco-Dive

The oldest dive shop around Amed, Eco-Dive is a well-staffed operation with several instructors and divemasters, who teach in several European languages. PADI open water, advanced diver, rescue diver, and dive master courses can be organised. Eco-Dive takes care to protect the environment by sponsoring beach clean-up operations conducted by local people, and waste recycling programs. The owners also sponsor education for local kids.

www.ecodivebali.com
info@ecodivebali.com
> In Jemeluk after the Diver's Café

Walks and Treks around Amed Beach

The hills and mountains behind Amed provide many opportunities for hiking. Just take a pair of good shoes and follow the little paths on the slopes of Mt Seraya.

Amed is also a good place to start treks to **Mt Agung**. Most hotels can arrange them for you, although it is likely to cost more than if you arrange it directly in Selat (approximately Rp500,000 for one or two persons).

The **Amed Café** in Jemeluk (T 0363-23 473) proposes a wide range of tours and guided walks, some of them include a picnic lunch and snorkelling (US$35 to 50 per person for a 4 to 5 hour trip).

Be very specific as to time of departure, the kind of equipment you'll be bringing, and the qualification of the guides. You'll normally leave in the middle of night, drive to the foot of the mountain and hike for four hours to reach the top of the mountain at sunrise. The hike is strenuous and demanding. The descent is even harder; make sure you are in a good shape. Bring a light pack with an ample supply of water, energy food, and a torch. Another good hike from Amed is the ascent of **Pura Lempuyang** through the village of Ngis (see the Amlapura-Tirtagangga section p. 223).

Taste the Five Waters of Uyang Bangle

> *The road to the springs starts from Bunutan, 500m east of Santai, and 1km west of Hotel Indra Udhyana. The small road follows a large, artificial waterway towards the mountain. You can walk from the start of the road, or drive 2km until you reach a small parking area on the left. It is better to park here as the road gets worse after this point. After another 2km, you'll reach the village of Bangle. From there, hire a local guide to find the way to the springs (guide costs Rp20,000 per person).*

An invigorating short hike, the visit to the five holy springs of Uyang Bangle provides a fascinating insight into Bali's animist cults. It takes about 1 to 1.5 hours through steep terrain, paddy fields, rivers, and forests. Bring good shoes or hiking sandals and a sarong to cover your legs – the springs are holy, and each harbours a small shrine where purification ceremonies are held every six months.

Most hotels can provide guides for this tour, but make sure they understand where you want to go. The Bangli Holy Waters, also called Toya Masam (acid waters) include a set of five springs, each with a different taste and reputed healing properties – curing ailments such as cancer, diabetes, kidney stones, stomach and skin problems. Make sure you taste every spring; as long as the water is flowing, it is safe to dip your lips into the water without swallowing it. The first spring tastes acid, the second surprisingly astringent, while the third one is supposed to be sweet, the fourth neutral and the last extremely bitter. The springs derive their tastes from the mineral-rich, volcanic rocks of Mt Seraya.

©The Natural Guide

Fishermen at sunrise

© The Natural Guide

The Hidden Life
of East Bali

Mt Agung rising over the salt fields

A Dream of Salt

In the back of a posh restaurant in Seminyak – a tourist area known for its hot parties – a ceremony is unfolding. With eager, hasty hands, the chef opens a small plastic bag brimming with whitish crystals. Pouring them onto a plate, he sticks a few grains to his finger, and raises them to his nostril. He inhales the fragrance, nods pensively, and then tastes the crystals with the tip of his tongue. "This seems like good stuff," he tells the dealer, eyes half-closed in appreciation. A waiter is called to bring a plate of the finest imported roast beef from the kitchen. More crystals are poured onto the juicy meat. The plate is passed around. Everyone chews slowly, awaiting the chefs' verdict. "This is the best salt I've ever tasted," he says. "Where does it come from?"

As it turns out, the coarse, slightly greyish crystals come from Amed Beach, a three-hour drive from the designer shops of Seminyak. They owe their delicate taste to the Indian Ocean. And because ocean waters and our bodies share the same combination of minerals - a tribute to our fishy ancestors – unrefined sea salt is the tastiest salt you can pour on your food. Unless, of course, you're afraid the white crystals will pump your blood pressure too high while dancing in Seminyak's nightclubs.

A Life Struggle

Without enough water to grow rice, the people of Bali's east coast carve a meagre living out of dry crops like peanuts, cassava, corn, tobacco, and beans. Fishing is the main source of income, but the catches are irregular; and local fishermen can't compete with modern vessels. Hotels provide a few jobs for the best educated of Amed's youth. Fishermen also get a side income taking tourists on boat tours. Like in most of Bali, they are organized in an association (seka) to make sure that each gets his turn in providing services to tourists. Yet in a good season, every fisherman sells only a few boat trips – not enough to make a living.

© The Natural Guide

Bringing water from the sea

A Pinch of Iodine
Villagers in Bali's eastern mountains are exposed to iodine deficiency disorder, leading to goitre and cretinism. Unlike seafood, sea salt does not necessarily contain iodine. The initial concentration of iodine in sea water is low. Traditional methods used to purify sea salt of bitter, laxative magnesium salts can wash iodine out. The amount lost depends on the process used: the greyer and more bitter the final product, the more likely it is to have retained magnesium and iodine. With the help of UNICEF, the East Bali Poverty Project is starting a program to add iodine in the local sea salt.

Back in Amed, Wayan doesn't have such worries. As the Seminyak party crowd goes to bed, she is out of bed and heading for the beach. On her shoulders, she carries a pole with two hanging containers made of roofing-tile zinc, looking like sagging accordions. "In the past, we used to carry water in baskets made of palm leaves. Now with the zinc, we lose less water, plus it lasts longer", she says proudly. Modernity, Amed style. Apart from this concession to efficiency, the way she turns water into salt has changed little over the years.

Toiling under the Sun

It is a cool 6:30am, and the morning sun hints at the heat to come. Wayan leans forward into the ocean, first to the right, then to the left, filling her zinc baskets with froth and water. Heavier now, she stumbles up the beach, amidst the *jukung* fishing boats. Oblivious to the beauty of Mt Agung rising from the mist, she carries 50kg of water on the back of her neck. Two hundred metres later, she reaches a roofless, cone-shaped, two-metre-high basket construction. The water containers swaying from her shoulders, she climbs a wobbly ladder leading to the cone's top. She pauses to breathe, and she sends the water splashing over, filling the cone. Then she is gone, quickly back to the sea. Over the next few hours she will carry about 500 litres, half a ton of water. Hardly "life on the beach", but necessary for the survival of Wayan's children.

Marine salt is a much-needed additional income for the poorest families of Amed. Three or four days a week, when the weather is sunny and dry enough, each of the *penggarap garam* – or salt workers – spends about four hours a day on the beach, men and women alike. In a good week they can fetch 70 to 100kg, worth Rp100,000 – enough to buy two salt-rimmed margaritas at a Seminyak bar. Or enough to buy rice to feed Wayan's family for the next two weeks.

Most salt farmers have to give half of their crop to their landlord – so there goes one margarita, or one week of rice. Following years of bad harvests and irregular fish catches, the poorest families in Amed have sold their land to wealthier people, who often don't reside locally. With tourism development, land prices have rocketed in the last five years. By selling the salt beach to hotel builders, the landowners – themselves not necessarily very rich – get more money than from the sweat of the salt workers. The smarter ones use the money to buy rice fields inland. Others burn the cash in cockfighting, and are left with bare hands and salty tears.

Slowly, as the beach gets taken over bit by bit, the small square salt fields and their strange conical contraptions are going too. People like Wayan lose their jobs and have little chance of finding a new one in a hotel. Her children may work in the tourism industry one day – but with a beach crowded with hotels, and without the peculiar spectacle of the beachside salt fields, will Amed remain as attractive to visitors?

© The Natural Guide

A cone-shaped basket to filter salt water

A Dream of Salt

This was young Nyoman's wonder when he returned to Amed, stunned at the changes in his native villages. The son of a salt farmer, he studied in Jakarta with the help of his foster father, a German environmentalist. Together they had a dream, developing an "eco-hotel" that would preserve the traditional salt fields and promote a better future for the farmers. For as Nyoman proudly explains, "salt is the soul of Amed." After one year, Café Garam – the Salt Café – was born, followed by Hotel Uyah – the Salt Hotel, which Nyoman dreams of turning into a salt museum.

So each morning, Kadek, or one of the other staff members of Hotel Uyah, guides tourists into the odd, salted landscape in front of the hotel. He shows them how farmers prepare the salt fields, little 5-by-5m squares, to receive ocean water. How after flooding one square, they leave it to dry, then collect the mixture of soil and salt, and pour it into a cone basket, where it is mixed again with sea water and filtered from its base

A Salt for All
Salt is produced in several of Bali's coastal areas. Each community has its own methods of extracting edible salt from the ocean, adapted to local conditions. In places like Jimbaran, with less intense sun than on the east coast, salt water is heated on wood fires to help evaporation.

© The Natural Guide

Salt drying on Amed beach

A hollowed coconut tree for salt collection

Salt baskets ready for sale

into a hollowed coconut tree – often replaced, nowadays, by pear-shaped cement reservoirs half-buried in the sand. From there, the water is finally poured into hollowed halved coconut trunks, aligned on stilts on the beach. In these drying pans, water evaporates under the scorching sun, leaving fine, square crystals in the middle.

Allowing four days for the whole process, the salt is ready for sale along Amed's roads. With a price of Rp1-1,500/kilo, each *penggarap* earns at best Rp5-10,000/day. It will be hard to convince the young generation that any man worth his salt should load water on their shoulders for less than a tip in a hotel. Some guides suggest handing money to the salt workers when visiting their fields. Yet turning the proud Amed people into beggars hardly seems desirable. What about, instead, valuing the tasty salt at a price worth its sweat content?

This is what happens at Café Garam, where more and more tourists come to learn about salt making, and stay to enjoy the good feeling of being in an "eco-hotel". The visitors are offered little baskets of salt made with local materials, for about the same amount that Wayan normally gets for 10 or 20kg of salt. The income is shared with the salt farmers. Every time a tourist buys a bag of salt, Wayan gets a better value for her toil.

The life of Amed farmers may get even better as chefs at trendy restaurants start using the salt in their cuisine. "I was dreaming of finding salt like this here", enthuses the French chef of the Warisan Restaurant in Kerobokan, north of Seminyak. "To find the same quality, you would have to import *fleur de sel* (literally "salt flower") from Brittany." As it turns out, Wayan of Amed produces *fleur de sel* under the cracks of her feet. The chef of the Bali Hyatt has also fallen prey to its unique flavour. As the value of her labour gets recognition, Wayan's life may become tastier – enough, maybe, to give her children reason for keeping the soul of Amed alive, and fulfil Nyoman's dreams.

© Tonozuka Dive & Dives

Diving Tulamben

Angelfish in Tulamben

> *To reach Tulamben from Amlapura or Amed, follow the main road going towards Singaraja after Culik. Tulamben is only 20min away from Amed or 1h from Amlapura. Bemos driving along the Amlapura-Singaraja coastal road pass through Tulamben – which you can also reach from Singaraja after a 2h-drive. Tulamben is small – once you are there, you can get around by foot.*

Driving from Culik to Tulamben, the road passes through an arid landscape of rocky grasslands and *lontar* palms (read end of section). The trip is enchanting in the afternoon, when the golden light lends grandeur to the cone of Mt Agung, its lava-covered slopes a stern reminder of the 1963 eruption. Streams that are nothing more than a bed of rocks in the dry season burst during monsoons. In 2002, rains flooded the coast – and part of the coral reef – under a mudslide of ash and rock.

Eight kilometres north of Culik, the road enters Tulamben, which consists mostly of a 500m row of houses, hotels, and shops along the coast. Poverty and lack of education take their toll on the environment; the sides of the roads are often littered with plastic waste. The beach is a narrow strip of black sand, gravel, and pebbles.

The main attractions of Tulamben are underwater, including some of the most awesome dive spots of Bali. Many divers, however, choose to stay in Amed, a mere 20 minutes away, with a wider range of accommodation and activities. Serious divers, however, will prefer to overnight in Tulamben to be underwater ahead of other divers.

Tulamben – Where to Stay – Where to Eat

Tulamben has many hotels, mainly along the sea front. Below is a small selection, each with a good restaurant.

A Divers' Resort at Tauch Terminal

18 Rm – Htw A/C Rst Bch Swp Div Trk Bcy Ckr T 0361-730 200 F 0361-730 201 resort@tulamben.com www.tulamben.com

> At the northern end of Tulamben.

This German-operated resort offers quality accommodation right on the ocean front. Relax in the pleasant outdoor restaurant facing the sea, or lounge by the pool on a sandy terrace overlooking the waves. The resort offers either bungalows or rooms with balconies in the main new building. Tauch Terminal is organized for diving, but also offers other attractions such as biking, rafting, trekking, and tours. The professionally-run dive shop offers courses for beginners or advanced divers, taught in Indonesian, English, or German. Once a month, the management organizes reef cleaning trips, sponsored by the PADI AWARE Foundation, during which guests can win free drinks by helping to clean the ocean.

30 Rm – Htw A/C Rst Bch Div Bcy T 0363-22 910 F 0363-22 917

> Near the southern entrance of Tulamben, after Mimpi Resort.

Paradise Palm Beach Bungalows is probably the best choice in the low price category, with simple rooms at various levels of comfort in a small garden. Try to get a room close to the sea front, and you'll spend an ultra quiet night soothed by the sound of waves. Besides its direct access to the sea, its biggest 'plus' is its friendly restaurant, full of divers exchanging endless…well, divers' stories. Underwater photographers come here to enjoy the reef.

29 Rm – Htw A/C Rst Bch Swp Div Trk Spa T 0363-21 642 F 0363-21 939 tulamben@mimpi.com www.mimpi.com

Travellers in search of luxury will appreciate *Mimpi Resort*. The rooms are rather small for this price range, but the beautiful, wide garden and pool facing the sea under the trees makes the resort attractive. The most comfortable rooms have a small garden and *bale* facing a private pond and the ocean. The quiet restaurant offers the best quality meal in Tulamben for about Rp50,000. Mimpi has a dive shop with a Japanese dive instructor and an English-speaking local dive master. Like most other resorts and dive shops in the area, Mimpi helps clean the beach every month.

Become an Underwater Naturalist

Tulamben is mostly known for its shipwreck. The Liberty, a U.S. nationality warship, was hit by a Japanese rocket in 1942. It laid stranded along the coast until the1963 eruption of Mt Agung pushed it into the sea, where it has remained to this day, less than 40m from the shore.

A thorny seahorse

This combination of man-made and natural disasters turned out to be an ecological miracle. The artificial cave created by the wreck became an ideal shelter for coral, gorgonians and sponges, themselves host to an incredible variety of fish. The mineral-rich waters running from the slopes of Mt Agung may also add to the fertility of this site. And indeed, although the *House Reef* coral in front of the beach were damaged by El Niño in 1998 and again by mudslides in 2002, they already show signs of recovery. During the last 15 years, some corals have also managed to grown from nothing in front of the Paradise Palm Beach Bungalows.

With quiet conditions suited to all divers and snorkelling, and impressive biodiversity, the Tulamben shipwreck is a perfect place to learn about marine life. Bring a good book about reef species or borrow one from your dive shop. As you swim around in awe, you'll become acquainted with petite blue ribbon eels, photogenic ghost pipefish, lionfish, bumphead parrotfish, swirling butterflies – and more creatures at play or fighting for life amidst giant clams, great sea fans, and an infinite collection of soft and hard corals.

Other sites of interest include the 30m-deep *Drop-Off* where sharks and other pelagic species might be spotted, or *Batu Kelebit*, which is suited to advanced divers and reachable by boat. Recently, new dive spots have been discovered in *Kubu*, 4km north of Tulamben. Indeed, new dive sites are continually being identified. Ask your dive shop for these new sites, which are less crowded than the better-known ones.

Tauch Terminal (see above) is the best-run dive shop in Tulamben. It has been operating in the area

Eco-Photographers

Underwater photographers worship the black sand of Tulamben, which lends dramatic colours to the fish in the foreground. Don't lose track of your buoyancy to take a snapshot; stay clear from the reef to avoid kicking corals. Resist the temptation to displace rocks or dig around your targets to make them stand out – take nature as it is. Likewise, don't feed the fish to attract them. It can harm their health, destroy their feeding habits, and unbalance the ecosystem.

Fan-shaped coral.

for more than ten years and knows the sites very well. All other dive shops in the island offer day trips to Tulamben.

Trekking the Slopes of Mt Agung

> *Turn inland at Kubu, following the sign towards Dukuh. A narrow asphalt road climbs up for 4km before turning into a trail of dirt and rocks. From this point, the whole trek takes about 6 hours up and down. If you are tired, friendly villagers may offer you a ride on the back of their motorbikes. To avoid getting lost, just go back along the same road.*

Besides its underwater wonders, you can also explore the fantastic landscapes behind Tulamben, on the arid lower slopes of Mt Agung. A good point to start is the village of Kubu, 4km north of Tulamben, where you can take a small road leading inland. After 4km, at the altitude of 300m, the asphalt gives way to a trail of dirt and rocks – if you have a car, it's beter to park it there. The path climbs up for another 6km towards the temple of **Pura Goran**, running along along a 50m deep canyon on one side and dry terraced fields on the other. As the river vanishes during the dry season, the villagers have to buy water from below, in exchange for mangoes, cashew nuts, or sugar and liquor from the *lontar* palm.

It takes two hours from the end of the asphalt road to walk to the first temple, *Pura Bingin*, a huge banyan tree of 30m diameter. Walk a few more minutes and you'll reach the second and main temple, *Pura Goran*, a simple platform with a breathtaking view of the sea. After this, the path becomes narrow and a bit slippery, winding upwards in fields, leading to a small forest, at an altitude of 680m. This community forest is sacred and has its own small shrine, surrounded by a bamboo fence. Villagers come here at the end of the dry monsoon to pray for rain and good harvests.

© Iskandar

*A **lontar** palm rising above the coast*

Lontar script

Antidotes to Poverty

The Palm of Abundance

The northern, lower slopes of Mt Agung would be barren were it not for the scattered round crowds of *lontar* palms. Their fan-shaped, blue-green leaves towering above the dry grass and lava rocks are a striking feature of the east coast. But the drought-resistant *lontar* does more than lend its grace to a desolate landscape. Throughout Balinese culture, from beer drinking to book writing, much is owed to this palm. And in east Bali, it is key to the survival of many communities.

Like the coconut tree, the *lontar* has something for everyone. Leaves and midribs are used to build houses and make fences or buckets. Split leaves are plaited into mats or plates for ritual offerings. Stem wood of old palms makes good construction material. Fresh sap and residue can feed pigs. But the best known uses of *lontar* are of the sap in making sugar and liquor, and of leaves for literature.

Writing or Drinking?

In Bali, the word *lontar* refers primarily to the manuscripts that were made from leaves of this palm, a practice originating in India. The leaves are dried, pressed and cut into rectangular slips. They are then ready to be inscribed, using a stylus to draw elegant characters in Sanskrit, old Javanese, or Balinese. The final step is to rub them with burnt tallow and bind them together in

801 Uses
Grown all around Asia in areas with marked wet and dry seasons, the lontar *(Borassus flabellifer; ental or rontal in Balinese) is at home in the drier parts of central and east Java, Bali, and the Lesser Sunda islands. This wonder palm, resistant to drought, is precious in semi-arid areas – a Hindu poem records more than 801 uses. Gandhi called it an "antidote to poverty".*

Chronicles and Comics
*Bali's most important chronicles on religion, medicine, and history have been written on lontar leaves. They are now kept in **Gedong Kirtya** in Singaraja, and in the Central Library of Balinese Culture in Denpasar. Very few young Balinese are able to read those manuscripts, and only a small number of artists keep the genuine tradition of writing lontar. Many shops, however, sell lontar manuscripts illustrating episodes of the Ramayana, crafted as decorative comics for tourists.*

"books". *Lontar* leaves have been used as a writing material longer than paper.

Making alcoholic drinks from the *lontar* sap may be an even older custom. Fermented sap from various palm trees, including the coconut, is popular in the tropics. Sap is obtained by tapping young, unopened flower clusters. Twice a day, the tapper climbs the palm to cut a slice of the flower bud and collect slow flowing sap in a bamboo tube. Each tree may produce 5 to 10 litres of sap a day during half of the year, and this for 30 years or more. Rich in sugars, vitamins C and B1 and a few proteins, the sweet palm juice (*tuak manis*) can be drunk fresh, or boiled into a thick syrup to extract brown sugar. Left to ferment, the *lontar* sap yields *tuak*, a mild brew with 5-6 percent of alcohol, which can be distilled into *arak*, a strong palm liquor popular throughout Bali. Sugar, *tuak* and *arak* production are important home industries in Karangasem, although they are threatened by an increasing lack of fuel wood.

The Missing Villages

And indeed, deforestation has taken its toll on the higher slopes of Mt Agung. The land there consists of steep, denuded sandy slopes constantly eroded by high winds and storms. The only crop that survives on this hostile terrain is sturdy cassava, and with it comes a host of problems. Cassava only contributes starch to the diet, lacking essential proteins, minerals, and vitamins. Even worse, the cyanides in cassava block the absorption of iodine, already rare in the mountains. Leading to multiple deficiencies, the cassava takes its toll on the health of local kids.

The rare travellers who venture on the north of Mt Agung come back haunted by visions of misery. Indeed, for the 11,000 people surviving on these slopes, life is a far cry from the glossy brochures of Bali. Some of these villages are not even mentioned on most maps.

"I wanted to help some poor communities in Indonesia", says David Booth, the founder of the East

Making a lontar script

Bali Poverty Project. "I did not expect to find people this deprived in Bali." With the help of local youth, international volunteers, and a few sponsors, including some hotels, David embarked on an ambitious program of community development. So far the project has provided education to more than 400 kids, while introducing better nutrition, hygiene, and health care.

Planting the Wonder Grass

But all these efforts would lead nowhere unless people could feed themselves and increase their income. "Since we're in Bali, my initial aim was to help the local communities develop eco-tourism," explains David. He soon realized that it would be counter-productive to bring visitors to communities not ready to handle their presence. Indeed, as can be seen around Lake Batur, the influx of money to isolated societies can have negative impacts, leading to internal conflicts or an over-aggressive pursuit of tourists. Moreover, as explained by Made Suarnata of the Village Ecotourism Network, "The drop in visitors' arrival after the 2002 terrorist attack reminded us that tourism is volatile. Communities have to be self-reliant before investing in tourism, which should only provide an additional income."

For the dwellers of Mt Agung, the priority is to grow fodder, legumes, and vegetables to get vitamins, minerals, and proteins. For this they need soil, and to keep soil from eroding they need vetiver, a sturdy grass known in Indonesia as *akar wangi* (perfumed roots), which makes a strong base against erosion.

In 2000, the villagers started planting vetiver, which proved to be well-adapted to the volcanic sands and arid climate – its roots can grow to more than 2m deep in a few months. Over the next seven years, the project hopes to transform 5,000 hectares of barren land into agroforestry gardens using organic fertilizer. And then, perhaps, the people of these villagers may invite travellers to their paradise, amidst mounds of fresh tomatoes and perfumed vetiver roots.

©The Natural Guide

Arid slopes below Mt Agung

The Root of Wealth

Much like lontar, vetiver is a crop of endless uses that grows well where nothing else survives. Its deep roots stabilise roads and farmland on steep slope. Its pleasant smell is also a good insect repellent. The wavy roots can be woven with linen into aesthetic, perfumed, insect-repelling blinds or mats sold in tourist shops. The leaves can also be used in basketry. Dried, old grasses make a good roofing material, while younger ones are used as fodder. Information and donations:
East Bali Poverty Project
T 0361-410 071
F 0361-419 741
www.eastbalipoverty project.org

Sidemen –
Mount Agung

© Leonard Lueras

*The Besakih complex of
temples on Mt Agung*

> *Coming from Klungkung
towards Amlapura, the road
to Sidemen is found on the
left as you leave town. You
can also reach it from
Amlapura, taking first the
road towards Selat and
Besakih, and turning left
after Putung. The road
through Sidemen is not in
great shape, but is passable
by cars or motorbikes, offering exquisite views of rice
fields and mountain slopes.
Bemos travel this road
regularly, but less frequently
after 2pm; it is worth
coming here with your own
vehicle. Alternatively, ask
your hotel to pick you up.*

♥ ♥ *As reminded by
Ida Ayu Mas Andayani,
owner of the Patal Kikian
Homestay and an active
promoter of the local
culture, "Sidemen is both
a centre for the arts, and
a place where the Balinese
environment is still in its
original state."*

Ever wondered why so many artists have been captivated by Bali to the point of never wanting to leave? Find the answers around **Sidemen**, at the foot of **Mt Agung**. The neighbouring village of **Iseh** was home to painter **Walter Spies** between 1939 and 1942. The most influential foreign artist living in Bali, Spies created dreamlike scenes with lush vegetation and surreal lighting. His paintings find a strong echo in the magic of Sidemen.

The same bamboo house was later occupied by **Theo Meier**, a Swiss painter known for his Gauguin-inspired portraits, who came to Bali in search of authenticity. **Urs Ramseyer**, a Swiss ethnologist and long-time supporter of Balinese culture, also selected this region as a base. Travellers staying in Sidemen will find occasions to learn about the making of fine **textiles** such as *ikat* and *songket*, discover sacred **dances,** and pay a visit to **Pura Besakih**, the holy centre of Balinese religion.

With its exquisite rice terraces and mountain views along the valley of the **Unda** river, nature lovers won't want to leave this area. The cool weather provides comfortable nights, with the lulling voice of millions of birds, insects, and frogs. Everywhere, gentle paths let you stroll amongst clear mountain streams, paddy fields and gardens of bamboo, *salak*, cacao, and coffee, shaded by trees bursting with flowers in all shades of purple, red, and orange. This is **trekking** and **rafting** country, and the ideal base from which to climb all 3142m of Mt Agung. But, more than anything else, Sidemen is a place where you can reconnect with nature and your soul.

Most of Sidemen's accommodation is found around **Tabola**. This peaceful village is located at the end of a little road starting on the left side of Sidemen's main road when coming from Klungkung; to find it, follow the signs leading to the hotels and homestays. Most of the local **pondok wisata** or **homestays** belong to the wives of the local prince. Located on unique sites with gorgeous views, they offer a charming atmosphere in traditional brick-and-carved-stone bungalows. Call before paying a visit to make sure someone is there to attend to your needs. Travellers who want to be closer to Mt Agung may want to stay in one of the little *losmen* around **Selat** or **Besakih**.

Where to Stay – Sidemen and Tabola

Live like a Prince at Patal Kikian

This enchanting homestay offers a choice of spacious, traditional brick and carved stone bungalows, each of them lodging two to four people. The three-bedroom suite is perfect for families. Each villa has a terrace facing boundless rice fields, under the eternal watch of Mt Agung's summit that plays hide-and-seek with the clouds. The surrounding garden feels like a small jungle in tones of red and green with a small pool. Meals can be prepared for US$5. As with all homestays, it is better to call first.

Ida Ayu Mas Andayani, who presides over Patal Kikian, works with Urs Ramseyer's Foundation to offer a special curriculum of arts to local school kids. Ask her staff to show you some of Sidemen's weaving units, to arrange dance performances for you, or to take you for walks in the area – including a six-hour walk which takes you through an old road to Padangbai. The photo album boasts picture of the owner with David Bowie, Mick Jagger, and other stars who visited this little gem.

A New Ashram

About 1km after the turn-off from Klungkung to Sidemen, look out for a statue of Ganesha. This elephant-faced Hindu god is the patron of arts and science, and a remover of obstacles. The statue was created recently by I Nyoman Labda, one of Bali's best sculptors, and marks the entrance to the Sevagram Ashram – a nascent community dedicated to Gandhian principles of non-violence, similar to the one in Candidasa.

© Titiek Pratiwi

Ganesha statue at Sevagram.

♥♥ ❸ ❹ 5 Rm –
Htw Swp Gvw Trk Cls
T/F 0366-23 005
> Indicated by a sign on the right side of the road, just after Sidemen when coming from Klungkung.

♥ ♥ ❸ 6 Rm – Htw
Rst Gvw Trk Shw Cls
T 0366-24 122
F 0366-21 444
(mark clearly: for Nirarta)
www.awareness-bali.com
> Located 1km after
Tabola village when
coming from Sidemen.

🐝 The staff of the Nirarta
Centre for Living
Awareness, which is the
complete name of this
resort, has been trained in
organic gardening. Enjoy
the tasty vegetables fresh
from the garden, which
harbours a collection of
130 medicinal plants.
Nirarta also works with
the local population to
reduce plastic waste, and
provides scholarships to
local kids; guests may participate through donations.

♥ ❹ 19 Rm –
Htw A/C Rst Swp Gvw
Div Trk Shw Cl Bcy Ckr
T 0366-24 330; 24 331
F 0366-23 456
sacredmt@indo.net.id
www.sacredmountainbali.com
> From Sidemen, follow
the signs leading to the
resort, which is located
west of Tabola on
the road to Luah.

Refresh your Soul at the Nirarta Centre

This marvellous retrat was founded by psychologist Peter Wrycza and his wife Ida Ayu, who comes from a local family of spiritual healers. Peter offers courses in meditation, self-discovery, and spiritual retreats. Twice a day, guests can join the staff for stretching and medita-tion in the yoga hall above the valley.

Travellers who simply want relaxation amidst gor-geous landscapes will also love Nirarta. Each of the bam-boo and grass-roofed bungalows is divided into two spa-cious rooms, with a soothing view of the rice fields and the mountains. At the bottom of the valley, the whisper-ing Unda river provides a natural pool and jacuzzi. The friendly staff will feed you with delightful, semi-vegetarian food.

Guided walks and vigorous hikes are offered, from 2 hours to a full day (US$5-12/person per half-day). Get up early for a three-hour hike to **Pura Sangkangunung** opposite Nirarta, and be rewarded with a humbling view over the valleys and the summits of east Bali. Discoveries of the regional culture are also available, including meetings with spiritual healers and priests, visits to weavers and farmers, or classes in Balinese dancing, music, and carving.

Hide in the Sacred Mountain Sanctuary Resort

Also known as *Tirta Sari*, this beautiful resort is located at the bottom of a pristine valley along the Unda river. The villas are made with environmentally friendly materials, some constructed entirely of bamboo and some combin-ing stone and thatch roofs. Most have no air-condition-ing, which is unnecessary in this cool mountain area.

The resort is a place for water lovers. Besides the river, it features an awesome 47m long, spring-fed swim-ming-pool, and the best villas have private dipping pools. Rafting can be organized, as well as diving and snorkelling on the east coast of Bali. Other activities include guided walks and treks, as well as numerous cultural classes such as Balinese costume, dancing, *gamelan*, and dance shows.

Located before Tirta Sari, *Lihat Sawah* is a perfect homestay for budget travellers. As indicated by its name, which means "Look at the Paddies", its simple bungalows overlook fantastic views of rice terraces. The staff can prepare food for guests. Lihat Sawah offers guided rice field treks (Rp30,000/hour, or Rp350,000 to ascend Mt Agung). Lihat Sawah is the perfect place to learn about the local textile cottage industry. Made, who is in charge of the homestay, runs a weaving business and employs 60 people from the area – she can take you to visit the looms and offers weaving classes. Dance shows can be organized for Rp100-200,000.

❶ ❷ 10 Rm –
Htw Gvw
Trk Shw Cls Bcy
T 0366-24183
> Find Lihat Sawah at the beginning of the road leading to Luah and the Sacred Mountain Sanctuary.

Another great homestay in the area is *Subak Tabola Inn*. Its spacious brick and carved stone villas are spread out in a lush garden, with a small pool in the middle of paddy fields and coconut trees. The wide terraces in front of each villa are perfect places to relax while admiring the superb view of the rice fields, with the summit of Mt Agung on guard in the back. The bungalows, however, are a bit neglected, and the place is sometimes empty, so it's worth making a call before thinking of a visit. The homestay arranges hiking to Mt Agung via Pura Pasar Agung for US$35/person, as well as other tours.

❷ ❸ 11 Rm – *Htw Rst Gvw Swp Trk Bcy*
T 0366-23 009
T/F 0366-23 015
> 200m after Tanto Villa in Tabola village, on the road to Nirarta. Take the steep road to the left for another.

Where to Stay – Selat and Besakih

Selat is the nearest village to **Pura Pasar Agung**, one of the starting points to climb Mt Agung. For travellers who want to sleept there, guides can arrange a night at a resident's house – without the amenities of a hotel, but with a unique chance to experience village life.

❶ 12 Rm – *Trk Bcy*
T/F 0366-23 037

Another possibility is to sleep in *Puri Agung Inn*, a simple place in a small compound along the main road in the heart of Selat. The pleasant café serves only breakfast. The hotel collaborates with friendly local guides to take you to the top of Mt Agung (Rp470,000 including transport) or for shorter treks around Selat. Ask for a sunrise breakfast in the *salak* forest, or a spring bath in Petung village.

❶ 7 Rm –
T 0366-92 675
> Look for the "Batik Keris Shop" sign in the front of Pura Ulun Kulkul.

© Ulung Wicaksono

Weaver at work

The Sacred Dance
Unlike other dance forms in Bali, **gambuh** *has not been transformed for tourist audiences. It can still be seen in its original form, a grand affair which involves about 45 dancers, musicians, and singers with elaborate, expensive costumes made of songket, a heavy cloth woven with silver and gold threads. The flute music, the strains of the rebab lute, the eerie singing, and the slow, stylized dance movements make it a hypnotic spectacle.*

Travellers visiting **Besakih** may stay at the friendly, budget *Losmen Dewi Sri* (the Rice Goddess's Homestay) within walking distance from the temple's gate. Balinese come here to meditate in the temples in the early hours of the day, or late at night when the temple is quiet.

Where to Eat – around Sidemen and Selat

You won't find any restaurants catering for tourists around either Sidemen or the Mt Agung area, but you'll be able to get good food from your hotel or from small warungs. The great semi-vegetarian restaurant in *Nirarta Centre* is worth a visit for its tasty semi-vegetarian, organic buffet (about US$5). The upmarket *Tirta Sari* (Sacred Mountain Sanctuary Resort) also has a good restaurant (min. Rp50,000 per meal). In Selat, a recommended, inexpensive local warung is *Pendawa*, about 200m to the west of Puri Agung.

Cultural Discoveries around Sidemen

Several shops along Sidemen's main road, in the centre of the village, advertise *ikat* (or *endek* in Balinese) and *songket* **weaving**. From there you can ask to visit the workshop of the weavers. Alternatively, this can be arranged from any of the hotels and homestays in the area. **Lihat Sawah** can even organize a **weaving** class from a one-day initiation to three weeks of deep learning.

A stay around Sidemen is also a chance to witness a performance of *gambuh*. This sacred dance, the oldest in Bali, is performed by only a few groups. One of the most reputable ones is based in **Padangaji**, a mountain village with a lively market above Muncan. Ask if your hotel plans a show, or have one arranged for you if you are in a group – it costs as much as Rp2,000,000.

Walks around Selat, Iseh and Sidemen

The pristine hills, valleys and rice fields in the area offer endless possibilities for walking and trekking. All the hotels and homestays listed offer a choice of guided walks lasting from one to several hours. Another alternative is to use one of the local guides available at Puri Agung Inn. Below is a selection of great walks.

Iseh-Selat Paddy Field Walk

This walk lasts only two hours through the vast rice fields of Iseh. The walk starts at the border (*wates*) between Iseh and Selat on the main Sidemen-Selat road. Around 50m south of the *wates* sign, a small path leads towards the west through the rice fields. Cross the Unda river and climb up the stony path passing vast paddies, then follow the path to Uma village – coming across farmers at work or resting in their huts near their pigpens and cow stalls, oblivious to the great rice terrace views. At Uma village, a small stony road will take you back northwards to the main Muncan-Selat road, which you will reach about 2km west of the Sidemen junction. From there take a bemo or an ojek back to your hotel.

A Three Hour Trek to Umasari

This easy walk has no tiring uphill stretches, but you'll need a guide to find your way. The trekking starts at Uma Village in Selat, with a gorgeous view of Sidemen and the hills of Sekoane and Buntah. After 30 minutes, you'll cross a small creek packed with swimming ducks. The path leads to the small hill of Antap in Umasari Kangin, then crosses a verdant agroforestry grove of cloves, coconut, palms, and durian, leading finally to the small temple of Pura Umagiang, built on top of a small hill with large *cempaka* trees (a local magnolia species) on both sides. The view over Sidemen and Iseh from the temple is stunning, with the small red brick house of the Swiss-born artist Theo Meier at the far end. The trek then leads to the big drainage dam of Sangkangunung, and crosses the Sempol river towards a lush bamboo forest.

Morning Climb to Puncaksari

The hike, for which a guide is needed, will take at least four hours from Padangtunggal to Iseh, climbing the 725m-high Puncaksari. Get started no later than 8am.

Contact for local guides: Wayan Tegteg, Nengah Kari, Wayan Sukre, Ketut Kari or Nyoman Nise, at Puri Agung Inn, T 0366-23 037

You will pass quite a few rivers and creeks along the treks; hiking sandals instead of running shoes are therefore advisable. Get a good guide from Puri Agung Inn to avoid getting lost along the small paths.

© Ulung Wicaksono

The Unda River

© Eric Penot

Mt Agung rising over rice fields

The walk starts through an enchanting, dense forest of bamboo and spiky *salak* palms, until you reach open ground with a plain temple, from which you can catch a glimpse of Candidasa and Padangbai. After passing three ancient stone temples, you'll finally reach **Pura Puncaksari**, which occupies an open ground at the hilltop, lined with massive *cempaka* and frangipani trees. From here, the view stretches as far as Mt Agung, Mt Lempuyang, and Nusa Penida. Rest a while on the fresh ground, listening to the sounds of bamboo flute fluttering in the breeze amidst the last of the mountain fog. The descending route curls slowly through vegetable fields and forest, ending up at the border of Iseh and Selat on the road to Sidemen, with a great view of rice terraces.

Mt Agung: Climbing the Sacred Mountain

Sidemen owes its spiritual quality to the proximity of Mt Agung. Often hidden from sight, especially during the rainy season, its summit shines a fearful aura as it suddenly materializes above the clouds. The 1963 eruption ripped apart the submittal cone, sending volcanic stone blocks 7km away, and killing more than 1000 people. The lava spared the Besakih temple, on the southern slope, reinforcing the perception that the tragedy was a divine intervention. Today, geologists are warning that Mt Agung is a disaster in waiting, as a fierce eruption is likely at any moment, and means of predetection are inadequate. Oblivious of the danger, Balinese have rebuilt their homes on its fertile slopes, and hikers come daily to enjoy the view from the top.

The easiest, most common route to Mt Agung starts *from Pura Pasar Agung*, a 30-minute drive from Selat. The climb starts around 2am, making it possible to reach summit at dawn after four hours of ascension. Beginning the walk in the dark, the path goes through the forest for a good hour before reaching the tree line. From there, the lights of coastal towns from Sanur to Padangbai glitter below the trekkers, matched only by

Arrangements to climb Mt Agung can be made from your hotel, or in Selat the day before. Enquire at Puri Agung Inn (T/F 0366-23 037) or at Gung Bawa Trekking (T/F 0366-24 379; M 081 238 407 52). Prices vary, but a good average is Rp300-400,000 per group of up to 4 people. The hike is within the reach of any trekker in good physical condition – however, it can be dangerous during the rainy season (Nov-March). Good shoes, water, snacks, a jacket for the chilly summit, and a hat are a must. Inquire first about Besakih ceremonies, when climbing Mt Agung is forbidden.

the stars above. After a struggle on the last, steep part of the slope, the edge of the crater is reached at around 6am. It is time for a short prayer to thank the gods, waiting for the sun to rise behind the Rinjani in nearby Lombok, slowly revealing the whole landscape of Bali below your feet. After 30 minutes of enjoying the stunning view, a bit chilled, the three-hour descent starts – by all accounts the most challenging section, as the steep slopes become slippery under exhausted feet. Wild raspberries (*gunggung*) picked along the way offer a sweet excuse for short rests.

Those who like a more sportive trek may prefer the other way, starting *from Besakih temple*. It is a long hike of nearly six hours, the first half of it through the forest, before reaching the summit. The descent along the same way lasts about four hours. Arrangements should be made directly with the guides at the temple. Each guide handles a group of up to three people for US$75, or US$50 for a single trekker.

Besakih: the Holy Navel of Bali

Built on the southern slopes of Mt Agung, at an altitude of about 1000m, Besakih enjoys spectacular views of the south of the island, especially from the back of the main temple, the **Pura Penataran Agung**. The panorama extends down to the sea through a forest-like scene of *meru*-shaped spires – the shrines standing in the open-air structures that make up the various temples of the complex. With the frequent presence of clouds, the temples can have an austere feel. Visitors get a real appreciation of the aura of Besakih through the coloured pageantry of majestic ceremonies.

The Rise, Fall and Rebirth of the Temples

Like many other temples in Bali, Besakih was built on the site of an ancient mountain sanctuary, predating the advent of Hinduism on the island. After the 14th century Majapahit conquest, it became the centre of royal ritual of the king of Gelgel. When the unitary kingdom split up

🦋 *Before trekking, guides will pray and present offerings at the temple. They will appreciate you joining them and showing respect – Mt Agung is a holy place, and guides expect good manner from every participant, to prevent any incident of supernatural origin. Menstruating women are not supposed to be on the sacred mountain. As acknowledged by the guides, these beliefs are of animist origin.*

© Leonard Lueras

Besakih in the moonlight

🦋 *Visit Besakih early, before the crowd of tourist buses and when the weather is still clear. Visitors are not allowed within the temple yards. Take a guide to avoid getting lost in the intricacies of the Balinese pantheon. Leave a tip of about Rp30,000 per group (up to 4 people). The temples are closed to tourists during major ceremonies.*

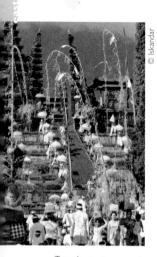

© Iskandar

Temple anniversary in Besakih

A Crowd of Guides
400 local people from Besakih village are employed as guides, taking a turn every four days – so 100 of them are present every day, with unequal knowledge of the temples. Those particularly interested in religion can ask if Made Suadnya is around. Take the time for an informal discussion with your guide, getting beyond standard explanations and trying to get his own perception of the temple, the rituals, or the changes going around Besakih.

in the late 17th century, the smaller kingdoms that succeeded it shared the cost of erecting the main building, Pura Penataran Agung ("The Great Temple of State"), and each king built his own shrine within the temple. Later on, Besakih fell into disrepair due to internecine discord. The earthquake of 1917 caused further damage to the remaining structures, and was seen by the Balinese as a punishment for this abandonment. The temples were restored in 1918 with the help of a Dutch architect, P.A.J. Moojen. Since then, new structures have been constantly added, with restoration work taking place in 1967, 1975 and 1999. Very few of the structures predate 1917.

A Stairway to Heaven

Today, the sanctuary encompasses 22 public temples, consisting of 298 sacred buildings symbolizing the divine universe, as well as 18 *warga* (clan) temples belonging to powerful families. God is worshipped here as the spirit of the living world. The temples offer a representation of the Balinese cosmos, a complex maze defying the understanding of Westerners.

Three of the temples point to the terrestrial elements: Manik Mas ("Beads of Gold") for fire, Bangun Sakti ("Awakening of Divine Power") for earth, and Basukian for water. Four temples known collectively as Pura Catur Daun ("the Four Lotus Petals") are dedicated to the four directions of the sky.

The main temple, **Pura Penataran Agung**, is dedicated to Shiva, the mightiest god of the Hindu pantheon. Its 57 structures are spread over seven terraces. According to I Ketut Wiana, a local guide, the layout is "a visualization of the concept of a spiritual staircase". The seventh level, with no building, represents the unifying, invisible divine presence. Above the topmost terrace one enters the abode of the gods, where no permanent houses may be built – as explained by one of the guides: "no one may be born or die above the temple."

Reordering the World

Almost daily, people come from all around Bali to perform some ritual in Besakih, notably post-cremation rites to send back the souls of the deceased to the ancestors' abode. Every year, crowds flock to celebrate the 10th month festival, when the gods give their "sitting audience". No one may climb Mt Agung during these rituals – who would dare to sit higher than the gods?

Yet the greatest of all Balinese rituals is the **Eka Dasa Rudra** ceremony, a purification rite held for the entire cosmos once a century, or when otherwise necessary. Two such ceremonies were held in the 20th century, in 1963 and again in 1978, since the course of the 1963 ritual was interrupted by the eruption of Mt Agung.

A Battlefield under a Volcano

Besides its role as a spiritual centre, Besakih is also a political arena – for religion and power still go hand in hand in Bali. Every political rivalry and religious disagreement has its echo in Besakih, and decisions made by the priests there apply to the whole of Bali. Powerful families compete to renovate their respective *warga* temples (*padharman*), thus showing off their wealth, prestige and rank. As observed by I Gde Pitana, Director of the Balinese Culture and Tourism Office: "most of the *warga* temples have now been renovated with fine elaborate carvings and paintings surpassing those of many public temples in Bali" (from *Bali – Living in two worlds*, edited by Urs Ramseyer).

In the past, a plan to turn the complex of temples into a cultural park was aired, and in 2001 the Minister for Culture and Tourism proposed it for registration as a UNESCO World Cultural Heritage site. Both proposals had to be abandoned in the face of fierce opposition from local religious and political leaders. For Besakih encapsulates the universe of the Balinese, who intend to preserve it like they would like to keep Bali – celebrated by visitors, but free from outsiders' control.

Animal Sacrifices

The guides at Besakih like to give an account of the 118 kinds of animals, representing all living creatures, that were sacrificed in 1978, despite frowning conservationists – specimens of endangered species, including rare birds and a baby tiger, were brought by Hindu believers from all the archipelago.

© Gilles Guerard

Back from the temple after a ceremony

*Entrance gate
to Pura Kehen*

© Godeliva D. Sari

Bangli

> *Bangli can be reached
by bemo from Gianyar or
Kintamani, or by mini-bus
or bus from Denpasar
(Batubulan terminal,
direction Kintamani).
Once in town, ojeks or
bemos are found
at the terminal
from 5am to 6pm.*

A Fateful Breakdown

*Like many visitors to Bali,
Scottish-born Muriel
Pearson had her life
turned around by chance.
Driving inland in search of
the "real Bali", she ran
out of gas in front of Puri
Denpasar in Bangli.
The king invited her into
the palace and adopted
her as a daughter,
giving her the name
Ketut Tantri. She even
dyed her red hair black at
the king's suggestion –
only leyak (witches)
have red hair on Bali.
There she wrote her book
Revolt in Paradise,
a fascinating tale of life
in Bali and Java
from 1932 to 1947.*

On the slopes of Mt Batur, the small, quiet town of Bangli offers a cool climate and, when the weather is clear, superb views of the volcano – its name comes from the term "*bang giri*", or "red mountain". With very little tourist presence, the district of Bangli is a friendly, easygoing region where you can experience the Balinese rural lifestyle at its best, amidst views of the mountains and the southern coast of Bali. Nature lovers will enjoy forests and cool waterfalls, while amateur anthropologists may explore traditional villages and scenic temples.

Based on a stela in its main temple, **Pura Kehen**, the town dates back to at least AD 1204. After being ruled by the Gelgel-based Majapahit dynasty, Bangli became Bali's most powerful upland court in the 19th century. Its influence, however, was limited by its lack of sea access. Bangli finally became a Dutch protectorate in 1909. Today, old royal houses can still be seen along the main streets. The only one open to the public is Artha Sastra Inn, which is used by the royal family as a guest-house to earn income – caste doesn't necessarily bring economic power in modern Bali, and many aristocratic families need extra funds for maintaining their rituals and palaces. Large ceremonies are held at **Puri Denpasar**, the palace of the last king of Bangli, which has been restored by his descendants.

Where to Stay – Bangli

The peaceful town of Bangli offers only a few accommodations. Once a royal residence, the *Artha Sastra Inn* is wedged into a family compound. The cheaper rooms are a bit run-down; the more expensive ones are located at the front next to the market, and can get a bit noisy during the day – which starts at 5am in Bali. There were water problems at the time of writing; try to call first before popping in.

Another choice is the *Bangli Inn*, which offers clean and simple rooms in a two-storey building with local-style bathrooms – no shower, just splash yourself with cool water from the traditional *mandi* water tub. In the centre of its courtyard is a small restaurant serving local food.

Where to Eat

Bangli has several warungs offering Balinese and Indonesian food, particularly at the night market (*pasar senggol*) near the terminal. Restaurant *Sari Ayu Nikmat* on Jalan Subakaya serves excellent *satay* (kebabs) and *gulai* (curry meat soup with coconut milk).

What to Do – Temples around Bangli

Pura Kehen is one of the most majestic temples on the island. Built on three terraces on the southern slope of the hill overlooking Bangli, its high platforms and megalithic constructions betray a link with the animistic terraced sanctuaries dating from early Balinese history.

As one approaches through the surrounding woods and coconut groves, the vivid carvings of the temple look like a set of *wayang* theatre puppets against a lush forest background. The entrance is decorated with two elephant-headed barongs and other carvings devoted to Shiva. Don't miss the *kulkul* (split drum) among the branches of a banyan tree in the outer courtyard – the priests have to climb the tree to beat the drum. On the wall to the entrance of the inner courtyard, decorative

❶ 9 Rm –
T 0366-91 179
> Near the bale kulkul, in front of the bemo terminal.

❶ 10 Rm –
T 0366-91 518
> 300m east of the Trimurti Statue, on the corner of Jl. Gajah Mada and Jl. Rambutan.

© Godeliva D. Sari

Elephant heads at the entrance to Pura Kehen

> Follow the road to Penelokan for 1km, then turn right at the T-junction and walk 300m, or take a bemo going towards Rendang and stop at the temples. Two friendly English-speaking guides are there to explain everything about the temple; leave a donation (about Rp20,000 per person).

© Godeliva D. Sari

*Decorative plates
in Pura Kehen*

plates show European folks riding horses and carts. Two statues of dragons and a big turtle head guard the entrance to the 11-tiered *meru*. Just opposite Pura Kehen, **Pura Penyimpenan** ("The Storage Temple") is used to keep the ceremonial equipment for the main temple.

Three hundred metres east of Pura Kehen, the spacious grounds of *Sasana Budaya Giri Kusuma* host cultural events like dancing and *gamelan* shows, as well as regular practices by local artists. Every year in May, a cultural exhibition is held to commemorate the anniversary of Bangli. Check the schedule of events at the tourism office next door (Jl. Sriwijaya No. 23; *T 0366-91537*).

Located 1km south of the centre of town, next to the detention centre (*Rumah tahanan*), is the **Pura Dalem Penunggekan** (death temple). As is often the case with death temples, outside panels show horror scenes of pleading evildoers impaled by arrows, boiled alive, devoured by demons, strung up from trees, or roasted over flames. Some are for adults' eyes only.

What to Do – Outside Bangli

© Elizabeth E. Listyowati

*Scenes of hell in Pura Dalem
Penunggekan*

The 12km stretch from Bangli to **Rendang** in the east, passing between Bunut and Bangbang Tengah, offers wonderful views of scenic rice terraces and deep gorges. From the main eastward road, you can walk along any small road leading to the south or the north to reach nearby villages. One pleasant short walk starts in **Bunut**, 2km east of Bangli, near the *Balai Perikanan* (Fisheries' Office). Take the narrow lane going north towards the village of **Kubu**, cutting through idyllic rice fields past the curious Pura Melanting and Pura Dalem of the *banjar*. After 4km, in Kubu, turn towards the west (left) and after less than 1km, you'll reach the main road going from Bangli to Kintamani, near the village of **Penglipuran**, which you can visit at the same time. Back on the main road, you can find a bemo to drive you home to Bangli, 4km to the south.

Penglipuran, the Bamboo Community

This village, with its traditional, pre-Majapahit housing style, was declared a "tourism village" (*desa wisata*) in 1992, as part as an official policy to develop cultural tourism. Yet it has kept a friendly atmosphere and doesn't get more than 10 to 50 visitors a day. Sadly enough, visitors usually come with guides from outside and most of the English-speaking youth, who could be local guides, have left the village looking for jobs.

Once past the parking lot and modern entrance, dwellings are constructed of earthen bricks, bamboo and wood in a neat, uniform style – admire the gracious bamboo tiling on the oldest pavilions. The first, unnumbered compound on the right on the main street is empty and open to visitors. Walk up to the great council temple (**Pura Bale Agung**) to admire its exquisite bamboo roofing. About 200m to the north stands a 75-hectare **bamboo forest** owned by the community. The tradition of bamboo weaving for making ceilings or partition walls (*bedeg*) is proudly maintained by the villagers; its quality is renowned all over Bali and beyond. All around the road before and after Penglipuran, craftsmen work along the road producing musical instruments and handicrafts made of bamboo. Another 3km north of Penglipuran lies **Kayubihi**, another Bali Aga village with a distinctive atmosphere.

Bukit Demulih, the Hill of No Return

Around 4km west of Bangli, the pleasant temple complex of Bukit Demulih offers one of the best **views** of Bali. From the centre of Bangli, follow the road to Tampaksiring, taking a left at the first fork. Proceed 1.5km further, past the iron bridge, and take a small asphalt road to the right, next to Pura Manik Mudera. Once in the village of Demulih, after the *kantor banjar*, a small paved road leads to **Bukit Demulih**. Park there and walk to the temples. The first temple along the path is Pura Tamansari. Newly renovated, it houses holy springs.

> Indicated by a sign, 4km north of Bangli on the road to Kintamani. A small entrance fee applies.

© Godeliva D. Sari

Penglipuran village landscape.

♥ **Yayasan Bambu** (the Environmental Bamboo Foundation, see p.160) promotes the conservation and uses of bamboo in Bali. It has supported Penglipuran village with workshop facilities and established a living bamboo collection on the right side of the temple. Craftsmen are now able to produce new designs using a recently introduced black bamboo variety. To be guided for a walk, contact I Wayan Arcana, who worked with the foundation (house No. 12 on the main street).

What's in a Name
Demulih — meaning "don't return" in Balinese — was once a parental plea to a Balinese prince. A man of many wordly appetites, the prince had been sent off to war in Java to calm his impulses. He later refused to return to Bali, until his parents lured him back by offering him a beautiful dehen — in Balinese, a pretty woman, but also or a hill. Instead of a wife, his parents granted him a fertile hill to quiet his hunger, so he would have no need to leave again to Java. The prince was later buried on his beloved dehen.

The Kuning waterfall

To its right, a set of steps leads to the three temple complexes on the top of the hill; the climb is a pleasant one through the midst of a dense wood. The temples are named after their locations: **Pura Puncak Kaja** faces the mountain, **Pura Puncak Tengah** is in the centre, and **Pura Puncak Kelod** faces the sea, with a gorgeous view over most of Bangli and Klungkung, down to the south coast and Nusa Penida. Take the small path next to Pura Puncak Kaja to descend to the village road, overlooking rice fields. The path ends up at the asphalt road in the middle of the village. Go east to return to the village entrance.

A Bath in the Kuning Waterfall

This 25m fall, with is refreshing pool, offers a pleasant bath in a quiet setting. From Bangli, drive south or take a bemo towards Gianyar. About 1.5km after the petrol station at the southern end of Bangli, get off from the bemo at the junction of a side road heading east to Kuning village. Continue on foot or on ojek for 1.5km on a small asphalt road, passing a village and rice fields. When the road splits, take a left and continue for another 400m to Kuning. Continue on foot to a small junction. Take a left turn and after 50m, a small dirt path on the left heads to the waterfall, passing fruit gardens and rice fields. At the end you'll find yourself on the edge of a sheer drop facing the waterfall. To reach the pool, take the rocky steps on your left and descend on the slippery path. Your efforts will be rewarded once you splash under a shower of spring water surging from under the black rocks.

Further south, another spot worth a visit is ***Bukit Jati***, located around 10km south of Bangli and 3km north of Gianyar. On the Bangli-Gianyar road, look for the petrol station at the village of Bunutin. Around 400m south of the petrol station, a small paved road leads to Bukit Jati. Just after the car park, continue on a dirt track up to the top of the hill. From here, the view is splendid, overlooking the southern part of Bangli out to Gianyar.

© Marion Lammersen

Mount and Lake Batur

Sunrise at Mt Batur

Climbing north from Bangli, the road meanders through bamboo forests, coffee groves, and gardens before reaching one of Bali's most dramatic vistas: the basin of **Lake Batur**, with the black cone of the active volcano smouldering behind it. In contrast to the evergreen land-scapes sculpted by rice growers, the **caldera** of Mt Batur is a realm of melted earth and raw telluric forces. The 1717m volcano is also Bali's second most sacred mountain. Its waters are the source of a dense network of rivers, some of them subterranean streams that resurface miles away as holy springs. The lake is revered as the source of life for all the *subak* (irrigation groups) of east Bali.

The area around Mt Batur is also rich in cultural heritage, with more than 50 villages proudly preserving traditions predating the 14th century influence of the Majapahit Empire. These so-called "Bali Aga" ("Mountain Balinese" or "Original Balinese") communities are caste-less. They maintain a council of elders ranked by seniori-ty, instead of elected representatives as in other Balinese villages. Their dwellings followed a typical pattern of wooden houses roofed with bamboo shingles, laid out along parallel streets – a now fading characteristic.

> *Batur is easy to reach by public transport from Ubud, Denpasar (**Batubulan** terminal), Amlapura, or Singaraja (**Penarukan** terminal); ask for buses or bemos to Kintamani. The main roads from Ubud or Bangli to Batur reach the rim of the caldera between Kintamani and **Penelokan** ("Place to Look" in Balinese). Dozens of restaurants, shops, guides, and vendors await tourists on this stretch of road, famed for its views. Alternatively, drive to Batur from **Rendang**, going through the forested shade of a quiet road before reaching the edge of the caldera on a more peaceful spot.*

© Dedok

Aggressors or Victims?

The arrival of tourists and money in an area previously shielded from the outside has resulted in an unpleasant ambiance around Batur's most visited spots. Lured by the glamour of the tourism industry, many villagers have left their lands in search of better opportunities. Lurking in front of popular viewing spots and at the foot of the volcano, persistent vendors, so-called guides, and swindlers of all kinds prey on visitors as soon as they alight from their vehicles. Although their presence can be obnoxious, one cannot help wonder whether they are not also sad victims of mass tourism – especially when the number of visitors dwindles as it did in 2003, leaving many Balinese empty-handed along their deserted vistas.

Travellers who want to enjoy Mt Batur despite this situation need to be ready – countless tourists have been cheated, robbed, and even assaulted after bitter discussions with guides or vendors. Avoid the busy tourist spots along the rim road, remain silent and calm, and keep a close eye on your car and belongings – there are stories of people discreetly unplugging a cable in an engine to be able to sell car repair services. As is typical across Bali, crowds of tourists and nagging vendors are concentrated in a small area. Along little back roads around the lake or inside the caldera, you'll encounter quiet communities where elders barely speak Indonesian and where villagers tend to ignore tourists.

Born in the Flames

Like Mt Agung, Batur was initially a sharp cone, pointing at 3,500m above sea level. About 30,000 years ago, a terrific explosion atomized its upper part, and collapsed the bulk of the mountain into the empty magma chamber, creating the present caldera. The hole was soon partly filled with a crescent-shape lake. In the middle of the caldera, a younger, smaller volcano – of the effusive rather than explosive type – grew out of the crater floor, rising 686m above the lake. The caldera's outer walls, remnants of the original mountain, range from

Beware of the Mountain

The only visible activity of Mt Batur is usually a wisp of smoke drifting across its lava-blackened slopes. With luck, you may be in Penelokan at night when the volcano erupts, spewing red fireworks of burning lava at regular intervals. Not all the volcano's manifestations are this enjoyable. Its last real fury was in 1917, when it destroyed 65,000 homes, 2,500 temples, and killed 1,372 people. During bouts of activity in 1926, 1959, 1963, and 1994, Batur emitted flows of lava that are still visible, belched poisonous gases that killed the lake's fish, and caused respiratory ailments all over Bali.

1,267 metres to 2,153m. The 11km by 13,5km caldera, one of the largest in the world, is actually divided into two smaller ones, one of them lying 120 to 300m below the other. It is worth taking a full day to explore the area. You can stay either in Penelokan or Buahan, on the quiet, southern end of the lake, or in Toyabungkah, at the foot of the volcano.

Mt Batur

Where to Stay – Penelokan and Buahan

The only quality accommodation in **Penelokan** is the *Lakeview Hotel and Restaurant*, cleverly designed like a mountain-top monastery hanging on to the caldera wall, with unique views from the terraces of its romantic rooms. Built with local volcanic stones, the building blends discreetly into the landscape, and the management makes constant efforts to minimize its impact on the environment. Alas, this exceptional setting is spoilt in the early mornings and afternoons by trucks carrying sand from quarries in the caldera.

Descending from Penelokan towards the lake, you can turn right at Kedisan, towards **Buahan** and **Abang**. Quarry trucks don't come to this corner of the caldera, so it is a good area in which to enjoy the lakeside in quiet. Those who like basic simplicity will enjoy *Baruna Losmen*, a slightly run-down budget guest house, isolated in a peaceful setting between the shore and the crater wall. A tiny restaurant is attached to the courtyard; the friendly lady in charge is a good cook and will be happy to offer you a taste of the local steamed fish.

Where to Stay – Toyabungkah

Turning left at Kedisan, the road leads to **Toyabungkah** ("Hot Springs"), a tiny settlement along the lake. It has a dozen plain guesthouses and a couple of resorts, surrounded by fields of shallots and vegetables thriving in the cool climate. Alas, these blessings come with a few plagues, such as the scores of flies that occasionally invade the area, and the 200 odd trucks carrying volcanic sand to Denpasar, usually in the early morning hours.

❸ 14 Rm – Htw Rst Gvw Trk Bcy
T 0366-51 394 ;
0366-52 525
T/F 0366-51 464
lakeview@indo.net.id
> Look for the entrance to the hotel at the bottom of a steep descent on the right, immediately after the junction of the main road from Bangli and the crater.

❶ 5 Rm – Rst Gvw Trk
T 0366-51 221
M 081 338 767 037

No less irksome are some of the aggressive local guides. Those who are not put off will enjoy quiet evenings along the lovely lakeside, baths in the fresh lake water or in the hot springs, and pleasant walks followed by delicious feasts of grilled lake fish (*ikan mujahir*). The most pleasant places to stay are located in the lowest part of the village, a right turn from the main street towards the lake shore, a bit away from the road and the trucks.

Under the Volcano III: a Love Story with the Lake

❤ ➊ 5 Rm –
Bch Gvw Trk
T 0366-51 166; 52 508
> Located on the left before the office of the guides association

These clean and plain bungalows, almost Spartan, are perfect for enjoying the grandiose setting of the caldera and the serene shores of the lake, under the spell of its changing colours. Take time to observe farmers and fishermen from the terrace, then stroll around the surrounding fields, ending up at the lake shore for a swim in the clear water. The same friendly family manages two other places, *Under the Volcano I* (in the village, along the main road) and *Under the Volcano II*, which is close to the lake with great views and a small garden.

➊ ➌ 9 Rm – (Htw)
Rst Bch Swp Gvw Trk Ckr
T 0366-51 249
F 0366-51 250
jero_wijaya@hotmail.com

Lakeside Cottages is another good option, with different types of rooms offering various levels of comfort. The most pleasant are the large cottages with hot water and pleasant verandas facing the lake, while the ones in the back have cold water only.

➊ 3 Rm – Htw

Travellers on a budget will appreciate the tiny *Ting Tong Cottages*, with its clean and quiet rooms, alas with no direct view to the lake.

Where to Eat

In **Penelokan**, the cosy restaurant of the *Lakeview Hotel* is worth a visit. It boasts a wide selection of quality local and international food served on a delightful terrace overlooking the lake.

Along the main rim road to Kintamani, several large restaurants cater to tourist buses, which stop there for the awesome view more than for the bland buffets. After Penelokan, in the direction of Kintamani, the *Puri Batur* restaurant is a bit quieter than its competitors, offering decent food in a peaceful environment on a balcony over the caldera.

In **Toyabungkah**, the *Volcano Breeze Café* (*T 0366-51 824*) is a perfect place to relax in an enjoyable environment, away from the frantic guides, enjoying grilled or roasted carp, or *mujahir* fish from the lake (about Rp50,000).

Boats waiting for passengers for Truyan

What to Do – Temples Around the Crater

The sacred site of Batur is surrounded by several remarkable temples. About 4km north of Penelokan, four temples stand in a row along the crater's rim. The most imposing is *Pura Ulun Danu Batur*, dedicated to the goddess of the lake, commander of the island's waters, who allied with the divinity of Mt Agung to create the fertility of the island. Just behind Besakih in terms of importance, this sanctuary hosts frequent ceremonies, which render a particular grandeur to the site as colourful rows of pilgrims march slowly in the mist over the caldera.

The original temple was actually located near the lake, near Pura Jati. Miraculously spared by the 1917 eruption, it was destroyed by the following one. Today, a smaller temple, *Pura Ulun Danu*, can still be seen after **Songan** on the north of the lake. Every ten years, live buffalos, pigs, goats, geese, and chicken, richly adorned with gold, are drowned in the middle of the lake with solemn grandeur to honour the lake's goddess. Since the temple was probably built on the site of a pre-Majapahit sanctuary, one can only fantasize about the quantity of wealth and death accumulated at the bottom of the lake over millennia of animist and Hindu worship.

On the northwest side of the caldera, Penulisan is the site of the highest temple on Bali, *Pura Puncak Penulisan*, also called *Pura Tegeh Koripan*. After an

What Not to Do

Although rather modern-looking, the Bali Aga village of Trunyan has kept an ancient tradition of letting corpses decay in a cemetery, without burial or cremation. This has attracted scores of voyeur tourists, willing to pay a lot to see little more than a few bones. The villagers invented wild rules to seize this tourist manna, imposing donations, setting a high-priced monopoly on boat travel on the lake, and sometimes extorting extra payments to take tourists back to shore. The resulting atmosphere is rather unpleasant; it may be safer to avoid this area.

ascent of 333 steps to 1745m, travellers are rewarded with an awesome view. Under an austere *bale*, a row of *linga, yoni,* and fragments of old sculptures contrast with finely wrought stone statues. Archaeological evidence indicates a sanctuary here as early as 1500 BC. The pyramidal complex, the site's 11 rising terraces, and its megalithic stones are typical of ancient mountain sanctuaries.

What to Do – To Climb or Not to Climb?

Most travellers believe it is a must to climb the summit of Batur. Think twice, however, before putting on your hiking shoes. The most common route to Batur is a rather easy two-hour ascent, in the company of many other visitors. The highlight is the cooking of eggs in the caldera's steaming water.

This oddity apart, it may just be as interesting to walk leisurely around the beautiful caldera without needing to summit the mountain itself – after all, the external walls are higher than the volcano. This will also save you the displeasure of dealing directly with the members of the Association of Mt Batur Trekking Guides (read side column).

If you climb Batur, it may be worth doing it through a hotel or agency, saving you the hassle of dealing with the guides. The longer itineraries are more interesting. While the shorter route takes you straight to the main crater and back in 4 hours (about US$20/person), the medium, 6-hour route lets you admire spectacular landscapes around the rim, and the 8-hour long route passes by all the craters of the volcano (US$30-40).

Besides roaming around Mt Batur, trekkers can also enjoy a pleasant walk through the third largest forested area in Bali, starting from Penelokan to the east, in the direction of *Mt Abang*. The climb to Mt Abang (2152m) can be arranged at the Baruna Losmen in Buahan.

After so much exercise, enjoy a dip in the Olympic-size pool or the smaller hot water pools of the new *Hot Springs* resort in the centre of Toyabungkah.

The Infamous Guides
Travellers who decide to climb Batur will have to go with one of the 100-odd members of the Association of Mt Batur Trekking Guides. Set in Toyabungkah and resented by many locals, it imposes its monopoly on anyone who wants to ascend the mountain. While the official price is set at a reasonable Rp150,000 per group, it is impossible to climb the mountain for less than Rp300,000 per group (4 persons max), or Rp150-200,000 per person. Attempts to bargain further or to climb on your own may result in nasty rows.

❈ Roijaya Wisata
at the Lakeside cottages in Toyabungkah can arrange climbs to Batur and Abang, as well as a good choice of treks in the area.
T 0366-51 249
F 0366-51 250
jero_wijaya@hotmail.com

Nusa Lembongan – Nusa Penida

© Waka Experience

The beach at Mushroom Bay

Initially "discovered" by surfers lured by its challenging barrels, *Nusa Lembongan* is now a popular getaway destination near Bali. Its main bay is a long stretch of white sand fringed by hotels in all price ranges, from backpackers' losmens in **Jungutbatu** to deluxe resorts in **Mushroom Bay**. Fishermen's boats, seaweed farmers, surfers, sailing cruisers, and the high-powered speed boats of "adventure" trip companies compete to take advantage of its turquoise waters. Yet a few steps behind this busy front, the island has kept the slow pace of a rural life of seaweed farming, and a serene coastline of white coves and mangrove-fringed bays.

Opposite Lembongan, the islet of *Nusa Ceningan* has no tourist accommodation, but it is great for walks, especially to the top for great views of the ocean.

Travellers in search of a real off-the-beaten-track experience will cross to the barren, larger island of *Nusa Penida*, which receives very few tourists. The hair-raising views from its western cliffs are matched only by the Bukit Peninsula in south Bali. Its arid landscapes are reminiscent of the wild Sunda islands, and if it wasn't for the presence of temples charged with mystic energy, you wouldn't feel like you were in Bali.

The accommodations of **Nusa Lembongan** are aligned along the main bay, which is where the boats land (be ready to be assaulted by hotel touts on arrival).

> Public boats to **Nusa Lembongan** leave from Sanur Beach at 8 and 10am (90min trip, Rp35,000); return boats leave around 7:30am from Jungutbatu. **Perama** also operates a shuttle boat to Nusa Lembongan (10:30am from Sanur, return trip at 8:30am, Rp50,000). Faster, private boats can be chartered for about Rp300,000.
> It is possible to travel to **Nusa Penida** from Padangbai (one hour, Rp30,000), or from Kusamba, a slower trip on traditional boats.
> To move between Lembongan and Penida, hop on one of the public boats leaving early from **Jungutbatu** (Nusa Lembongan) to **Toyapakeh** (Nusa Penida). Alternatively, a chartered boat from Lembongan to Penida and back costs about Rp150,000.

The Pontoons

As you land in the bay of Lembongan, you'll notice two pontoons belonging to "adventure" trip companies. The smaller one, carefully installed in an area without coral, belongs to Bali Hai. The most visible is the two-storey yellow structure of Bounty Cruises. On a busy day, scores of loud speed boats shoot from the 48m long raft. "Guests complain that it ruins the landscape," explain local hotel owners, "but it belongs to well-connected people, and we were not strong or united enough to resist it." Quicksilver also installed two metallic pontoons near Penida. The rafts employ a few local staff, but are mainly used for day cruises, with little profit for local people. Their anchor chains threaten the coral.

© The Natural Guide

A pontoon in front of Celengimbai

❶ ❷ *12 Rm –*
Htw A/C Rst Bch Bcy Trk
T 0366-24 487
M 081 239 547 25

On the northern end, the village of *Jungutbatu* has a dozen budget *losmen* with restaurants facing the beach – a narrow strip of white sand shared with fishing boats and seaweed farmers. At night, it becomes animated with music from the bars and guitar players, and has a laid-back surfers' and backpackers' atmosphere.

Further south, in the corner of the bay, *Celengimbai* is a lovely hideaway with slightly more comfortable accommodations, and a small, peaceful beach. Unfortunately, the beach faces the bulky pontoons used by day-trip operators. On the western end of the main bay, the secluded *Mushroom Bay*, trimmed with rather luxurious resorts, would be idyllic if it wasn't for the noisy ballet of motorboats pulling banana-shaped dinghies and their haul of excited tourists.

Travellers wanting to visit **Nusa Penida** can do it in a day tour from Lembongan, but it is really worth spending at least a night in one of the small homestays in *Sampalan* to explore this wild-looking island.

Where to Stay – Jungutbatu

Most of the bungalows along the shore offer decent rooms for Rp30-70,000 (not including breakfast). They have plain bathrooms with cold water in concrete or wooden buildings, often rather run-down. The upper rooms with a veranda are usually better, but can get noisy as you can hear the cockerels, motorboats, and music from the bars. The ones facing the sea are slightly more expensive and often full. It is difficult to predict which place will be the best – new operations may quickly run down, while older ones may undergo renovations. At the time of writing, the cleanest, best value rooms were found at the *Linda's Bungalows*, at the northern end of Jungutbatu, with 15 rooms in a white concrete building. Next door, *Puri Nusa* (*T 0366-24 482*) offers a good choice of 19 rooms surrounding a small garden.

Further south, next to Mainski Inn, *Ketut Losmen* is slightly more upmarket than the other places. It offers comfortable rooms in brick-and-bamboo bungalows, along a narrow strip of garden perpendicular to the beach. The ones in the back have very large beds and hot water; the restaurant in the front, shared with Two Thousand Bungalows, is a pleasant place to relax.

The best places to stay in Jungutbatu are at the southern end of the beach, about 500m from the main herd of bungalows – a quiet spot within walking distance from the animated cafés. *Pondok Baruna* is a good address for divers, with an alignment of charming, spotless rooms tastily decorated in white and blue, each with a tiny terrace facing the ocean. The friendly staff proposes a wide range of activities, including underwater sports in the attached, eco-friendly World Diving Centre. Further south, *Bungalow No. 7* offers clean rooms in traditional, well-decorated brick-and-bamboo cottages along a well-tended garden. The front cottages have a large veranda on which to lounge in front of the ocean.

♥ ❶ 8 Rm – Rst
Bch Div Bcy
M 081 239 409 92
F 0366-24 486
info@world-diving.com

❶ 14 Rm –
Rst BchTrk Bcy
T 0366-24 497
putuyasa7@hotmail.com

Where to Stay – Celengimbai

This small beach, located in the corner of the main Lembongan Bay, south of Jungutbatu, offers more privacy than the bungalow-packed area in the north. To reach it from Jungutbatu, walk along the beach, pass the Coconut Beach resort and then walk up the small corniche. You can also charter a boat, or drive on a motorbike through the village of **Desa Lembongan**.

One of the oldest hotels on the island, *Villa Wayan* is a friendly resort with clean, well-decorated rooms spread over two main buildings with a wide terrace overlooking the bay. The breezy restaurant has direct access to the white sand beach – beware the stones and corals at low tide. The menu offers an ample choice of salads, sandwiches, grilled fish, and local specialities, such as the mouth-watering Lembongan curry, cooked in coconut and lemongrass. Ask the staff about walks and boat rides around the islands.

Behind Villa Wayan, the three bungalows of *Morin* are cleaving to the rock between the two coves of Celengimbai and Coconut beach. The clean, bamboo-

❸ 6 Rm – A/C Rst Bch
Gvw Trk Bcy
T 0361-271 212
F 0361-287 431
villawayan@dps.centrin.net.id

❷ ❸ 6 Rm – Rst Bch
Gvw Div Trk
T/F 0361-288 993
M0 0818 356 804
wayman40@hotmail.com

walled bungalows are tastefully decorated, each with a small terrace facing a breathtaking view of the bay. At the front, a tiny restaurant welcomes guests on a romantic sand-floored terrace. The friendly owner proposes a program of walks, boat tours, snorkelling, and diving.

Where to Stay – Mushroom Bay

This wonderful cove derives its nickname from its mushroom coral; its original name is Sanghiang Bay. It gets busy during the daytime, with a swarm of motorboats carrying the clients of Bali Hai and other adventure companies. To find some calm, walk down the cliff to the smaller, lovely cove located just before Mushroom Bay.

> *Mushroom Bay can be reached on motorbike from Desa Lembongan or by boat from Jungutbatu. It is also nice to walk from Celengimbai: pass through the Tamarind Hotel, climb on a small path, follow the cliff and go down to the bay through the Mushroom Beach Hotel.*

♥ ❹ ❺ *10 Rm –
Htw A/C Rst Bch Swp Div Trk Byc Ckr Spa
T 0361-723 629
F 0361-722 077
www.wakaexperience.com*

Of all the upmarket resorts crammed on the bay, the most discreet one is *Waka Nusa*. Virtually invisible from the beach, it features stylish, round-shaped bungalows with grass roofs – perhaps a bit too close too each other. The garden is a minimalist, elegant blend of pandanus, blossoming frangipani, and palms growing on the white sand. These species are well-adapted to the coastal environment and need little water, thus sparing the scarce water resources of the island. The resort has a small pool and a restaurant, serving good local and international food (Rp80-100,000). Cruises and sailing trips from the mainland can be arranged on the awesome, 23m-long **Waka Louka** catamaran. Glass-bottom boat tours, snorkelling, diving, and canoeing are also offered.

❺ *12 Rm –
Htw A/C Rst Bch Swp Gvw Div Trk Bcy Ckr Spa
T 0361-725 864
F 0361-725 866
www.nusa-lembongan.com*

At the western end of the bay, dominating the beach with its imposing restaurant, the *Nusa Lembongan Resort* features luxurious stone and wood villas in a terraced garden. Seven secluded teak decks overlook the bay, enabling guests to sunbathe or have a romantic candlelight dinner with fine food served from Jojo's restaurant (Rp80-100,000). A wide range of activities are offered by the resort in order to discover Nusa Lembongan and Penida. Guests can reach the island on the elegant sailboat owned by the resort. The resort provides help to local schools.

Where to Stay – Nusa Penida

Perhaps because of its *angker* (haunted) reputation, Nusa Penida has been spared by hotel developers – a proposal to establish a casino on the island has been put on hold, due to public outcry that it would soil the spirituality of the place. The only tourist accommodations are in **Sampalan**. Our favourite is the adorable *Made Homestay*, which hides spacious, traditional brick bungalows with carved doors in a family compound, around a lush garden livened up by red hibiscus. Ask the friendly family members to arrange motorbike rentals and guided tours around the island.

A bit further down the road, in another alley, *Nusa Garden Bungalows* crams a few clean brick cottages in a small garden featuring odd painted concrete castings of herons and deer frolicking on the lawn.

None of these places have a restaurant, but they can prepare or order food for you, unless you prefer to walk to the nearby colourful market or pick a local warung – *Kios Dewi* is a favourite with travellers.

Sampalan is a perfect base to explore Nusa Penida, which can take at least one or two days. To get really immersed in the local culture, ask to sleep in friendly villagers' homes along your journey.

❶ 4 Rm –
> In a little alley off the left side of the road when entering Sampalan from Toyapakeh.

❶ 5 Rm –
T 0361-418 338
M 081 283 018 03;
081 338 557 595

Where to Eat – Nusa Lembongan

Let's face it, no one comes to a surfers' island for fine dining. Jungutbatu beach is predictably lined up with friendly, inexpensive cafés offering a standard menu of fried noodles or rice, pasta, grilled fish, salads, and sandwiches. On the northern end of the beach, between Linda Bungalows and Puri Nusa, the *Kainalu Surf Café* serves a wider choice of seafood, Indonesian, Chinese, and even Mexican dishes, on a quiet terrace overlooking the sea (Rp15-35,000). For something different, try the modest *Ketut's Warung*, hidden 200m away from the beach behind Agung and Lembongan bungalows. Its dining room has a friendly warung atmosphere, and a small but tasty choice of local and Thai dishes (Rp10-25,000).

The Knowing Hands
The owner of Ketut's warung offers a great therapeutic-massage-cum-foot-reflexology, probing your feet and back for tensions and jammed nerves. Tell him where you feel pain; he'll do his best to relieve you with his magic hands and sandalwood oil. At Rp75,000 for 45 minutes, this is more expensive than a beach massage but worth the experience.

Mangrove on the coast of Nusa Lembongan

© Ujung Wicaksono

Manta rays can be spotted around Lembongan and Penida. Watching them fly around you with their ample, dark wings is an exhilarating experience. Don't panic as they rush towards you with their gaping mouths, they feed only on microscopic plankton. Avoid direct contact so as not to scare them.

Grey nurse shark in Nusa Penida.

© Tonozuka Dive & Dives

Travellers in for a treat can hop to **Mushroom Bay**. There, for Rp 80-100,000, they can get a gourmet meal in the deluxe *Waka Nusa* or at *Jojo's* restaurant in the Lembongan Resort.

What to Do at Sea – Lembongan and Penida

Boat trips are a great way to discover these fantastic islands. Start at sunset with a short tour around the Lembongan **mangrove** on a fishing boat (Rp50,000). In clear weather, you can see Mt Agung in the background. You can also charter a boat for the day (Rp200,000) to circle around **Nusa Penida**. Pass along its **southwest coast** to admire a succession of green coves secluded between stern, limestone cliffs – look out for the *batu bolong*, a hollow rock which arches into the ocean.

Divers and *snorkellers* have an endless choice of great spots around Lembongan and Penida. There are strong currents, so if you are snorkelling, stay close to your boat. If you are diving, pick a professional dive shop with safety-minded instructors.

Good snorkelling and easy dives can be accessed from a fishing boat at the southern end of the main bay of **Lembongan** or in **Mushroom Bay** (about Rp25,000 per boat for snorkelling). Beware of the currents as soon as you swim out of the shelter of the bays.

For a greater variety of marine life, it is worth chartering a boat to **Crystal Bay**, in the pass between Lembongan and Penida, or to the sites of **Toyapakeh**, **S.D. or Sekolah Dasar** ("Elementary School") and **Pura Ped** on Penida's north coast. All have good snorkelling and are suited for divers of all levels.

A few other sites, such as **Manta Point** at the southern end of Penida or **Jurassic Point** in the north of Jungutbatu, have strong currents and are only for experienced divers. In their great guide book *Diving Bali,* David Pickell and Wally Siagan commented that a trip to this area could become "your worst, your best, or your last dive".

Most operators on Bali's south and east coast will take you for a dive trip to Penida. From Lembongan, the best operator is the eco-friendly *World Diving*, with several dive masters, a dive instructor, and good equipment. They protect the coral during dive trips, participate in beach clean-ups and local environmental education activities, and cooperate with the WWF's Reef Check program. World Diving can take clients to no less than 18 different sites around the islands, including sites that are rarely visited by other divers. Excursions can be arranged on one of their boats (US$20 to 30 per dive).

Surfers appreciate the good barrels of Nusa Lembongan during the dry season (May to Oct), although the waves can get a bit crowded around July and August. The most challenging ones are right in front of Jungutbatu near the **Shipwreck**. Another famous point is called **Lacerations**, since it has brought a few surfers to rough landings on shallow corals. Beginners should stick to the easier **Playgrounds** on the western end of the bay. Alternatively, ask to be taken by boat to **Secret Point** in Nusa Ceningan (Rp150-200,000 per boat, max 4-7 persons). It is better to bring your own board and repair kit, however, surfboards can also be rented at the Two Thousand Café (Rp 35-50,000/day).

Biking or Walking around Lembongan

The island is a great place for biking, as there are not many other vehicles and only a few steep spots to test your stamina or your rented bike's brakes. Travellers with sensitive rear ends – the local push bikes are not too comfortable – can circle the island on foot in about two hours. However, it is better to allow for at least half a day, taking time to enjoy various places of interest.

Starting from Jungutbatu, set off towards the south (turn right as you leave your *losmen*, facing away from the sea). The road will take you to the picturesque village of **Desa Lembongan**, with its huge banyan tree and its colourful temples.

M 081 239 006 86
F 0361-288 500
www.world-diving.com
> At Pondok Baruna, in the south of Jungutbatu.

© Wisnu Foundation

Ceningan coast

There are few vehicles on Lembongan. With motorbike rentals at Rp25,000 per hour, it is best to walk or rent a pushbike (Rp25-35,000 per day). Boats can take you from Jungutbatu to Celengimbai or Mushroom Bay for Rp30-50,000.

*The **Two Thousand Café** is a good place to arrange snorkelling and boat tours, chartered transportation to Nusa Penida or Sanur, pushbikes, surfboards and motorbikes. Ask for Made Lembongan, who will be glad to explain how to reach the various points of interest around. The nearby **Mainski** has an **Internet café**.*

© Waka Experience

Fishing boats above seaweed farms

♥ Visit Ceningan with the Locals

The Village Ecotourism Network proposes a trip to Ceningan on a boat owned by a fishermen cooperative. You can stay on the island in a villagers' home, in simple but friendly conditions. Taste a traditional dinner, and then trek with a local guide, or try snorkelling and fishing (around US$65-120 per person, all inclusive). T/F 0361-735 320 jed@denpasar. wasantara.net.id

In the village, on the right in the descent towards the Ceningan bridge, you may stop at the *underground house* built by Made Byasa between 1961 and 1976. This Hindu priest wanted to emulate the great Pandawa family from the Mahabharata epic, who hid 12 years in a forest cave while fighting their cousins, the Kurawas. Crawl in this labyrinth of galleries, featuring a small kitchen and two "bedrooms" – austere alcoves dug into the limestone. Go with a guide to find your way, and pay a Rp10,000 fee to the owner.

For natural wonders, go to *Dream Beach* in Lebaoh Bay, turning right to the south at the entrance of Lembongan. Its fierce waves are not ideal for swimming, but you'll enjoy the view of the small white beach from the terrace of the **Pandanus Café** above. The nearby *Devil's Tear* is a 30m-diameter cove in the rocks, where waves crash at full power from all directions, pushing water until it sprouts out as a high-pressure spray, like the fumes of an angry dragon.

Coming back towards Desa Lembongan, turn left (westwards) and follow the road down to the coast, where you can stop and have a look at the mosaic of green and blue *seaweed farms*, separated by little posts and ropes on which algae are tied up to grow. Since the mid-1980s, nearly all the community lives off seaweeds, which are exported to the rest of Asia for the cosmetic and food industry. Every household can make one to two million rupiah a month from the red and green algae – just enough to survive on these islands, where everything has to be brought from the mainland at high cost.

From the southern end of Lembongan, you can cross over on a suspended bridge to *Nusa Ceningan*. Circle around this small island and climb to its top to admire the views of Lembongan and Penida. Back on Nusa Lembongan, continue towards the north on the flat, peaceful coast road along the mangrove. On your way, stop at a little house with a sign saying "**Wood Carving**". The friendly artist, an old man with gleaming eyes, will proudly show you his collection of unique pieces, carved from pieces of wood collected in the roots of the mangrove. "Sometimes I keep a piece of wood for months, getting inspiration during meditation. I exploit the shapes given to the tree roots by water, sand, and wind to mimic fantastic creatures from ancient Hindu sketches," explains the old man, with the help of his sons for translation. From his house, it's another 30 minutes of pedalling back to Jungutbatu through dense coastal vegetation.

Off the Beaten Track in Nusa Penida

This tour of Nusa Penida can be done in one or two days on a motorbike. Start from **Toyapakeh** and drive eastwards to **Sampalan** where you can visit the market and grab local food in one of the warungs.

Before Sampalan, 5km after Toyapakeh, stop at the *Pura Dalem Penataran Ped* (or Pura Ped). Built almost entirely of volcanic sandstone and limestone, with rough *paras* carvings and guardian statues, the temple is dedicated to Jero Gede Macaling, the most fearsome deity of the Balinese pantheon. This fanged (*macaling*) monster is believed to cross over to Bali regularly, landing on the beach of Lebih near Gianyar, and threatening to bring floods, diseases and other disasters. Yearly ceremonies are conducted to bring the deity back to Nusa Penida.

Like everything in the Balinese world, Macaling is not inherently bad or good. If properly addressed, his powers can bring good fortune – hence Balinese never miss an occasion to pray at the Pura Ped. This ambivalence is symbolized in the *poleng* cloth adorning the temple. The chequered black-and-white pattern represents the balance between good and bad, with the grey parts symbolizing the transition between both. *Poleng* clothes are usually put in places where strong spirits are lurking, to balance their possible bad influence.

Leaving the temple, the road winds above the coast, passing fishing villages and revealing good glimpses of the

☙ *The best way to get around Nusa Penida is by motorbike, which can be rented for Rp50,000/day at Toyapakeh. Test your vehicle first. The roads of the interior are steep, winding, and deserted. You need a reliable engine, good brakes and a full tank. If you're not sure of your driving abilities, get a driver or guide and hop on the back.*

© The Natural Guide

Poleng *cloth at Pura Ped*

> Find the cement stairs leading to the cave on the left side of the road, indicated by a sign saying Pura Gili Putri Goa in front of a little shop. Put on a sarong to visit the holy cave and leave a donation.

© The Natural Guide

A shrine in Goa Karangsari

The peculiar, karstic relief of Penida is due to its limestone ground, which it shares with the Bukit peninsula in the south of Bali. Limestone is easily dissolved by rainwater, which carves its way deep into the plateau, out of the reach of people, plants, and animals. After travelling underground, digging strange holes and caves, the water surges out from the rock in awesome waterfalls or springs, often hidden at the bottom of the plateau and cliffs.

shore, which are lined with seaweed farms. About 10km south of Sampalan, you'll reach the limestone cave of *Goa Karangsari*. Climb the cement stairs and crawl into the entrance of the cave with a local guide until you reach an enormous cavern – best avoided if you have a phobia of bats. Two shrines are set in the grotto, and a last one guards its back exit, above a hidden valley. People come from all over Bali to pray or meditate in week-long fasting retreats in this huge, natural shelter.

After leaving the cave and admiring the ocean view from its entrance, continue eastwards to the colourful fishing village of **Sewana**, passing the temples of Pura Puseh Yehulaten, a seven-roofed *meru* perched above the ocean, and the discreet Pura Songaya, with its two small *meru* hidden against a small hill. Just after this temple, a small road leads to the left towards **Semaya**. It will take you past *Pura Batu Medau* and its impressive, newly-built carved door. Further down the road, don't miss the impressive *Pura Batu Mas Kuning* ("Temple of the Golden Stone") with its explicit golden statue of a naked male deity, its great view over the coast, and its peaceful *Pura Dalem* (Death's Temple) hidden below majestic trees. From there, go back to the main road and continue southwards to **Tanglad**.

The road from Sewana to Tanglad is one of the wildest of Bali as it climbs through stone terraces bearing cacti and crops of cassava, banana, and forage. It also overlooks the ocean with Mt Agung and Lombok in the background. Gone are the ubiquitous rice paddies of Bali – it seems like you have landed in the arid hills of some Mediterranean country. Near Tanglad, you'll notice a few T-shaped or round reservoirs made of concrete, used to store water above or under the ground.

Tanglad is a picturesque village where you can admire the local *weaving* industry. At the T-junction after the village's entrance, take a left and go down to the village's open ground, with its volleyball field. From there, ask anyone if you can visit one of the 25 or so

homes of **tenun cag-cag** weavers. The manual loom
is perched on a woman's knees, on which she produces
traditional **kain cepuk** in bright reds, pinks, and yellows.

The most impressive site of Tanglad is *Pura Tunjuk
Pusuh* ("Temple of the Sprouting Bud"), which you'll find
at the end of a narrow 2.5km road starting on the left
just after the village's gate. The temple itself is a simple
walled ground with three *meru*. It owes its sanctity to its
location, on the top of a mount covered with a patch of
forest sprouting from a hidden spring above the barren
hills. The place oozes with peace, and the tiny road
looks over the most fantastic view of Nusa Penida's
cliffs. The road is steep and damaged, so you may want
to leave your motorbike at the village and walk to the
temple, a fantastic two-hour trek back and forth.

After Tanglad, just after the stone marking the
entrance to **Batukandik**, take the road to your left
towards the *Guyangan spring*. The road winds through
the arid hills for about 7km; passing a temple on the left,
until it reaches the edge of the island – a 200m vertical
cliff falling towards the ocean. If you're brave enough,
you can start walking down the rock face on narrow
concrete steps and a blue metallic ladder. Don't venture
too far down alone, for a wrong step will send you
straight for a fall. By walking down the first few metres,
you can catch a spellbinding view of the cliffs and the
purest blue-green ocean. Against the limestone, you'll
notice a series of pipes carrying water from the spring
at the bottom of the cliff.

From the spring, return to Batukandik and continue
towards **Batumadeg**. Here you can stop at the
Sebuluh waterfall, and continue towards the sea to
admire more steep cliffs and rock pinnacles eroded from
the limestone, which shoot straight up from the ocean.
From Batumadeg, the road goes to Klumbu and Puncak
Mundi, the highest point of the island (512m). From
Klumbu, you can follow the main road back to
Toyapakeh or turn right to cut towards Sampalan.

*Support the local
weavers by buying one
of their pieces – Rp50-
75,000 for a standard
size, Rp150,000 for the
biggest. You can also
arrange to learn weaving,
but you'll need a Balinese
interpreter.*

*Hair-raising stairs descending
towards the Guyangan spring*

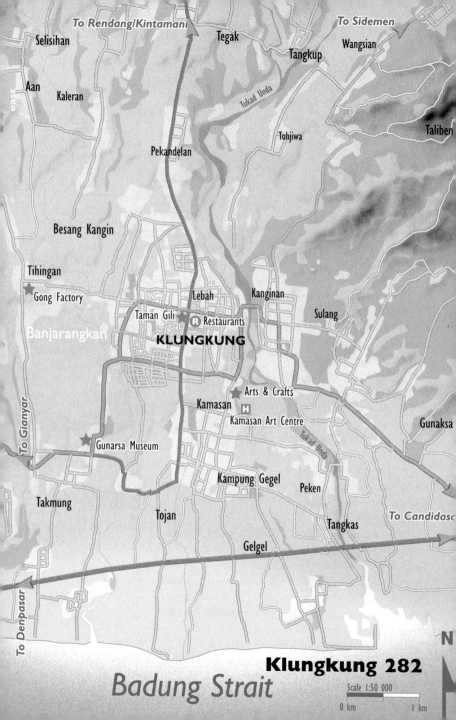

To Rendang/Kintamani

To Sidemen

Selisihan

Tegak

Tangkup

Wangsian

Aan

east

Kaleran

Tukad Unda

Taliben

Tohjiwa

Pekandelan

Besang Kangin

Kanginan

Tihingan

★ Gong Factory

Lebah

Sulang

Banjarangkan

Taman Gili

Ⓡ Restaurants

KLUNGKUNG

Arts & Crafts ★

Kamasan

Ⓗ

Kamasan Art Centre

Gunaksa

Tukad Unda

Gunarsa Museum ★

Kampung Gegel

Peken

Takmung

Tojan

To Gianyar

To Candidasa

Tangkas

Gelgel

To Denpasar

N

Klungkung 282

Badung Strait

Scale 1:50 000

0 km   1 km

east

To Culik/Tulamben

Kalangsari

Wates

Asahdulu

Tegallinggah

Linggawana

Ancut

Gulinten

Laga Kaler

Tistagede

Kertamandala

Sege

Asah

Pura Lempuyang

Lempuyang Kaja

Pidpid

Abang

Ngis

Lempuyang Kelod

Dauh

Trek Pura Lempuyang

Basangalas Kangin

Batur Indah

embah Dukuh

Villa Gangga

Bias

Ababi

Good Karma

Tiyingtali

Bukit

Puri Sawah & Cafe

Genta Bali

Rijasa

Cabe Bali

Tirtagangga

Tirta Ayu & Restaurant

andan House

Temega

Dauma

Panaban

Karangsasak

Bukit Kelod

Batannyuh

Tibulakabali

Kaler

Dausa

Tegallinggah

Seraya

To Amed

Padangkerta

Pesuguhan

Bungkulan

Puri Agung

AMLAPURA

Villa Amlapura

Market

Pisiatin

Bungaya Kangin

Yehkali

Damakarya

Subagan

Genteng

Buddhist Monastery

Gerobog

Pura Kebon Bukit

Taman Ujung

N

To Candidasa

Jasri Kauh

Ujung

Tenganan

To Irene's Hotel

Scale 1:75 000

0 km   1.5 km

Puri Bagus Manggis
Kajanan

Tk. Patuawan

Desa

Tk. Bulu

Asak Kangin

Bukit Tengah

Tenganan

Pegeringsingan

Pertima

Bukit Kangin

Timbrah

Dauhtukad   Kanginan

Perasi Tengah

Pekarangan

Kauhan

Karangasem

Bugbug

Caluk Kauh

Nyuhtebel

Tauman

Catuk Kangin

Tengah

Sengkidu   Subagan   Karanganyar

Candidasa

Nirwana Cottage

Dasawana
Kedai

Pura Gumang

ira

Watergarden
Kubu

Astawa

ok Pisang

Flamboyant Beach

Lotus Seaview

Toke

Sindhu Brata

Yos Diving

Ida's

Sekar Orchid

Kelapa Mas

Gandhian Ashram

Puri Bagus Candidasa

Asmara Dive Resort

To Amlapura

To Pasir Putih

east

Mimpang

Gili Tepekong

Lombok Strait

Padangbai – Candidasa 284-285

N

Scale 1:50 000

0 km   1 km

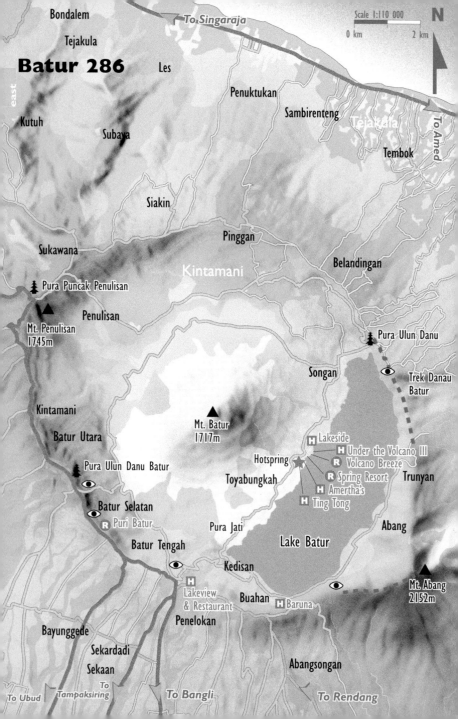

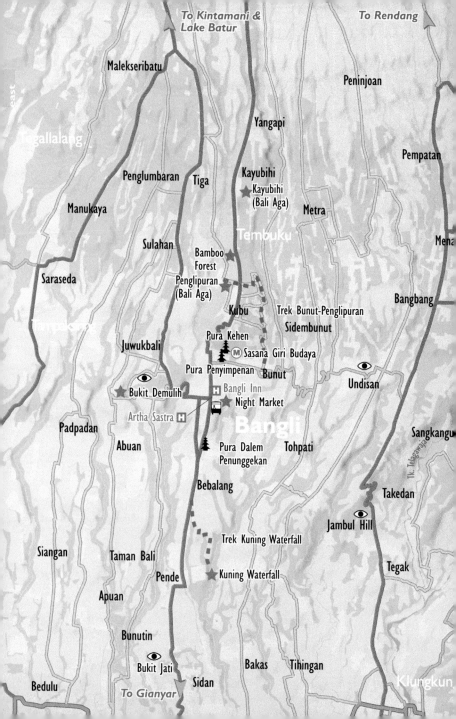

Puri Nusa 🅗
Linda's 🅗
Ketut Losmen 🅗
Pondok Baruna 🅗
Bungalows No. 7 🅗

Surf Shipwreck ★

🆁 Ketut
🆁 Kainalu Surf

Surf Lacerations ★

Nusa
Lembongan

🅒 Jurassic Point

S.D.
🅒🅒

Pura Dalem
Penataran Ped
🌲

Coconut Beach ★
🅒 World Diving Jungutbatu
★ Celengimbai

Nyuh
Ped

Mushroom Bay ★
Nusa Lembongan Resort 🅗
🅗 Morin
Wayan 🅗

Toyapakeh 🅒🅒

Toyapakeh
Toyapakeh

Jojo 🆁
🆁 Pandanus
Waka Nusa 🅗 Pandanus ★
Seaweed Farming

Crystal Bay Anyar
🅜 Suspended Bridge
🅒🅒

Biaung
Seran

Ceningan
Toyapakeh Strait
Sakti

Penaga
Kl

Penina
Pangkot

Sampang
Bungamekar
Penutuk

Penangkidan

Gahing
Batumadeg
Manta Point 🅒🅒
Sebuluh Watefall ★
Pangkur

Cacah

Semuputeh
Peguy

Indian Ocean

N

Nusa Lembongan –
Nusa Penida 290-291

Scale 1:110 000

0 km   2 km

Lombok Strait

east

Dewi
Made
Sampalan
Nusa Garden
Telaga
entral
Kutampi
Jepun
Batununggal
ning
Goa Karangsari
Karangsari
Pura Puseh Yehulatan
Iseh
Ponjok
Suana
Nusa Penida
Pura Batu Medau
Semaya
Pura Batu Mas Kuning
Salang
Pejukutan
atukanduk
Karanggede
anjung
Caruban
Karangbilis
Tektekan
Belatu
Tanglad
Weaving
Pura Tunjukpusuh
Bungkil
Tebe
atukanduk
ngan Springs
Sekartaji
Wates

North Bali
in a Nutshell

© Leonard Lueras

*Pura Ulun Danu
at Lake Tamblingan*

The Other Side of Bali

North Bali consists of a single administrative district, the former kingdom of **Buleleng**, stretching along the full length of the island's north coast. This rough strip of land, 2 to 20km wide, is wedged between the sea and the volcanic chain that runs parallel to the coast. This natural barrier has partially insulated the north from the southern kingdoms, giving birth to a unique culture.

Oriented towards the northern sea trading routes, Buleleng and the ports of the northeast coast were for centuries the main gateway for external influences to Bali. Indian pottery shards dating back 2000 years were discovered in Pacung, 40km east of Singaraja – indicating that Indian traders may have reached Bali in the first century AD. Around AD 400, China joined this network of trade relations, and Buddhist pilgrims started to make their way to the north coast of Bali on merchant vessels. Today, Bali's main Buddhist monastery is located west of Singaraja. Later, Arab merchants carrying spices and aromatic wood to the Mediterranean joined the trade, bringing Islam to Indonesia. Finally the Dutch, being first traders and seafarers, made the northern town of **Singaraja**, near Buleleng's harbour, their base in Bali.

Perhaps because of their long history of contacts with the outside world, the people of north Bali are reputed to be more straightforward and egalitarian

Hard Facts

- *1365 sq.km – a quarter of the area of Bali*
- *Capital: Singaraja (approximately 100,000 inhabitants)*
- *580,000 inhabitants in 127 villages and 467 hamlets*
- *400 people per sq.km*
- *125km of coastline*
- *Highest peak: Mt Catur, 1865m*
- *Two lakes, Danau Tamblingan and Danau Buyan.*

than those of the south. With its colonial houses, Chinese shops, neo-Balinese government offices and Muslim neigh-bourhoods, Singaraja bears more resemblance to the har-bour cities of Surabaya in East Java, or Makassar in Sulawesi, than to the old towns of south Bali.

The Fallen Kingdom of Buleleng

In the 14th century, north Bali, like the rest of the island, fell under the rule of the Javanese kingdom of Majapahit – although the hinterland harbours a few Bali Aga villages, which have retained traditions pre-dating Majapahit. After the fall of Majapahit at the end of the 14th century, Buleleng remained under the power of Gelgel, the unified kingdom which dominated Bali until 1560. When Gelgel felt apart, Buleleng rose to prominence under the rule of Pandji Sakti (1650-1710), extending its domination until Blambangan in East Java. It later fell under the control of Karangasem, only regaining its independence in 1823. This freedom was short-lived, for the Dutch were soon to tighten their grip on Bali's shores.

Like the previous visitors to the island, the Dutch initially came to north Bali as traders. During the first half of the 19th century, however, they were moving towards direct colonization. Around 1840, the Dutch had become nervous about their lack of control over the Balinese kingdoms. They worried that other Europeans might get a foothold on the island. Tensions escalated in 1845, when the kings of Buleleng and Karangasem formed an alliance with the possible aim of conquering other kingdoms and resisting the Dutch.

In 1846, the Dutch took the pretext of a dispute over a shipwreck to launch their first attack on north Bali. The Balinese were led by a coalition of princes commanded by Gusti Ketut Jelantik, renowned for his brilliant fighting tactics. Today, local storytellers recount with pride how Jelantik's troops, armed only with daggers and spears, defeated the invaders by filling hidden holes with sharp bamboo poles – a technique used across the

Islam in North Bali

Don't be surprised to hear the muezzin *making the pre-dawn call to prayer near Lovina Beach.* About 37,000 Muslims live in north Bali. Some are descendants of Javanese soldiers who came in the 17th century to serve the king of Buleleng. Others are ethnic Bugis, whose ancestors came from Sulawesi as mercenaries and sea traders; most of them are now fishermen. Since 1970, Muslims have been coming from all over Indonesia, especially Java and Lombok, to work in tourism-related businesses. These Balinese Muslims live in peace with the Hindu majority, combining local first names with Islamic names – as in Ketut Ahmad Ibrahim. Some perform Hindu-Balinese ceremonies to ensure the fertility of their crops. The young generation, however, is often studying in Islamic boarding schools in Java or Lombok, where education is cheaper and stricter than in local schools. (based on an article by Bodrek Arsana in *Latitudes* magazine).

From Durians to Wine

*Despite its relatively dry climate, the hinterland of Singaraja and Seririt boasts stunning rice fields, fed by rivers from Mt Batur and the lakes area. Drier slopes in the north-east and northwest are cultivated with corn, beans and peanuts. Everywhere, orchards yield an endless feast of cloves, copra, coffee, cocoa and fruits, including, near **Munduk**, the island's best durians – the stinking king of Asian fruits. The sunny hills behind Pemuteran are home to the sweetest grapes in Bali, cultivated on bamboo frames to produce wine.*

© Djuna Ivereigh

Harvesting grapes in north Bali

archipelago to kill wild pigs. The Dutch renewed their attack two years later, gaining control of north Bali in 1849 after the battle of Jagaraga. Thus, 50 years before the southern kingdoms fell to the colonial powers, Buleleng became the first Dutch regency in Bali, and the administrative centre of the island.

It was only around 1960, 15 years after Indonesian independence, that the new national government moved the administrative head of Bali to the southern city of Denpasar. The building of the airport near Kuta stripped Buleleng of its role as the gateway to Bali. Today, how-ever, Northern Balinese are fighting to re-establish some of their lost pre-eminence. They display their creativity in the cultural realm, preserving and elaborating their musical and dance traditions, including unique *gamelan* orchestras, *wayang wong* and *baris gede* dances, and the popular ***joged***, a raunchy dance contest that has spread across the island (read our story on p. 304).

Living Off the Sea

Although north Bali is one of the main fishing grounds of the island, its fishermen are among the poorest of the poor. Fishing communities, which harbour many immigrants, are regarded with a degree of disdain by inlanders. During the last decade, over-harvesting, destructive fishing methods, pollution and uncontrolled tourism have also caused degra-dation of coral reefs and a drop in catches.

Yet local villagers are bringing their traditional insti-tutions into play against this trend, sometimes with the help of NGOs (read our story of the village of **Les** in the section on Air Sanih-Tejakula). And because corals are one of the best selling points of north Bali tourism, dive shops and hotel owners are now helping to protect and rehabilitate coral gardens. The pioneers of such efforts are found in **Pemuteran** in the northwest tip of Bali. Meanwhile, communities and foreign investors are find-ing new ways to exploit the coast, from shrimp cultiva-tion to pearl farming.

Sea Shores and Mountain Lakes

With 125km of coastline, north Bali is a destination for sea lovers. Total peace is found in the northeast, between *Air Sanih* and *Tejakula*. The coastland, alas, is a narrow beach of black sand, pebbles and rocks, which in some places is eroded, and has been replaced by a concrete wall against which small waves crash. Several eco-friendly resorts catering to travellers in search of tranquillity have been developed recently. This is also a good base to visit the unique **temples** of Meduwe Karang, Jagaraga and Beji and the traditional villages in the hinterland.

© Ulung Wicaksono

Lake Buyan

Just west of Singaraja, *Lovina* is the name given to a 10km long beach area centred around **Kalibukbuk**. This fishermen's village became an alternative destination to Kuta at the end of the 1980s, which led to the construction of more than 60 hotels, many of them are now run-down and empty. Yet Lovina has kept a laid-back atmosphere and will be appreciated by travellers in need of shops, amenities, inexpensive rooms and restaurants. It provides a good access to the beautiful hills and mountain areas in the hinterland.

Nature and **mountain** lovers will enjoy the cool slopes between *Seririt* and *Munduk*, near the twin **lakes** of **Tamblingan** and **Buyan**, under the skirts of 1860m high **Mount Lesong**. This is the first place in Bali to feature a resort dedicated to eco-tourism, which proposes an endless choice of **trekking** tours, as well as **cultural activities** from dancing classes to weaving or wood carving. Good accommodation is found in traditional style cottages or homestays.

Besides its natural attractions, Buleleng has distinctive cultural sites: sophisticated temples with vivid carvings featuring colonists and early tourists near Sangsit; a collection of lontar palm leaf manuscripts in the **Gedong Tirtya** library in Singaraja; or a Buddhist temple in Banjar.

In the extreme northwest, quiet black-sand beaches await the traveller around *Pemuteran* – a perfect area to relax far from the crowds, and the entry point to some of the island's finest **diving** in **Menjangan Island**. This is also a good base to trek in the **West Bali National Park**. Although not cheap, Pemuteran has a few good eco-friendly hotels with gorgeous gardens near the beach.

north

Getting there

The main route *from the south* runs from Denpasar to **Singaraja** through the misty, vegetable-growing terraces around **Bedugul**, offering views of Lake Beratan and Lake Buyan (80km, 2-2h30min by car, 3-4h by public transport). For better views and less traffic, drive through Tabanan and Seririt, with breathtaking views of paddy fields around **Pupuan**. Alternatively, get a view of Mt Batur by driving from Denpasar or Ubud through **Kintamani**. A less well-known route goes from Sangeh, west of Ubud, to Penulisan and Kubutambahan, east of Singaraja, through quiet rural areas.

Travellers coming *from the east* can try the east coast road from **Tulamben**, which drives through a moon-like, arid landscape behind Mount Agung. Mountain lovers will prefer the beautiful road from **Amlapura** to Rendang and Kintamani.

Public *buses* and mini-buses to Singaraja can be found at the **Ubung Terminal** in Denpasar. They drive either through Tabanan and Pupuan, or through Batubulan and Kintamani. You can also get buses from Amlapura to Kintamani and Singaraja, and bemos along the east coast road. **Perama** buses will take you more comfortably to Singaraja and Lovina from most tourist areas (US$7 from Kuta, head office *T 0361-751 551; 751 875*; www.peramatour.com).

Getting around

Singaraja has three public transport terminals. Sukasada, also called Sangket, serves the south. Banyuasri serves the west (Lovina: 20min, Pemuteran: about 2h), Kampung Tinggi-Penarukan serves the east (Air Sanih: 30min, Kintamani: 1h30min, Amlapura: about 3h). Bemos run between the terminals. Once on the north coast, you can get around by bemo or ojek, however, they become scarce after 3 pm, especially in the interior. Cars, motorbikes and push bikes can be rented in Lovina; most hotels elsewhere will be able to arrange a car or bike rental.

Practicalities

*Banks, postal services, and Internet access can be found in Singaraja and Lovina. The BCA **bank** in Singaraja (Jl. Dr. Sutomo, T 0362-23 761, 8am-3pm) changes money and has an ATM. A 24h **telephone** office (Telkom) is found near the Singaraja post office, and **wartel** phone services are all around. There are money changers, ATMs and good **Internet** cafes in Kalibukbuk (Lovina). For **medical services** in Singaraja, try the private hospital (Rumah Sakit Kerta Usada, Jl. Cendrawasih #5, T 0362-26 277; 26 278) or contact Dr. Handra (I Gde Putra Kartika), Jl. Bukit Indah #1 T 0362-23 798 M 081 23 60 57 33 7-9am or 6-9pm.*

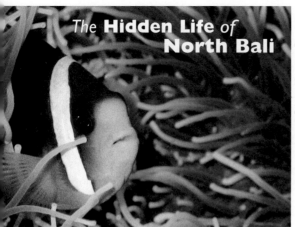

The **Hidden Life** of **North Bali**

© Bahtera Nusantara Foundation

A clown fish hiding in anemons

Endangered Seas

By Degung Santikarma

From Kuta to Nusa Dua – and later Lovina, Amed and Pemuteran – much of Bali's tourism industry has built up around the sea. Attractions range from surfing, scuba diving, sailing, and luxury cruises to walking underwater while wearing a spaceman-like oxygen helmet or spotting whales and dolphins. Bali's beaches have become symbols of holiday hedonism and tropical adventure.

But for the Balinese, the beach is more mysterious. Balinese use a sacred geography that positions volcanic Mount Agung at the *kaja* compass point, and the sea at the opposite *kelod* pole. The mountain is the abode of the gods, while the sea is the home of assorted deities and demons including Baruna, the god of the sea. Like all powerful forces, the sea has good and bad, sacred and profane aspects. With its strong currents and angry waves, the ocean can kill and the supernatural beings that inhabit it can bring physical or mental illness, but its waters contain life. It is believed to be able to absorb human and spiritual pollution, including the ashes of cremated corpses, and still remain pure. Seawater is used in many Balinese ceremonies, including rituals to

Not a Playground
With the exception of kids and Kuta-surfing "beach boys", most Balinese do not see the sea as a playground. Fishermen who must brave the waters make offerings to the gods and demons to ensure their safety. In seaside villages, beachfront land was long considered the least desirable for human habitation. Not many Balinese can swim, and most of those who can learn from necessity. Indeed, the fact that tourists spend their free time lying on the beach or playing in the waves is considered by some Balinese to be a possible reason for their generally weird behaviour.

north

maintain the magical potency of shadow puppets, *gamelan* instruments, dancers' headdresses and masks.

Today, both tourist and Balinese mythologies of the sea are being threatened by a new reality: environmental destruction. Runoff from agricultural chemicals, pollution from small industries and hotels, destructive fishing methods and – ironically enough – marine tourism itself all have done their share to damage Bali's underwater world.

Not Without my Corals

The backbone of Bali's coastline is the coral reef: a massive structure of limestone built by tiny living creatures which are extremely sensitive to the slightest changes in the light, temperature and chemical composition of their surroundings. Besides being beautiful, coral reefs provide shelter to 25 percent of marine species, protect shorelines from erosion and serve as nurseries for growing fish. The reefs that ring Bali are home to one of the most diverse varieties of sea creatures anywhere on earth. They also sustain the sea life on which fishing communities depend, and they bring funds to villages in the form of marine tourism.

Today, however, over 80 percent of Bali's coral reefs are moderately or even severely damaged. Like coral reefs elsewhere on the planet, Bali's corals have been hurt by global warming. A rise in the ocean's temperature of only a degree or two can cause bleaching and even the death of corals. In 1998, the El Niño phenomenon led to bleaching of over 75 percent of the corals around the West Bali National Park

Bleaching Corals

To the naked eye, corals may resemble rocks (hard coral) or plants (soft coral). But looks can be deceiving, for corals are composed of thousands of polyps, tiny animals that are cousins of jellyfish. In hard corals, polyps extract calcium carbonate from seawater to build external limestone skeletons. These in turn shelter microscopic algae, the Zooxanthellae. *In a symbiotic relationship, the algae provide oxygen and food for the polyps. They are also responsible for the corals' bright colours. Yet environmental stresses, such as a 1-3° change in water temperature, or a change in salinity, pollution levels or light, can cause the polyps and algae to end their partnership. The immediate result is a change in coral colour to bleak white. Without their life partners, most corals cannot survive for long. Like a dead tooth, they become brittle and are quickly destroyed by currents or human intrusions.*

By Titiek Pratiwi

Corals and star fish

© Tonozuka Dive &Dives

and Tulamben in east Bali. Some of them have started to recover, but the remainder still suffer.

Your Ocean, my Dustbin

The most immediate threats to the corals come from local causes. Increasing amounts of waste and poor garbage management damage the marine habitat. Without properly administered facilities to handle the growing number of cans, bottles, plastic bags and other inorganic matter that an increasingly well-off Balinese population and their tourist guests consume, much of the island's refuse is either burned or dumped in the sea.

With little government attention, individuals and businesses are left to devise their own solutions to problems that impact an entire island. "Many hotels don't have sufficient waste management facilities and programs in place," explains Made Widiasari from Bhakti Wahana Bali, a local organization involved in community-based environmental activism. "Some hotels route the waste from their bathrooms and kitchens directly into the sea." With competition for guests so tight, some tourist facilities are reluctant to invest in technologies to protect the environment – even if this means a long-term erosion of Bali's ability to attract tourists.

Victims of Growth

Economic growth has also led to environmental challenges. The garment industry, which often uses toxic dyes, frequently releases its industrial by-products into rivers that empty into the sea. The new varieties of hybrid rice introduced to Bali by the Indonesian government in the 1970s as part of the so-called "Green Revolution" produce higher yields but require frequent application of pesticides and modern fertilizer. Pesticides run off into the sea, contributing to the death of fish and corals. Fertilizer in the water lead to excessive growth of algae, which chokes the corals, and to toxic algae blooms, which can kill fish and make

Not a Recycling Bin
Traditional Balinese thought sees the sea as a kind of cosmic recycling centre, able to transform the refuse of human existence into clean water. But no sea, Bali's included, can accommodate all the by-products of human "progress," much less uncontrolled tourism development.

© The Natural Guide

A retaining wall to curb coastal erosion

north

Sea Lovers can Help!

Don't:

• *Anchor boats on reefs*

• *Step on corals, touch anything under water or feed fish*

• *Remove anything, living or dead, from the sea*

• *Patronise restaurants that serve live fish, especially grouper, Napoleon wrasse and lobster, often caught with cyanide*

• *Patronise restaurants that serve turtle meat*

• *Eat shark fin*

• *Buy live tropical fish for your aquarium, unless it comes from a certified source guaranteeing it has not been caught in a destructive way*

• *Buy objects made out of turtle shell, coral or seashell*

• *Throw away waste except into designated containers*

• *Participate in "dolphin watch" tours that involve chasing dolphins with motor boats.*

shellfish poisonous to consume. Coastal development and deforestation also contribute, sending sediment that blankets the corals, depriving them of the light needed for their survival.

Bali's corals have suffered greatly from fish bombing, in which sea creatures are stunned or killed with home-made explosives, usually empty soda bottles filled with potassium nitrate. Exporters have also encouraged fishermen to use cyanide to catch reef fish (read more about this in the story of Les village p.315). Not only does poison kill the corals, divers often add to the damage by enlarging crevices in which stunned fish may be hiding.

These destructive practices may be quicker than traditional fishing methods, but the environmental and human costs are extremely high. Coral reefs can take fifty years to recover from the damage caused by bombs and chemicals, leading to a vicious cycle in which fish become more scarce, catching them with hooks and simple nets becomes more difficult, and more people are encouraged to destroy the reefs in search of immediate gains. Traders get the bulk of the profit, while local fishermen, who desperately need the catch to feed their families, may get at most US$2 or 3 per kilo of fish.

A House of Coral

Coral is also used as a building material in Bali. In the days before tourism, Balinese collected dead corals and other materials from the coast, such as sand and rocks, to use in making walls and temples. Because the scale of such construction was small, the reefs suffered little damage. But with economic development, the use of coral in building has increased, especially in tourist areas – as sadly witnessed in Candidasa, east Bali, where the depletion of corals has led to the invasion of the beach by the sea. Some wealthy Balinese who use their money to renovate homes and temples still choose coral for its strength and durability or to advertise their traditional status. Meanwhile, poor fisherfolk in places like Serangan

Island, off Bali's coast, who have lost their fishing grounds to tourist development and reef destruction, now make their living by selling chunks of hard coral for around US$1 per 30 x 15cm slab. Laws banning the use of coral for building in Bali have done little to slow the flow of destruction.

Loving the Sea Too Much

Even excursions by tourists to witness the wonders of the underwater world can threaten its fragile balance. Dive boats that drop anchor on delicate reefs, as well as divers who step on the corals or touch them with their equipment, cause myriad tiny breaks, each of which may take years for new coral growth to repair. Careless "dolphin watch" tours chase dolphins aggressively, disturbing their feeding and mating.

Marine enthusiasts on the other side of the world may also contribute to the destruction of the reefs by buying colourful aquarium fish caught with poison. Although there are export regulations banning the sale of live corals, aquarium owners in Indonesia often buy corals for up to US$50 in urban markets. These corals are collected by divers using chisels and hammers, and obtaining a 10cm ornamental coral can involve the destruction of a square meter of reef.

Exotic food lovers often unwittingly encourage environmental destruction; eating fish displayed in restaurants' aquariums may mean supporting poison fishing. Shark fin soup consumers beware: sharks are caught in large quantities only to have their fins cut, and be thrown back alive into the sea. A few restaurants in and outside Bali are still serving turtle meat, a total no-no given how endangered this species is.

Even the recent fashion for seashell-decorated accessories, sold in shops in Kuta and around the world, leads to the depletion of sea life. Unfortunately not all these shells are collected dead on the beach. Large quantities are also caught with nets, disturbing corals and removing needed food for other sea creatures.

Sea Lovers can Help!

Do:

• *Use mooring buoys*

• *Learn to control your buoyancy when diving, so you don't touch corals accidentally*

• *Make sure your diving equipment is securely attached to your body*

• *Avoid the use of plastic bottles and bags, refill and reuse them when possible*

• *Make donations or volunteer to help marine conservation organisations*

• *Before booking a cruise, a dolphin watch tour or a dive, ask dive shops and boat operators about the steps they take to protect the environment*

• *Patronise tourist facilities that take care to protect Bali's precious marine habitat – look for our ♥ or ♥ ♥ favourites!*

© Godeliva D. Sari

Signboard in Pemuteran

A Line of Hope for the Fish

Local and international NGOs have been working to protect Bali's marine environment. Programmes to monitor the health of the coral reefs and to encourage appropriate coastal management have been able to stem some of the tide of reef destruction. Initiatives to enforce environmental protection laws and build local awareness of the importance of the sea as a living resource have made some progress. Some NGOs have even been experimenting with building coral nurseries and artificial reefs to help replace coral that has been destroyed. But coral, which grows only 0.2 to 4cm a year, has a hard time holding its own against the pace of human destruction.

Conservation remains a challenge in Bali. Resources to enforce laws are limited, and despite educational programmes, some Balinese either do not yet understand the long-term implications of damaging the marine ecosystem – or they are too caught up in their own economic struggles. Some poor fishermen and tour operators argue that they need whatever advantages they can get to compete with wealthier, foreign-financed outfits, although most of them now realize the long-term impact of destructive practices.

Yuyun Ismawati, Director of Bali Fokus, a local organisation that works to protect coastal areas and to halt the spread of land-based pollution that can leak into the sea, explains that poor Balinese are often left with little choice but to exploit the reef to meet their daily needs. "Cutting corals is hard, awful work," she explains. "People would rather do something else if given the opportunity. The challenge for those who care about the environment is not to just pass laws banning destructive practices, but to provide income-generating alternatives for people who desperately need them."

Sea Lovers can Help!

You can support these organisations – become a member, make donations or participate in volunteer work such as the "reef check" program run by the WWF, in which divers monitor the reefs' condition.

Friends of the Reef-WWF Indonesia
T 0361-247 125; 0361-236 864
F 0361-236 866
www.wallacea-wwf.org

The Nature Conservancy
T 0361-270 793; 0361-287 272
F 0361-270 737
tncbalistaff@tnc.org; tncseacmpa@attglobal.net;
www.nature.org

Bali Fokus
T 0361-743 57 96;
F 0361-757 981
www.balifokus.or.id

Bhakti Wahana Bali
T/F 0361-464 429
M 081 83 44 654
ybwbali@yahoo.com
nimadewidiasari@yahoo.com

Wisnu Foundation
T/F 0361-735 320
wisnu@wisnu.or.id

Conservation and Business

Conservation also confronts big business and government in its attempts to secure the future of Bali's seas. "Trying to educate the community can be easier than trying to make people in the government care," says Suarnatha, Director of Wisnu Foundation, a local environmental NGO. "Because of corruption, there's not enough accountability toward those in the community who do care about the environment."

Organizations like Bali Fokus struggle to make the business community, especially in those involved in tourism, committed towards better environmental management – moving from promises and public relation declarations to real change and help.

It remains to be seen whether Bali's sea world can survive and if humans – the good and the bad, the selfish and the well-intentioned – can create workable ways of living with their environment. In the meantime, visitors to Bali can do their part by not supporting the trade in endangered species, stepping lightly around the corals and supporting tourist facilities and organisations that protect Bali's marine habitat.

© Leonard Lueras

A fisherman on the beach

© Djuna Ivereigh

Jukung *fishing boats*

Shake it on Stage with *Joged* Dancers

By Bodrek Arsana

Travellers tired of stale hotel numbers can share popular Balinese fun by attending a joged *dance show. Unlike the* kecak, barong *and* legong *dances,* joged *is rarely performed for tourists. It is especially popular among the people of north Bali, but all around the island, villagers try to attract the best groups from Singaraja or Bangli. In north Bali,* joged bumbung *groups are usually invited for ceremonies celebrating a baby's third month birthday, as well as weddings, New Year, village and youth groups' anniversaries.*

Saturday night is getting underway in a village near Lovina. A crowd of all ages gathers around a simple, dimly-lit stage decorated with young leaves. A few tourists sit down in the front row on shaky bamboo chairs, nervously clutching their cameras. A *gamelan* orchestra fills the air with soft beats, which are soon drowned out by applause and whistles as hundred of local viewers, shaking with excitement, push and shove to get closer to the stage.

The stage curtain shielding the backstage area starts to quiver. As the orchestra's intensity rises, a heavily made-up dancer weaves out from behind the curtain, alluringly spinning her fan while staring at the audience, her pupils twitching from side to side. Her fast, rhythmic writhing matches the dynamic percussion. As flashes from the tourists' cameras bounce off the dancer, the impatient audience start yelling her name, holding their hands out to the stage. The most daring wave to the tourists, contorting their faces to be immortalized by the foreigners' cameras.

© Dedok

The dancer searches for the first man to be *dijawat* – pulled from the audience to be her dance partner. All the men near the stage reach out, only to be disappointed when she points at an old foreigner, who heads up to the stage accompanied by a burst of catcalls. The dancer's hip thrusts get more energetic as she circles the grey-haired traveller, who laughs embarrassedly as the audience scream: "Break-dance, Sir! Monkey dance, Sir! Rock'n'roll, rock'n'roll!" Inspired, the man starts an imitation of Elvis Presley, while the delighted viewers clap, laughing at his attempts to match the girl's grace and energy. After a few minutes, the sweating victim is sent back into the crowd, replaced by another *pengibing* (male partner). As the night progresses, different men are given their chance to show their talent onstage, competing to throw their hips at the dancer, who mockingly escapes or pushes them away.

© Dedok

Joged bumbung used to be entertainment for hard-working farmers, part of the thanksgiving celebrations after rice harvests. It is said to have originated in the fertile area of Munduk in north Bali. *"Joged"* refers to folk dances, usually those that allow audience members to participate, and *"bumbung"* is the bamboo *gamelan* that backs up the dancers. Similar dance forms are popular on neighbouring Java.

65-year-old Putu Regep has managed the *sekehe joged* (*joged* association) in his village for decades. His *Lestari Budaya* ("Everlasting Culture") group was born in 1979, and now has 27 members, including 4 dancers and 18 *gamelan* players, plus makeup artists and support personnel. A winner of countless local trophies, the group services large events like the Bali Arts Festival and also temple rituals or family celebrations. It has performed in almost every hotel and village hall in Bali.

Fees vary from around Rp700,000 a night for a performance in a village or a small hotel in north and east Bali, to Rp1.5 to 2 million in the main tourist areas of Kuta and Nusa Dua. The prices aren't fixed, however.

Joged bumbung is usually performed in a public space like a village hall (bale banjar) or an open field. Tourists can ask local people when and where these performances are held. They are often accompanied by game playing, gambling, and even cockfighting. Ask a local guide to explain appropriate behaviour. If in doubt, just watch the crowd and do as the Balinese do. As not many tourists patron joged shows, your presence will be a lasting source of entertainment – especially if you're called on stage to shake your butt with the dancer.

Talent and Taksu

After a few weeks of study, dancers are ready to perform and are prepared for their initiation (upacara melaspas). This ritual is meant to purify the dancer and liberate her taksu, or mystical power, needed to do justice to the dances and attract audiences. In the past, this initiation was mandatory for new members of joged groups, along with other steps to ward off bad fortune. For example, dances had to be performed by a virgin, and menstruating women were not allowed to perform. These rules are now often broken as joged *becomes more commercial.*

"We're not just after money, we want to preserve our cultural heritage and traditional dance forms," explains Putu Regep. "For performances related to religious rituals, we let the temple priests decide on their contribution – it's part of our *ngayah*, our service to the gods."

Twenty-two year-old Ni Kadek Wartini, one of Lestari Budaya's most senior dancers, has become a symbol of the group. She clearly isn't in it for the money. "The income is very small. I get about Rp20,000 each time I perform," she explains. Most dancers start out young and inexperienced. The group trains them, and has agreed upon rules to ensure that their investment pays off. Each member commits to not marry for three years after joining the troupe. If they break this promise, they have to pay 300kg of rice or Rp900,000. However, explains Kadek, "dancers usually last at most five years in our group. This ensures a faster regeneration."

Joged bumbung has gone through many changes. It has been combined with other dances, such as the Indian and Arabic-inspired Malay *dangdut* or the Sundanese *jaipong*. In Buleleng, there is even a trend of *joged porno*, in which the dancer's rear end becomes a main attraction. These erotic wrigglings are recorded and sold on video CDs. "*Joged* has become too commercial, they're forgetting the artistic element to chase money and fun," chides Putu Regep.

But for Kadek Wartini, the sexy movements are the key to her dancing. "What would *joged* mean without that?" she asks. "It's natural, and there's no reason to deny the changing times. Also, this is what the audience wants. If we don't really work it, they throw stuff at us or ask us to get off the stage!" Dancers' shaking hips and audiences' roving hands are the spices that gives *joged bumbung* its unique flavour. "The important thing is that the audience is satisfied. *Joged* was made to have fun," Kadek concludes. Around the stage in Lovina, tourists and locals are living out her words, whistling, clapping and twisting into the wee hours of the morning.

© Dedok

© The Natural Guide

Bas-relief on Pura Meduwe Karang

The spectacular coast east of Singaraja features a long, narrow beach of black sand, pebbles and rocks buffeted by gentle waves. In the hills, winding roads offer stunning views of steep canyons and clove gardens covering arid slopes. After nightfall, everything comes to a standstill. This is the perfect place to escape the crowds, then hike to timeless villages like **Sembiran** and pristine **waterfalls** like **Yeh Mampeh** – or discover bizarre **temples** with erotic bas-relief, carvings of Dutchmen riding bicycles and other exotic monsters. The choice of accommodation is limited. The less expensive hotels are found around **Air Sanih**. Further east, around **Tejakula** and **Sambirenteng**, a few more upmarket resorts offer a perfect escape while trying to preserve the beautiful environment of this isolated coast.

Visitors to the northeast coast may prefer to stay in Lovina, where they can charter a vehicle and make a day trip to the villages and temples east of Singaraja. If you use public transport, ride first to the Panerukan bus terminal, located at the eastern end of Singaraja, just before Sangsit. From there, you can catch a bemo to any of the eastern villages.

Where to Stay – Air Sanih

Air Sanih is known for its spring water baths – a set of pools stuck between the coast and the main road, with a lively crowd of locals in the afternoon. The baths can offer a fun experience, but don't expect anything pristine. A few hotels are found between the road and the beach. Here budget travellers can find inexpensive backpackers' places such as **Puri Rena**, **Hotel Tara**, or **Wira Bali**, most of them rather run-down.

❸❹ *4 Rm – Htw A/C*
Bch Shw Bcy
T/F 0362-26 561
www.ciliksbeachgarden.com
> *Indicated by a sign
on the beach side
of the road.*

In a higher price range, *Cilik's Beach Garden* offers stylish, spacious villas with terraces in a large garden along the beach. Each villa has a romantic, high *alang-alang* grass roof, and is tastefully decorated with ethnic textiles. Only one room has air-conditioning, but the design and location of the bungalows provide enough breeze. Free Internet access and snorkelling equipment is provided; the staff can organize things like massages or dolphin tours. No restaurant, but guests can order good Indonesian food at reasonable prices.

Where to Stay – Pacung/Lower Sembiran

❶ *16 Rm – Htw A/C*
Rst Bch Swp
Div Trk Shw Bcy
M 086 812 103 677;
081 24 63 79 79
T/F 0362-24 437
> *Indicated by a sign on
the main road, 250m west
of the petrol station
in Pacung.*

Further east, *Pondok Sembiran Bungalows* is a good value in a quiet location, set far enough back from the road. It has four rooms near a flower-filled garden that surrounds a small, spotlessly-clean pool. Each room has a small ensuite living room with bathroom, with connecting doors to the next room, making it convenient for families. Further down, six seaside bungalows ringing a small garden offer a great view of the rocky black beach. Trekking to Sembiran can be arranged.

Where to Stay – Tejakula to Tembok

Over the last few years, the Tejakula area has seen the development of environmentally-friendly resorts in the mid- to up-market category, catering to travellers in search of comfort and peace, with good diving opportunities.

Awaken your Soul at Gaia-Oasis

♥ ❸ *29 Rm – Htw Rst*
Bch Swp Gvw
Div Trk Cls Spa
M 081 23 85 33 50
F 0362-28 414
paradise@gaia-oasis.com
www.gaia-oasis.com
> *From Tejakula, follow
the signs to a path towards
the beach. After 200m,
park your vehicle and walk
another 300m; staff will
fetch your luggage.*

This alternative resort was created to fulfill a vision – providing a natural setting in which to "make friends with yourself and others." Hidden below the wild, arid slopes of Tejakula, Gaia-Oasis is set in several hectares of coconut groves, in front of an endless palm-fringed beach of black sand and pebbles. The tasteful, simple bungalows each have three beds and a small terrace, and are set far apart from each other. Another cluster of rooms is located in the hills, overlooking the ocean. Gaia-Oasis caters to groups conducting meditation or other spiritual retreats, with two workshop rooms. Individuals who simply want to relax are also welcome.

The wellness centre features a program of massage or beauty treatments. Budding artists can develop their creativity in a small painting studio. The restaurant serves vegetarian food and fish; guests get free refills of teas, coffee or mineral water (no plastic bottles!). The local staff have been trained in waste separation. Dive classes can be arranged with a local dive shop, as can snorkelling, dolphin tours or boat trips to the Kangean archipelago, a wild set of islands north of Bali.

Indulge in Luxury at Agung Bali Nirwana

Three large, modern-style villas, decorated with well-selected antiques and furniture, and fully equipped with modern amenities, are set in a small garden surrounded by the coconut groves of a fishing village. Advertising itself as eco-friendly, Agung Nirwana minimizes the use of chemicals in the rooms, garden and swimming pool, and has started a coral growing experiment. A cute wooden spa faces the ocean – alas, there is not much of a beach left, as the coast is eroded and a wall has been built to protect what remains. Various activities are offered, from snorkelling to diving to short hikes, as well as an introduction to sugar-making in the nearby village.

Forget It All at Alam Anda

Alam Anda ("Your Nature") is a great getaway on the northeast coast, with a few comfortable, traditional bamboo bungalows, each with its own terrace in a lush garden facing the ocean. Guests can take cooking classes, which include a shopping tour of the nearby village, or choose between health massages, sailing trips and tours of Bali. Alam Anda has a professionnally-run dive shop and a good reef for snorkelling, set just in front of the restaurant's terrace and protected from destructive fishing with the cooperation of local villagers. The resort also sponsors educational programs to raise the awareness of local communities on environmental issues.

Guests may become shareholders – Gaia-Oasis is owned by a group of people sharing the same vision of peace, spirituality and closeness to nature. Investors can build their own bungalow and use it or rent it at their convenience.

♥ ④⑤ 9 Rm – Htw
A/C Rst Bch Swp
Div Trk Shw Cls Spa
M 081 23 84 39 38;
081 23 94 73 08
F 0362-23 109
www.agung-bali-nirwana.com
> Indicated by a sign along the main road, on the beach side, in Sambirenteng.

♥ ③④ 16 Rm – Htw
Rst Bch Swp Div Shw Cls
T 0361-75 04 44
T/F 0362-22 222
M 081 24 65 64 85
alam-anda@indo.net.id
www.alamanda.de
> Indicated by a sign along the main road after Sambirenteng.

Further down the road towards the east, in the village of Tembok, *Poincianna Bungalows* caters to travellers in search of lower-priced accommodation. This small, clean, newly built resort has a few modern-style bungalows facing a small garden and a swimming pool located on the edge of the ocean, behind a fishing village. A restaurant is being added.

Where to Eat

Apart from a few warungs selling plain local food in front of the springs in Air Sanih, there are not many restaurants along the coast, hence you may often resort to eating in your hotel. However, while in the area, don't miss *Puri Bagus Ponjok Batu* Seafood Grill and Restaurant. Set on a hill above the main road, it offers excellent local cuisine based on fresh vegetables and seafood plus an ocean view from open bamboo cottages – all for about Rp30,000 per person. Try the Balinese ferns (*urab paku*), the tumeric rice or the fish kebabs (*satay lilit*). If you dread spicy food, ask for your dish to be cooked *tidak pedas* (not hot). Reservations can be made through Hotel Puri Bagus Lovina.

> *Indicated by a sign on the main road, between Pacung and Air Sanih.*

Puri Bagus works with local farmers towards the development of organic, chemical-free agriculture.

What to Do – Intriguing Temples of Northeast Bali

The northeast has a few unusual temples – each of them with distinct attractions, bearing witness to the multiple external influences that have shaped the culture of north Bali, from the Indian to the Chinese and the Dutch.

Coming from Singaraja, the first temple is the exquisite *Pura Beji* in **Sangsit**, a *subak* temple dedicated to maintaing the balance of irrigated rice cultivation. Made of a slightly pinkish sandstone, the temple's lively carvings exhibit a softness that contrasts with the black lava used in other temples.

> *Wear a sash and a sarong when visiting temples; they can be borrowed at the entrance. Leave a donation of at least Rp5,000 per person; it is used to pay the guides and maintain the temples.*

> *Find the sign to Pura Beji on the northern side of the main road, 300m before the end of Sangsit, opposite a small road indicating "SMP Sawan".*

While there, don't miss the nearby *Pura Dalem* – death temple – with its carvings representing the punishments of sinners in hell. Take a walk further down the road, going from Pura Beji towards the coast, pass a walled compound, then turn to the right across the rice fields. The inner courtyard exhibits popped-eye statues of the mythical witch queen Rangda pressing her gargantuesque breasts in her claws, her snake-like tongue hanging down to her feet. The outside wall is adorned with bas-relief depicting sinners stabbed with *keris* knives, along with complicated erotic scenes.

About 4km up in the interior, just before Sawan you'll find **Pura Dalem Jagaraga**, a fascinating reminder of the violent history of colonization in Bali. "Once upon a time," starts the temple's story, "the nearby village of Menyalih was plagued by ants." Ants? "Yes," insists the local guide, "our people were killed by demonic ants, and at each temple anniversary, at least one villager would fall dead from their bites." According to the myth, the people of Menyalih offered the land which is now Jagaraga to whoever could defeat the treacherous insects. Two local heroes took up the challenge, and rid the village of the plague using magic powers – DDT had not been invented at the time. Owing to the fertility of the land, they called the village Jagasari ("watch out for your crops").

The bountiful crops soon attracted a new plague in the form of Dutch colonizers. "We welcomed the Dutch when they were just traders, but during the 19th century they were lured by our fertile fields; they tried to tax our crops and force us to cultivate the land for them," explains the guide. After two battles won by the Balinese in 1846 and 1848, the final one took place in Jagaraga in 1849. The destruction and casualties were intense – the local resistance had built an entrenchment, and most of the area and its temple were destroyed. In fact, this can be considered as the first of the *puputan* battles (fights to the end) between the Dutch and the Balinese. The wife and servants of Gusti Ketut Jelantik, the leading prince of the resistance, marched to their deaths in a

© The Natural Guide

Sculpture of Rangda in Pura Dalem Sangsit

> The road to Sawan and the Jagaraga temple is indicated by a sign a few hundred meters east of Sangsit. Sawan can also be reached by bemos departing from Singaraja's **Panerukan** terminal.

 The local guide attending the temple is ready to provide enthusiastic explanations of the temple and its history. Leave a contribution.

hail of Dutch bullets – although Jelantik escaped alive and retreated to Karangasem. In memory of this traumatic event, the villagers rebuilt their death temple and renamed the village Jagaraga ("watch out for yourself"). In the 20th century, its external wall was adorned with bas-reliefs depicting scenes of the colonial era: an invader in a car being held at gunpoint; a foreigner smoking a pipe on his terrace; airplanes falling from the sky above bicycle riders and Balinese attending to their coconut trees.

Once in Jagaraga, continue further up the road to the village of **Sawan,** where you can visit a *gamelan gong* factory (actually, it is a tiny workshop where local craftsmen melt copper in a small charcoal foundry). In Sawan, take a nice walk to *Pura Batu Bolong* (Temple of the Hollow Stone), set above a huge banyan tree and some holy springs where villagers like to bathe. It is forbidden to climb the stairs to the temple, but you can use the spring water baths with the villagers – hence creating a sensation, since this area doesn't see many tourists. To minimize stares, don't go with a bathing suit; bathe with a sarong like the locals.

Find Batu Bolong street on the left side of the road, just after Sawan's main schoolhouse. Walk about 300m, then turn to the right. A little road goes dow about 1km past charming countryside until you reach the temple.

Descending from Sawan and continuing further down the coast towards the east, you will find *Pura Meduwe Karang* (Temple of the Land's Masters) on the northern side of the main road in Kubutambahan. While Pura Beji celebrates irrigated rice cultivation, this temple is dedicated to dry crops (*tegalan*). The dark stone temple is particularly beautiful in the late afternoon, when the setting sun shines glorious light on the frangipani trees that guard the gate.

The main attraction here are the carvings representing Hindu gods, a *legong* dancer, and the lion king of Singaraja (*Singa Raja* = Lion King), which is said to embody the boldness and frankness of the northerners. The most famous bas-relief represents the first eco-tourist to the island, riding a bicycle with a flower-shaped wheel amidst rats and dogs. He is said to be the painter W.O.J. Nieuwenkamp, who rode around

© The Natural Guide

Entrance gate of Pura Meduwe Karang

Bali in 1904. Kids flock to the temple to guide you around, adorning the bicyclist's ear with frangipani flowers. Don't feel obliged to give them money – it encourages begging, which is not much appreciated by Balinese.

You can complete your tour of the northeastern temples with a trip to *Pura Ponjok Batu* (Temple at the Rocky Corner), found 15km to the east of Kubu-tamba-han in the village of **Pacung**. The temple is built on a special site oozing with energy, just above a small promontory beaten by the waves. Mystical stories and archaeological discoveries attest to the importance of this location. According to one of the local guides, Pura Ponjok Batu was built at a time when the high priests believed that there needed to be a new temple on the north coast to maintain a balance of sanctuaries across Bali. Long before, however, the site of Ponjok Batu was already used for sacral purposes. An ancient sarcophagus was recently found in the area; it is displayed in a shrine outside the temple.

The temple is now dedicated to Danghyang Nirartha, the Javanese priest who exerted a great influence on the Balinese religion in the 16th century. He is said to have liked to sit on these rocks and pray, meditate or write poetry, inspired by the energy of the waves. The story also says that one day, the local villagers witnessed lights radiat-ing up from the ground in the area. During his meditation, Nirartha forecasted the wreckage of a ship. Soon enough, a boat landed on the beach and the holy man brought the dying seamen back to life using fresh water from a spring that magically appeared on the beach. A statue of the ship can be found on a small rock amidst the waves, just below the temple. Another, smaller shrine in front of the beach marks the site where the sacred spring can be seen at low tide. At the entrance of the temple, yet another shrine is set in front of a giant tree. This devotion to rocks and springs attests to the animist spirit that runs through the Hindu Balinese religion.

© The Natural Guide

Pura Ponjok Batu in Pacung

♥ *Pura Ponjok Batu Temple is not visited by many tourists. Owing to the sacredness of the site, a strict dress code applies. Don't walk around in a beach singlet; wear a decent, shoulder-covering shirt or clean t-shirt, a sarong and a sash. A priest will perform a purification ceremony before admitting you into the temple. Kneel down in front of him on a mat, and do as told – you will be sprinkled with holy water, then asked to offer your cupped hands, which will be filled with water in which to dip your lips. The priest will then glue sticky rice to your forehead and chest. A local guide is ready to take you on a tour of the temple, providing explanations in decent English. Leave a donation.*

The Wild Hinterland of Northeast Bali

The back roads of the northeast offer fascinating trips through one of the wildest areas of Bali. Behind Sangsit, the gentle, terraced slopes of Sawan are among the most fertile areas of Bali. As soon as you begin to ascend, especially in the eastern area behind Pacung and Tejakula, the roads start to wind through clove gardens so dense that their sweet smell lingers with you throughout your trip. Occasionally, a turn of the road gives a glimpse out towards the ocean and its coconut fringed coast.

Hike towards Sembiran

This is a pleasant way to discover the countryside. The quiet road to Sembiran climbs for 4km in sharp curves through arid slopes, revealing stunning views of the coast. It can be done by car or bemo, but walking is more enjoyable. It also makes a good motorbike trip. The village of Sembiran is a large Bali Aga community, spread out over several hills. Walk around the little streets past stone walled houses – temples are everywhere, and it feels as if time has stopped. The friendly villagers do not see many tourists. It is great to be there at the end of the day when they are sitting in front of their porches, relaxing and gossiping. If you feel like more hiking (or driving), you can continue for 8km towards Tajun, where you can join the main road going to Kubutambahan. From Sembiran to Tajun, the road passes through quiet countryside filled with trees.

Bathe in the Yeh Mampeh Waterfall

Just after Bondalem, near Tejakula, 18km east of Air Sanih, the fishing village of Les hides the wintry, 40m high fall of Yeh Mampeh, showering from a crack in the black-rocked hills of Bangli. You will find a sign leading to the waterfall along the main road in Les; take the side road heading inland. The asphalt road continues for about 1km, followed by a 2km dirt path through coconut and rambutan fruit plantations. Finish the walk with a bath in the deep, quiet pool below the fall.

The small roads in the interior are perfect for hiking, with few vehicles to disturb you. Bemos travel on the main road and service the main villages of the interior. A hardy motorbike can also be used to explore the steep winding roads, which are not in good shape.

The road to Sembiran is indicated by a sign in Pacung, along the coastal road. Watch for it just after Pacung, less than 1km east of the petrol station. If you are on public transport, take a bemo to Pacung and indicate you want to get off at the Sembiran junction.

Tejakula is fishing country – at night, there are so many boats on the water, using lamps to attract their prey, that it feels like there is a whole city on the ocean. The sea life has been damaged by destructive fishing practices, but in the small village of Les, fishermen are reversing this trend (read next page).

Fishermen without a Net:
The Story of Les Village
by Titiek Pratiwi

Without his gun, how could a cowboy chase crooks? He might settle for whirling a rope or throwing a knife. Without nets, what can fishermen in Bali do to catch fish? Less eye-catching than the whirling rope, yet more harmful than a flying blade, they settle for using cyanide.

Located in Tejakula subdistrict, 28km east of Singaraja, Les is a traditional fishing village. More than half of its 200 fishermen specialize in catching ornamental fish. This new business was introduced in Les in the early 1980s, following the flourishing example of Java. With financial support from exporters in Denpasar, it expanded as far as Lombok and Sulawesi. Many fishermen opted to catch the colourful aquarium fish for the decent daily income of this low-cost activity.

A young fisherman

"When we started to catch ornamental fish, we used nets similar to the ones we used to catch *pelagis*," says Nengah Artiawan, a fisherman in Les, referring to the pelagic species of table fish common in north Bali. "The nets for aquarium fish are different; they should have a fine, 5mm mesh, adequate for trapping small fish without damageing their scales."

However, around 1985, this type of net disappeared from the market. Ironically, according to the fishermen, this was partly a consequence of the ban on trawl fishing – a destructive method in which fine mesh nets are dragged by boats. Exporters suggested using cyanide instead; available in local markets for less than US$4/kg, it is lighter and easier to use than nets.

To catch their colourful prey, fisherman start at dawn around six. Their experience enables them to spot particular sites, like coral gardens, where the fish like to hide. They plunge into the water, squirt the poison around the corals, swim back up to their boats, and wait until the fish are floating on the surface to collect them. They often have to race with predator fish which see a chance for a floating feast, unaware of the extra cyanide marinade.

Killing Fish and Fishermen

Unaware of its harmful impacts, the fishermen regard cyanide merely as a lightly soporific substance for fish. It never crossed their mind that it may endanger small fish, coral and their own health. "Many times we broke the cyanide lump with our teeth – it's like cracking a piece of brown sugar, only much more bitter," recalls Gede, another fisherman, unaware that a few mg of cyanide may lead to his permanent rest in peace. Now he recognizes his bold habit of cyanide chewing as a possible reason for his frequent fevers and breathing difficulties.

Lacking Alternatives

"After cyanide was banned in 1995, we started to wonder if it was the best solution," confesses Nengah. *"But nobody ever explained the reason or came up with an alternative. Despite our fear of being caught, we had to keep feeding our families."* Some converted to low-paid construction jobs, while others returned to catching table fish — which brings a lower income. The others play hide-and-seek with the marine patrols, a losing game in which they often end up paying fines of US$1000 to 3000 per person, or spending a few months in jail.

Inquiries, information and help:

Bahtera Nusantara Foundation,
Denpasar, Bali
T/F 0361-242 405
bahteranusantara@
indo.net.id

Marine Aquarium Council
www.aquariumcouncil.org

In October 2001, members of the Bahtera Nusantara Foundation, an environmental NGO working in the coastal areas of Bali, started to assist the fishermen of Les in finding a healthier solution. Working with the local authorities and *kelian adat* (traditional chiefs), Bahtera tried to remind the fishermen of their long-forgotten buddy, the net, as a method for catching ornamental fish. They tried out nets obtained through partner NGOs in the Philippines, along with the fishermen's hand-crocheted nets. Demonstrations of direct application of cyanide solution to corals and fish under the eyes of fishermen enabled them to understand its destructive impacts. Soon, as the fishermen's knowledge broadened, cyanide use was regarded as fishy.

Both Gede and Nengah reckon that their daily catch today, after switching back to nets, is about the same as when they used cyanide — their income has not decreased as they initially feared. Besides, the mortality rate of the ornamental fish they catch has dropped from thirty to ten percent. Since exporters charge them for the loss of dead fish arriving in their storerooms, this means increased earnings. Still, large exporters do not reward them with a better price for their cyanide-free fish.

The fishermen in Les are now going one step further by nursing the cyanide-bleached corals along their shores, using a simple transplantation method introduced by Bahtera. A modest edifice is under construction to attract eco-friendly snorkelling and diving to the village as an alternative income source. An initiative to acquire an official cyanide-free certification for their fish, in collaboration with the Hawaii-based Marine Aquarium Council (MAC), is also on the go.

Yet for the fishermen of Les, the biggest snag is the unavailability of fine nets, the tool they need to continue fishing without poisoning the corals. They are looking for information and contacts to acquire such nets. Any help will be generously rewarded by their sincere friendship and a cup of delicious Balinese coffee.

© A. A. B. Dianatha K.

Fishing boats on the beach of Lovina

> *Lovina is easy to reach by public transport from the Banyuasri terminal in west Singaraja. Make sure to tell the bemo driver which village you are going to.* **Perama** *buses and shuttles service Lovina from most other tourist areas of the island (T 0361-751 551; 751 875).*

Lovina is the name given to a string of villages centred around **Kalibukbuk**, from **Pemaron** in the east to **Temukus** in the west. This romantic name contributed to the appeal of what was hoped would become an alternative to Kuta – a tranquil beach resort for tourists interested in peace and dolphins. Alas, Lovina has been a victim of its own success. Its grey-sand beach and busy main street lined up with hotels and restaurants no longer offer a pristine experience. Like in Kuta, eager vendors patrol the roads and the beach offering "transport" services and handicrafts. Travellers in search of total peace along the coast will have to push as far as Pemuteran to find what Lovina used to look like.

Yet Lovina remains a convenient base to explore north Bali, especially for travellers on a budget and without a vehicle. It offers a wide range of accommodation and restaurants, especially in the lower price range. Lots of transport options are available, including bemos and shuttle buses, as well as motorbikes, bicycles and car rentals or guided tours. Lovina also has **postal services**, numerous wartel **phone kiosks**, **Internet** cafés, and two **ATMs**. Most of these services are concentrated around **Jalan Bina Ria** in Kalibukbuk, which is easily identified by a sign indicating the way to Hotel Angsoka. This is where the heart of Lovina beats, and where you'll find most inexpensive hotels and restaurants, as well as Lovina's nightlife – a few relaxed street-side cafés with live music performed by eager local bands.

What's in a name?
"Lovina" was the name given by Pandji Tisna, the last king of Buleleng (1908-1978), to a homestay he built in Kaliasem in 1953. It is said to mean either "Love Indonesia" or, in a more ecumenic version, refers to the "love" contained "in" the heart of all people. The international reputation of Pandji Tisna as a novelist and columnist attracted guests to his bungalows, which are now the Lovina Beach Hotel. Soon other hotels were added, and as north Bali became popular, the successful Lovina brand name was used throughout the area.

Fighting for Pemaron
The beaches and fish-filled corals of Pemaron are threatened by the construction of an oil-powered electricity plant. This controversial project is allegedly needed to meet Bali's growing energy demand, but is singularly ill-located near a fishing village and tourist destination. Local sea lovers, community members and tourism enterprises have organised a forum to protect their environment and livelihood. To support them, contact:
www.bali-in-danger.net

Many of the hotels of Lovina were built in the 1970s and 1980s and have not aged well. We selected a few options which offer a quiet experience in quality settings.

Eastern Lovina, only a ten minute drive past Singaraja, includes the villages of **Pemaron**, **Tukad Mungga** and **Anturan**, which are less crowded than the centre of Lovina.

Central Lovina, which covers the villages of **Kalibukbuk** and **Kaliasem**, is the ideal choice for travellers who want to avail themselves of a range of facilities, restaurants and bars.

Western Lovina refers to the village of **Temukus**, which is still relatively underdeveloped, but unfortunately offers only a narrow strip of land between the main road and the seashore.

Above Lovina, peace fanatics will find ideal places to stay in the hills of **Selat** or **Kayuputih** – no direct beach access, but fabulous views are guaranteed.

Where to Stay – Eastern Lovina

A Deluxe Stay at Puri Bagus Lovina

💙 ❹ ❺ *40 Rm – Htw A/C Rst Bch Swp Div Trk Cls Bcy Ckr T 0362-21 430 ; 21 403; 21 487; F 0362-22 627 www.bagus-discovery.com*
> *Indicated by a sign on the beach side of the main road in* **Pemaron**.
For sea lovers, Puri Bagus offers romantic sunset or dinner cruises on a spacious wooden boat.

Set in a spacious garden, Puri Bagus's light-stone walled bungalows, tastefully decorated and equipped with romantic open-air bathrooms, provide calm and comfortable shelters. Puri Bagus offers numerous activities, from snorkelling, diving, fishing, canoeing and dolphin-watching to trekking, bicycling and cooking classes. An innovative walks program lets guests discover traditional methods of making coffee, coconut oil, brown sugar and *arak* liquor, as well as visit vegetable gardens and the delicious restaurant of *Ponjok Batu* near Air Sanih. The owners have embarked on programs to separate waste and train villagers in organic farming.

❷ ❸ *28 Rm – Htw A/C Rst Swp Div Trk T 0362-41 039 F 0362-41 379 celukabc@singaraja. wasantara.net.id*

Further west after the petrol station, *Celuk Agung* offers bungalows in the middle of a nice garden, with a poolside restaurant serving Balinese and Indonesian food. Prices can be negotiated. Ask the owner or the staff for trekking and diving programmes.

> *Rumah Cantik is well hidden, so call before making a visit. Turn towards the hills in **Kaliasem**, just after the Octopus Garden. About 500m inland, a small path to the left leads towards Rumah Cantik. Since the owner was born in the village, the locals know the place as "Rumah Kletak" – Kletak's house.*

❷ ❸ *30 Rm – Htw A/C Rst Swp Div Trk*
T 0362-41388
F 0362-41057
rambutanlovina@hotmail.com
www.rambutan.org
> *Jl. Mawar (a.k.a. Jl. Ketapang), starts opposite Khi Khi restaurant and the Lovina Clinic.*

❷ ❸ *24 Rm – Htw A/C Rst Bch Swp Div Trk Bcy*
T/F 0362-41 219
www.bayukartikaresort.com

❶ ❷ ❸ *44 Rm – Htw A/C Rst Swp*
T 0362-41 841; 41 268
F 0362-41 023
angsoka@singaraja.
wasantara.net.id
www.baliweb.net/angsoka

❶ ❷ *6 Rm – Htw A/C Rst Bch Swp*
T 0362-93 407
F 0362-93 406
> *On the main road in Temukus*

The ones upstairs are our favourites for the views of treetops and rice paddies.

Owners Jette and Kletak, along with their faithful staff, will take care of you, arranging meals and breakfast with home-made bread. On a lazy day you can choose between dreaming in the garden's *bale,* getting a massage or walking 200m to the beach. If you are after more activity, ask your hosts to take you on a tour of north Bali, a visit to the market in Singaraja or a walk in the lovely countryside. The owners take care of the environment and will give you a free refill of water to limit your use of plastic bottles.

Among dozens of hotels around Lovina, *Rambutan Cottage*, in Jalan Mawar, is worth a mention for its spacious garden, nice pool and friendly staff. In addition to its rooms, it has three comfortable villas in a well-tended garden. The biggest ones have small kitchens and a playground for children. Every Friday, traditional dance is performed in the thatch-roofed restaurant. Ask the staff for programs of diving, snorkelling or trekking with local guides. Further down toward the beach, at the end of Jalan Mawar, is *Bayu Kartika Beach Resort*, offering spotless bungalows along a vast garden facing the beach and fishing boats. After a half-day trekking or a dive, try a Balinese massage on the beach for about Rp50,000 – or lounge by the pool under a lush canopy of mango trees.

Travellers who want to stay in the centre of Lovina for convenience will enjoy *Angsoka*, strategically located on Jalan Bina Ria. It offers good value accommodations, with a choice of rooms or bamboo bungalows providing various levels of comfort in a wide price range (from Rp40,000 to 400,000 per room), all set in a large garden.

Where to Stay – Western Lovina

If you're ready to escape the centre of Lovina drive 2km to the west towards Temukus, the clean and quiet *Bagus Homestay* is excellent value. It offers spacious bungalows in a good-sized garden, with an elegant small pool and a restaurant facing the beach.

A bit closer to Lovina lies *Agus Homestay*, which belongs to the same owner. It is even cheaper, but it does not offer the same nice garden and pool, and it has a seafront terrace instead of a beach.

Where to Stay – Above Lovina

Soothe your Soul at Sananda "Centre of Light"

This wonderfully different place features three large bungalows spread out over a sloping garden. High ceilings, sober decorations and semi-open bathrooms contribute to a serene atmosphere, dominated by the pervasive vegetation, the song of birds and the sight of the Lovina bay. A profusion of ornamental and useful plants grow under mango and neem trees, some of them flourishing in a waste water garden – one of the latest concepts in smart waste treatment for nature-friendly hotels in Bali.

Located in Selat, about 2km from the main road and 5km from the centre of Lovina, Sananda is ideal for adepts of meditation, but also for hikers. There is little chance of encountering other tourists along the small roads leading uphill amidst gardens and forest. Tours with car and driver can be arranged. The caring staff prepare breakfasts and Balinese meals with fresh vegetables, making you feel like you are part of their family. Cooking classes can be arranged with Warung Bambu in Pemaron. Besides taking care of the environment, the concerned owner supports the schooling of local children.

A Deluxe Mountain View at The Damai

"Hard to find, hard to leave" is The Damai's motto, and it stands true for the lucky guests who can afford to stay in this unique hideout, nestled in the hills above Lovina. Facing a quiet valley of rice fields and orchards are clustered spacious bungalows – perhaps a bit too close together for total privacy. Decorated with selected antiques and rare Indonesian textiles, each room features a spacious open-air bathroom, some of them with their own spa. A small pool boasts a stunning ocean view, with dim night-lighting lending a touch of mystery.

❶ 7 Rm – Htw A/C Rst
T/F 0362-41 202

♥♥ ❷ 3 Rm – Htw Trk
M 081 23 64 17 81
ginamenegola@yahoo.de
www.sananda-bali.ch.vu
> Take a small road going uphill next to the petrol station in Anturan.
After 1km, turn left at the T-junction, then turn right again after 200m, going towards Selat in the mountain. Sananda is found 1km after Anturan on the Jalan Raya Anturan-Selat road. Ojek drivers can lead you there from the main road.

♥ ❺ 8 Rm – Htw A/C
Swp Gvw
Div Trk Cls Bcy Ckr Spa
T 0362-41 008; 41 501
F 0362-41 009
resort@damai.com
www.damai.com
> Look for the Damai sign along the main road in Lovina, and follow the road for about 4km up the mountain slope.

The Damai advertises an impressive menu of tours and cultural activities, including lessons in Balinese music, dance, cooking and traditional dressing. Romantic picnics on Lake Tamblingan are among the guests' favourites. Active types can choose from nearby walks, diving, biking, horse riding, tennis, and water sports. Tired muscles can be relieved by a massage in the spa, which overlooks the valley. Prices for these activities are in line with the hotel's rate – they are not cheap by local standards; but the activities are well appreciated by delighted guests.

Lovina – Where to Eat

There are countless inexpensive restaurants in the centre of Lovina, especially on Jalan Bina Ria. Try the excellent picks below to step out of the usual "burger-pizza-mixed rice" routine.

Warung Bambu Pemaron: a Balinese Experience

♥ ♥ *Rst Shw Cls*
T 0362-31 455
T/F 0362-27 080
warungbambu@gmx.net
➤ *In Pemaron, indicated by a sign on the main road. Turn onto a small road leading towards the sea and Hotel Puri Bagus.*

Ever wondered what excellent Balinese food tastes like? If so, make sure to spend a night in Warung Bambu. The *nasi campur* (mixed rice) is a bounty of fresh vegetables, soybean cake (*tempe*), brochettes (*satay*), fish and chicken, with a unique blend of local spices. The curries, cooked with love in coconut milk, are authentically delicious, but the most special is the *pesan* – fresh tuna fillet marinated in spices and cooked in a banana leaf. A wide range of grilled fish and seafood is also available. Even the fruit basket is a feast for the senses, including local fruits such as the astringent *salak* or the honey-sweet *sawu*.

❀ *Beate and Nyoman, the tireless owners of Warung Bambu, are fighting for a clean environment, and have created a waste management project working with local communities called CV Sapulidi. They also run original **tours** around the area (see p. 327), and are ready to share their culinary miracles in their **cooking classes**.*

Warung Bambu is also a mini-gallery, displaying original paintings that add colour to the homey atmosphere created by the bamboo tables and the deck opening onto the rice fields. Culture lovers should make sure they don't miss the **dance shows**, which are offered twice a week on Wednesdays and Sundays – these are original choreographies based on Balinese tradition, performed with feeling and creativity by local artists. **Dance classes** can also be arranged.

Dinner with a Sea Breeze at Warung Bias

Located a few meters from the seashore and open to the lush green vegetation, this pleasant warung offers international food – try the sandwich made with home-made bread or the prawn thermidor – but also a great choice of tasty local food, such as the traditional grilled village chicken with chilli sauce or the prawns cooked in banana leaves. Warung Bias is run by the owners of Saraswati, one of our favourite places to stay in Lovina, and it puts the same emphasis on cleanliness, friendly service and environmental concern as the homestay.

> Located in Kalibukbuk, near the end of Jalan Pantai Banyualit (follow the sign towards Hotel Banyualit).

Thai Delicacies at Jasmine Kitchen

This newly opened restaurant occupies a small two-storey building with a smart choice of furniture and paintings. The MSG and preservative-free dinner menu, ranges from a piquant Tom Yum soup to smooth fish cakes or refreshing homemade lime and chile sorbet. At lunchtime, a set menu of appetizer, main course and dessert is offered for Rp25-30,000. A soothing lemon-grass tea provides the perfect ending to your feast.

> On a small lane on the right side of Jalan Bina Ria. Jasmine Kitchen cares about the environment, participating in local waste management initiatives and shunning plastic bottles – guests can refill their glasses and bottles from the mineral water container.

A Gourmet Dinner at The Damai

When famous Danish Chef Per Thoftesen was invited to teach The Damai's staff how to make bread, he fell in love with the gorgeous mountain setting: "I came for one month and stayed two and a half years, of which nine months were spent training the local staff," he explains with a smile. This gave him the occasion to work with his local counterpart, I Ketut Tangkas, to create a blend of European and Asian flavours that is now the signature of this romantic restaurant. Most dishes are based on products sourced from local farmers and fishermen, including vegetables cultivated on The Damai's grounds, where efforts are being made to reduce chemical use and move towards organic farming. Lunch main courses cost about US$10, Gourmet Dinners range from US$25-50 per person.

> T 0362-41 008
F 0362-41 009
resort@damai.com
www.damai.com
> Look for the Damai sign along the main road in Lovina, and follow the road for about 4km into the mountain slope.

The cooking classes provide a great opportunity to discover local markets and learn all sorts of creative, colourful and spice-rich recipes.

On the Beach at Café Spice

T 0362-41 969
> Follow the sign from the main road in Kaliasem.

Perfectly located in front of a quiet beach spot, this relaxed and friendly place serves affordable international and local food and snacks, including great breakfasts. It belongs to the same environment-loving owners as Spice Dive.

T 0362-41 144; 41 344
> On Jalan Bina Ria, the main street of Kalibukbuk.

Other recommended places in the area include *Kakatua*, with its impressive menu offering cuisine from around the world, including Balinese, Mexican, Indian and Thai, in a pleasant setting on the main street of Lovina.

T/F 0362-41 548
> On the main road in Kalibukbuk, near Jl. Damai.

We also like *Khi Khi*, which offers simple Indo-Chinese dishes and fresh seafood prepared in its open kitchen, with an ample choice of fruit juices.

T 0362-42 031
> Easily spotted on the main road in Kaliasem.

Locals often recommend the *Octopus's Garden*, which offers an interesting combination of local food, seafood (don't miss the famous octopus salad), Italian and Japanese food.

Lovina – What to Do at Sea

Lovina is a beach resort and the main activities are centred around the sea. The coral reefs around Lovina are not the most spectacular on the island, and are more suited for introductory dives, training and night dives. Serious divers can use Lovina as a base from which to explore more exciting spots like Menjangan, which is only an hour away.

Snorkel with the Fishermen

© Dwi Rahmad Muhtaman

Sorting the fishing nets

The corals near the beach are not in prime condition, hence it is better to arrange a snorkelling boat trip with one of the fishermen for Rp30,000. Your hotel can arrange it for you, but you'll get a cheaper price by booking directly with one of the boat owners on the beach. They all belong to a local village association, which has its own internal rules allowing boat owners to take turns working with tourists.

Take a Spice Dive

A Padi 5-star dive centre, Spice Dive has qualified international instructors and dive masters who are known
for their friendliness. Dive trips can be organised from
Menjangan in the northwest to Amed in the east.
Specialty courses are offered, as well as night dives
around Lovina. Spice Dive is committed to protecting
the marine environment, and takes part in clean-up programmes, reef regeneration, and environmental awareness programs with the local community.

Get Wet at Spice Watersports Centre

A wide range of other water sports are also offered at
Café Spice by the operators of Spice Dive. If you care
for the environment, it is better to avoid anything using
noisy motor boats, such as water skiing, and enjoy unob-
trusive activities like **wind surfing** or **canoeing**.

The nearby *Indiana* massage center also advertises
canoeing.

Encounter Dolphins in a Gentle Way

For better or worse, dolphins are an icon of Lovina;
immortalized on statues at the end of the main street.
Dolphin watching – or shall we say dolphin chasing? – is
the most popular tourist attraction in Lovina. For
Rp30,000, you can hop on a boat at 6am with a local
fisherman for a chance to spot a group of dolphins, or,
very rarely, even a whale.

The local fishermen have an ambivalent relation
with these smart sea mammals. They appreciate the dolphins as fishing guides – their presence often means that
a lot of fish are around – but resent them when they get
trapped in their nets, causing a lot of damage. However,
fishermen have always respected them and freed them
from the nets; they are not part of their catch.

♥ ♥ ⚲
T 0362-41 305; 41 509;
0362-41 512;
F 0362-41 171
spicedive@
balispicedive.com
www.balispicedive.com
> *Spice Dive has an outlet on
the main road in Kaliasem,
west of the mosque, and
another one on Jalan Bina
Ria, the main street of
Kalibukbuk.*

✄ T 0362-41 969
> *From the main road,
follow the directions to
Café Spice or enquire at
Spice Dive.*

*Dolphin statue with sacred
poleng cloth*

© Godeliva D. Sari

♥♥ *The guidelines on these pages have been developed for Indonesia by APEX Environmental based on internationally recognised standards. They are are also endorsed by the local programs of The Nature Conservancy and the World Wildlife Fund. For more information contact: Benjamin Kahn, Director APEX Environmental, Indonesia Oceanic Cetacean Program: www.apex-environmental.com.*

© Dedok

The Dolphins and Lovina

When Lovina's popularity increased in the 1980s, fishermen discovered that tourists were ready to pay for a chance to spot the cetaceans. They started to offer their services to tourists, taking them on sunrise trips to watch dolphins jumping in the water. Soon enough, the number of boats and tourists increased, and on an average day, it is standard to see more than 20 boats gathered around the dolphins' favourite hangout spots.

Commercial competition and the eagerness of tourists to add a new thrill to their list of adventures in Bali soon turned innocent watch tours into aggressive chases. As stated by Dewa Made Suarsana, the head of the Local Fishermen's Association, "We normally don't want to chase the dolphins. We would be very happy to just stop our engine and stay at least 50m away from the animals. But many tourists insist that we get closer so they can take better pictures. Some even want to touch the dolphins or swim around them. We don't like it; it can be dangerous and we have no insurance. But have to do what our customers ask; some of them request a rebate or refund if they don't get to see the dolphins."

The Dolphins and You

Don't believe it if you're told that dolphins enjoy the experience, or are not disturbed by it since "they keep coming over to the area anyway." As stated by marine ecologist Benjamin Kahn: "There are many reasons why dolphins may gather in an area. It may be a good feeding ground, a favourite resting area away from predators, part of a migratory route, or even a mating area. Hence they will come back because they need the environment and its resources, but being chased by boats may disturb activities which are essential to their biological cycle." In other words, imagine being surrounded by 20 motor vehicles full of gaping intruders while in your favourite restaurant or while honeymooning, and you'll have an idea of what dolphins endure in Lovina.

So what to do as a nature lover? Dolphin watch tours are a good side income for fishermen, and give them an incentive to preserve the marine life. If you decide to book one of them, explain to your boat driver that you do not want to chase the dolphins. When you see a group of dolphins, ask him to stop his boat and wait. You may not see the animals as close as the other boats running after them. But it is better than disturbing these lovely creatures, and it will show the local fishermen that not all tourists are disrespectful of sea life. By allowing the dolphins to behave in a natural way, you may even get a chance to witness something special, like hunting, feeding, mating or the birth of a baby dolphin – which won't happen when animals are being harassed.

Cetaceans are sensitive, intelligent and curious. If approached in a gentle way, they are likely to come close to a boat, but the encounter should take place on the animals' terms:

- *Minimise speed and noise; avoid sudden changes in speed, direction and noise.*

- *Stay at least 50m away from dolphins, 100m from whales.*

- *Never pursue, encircle or separate the animals; don't approach directly from the front or back.*

- *Don't feed the cetaceans or throw rubbish overboard.*

- *Allow the animals to control the nature and duration of the encounter.*

- *Don't try to have a closer look at special behaviours such as feeding or mating.*

- *Don't join if they are already too many boats around the dolphins.*

- *Don't run through groups of dolphins to solicit bow-riding. Don't accelerate if dolphins start to bow-ride.*

© Dedok

Tours and walks around Lovina

An Alternative Discovery of North Bali

The energetic owners of Warung Bambu in Pemaron never run out of ideas for taking people to discover the hidden life of north Bali. As the Lovina counter of Bali Discovery Tours, they offer unique opportunities to discover the culture of the region they love. Try, for example, the **Secrets of North Bali** tour, which will take you through splendid stretches of rice fields and natural

💛 *Contact: Warung Bambu Pemaron, or Bali Discovery Tours T 0361-286 283 F 0361-286 284 info@balidiscovery.com www.balidiscovery.com*

> *In Pemaron, indicated by a sign on the main road; turn onto a small road leading towards the sea and Hotel Puri Bagus.*

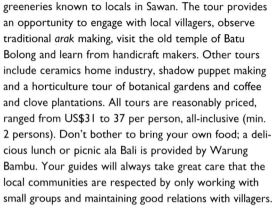

© Dedok

🐾 *Contact: **Ibu Sila** via Sananda Homestay M 081 23 64 17 81; her husband will guide you to the waterfall. Or go directly to Selat vilage and after passing the elementary school, hidden in the hillside opposing a simple wooden warung, you'll find the small path leading to the waterfall.*

greeneries known to locals in Sawan. The tour provides an opportunity to engage with local villagers, observe traditional *arak* making, visit the old temple of Batu Bolong and learn from handicraft makers. Other tours include ceramics home industry, shadow puppet making and a horticulture tour of botanical gardens and coffee and clove plantations. All tours are reasonably priced, ranged from US$31 to 37 per person, all-inclusive (min. 2 persons). Don't bother to bring your own food; a delicious lunch or picnic ala Bali is provided by Warung Bambu. Your guides will always take great care that the local communities are respected by only working with small groups and maintaining good relations with villagers.

Touring the Hills behind Lovina

You don't need to go very far to escape the tourist crowds of Lovina and find total peace. The hills and slopes of the interior offer beautiful landscapes of rice terraces and mixed agroforests of coffee, clove and fruit trees. You can explore this area on foot or by car – the best way is probably to rent a motorbike for a day or charter an ojek if you don't want to drive yourself. The best landscapes are found behind Anturan and Kaliasem, and around Kayuputih (just follow the signs leading to The Damai from the main road in Kalibukbuk) and Selat.

Easy Hike to Sipoklabuh Waterfall – Anturan/Selat

A good option for a pleasant walk in Anturan is the hidden path leading to the Sipoklabuh waterfall. The 15m waterfall, impressive during the rainy season (December-March), turns into a trickle during the dry months, but the walk and the view are still worth a try. During the 30-minute stroll, you will traverse fruit gardens, coconut groves and wild vegetation, with the tall green hill towering on the other side. At the end of the path, cross a small stream before coming to the waterfall. Lay down on the surface of a flat rock while enjoying fresh breezes and the quietness of the area.

A Coffee Hike From Selat to Asah Gobleg

This 10km, 4-hour long hike will make you sweat through one of the most charming back roads of Bali. You can do it without a guide, walking uphill on a small, damaged asphalt road and going back downhill on an ojek. Get on the road around 7 or 8am, with an ample supply of water and energy snacks.

© A. A. B. Dianatha K.

Coffee flowers

Start the walk from the *Balai Dusun* (village hall) in Selat, or from the beginning of the road leading to Gobleg in Selat. If in doubt, check with the locals if you are marching in the direction of Asah Gobleg (or Gobleg plateau). They may think you're mad to do this on foot, but will just add this to the endless list of reasons why tourists are a bit odd. If asked why you are doing this to yourself, just answer "*olahraga*" (exercise) – sports are becoming popular throughout Indonesia, and on a week-end, you may even meet groups of kids walking and jog-ging on this road. After the Balai Selat, the road goes down for a few hundred meters, before the actual hike starts. From there on, it's uphill for about 9km, during which you'll climb from 300m to 1300m.

The first half of the hike winds through villages, and you may occasionally encounter motorbikes climbing up with a whole family loaded on the back, amidst lots of noise and fumes. Some may even offer to take you on board, so if you are too tired and want to give up, there is always an option. After 4km, the road enters a beautiful and deserted forest area, followed by an amazing countryside of steep gorges covered with coffee bushes. If you have the chance to be there when the coffee trees are blooming, you will be soon dizzied by the honeysuckle-like fragrance of their white flowers. You won't meet many human souls there, apart from farmers carrying monster loads of cut grass and leaves on their heads, wondering with huge smiles why any-one with no cattle to feed would want to walk up this road – the notion of *olahraga* is still alien to these older, hard-working folks.

> To start out on this hike, arrange for a vehicle or an ojek to drop you at the beginning of the road leading from Selat to Asah Gobleg. To find it, drive first from Anturan inland towards Selat. After you pass Sananda Homestay on your right, continue for another 3km uphill, and you'll encounter the junction where the road to Asah Gobleg starts. You can also asked to be dropped further up in front of the *Balai Dusun* (village hall) in Selat.

Flowers for the Gods

Millions of flowers are used every day in Bali for offerings. While most Balinese pick flowers in their backyard, the busy urban middle class can't be bothered to spend hours hunting for the right combination of coloured petals. Hence there is a growing demand for flowers to be sold as do-it-yourself or ready-to-use offerings in the markets. The fertile, cool areas around Lake Tamblingan are the perfect ground for these good looking crops. There you'll see many vehicles full of pale blue hydrangeas, which sell for a few thousand rupiah a kilo.

T 0362-41 305; 41 512
F 0362-41 171
www.balispicedive.com
Enquire at Spice Dive or at the Cyber Spice Café on Jalan Bina Ria in Lovina.

The road ends up in Gobleg plateau amidst a bizarre landscape of flower fields, and you will see hectares of orange and blue petals blossoming between pine trees.

As you reach the stone board indicating the entrance to Asah Gobleg, just follow the road to the right. After 1.5 km of mildly uphill road, take a left turn towards Wanagiri and Bedugul. There you can start to enquire about ojek to bring you back down to Munduk. You can also walk another km and reach another fork, where ojeks are usually waiting. Ask them to take you to Munduk along the road going left. After 5km, you'll reach the main asphalt road above Tamblingan Lake. Another left will bring you to Bedugul, while the right goes down to Munduk. Your ojek should be able to take you down to Munduk for about Rp10,000. Ask to be dropped at the market *(Pasar Munduk)* where you will find a bemo to take you back down to Seririt, and from there to Lovina. Make sure you reach Munduk before 3pm – later than this you may not find vehicles easily.

Put Some Spice in your Trekking

Besides its well-known program of waters sports and scuba diving, *Spice Dive* had a thought for those of us who don't want to get in the water. They offer a good choice of walks around north Bali, lasting from three to five hours or more, taking you through bamboo forests and hidden rivers. You may still get wet from the sweat or from a sudden shower in the hills, but you're guaranteed to enjoy the trip.

© Jean-Marie Bompard

Flowers on sale in the market, ready to make offerings

© Ulung Wicaksono

Rice fields and agroforestry in Mayong

A mere 12km from Lovina, the small, coastal market town of **Seririt** has a busy atmosphere. Just east of Seririt, travellers appreciate the quiet Buddhist monastery and the hot springs of **Banjar**. Seririt is also the gateway to the spectacular rice fields of **Bestala**, **Mayong** and **Munduk**. Slowly climbing from the north coast to the romantic **lakes** of **Tamblingan** and **Buyan**, this area is home to nature lovers. Trekkers will find an endless choice of rice field walks, forest hikes, garden tours and waterfalls below the 1860m-high **Mt Lesong**. There are cultural and historical wonders galore, from hidden temples and ancient Bali Aga villages to vestiges of the Dutch colonization.

Recent archaeological discoveries suggest that the Tamblingan area has been populated for about 2000 years. It was known as a cultural and spiritual centre in the 10th century, long before the Majapahit presence in Bali. Lured by the cool climate of Munduk, the Dutch established their first guest-house – or more exactly "rest house" – there for officials and visitors in 1903, 25 years before the opening of the first hotel in Denpasar.

Seririt, Banjar and Munduk offer a few cottages and homestays, all designed to offer tranquillity in lovely rural settings, with a great choice of tours and guided walks. Discover them here, from the coast to the interior.

> Like most areas away from mass tourism, Seririt and Munduk have a limited choice of places to stay for the budget traveller; cheaper accommodation can be found in nearby **Lovina**.
> Getting around can also be a bit difficult. You'll find bemos and ojeks in **Banjar**, **Seririt** and **Munduk**, but there are not many in the interior after 3pm. For long excursions, charter a vehicle or ask your hotel to arrange transport.

♥♥ **Munduk** is the centre of an eco-tourism project dedicated to maintaining the cultural heritage and the ecological balance of the area around lake Tamblingan – the lake and the surrounding mountains play a key role in regulating the flow of water to the downstream areas.

north

Where to Stay – Seririt and Banjar

A Blue Symphony at Zen Lifestyle Energy Resort

 **3** 7 Rm – Htw A/C
Bch Swp Gvw Div Spa
T 0362-93 578
F 0362-93 579
contact@zenbali.com
www.zenbali.com
> The road to the resort
is found 2km west of
Seririt on the main road
from Lovina to Pemuteran.

The design of this resort is a love story between the landscape, the sky and the sea joining in a symphony of blues. The tasteful rooms are well spaced, each with its own veranda facing the garden, pool and sea. Every morning your terrace will be decorated with a mandala made of flowers. Peace is the priority in Zen: there is no television or phone; children under 14 are not allowed. Besides the soothing music – classical in the morning, meditative in the afternoon – the only noise comes from birds nesting around the swimming pool. Spot the metallic blue of a kingfisher, or receive the visit of a cockatoo.

In the morning, you can join meditation sessions or indulge in spa treatments inspired by the spice and flower-based recipes of the 17th century Javanese court. Health therapies, yoga classes and ayurvedic massages are also on the program. Guests are offered guided tours to discover the beautiful hills and rice fields of the area, visit the Seririt market before a cooking lesson, or sail with local fishermen. The quiet beach is only 200m away. The *table d'hôte* offers healthy, local meals for Rp50-75,000.

Escape it all in Ratu Ayu Villas

4 3 Rm – Htw
Rst Gvw Div Trk
T 0362-93 612
T/F 0362-93 437
lumbung@dps.centrin.net.id
> Take the road leading
to Zen Resort. After 1km,
take the rocky left turn that
leads to Ratu Ayu Villas.

Nestled in two hectares of verdant garden, these plain thatched roof and *lumbung* (rice barn) style cottages overlook a picturesque panorama of vineyards, green hills and the vivid blue sea. The beach is in walking distance, so ask the staff to take you fishing with a *jukung* boat, or grab the free snorkelling equipment and enjoy the calmness of the sea and the black-sand beach.

Trekking, diving and guided tours can be arranged with **Puri Lumbung Cottages** in Munduk, which owns Ratu Ayu. A refill of mineral water can be provided for free for guests of the hotel or restaurant.

For travellers looking for a more affordable alternative, *Pondok Wisata Grya Seri* in **Banjar** has a few plain brick and carved stone bungalows in traditional Balinese style, with small terraces facing the surrounding lush vegetation. The standard bungalows are reasonably clean and have pleasant open-air bathrooms; the suite has a great terrace but a run-down bathroom. Travellers can eat in the small restaurant, or at the spring's restaurant nearby. This is a good base for walks and hikes around.

❶ ❷ 14 Rm – Rst Trk
T 0362-92 903
F 0362-92 966
> *Located just before the **Banjar hot springs** (see below, p.336).*

Where to Stay – Munduk

An Eco-Tourism Centre at Puri Lumbung

The first of its kind in Bali, Puri Lumbung Cottages is more than a hotel – it is an eco-tourism project dedicated to the discovery, conservation and enhancement of the unspoiled area around Munduk and Tamblingan. Nyoman Bagiarta, the visionary founder, has been working with local communities and tourism schools, training guides to offer an amazing variety of ways to discover the local landscapes and culture. Puri Lumbung has received international aid and support from artists.

♥ ❸ ❹ 20 Rm – Htw Rst Gvw Trk Shw Cls
T 0362-92 810
F 0362-92 514
lumbung@dps.centrin.net.id
> *Easy to spot along the main road climbing above Munduk towards the Tamblingan Lake.*

Set in a lush flowery garden, the cottages – unfortunately located a bit too close to each other – are replicas of the local *lumbung*, or rice granaries. They offer either great rice field views or simple garden views.

Puri Lumbung has helped the local villagers establish several **guesthouses** in Munduk, offering cheaper accommodation in Dutch colonial style houses with a family atmosphere. One of them is *Guru Ratna Homestay*, which has plain rooms, some of them with verandas offering great views onto the valley. The panorama can also be enjoyed from the dining area where local cuisine is served. Learn how to cook the local specialities (like the *lak-lak* pancake served for breakfast) or how to make ritual offerings with the owner's family. Excursions can be organized, with packed lunches wrapped in eco-friendly banana leaves instead of plastic. Babysitting can be arranged.

♥ ❶ ❷ 5 Rm – Gvw Trk Cls
T 0362-92 812
M 081 33 85 26 092
> *Along the road in the centre of Munduk 200m above the market or 1km below Puri Lumbung.*

❷ *4 Rm – Htw Rst Gvw Trk Cls*
T 0362-92 811
F 0362-92 514
lumbung@dps.centrin.net.id

❸ ❹ *9 Rm – Htw Rst Gvw Trk Bcy Cls Spa*
T/F 0362-92 818
lumbungbali@hotmail.com
www.lumbungbali.com
> Along the main road above Munduk, about 200m south of Puri Lumbung.

❹ ❺ *2 Rm – Htw Gvw Trk*
M 081 24 64 78 47
Singapore office:
T +65-64 74 16 28
F +65-64 79 30 55
nealnet@singnet.com.sg
www.vilasangkih.com
> In the hills south of Munduk, above the village of **Umejero**. Make a booking first, and a driver will pick you up.

Another alternative in the same style is *Meme Surung Homestay*, which is run by Puri Lumbung Cottages, and has plain rooms in an old Dutch colonial house overlooking the valley.

At Peace in the Mountains at Lumbung Bali

This copy of Puri Lumbung offers the same traditional granary style bungalows, albeit with more space, comfort and privacy. The balconies overlooking the well-tended garden offer stunning views of the clove-covered mountains. The small restaurant serves great local specialties – don't miss the Balinese breakfast with fried bananas and local cakes. The friendly staff offer activities from traditional top spinning to weaving or wood carving; as well as guided tours and treks to local temples, waterfalls and mountains.

A Deluxe Sunset View at Vila Sangkih

Superbly designed and furnished, this modern Balinese style villa is hidden in a three-hectare clove and coffee farm at 750m above sea level. A fully equipped kitchen is at your disposal; the cook can prepare traditional cuisine and western dishes. After a jacuzzi, enjoy the dramatic views and sunsets from comfortable loungers in the large open terrace, surrounded by graceful lotus ponds.

The villa is managed by Nyoman Sutarya, a great guide who can arrange a personalised discovery program, such as treks to historical and spiritual sites (you can also contact him at Puri Lumbung or Guru Ratna Homestay). The landlord promotes organic farming in the area.

Where to Eat

Apart from local warungs, there are not many restaurants in the area, but all the hotels listed have their own restaurants or *table d'hôte* with good healthy food. However, make sure you don't miss the two little gems below – good food, great views, wondrous welcomes and two occasions to know more about the region.

More than Just Food at Mayong Bali Panorama

Travelling from Lovina and Seririt to Munduk, the view over the valley is stunning when approaching the village of Mayong. There, Made Murjasa and his wife Karsini, both in their late twenties, will welcome you on the flowered roadside in front of their warung – three puppet-sized bamboo tables on a frail wooden balcony, facing a grandiose panorama. The fresh fruit juices are the best of the island thanks to the fertile slopes around, and the healthy food is mostly organic. Try the *dadar Bali*, a sweet roll flavoured with leaves of fragrant screwpine, and filled with grated coconut and palm sugar.

Made and Karsini dreamed to offer more than just great food and are always ready to help you discover the countryside. Walking down towards the village of Bestala, they will introduce you to the amazing diversity of fruits grown there, especially the magic durian (see p. 340), or take you for a cool walk to the waterfalls near Banyuatis.

Grind your own Coffee at Ngiring Ngewedang

This inviting restaurant – its name means "please stop by and come in" – offers great local and international food, with crispy fresh vegetables from the area.

This is also a *warung kopi* (coffee shop), which has been turned into a small museum where you can observe traditional coffee roasting and grinding instruments. The friendly staff will disclose the secrets of coffee making, and show you how to differentiate the strong *robusta* beans from the smooth *arabica* – the local powder is a balanced mixture of both.

What to Do – Around Seririt and Banjar

Just before Seririt, the large village and market centre of Banjar – 10km away from Lovina – offers a few interesting attractions. This is a good starting point to explore the scenic routes of the interior.

♥ ♥ *Rst Gvw Trk*
M 081 75 63 007
081 338 630 449
mayong_bali@yahoo.com
> *On the left side of the road when driving from Seririt to Munduk, 8km after Seririt.*

Besides disclosing endless stories about the magic of their village and its Eden-like gardens, Made and Karsini love to share their vision for Bali's ecological balance: "we can destroy Bali or make it better... it depends on all of us."

♥ *Rst Gvw Cls Shw*
T 0362-41 126
M 082 83 65 146
F 0362-41 840
> *On the side of the main road above Lake Tamblingan.*

The local coffee, sold for about Rp10,000 per pack, makes a great present. Drink it Turkish style – no, Bali style – without filtering it. Just put a spoon at the bottom of your cup with sugar, stir, let rest, enjoy!

> Drive to the village of Banjar, then follow the signs leading to the market, 2km away, and then to the hot springs (1km from the market, a nice walk through quiet countryside). Bemos will drop you at the market or the entrance of Banjar – from there you can find an ojek to the market or the springs.

> The road to the Vihara starts just before Banjar. At Dencarik, turn towards the mountain, then after 2km turn right, following the sign towards Banjar and the Vihara. Bemos can drop you at the Dencarik junction on the main road; from there an ojek will take you to the Vihara.

The *Banjar hot springs* (air panas Banjar) have been arranged in a set of swimming pools. Carved lion faces spit warm water with a high content of sulphur, falling straight from the volcanic rocks uphill. Don't expect an all-natural experience – you'll have to walk 300m past vendors offering cheap bikinis, sarongs and cold drinks. The pool attracts quite a number of tourists, and is equipped with a changing room, lockers and toilets. Yet the warm water and the profusion of vegetation, in all tones of green, yellow and reds, make it a pleasant stop. The warm water is particularly soothing after a hike or a day on a motorbike. A restaurant is ready to welcome hungry travellers just above the pool.

As you come down from the hot springs, turn right to get to the road leading to the *Brahma Arama Vihara*, the most important **Buddhist monastery** in Bali. Offering a gorgeous view over the valley, it has a peaceful atmosphere with incense-filled prayer rooms and golden Buddha statues. The Vihara, however, is not meant to be a tourist site. If you decide to visit it, a number of rules apply: dress modestly (cover your legs and shoulders); walk around silently without smoking, drinking or eating; don't try to enter closed areas; and leave a donation. Travellers can ask to participate in the Vipassana sessions, a plain meditation technique in which clarity of mind is reached by concentrating on one's breathing.

Day Tours starting from Banjar

The roads behind Banjar offer perfect opportunities to discover beautiful rural landscapes. The tours below can be done on foot if you leave early and enjoy walking, or by motorbike. They can also be done with a small 4x4 vehicle. The roads are steep and not in good condition.

A 20km tour through Pedawa

This tour starts from the **Vihara** (see above): just follow the quiet asphalted road uphill after the monastery, climbing past villages, terraced gardens and great views

© Dedok

of steep valleys. At the sixth kilometre you'll enter the village of **Pedawa**, where the road hides below Eden-like gardens of clove trees, coconuts, cocoa and coffee bushes. 2km further, turn right at the T-junction towards **Banyuseri**. Soon after, the road starts winding down towards the west, offering wonderful glimpses of a wide valley floored by rice fields.

The last part takes you through terraced hills, which become drier as you get closer to the sea – it can be quite moon-like in summer, with yellow conical hills towering in front of the ocean. After 20km you'll finally reach the **Banjar market**, where you can get food and drinks. Tired legs can be relieved at the nearby hot springs (see previous page). From Banjar, transportation is available. You can also ask a vehicle from your hotel to wait for you at the hot springs around 3pm.

*If you do this tour on foot, get dropped at the **Vihara** by an ojek, car or bemo – you may arrange it from your hotel the day before. Start walking not later than 7am, to enjoy the first three hours, which are uphill, during the cool hours of the day. Bring a good hat and sunscreen, an ample supply of water and a packed lunch. The road is paved so all you need is comfortable walking shoes. Total length: 20km (9km uphill, 11km downhill).*

A Panoramic Hike through Bestala and Banyuseri

This smaller tour takes you through some of the most scenic areas of Bali on a tiny, badly damaged asphalt road. The road starts downwards for 1km towards the village of **Bestala**. Down in the valley, turn left at the first fork, and follow a small road that goes to the opposite slope, revealing exquisite rice fields on the way. Then go upwards for 1km on the other side through gardens and groves. At the next T-junction, stay on the main road, which turns to the right, and continue climbing for another 3km past stunning views of forested valleys, blue mountains and rice fields. At the next fork, follow the sign towards **Banyuseri** on the left and continue for 1km, until you'll reach another T-junction, where you'll meet the main road that goes down towards the coast. Take a left and follow the road down towards the **Banjar market**, which you'll reach after another 8km.

From there, you can visit the hot springs and find transportation to anywhere in the area.

*Start no later than 7am from your hotel. Arrange for a bemo or an ojek to drop you at the start of the road to **Bestala**, which is found on the left side of the road, just before **Mayong Bali Panorama** (approximately 6km south of Seririt on the road to Munduk). Total length: 14km (5km uphill, 9km downhill).*

In the more affordable category, *Kubu Lalang* keeps alive the relaxed atmosphere that made Lovina attractive in the 1980s. It has one bungalow in the back and two rooms with small verandas, bordered by the terrace of its small beachfront restaurant. The simple rooms are decorated with bright textiles in a laid-back hippy style. Budget travellers who want to treat themselves to a calm retreat will be right at home. The terrace of the restaurant is perfect for snoozing in a hammock, in the company of colourful fishing boats perched on the black sand. Free boat transfers are provided for guests to enjoy lunch or dinner in Lovina.

① ② *4 Rm – Bch*
T 0362-42 207
kubu-lalang@cu-media.com
www.kubu.
balihotelguide.com
> In **Tukad Mungga**, at the end of an earth road crossing through rice fields next to the Bali Taman Hotel.

❀ Sea activities (snorkelling, night snorkelling and sailing) can be arranged for around US$10-15.

Where to Stay – Central Lovina

At home in Saraswati

This green, tasteful homestay offers total peace near the centre of Lovina. Hidden in the coastal coconut fringe, the compound is bordered by a small stream edged with undulating bamboo groves. The beach is a short walk away, through a path leading to a tiny settlement of fishing huts. You can laze on the terrace of your spacious bungalow or sunbathe in the garden, watching the river flow and the coconuts grow.

A separate kitchen is available; guests can order or prepare breakfast, helping themselves to hot and cold drinks, fruits and home-made bread. Delicious food can be enjoyed at the nearby **Warung Bias** or ordered at any time. The helpful, discreet staff make guests feel totally at home. Saraswati is ideal for families, especially those with young children. Airport pickup, excursions to Munduk and other trips can be arranged.

♥ ♥ **② ③** *3 Rm – Htw*
T 0362-41 867
burgel_schaefer@yahoo.com
www.saraswati-bali.com
> Indicated by a sign on the beach side of the road, 2km east of the centre of Lovina, in **Celuk Buluh**.

❀ Burgel and Made, the owners, take care of their environment in every way possible. They use solar heaters and rechargeable batteries, turn organic waste into compost, and supply drinks in glass bottles that can be reused.

Rumah Cantik, the House of Beauty

Find this fantastic homestay, hidden amidst luxuriant vegetation between a village and rice fields, and you'll never want to leave. The two comfortable villas are decorated with taste. Each of them has two bedrooms with fan or air-conditioning and private balconies or terraces.

♥ **③** *4 Rm – Htw (A/C)*
T 0362-42 159
F 0362-41 171
info@lovinacantik.com
www.lovinacantik.com

The Munduk waterfall

© A. A. B. Dianatha K.

♥ ♥ 🐾 (≡) 🦉

T 0362-92 810
F 0362-92 514

© Dedok

♥ 🐾 🦉

T/F 0362-92 818

What to Do – Around Munduk and Tamblingan

Mountain- and nature-lovers could spend two weeks in Munduk without exhausting its attractions. Make sure you follow the scenic route above Lake Tamblingan and Lake Buyan, and from there back down to Munduk – this is one of the most romantic landscapes of the island. Sights of interest along the Tamblingan to Munduk road include the **plastic pyramid** and the spectacular Munduk waterfall, indicated by a sign along the main road, 4km below the Ngiring Ngewedang restaurant. Serious trekkers should try the eight-hour hike to the 1860m peak of Mount Lesong. For most tours you will need a guide, which you can get at any hotel or homestay in Munduk.

Treks and Cultural Discoveries in Munduk

True to the spirit of eco-tourism, *Puri Lumbung Cottages* proposes an endless menu of **treks and tours** to waterfalls, bird watching areas and historical sites. Choices range from an easy two-hour walk in nearby clove and coffee plantations, to a more challenging seven-hour walk from the Tamblingan Lake to Jatiluwih – this beautiful trek will take you through natural forest along an ancient trade path, linking the uplands to the southern slopes of Mt Batukaru. Another favourite is an easy walk through rice terraces to learn about the traditional *subak* irrigation system. Eco-friendly lunch boxes made of bamboo are provided. Walks cost from US$3-8.50/hour depending on the experience and English language skills of the guide. Ask for a massage afterwards.

A wide array of **traditional activity classes** is also available at Puri Lumbung, including weaving, painting, wood carving and playing local musical instruments. You can also ask for boat trips on the nearby lakes.

Lumbung Bali also offers a good choice of trekking and cultural activities, albeit more limited, for Rp25-50,000/hour (the latter for fully English speaking guides).

A Forest Walk to the Temples of Tamblingan

The forest bordering lake Tamblingan harbours a series of temples which provide a great pretext for a pleasant walk around the area. Start at **Pura Pekemitan Kangin**, on the Munduk to Wanagiri road. From Munduk, take the road east for 3km. At the T-junction to Gobleg, go straight on towards Denpasar; the temple is located 300m further on the lakeside. This is the traditional entrance to Lake Tamblingan and Bukit Selat region. Take the steep, narrow stairways down towards the lake, adjacent to the temple. Watch your surroundings for wild animals. If you keep silent, you may encounter monkeys, woodpeckers and small squirrels.

The second temple of **Pura Sangiang Kangin** is situated above the lake, at the end of a cemented stairway. From there, follow the slippery path for 40mn through dense forest towards **Pura Dalem Tamblingan** (Death Temple). Watch out for the hand-like leaves of *lateng*, a shrub no more than 50cm tall that is very itchy. Once at the temple, take a break by the lake to admire the dark blue water and the deep green forest. The path then crosses an open area and climbs up steeply eastward to **Pura Endeg**. This newly renovated temple (previously called **Pura Kentogumi**, which means prosperity in old Balinese) is famous for its symbols of good fortune. Local businessmen come here to pray during the Chinese New Year.

From there on, a 15mn downhill walk leads to the edge of Lake Tamblingan, with **Pura Ulun Danu Tamblingan**, the Lake's Temple, close to the village. Take a leisurely walk around the lake, meet the local fishermen, or take a sip of Balinese coffee in one of the small warungs while stretching out your legs on a long bamboo seat. The fresh breeze from the lake with its sweet smell of the forest will lull you for a while until heading back to the road.

> This tour can be arranged from Lumbung Bali or Puri Lumbung.

♥ While coming down from Lake Tamblingan, you may notice the **plastic pyramid**. Created in 1993 by Teguh Ostenrik, a Jakarta-based artist, the monument carries a message: "The bricks are made of compacted plastic waste. This is to motivate people to not throw away plastic bags, and appreciate their value." The building process was discussed at a public meeting, which became the catalyst for the formation of the **Wisnu Foundation**, an organisation promoting environmental care in Bali.

© A. A. B. Dianatha K.

The plastic pyramid

4 10 Rm – Htw Rst
Trk Ckr Spa
T 0361-419 606
F 0361-413 060
sales@thekalaspa.com
www.thekalasapa.com
> Along the main road
above Lake Buyan.
Book and choose your
package before arriving.

A Health Package at the Kalaspa

Travellers who want to be pampered will be happy in this deluxe spa and health retreat. The main building is a slightly austere structure leading to an open garden in which ten exclusive, well furnished villas are set above a landscape of vegetable farms. The spa centre includes a jacuzzi, sauna and meditation room. Packages include a unique hot and cold black stone massage, aromatherapy and herbal therapy using local plants. Walks and boat tours on the lake can also be organized for a healthy stay.

Durian Anyone?
By Jean-Marie Bompard

Intoxicating and
Addictive

Despite its repelling smell, the taste of the creamy flesh inside a durian is a divine surprise. Eating it "grows on one like opium smoking," as a 19th century British naturalist once noted. Even elephants, tigers, monkeys and tapirs are drawn to the magic fruit. Durian has a "warming effect" on the body and can leave one feeling hungover – the antidote consists in drinking water from empty husks. Locals warn against mixing durian and alcohol, although scientific tests conducted in Singapore indicated that mice fed with a mixture of durian and alcohol had a more steady gait than those fed with only brandy...

Seen from the road leading to Munduk, Bestala looks like any other Balinese village nestled among rice fields. Yet it prides itself on being home to the island's best durians, which grow from ancient trees located on the fertile, well-drained slopes above the village. The name of this yellowish fruit is derived from the Malay word *duri*, or thorn, alluding to its spiky armour. The fruit, as big as a coconut, can weigh up to 3kg and hangs from trees reaching 40m high – turning a garden stroll into a major hazard. But the true power of durian is of a different nature: its soft flesh contains no less than 63 volatile compounds, which contribute to the haunting fragrance, at once repulsive and fascinating, of this king of Asian fruits.

Durians in the market, topped with a small offering of flowers

Unlike the modern cloned varieties imported from Thailand, local durians are grown from local tree varieties selected over centuries, each producing fruits with distinctive colours, shapes, texture and taste. As explained by Karsini from Mayong Bali Panorama: "Some durians are for beginners – they have a soft flavour. Experienced fans prefer the really pungent ones." In Bestala, villagers recognize instantly the tree any fruit comes from. Each mature tree receives a name, referring to its features or to its fruits: "*I tegeh*" means the tall one, "*I tebel*" means the thick one, etc. Indeed, Bestala villagers believe that if a tree is not given a name it may "feel estranged" or "excluded from the community", and may take revenge by dropping its fruits on its owner's head.

Durians are celebrated during the local ritual of *Tumpek Pengatag*, which means invitation or request. Praying for abundant harvests, farmers make offerings to special shrines in the middle of the groves, and to special coconut, durian, clove or mangosteen trees, which represent the rest of the plantation. Unproductive trees also receive offerings, in the hope that this will make them more generous.

There is an economic logic behind these animistic rituals. Durians sell for Rp5-10,000 along the road. A single tree bearing 300 fruits can yield one million rupiah to its owner; with a handful of trees, a farmer can earn much more than a hotel's employee. The harvest is also not especially hard work, requiring nothing more than watching the trees and waiting for the fall of ripe fruits. Indeed, local customs forbid climbing durian trees to pick the fruits. This is believed to jeopardize the next harvest, preventing the durians from falling naturally to the ground and instead causing them to open on the branches, looking like smiling faces mocking the poor farmer, who sees his crop eaten by birds and squirrels.

To enjoy rural Bali at its best, walk with a villager under the durian trees, watch your head and enjoy the unique feeling of peace and abundance surrounded by smiling faces – if not by smiling durians.

A Nourishing Aphrodisiac

In addition to its inimitable taste, the appeal of durian lie in its alleged aphrodisiac properties. Some locals say this comes from the smell, and recommend placing a fruit under one's bed. However, any stimulant virtues of the King of Fruits may simply be due to its energizing power – durians are packed with sugars, proteins, fats, vitamins and minerals. In June 2003, the introduction of durian-flavoured condoms by an AIDS prevention organization in Indonesia was a big success, with 130,000 durian condoms snatched up in the first week of sales.

© Godeliva D. Sari

Sunrise over Pemuteran

> *You can reach Pemuteran by public transport from Lovina, or from the Banyuasri terminal in west Singaraja – look for a vehicle going towards* **Gilimanuk***. If you come from the south with your own vehicle, drive through* **Pupuan** *to admire the rice fields. If you wish to visit west Bali first, you can reach Pemuteran through* **Negara** *and Gilimanuk, although this road is far less attractive. Buses and bemos service the busy road along the southwest coast, from Denpasar to Gilimanuk. From there, catch a bemo to Pemuteran.*

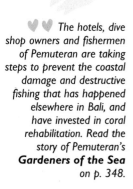

The hotels, dive shop owners and fishermen of Pemuteran are taking steps to prevent the coastal damage and destructive fishing that has happened elsewhere in Bali, and have invested in coral rehabilitation. Read the story of Pemuteran's **Gardeners of the Sea** *on p. 348.*

Isolated at the western tip of Bali, under the watch of majestic, arid mountain slopes, Pemuteran has a peaceful, soothing atmosphere. Less well-known than Lovina's, its black-sand beaches attract smaller numbers of travellers. Divers appreciate its quiet waters devoid of current and its proximity to the wonderful coral reefs of **Menjangan Island**.

The northwest is one of the poorest parts of Bali; many villagers have difficulty finding water during the driest months. The hills behind Pemuteran would be mostly barren if it were not for grapes, which grow all year long on these sunny slopes. This is your only chance to visit a vineyard in Bali and taste the local rosé wine directly from the producer (read our story on p. 346). **Trekking** in the nearby **West Bali National Park** can be organized by most hotels for Rp150-300,000 (see also p. 409). Culture lovers will appreciate the **temples** along the 20km long coastal road from Banyupoh to Pemuteran.

As in all areas yet spared by mass tourism, accommodation is scarce and mostly in the middle to upper price range. Below are some selected places to stay from east to west. All are located along the main road and are easily spotted by their signs.

Where to Stay – Banyupoh

Located 28km west of Seririt, *Segara Bukit* is the first place to stay from the east, and the cheapest in the area. Its thatch-roofed bungalows are set up around an open garden; choose the quieter beachfront rooms to avoid the noise from the neigbouring fish farm. After diving, snorkelling or trekking, stretch out on the clean beach or enjoy the small pool bordered with frangipani trees. The restaurant serves meals for Rp30-40,000, and lets you refill your bottle of mineral water.

❶ ❷ *12 Rm –*
Htw A/C Rst Bch Swp
Div Trk
T 0362-94 749
F 0362-22 471

Where to Stay – Pemuteran

A Garden Life at Pondok Sari

Set in a spacious garden with a lush vegetation of pandanus and frangipani, these comfortable bungalows provide calm and cosy shelters. Enjoy the quiet beach, which is cleaned everyday by the staff and protected for snorkelling and diving. The relaxed beachfront restaurant serves good food at reasonable prices.

Pondok Sari also provided facilities for the first coral reef rehabilitation project in the area, initiated by Yos Diving Centre. The hotel supplies electricity power for the project, as well as donations for the sea guards.

♥ **❸** *22 Rm –*
Htw A/C Rst Bch Swp Div
Trk Bcy Spa
T 0362-94 738
F 0362-92 337
contact@pondoksari.com
www.pondoksari.com

Fight for the Corals at Taman Sari

The spacious cottages of this slightly upmarket resort are set up in a pretty garden with a beachfront pool. The beach is spotless thanks to the staff's daily clean-up program. Savour the cool breeze while enjoying local and Thai dishes for Rp65-75,000 in the thatched restaurant, next to the small library.

Diving and glass bottom cruises are arranged with **Archipelago** or other local dive centres. Make sure you go for a dive in the coral reef rehabilitation site, a few hundred meters from the shore, one of the largest in the world. For snorkelling, boats and equipment can be rented from local villagers, which provides them with additional income.

♥ ♥ **❸ ❹** *31 Rm –*
Htw A/C Rst Bch Swp Div
Trk Shw Bcy
T 0362-93 264; 94 755
Sanur Office:
T 0361-281 241
F 0361-286 879
tamanri@indosat.net.id
www.balitamansari.com

✂ *A description of the coral reef rehabilitation project, including how to make contributions, is on hand in each room.*

Your own villa at Puri Ganesha

❺ 8 Rm – Htw A/C
Rst Bch Swp
Div Trk Shw
T 0362-94 766
F 0362-93 433
www.puriganeshabali.com

> At the western end of
Pemuteran. Book first by
phone or internet.

This luxurious resort consists of four large, two-storey villas, each with a spacious veranda and private seawater swimming pool on 400sq.m of beach front, ideal for families. The cosy restaurant serves healthy food using organic vegetables. Great discovery tours are proposed – like the rice and spice adventure, a culinary experience including cooking classes and visits of markets and village kitchens.The owners collaborate with the Bali Cancer Society to provide free cancer tests for local women.

❸ ❹ 26 Rm – Htw A/C
Rst Bch Swp Div Trk Spa
T 0362-94 798
F 0362-94 799
anekabagus@dps.
centrin.net.id
www.anekahotels.com

At the eastern side of Pemuteran, 1km from the temple of Pura Pulaki, *Aneka Bagus* offers standard rooms in a two-storey building. The more comfortable, thatch-roofed bungalows are set well apart around the garden. Enjoy diving, snorkelling, tours and trekking, or get pampered at the Tropical Spa for US$17-20, while waiting for your dinner.

❺ 32 Rm – Htw
A/C Rst Bch Swp Div
Trk Shw Cls Spa
T 0362-92 312
F 0362-92 313
mbr-bali@indo.net.id
www.matahari-beach-
resort.com

The more luxurious *Matahari Beach Resort and Spa* lets guests learn Balinese culture – from dances, wood and stone carving to local cooking secrets. Walk around the garden to discover the small *wayang* museum displaying a full set of shadow puppet characters, or the exhibition of farmers' tools in the *lumbung* (granary). Local handicrafts or paintings are available at the gallery. After a day under the sun, try massage in the spa or blend your own cup of tea at the traditional teahouse. When the sun goes down, head to the restaurant with its traditional firewood stove (Rp140-225,000).

❹ ❺ 12 Rm – Htw A/C
Rst Bch Swp Div Trk
T 0362-94 746
F 0362-93 449
selinibalipmt@yahoo.com
selini_bali@nangura.net
www.tamanselini.com

At *Taman Selini Bungalows*, accommodation is in comfortable thatched bungalows encircling a flower garden. Only a short walk from the beach, a large pool lets you lounge about and enjoy the sea breeze. For lunch, choose between local dishes or Greek food for Rp40-50,000. Take a *jukung* boat ride with local fishermen, or consult the diving or trekking program. Local masseurs can be called for Rp30-40,000. The staff are trained to separate waste and use it for composting.

Along the coastal side road in **Banyuwedang**, 5km from the Wisnu Airstrip in Pemuteran, *Mimpi Resort Menjangan* covers a large site stretching down to the mangrove-fringed beach. The rooms have a stark and simple design, with open-air bathrooms and a hot-spring tub in the highest priced villas. All the guests can enjoy the lovely, natural hot spring pools filled with thermal water from the Banyuwedang spring. At the western end is the ocean view swimming pool, and a spacious restaurant with a wonderful view of the bay, serving local and international dishes for a reasonable price. The resort has its own dive centre (dive trips cost US$100 for two dives). Trekking can be organized with the **West Bali National Park** for Rp200-350,000.

❹ ❺ *54 Rm – Htw A/C
Rst Bch Swp
Div Trk Bcy Ckr Spa
T 0362-94 497
F 0362-94 498
menjangan@mimpi.com
www.mimpi.com*

An adult turtle at Reefseen's hatchery

© Godeliva D. Sari

Pemuteran – What to Do at Sea

More than just a Dive at Reefseen Aquatics

One of the first dive shops in the area, Reefseen will take you to the most elusive sites in Pemuteran. Two dives cost US$55, and a two-dive trip to Menjangan US$70. Don't miss Kebun Chris (Chris's Garden, named after the owner) in front of the diving counter. This rich coral area, protected from destructive fishing owing to the assiduous care of local divers, is perfect for night dives and snorkelling. A **glass bottom boat** tour allows you to enjoy the underwater world without getting wet.

For a new outlook to north Bali, try **horseback riding** in the mountain or along the beach (US$30 for 1.5 hours). End your visit in the turtle hatchery, where baby **turtles** are happily swimming in small basins before being released to the sea. The eggs are purchased from local villagers, who thus get an incentive to stop eating them and preserve the mature turtles who will later return to lay more eggs. Make a donation to fund the release of a hatchling.

On Saturday nights, **Balinese dances** performed by enthusiastic local youngsters, trained and sponsored by Reefseen, warm up the atmosphere.

*T 0362-92 339
T/F 0362-93 001
dive@reefseenbali.com
www.reefseen.com*

> *opposite* **Pondok Sari**
M 081 338 77 99 41
or c/o **Aneka Bagus**
T 0362-94 798
Tanjung Benoa Office:
T 0361-773 774;
0361-775 438; 775 440
F 0361-775 439
yosbali@indosat.net.id
www.yosdive.com

c/o **Taman Sari**
M 081 24 64 13 70;
081 24 67 94 62
info@archipelagodive.com
www.archipelagodive.com

*Archipelago participates
in the artificial reef
program of Taman Sari,
and conducts talks with
fishermen to prevent
destructive fishing.*

Bali Discovery Tours
*arranges a visit to the nine-
hectare Hatten vineyard in
Sanggalangit for US$60,
including a picnic lunch.
Ask to walk to the southern
part of the vineyard to enjoy
the mountain panorama.*
T 0361-286 283;
F 0361-286 284 (Sanur)
T 0362-31 455 (Lovina)
info@balidiscovery.com
www.balidiscovery.com

A Heart for Corals at Yos Diving Centre

Owned by Yos Amarta, a keen environmentalist, this dive shop initiated coral rehabilitation in the area. Managed by one instructor and four dive masters who speak English and German, Yos Diving has an excellent reputation for safety and professionalism. The operator offers courses from discovery to rescue diver, and a wide choice of diving tours for certified divers. Onshore dive costs US$20, while two dives to Menjangan, Secret Bay and Tulamben cost US$60-95 including lunch. If you don't want to get wet, the counter offers trekking packages in the West Bali National Park (from Rp120,000 for 1-2 hours to Rp300,000 for 5-7 hours, for 1-2 persons).

Based in Taman Sari Hotel, *Archipelago Dive Sarana* is another good international dive centre in the area. The local and friendly staff, which includes an instructor, a rescue diver and a dive master, will show you the most interesting sites in Pemuteran for US$35 per dive. Diving trips to Menjangan or Tulamben can also be arranged for US$70-100 per two dives. PADI courses range from initial discovery to dive master, and can be taught in English and Indonesian. Since "dive safely" is the motto of Archipelago, they offer a maintenance service where you can drop your own equipment for a check-up before getting wet.

A Picnic Lunch at Hatten's Vineyard

Viticulture was introduced to north Bali as early as the 16th century by Portuguese traders, enabling local farmers to take advantage of the sunshine and cool coastal breezes to grow grapes all year long. However, wine-making is a recent introduction.

Rai Budiarsa, the founder of Hatten, was managing the traditional rice-wine making business of his family when he had the idea to produce wine...from grapes. A graduate in agriculture, Rai Budiarsa saw an opportunity to turn the great grapes of north Bali into wine that would suit the tastes of tourists – a smart business move, considering the heavy taxes on imported wine. In 1994, he launched Hatten Wines with the help of French winemaker Vincent Desprat, who found a way to turn the Muscat-tasting varieties grown locally into a good rosé wine, which goes well with the warm climate of Bali. Try it after a pleasant tour of the sunny slopes.

Temples of the Northwest Coast

The main road from Seririt to Pemuteran is lined with a few temples, wedged between the arid mountains and the black-sand coast. Each holds a different symbolic function related to the life of the region.

The first from the west, *Pura Melanting* is also known as the "main market temple" (Pura Pasar Agung) around Pemuteran; visitors come here to pray for good fortune in trade. Along the main entrance is a dragon statue with a lotus flower on its back, representing the path of the temple's protecting goddess. The black-stone temple looks particularly impressive during the rainy season, with the grassy hill in the background. Ask the *pemangku* (priests) for permission before entering the inside gallery, as a short purification is required first.

Known as the key temple of Pemuteran, *Pura Pulaki* is built at the foot of a black-stone hill facing the beach. It is devoted to Danghyang Nirartha, the great religious leader of the 16th century. The view is wonderful at dusk when the sun falls gracefully on the front side of the temple, creating an almost surreal atmosphere. Oddly, Chinese style ornaments were added to the building during a recent renovation. Just opposite the Pulaki Temple stands *Pura Pabean*, dedicated to the dearest wife of Danghyang Nirartha. The site used to be a port for trading boats needing to refill their provisions. Small boat still stop here to pray for a safe journey. The temple lies on a spacious ground near the ocean, in a cool and serene atmosphere. Below the main temple, the older *Pura Segara*, a few piles of raw stones with weird human-like shapes, is still guarding the shore.

> Surprise your friends! Bring back home a bottle of rosé wine from Bali, available in supermarkets for about Rp75,000.

© Godeliva D. Sari

Ancient stone statues at Pura Segara

> Pura Melanting is located 1km west of Segara Bukit Cottage in Banyupoh. From the main road, follow the hillside road for another 300m to the parking lot. The dark red bemos driving from Singaraja to Gilimanuk can drop you on the main road in front of the temple. From there you can walk to the temple or take an ojek for Rp3,000. Pura Pulaki is on the Seririt-Pemuteran main road, 900m east from the border of Pemuteran and 1.2km west of Pura Melanting.

Gardeners of the Sea
By Titiek Pratiwi

Until 1990, Pemuteran was a small fishing village and one of the poorest communities in Bali. "The land here is so dry and poor that most people even refused a free parcel of land in Pemuteran" recalled Putu Suyasa, the *kelian adat* (traditional village head).

Things started to change in the late 1980s when a tour operator, Agung Prana, decided to build a hotel in the area to take advantage of the unspoiled marine environment. "The people, like its land, were poor and tourism brought another option for them to improve their lives," says Prana. Through informal talks, he consulted the leaders of the community. Wanting his staff to consist mostly of local people, Prana provided them with training in English and tourism. The next step was to initiate simple, down-to-earth beach cleaning and the planting of trees to provide shade. "It took some time to get into the heart of the people, and longer to make them set for tourism and environmental conservation." Gradually, other tourist operators followed to the area.

Yet, even though more visitors came to Pemuteran to enjoy its marine life, the coast started to suffer from environmental degradation as elsewhere in Bali (read "Endangered Seas" on p. 297). Destructive fishing using bombs or cyanide became increasingly frequent, and in 1998, the ocean warming brought by El Niño turned rich corals into deserts of rubble. As fish disappeared from the dying area, fishermen and tourism operators saw their income dwindle.

The Sea Wards

The community was prompt to react. In 1998, the villagers, with financial support from tourist operators in the area, formed a group of *pecalang laut* (community marine patrol), the first of its kind in Bali. For several months, they managed to contain blasting and cyanide use. Yet, as the destructive practices lessened, so did the motivation of the villagers. Weak management brought

Coral growing on a metal structure

© Karang Lestari Foundation

the marine patrol to an halt. "The boat used for patrolling was broken and the money to buy gasoline and salaries was spent for other uses," recalls Narayana Deva, manager of the local *Karang Lestari* (Coral Conservation) Foundation. Soon the bomb and cyanide users were back near the shores of Pemuteran.

In June 2000, concerned with the damage, Yos Amerta, a local dive shop owner, embarked on a coral rehabilitation project with support of scientists from the Global Coral Reef Alliance (GCRA). The success of a first trial encouraged Prana and Narayana to broaden the program. Enlisting the support of the GCRA, they developed a 270m long rehabilitation area, covering an area of 2 hectares – which the GCRA says is the largest of its kind in the world.

To gain the support of local people, the promoters of the project used art performances such as *wayang wong* (stage shows with themes from shadow puppets stories), dances and traditional music to convey the importance of environmental conservation. "It didn't take long to gain local support since the community had experienced the full impacts of marine destruction," admits Prana.

To the delight of fishermen, the installed structures brought back fish and tourists to the previously destroyed areas. Even dolphins have returned. This motivated villagers to revive the local marine patrol. The village head even issued a traditional decree (*awig-awig*) to protect the coral reef structures, forbidding ornamental fish catching and all destructive fishing methods in Pemuteran area. Punishments for breaking the decree start from a fine of 200kg of rice and can go as far as banishment from the village. In June 2002, Prana and his business partner Narayana, along with the community of Pemuteran, formed the *Karang Lestari* Foundation to ensure their project's sustainability. As Narayana put it, "the long-term goal is to switch from hunting fish to farming them, secure sustainable fisheries and provide tourism attractions for future generations."

Electrifying the Corals

While coral rehabilitation is usually promoted by immersing artificial reefs made of concrete, the method used in Pemuteran adds a bit of a twist. Cage-like metallic structures are charged with a low voltage current to accelerate the growth rate of coral, and increase its chances to survive environmental stress. The nursed corals, especially soft corals, grow more rapidly than normal, forming dense arrays of branches with dazzling colours. Some coral species grow particularly fast, up from the usual one centimetre per year to around one centimetre per month.

Enquiries and Donations:
Karang Lestari Foundation
(contact person: Putu Yasa)
c/o Taman Sari
0362-93 264; 94 755
narayanadeva2000@ yahoo.com.

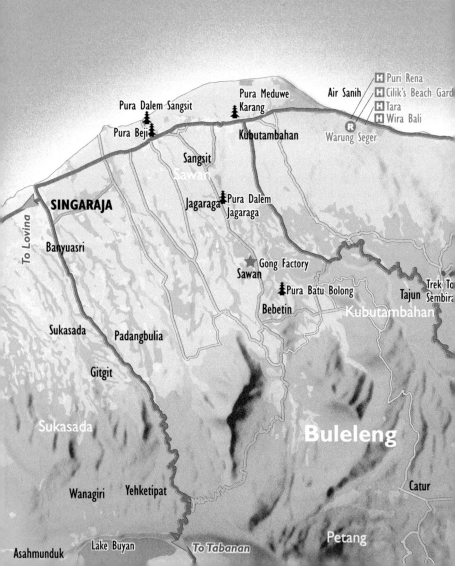

Bali Sea

north

Pura Dalem Sangsit

Pura Beji

Pura Meduwe
Karang

Air Sanih

H Puri Rena
H Cilik's Beach Gard
H Tara
H Wira Bali
R Warung Seger

Kubutambahan

Sangsit

Sawan

SINGARAJA

Jagaraga

Pura Dalem
Jagaraga

Banyuasri

Gong Factory

Sawan

Pura Batu Bolong

Tajun

Trek To
Sembira

Bebetin

Kubutambahan

Buleleng

To Lovina

Sukasada

Padangbulia

Gitgit

Sukasada

Catur

Wanagiri

Yehketipat

Lake Buyan

To Tabanan

Petang

Asahmunduk

Scale 1:160 000

0 km   2 km   4 km

N

north

uri Bagus Ponjok Batu

Pura Ponjok Batu

Pondok Sembiran

cung

Bondalem

Gaia-Oasis

Tejakula

Sembiran

Sembiran Bali Aga

Tejakula

Tejakula

Agung Bali Nirwana

Les

Trek to
Yeh Mampeh

Sambirenteng

Poincianna

Alam Anda

Kutuh

Penuktukan

Tembok

Subaya

Yeh Mampeh
Waterfall

To Amed

Dausa

Sukawana

Kintamani

Daup

Songan

anga

To Bangli

Toyabungkah   Lake Batur

Trunyan

Scale 1:110 000

0 km   2 km

north

Kubu Lalang Ⓗ

Bayu Kartika Ⓗ
Angsoka Ⓗ
Jasmine Ⓡ
Kakatua Ⓡ
Spice Diving Ⓞ
Cyber Spice Ⓜ
Agung Massage Ⓢ

Celuk Agung

Tukad
Mungga

Warung Bias Ⓡ
Sol Lovina Ⓗ
Saraswati

Rambutan

Kalibukbuk

Anturan

Spice Cafe Ⓡ Ⓡ Khi khi
Indiana Ⓢ Ⓡ
Ⓡ Octopus Garden
Agus Ⓗ Rumah Cantik
Ⓗ Bagus Ⓞ Ⓗ
Spice Water
Worlds
Temukus ★ Sapi Gerumbungan
Kaliasem

N

Scale 1:60 000

0 km   1 km

Lovina Be ★

Temukus

Bali Sea

Ratu Ayu Ⓗ
Zen Ⓗ
Ume Anyar

Tukad Saba

Seririt

Dencarik

Kalianget

To Pemuteran

Kalopaksa

Petemon

Bubunan

Banjar

Grya Seri Ⓗ ★ Buddhist Monastery
★ Hot spring   Sidetapa

Corot

Cemp

Pangkungparuk

Ringdikit

Trek Vihara-Banjar

Trek Bestala-Banjar

Ularan

Mayong

Mundukbestala

Banyuseri

Busungbiu

Bestala

Unggahan

👁 Ⓡ Mayong Bali
Panorama

Tirt

Busungbiu

Titab

Pelapuan

Bany

To Tabanan

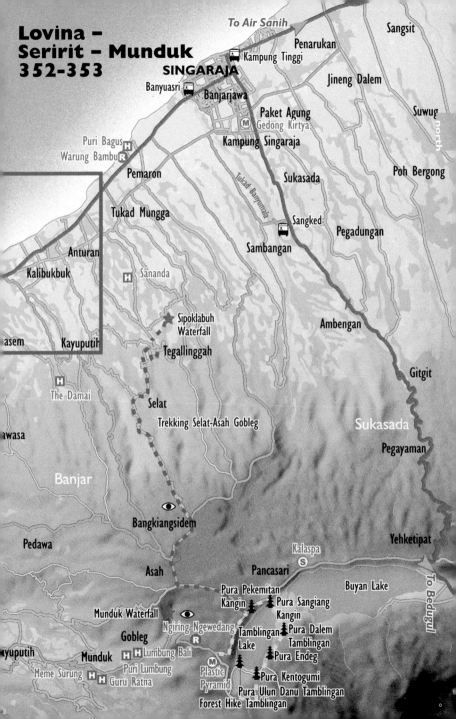

Lovina –
Seririt – Munduk
352-353

To Air Sanih

Sangsit

Penarukan

Kampung Tinggi

SINGARAJA

Jineng Dalem

Banyuasri

Banjarjawa

Suwug

Paket Agung

Gedong Kirtya

Kampung Singaraja

Poh Bergong

Puri Bagus
Warung Bambu

Pemaron

Tukad Banyumala

Sukasada

Sangked

Pegadungan

Tukad Mungga

Sambangan

Anturan

Sananda

Kalibukbuk

Ambengan

Kayuputih

Sipoklabuh
Waterfall

Gitgit

asem

Tegallinggah

The Damai

Selat

Sukasada

Trekking Selat-Asah Gobleg

Pegayaman

awasa

Banjar

Bangkiangsidem

Yehketipat

Pedawa

Kalaspa

Asah

Pancasari

Buyan Lake

To Bedugul

Munduk Waterfall

Pura Pekemitan
Kangin

Pura Sangiang
Kangin

Ngiring Ngewedang

Gobleg

Tamblingan
Lake

Pura Dalem
Tamblingan

Lumbung Bali

Munduk

Pura Endeg

ayuputih

Puri Lumbung

Meme Surung

Guru Ratna

Plastic
Pyramid

Pura Kentogumi

Pura Ulun Danu Tamblingan

Forest Hike Tamblingan

north

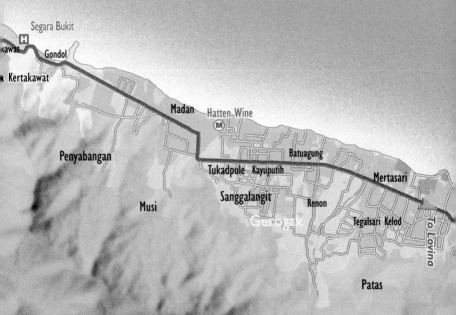

Scale 1:110 000

0 km   2 km

N

north

Segara Bukit

kawat

Gondol

Kertakawat

Madan

Hatten Wine

Penyabangan

Tukadpule   Kayuputih

Batuagung

Mertasari

Sanggalangit

Renon

Musi

Gerogak

Tegalsari Kelod

To Lovina

Patas

Mendoyo

Yehembang Kauh

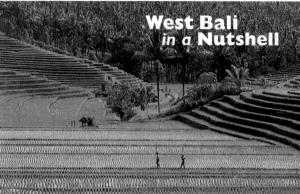

West Bali
in a **Nutshell**

© Leonard Lueras

Rice terraces near Pupuan

Hard Facts

- *1680sq.km – 30 percent of the area of Bali*
- *600,000 inhabitants – a fifth of Bali's population*
- *Two districts: Jembrana (capital: Negara) and Tabanan*
- *360 people per sq.km (465 in Tabanan, 260 in Jembrana)*
- *30,000ha of rice fields (40 percent of Bali's rice area)*
- *50,000ha of forest (40 percent of Bali's forests)*
- *Highest peak: Mt Batukaru, 2276m*
- *Largest lake: Danau Beratan, 37sq.km*
- *The remains of people living on the coast 2,000 years ago were found near Gilimanuk.*

Fertile Crops and Dark Forests

Heirs to the kingdoms of Tabanan and Jembrana, the two western districts of Bali control much of the island's natural wealth. Covered by thick forests, the dome of Mt Batukaru towers over **Tabanan**. Together with Lake Beratan, the sacred mountain provides water to a vast domain of gentle slopes converted to fertile rice terraces. The upper hills nourish famed coffee plantations.

At the western tip of the island, the rugged mountains of **Jembrana** are mostly forested, and home to the **West Bali National Park**. Close to Java and underpopulated, this region has always attracted outsiders, some seeking a livelihood, some fleeing natural disasters, some hiding from political or religious persecution. In 1930, the opening of the ferry between East Java and **Gilimanuk**, at the western end of Jembrana, reinforced its role as a gateway to Java. Large communities of Chinese, Javanese, and Bugis have settled in the area, leasing land from the local lords to establish cash crops. Jembrana also harbours several Christian villages, and the largest Muslim population in Bali (45,000 people). Taking advantage of its large tract of unoccupied land, the government used Jembrana to relocate refugees from the 1963 eruption of Mt Agung, as well as landless farmers from overcrowded areas of Bali.

The Forgotten Kingdoms

Very little has been written about the early history of Tabanan and Jembrana. According to royal chronicles, **Tabanan** came under the suzerainty of King Airlangga in 1037 AD. Then it is said to have been ceded to one of Prince Gajah Mada's generals, Arya Kenceng, after the invasion of Bali by the Javanese Majapahit army in 1343 AD. Arya Kenceng established his court in the village of Pucangan, and his son later moved it to what is now the town of Tabanan.

At the beginning of the 18th century, the kingdom of **Mengwi**, Tabanan's eastern neighbour, progressively gained control of west Bali, extending its rule as far as the Hindu kingdom of **Blambangan** in East Java. The visionary rulers of Mengwi mobilised their people to build the irrigation networks and terraced rice fields which make Tabanan the rice bowl of Bali.

In the 19th century, constant struggles with its neighbouring kingdoms ended in the final defeat of Mengwi, which was brought down by Tabanan, Badung, and Klungkung in 1891. In grand Balinese fashion, the king of Mengwi committed *puputan*, marching into death during the final battle rather than surrendering to his enemies.

Having gained its independence, Tabanan was soon to lose it to the Dutch. One of the last kingdoms to capitulate, Tabanan fell to the colonisers in 1906. The Dutch meted out harsh punishment to the kingdom for having allied itself with Badung, their fiercest enemy, and razed the royal palace of Tabanan. Today, only the subsidiary courthouse of **Kerambitan** can be seen.

Mostly covered with forested mountains, the sparsely populated **Jembrana** has remained marginal in Balinese history. It was the second Balinese kingdom to fall to the Dutch, immediately after Buleleng, in 1850. Like the other settlers before them, The Dutch established large plantations of cotton, cacao, coconut, coffee, teak, and tobacco in Jembrana.

Suicide by Overdose

In 1903, the Dutch were at odds with the rulers of Tabanan over the issue of suttee. Following this old Indian custom, the widows of the deceased raja threw themselves onto his cremation pyre, drawing protests from humanists in Holland. But as the new king and his son came to negotiate this matter with the Duch officials, they were thrown in jail. Painter Nieuwenkamp recounted with indignation how they were kept in a dark cell without food. Threatened with exile, both men took their lives – the son by an overdose of opium, and the king by stabbing himself in the throat with a betel nut chopper (in W.O.J. Nieuwenkamp: First European Artist in Bali, by Bruce Carpenter).

Ceremony in Taman Ayun, Mengwi

Land and Freedom

Tabanan and Jembrana, for opposite reasons, were among the few Balinese districts under direct Dutch rule – Jembrana because it was among the first conquered, and Tabanan because it had fiercely resisted the colonisers. In Tabanan, the Dutch confiscated the land under the domain of the kings, and distributed it to the *banjar*, or local communities. Hence, while in the rest of Bali the land remained controlled by a few landlords, the peasants of Tabanan had greater control over their rice fields. This may have contributed to making Tabanan the most productive rice area of Bali.

Land reform came again to the forefront in west Bali after World War II and Indonesian independence. Conservationist and revolutionary movements fighted each other from 1950 to 1965. At stake was the very basis of Balinese social order – whether or not Bali should remain a feudal caste society. The revolutionaries, led by the Indonesian Communist Party (PKI), advocated seizing the land from the aristocracy and distributing it amongst the peasants.

Their leader, Suteja, then Bali's governor, was a minor member of Jembrana's royal family, while his main ally, Gede Puger, was from Buleleng in north Bali. The leftist movements were strongly anchored in the northern and western regencies. In these areas opened to external influences, the people are said to be more keen on democracy than southern or eastern Balinese, and less ready to conform to the caste system.

The land reform movement came to a tragic end in 1965, when an aborted coup d'état in Jakarta was attributed to the PKI. This provided justification for the massacre of all those suspected of sympathising with the communists. The palace of Jembrana was reduced to rubble. Yet in the following years during the rule of Soeharto, the people of Tabanan were among those most active against the attempts of the government to take control of rice cultivation (read side column).

The Rice Strike

The Balinese tried to resist the attempts of President Soeharto's New Order government (1966-1998) to control their rice production, in the name of modernisation, through the so-called "green revolution" (read the Subak feature on p. 361). One of these policies requested that farmers sell all their harvest to a state agency. The subak (rice growers' associations) of a whole river basin of Tabanan refused this order and, to show their determination, ceased to plant rice during three consecutive seasons.

© Djuna Ivereigh

Ploughing a rice field

Best Kept Traveller's Secrets

The two western districts and former kingdoms of Tabanan and Jembrana are a traveller's dream, offering the best of traditional rural Bali with very few visitors. The only areas where you are likely to feel a dense tourist presence are around Lake Beratan and the sea temple of Tanah Lot. Outside of these well-known sites, you'll be in the sole company of local farmers or wild animals while admiring the best rice terraces in Bali, walking along endless beaches beaten by fierce waves, dreaming in front of sunsets on top of hidden cliffs, and trekking up jungle slopes to mossy temples. In Jembrana, you can also watch spectacular *jegog* dances featuring giant bamboo instruments, or visit temples, mosques, and churches in a single day.

© Dominique Clarisse

The temple at Lake Beratan

When driving towards the western tip of the island, the proximity of Java and the presence of migrants are felt more and more. In a subtle grey area around Negara, the landscape starts to fill with mosques, men wearing *peci* (a round, black velvet hat worn by Indonesian and Malay Muslims), restaurants serving *nasi padang* (the spicy, curry-based cuisine from West Sumatra popular throughout Indonesia) and Javanese-style wooden carts pulled by plodding water buffalo.

Coming from the south, the heavily-trafficked road heading west towards Gilimanuk leads first to the busy district capital of *Tabanan*. Most tourists pay only a brief visit to this area for the famed **Pura Tanah Lot**, perched on an isolated rock with gorgeous sunset views – expect to share this icon of Bali with hundreds of other visitors and the usual swarm of vendors preying on tourist sites.

Beyond Tanah Lot, the surroundings of Tabanan offer interesting cultural sites, such as the **palaces** of the Tabanan princes, the ceramic village of **Pejaten**, and the **Subak Museum** dedicated to rice cultivation. Good accommodation in all price ranges can be found along the quiet coastline, or in the interior.

Getting There and Around

The westbound highway from Denpasar passes through the town of **Tabanan**, *then follows the coast through* **Negara** *before reaching the busy transit harbour of* **Gilimanuk**, *where car and passenger ferries can be boarded to Java. Buses from Denpasar's* **Ubung** *Terminal depart every hour towards Gilimanuk (about 1h to Tabanan, 3h to Negara, 4h to Gilimanuk). The densely-populated area around Tabanan is served by bemos. In the rest of the countryside, public transport is scarce, and you'll have to rely on ojeks. The best option is to rent a vehicle. Alternatively, ask your hotel to provide transport.*

Practicalities

West Bali has few facilities for tourists. ATMs and money-changing services can be found in the main towns of Tabanan, Negara, and Gilimanuk. Along the road and in the towns, private telecommunications offices (wartel) provide telephone and fax access, and occasionally internet connections (warnet). For a good internet access, stop at the Bali Camp, a modern software company hidden in the hills near Baturiti (read Bedugul and Lake Beratan on p. 385).

Climbing above Tabanan, small roads lead to *Mt Batukaru* and *Jatiluwih*, where farmers are still growing beautiful, long-stemmed native rice which has disappeared elsewhere in favour of modern varieties (read the story about *subak*, next page). This is an endearing area for nature lovers, with great eco-friendly lodgings from where you can set out trekking or bird-watching. Besides **Pura Batukaru**, one of Bali's holiest sanctuary, the mountain slopes harbour many hidden temples, including a mysterious **temple of thieves**.

Further north, *Bedugul* and *Lake Beratan* are popular with local tourists, who come here during week-ends to relax in the cool, misty atmosphere of this mountain area and savour the fruits and vegetables grown on its slopes. The area lacks good lodgings, except for a few resorts around Pacung. Its main attractions are the romantic lake temple of **Pura Ulun Danu Batur**, and the forested **Botanical Garden** (*Kebun Raya*).

West of Mt Batukaru, the mountain road from *Antosari* to *Pupuan* and the coastal area near **Lalanglinggah** offer awesome landscapes of rice fields undulating on the horizon, coffee plantations, and waterfalls. Rarely visited by tourists, it has exquisite boutique hotels in the middle-to-high end of the price range – a honeymooners' paradise.

Driving further west, the coastal road passes through *Jembrana*, a sparsely populated district with quiet beaches and good **surfing**, catholic **churches** in the mountains, and Hindu **temples** by the sea. It offers a limited choice of accommodations, from inexpensive homestays and good bungalows near the beaches around **Medewi** and **Negara**, to a luxurious mountain resort near **Lake Palasari**.

At the northwestern end of Bali is the *West Bali National Park*, created to protect the nearly-extinct Bali starling (read the story on p. 414). This area is perfect for **bird-watching**, **trekking**, and **diving**, but it lacks decent accommodations and is best accessed from Negara or **Pemuteran** in north Bali.

© Elizabeth E. Listyowati

Rainforest in the Botanical Garden

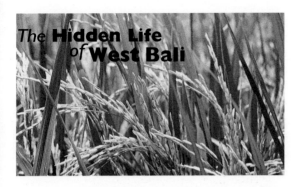

The Hidden Life of West Bali

Subak: the Green Democracy
By Degung Santikarma

A Story of Frogs and Kites

I am the grandson of a rice farmer from Denpasar. I remember as a boy how my grandfather would take us kids to his rice field in the afternoons, where we would fly kites, catch eels, frogs, and small fish, and help pull out the weeds. I especially loved planting season, when my grandfather would let me sit on the back of the buffalo as it pulled the iron plough through the rich, dark earth. When it was time to transplant the delicate green shoots, however, we were shooed away. Only when the rice had turned tall and heavy would we be allowed back, to wade and cavort in the muddy water.

My grandfather passed away before I was old enough to realise what we were losing. For now that our grandfathers are gone, we are leaving their way of life. We become office workers, traders, and tour guides. Prime rice fields are being converted into shopping arcades, resorts, and golf courses. And as industries and hotels swallow gallons of water, rice paddies become dry, destroying the very landscapes that tourists come to admire.

Besides being a farmer, my grandfather was also a *pekaseh*, a head of a local water-use group called a *subak*. Each of these groups are comprised of a hundred or so farmers sharing the same source of water. They are responsible for maintaining Bali's complex network of irrigation structures, while coordinating planting and harvesting times to maximise water availability while minimising the spread of pests. And because water is the holiest resource on Bali, they are also in charge of organising the cycles of ceremonies connected with rice cultivation.

Engineers and Priests

Traditionally, *subak* groups were independent of other social units such as the village, the royal court, or the family lineage. In the era of warring kings, the *subak* stood aside, beholden only to solidarity among rice growers, whether they were landowners or tenants. Heads of *subak* were not chosen based on their lineage, but for their experience in rice farming, their knowledge of the Balinese calendar, and their honesty and diplomacy. For besides the flow of water and rituals, *subak* heads must maintain smooth social relationships, coordinating planting calendars among dozens of people and supervising the maintenance of kilometres of waterways. They mediate conflicts over water use and levy fines on *subak* members who violate the group's rules.

Modern-day *subak* heads struggle under different challenges. I recently took a walk through my neighbourhood with Kak, the last rice farmer on our street. He explained that so many people had stopped farming in the area that four local *subak* groups had been combined into one. As we walked, Kak pointed out water channels that constantly jam and overflow. Balinese consume more and more plastic, and without proper waste management, most of the island's garbage gets dumped in waterways. Kak also bemoaned the fact that factory runoff, pesticides, and detergents had killed most of the frogs, eels, and fish that used to make up a large part of his family's diet.

The New Rice, from Miracle to Disaster

Kak's problems started in the late 1960s, when the Indonesian government got on board the "Green Revolution", which promised to increase rice yields

© Ujung Wicaksono

A shrine in the rice fields

Subak *Temples*
Each subak *has its own temple, as well as smaller field shrines called* bedugul. *In larger sanctuaries, such as* **Pura Batukaru** *or the lake temples* (**Pura Ulun Danu**), *priests traditionally conducted rituals for hundreds of* subak, *and scheduled water flows and planting times across huge watersheds.*

through new varieties, continuous planting, the use of fertilisers and pesticides, and the "rational" management of irrigation. In 1967, backed by oil funds and international aid, the Indonesian government launched a program called "Massive Guidance", which directed farmers to stop planting traditional Balinese rice and to begin planting the new varieties. Because these rice strains are fast-growing, enabling three harvests per year rather than the traditional two, increased prosperity was expected.

The government, with assistance from foreign experts, also took over from the water temples the responsibility of determining irrigation flows and of scheduling planting times. Leaving such important matters in the hands of priests was thought to be foolish at best backwards, and superstitious at worst.

At first, rice yields indeed rose, but the chemical inputs necessary to grow the new rice were offsetting much of the farmers' profits. By the mid-1970s, farmers were reporting plagues of pests, as well as confusion and conflict over water use. Scientists and bureaucrats did not recognise that over hundreds of years, Balinese had worked out a complex irrigation and planting scheduling system. Besides maximising water availability for everyone, they coordinated planting times to starve rice pests during fallow periods. Instructed to keep planting continuously, farmers had to use ever-increasing amounts of pesticides, and pests became increasingly resistant to the chemicals.

The technocrats also failed to appreciate how *subak* rice management was intimately woven into social life. As the government constructed new water works with little regard for ancient water-sharing agreements, conflicts broke out between *subak*. Farmers switched from collective management to *tulak sumur* ("every man for himself") and pests spread easily between fields planted without coordination. The mechanisation of farming forced many women out of agriculture, ignored the ideals of social solidarity of the *subak*, and gave the government unprecedented control over people's lives.

The Lost Granaries

The lumbung, *or rice granary, was an attribute of Balinese houses until the 1970s. Their shape varies from area to area, but the best-known is a small structure with a grass roof in the shape of a horseshoe, built on stilts to ward off rats, over a wooden work platform. The Green Revolution pushed farmers to sell their crop to a government agency instead of keeping it. Increasing cash needs also led farmers to rely on the market to buy and sell rice. Traditional* lumbung *can still be seen in mountain areas — and in the many hotels which have adopted their name and shape as a trademark.*

© Elizabeth E. Listyowati

Traditionally-harvested rice

© IThe Natural Guide

A modern irrigation gate

Green Chips

An American anthropologist, Stephen Lansing, created a computer model to gauge the effectiveness of various methods of irrigation control. He found that when water temples set the cropping patterns for the subak, *water stress and pest damage were minimised, and yields were maximised.*

Controlling Rice, Controlling Lives

Kak invited me to talk to Pak Wayan, now the head of our area's *subak*. He told me how, several years into the Green Revolution, some farmers decided they had had enough. "We didn't want to plant the new rice anymore. It was expensive to buy the chemicals and we had to go into debt. The old rice was not only naturally pest-resistant and able to withstand drought, it stored better and it didn't get beaten down by the rains. Sure, we grew less of it, but what we grew tasted a lot better." But when Pak Wayan planted his field with old Balinese rice, the police came and tore it up. "They said we were backwards and against the development of Indonesia."

One of Pak Wayan's friends, Raka, chimed in, explaining that the "New Order" government, which ruled Indonesia between 1966 and 1998, never liked the *subak* groups. "They said that the Green Revolution was meant to help the farmers, but in fact it was also an opportunity to control us." Raka argued that the *subak*'s tradition of autonomy and democracy, and its ideal of providing water to its members according to their needs rather than their class or caste status, was more than President Soeharto's autocratic regime could swallow.

Revenge of the Subak

By the 1990s, even government officials and international aid agencies were acknowledging the problems caused by government management of irrigation. The Asian Development Bank recommended returning the control of irrigation to the *subak*, with the government merely providing funds to maintain the water channels. The water temple priests, once seen by the technocrats as symbolic of primitive, pre-rational thought, were again viewed as masters of the art of large-scale irrigation and natural pest control. A new project funded by the World Bank advocated "Integrated Pest Management", encouraging farmers to do what they had been doing for centuries, i.e. using a careful balance of mostly natural means to control rice pests.

The Road Ahead

The fall of President Soeharto in 1998 and the changes at work since then may – or may not – bring renewed hopes for the *subak*. A law passed in 2000 increases the autonomy of local governments. Across Indonesia, people are searching for ways to revive old institutions to manage natural resources. But they do it with different agendas, mixing genuine hopes for strengthening local democracy with disguised attempts at seizing new sources of power and money. Meanwhile, the World Bank is pushing for "reforms" aimed at privatising water management, amidst protests from NGOs.

Since 1998, long-suppressed environmental organisations have more room to fight for better uses of the embattled natural resources of Bali. Groups like Bali Fokus and Bhakti Wahana Bali push hotels to reduce water use, and government to pass waste management bills. But some changes will be hard to reverse. Made Suarnatha of the Wisnu Foundation explains: "It would take strong will on the part of communities to revitalise the *subak*. The tourism and market economy has taken many young people and resources away."

When tourism arrivals dropped after a bomb exploded in a nightclub in 2002, it became popular to "reconsider agriculture as a priority", as stated by Ida Ayu Agung Mas of the Sua Bali Foundation – who had for long questioned an economy over-dependent on tourism. Bali Governor I Dewa Made Beratha declared 2003 as the year to promote agriculture. How much this will be followed by actions benefiting *subak* remains to be seen. Many young people in Bali are not necessarily ready, or willing, to go back to farming – nor is it clear where they would find the land and the means to do so.

Standing at the crossroads, pulled in different directions by rapid social, political, and market changes, the grandsons of rice farmers are facing tough choices. Only they can decide whether to either sell away, or to find a new life for a centuries-old heritage of fine-tuned management of the holiest resource of the gods' island.

A Project for Whom?

In 1997, the Asian Development Bank, which had loaned Indonesia US$33.6 million for a Bali Irrigation Sector Project, concluded in its Project Evaluation report: "The designers' limited understanding of farmer-managed irrigation resulted in shortcomings in the Project. Equitable sharing of water and watershed concerns were overlooked. Subak's capacities for operation and maintenance were weakened. None of the beneficiaries reported a perceptible gain in output from the Project."

Water flowing through a bamboo pipe

© Dominique Clarisse

Sunset at Pura Tanah Lot

Tabanan

> *Tabanan can be reached by bus in about one hour from Denpasar's **Ubung** terminal. To get around Tabanan, take one of the bemos awaiting passengers from 4am to 6pm at the **Pesiapan** terminal in the northwest part of the town. The villages around Tabanan are easy to reach by bemo or ojek. However, the beach areas at the end of small roads are rather isolated, so it is better to have your own vehicle if you stay there.*

Arriving from the south, most travellers pay a visit to **Pura Tanah Lot**. Rising from the ocean at the southeast of Tabanan, this temple has become an emblem of Bali and is predictably packed with shops and tourist buses. Further west, facing a revitalising landscape of strong waves, the coast around **Yehgangga** and **Pasut** is a perfect escape from the crowds, with a good choice of accommodations at various prices.

In the heart of Bali's rice belt, **Tabanan** is a medium-sized town bustling with small industries and Chinese-owned shops. East- and westbound traffic streams in and out, connecting the south of Bali with the port of Gilimanuk, the gateway to Java, at the western end of the island. Travellers who want to stay near Tabanan can find good accomodations in **Kerambitan** or **Umabian**. This densely-populated area offers few natural attractions, apart from **walks** along the beach or to the **monkey forest** of **Alas Kedaton**. Visitors interested in culture and history can choose between a tour of the royal family **palaces** in **Kerambitan**, a visit to the ceramic makers of **Pejaten**, or an immersion into the complexity of rice cultivation at the **Subak Museum**.

Where to Stay – Along the Coast

Coming from Tabanan, a small road turns towards **Yehgangga** – follow the signs to the Waka Gangga resort. This beautiful beach is located at the end of a sacred river (its name means "Gange Waters" in reference to the Hindu holy river). It is popular with local people who come here for ceremonies or, more simply, to relax. Despite its holy name, the entrance to the beach can be dirty at times with waste discarded by local visitors or carried by the river.

A Night in the Paddies at Waka Gangga

This resort is designed to let visitors experience the magic of rice fields to the fullest. Each of the luxurious bungalows is a circular, thatched roof wooden hut, with large windows facing boundless rice terraces descending towards the ocean. The large bathrooms are perfect for honeymooners.

In homage to the *subak* heritage, rice grows at the foot of each hut and small paddies circle the teak decks in front of each room. The simple, elegant design uses natural element such as stones, coconut wood, and white cotton, and gives the priority to recycled timber – from old electrical poles to carved temple beams. The resort features a large pool and a cosy spa decorated with antiques. Built above the beach, the hut-shaped restaurant serves excellent local, Asian, and international cuisine (about Rp100-150,000). Ask for guided tours and sunset walks of the surroundings.

In a more affordable price range, *Bali Wisata Bungalows* is a simple, friendly, and comfortable place nestled above a lovely stretch of quiet beach near **Yehgangga**. Its spacious cottages face a wide garden and a wonderful landscape of rice paddies, dark sand, and rocky cliffs. It's a good base for walks along the beach – a two-hour walk to Tanah Lot and a one-hour walk to Klating beach. Above the pleasant, wide pool, a small restaurant facing the sea serves good local food.

Further west, the friendly *Bibi's Cottage* is tucked into a remote corner in **Tibubiyu**, near **Pasut Beach** – a long, large, quiet stretch of grey sand with strong surf. The simple, bamboo-walled bungalows have wonderful views of the rice fields and ocean. When tired of admiring

♥ ⑤ 10 Rm – Htw
A/C Rst Bch Swp Shw Spa
T 0361-416 256;
0361-416 257
F 0361-416 353
wgr@wakaexperience.com
www.wakaexperience.com
> From Tabanan, take a small road to the left indicating the resort. You'll find Waka Gangga at the end of the road, after crossing the river.

❷ ❸ 12 Rm – Htw
Rst Bch Swp
T 0361-744 35 61
F 0361-812 744
mailbwb@baliclick.com
www.baliwisatabungalows.com
> On the right side of the road to Yehgangga, 1km before Waka Gangga.

❶ 5 Rm – Trk
T 082 361 09 14

> In Kerambitan, follow the sign to Pasut Beach. Turn right at the fork in front of Puri Agung, then find the sign indicating Bibi's cottage after 7km — or take a bemo from Pesiapan to Tibubiyu (before 2pm).

❸ 8 Rm – Htw A/C Trk Rst Shw Cls
T 0361-281 421
F 0361-286 879
T/F 0361-261 420
puritamansari@yahoo.com
www.balitamansari.com

> From Mengwi, head north towards Bedugul. After 6km, follow the sign towards Alas Kedaton and after 200m, turn left towards Desa Wisata Umabian. 500m further, after the village, turn right to find the hotel on the left.

❸ 8 Rm – Shw Cls
T 0361-812 668
F 0361-810 885
gps@dps.centrin.net.id

> From the centre of Tabanan, head west for 3km on the bypass to Gilimanuk, then turn left at the traffic light and continue for 4km. Alternatively, take a bemo from Pesiapan to Kerambitan.

the surf, take a walk in the wonderful rice growing areas nearby or explore a longer beach path to Yehgangga (see next page). Art lovers should have a look at the works of the owner, who is a dedicated painter. A small gallery is under construction. The guests-only restaurant serves lunch and dinner on request.

Where to Stay – Inland

A Countryside Retreat in Puri Taman Sari

This comfortable hideaway is tucked away in the farming village of Umabian. The restaurant and the most expensive bungalows have serene, uninterrupted views of the rice paddies. Tools used for traditional agriculture are exhibited in a small *bale* near the restaurant. Two bamboo gazebos set amidst the rice fields are perfect to laze and daydream. The staff also offer tours to discover the region — for example a half-day trip to Blayu or to the **monkey forest** of **Alas Kedaton**, which includes a two-hour walk (US$20 per person). Should you need a peaceful place to relax or meditate, ask for the path to **Pura Tungkeb**, a pleasant 30-minute walk.

The owner provides free dancing lessons for locals, and guests are welcome to join their practice in the *bale banjar* (village hall). Dancing and cooking classes are also available.

A few minutes drive after Tabanan, *Puri Anyar* ("The New Palace") offers guests a chance to stay in the royal family compound of Tabanan in **Kerambitan**. The cottages are richly decorated with paintings and Balinese crafts, while the doors and the roof trim are carved and painted in gold and bright colours. A spacious courtyard holds a wooden cart used for religious ceremonies and weddings. The owner proposes a large cultural programme, from dance classes and cooking lessons to dance performances or wedding ceremonies. Should you stay when a ceremony is being held in the *puri*, you are welcomed to join in; the owner will provide proper dress for the occasion.

Where to Eat – Tabanan Town

There are several warungs along the Tabanan-Gilimanuk bypass, serving *nasi campur* and other local dishes for Rp15-20,000. Two restaurants proposing Lombok specialities are worth a try. The first one, *Taliwang Bersaudara*, is indicated by a sign along the main road at the eastern end of Tabanan, next to the Subak Museum (take a bemo from Pesiapan towards Kediri). It offers meals for Rp30-40,000. At the western end of town, on the Tabanan to Gilimanuk bypass, *Kayanti* charges Rp15-25,000. Both serve tasty *ayam taliwang* (grilled or fried chicken with a strong, richly-flavoured sauce) and *plecing kangkung* (water spinach in a spicy sauce).

Where to Eat – Tanah Lot

In the middle of the hurly-burly of small shops and tourist traps crammed near the entrance of Tanah Lot, *Dewi Shinta* is a pleasant surprise and good value. The table at the back of the restaurant offers the quietest spot facing a small garden. Meals cost Rp30-50,000 with a buffet menu option at Rp50,000.

© Elizabeth E. Listyowati

Coconut leaf plates used for temple offerings

What to Do – Beach and Forest Walks

A Beach Walk around Yehgangga

This easy ten-kilometre walk takes you from Yehgangga to Tibubiyu and back. Start from the Yehgangga beach, heading westward for 3km until you reach a small temple perched on a cliff, with a superb view of the coastline. Look for a small path behind the temple, and walk west on this path for 2km towards Tibubiyu. Tucked under a pair of coconut palms, a sign indicates Bibi's cottages. This will lead you through vast rice fields to the village – if you miss the board, just continue to walk until a small road on your right leads to Tibubiyu. After Bibi's cottages, you will reach the main Tibubiyu-Klating road; continue to your right on the road towards Klating. Then turn down to Klating beach and walk back on the beach towards Yehgangga.

> From Tabanan, follow the signs to Waka Gangga. Yehgangga and Tibubiyu can be accessed by bemo from Pesiapan.

The walk can be done in reverse, from Tibubiyu towards Yehgangga. You can shorten it by taking an ojek in Yehgangga village.

> From Mengwi, head north towards Bedugul. After 6km, follow the sign towards Alas Kedaton and start walking at the beginning of the road to Jebaud village. You can come back on an ojek from the temple.

As is often the case in Bali, this forest is dotted with macaques. Unlike the ones in Sangeh or Uluwatu, which have seen too many visitors, these ones are relatively well behaved and will not try to steal your belongings — make sure you don't encourage bad habits by feeding them.

Walk to the Monkey Forest of Alas Kedaton

This short walk takes only 90 minutes to **Pura Alas Kedaton**. The walk is more interesting than the temple itself, which is packed with small shops — exactly 202 stalls, as explained proudly by a local guide. Start at the beginning of the road that leads to the small village of **Jebaud**. Walk on the asphalt road until you notice the *bale banjar* (village hall) on the right. Look for a small path just after the *bale banjar* and head east towards the rice fields until you notice the dense foliage of **Alas Kedaton** (*alas* means forest in Balinese). Follow the path towards the forest; on a clear day you will enjoy a wonderful view of Mt Batukaru to the north. After 20 minutes, the path reaches the small river of Yeh Ge. Cross the river, then look for a small path leading to the asphalt road on the west side of the Kedaton forest. Follow the road until a small gate on the right leads to the temple. Except for religious activities, it is forbidden to enter the temple.

On your way from or to the temple, stop at Umabian to visit the **weaving shop** located 100m after the turn towards Alas Kedaton. The handmade textiles from this area are quite well-known by the locals. They are woven mostly in bright colours of yellow, green, and red, and are handsomely ornamented with gold patterns. The owner will show your her collection of fine silk scarves that take more than two months to be completed. You can see the weavers at work in an open *bale* nearby.

A Cultural Journey around Tabanan

A Backroad to Tanah Lot

Located on an outcrop of rock eroded from the western coast, **Pura Tanah Lot** ("Temple of the Land and Sea") is a key sanctuary allegedly built to guard the coastline by Danghyang Nirartha, the Javanese priest who travelled through Bali in the 16th century, bringing a wave of renewal to the local Hinduism.

Meditating in Tanah Lot

© Ulung Wicaksono

Acccording to one legend, Nirartha was asked to leave the area by a local religious leader jealous of his popularity. Using his powers, Nirartha left by simply moving the rock upon which Tanah Lot is built from the land into the sea, changing his scarf into the sacred snakes that are still said to guard the temple.

Tanah Lot is easily accessed by road from Denpasar or Tabanan (follow the signs to the temple), or by bemo from Tabanan through Kediri. Rows of dilapidated shops and small restaurants vying for more than 600 visitors a day make it difficult to feel any serenity in the area. The temple can be best appreciated in the early morning, around 8 or 9am, before the crowd of buses starts to swamp the place.

Instead of passing through the busy main access, go to the back end of the parking lot where the asphalt road splits, going right towards the exit and left towards the sea. Head towards the sea until the end of the asphalted road, then take a small path to the left, where there are a few newly-built villas on your left. Along the path, there are several small temples perched on each neck of land. The first is **Pura Batu Mejan**, locally known for its holy spring used for religious ceremonies, then **Pura Batu Bolong** ("Temple of the Hollow Rock") perched on an odd rock with a hole in its middle, and **Pura Galuh** at the eastern end. The path ends at a small garden just north of Pura Tanah Lot. When the tide is low, you can climb down the cliff and walk along the sand to access the main temple.

A Ceramic Cottage Industry in Pejaten

To see ceramicists at work, head to the village of Pejaten in the south. Home to a small ceramics industry, it is packed with wares made of painted clay, ranging from roof tiles to plates and bowls to vases in all shapes and sizes. As you enter the village, you'll notice stacks of coconut husks along the road, ready to fuel the kilns. At the southern end of the village, pay a visit to **Tanteri Ceramic**, which offers a wide selection of bowls, cups, pots, bottles,

The True Bali

In 1994, the government authorised the building of a 100ha, 300-room golf resort near Tanah Lot. The project violated a 1989 decree forbidding such developments within 2km of a sacred site, and brought dissent in Bali. The army suppressed protests about the project and the local Hindu authorities finally caved in. To make villagers sell their land, the government cut their irrigation water, turning their rice paddies into low-value dry fields. Today, the resort advertises itself as "a true Bali experience" where "water is a predominant feature" with "an affinity for the natural surroundings of rice terraces".

Making pots in Pejaten

© Murdani Usman

> Pejaten is located 4km south of Tabanan – turn left from the main road to Gilimanuk near the petrol station, or take a bemo from Pesiapan to Bongan and get off at Pejaten. T/F 0361-831 948 www.tanteri-ceramic.com

> Located 2km east of the centre of Tabanan, in the village of Senggulan, the museum is passed by bemo on the Tabanan to Kediri route.
Open daily 8am-8pm, except Sundays and national holidays. A small donation is requested.

✿ Most displays have English explanations, however, it is better to ask one of the museum staff to guide you during the visit to get further information.

A scarecrow in the rice fields

© Ulung Wicaksono

and other objects. In the typical style of Pejaten, they are ornamented with figurines of geckos or dragonflies, and painted in soft, pastel hues of green, beige, taupe, or pale blue. The well-stocked warehouse offers crafts at better prices than in shops. Ask the staff for special wrapping for wares to be shipped or sent by plane.

Getting Into Rice at the Subak Museum

This unusual museum is worth a stop for agricultural enthusiasts. At the end of the visit, one will realise that behind every beautiful rice terrace there is a complex and delicate system. The museum stands on spacious grounds and may feel rather deserted. Start the visit from the contemporary statues of two boys riding buffaloes near Dewi Sri (the rice goddess); then continue clockwise to the right.

The exhibition starts with a history of the *subak* system written in old inscriptions on *lontar* palm leaves, and ends with a set of traditional tableware to serve cooked rice. In between, it displays wooden boards used to calculate planting or harvesting times, wooden threshers, a miniature mock-up of a *subak* system, and a coconut wood timer which was once used to allocate speaking time in *subak* meetings. Contemporary concerns of the shrinkage of agricultural land, water shortages, and rice price problems are hardly mentioned. It feels like time has stood still, bringing you back to when farming was a matter of buffalo and wooden scarecrows.

The Royal Palaces of Kerambitan

Two palaces of the royal family of Tabanan can be admired in the centre of Kerambitan, 6km west of Tabanan. **Puri Anyar** covers 2.5ha, with several pavilions used for royal dwellings or religious ceremonies. It serves also as a guesthouse (see above, Where to Stay). Surrounded by spacious grounds, **Puri Agung** ("The Great Palace") houses many pavilions that can be visited. These buildings look more faded than the temple of Puri Anyar. The "must see" quarters are the family temple, the *bale* used for tooth filing ceremonies, and a few large *bale* decorated with *wayang*-style paintings and carved doors.

According to legend, these palaces were erected by a son of the 13th king of Tabanan. Having no descendent from his wife, the king swore to crown his firstborn son. Soon, one of his concubines gave him an heir – followed a few months later by a son born to the queen. This second child should have been heir to the throne but the king kept his word, and crowned the son of his concubine instead. The bereft queen's son went to the mountains where he studied spirituality until his family asked him to come back and offered to erect a royal house at the first place where he would see "billowing smoke". This palace became Puri Agung Kerambitan. Later, the prince's son erected the palace of Puri Anyar.

Today, as if history wanted to avenge the prince without a crown, the royal houses of Kerambitan are the only ones that remain, since the Dutch destroyed the main royal palace of Tabanan.

> From the centre of Tabanan, head west for 3km towards Gilimanuk, then turn left at the traffic light and continue for 4km. Alternatively, take a bemo from Pesiapan to Kerambitan.

Coffee and cakes with a Balinese Prince

Based in Umalas, near Denpasar, **Matangi Tours** propose an original way to discover the culture and history of Tabanan. The Matangi team takes guests in comfortable vehicles through winding country roads to a small village, where it is possible to trek and have lunch in a comfortable *bale* erected with the help of the local community. This is the occasion to meet the priests, artists, craftsmen, and farmers of this traditional community.

One of the highlights of the tour is the royal palace visit, where an informal meeting with the prince of Tabanan can be arranged. Here you can share coffee and cakes, as well as insights on Balinese history, with this heir of the royal family. Each tour normally accommodates no more than five guests to keep its impact low and allow good contact with the villagers. Matangi respects the way of life of communities, and works with them to improve the village's traditional infrastructures so they also benefit from the tours.

© Dedok

♥ 🍡

T 0361-739 820;
0361-731 402
F 0361-731 403
matangi@idola.net.id

© Ulung Wicaksono

Rice terraces in Jatiluwih

Batukaru – Jatiluwih

The Morning of the World

> This area can be accessed from Tabanan, following the road north to Pura Luhur Batukaru, or from Mengwi, following the busy road towards Bedugul and Singaraja. To reach it by public transport from south or west Bali, take one of the many buses plying the route between Denpasar and Gilimanuk, getting off at Mengwi to catch a bemo to Baturiti. Once in the area, local transport can be difficult. Ojek are available at the Baturiti market. You can also ask your hotel for transport.

Above the busy town of Tabanan, little roads climb to the north towards 2276m-high *Mt Batukaru*, crossing villages where the quiet is broken only by colourful ceremonies. The slopes of Mt Batukaru are the most humid region of Bali. Clouds often obscure the views around noon; mornings are superb. Walking around Jatiluwih and Batukaru in the very early hours of the day, one realises why Bali was dubbed "the morning of the world".

On the upper slopes, **Pura Luhur Batukaru**, one of Bali's most important and least-visited temples, is nestled at the edge of a deep forest. This is a realm for meditation, endless **forest hikes** or **bird-watching**. Heading eastward, the flank of the mountain nourishes the **rice fields** of *Jatiluwih*, a stunning man-made wonder of boundless rice terraces facing the ocean. For a long time, bad roads have kept this peaceful village known only to a few initiates. The roads are now better maintained, and Jatiluwih is gaining international recognition – UNESCO is considering turning it into a World Heritage Site. Narrow roads still limit the access of large tourist crowds to this area. Jatiluwih also shelters a few fascinating, **secretive temples** accessible by walking through the rice fields, including a unique temple dedicated to thieves.

Where to Stay – Batukaru and Jatiluwih

This area offers great accommodations in eco-friendly mountain resorts or inexpensive losmens facing rice fields, but with a limited number of rooms. It is advisable to book in advance, especially during the peak season.

Driving from Tabanan towards Mt Batukaru, travellers can stay at the *Yeh Panas Hot Springs Resort*. The eight comfortable bungalows, with slightly run-down showers, are widely spaced in a pleasant setting by the river. Pools of bubbling hot water from the nearby springs are found in the well-tended garden. Balconies offer nice views of the river and rice fields.

❸ *16 Rm – Htw A/C Rst Swp Gvw Spa*
T 0361-262 356
Reservation Office:
T 0361-484 052
F 0361-271 296
spayehpanas@ telkom.net.id

An Eco-Lodge at Sarinbuana

Feel like hiding in a lush forest where the most likely beings you will meet are monkeys, eagles, squirrels, and a friendly owner obsessed with protecting the fragile ecology of Bali? Then climb up to the cosy bungalows of Sarinbuana Jungle Lodge, a home for nature lovers and bird-watching fans. To reach the lodge, one must climb down stone steps for 50m, passing a lush cocoa plantation. The wooden bungalows hug the contours of the valley, facing west towards forests and orchards. On a sunny day, the view stretches out as far as the coast of Uluwatu, over a landscape of dense foliage highlighted by a waterfall.

♥ ♥ ❷ ❸ *4 Rm – Htw Rst Gvw Trk Bcy Shw Cls*
M 081 747 159 16
ecolodgebali@yahoo.com

> *Head west on the main Tabanan-Gilimanuk road for 15km, then turn right after the market of, Bajera heading north to Wanasari. Continue for another 13km to Sarinbuana village and look for the lodge's sign on the left.*

The owner, a dynamic environmental activist, has built a smart system for recycling waste water into an organic vegetable garden. He does a lot to help guests enjoy the pristine nature around the lodge. Local youngsters trained as guides are ready to take you on trekking routes ranging from a short 5km walk to a one-day long forest hike to **Puncaksari** – unless you prefer to combine a visit to the bat cave in **Soka Beach** with a trek around the **Wanagiri** and **Pupuan** areas. A 30m bird-watching tower is under construction with the cooperation of the local community; binoculars are available for guests.

A Mountain Retreat at Prana Dewi

♥♥❸ 4 Rm – Htw
Rst Gvw Trk Cls
T/F 0361-736 654
M 081 338 660 154
franzisca_rapp@
hotmail.com
www.balipranaresort.com

> From Tabanan, follow
the road towards Pura
Luhur Batukaru.
The resort is marked
by a small sign a few
hundred metres after the
village of Wongayagede,
3km before the temple.

On two hectares of land at the base of Mt Batukaru, Prana Dewi offers uniquely-designed bungalows set within private landscaped gardens featuring fish ponds, organic rice fields, and small waterfalls. Each of the clean, comfortable bungalows is artistically different, combining modern and traditional Balinese architecture. No air-conditioning is needed in this cool mountain area. The design of the bungalows and the restaurant is perfectly integrated into the surrounding rice fields and gardens.

The owner of Prana Dewi, Pak Dehan, is devoted to the local community of Wongayagede. The friendly staff come from the nearby village and are encouraged to learn about forgotten forms of traditional agriculture and organic farming. Ask them for a tour of the organic garden, or for walks in the nearby area. Yoga courses are organised twice a month for three to six days, or upon request for groups (US$50 per day, including shared accommodation and meals). The lovely restaurant serves mostly locally-grown organic food.

A Rice Field View at Galang Kangin Inn

♥❶ 8 Rm – Gvw Trk
T 0361-815 240
M 081 138 94 19

> A few hundred metres
beyond Café Jatiluwih
along the road to
Gunungsari. The losmen
is not indicated by any
sign in order to "preserve
the village atmosphere".

This charming losmen, whose name means "Sunrise Inn", is the only accommodation around **Jatiluwih**, and the only good one in the budget category in the whole area. From the terraces of the road front bungalows, the view encompasses the entire valley, casting such a spell that one is ready to forget everything else, including the few vehicles passing on the road during the day. The rooms are simple and clean. The nearby café is closed after 4pm, but the owner's wife can cook a simple and copious dinner if asked in advance. Her husband will introduce you to the life of Jatiluwih villagers, including their work in the fields and their ceremonies in the temples.

Where to Eat – Batukaru and Jatiluwih

Starting from Mt Batukaru, *Prana Dewi* Mountain Resort has a small, friendly restaurant serving healthy organic food, including a good choice of vegetarian dishes.

Try the "Tempe à la **Prana Dewi**", fermented soy cake with coconut stewed ferns and other local leafy vegetables, served with a deliciously spicy *sambal* bongkot (chilli, onion, garlic, and torch ginger flower). Most of this food has been grown on the grounds of the resort or harvested in surrounding gardens and forest. This is a perfect stop on the way to the temple and the mountain.

Ideally situated, the open-air pavilion of *Café Jatiluwih* pays homage to the grandeur of the views. The few guests are usually absorbed in the panorama of celebrated rice fields, distracted only by flocks of egrets enjoying a picnic of frogs in the paddies. The food is simple, in accord with the rural setting. The red rice served is a local variety grown in the fields that stretch out in front of the diners. Have a taste of the grilled or fried chicken with a deliciously fresh *sambal cicang*, a spicy sauce made of torch ginger flower minced with chilli, onion, garlic, and shrimp paste (*ayam bakar/goreng sambal cicang*).

Organic Luxury at Big Tree Farm

For a romantic treat on the slopes of Mt Batukaru, above the Jatiluwih rice fields, spoil yourself with one of *Big Tree Farm's Firefly Supper Series*. You will be picked up at your hotel in the afternoon, in time for a scenic trip to Jatiluwih where you can enjoy your dinner among the rice fields, and then sent back safely to your hotel after dinner (Rp400-600,000, inclusive of supper, wine, and transportation).

During the day time, you can also visit Big Tree's **organic farm** near the Petali temples in Jatiluwih. Ben and Blair, the dedicated owners, have set up a 2.5ha farm on land contracted to local villagers. Instead of using pesticides, they employ workers to remove slugs and other bugs manually, one by one, from their neat fields. With more and more tourists and expatriates in Bali craving healthy, organic food, Big Tree Farm has become the supplier of many a famous hotel and restaurant on the island.

♥ ♥
T/F 0361-736 654
M 081 338 660 154
> In Wongayagede (see above, Where to Stay).

♥ T 0361-815245
> Above the Jatiluwih rice fields.
Open 9am-5pm

✿ Local red rice and roasted coffee beans are for sale at the counter. Ask the friendly staff to show you the torch ginger flower (cicang or bongkot) used as a local spice.

♥ T 0361-742 44 16
T/F 0361-974 294
office@bigtreebali.com
www.bigtreebali.com
Open 8am-5pm

© Djuna Ivereigh

Offerings to the rice gods

What to Do – The Magic of Mt Batukaru

Pura Batukaru

A Natural Spa at Yeh Panas Hot Springs

On the way to Mt Batukaru, or on your way back after trekking, you may like to relax sore muscles at this hot springs resort. The outdoor, hot bubbling pool enclosures can accommodate four to eight people. The smallest pool for two persons is a favourite among the local clientele who come here on weekends.

The naturally hot water from the springs contains sulphur, potassium, sodium and small percentages of minerals, with no additives except an occasional dose of chlorine. The water is said to relieve itching and heal skin diseases. After a hot bath, you can relax in the fresh water swimming pool, while children can enjoy the kids' playground. The restaurant serves Indonesian-Chinese and Western food (approximately Rp80,000 per meal).

Pura Luhur Batukaru, a Temple in the Forest

This awesome temple is one of Bali's six major temples (*sad kahyangan*), each of them dedicated to a direction of the compass – Pura Batukaru guards the west. It is visited by endless processions of Balinese during religious festivals. Surrounded by pristine mountain forests, the temple lies at the bottom of holy Batukaru mountain and exudes spirituality. The sanctuary itself is quite simple; the thatched *meru* blend into the surrounding environment. The temple is well managed and it has been protected from commercial enterprise. A great view of Mt Batukaru looming in the background can be seen from the entrance gates. The best time to see the temple and the mountain is early morning, before thick clouds descend upon the slopes after midday.

Pura Luhur Batukaru is thought to have been established in the 11th century when the saint-architect Mpu Kuturan built towering *meru* at the base of the mountain. The temple was then consecrated by the kings of Tabanan, who made it their state temple and dedicated the shrines to their ancestral gods. In the 16th century, the shrines were ransacked and razed by a rival raja thought to have come from Buleleng. While devotees continued to worship at the area, the temple was not restored until 1959. Thatched *meru* standing in the inner sanctuary of the temple continue to honour the defiled kings of Tabanan. The most important shrine is the seven-tiered pagoda, dedicated to Mahadewa, the god of Mt Batukaru.

For a nice stroll, walk to the east of the temple where a large pond honours the gods of nearby Lake Tamblingan. A shrine lies on a small island in the middle of the lake; only local priests are allowed onto the island.

© Waka Experience

Carrying palms and flowers for offerings

A Forest Hike to Mt Batukaru

This mountain, whose name means "the coconut shell rock", is the second highest in Bali (2,276m). On its flanks you can walk through the dense forests of a 1,800ha nature preserve, in the sole company of birds, reptiles, and monkeys. A small temple dedicated to the mountain will welcome you when you reach the peak of the summit. A casual walk up the mountain will take around six to seven hours, and four to five hours to return to ground level. If you wish to undertake this walk in one day, you will need to depart at sunrise. Alternatively, you may choose to camp at the summit – this can be arranged with the help of Prana Dewi Mountain Resort if you don't have your own tent.

Walks from Wongayagede Village

For less demanding treks, inquire at Prana Dewi Mountain Resort. One of the walks will take you across the Mawa river, through tall bamboo and agroforests containing fruit trees, cacao, sugar palm, and coffee. Have your bathing suit ready for a dip in the clear river. From there, you'll reach the base of the mountain, where a small shrine can be found. Return by way of the back of the Pura Luhur Batukaru temple. This walk can take around two hours,

Wear good shoes as the slopes are steep and slippery. Consider wearing long sleeves, trousers, and insect repellent to guard against small leeches. The hike to the summit should be attempted with a guide, to avoid getting lost in the forest, and only during the dry months of April to October. Most hotels in the area can arrange a guided hike for around US$50, and guides may also be found at the Pura Luhur Prana Dewi.

with plenty of time left over for swimming and eating local produce such as *salak* fruit.

Another walk goes down across the nearby river, into exquisite rice fields (be prepared to get a bit muddy) and forested valleys. This three to four hour walk is slightly more demanding than the previous one, but the view is well worth it.

A Hot Springs Walk to Belulang

This walk takes you through the spectacular Jatiluwih rice fields to the outskirts of Belulang village, where you can bathe in hot spring water. It is also nice to do on a mountain bike or a motorbike. The walk takes about 2.5 to 3 hours each way, starting from Wongayagede. From the main road, take the small, quiet asphalt road going towards Jatiluwih, passing through beautiful rice fields. Follow the road up the hill and turn right at Vila Naga Puspa restaurant, then walk down the road through the pretty village of Mengesta. At the end of this road, turn left at a path, which takes you through stunning rice fields to a river. Cross the river and follow the path up the hill. At the top of the hill you will see the hot springs and Belulang village in the next valley. There is a small entrance fee for the springs (about Rp4,000).

© Elizabeth E. Listyowati

Hot water spring in Belulang

The hot springs consist of a small pool and a number of bathing areas where you can stand under the water as it comes out of the earth. They are surrounded by friendly warungs eager to sell you drinks and snacks. Some of them (such as **Warung Ari**) provide great rest spots where you can take in the view and relax after your bath.

Rice Fields and Hidden Temples in Jatiluwih

The road to Jatiluwih branches east from Wongayagede about 2km south of Pura Luhur, and then proceeds to Jatiluwih, "the eminently beautiful", nestled at about 700m at the foot of three imposing mountains, Mt Batukaru (2,276m), Mt Sengayang (2,087m) and Mt Adeng (1,826m).

✿ *Walks around Jatiluwih can be arranged at Galang Kangin Inn, or ask at Café Jatiluwih.*

The surrounding rice fields are considered to be one of the most ancient and elaborate samples of traditional rice irrigation systems (*subak*), and have been proposed by the government as a possible UNESCO World Heritage Site. No construction is allowed in the area. Here you will discover an expansive panorama stretching out over broad and gently sloping terraces sculpted from the south-facing hillsides. At points, you can even glimpse the sea on the distant blue horizon. In the south, the tiny and isolated Sangeh forest looks like an elevated island above the surrounding flat region. Jatiluwih rice fields are at their best in the very early hours of the day – the sky often gets cloudy in the afternoon.

It is worth spending the night in Jatiluwih for the pleasure of waking early and walking in the rice fields when the light and the air are at their best. You can stroll around aimlessly, exploring little paths, or ending up at the *subak* temple situated not far from the road near Gunungsari. For a glimpse of a few hidden aspects of the Balinese religion, explore the secret temples around Jatiluwih.

The Last Tall Rice

The farmers in Jatiluwih are still cultivating tall rice varieties, which grow from 1.20 to 1.50m – like in old Balinese paintings. Unlike the short, modern varieties, they can be planted only once or twice a year. Only the spikes are harvested, and then tied up in small bunches and stored in traditional lumbung. The straws are ploughed back into the ground, reducing the need for fertilisers. This rice is mostly for local consumption – farmers like its soft, nutty taste. Behind the pretty rice fields, a lot of the farmers' income actually comes from poultry and vegetable farms.

The Rival Temples of Jatiluwih

Ignored by most visitors, a pleasant paved lane climbs up above Jatiluwih Kangin. It is bordered by a string of four temples, located about 1km above the village, half-hidden in the tree gardens and coffee plantations.

I Wayan Miora, a member of the local community, explains their origin as follows: "Once upon a time, the kingdom of Gelgel, now known as Klungkung, was plagued with disputes and diseases. In despair, the king asked for help from three advisor-priests, representatives of the three priestly lines of Brahmana Mas, Bujangga Wesnawa, and Arya Wang Ban. All three embarked on a meditation journey. Arriving deep in the forest, they stopped on the southern slopes of Mt Batukaru, above Jatiluwih. In this secluded sanctuary, close to the Holy Mountain, they received inspiration

© Waka Experience

Traditional rice ripening

and revelation from the Supreme Force on how to over-come Gelgel's difficulties. Order and prosperity could be restored in the kingdom, and four temples were erected to remember their holy sojourn in this place – one for each priestly line, and one for the Supreme Deity."

Centuries later, it seems that the lesson of unity in adversity taught by this story has been forgotten, as the various religious groups compete to overshadow each other through flamboyant renovations of their respective temples – reflecting the struggles for status at work behind the aesthetic front of the Balinese religion.

Today, the most important and largest sanctuary is **Pura Luhur Petali** or **Kahyangan Jagat** ("Temple of the Realm"), dedicated to the ancestors of the Arya Wang Ban clan of Tabanan. The cost of its renovation and enlargement has amounted to some US$250,000; an additional US$100,000 was spent on the inaugural cere-mony in 2002. Only the central shrine has remained untouched. A grand, holy *bunut* fig tree stands above the temple, its roots clasping the ageless stones, while a pink-flowered *Medinilla*, symbolising the heavens, grows above the left upper part of the shrine.

Every 210 days, an important ritual ceremony, the *Petoyan*, draws devotees from the whole region – this is the occasion to witness the sacred *Wali Pendet* dance, gracefully performed by young girls holding basket of flowers as offerings. Farmers believe that the exceptional harmony of the rural landscape around the temple reflects the presence of the gods, as if nature and sculpt-ed rice terraces became an endless shrine devoted to the world's beauty.

About 500m higher up is the ancestral temple of the **Bujangga Wesnawa**, a group of followers of Wisnu, the Preserver and God of Water (read side column). A lofty, brand-new and sumptuously decorated 11-tiered *meru* stands in contrast with the surrounding countryside. Erected in April 2003, this is probably the first *meru* in Bali built on a metallic framework able to resist the

> *From the centre of Jatiluwih Kangin, leaving the road to Wongayagede on the left, take the little road that heads up behind the main village temple. Ask for directions to **Pura Petali**.*

The Dissident Priests

Balinese Hinduism is not a homogenous body. The Bujangga Wesnawa, who are found in Gunungsari near Jatiluwih among other places, are an example of a group challenging the domination of the Brahmana priests. These casteless people trace their doctrine to pre-Hindu Vedic concepts. In India, Wesnawism was a reaction to the abuses of high caste Hindus. In Bali, in a kind of compromise, a triumvirate consisting of priests of the three main groups (Brahmana Siwa, Brahmana Boda, and Bujangga) holds court at major ceremonies. The Bujangga are seated on a lower platform, but they are given special responsibilities during purification rituals.

strong local winds. It may be also the most expensive one. A single wealthy devotee spent more than US$125,000 to have it built. The structure is adorned with carved wood and stucco, painted in vivid colours and covered with gold leaf. A bit higher up is **Pura Rsi Brahmana Mas**, after which the grassy lane climbs to **Pura Taksu Agung**, dedicated to the Supreme Force that bestows super-natural powers.

In Search of the Temple of Thieves

Based on a story by Bodrek Arsana in Latitudes *magazine*

A pleasant walk will take you through the terraced rice fields down to mysterious temples hidden on a ridge top near the village of Utu, 3km away as the crow flies. The main temple, albeit of modest dimensions, consists of several renovated shrines. In a corner, the most important one, keeps the austere, ancestral shape of a terraced pyramid.

The temple is topped by a small megalithic *linga*, wrapped in white and yellow fabrics, which is said to be circled by a rim sounding like a metallic bell when struck, – hence the temple's name: *Pura Besi Kalung*, "Temple of the Iron Necklace". Villagers also attest that the stone has the power to shift to announce critical times. "The last time it happened, I witnessed it myself," says Komang, a teacher in nearby Babahan. "It was two weeks before President Soeharto's fall. I even sent a message to warn the governor."

Outside the main temple is a smaller one, modest in appearance. A few offerings accumulate near the three mysterious egg-shaped stones placed on the shrine. From time to time, often at night, discreet devotees come to worship here. This is *Pura Sanghyang Maling*, "the Temple of the Great Thief". As explained by a local villager, "God created thieves, hence they should have their temples, too." The local story says that the temple got its reputation after a famous thief, caught in the act and chased by angry villagers, ran into the temple where he

> Utu can be accessed by road from Senganan. Follow the road southward to Bolongan, then take a smaller road which plunges into the valley toward the right. Cross the bridge above the river and the hot spring before climbing up to Utu.

You can go there by yourself but it is better to get a local villager or priest to guide you. Go first to Babahan where several priests of the Utu temples live. Stop at a warung and ask around for a temple priest (pemangku Pura Utu). One of them or a villager will be able to guide you to the temple. Pay a fee and leave a donation for the temple.

© Dedok

vanished mysteriously. According to one of the temple's priests, a variety of devotees come to the temples – including would-be thieves, but also businessmen asking protection from crime and government officials hoping to protect their jobs. Because of the dubious image of a thieves' temple, some high Hindu or village officials prefer to call it "Pura Maeling" ("Temple to be Remembered") or "Pura Mahaling" ("Temple of the Invisible").

Trekking the Ancient Rice Road

Until the turn of this century, the forest trail going through the mountain range from Jatiluwih to the **Tamblingan Lake** was the unique way for Jatiluwih farmers to trade their rice surplus to the north coast. These days, only few villagers expert at hunting deer – an offering required for major temple ceremonies – dare to venture in the dense forest. For nature lovers, trekking **from Jatiluwih to Tamblingan** is an exciting opportunity to discover ancient forests and unique mountain views. After starting from Jatiluwih (750m) at 7am, a one-hour walk in the gardens followed by three hours in the forest will take you to the caldera known as *Lubang Nagaloka* ("the Dragon Hideout"), at 1,688m up the slopes of Mt Lesong. From there, the path goes down to the serene Tamblingan Lake where the expedition ends at dusk.

Luxury Explorations with Waka Land Cruises

For travellers hoping to discover Jatiluwih and Mt Batukaru in comfort, Waka Land Cruises offers day tours in a 4-wheel drive vehicle for US$83 per person. The tour will take you to hot springs, local farmers' houses and traditional sites, such as a quarry where stones are cut by ancestral methods to build temples. The trip includes a quality lunch based on local ingredients, some from the rainforest, accompanied by wine and cognac – which you will enjoy in the forest on a bamboo terrace built by local craftsmen.

The trek from Jatiluwih to Tamblingan needs to be planned two days in advance. It can be arranged by Pak Miora, the owner of Galang Kangin Inn (T 0361-815 240) at about Rp250,000 per trip (transport back from Tamblingan not included). An English- or German-speaking guide is sometimes available. Porters can be hired. The same trek can be done in reverse from Puri Lumbung in Munduk (north Bali).

© James K.Jarvie

Carrying alang–alang

T 0361-426 972
T/F 0361-426 971
www.wakaexperience.com
wakalandcruise@
hotmail.com

© Djuna Ivereigh

Pura Ulun Danu Beratan

In the Mist

From Mengwi, the main road leading north to Singaraja leaves the dense villages of the plain, climbing to the foot hills through a cocoa and fruit growing area. Past Luwus at 500m a.s.l., rice fields are replaced by neat fields of cabbage, carrots, or chillies, sometimes mixed with newly-established tangerine orchards.

Approaching the hill resort of *Pacung*, the views of the valleys become more scenic. Further up, the market of *Baturiti* buzzes with small trucks loading vegetables to be sold in the lowlands. Most visitors pass quickly through this area on their way to the mountain resort of Bedugul, which many leave after a stop at **Lake Beratan**. Yet Pacung and Baturiti offer both fine panoramic views of the valleys and mild temperatures, which can be enjoyed from the restaurants along the road. This can be a pleasant stop on the way to north Bali, or a base from which to visit Jatiluwih and Batukaru in the west, or the vegetable and coffee growing areas in the east.

Around the lake, the cool resorts of *Bedugul* and *Candikuning* are popular with local tourists. The area tends to be foggy and the vegetable slopes, covered with villas and restaurants, have lost their natural charm. Yet it does offer a few points of interest such as the romantic temple lake of **Pura Ulun Danu Beratan**, or the unique **Botanical Gardens**.

> Lake Beratan is a one hour's drive from Denpasar or Singaraja, on the busy north-south axis. As usual, small roads are more pleasant – try driving from Denpasar and Mengwi to the north through Sangeh and Petang, on a peaceful road going through colourful villages. Alternatively, drive from Tabanan through the slopes of Mt Batukaru, passing Wongayagede and Jatiluwih. Pacung and Bedugul near the lake are easily reached by bus or mini-bus from Denpasar (Ubung terminal), Mengwi, or Singaraja (Banyuasri terminal).

Bring a jumper and rain jacket – above 1,000m, average temperatures range from 18-24°, and occasionally cool down to 11° at night. Fog and small rains are frequent.

Where to Stay – Pacung-Baturiti

Although very few tourists stop there, Pacung offers a handful of hotels and restaurants in quiet, scenic surroundings, and is less crowded than Bedugul.

On the steep slope below the main road from Mengwi to Bedugul, the luxury *Pacung Mountain Resort* hides quiet rooms that look over a valley of gardens and rice terraces, with misty mountain ranges in the background. The ten bungalows nestled at the bottom of the valley offer the most secluded rooms. On weekends, tourists from Jakarta and Denpasar make the most of the cool climate. Guests can join a walk through gardens and rice fields (US$17.50/person); part of the fee goes to the villages visited.

Meditation adepts can participate in the retreats held in the Pacung Mountain Resort by Merta Ada. This Chinese-Balinese healer from the Sanur-based **Bali Usada Meditation Centre** claims to use techniques based on ancient *lontar* palm manuscripts and teachings from traditional healers and doctors. Participants are encouraged to learn self-healing methods.

On the other side of the road, the *Pacung Indah Hotel and Restaurant* has only three rooms, decorated to yield an intimate yet rustic, colonial cottage atmosphere. They are located in a rather wild garden at the back of the restaurant. A bit of noise from the road can be heard, although the area is generally quiet. The most comfortable "suite" and the terrace of the restaurant offer a great sunrise view of Mt Agung.

Further up, the charming *Hotel Villa Baturiti*, our favourite in the area, offers comfortable, tastefully furnished wooden cottages. The mountain chalet atmosphere is a perfect match to the gorgeous views of the valley. The resort is rather well isolated from the the road by a hill; quiet nights are interrupted only by cock-crows from the valley's farms. The only sad note is the caged birds greeting visitors. Simple meals are served on the small terrace.

❹ ❺ 35 Rm – Htw
Rst Swp Gvw Trk Spa
T 0368-21 038
F 0368-21 043
> *Just before Pacung, on the right side of the road when climbing from Mengwi, approximately 8km before Bedugul.*

Bali Usada Meditation
Baturiti Office:
T 0368-21 107
Sanur main Office:
T 0361-289 209
F 0361-287 726
www.balimeditation.com

❷ ❸ 3 Rm –
Htw Rst Gvw
T 0368-21 020
F 0368-21 964
david@pacung.com
www.pacung.com

❷ ❸ 15 Rm –
Htw Swp Gvw
> *On the left side of the road, approximately 3km after the Baturiti market, or 5km before Bedugul when climbing from Mengwi.*

Where to Stay – Bedugul-Candikuning

Bedugul usually refers to the villages located on the western shores of Lake Beratan, at the foot of Mt Tapak (1,909m). The lake sits inside the wide and now some-what unclear crater of a volcano, bordered by Mt Penggilingan (2,153m) and Mt Catur (1,865m) on the northeast. This is a favourite destination for local city weekenders, who appreciate its cool weather and the quality of its flowers, vegetables, and fruits. On rainy days, the mist often blankets the lake, wrapping the base of the 11-tiered *meru* in a romantic haze. Far above tropical Bali, the mountain sights and cool temperatures evoke the atmosphere of alpine lakes.

This peaceful landscape, however, has been invaded by herds of hotels, restaurants, sellers, and food stalls catering mostly to local visitors. Foreign travellers gener-ally stop to visit the famous **Pura Ulun Danu** temple and its trademark *meru* built on a tiny island on the lake. Other areas of interest include the less famous **Pura Puncak Mangu** and the **Botanical Gardens**. If you have a vehicle, it is more pleasant to overnight in Batukaru, Pacung, or Munduk (north Bali) and visit these sites on a day trip. If you need to stay around Bedugul, the area offers hotels and hill resorts, including an inter-national golf resort. None of these are particularly appealing to nature lovers – they are either too close to the road or to the busy recreation spots around, or very expensive.

Several inexpensive homestays are found along the road to the Botanical Gardens, some of them closed during the off-season. Located on a lane in the back of the road to the Botanical Gardens (Kebun Raya Candikuning), *Permata Firdaus Homestay* offers clean rooms at a moderate price.

Another option, slightly more comfortable, is *Hotel Bukit Permai*. Time seems to have stopped here in the early 1980s. The spacious bedrooms are simple. The adjoining bathrooms could use a facelift, and a bit of

Balinese Muslims

The six villages around Lake Beratan are home to strong Muslim communities, as attested by the large mosque erected on a hill opposite the Pura Ulun Danu. These Muslims are the descendants of farmers from Karangasem and Lombok, who came in the early 1900s to clear the forest. They coexist in peace with local Hindus, who call them "Bali Muslim"; both groups participate in each other's religious celebrations. Relations, however, may become more strained with newly arrived, more orthodox Muslims from Madura, Java, and Lombok.

❶ *6 Rm – Trk*
T 0368-21 531

❶ *13 Rm – Htw Gvw*
T 0368-21 443

> On the last turn before entering Candikuning, on the left side above the main road.

❸ ❹ 23 Rm – Htw Rst Gvw Trk Spa
T 0368-21 491
F 0368-21 022

noise can be heard from the road below. Still, the resort retains some nostalgic allure, as it is nicely set on the upper slopes of Bedugul, bordered by trees, with amazing views over the southern plain. Its isolation leaves plenty of time to learn about the local history from H. Mohd Ali Bick, one of the hotel's managers, who is the leader (*kelian adat*) of the Muslim community in Candikuning Dua. He can help find a guide for local trekking.

In a higher price range, **Enjung Beji Resort Hotel** in Candikuning is the most pleasant hotel around. On the left side of the Ulun Danu temple, this quiet resort offers spacious, clean rooms in a 3.5ha garden along the shore of Lake Beratan, with Mt Mangu and Mt Penggilingan in the background. Although not far from the main road, the resort is as sleepy as the lake, and will satisfy travellers or families in need of total peace. The restaurant is adjacent to the lake and the temple gardens, which can be entered at will. The staff can also show you the nearby vegetable and strawberry fields. Pak Ketut Paseh, one of the security guards, knows the forest well and can guide travellers to climb Mt Mangu. He is usually available on Wednesday and Sunday (Rp300,000/half day).

Where to Eat – Pacung and Baturiti

This scenic stretch of road is perfect for a lunch stop in one of the restaurants of the local resorts.

The restaurant of **Pacung Mountain Resort** caters to tours, and offers a buffet with a selection of Indonesian, Chinese, and international food (Rp65,000).

On the other side of the road, **Pacung Indah** has a pleasant restaurant with a great view facing Mt Agung, though a bit too close to the road (buffet Rp55,000 or à la carte meals for about Rp80,000). Try the *ayam bekaka*, a specialty of fried chicken with local spices.

Travellers searching for a simple and inexpensive local meal will find many warungs at the Baturiti market.

© Elizabeth E. Listyowati

Chilli farm near Baturiti

Where to Eat – Bedugul and Candikuning

The *Ulun Danu Restaurant*, inside the well-kept temple grounds overlooking the lake, offers a buffet for groups as well as à la carte Chinese, Indonesian and Italian food (until 5pm). The terrace is pleasant when visitors are few. From the restaurant, walk under the canopy of a huge banyan tree past a satin-like lawn and gorgeous gardens with trumpet-flower trees and gladioli – a scene of placid beauty.

Strategically located at the point where the main road reaches the lake shore, *Mentari* is a large restaurant catering mostly to groups. As in most buffet-style restaurants in heavily frequented spots, the price of a buffet lunch (about Rp50,000) includes a 30% commission for your driver or guide. Open until 5pm only.

Several local warungs serve spicy halal specialties from Lombok. One of them is *Warung Barokah*, just opposite the entrance of the temple. A simple meal costs about Rp15,000.

Lilies near Pura Ulun Danu Beratan.

What to Do – Rural Landscapes near Baturiti

On the way to Baturiti, between Luwus and Mekarsari, the stalls along the road are worth a stop during the fruit season – discover the exotic tastes of feshly harvested mangosteens, rambutans, durians or even the rare sweet lychees grown in the area.

Further up, in **Mekarsari**, a small white sign on the right side of the road reads "Waterfall 1,500m". The lane leads to the hamlet of Kerobokan, from where you can follow a little path ending in lovely views, with a small *waterfall* along the river flowing through the gorge.

The best landscapes are found around the scenic little road going westwards from Baturiti to **Antapan**, where you can explore villages where vegetables and flowers are grown. If you continue southward, a T-junction brings you to a scenic country road, winding its way in steep curves from **Sangeh** in the south towards **Pelaga**, **Catur**, and **Penulisan** in the northeast.

The Bali Silicon Valley
*Besides cabbage, carrots, and coffee, the cool hills of Baturiti are now yielding software. **Bali Camp**, a young local company, caters to banks and corporate clients from all the world. Its pleasant, modern, and efficient atmosphere is meant to seduce dozens of young staff and make them forget the cities' lights. Located a few hundred metres on the left, above the Pacung Mountain Resort, it offers free internet facilities to travellers and local youths.*
T 0368-21 919

In **Pelaga**, take the opportunity to visit some of the best *coffee plantations* on the island, a gorgeous sight when the white, fragrant flowers are blossoming on the shiny, dark green leaves of coffee bushes. Most of the coffee grows on steep slopes, shaded by light trees, and has a pleasant agroforestry atmosphere. Very few pests are present at this altitude and with fertile mountain soils, chemical fertilisers are not necessary. Hence most of the coffee is organic or semi-organic – grown with no chemicals, or with very small quantities.

Contact some of the local villagers trained by the Village Ecotourism Network to learn all there is to know about coffee making, to taste or buy freshly ground beans, or even to overnight in a farmer's house or trek through the coffee plantations.

♥ ♥ 🐾 ***Village Ecotourism Network***
T 0361-735 320
jed@denpasar.
wisantara.net.id

© Waka Experience

Ripening coffee cherries.

Temples and Treks around Bedugul

On the way to the cool mountain resort of Bedugul, the road passes by Taman Rekreasi Bedugul, a huge hotel abandoned soon after it was built in the 1990s, and which is apparently being renovated.

Upon reaching the pass, the main road goes through Candikuning Dua (two) then Satu (one), a marketplace close to the Pura Ulun Danu Beratan temple and the Botanical Gardens. The road then goes on along the lake for about 5km to Pancasari, passing patches of vegetables and villas surrounded by colourful gardens filled with canna lilies, gladioli, and dahlias. Beyond, a marvellously scenic and tranquil road on the left branches westward to Munduk. It follows what was once the rim of the crater, offering wonderful views over Lake Buyan and, above all, the amazingly preserved Lake Tamblingan (see p. 331).

Heading northward, the main road winds steeply up to the pass to Singaraja, amidst luxuriant forests inhabited only by monkeys that you may spot wandering on the roadside.

✂ *Although the Beratan temple can be accessed directly from the road, amateurs of romantic boat trips can access it from the lake by taking a sampan dayung (row boat) for Rp35,000/half hour.*

The Temple of the Lake's Goddess

Set in a well-kept garden, *Pura Ulun Danu Beratan* is dedicated to the lake goddess, Dewi Danu, who is believed to regulate the flow of water for all the *subak* farmers' associations in southwest Bali. As is often the case with Balinese temples, the fine location by the lake is more impressive than the building itself. The temple is easily accessed from the main road going from Bedugul and Candikuning – turn right into the parking lot, which is home to many tourist buses and faces the usual row of gaudy souvenir shops and pushy vendors. The courtyards are closed to visitors.

The temple is said to have been built by the *pande* or blacksmiths, a clan responsible for forging the powerful *keris*, the daggers of warriors and kings. Their mastery of fire and metals is viewed by Balinese as supernatural, and has traditionally put them outside the usual caste hierarchy. They established themselves along the lake where they were able to find the water necessary for their craft, but were later wiped out by the troops of East Java's Majapahit Kingdom.

Passing under the banyan tree in the midst of the garden, a large Buddhist stupa looks out of place in this Hindu sanctuary. It was erected in the 1950s by a dissident group of *pande* from Singaraja, who declared themselves Buddhist devotees. From here, looking back toward the hills, one can see the grand mosque of Bedugul above the main road. The elegant 11-tiered Hindu *meru* sitting on an islet, with the Buddhist stupa and the mosque's dome in sight, reflects the peaceful coexistence of these three religions on the lake's shores.

Hiking to Pura Puncak Mangu

This remote temple is located on the top of Mt Mangu (*puncak* means summit) along the rim of the caldera above Lake Beratan. It is one of the six *sad-kahyangan* temples of Bali, dedicated to various cardinal points –

A Holy Barn for Rats

In the front court of the temple, you may notice sparrows flying about the rusty corrugated iron roof of a barn. Twice a year, the subak farmers' groups affiliated to the temple bring a symbolic part of their rice harvest to the temple's barn, where it becomes the feast of birds and rats. "Feeding the birds and rodents in the temple courtyard prevents them from devastating the rice fields," explains the local priest. In the past, each subak would bring a symbolic quantity of rats, to be burnt in a big ngaben (ritual cremation) to exorcise the plague.

© Dedok

🐾🐾 *To hike towards* ***Pura Puncak Mangu***, *turn first right at the fork before Bedugul, going towards Taman Rekreasi Bedugul on the southern shore of the lake. From there, it's a 30min walk to the Goa Jepang caves, where the path starts. The caves can also be accessed by a boat hired from the pier near the Pura Ulun Danu temple. Get a guide from the ranger's station at the start of the climb or ask your hotel to provide one. You can also ask Pak Ketut Paseh, the security guard at Enjung Beji Resort Hotel in Candikuning, to guide you on Mt Mangu for about Rp300,000.*

this one marks the northwest. Despite its importance, access is difficult and it remains relatively unknown. For travellers in reasonably good shape, the 6km hike along the northeastern edge of Lake Beratan requires about 2.5 hours of hard climbing through canopied rainforest. The trail, however, is often littered with plastic bottles and discarded wrappers, mostly left by local tour groups and schoolchildren.

The rim trail to Mangu Pass starts from **Goa Jepang** (the Japanese caves), that were dug for the Japanese by Indonesian prisoners during WWII. The first segment of the trail is a gradual incline, winding through bean and cabbage patches, then climbs through a dark forest of *lantana* and *pandanus* with glimpses of the lake below.

A steep and slippery muddy slope, the last section of the climb is physically demanding, requiring you to sometimes pull yourself up by the roots of trees. At the top, you are rewarded by stupendous views of Mt Batur, Mt Abang, and the mountains of west Bali visible through gaps in the dense forest. Unless a festival is taking place, monkeys will likely be your sole companions.

Built by the first raja of Mengwi, the temple itself is simple, with a *padmasana* (throne of Surya, the sun god) a *linga*, some nice bas-reliefs, and two *meru*.

The Sleeping Beauty: Bali Botanical Gardens

Also known as ***Kebun Raya Eka Karya Bali***, this park is set on 154 hectares on the slopes of Mt Tapak between 1,250 and 1,400m a.s.l. Despite its name, it is in fact a forest – a paradox in the garden island of Bali – home to 1,753 plant species, including a collection of conifers. It is an attractive place for relaxing walks without too much adventure. The park gets busy on the weekends, when Balinese families picnic on the lawns near the entrance.

Originally designed as a conservation area, the park functions as a leisure and research area. It is owned by the Forestry Department and managed by the Institute

© Elizabeth E. Listyowati

The Botanical Gardens; next page: pink frangipani flowers

of Sciences. This twofold bureaucracy is hampering efforts to promote interest among the 260,000 yearly visitors, most of them local youths.

Information about the plants and suggestions for walks are given in the booklet, *Six Guided Walks in the Bali Botanic Gardens*, sold at the entrance for US$3 as a substitute for the general lack of signs – labels are scarce and often in great need of painting. The walks let you discover the important plants used in Balinese rituals, the diversity of ferns, the orchid and cactus collections, and the local mountain forest species. Quite interesting are the trails behind **Pura Meringgit**, where you can discover a luxuriant forest undergrowth of palms and ferns.

Besides plant species, the booklet offers amateur **bird-watchers** a checklist of about 100 species and a guide to some 20 easily-seen birds according to their habitat. The staff of the Botanical Gardens can also arrange a half-day trek to Mt Tapak (1,870m) starting from the Gardens and arriving at the Pancasari strawberry farm, with a guide from the village. The trek requires a permit from the Forestry Department and needs to be planned one week in advance (Rp250,000).

Fruits and Flowers at the Candikuning Market

On the way back from the Botanical Gardens, if not perturbed by the haranguing of sellers, catch a glimpse of the amazing variety of fruits and ornamental plants on sale at the *Candikuning Market* along the main road. Stalls packed side by side tempt visitors with tropical and temperate species grown in the lowlands (grape, watermelon, mangosteen, durian, etc.) or in the mountains (tamarillo, passion fruit, tangerine, and even strawberries). However, you will need to bargain very hard if you are tempted. Avoid buying any plants collected from the wild – in particular rare orchid species gathered by local youths. Although these species are protected by local regulations, the authorities of the Gardens seem to do little to control the illegal trade or warn potential buyers.

T/F 0368-21273
krielipi@singaraja.
wasantara.net.id

>*Entering Candikuning from the south, take the left lane at the corn knob statue and follow it for about 3km. Guided visits can be organised by the staff (call in advance, Rp100,000 for 2 hours).*

© Troy Davids

Flower Power

More than 300 plant species are used in Balinese rituals. A symbol of sincerity and purity, flowers are a basic component of offerings. The white or pink flowers of frangipani trees (jepun jawa or Plumeria), the yellow or white cempaka (Michelia) lend their sweet fragrances to every compound. Jempiring, a species of Gardenia with porcelain white flowers is often planted in holy sites. The greenish or yellowish ylang-ylang flowers (sandat, Cananga odorata) develop their scent even when wilted or dried. A network of plant lovers thrives to conserve this green heritage, especially the rare species, and related knowledge.

Antosari – Pupuan

© James K. Jarvie

Rice terraces

A Vision of Abundance

As you drive toward the west from Tabanan, reaching the intersection of **Antosari**, the road becomes less busy. Soon, boundless waves of rice fields on both sides of the road are the only signs of human presence. From Antosari, the main road continues to the left towards the coast, while a smaller road climbs up towards **Pupuan** and **Seririt** in the north. This western end of the district of Tabanan has fewer inhabitants than the east, and even fewer tourists. Yet mankind has conspired with nature to turn these slopes into rice fields, orchards, and coffee groves bursting with cherries in all nuances from green to red. Off the beaten track, forests with pristine waterfalls and hidden temples await nature lovers. This is an area to fill your eyes with awesome memories of great landscapes, shared with no one else but friendly farmers.

Like most areas with few tourists, the coast west of Antosari and the mountain road to Pupuan have only a few hotels, in the middle-to-high end of the price range. They offer quality lodgings in exceptional settings, and are worth the expense for travellers willing to indulge a little. Another option is to stay in one of the more affordable bungalows near Yehgangga or Pasut Beach in the Tabanan area. Pupuan is also within easy reach of Lovina, Seririt, or Munduk in north Bali.

> The road from Denpasar to Gilimanuk passes through **Antosari** and then continues on the coast towards **Balian Beach, Soka Beach, Lalanglinggah,** and **Suraberata**. This road is frequented by many buses and bemos. The road towards **Pupuan** is also used by bemos, although mostly only until 2pm. It is worth hiring your own vehicle to explore the area. A motorcycle is the perfect way to enjoy the great vistas and the fresh air from the ocean and the mountains.

Where to Stay – On the Coast

Hiding in Bliss at Gajah Mina Resort

One of the best resorts in Bali for surroundings and comfort, Gajah Mina is worth the trip to west Bali, especially on a honeymoon. The resort is at the end of a tiny village road winding through rice fields shaded by coconuts, with the deep blue line of the ocean in the background. After a last breathtaking turn, a majestic stairway lets you access a refuge of elegance from out of this world. Each of the villas offers total secrecy in small gardens surrounded by thick walls. Private terraces invite you to lounge amidst the clouds and the crowns of palms.

Tucked in between rice fields, the wide pool is built around the shape of a rice terrace and uses electrolysis to keep the water clean without chemicals. A walk towards the ocean leads to a small cape covered by thick *alang-alang* grasses, ending on a cliff from where dramatic views extend towards both ends of the island. You can also visit grottos accessible at low tide below the cliff, with mysterious carvings, or walk endlessly on the 30km long beach – beware of the very strong surf.

For light exercise and fun, ask to be taken with mountain bikes to the top of a steep road, from where you can descend amidst great landscapes of rice paddies. To relieve sore muscles, get a fantastic massage from a well-trained local villager.

Near Balian Beach, *Sacred River Retreat* proposes a retreat for meditation and yoga fans in a lush garden compound. Guests are welcome to join morning and evening 90-minute yoga and meditation sessions. The staff can also arrange tours to nearby temples, to provide different experiences of meditation. In the centre of the retreat, a small pool with a rock cave is perfect for relaxation. If you are interested in more sportive programs, head for a trek to Lalanglinggah, a walk to Balian Beach, or ask for guided tours to Singaraja or Pupuan. Cultural classes available include silk painting (US$50/person), dancing and *gamelan* music (US$10/person/hr).

❹ 9 Rm – Htw A/C Rst Bch Swp Gvw
T 0361-733 646;
0361-730 084
M 081 238 116 30
F 0361-731 174
www.gajahminaresort.com
> Indicated by a sign on the right side of the road in Suraberata, about 2km after Balian Beach.

❸ 10 Rm – Htw A/C Rst Swp Trk Bcy Shw Cls
T/F 0361-814 993
www.sacred-river.com
> Indicated by a sign on the road from Tabanan to Gilimanuk. The resort gets its name from the Balian River, where a famous balian (traditional healer) used to meditate.

Where to Stay – Belimbing and Pupuan

In the Rice Paddies at Cempaka Belimbing

♥ ❸ ❹ 16 Rm –
Htw A/C Swp Rst
Gvw Trk Shw Bcy Cls
T 0361-753 174
T 082 836 09 05
T/F 0361-754 897
F 0361-754 934
purwa@kcb-tours.com
www.cempakabelimbing.com
> Indicated by a sign at the
junction of Pupuan-Antosari
and on the main road,
10km north of the junction.

Located in one of the most scenic areas in Bali, Cempaka Belimbing Villas offers a peaceful stay and wonderful walks. The bungalows are built in line with the original terraces to enhance the views of the rice fields – the ones on the right side of the road have the most fantastic vistas. The treks, from two to four hours, let you discover rice paddies, farming villages, spice gardens, or small streams. At the end of the trek, get ready for a Balinese massage (US$10) in a small bamboo cottage next to the crystal-clear pool. The owner cares for the exceptional environment of the resort, and has trained the staff in waste management techniques, such as composting and reusing organic waste. The hotel supported the establishment of local dance and *gamelan* groups.

A Planter's life at Sanda Butik Villas

♥ ❸ ❹ 8 Rm –
Htw A/C Rst Swp Gvw Trk
T/F 0828 369 137
T 0817 355 481
www.sandavillas.com
> Indicated on the right
side of the road in Sanda,
before Pupuan when
coming from Antosari.

Opened in 2001, Sanda was built on a coffee plantation – and most of the coffee groves are still to be found, extending their branches full of green, yellow, and red cherries to greet visitors. Everything in Sanda is exquisite, from the refreshing pool facing an airy view of the mountains to the well decorated rooms, with their private reading cabins where you can lounge in comfort in front of rice fields. At about 700m above sea level, the air is cool and the nights quiet. The charming owners care for the environment, and like to encourage visitors to discover the nearby **Blehmantung waterfall**, unless you prefer to hire a local guide (about Rp200,000) for a four-hour trek to **Mt Batukaru** at sunrise.

Where to Eat – Antosari to Pupuan

This area is perfect for gourmets as boutique hotels offer refined cuisine in the most marvelous surroundings, with prices usually ranging between Rp35,000 for a simple dish and Rp70,000 for a full meal. For locations, look up the corresponding hotels above.

The *Naga Restaurant* of *Gajah Mina Resort* in Suraberata features great Asian and international cuisine using local produce – make sure to try some of the Thai dishes, the fresh vegetables soups or salads, or the seafood specialities. Set above the rice paddies, the location is truly exquisite.

At the *Sacred River Retreat* near Balian Beach, *Café Louisa* serves local and Western food with a great choice of vegetarian dishes. It boasts a unique "green dragon juice" made of cinnamon leaves and pinneaple (no dragon meat) to heal any mild stomach problems.

On the road to Pupuan, *Warung Kopi Sedap Malam* at *Cempaka Blimbing* offers Indonesian food and several choices of steaks in a spacious open *bale*. Overlooking a lush view of rice fields, the ambiance is laid back and relaxing. In the high season, dance performances by local children, held twice a week, add to the ambiance during dinner.

Further up in the mountains, *Sanda* is another gourmet stop, with a spacious restaurant terrace featuring a small library, in a romantic atmosphere above the exquisite pools and amongst the coffee trees. The restaurant offers one of the most delicate combinations of Asian and international cuisine around. A pick-up can be arranged for a romantic dinner excursion.

© Jean-Marie Bompard

Rice fields near Antosari

What to Do – Near the Coast

The coast from Soka Beach to Lalanglinggah has endless beaches with grey sand and gorgeous waves that make for romantic sunset walks. Swimming is hazardous as the surf and the current are strong. **Balian Beach**, at the mouth of the Balian River, is a good, rather easy *surfing* spot, with great swimming upstream in the calm river. The water, however, can get muddy from the runoff.

© The Natural Guide

The coast at Suraberata

Rice Field Walks around Lalanglinggah

The 7km stretch of coastal road from Soka beach (where the main Tabanan-Gilimanuk road joins the coast)

The Magic Grass

Lalanglinggah takes its name from the ubiquitous alang-alang grass. This tall, rough herb is considered in most of Asia to be a noxious weed. But for Balinese, it was the first plant to appear after Creation, and they believe it can purify and even replace water used for rituals. If holy water is missing for a ritual, Balinese will walk over to the nearest building with a lalang roof and touch it with the right hand. A high-maintenance, traditional roof thatching material now mostly used for tourist accommodation, alang-alang *is grown on dry hill tops, or brought from other islands as local production is insufficient.*

to the Balian River and Suraberata hides a hinterland of thick-layered rice paddies hiding clusters of farm houses. Although the name of the main village, Lalanglinggah, means "The Wide Grassland", this is where you can find some of the most amazing rice field landscapes in Bali. Get a good map of the area and start walking or biking on any of the small roads leading inland from the main road. You can create you own itinerary anywhere between **Lalanglinggah**, **Antosari**, or the villages of **Antap** and **Lumbung** ("Granary"). Start early in the morning to avoid the searing heat and to have a better chance to meet farmers in the field. Don't hesitate to ask the farmers about rice cultivation – gestures and smiles can break through any language barrier.

To get you started, below are directions for an easy four-kilometre walk which will take you through a small road going north to the village of Lumbung. You'll find the beginning of the road at the hillside of the main Tabanan-Gilimanuk highway, at the border between the villages of Antap and Lalanglinggah. Look for a small white cemented board which reads "*wates Desa Antap*" ("boundary of Antap Village"), and from here start climbing north on the small hillside road. Soon the road passes through vast rice terraces dissected by narrow paths. After 2km, the asphalt road ends at the small village of Pengererengan. Continue on the dirt road for 50m, and look for a small path on the right just after a coconut grove. The path forms a beautiful arch in the middle of a wide rice field, then goes up to a small stream bordered by a bamboo grove. Cross the stream and continue up to the trail heading to the asphalt road at Tireman village. Turn right and go south to the main road, where you can catch a bemo to take you back to your starting point.

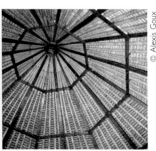

© Alexis Goux

Traditional alang–alang *roof*

Goa Lawah, a Bat Cave at Soka Beach

You'll find Goa Lawah ("The Bat Cave") hidden on the shore just west of Soka Beach. From the entrance of Soka Beach, walk 200m on the main Tabanan-Gilimanuk highway, passing two small bridges along the way. On the beach side, look for the Pura Luhur Srinjong signboard and follow the path to the temple – the temple itself is open only for religious activities. For a better view, follow the weather-beaten path on the left side of the temple down to the beach. Unless there is a ceremony, your only onlookers will be the local lizards and birds. Turn right at the beach to reach the cave, which you are not allowed to enter, as it is regarded as sacred, as indicated by a small shrine guarding its entrance. Nonetheless, you can appreciate the cave from the outside, avoiding the overpowering smell of bats that lurk deep inside. As you walk or swim along the beach, beware of the strong, dangerous current.

> *Take the bus or a bemo on the Tabanan-Gilimanuk route, get off at Soka Beach, then walk to the Pura Luhur Srinjong temple.*

© Bali-photo

Bats in Goa Lawah.

What to Do – On the Road to Pupuan

The road from Antosari to Pupuan is one of the most quiet and scenic in Bali, and a good way to reach the north coast.

A Hidden Temple in the Forest

Pura Luhur Mekori is worth a visit for the serenity of the surrounding Mekori Forest (*Alas Mekori* in Balinese). The temple is located 15km north of the Pupuan-Antosari junction, just after Belimbing. As you climb up the road from Antosari, a sign indicates the temple on the right side of the road, opposite a small market. From the main road, follow a path to the heart of the forest towards the temple under a dense canopy where tree ferns, mosses, and lichens grow as much in the trees as on the ground.

The complex has an outer courtyard populated with long-tailed macaques that flee at the sight of a visitor. The *pura* itself is a simple seven-tiered *meru* made of carved wood and stone. Take the path on the left side of the temple. After a few minutes, this leads to a giant banyan tree with octopus-like strangling roots. A small shrine stands beside the tree. Walk behind the tree to admire wild orchids and small poles covered with thick layers of moss.

> *The Mekori temple can be reached by bus or bemo on the Tabanan-Pupuan-Singaraja route – ask the driver to stop at Pura Luhur Mekori.*

As the Mekori temple is not often visited, take care to respect its sanctity. Put on a long sleeve shirt, a sarong and a sash. Leave a small donation to help preserve the pura.

A Gentle Hike to the Blehmantung Waterfall

This short hike is easy and will take you through a lovely landscape of rice fields, forest, and coffee farms. Start from the village of Pupuan, where a blue sign advertises the start of the road to the waterfall. Follow a rocky road, which can be used by motorcycles, passing village houses, rice fields, and coffee plantations, until you can go no further. There you'll find a small house on your left and some concrete steps on your right, which will lead you to an irrigation channel.

Follow the channel past a big boulder until you reach a small dam, above which a first, small waterfall shimmers on a dark, forested cliff. From here on, a concrete staircase to your right ends up on a narrow dirt track winding through a coffee plantation. A couple of hundred metres more and you'll reach the second waterfall, a 50m high fall cascading into a small pool where you can swim in cool refreshing water – the perfect place for a picnic. The whole area has a mysterious atmosphere, enhanced by the presence of mossy wooden shrines guarded by erect rock blades.

The 1.5km walk to the waterfall takes 30 to 45 minutes. Bring comfortable hiking sandals or running shoes. Don't forget an empty plastic bag to collect garbage left behind – even by other people! You can get a map to the waterfall at Sanda Butik Villas.

© The Natural Guide

The Blehmantung waterfall.

Rice Field Vistas in Pupuan

Continuing north after Sanda, the road goes through dazzling rice fields near Pupuan, and between Pupuan and Mayong – perhaps the best rice field views of Bali. It is worth coming here with your own vehicle to stop at will, and admire the dramatic landscapes that change at every bend and make great photographs.

Towards the North

Continuing from Pupuan to the north, you reach **Seririt** on the north coast. From there, you may decide to explore the beautiful area between **Seririt** and **Munduk**, continue westwards to the quiet beach and awesome corals of **Pemuteran** and **Menjangan**, or drive east towards **Lovina**, **Air Sanih**, and **Tejakula** – refer to our north Bali chapter for a natural discovery of the "other side of Bali", as the north coast is often called.

Jembrana

The Wild West

Although Jembrana, or *jimbar wana* ("the great forest") is mostly known for its forested mountains, it is also a landscape of fertile **rice fields and plantations**, with a pleasant **water reservoir** and stretches of **black-sand coastlines** that make for easy **surfing**. The area is home to Christian communities in Blimbingsari and Palasari, as well as mixed Muslim communities of Javanese, Madurese, and Bugis. The coast of Jembrana also houses two impor-tant Hindu temples dedicated to the legendary priest, Danghyang Nirartha, who arrived from Java on this shoreline. Don't miss the wooden **horse carts** in Negara and a **hollow banyan tree** in Manggissari.

Since few tourists make it all the way to Jembrana, the choice of accommodations is limited. *Medewi Beach* has inexpensive losmen and good middle-range bungalows. Travellers will also find a choice of simple hotels and homestays in *Negara* and on the beaches nearby. For a luxurious retreat, tuck yourself away in Taman Wana, in front of the *Palasari Dam*.

Where to Stay – Medewi Beach

Located halfway between Tabanan and Gilimanuk, the small beachside village of Medewi has several inexpensive homestays that often play host to surfers. In the more upmarket category, *Puri Dajuma Cottages* has com-fortable bungalows in front of the beach in **Pekutatan**, as well as a spa and sauna in a corner of the garden.

> The main Denpasar-Gilimanuk highway runs along the coast of Jembrana, passing through the centre of Negara, the district capital. Daily buses from Denpasar (**Ubung** terminal) to **Gilimanuk** serve the road. Ojeks can get you onto small inland roads. Around the town of **Negara**, try the dokar, or traditional wooden carts pulled by small horses (about Rp10,000 for a tour of town).

Negara, the capital of Jembrana, is well-known for its bull races (mekepung). Many travellers, however, are repelled by the harsh treatment suffered during the race by the buffalo, which are often whipped until they bleed.

20 Rm – Htw A/C Rst Bch Swp Trk Bcy Ckr Spa
T 0365-43 955
F 0365-43 966
www.dajuma.com
> Indicated by a sign along the main road before Pekutatan market (pasar).

The black-sand beach dotted with traditional *jukung* boats is perfect for a relaxing stroll, while next to the restaurant is an inviting seawater pool. The hotel staff can take guests for a two-hour walk to nearby clove plantations, and can arrange treks in the West Bali National Park as well as sailing trips.

Where to Stay – Negara and Around

Few travellers stay in Negara, except in August when the town springs to life for the annual bull race (*mekepung*). It is a good base, however, to explore the region.

Travellers in search of a peaceful environment will appreciate *Taman Carik*, further north in Sawe Rangsasa. The red brick bungalows are stretched throughout rice fields, with very basic rooms and local-style, cold-water bathrooms (*mandi*).

🚩 *9 Rm – A/C*
T/F 0365-44 249
M 081 239 503 27
> *Indicated by a sign on Jl. Ahmad Yani, 200m west of the traffic light to Kota Negara.*

Another inexpensive option is to stay on the beach at *Delodbrawah*, which has smaller waves than Medewi and is popular with locals. A few *homestays* spread out along the coast or on the roadside offer basic accommodations with simple *mandi* for the price of Rp30-40,000. The most pleasant are **Segara Agung**, **Taman Asri**, and **Mustika**. For meals, a short walk brings you to the nearby cafés serving dishes for Rp10-15,000.

> *Turn south to Delodbrawah 7km east of Negara, then follow the signs to the beach.*

Further west in Balukrening Beach, *Bali Warna Lokal* has rather shabby standard rooms, but the bungalows overlooking the sea are a good value. The open *bale* in the compound is for breakfast and coffee only. For meals, you can either go to town or to the nearby **Ha Pel** restaurant.

🚩 *8 Rm –*
> *Follow the sign to the Ha Pel Hotel at the Cupel-Gilimanuk-Negara junction, 1km west of Negara.*

A Lakeside Hideaway at Taman Wana Villas

At the border of the Palasari dam, this resort offers luxurious villas constructed from wood and marble with thatched roofs. Hidden in the lush greenery, they overlook the forest and rice fields.

Guests are offered a wide range of activities, from walks in the rice fields, village tours to see traditional sugar making, temples, and churches, or more

Top of page:
Dokar horse carts in Negara

adventurous forest walks. Don't miss morning boating on the Palasari Reservoir. The dam serves irrigation needs in the area; you may spot farmers walking around the hotel to attend to their rice fields or examine their *subak* waterways. To bring an active day to a relaxing close, take a dip in the small whirlpool a few metres above the lake, or catch the breeze in the wooden spa, dreaming that you're the nymph of the lake.

💙 ❹ ❺ *27 Rm –
Htw A/C Rst Swp Gvw
Trk Ckr Cls Spa
T/F 0365-40 970
twfv@dps.centrin.net.id
twvs@dps.centrin.net.id
www.bali-tamanwana-
villas.com*

Where to Eat – Medewi – Negara

Many warungs and restaurants along the road offer various types of Indonesian food. This is your chance to taste the hot chilli curries of Padang cuisine, originally from West Sumatra and popular throughout Indonesia. Migrants from Madura at the eastern tip of Java have brought their specialties of crispy *sate kambing* (goat kebabs).

For something less spicy, *Warung Bidadari* on Jl. Ngurah Rai serves a tasty *nasi campur* (mixed rice). Further down the road, in front of Hotel Wira Pada, *Café Nathalia* serves noodles and Chinese food. You can also try *ayam-panggang-goreng* (grilled-then-fried chicken) at *Rumah Makan Puas*, 200m east of Café Nathalia.

What to Do – Beaches and Surfing

As elsewhere along the southwest coast of Bali, the shores of Jembrana are dotted with quiet, black-sand beaches with strong waves. Always remain close to the beach when in the water, as currents can take even good swimmers away in an instant.

The first beach on the way from Tabanan is *Medewi Beach*, which is better for **surfing** than swimming. Some surfers say it has the longest lefthand wave in Bali, reaching 50 to 150m on a normal day, and 400m during the best days. It is suited to all surfers, including beginners, as the swells are not too high (1 to 2.5m at most) and the landing is on sand and boulders instead of reefs. There is no surf shop, so bring your own gear and befriend local surfers to learn about the best spots and surfing times, usually early morning.

© Dedok

Coconut plantation around Medewi

For smaller waves, go further west to *Delod-berawah*, just before Negara. The beach is popular with locals and has a few friendly cafés and lodgings. The clean, black-sand shore is ideal for quiet morning walks. Go for a walk to rice fields following the side road, 100m inland, heading west to Yehkuning. A quieter place to laze away a few hours and enjoy the gentle sea breeze is *Balukrening*, located around five kilometres west of Negara. Less frequented by locals because of its isolated location, the beach offers gentle waves and an ambiance of pure calm.

What to Do – On the Steps of Nirartha

According to the legend, Danghyang Nirartha landed in Negara around AD 1546, crossing the straits from Java on the broad leaf of a bread fruit tree (*keluwih*). He landed near Negara, where he took a rest under the shade of an *ancak* tree. There, his followers later commemorated this event by building Pura Ancak, a beautiful limestone temple now known as *Pura Gede Perancak*, sitting by the river's edge near the harbour.

> *Perancak is located on the coast south of Negara. Several routes lead to the temple. The most exciting one goes through vast rice fields from Dauhwaru past Budeng and Samblong. To find it, turn left at the first junction indicating Kota Negara, at the eastern entrance of the town, then just follow the road signs to Perancak.*

Travelling around the island, meditating, and building temples, Nirartha is said to have impressed the Balinese with his magical powers. He contributed to incorporating Buddhist elements into the local religion, and added the *padmasana* to Balinese temples – a lotus-shaped throne made of stone and believed to be the seat of Sanghyang Widi, the Supreme Being, or Surya, the sun god.

After a pilgrimage to the temple, stroll around the *Perancak harbour*, where traditional fishing boats, bigger than ordinary *jukung* and painted in bright colours, bob leisurely on the waters at the mouth of the Perancak River. Every morning from 5 to 9am, a busy *fish market* is held on the beach. Fishermen and fish buyers sing boastingly of the day's choice catches, with *dangdut*, a popular music style heavily influenced by Indian and Arabic tunes, roaring in the background.

© Dedok

While in the area, pay a visit to the *turtle conservation site* of Kurma Asih. The turtle project began in 1997 with the support of the WWF, involving most of the fishermen who caught turtles for ritual and commercial purposes. The WWF made fishermen aware of the growing rarity of turtles and looked for ways to provide them with incentives to protect this endangered species. The project is now run by a group of locals. They purchase turtle eggs from villagers, then nestle them in a quiet part of the beach in Perancak. In another corner is the turtle hatchery, where young turtles are cared for before being released into the sea.

The turtle hatchery needs help to sustain its activities. Visitors can support the program by making a donation or adopting a turtle nest. Contact: Pak Anom Astika Perancak Village T/F 0365- 43 702

Further east along the coast, *Pura Rambut Siwi* ("Temple of the Worshipped Hairs"), like other sanctuaries allegedly built by Nirartha, is located on a remarkable site. The temple sits on the border of the sea in Yehembang, offering a clear view of Java and a peaceful landscape of rice fields, with verdant mountains in the background. The serene atmosphere exudes the spirituality attributed to the great Javanese priest.

Legend has it that a small temple already existed here when Nirartha arrived in Negara. Following the insistent demands of the guarding priest, he offered up prayers at the temple, which then crumbled to the ground. Nirartha rebuilt the temple and gave a lock of hair to the local priests. The hair was enshrined and locked up in the three-tiered *meru* in the inner courtyard, which can only be accessed for praying.

Pura Rambut Siwi is indicated by a sign on the main road, around 16km west of Medewi. You will see many buses and trucks whose drivers have stopped for prayers. Wear a sash and give a donation before going around the temple with the local priest. Ask the priest to show you the carvings on a red brick bale, telling the story of Nirartha and his fight with a dragon-snake.

Going down the coastline, you can find another group of shrines – **Pura Tirta**, dedicated to a source of holy water, **Pura Penataran**, and the cave of **Goa Mayan Sati** ("The Powerful Tiger Cave"). Local people like to tell travellers that the cave has a secret walkway that leads all the way to Pura Pulaki on the north of Bali. As you take in the stillness and superb sight of southeast Java, it becomes clear why Nirartha chose this area to build his sanctuaries.

Walks Around Christian Bali

A Balinese Christmas

"The Gospel is like water: it can be held in a glass or in a coconut shell." (Dr Mastra, head of the Balinese Protestant Church, quoted by F.B. Eiseman in Sekala dan Niskala). *And indeed, Balinese have integrated Christianity into their own culture. They practice Balinese dances and combine local names with Christian ones – as in Made Veronica. Angel statues wear Balinese costumes and at Christmas, Palasari fills with penjor – the graceful bamboo archs decorating Balinese villages during festivals. Women attend mass in a kebaya (brocaded blouse) and men wear their destar (head cloth). The sermon is delivered in Indonesian, and attendants sing hymns in Balinese.*

Palasari and Blimbingsari are home to the largest Christian communities on Bali. The settlements date back to 1939. Despite the fact that there were only a few hundred non-European Christians on Bali at the time, the Dutch feared that missionaries would corrupt the local culture. They wanted to make sure that Bali remained unaltered as an attraction for tourists and a showcase for enlightened colonialism. The colonial government asked that the missionaries and their followers relocate to these remote areas. The Catholics settled in Palasari, while the Protestants settled further west in Blimbingsari – which they turned into a training centre for missionaries bound for jungle postings.

A peaceful village with the biggest Catholic church in Bali, Palasari is a good start for walks in the gorgeous countryside. Constructed from 1954 to 1958, the white building is adorned with Balinese carvings and charming black roofs at the rear, and surrounded by a well-kept garden. To visit the church, go to the back and ask permission from the friendly priest. On the northern side of the field is an orphanage founded by a nun, Maria Goretti, and run by the church.

The junction to Palasari is found 17km west of Negara (follow the signs to Taman Wana). If you go by bus, get off at the junction and ask an ojek to take you to Palasari. From the church, take the small road heading east, following the sign to Taman Wana. The view along this road is superb, over extensive rice fields and the green hills of Mt Melaya and Mt Jatukangsa in the distance. After 1km, the road starts to climb and turns sharply. From here the view of Palasari church in the greenery is not to be missed. Walk down the road and take a small tour in the vastness of the rice fields. Take a break in a simple resting *bale*, enjoying the quiet and fresh air. About 200m before the villas, when the road starts to climb again, look for a small path on your left.

© Murdani Usman

Mass in Palasari

This leads to the southern part of the **Palasari Reservoir**. Climb up to your right and head for the small artificial lake. After the irrigation office, the asphalt road goes to an open field with a *wantilan* (public pavilion). At this junction, follow the road to the left leading back to Palasari village at the northern part of the church. Turn right on the asphalt road to the intersection of Ekasari and take an ojek to go back to the main road.

© Titiek Pratiwi

Hollow Trees and Giant Bamboo Pipes

On the northern side of Medewi, a twisting road climbs from Pekutatan up through Tista village and towards Pupuan. Around 10km from the junction, in Manggissari, the road passes through the base of a giant banyan tree, known as *Bunut Bolong* ("the hollow banyan"). Locals believed that the *bunut* tree has been there since the first settlement of Manggissari in the mid-1920s. Passing under the tree seems like passing through an antique doorway; old, yet vigorous, and wonderfully carved by nature, a silent witness to the local history.

Bunut Bolong, the hollow banyan tree

Continue on the road until it splits at the small village of Tista. Take the right turn and follow the road southwards for 6km to *Juwukmanis* ("sweet oranges"). The village has two **waterfalls**, located on both sides of the road. Both are around 6-7m high, and cascade into refreshingly cool pools 3-4m deep before joining two small rivers. For the eastern waterfall, go to the *bale banjar* (village hall), marked with the statue of a farmer in the front. Follow a small path at the back of the building, walking steeply down to the waterfall through a dense coffee plantation. For the western waterfall, look for a path on the opposite side of the *bale banjar*. Along both paths are green valleys, with a dense covering of cloves and coffee, the air thick with pungent aromas of both plants. Make sure to wear good footwear as the paths can be slippery. The walk down takes only half an hour, and a bit longer to climb up back to the main road.

❀ *For a good local guide, ask for Pak Ketut Agus at Juwukmanis village. There is no public transport to Juwukmanis, so it is better to rent an ojek. From Juwukmanis, the road winds down to Pangyangan through a vast clove plantation. Stop at Pondok Bambu, a viewing point with a few bale, around 4km south of Juwukmanis. The view is superb, stretching down to the southern coastline.*

A Jegog Performance in Juwukmanis

For jegog shows, contact:
I Ketut Surung
Suar Agung Foundation
Puri Gamelan Suar Agung
Sangkaragung Village,
T 0365-40 674;
or in Denpasar:
I Ketut Suwentra
T 0361-232 765
F 0361-224 908
www.jasatours.com

The name *jegog* comes from the word *nyegogog*, meaning "the biggest" in Balinese. It refers to instruments made from giant bamboo tubes decorated with colourful carvings. They produce a deep, thunderous sound. They are so large (up to 2m long and 65cm in diameter) that the musician has to sit on top and play them with heavy mallets. Don't hesitate to sit under the *jegog* during the performance to appreciate the full resonance it can generate.

Like the *kulkul* (split wooden drum) used in most Balinese village halls, the *jegog* was initially used to call people to collective work for the community (*gotong royong*). In 1912, Kiyang Geliduh, a local artist, incorporated them into the *gamelan* orchestra with smaller bamboo instruments. This new *gamelan jegog* accompanies Jembrana's traditional dances created for the *mekepung* (buffalo race), as well as the local *leko* dances (sitting dances).

The best performances are the *jegog mebarung*, during which two or three groups of musicians compete, including an enthusiastic group of children aged 8 to 14. **Yayasan Suar Agung**, a local foundation, shows regular performances in **Sangkaragung** village, where there is a private museum displaying *jegog* instruments (the entrance fee – negotiable – is US$35/person, and is used to sustain the activities of the foundation).

© Supardi Asmorobangun

The Juwukmanis waterfall

© Yayasan Suar Agung

A jegog performance by children

West Bali National Park

© Djuna Ivereigh

The large deer (menjangan)

Jungle, Birds and Corals

Beyond manicured rice fields and temples, Bali is also home to the 19,000ha West Bali National Park, stretching across the two districts of Buleleng and Jembrana. A large part consists of marine and coastal areas housing rich coral, while the rest is covered with monsoon forest and rainforest. An additional 55,000 hectares of buffer zone, covered with plantations and forest, encircle the park. The road from Cekik to Pemuteran crosses the park, passing the village of Sumberklampok, an inhabited enclave within the protected area.

Though most of the park is set for research and conservation purposes, a few **trekking** routes are open to visitors. With the assistance of skilled guides, visitors may spot birds and wild animals. Within the park, the tiny, uninhabited **Menjangan Island** is one of the best **diving** sites around Bali. All the dive shops in Bali can organise trips to Menjangan. The nearest ones can be found in Pemuteran (north Bali). Apart from some upmarket resorts, the area has few accommodations. Visitors to the Park may stay in Pemuteran or Negara (Jembrana).

Where to Stay – Cekik and Gilimanuk

It is possible to camp at the park's camping area in Cekik, but the open ground, close to the busy main road, is not very interesting. Travellers may also

> *Daily buses from Denpasar to Gilimanuk pass in front of the park's headquarters in* **Cekik** *(Denpasar-Gilimanuk: about 4hrs from Ubung Terminal). The island of* **Menjangan** *can be accessed by boat from the small harbour of Labuhanlalang. To reach the harbour, catch a bemo at the junction in front of the headquarters, heading to Banyuwedang.*
> *From the north, buses from Singaraja to Gilimanuk pass in front of the park's offices in Cekik and Labuhanlalang (Singaraja-Gilimanuk: about 3hrs from Banyuasri Terminal).*

> *West Bali National Park Headquarters, Cekik: T 0365-61 060, open 7:30am-3:30pm. Labuhanlalang Office, open 7:30am-3:30pm.*

❶❷ 22 Rm – Htw A/C
T 0365-61 264
F 0365-61 265
> Indicated by a sign
on the main road,
1.5km west of Cekik.

♥ **❹❺** 16 Rm –
Htw A/C Rst Bch Swp
Div Trk Spa
T 0361-484 085
F 0361-484 767
www.wakaexperience.com
> Accessible by a
15min boat ride from
Labuhanlalang. Book
ahead to arrange trans-
portation. Trekking in the
park can be arranged, as
well as diving in
Menjangan. The resort
has a good library on the
park and Bali's environ-
ment. To protect the
park's fauna, it is forbiden
to bring animals.

overnight in the busy harbour of **Gilimanuk**, where
people stop on their way to cross the Bali strait by ferry.
Lodgings in town are mostly intended for the overnight
stay of truck drivers. Most are not very traveller-friendly,
especially for solo women. *Hotel Sari* has decent
bamboo-walled rooms in quiet quarters off the main road.
The standard rooms are a good value. No restaurant,
but there are many warungs on the main road.

A Deluxe Jungle Hut at Waka Shorea

This romantic resort is built on an eight-hectare "ecotourism" concession in the National Park. Consistent
with their philosophy to respect natural landscapes, the
designers made an effort to protect the park's environment and have not displaced or destroyed any trees.
Wooden bungalows on stilts, decorated with style, are
hidden amidst thick vegetation, making you feel like you
are part of the jungle. On the white beach fringed by
crystal clear water, two deluxe villas are surrounded by
small gardens, where the wild vegetation of dry herbs is
allowed to grow freely. Due to the proximity of the
highly-populated island of Java, the waves bring a lot of
plastic waste, but the resort's beaches are kept clean by
the dedicated staff.

The lovely pool, in the shape of a half-moon, contains few chemicals, so that it can be used as a drinking
spot by wild animals during the dry season. By keeping
quiet while sipping your own drink, you may spot boars
and small deer coming here to clench their thirst. Above
the pool, the restaurant and spa, where water use is limited, let you admire the peaceful landscape.

Where to Eat – Gilimanuk

Bodrek Arsana, editor of *Latitudes* magazine, chose
Warung Men Tempeh as one of the top warungs of
Bali. Open from 10am to 4pm in the busy Gilimanuk bus
terminal, it serves the best *ayam betutu* in Bali – chicken
simmered in an exotic mixture of garlic, galangale,

shallots, laos root, turmeric, ginger, hot chillies, and shrimp paste. This is your chance to have an authentic Balinese food experience, side-by-side with locals on their way to Java, in the dusty ambiance of the terminal. Expect to have your tongue severely bitten by the hot chilli sauce, which is not made for tourist palates. For less piquant food, go to restaurant *Lestari* on the main road to Gilimanuk, 1.5 km west of Cekik, or eat at one of the warungs serving *nasi campur* near the terminal.

The jetty in Labuhanlalang

Where to Eat – Labuhanlalang

There are several cafés at the Labuhanlalang jetty serving the usual local menu of *nasi campur* or noodles, sandwiches, pancakes, and spaghetti. One of the first warungs in the area, *Warung Ibu Dewa*, is worth a try for its tasty *nasi campur* and friendly service.

What to Do – Trekking and Bird-Watching

There is no entrance fee to drive through the park, but you need a permit and a licensed guide to enter the park and visit any site within. You can obtain the permit and arrange guided trekking or camping at the park headquarters in Cekik. It has a small visitors' centre displaying information on the park's flora and fauna. Another option is to head north for another 10km to the visitors' centre in Labuhanlalang, especially if you want to go directly to Menjangan island.

The park offers several trekking routes ranging from a 2-hour walk, recommended for bird spotting, a 3 to 4-hour walk to Telukterima, or a 6 to 7-hour hike to Mt Klatakan. Ask your guide if you want to spot particular animals, birds, or plants. Below are two recommended trails.

> Drive to Tegalbunder or take a bemo from Cekik or Labuhanlalang, and walk to the ranger point in Sumberklampok. Go only with certified English-speaking guides registered with the park. They know the area very well, and are eager to provide information on the plants and animals. Some speak German, Dutch, and Japanese. Every Friday, the guides clean up the beach as part of the Bali Clean-Up campaign.

A Two-Hour Walk for Bird Watchers

Although the National Park was set up to protect the **Bali starling** (*jalak Bali, Leucopsar rothschildi*) there are so few of them left in the wild that your only chance to spot them is in captivity.

© Djuna Ivereigh

The Bali starling

The guide fees for this two-hour trek are Rp65,000 for 1 or 2 persons, or Rp104,000 for a group of 3 to 5 persons.

Macaques in the forest

© Bali-photo

The guide fee for the trail is Rp207,500 for 1 or 2 persons, or 310,000 for 3 to 5 persons. It is also possible to shorten this walk to 4 hours (Rp95,000 for 1 or 2 persons, 152,000 for 3 to 5 persons). For the shorter version, start at Klatakan village and climb the trek up to the peak of Klatakan, then go down to Ambyarsari where you can take an ojek back to Cekik.

Near Sumberklampok, a pre-release centre keeps a few couples for breeding before setting them free in the park. You'll have to get a permit and pay a conservation fee of Rp300,000 per person to see the caged starlings – a good incentive for the park authorities to protect the birds, but probably excessive for most travellers, unless they are serious bird fans.

To spot birds in the forest, ask a guide to take you on the **Tegalbunder** trail, a 2-hour walk through the monsoon forest near the pre-release centre. Try to start in the early morning, around 6am, to have more of a chance to see a good variety of birds. Species that are likely to be spotted are the chattering yellow-vented bulbul, common throughout Indonesia; the pretty black-napped oriole, with its bright yellow body; the black or ashy drongo, which likes to feed on insects; the restless pied fantail; and the barn owl, which hides in dark places during the daytime. You may also hear the high-pitched chirps of olive-backed sunbirds or the monotonous tweet of the brown-throated sunbird. Bring a pair of binoculars and a good book about Bali's birds.

A Seven-Hour Hike to Gunung Klatakan

This trail is the most strenuous, yet most interesting, hike in the park. Expect the walk to take 6 to 7 hours and put on comfortable shoes. The walk starts at the ranger point at Sumberklampok, passes through the forest and then goes down to the main road near Mt Klatakan. In the dry season, you may ask permission to overnight in the park with your own camping equipment.

During the walk, you will pass the tropical rainforest area, and see protected plant species such as the *sawo kecik (Manilkara kauki)*, the *bayur (Pterospermum javanicum)*, rattan, and rare orchids. Although you may not always spot them in the dense foliage, you will likely hear the voices of black monkeys, long tailed macaques, or the harsh cackle of the Asian pied hornbill and the wreathed hornbill. Watch closely for black giant squirrels leaping

on tree branches or the occasional appearance of small
kancil (barking deer).

Diving Pulau Menjangan

This tiny island made its way onto the diving map following
a camping party of the Indonesian navy in 1978. Since
then, it has become one of Bali's most appreciated dive
sites along with Tulamben. The island used to be known
for its deer (*menjangan*), now absent from the island due
to poaching. Menjangan is now famous for its calm and
clear water, where diving can be done most of the year
– although the sea can be too rough in January and
February. It is also popular for its many gorgonians and
soft coral, and its wall full of caves and crevasses. The
site is also loaded with reef fish such as the angelfish,
butterfly fish, anthias, and gobies. Try the rarely-visited
tiny wreck ship known as **Kapal Budak** (slave ship).
On this calm spot, full of *acropora* and gorgonians, you
may have the chance to swim with green turtles. As you
follow the 30m-long wall to the wreck, you may also
come face to face with a white-tip shark lurking at the
deep corner of the old ship.

A Temple of Love at Jayaprana's Grave

This simple temple offers a great view of the north coast
and Menjangan island floating above the clear ocean, with
the blurred shapes of coral reefs beneath. The temple
was erected on ground believed to be the grave of
Jayaprana and Layonsari, the Balinese heroes of love.
According to the story, Jayaprana was a foster son of the
king of Kalianget, who wanted to steal his beautiful wife.
The jealous king sent Jayaprana on an expedition
to repel brigands, and then set an ambush to kill him.
Jayaprana was buried on what are now the temple's
grounds. Upon learning of his death, Layonsari, his wife,
chose to follow him to his grave instead of bowing to
the king's wish. A simple temple was erected on the site
and people come here to pray for love.

*Dive trips to
Menjangan can be
arranged from any dive
centre in **Pemuteran** or
around Bali. It takes 30
minutes to reach the
island by boat from
Labuhanlalang.
A 10-person boat costs
Rp250,000 for 4 hours,
and Rp20,000 for each
additional hour.
Add the park's entrance
fee (Rp2,500/person)
and Rp60,000/boat
for the guides and
conservation fund.*

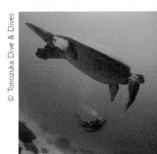

© Tonozuka Dive & Dives

*Green turtle near
Menjangan Island*

> *Around 12km east
of Cekik or 1km west
of LabuhanLalang. The
temple, Pura Jayaprana,
is located on top of a
stone stairway 15 minutes
away on foot from the
main road.*

Bali starlings (Leucopsar Rothschildi) *in captivity*

© Djuna Ivereigh

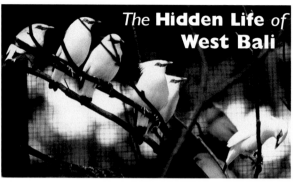

The **Hidden Life** *of* **West Bali**

Threatened Birds, Confused People

By Titiek Pratiwi

A Park for a Bird

The West Bali National Park was set up to preserve the Bali starling and its forest habitat. International experts proposed a 77,000ha area, but the provincial forest service, eyeing possible profits from forest exploitation, never agreed to the proposal. The park remained at a mere 19,000ha – its original size when it was set as a game reserve by the Council of Kings in 1946. Conservation specialists have it that this is too small an area to maintain a viable bird population.

"The Bali starling? We used to spot it all the time on our roof tops, it was nothing special – like a pigeon, only a bit prettier," explains Pak Misnawi, a dweller of Sumberklampok. A human enclave in the West Bali National Park, this village has been at the centre of a bird-versus-people controversy for the last 30 years. Its history, and the tragedy of the "prettier-than-pigeon" starling that is Bali's only endemic bird, illustrate the vagaries of conservation in poor countries.

According to Pak Misnawi and his neighbours, the Bali starling (*jalak Bali*) started to disappear in the wild after 1977, when it was declared an endangered species by the International Union for the Conservation of Nature. "Nowadays, the bird cannot be found in the wild. I think it is probably because it is 'protected' in captivity," adds Pak Misnawi.

Don't jump to the conclusion that the old man mistook the cause for the effect. There are other cases of animal and plant species whose trade value rocketed after they were declared endangered, attracting hordes of poachers. In fact, declaring a species as "protected" without providing the means for its effective protection can be a sure way to contribute to its extinction.

© Dedok

All the Pretty Birds

In the 1920s, the small white bird with its distinctive blue-striped eyes roamed around the whole northwest of Bali, from Seririt to Labuhanlalang. A combination of hunting and destruction of its habitat for agriculture and plantations dwindled its numbers to 112 in 1974, far below what biologists consider a viable population.

Numbers continued to fall after the Bali starling's habitat was declared a protected area in 1985. From 105 birds in the wild in 1980, the population fell to 36 in 1991, and has remained below 30 since 1994 – reaching dramatically low counts of 6 or 8 in 2001 and 2002. The guards know very well why. Since the bird has been known worldwide as endangered, its prices have reached US$6000 in the United States or Europe and US$2000 locally. A guard interviewed by *Kompas* in 2001 stated half-jokingly that the bird is worth more than the life of the park's security personnel. Paid less than US$150 per month, with no proper facilities, poor management, and widespread corruption, guards have little incentive to risk their lives for a pretty pigeon.

Poachers don't need to hunt the birds far. The park keeps a few – from a handful to several dozens – in captivity, buying them from zoos and breeding them before releasing them in the wild. Though the cages seem as heavily safeguarded as Fort Knox, this is not enough to dishearten high-spirited burglars. In February 1999, a group of thieves managed to break into the pre-release centre, took the guards hostage, and ran away with 39 birds. In August 2000, 13 more birds were stolen from the cages, and 15 more in February 2004. The statistics of the pre-release centre fail to account for the loss of many others, some of which may be stolen.

In a classic game found throughout Indonesia and other poor countries with illegal logging and poaching issues, the powers-that-be and the local population blame each other for the bird's demise. For the park's authorities, local villagers are to blame for hunting and

The Migrants

Sumberklampok is home to Javanese and Madurese who moved to west Bali in the 1930s to work in teak and coconut plantations set up by the Dutch. People from east Bali were also relocated here after the eruption of Mt Agung in 1963. After independence, the plantations were leased by the government to local private corporations, but were abandoned in the 1990s. Having lost their jobs, the villagers turned to fishing, dry land farming, and logging timber – most of it from the deserted plantations and degraded forests surrounding the park.

© Leonard Lueras

Forest in the National Park

stealing the birds. Local community members accuse outsiders working with the complicity of the park's guards. In all cases, the elegant blue-striped bird will remain threatened as long as the law is not enforced, especially if local villagers have no incentive to protect it.

No Land for the People

© Bali Bird Park

As for the residents of Sumberkelampok, they have more pressing issues at hand. "The authorities didn't explain how the National Park functions and for what reasons," stated Made Indrawati, a local village leader. "Before the park was set up, we used to collect firewood and fruits in the forest. Fishermen looked for a catch in what is now the protected area. The National Park limits their access to the natural resources they depend upon." After the opening of the park, the government proposed to relocate the people to Sulawesi, 1000km away from Bali, with promises of a better life as part of a national resettlement program called "transmigration".

"The authorities said that our area would be reforested for conservation purposes," said Made Indrawati. Then we heard that a Jakarta-based group planned to build a huge tourist resort near Sumberkelampok. We refused to leave, and decided to fight for our rights." The community conducted protests as far away as Jakarta to defend their settlement. As of today, no final decision has been taken and the legal status of Sumberkelampok remains unclear.

A Bali starling couple

Fighting for Tomorrow

Nevertheless, the villagers mobilised themselves to conserve their natural resources and to find new ways to meet their needs. Made Indrawati, along with other local leaders, initiated the Sumberkelampok Cooperative (KUB Sumberkelampok). They started by mapping areas where villagers can collect forest products without endangering them. Other projects followed to test organic farming, improve water supply, and plant fruit and firewood trees.

To increase their income without depending on the forest, the villagers decided to try seaweed farming – but their site falls within the park's marine area, and the authorities have yet to agree to revise the park's boundaries to allow this development. Local farmers are now wondering why two tourism resorts (the 8ha Waka Shorea and the 200ha Menjangan Jungle and Beach Resort) could obtain a concession from the park while they can't use a few hectares of coastal area to make a living. As long as money will remain the main motivation of the powers that be, evicted humans and little hunted birds will have a hard time to survive.

WWF: Marine Conservation in West Bali
By WWF Indonesia

Active in Indonesia since 1962 as part of the WWF global network, **WWF Indonesia** *fights to conserve the archipelago's biodiversity for present and future generations.* **WWF's Marine Program** *works in Sumberkima village on Bali's west coast to promote sustainable methods of catching aquarium fish, and eradicating destructive practices such as the use of cyanide. Fishermen co-designed aquarium fish aggregation devices, suitable fishing nets, and fish decompression buckets.*

The Marine Program supported community organisation to transfer information about eco-labelling programs. After linking with two exporters in 2003, the fishermen were able to export more than 20,000 fish and are now ready for certification by the Marine Aquarium Council, which will verify that the fish is harvested in a sustainable manner – a big plus with eco-sensitive consumers.

WWF's Endangered Species Program also developed a campaign to raise awareness of the need to protect green turtles in Bali, supporting the establishment of a Turtle Centre in Serangan Island. **WWF's Climate Change Program** *uses stories on the importance of reef conservation for poor coastal communities in west Bali to inform citizens of rich countries of the need to curtail CO_2 emissions, responsible for global warming and the death of coral.*

With a Little Help
WWF Indonesia has facilitated the development of a Community Forum to take care of the coastal areas near the National Park, grouping fishermen, local enterprises (including dive resorts), and the Cooperative of Sumberkelampok. The Forum encourages non-destructive fishing methods, helps guard the marine protected area, and cleans up the coasts. The Forum also initiated seaweed farming as an alternative source of income for local people.

Contact: Forum Komunikasi Masyarakat Peduli Pesisir (Coastal Care Community Forum), c/o WWF office: T 0365-61 536 fkmpp_tnbb@yahoo.com

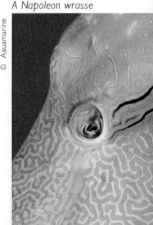

A Napoleon wrasse

© Aauamarine

Mundeh

To Pupuan

Pupuan Sawah

Margatelu

Pekutatan

Tiyinggading

Antagana

Lumbung Kauh

Angkah

Loyanan

west
To Negara

Lumbung

Surabereate

Sacred River
Retreat & Cafe

Lalanglinggah

Badegede

Gajah Mina & Restaurant H

H

Antosari

Trek Lalanglinggah

Bajera

Selemadeg

Balian Beach
(Surfing)

Tireman

Antap

Selemadeg

Goa Lawah

Soka Beach

Tibubiy

Bibi's Cottage H

Pasut Beach

Klating Beac

Indian Ocean

N

Tabanan – Antosari 418-419

Scale 1:130 000

0 km   1.5 km   3 km

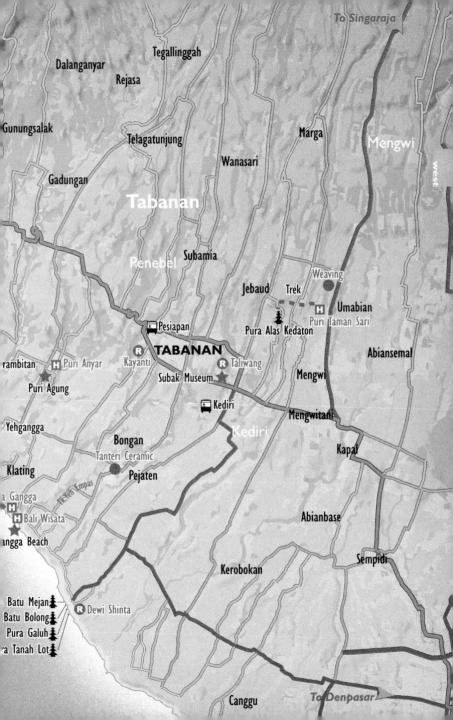

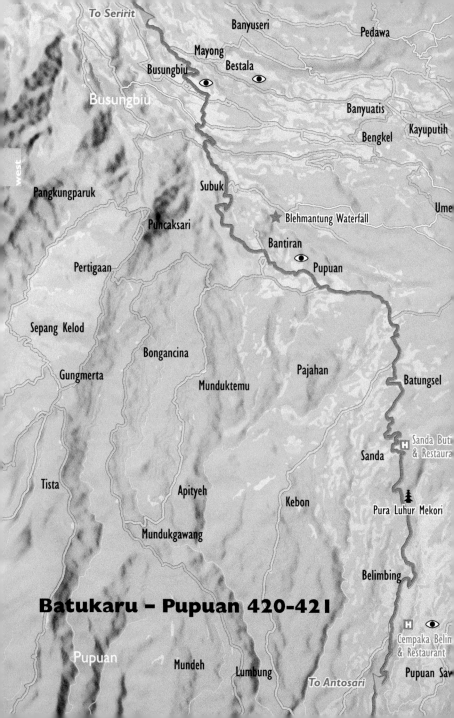

To Seririt

Banyuseri

Pedawa

Mayong

Busungbiu

Bestala

Busungbiu

Banyuatis

Bengkel

Kayuputih

west

Subuk

Ume

Pangkungparuk

Blehmantung Waterfall

Puncaksari

Bantiran

Pupuan

Pertigaan

Sepang Kelod

Bongancina

Pajahan

Gungmerta

Munduktemu

Batungsel

Sanda Buti
& Restaura

Sanda

Tista

Apityeh

Kebon

Pura Luhur Mekori

Mundukgawang

Belimbing

Batukaru – Pupuan 420-421

Cempaka Belin
& Restaurant

Pupuan

Mundeh

Lumbung

Pupuan Sav

To Antosari

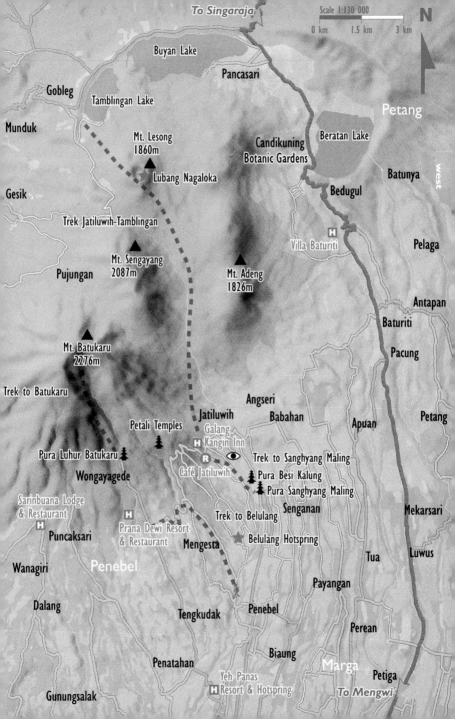

Blimbingsari

Melaya

Palasari Reservoir

Palasari Church

Palasari

Taman Wana Villas

Ekasari

Batu Agung

Jembran

Manistutu

To Gilimanuk/WNBP

west

Dauhwaru

Pendem

Taman Carik

Kaliakah

Balerbaleagung

Banyubiru

Balukrening

Ha Pel

Bali Warna Lokal

Puas

Bidadari

NEGARA

Sangkaragung

Cupel

Loloan Barat

Nathalia

Loloan Timur

Samblong

Jegog Museum & Show

Taman Asri

Budeng

Mustika

Segara Agu

Pura Gede Perancak

Yeh Kuning

Perancak Harbour
& Fish Market

Turtle Conservation

Delodbrawah Beac

N

Jembrana 422-423

Scale 1:170 000

0 km   2 km   4 km

Penyaringan

west

Pangkungparuk

Mendoyo

Pekutatan

Yahembang

Bunut Bolong

🌲 Pura Rambut Siwi

Pulukan

Manggissari   Waterfalls

Yehsumbul   Medewi

Juwukmanis

🌲 Goa Mayan Sati

Pondok Bambu ◉

🌲 Pura Tirta

🌲 Pura Penataran

Pangyangan

⭐ Medewi Beach
(Surfing)

Ⓗ
Puri Dajuma

Indian Ocean

To Tabanan

West Bali National Park 424

Bali Strait

Menjangan Island

West

Waka Shorea H

Mt. Prapat Agung
322m ▲

Mimpi Menjangan H

WBNP Office M
Pejarakan
Labuhanlalang M R Warung Ibu Dewa
Banyuwedang
Teluk
Terima
Labuhanlalang
Pura Jayaprana
Sumberkima
Sumberkelampok
To Pemuteran
Men Tempeh R
Gilimanuk M
Sari Museum
Lestari H R
Tegalbunder
M WBNP Headquarter
Cekik

Ekasari

Mt. Jatukangsa ▲

Mt. Sangian ▲

Klatakan

Warnasari

Tukadaya

Ambyarsari Blimbingsari
Palarejo
Sumbersari
Palasari Reservoir
Manistutu
Berangbang

N

Melaya

Nusasari

Candikesumah

Scale 1:160 000

0 km   2 km   4 km

To Negara

Bedugul – Lake Beratan 425

Books

Bali has inspired countless writings, from thorough academic studies to racy novels and gaudy coffee table books. This is only a small selection to get you started. Nearly all the books (new, used or out-of-print) listed here can be ordered from Internet book dealers, easily identified by using search engines such as **www.fetchbook.info** or **www.bookfinder4u.com**. Locally published books may be found in good local bookshops such as Ganesha (**www.ganeshabooksbali.com**) or Ary's in Ubud. All the Periplus editions are easily found at the many Periplus corners in Kuta, Seminyak, Ubud and at the airport. For mail ordering of books on Balinese culture, check out **www.murnis.com**. A few titles may be available only from Select Books, the Southeast Asian book specialist based in Singapore, **www.selectbooks.com.sg**. For additional nature field guides, check the thematic lists of Natural History Bookstore (UK), **www.nhbs.com**. Antiquariaat Gemilang, The Netherlands **www.antiquariaten.com/gemilang** has an annotated catalogue of 275 rare and out-of print books on Bali, and other thematic catalogues mostly on South-East Asia.

Ecotourism

Ecotourism: Principles, Practices and Policies for Sustainability – M. E. Wood. United Nations Publications, 2002.

Handbook: Tri Hirta Karana Tourism Awards and Accreditations – B. Ashrana & Jackie Ingham. Bali Travel News, 2002.

Ekowisata Rakyat. Lika-liku Ekowisata di Tenganan, Pelaga, Sibetan dan Nusa Ceningan, Bali – Ida Bagus Yoga Atmaja. Wisnu Press, Bali, 2002.

Nature-Ecology

The Ecology of Java and Bali (The Ecology of Indonesia Series, vol. 2) – Tony Whitten, Roehayat Emon Soeriaatmadja & Suraya A. Afiff. Periplus Editions, 2000.

The National Parks and Other Wild Places of Indonesia – Janet Cochrane & Gerald Cubitt. New Holland Publishers, 2000.

Bali, Balancing Environment, Economy and Culture – Edited by Sugeng Martopo & Bruce Mitchell. Univ. Of Waterloo, 1995.

Flora

Flowers of Bali – Fred & Margaret Eiseman. Periplus Editions, 1988.

Fruits of Bali – Fred & Margaret Eiseman. Periplus Editions, 1994.

Birds

A Field Guide to the Birds of Java and Bali – John Ramsay MacKinnon & Karen Phillipps. Oxford Univ. Press, 1993.

Birding Indonesia – Edited by Paul Jepson & Rosie Ounsted. Periplus Editions / BirdLife Indonesia, 1997.

Birds of Bali – Victor Mason & Frank Jarvis. Periplus Editions, 1998 (4th print.).

Marine Life

Handy Pocket Guide to Coral reef Fishes of Indonesia – Periplus Editions, 2004.

Marine Fishes of South-East Asia. A Field Guide for Anglers and Divers – Gerry Allen. Periplus Editions, 2000.

South-East Asia: Tropical Fish Guide – Gerry Allen & Roger Steve. Periplus Editions, 1994.

History

Historical Atlas of Indonesia – Robert Cribb. Univ. of Hawaii Press, 2000.

A Short History of Bali – Indonesia's Hindu realm. Robert Pringle. Allen & Unwin, NSW, Australia, 2004.

Negara, The Theatre State in Nineteenth-Century Bali – Clifford Geertz. Princeton Univ. Press, 1980 (1990 ed.).

The Dark Side of Paradise, Political Violence in Bali – Geoffrey Robinson. Cornell Univ. Press, 1995.

Bali Chronicles: A Lively Account of the Island – Willard A. Hanna. Periplus Editions, 2004.

Bali 1912 – Photographs and Text by Gregor Krause. January Books, 1920 (1988 ed.).

Bali: A Paradise Created – Adrian Vickers. Periplus Editions, 1996.

Bibliography

Bibliography of Bali: Publications from 1920 to 1990 – David J. Stuart-Fox. Koninklijk Instituut Voor de Tropen, Bibliographical Series 19, Leiden, 1992.

Indonesian Heritage Series

Indonesian Heritage (10 vols: Ancient History, Human Environment, Early Modern History, Plants, Wildlife, Architecture, Visual Arts, Performing Arts, Religion and Ritual, Language and Literature) – Edited by Tony Whitten & Jane Whitton. Archipelago Press, 1996–2003.

Contemporary issues

Bali: Cultural Tourism and Touristic Culture – Michel Picard. Archipelago Press, 1996.
Staying local in the global village: Bali in the twentieth century – Edited by R. Rubinstein & L.H. Connor. Univ. of Hawaii Press, 1999.
Bali, Living in Two Worlds. A Critical Self-Portrait – Edited by Urs Ramseyer & I Gusti Raka Panji Tisna. Museum der Kulturen and Verlag Schwabe & Co, Basel, 2001.
In The Arms of The Angels. Memoirs of a Medical Volunteer, Bali October 2002 – Kim A. Patra. Saritaksu Design Communication, 2003.
Who Did This To Our Bali? – Dewi Anggraeni. Indra Publishing, 2003.

Culture & Society

People in Paradise. The Balinese – Hugh Mabbett. Pepper Publications, 2001.
The Balinese – J. Stephen Lansing. Harcourt Brace College Publishers, 1995.

The Peoples of Bali – Angela Hobart, Urs Ramseyer & Albert Leemann. Blackwell Publishers, 1996.
Island of Bali – Miguel Covarrubias. Periplus Editions, 1937 (1999 ed.).
The Balinese People: A Reinvestigation of Character – Luh Ketut Suryani & Gordon D. Jensen. Oxford Univ. Press, 1992.
Bali: Sekala and Niskala (vol. 2 Essays on Society, Tradition, and Craft) – Fred B. Eiseman. Periplus Editions, 1995.
Priests and Programmers: Technologies of Power in the Engineered Landscape of Bali – J. Stephen Lansing. Princeton Univ. Press, 1991.

Religion

Bali: Sekala and Niskala (vol. 1 Essays on Religion, Ritual and Art) – Fred B. Eiseman. Periplus Editions, 1996.
Trance and Possession in Bali – Luh Ketut Suryani & Gordon D. Jensen. Oxford Univ. Press, 1993.
Turtle Island: Balinese Ritual and the Green Turtle – Charles Lindsay (photographer) & Lyall Watson. Takarajima Books Inc. N.Y., 1995.
Religion and Ecology in India and South East Asia – David L. Gosling. Routledge, 2001.

Rituals & Ceremonies

Offerings, The Ritual Art of Bali – Francine Brinkgreve (photographed by David Stuart-Fox). Image Network Indonesia, Sanur, Bali, 1992.

Guidebook for Balinese Prayer – Terry Satterthwaite & Ketut Rusni. Wholistic Creations, Bali, 1996.

Arts

The Art and Culture of Bali – Urs Ramseyer. Museum der Kulturen and Schwabe & Co, AG Verlag, Basel, 2002.

Dance

Balinese Dance, Drama and Music – I Wayan Dibia, Rucina Ballinger & Barbara Anello. Periplus Editions, 2004.
Dance and Drama in Bali – Walter Spies & Beryl de Zoete. Periplus Editions, 1938 (repr. 2002).
Dancing Out of Bali – John Coast. Periplus Editions, 1954 (ed. 2004).

Music

Balinese Music – Michael Tenzer. Periplus Editions, 1991.
Gamelan Gong Kebyar: The Art of 20th-Century Balinese Music (book & CD) – Michael Tenzer. Publisher Press, 2000.

Painting

Balinese Paintings – A.A.M. Djelantik. Oxford Univ. Press, 1986.
The Development of Painting in Bali: Selections from the Neka Art Museum – Suteja Neka & Garrett Kam. Yayasan Dharma Seni Museum Neka, 2000 (3rd revised ed.).

*Images of Power: Balinese
Paintings made for Gregory
Bateson and Margaret Mead*
– Hildred Geertz. Univ. of
Hawaii Press, 1995.
*Reflection of Faith: The Art of
Painting in Batuan, 1834–
1994* – Klaus D. Höhn.
Pictures Publications Art
Books, The Netherlands,
1997.
*W.O.J. Nieuwenkamp: First
European Artist in Bali* –
Bruce W. Carpenter.
Periplus Editions, 1998.

Architecture

*Introduction to Balinese
Architecture* – Julian
Davison. Periplus Editions,
2003.
*Monumental Bali, Introduction
to Balinese Archaeology and
Guide to the Monuments* –
A.J. Bernet Kempers.
Periplus Editions, 1991.
*Architecture of Bali: A Source
Book of Traditional and
Modern Forms* – Made
Wijaya. Archipelago Press
& Wijaya Words, 2002.

Gardens

*Tropical Garden Design. Made
Wijaya (Michael White)* –
Archipelago Press & Wijaya
Words, 2003.
Balinese Gardens – By William
Warren, photographs by
Luca Invernizzi Tettoni.
Periplus Editions, 1995.

Other Arts

*Balinese Masks: Spirits of an
Ancient Drama* – Judy
Slattum, photographs by
Paul Schraub. Periplus
Editions, 2003.
*Perceptions of Paradise: Images
of Bali in the Arts* – Garrett
Kam. Yayasan Dharma Seni
Museum Neka, 1993.

Balinese Textiles – Brigitta
Hauser–Schäublin, M. L.
Nabholz–Kartaschoff & Urs
Ramseyer. Periplus Editions,
1997 (2nd printing).
Ramayana in the Arts of Asia
– Garrett Kam. Select
Books, Singapore, 2000.
*Illuminations: The Writing
Traditions of Indonesia* – Ann
Kumar & John H. McGlynn.
The Lontar Foundation,
Jakarta / Weatherhill Inc.,
New York, 1996.

Food
Cookery and Food

*Bali Unveiled: The Secrets of
Balinese Cuisine* – Heinz von
Holzen. Times editions,
2004.

Coffee

A Cup of Java – Gabriella
Teggia & Mark Hanusz.
Equinox Publishing, Jakarta-
Singapore, 2003.

Kretek

*Kretek: The Culture and
Heritage of Indonesia's Clove
Cigarettes* – Mark Hanusz.
Equinox Publishing, Jakarta-
Singapore, 2002.

Literature
Children's Stories

*A Club of Small Men: A
Children's Tale from Bali* –
Colin McPhee (illustrated
by Trina Bohan Tyrie).
Periplus Editions, 1948
(reprint 2002).
*The Naughty Toad and Other
Tales from Bali* – Selected
and retold by Victor
Masson, illustrated Pengo-
sekan artists. Bali Art
Printing, Sanur / Hamlyn,
Sydney, 1975.

*Balinese Children's Favourite
Stories* – Victor Mason,
Gillian Beal & Trina Bohan-
Tyrie. Periplus Editions,
2001.
*Sadri returns to Bali: A Tale of
the Balinese Galungan
Festival* – Elizabeth
Waldmeier & Susan Tuttle.
Periplus Editions, 2002.
*Gecko's Complaint: Balinese
Folktale* – Ann Martin
Bowler & I Gusti Made
Sukanada. Periplus Editions,
2003.

Poetry

*The Morning After, Poems
about Bali by Bali's major
poets* – Edited by Venn
Cork. Darma Printing,
NSW, Australia, 2000.

Fiction

The Rape of Sukreni – Anak
Agung Pandji Tisna.
Published in Indonesian in
1936 (translated by George
Quinn). Lontar Foundation,
Jakarta, 1998.
A Tale from Bali – Vicki Baum.
Editions, 1937 (ed. 1999).
Twin Flower, a Story of Bali –
G.E.P. Collins. Oxford Univ.
Press, 1934 (1992 ed.).
*The King, the Witch and the
Priest, a Twelfth Century
Javanese Tale* – Pramoedya
Ananta Toer (transl. Willem
Samuels). Equinox Publishing,
Jakarta-Singapore, 2002.
*The Sweat of Pearls. Short
Stories about Women of Bali*
– Putu Oka Sukanta (transl.
Vern Cork). Indonesiatera,
Magelang, 2004.
*Bali Behind the Seen, Recent
Fiction from Bali* – Edited by
Vern Cork. Darma Printing,
NSW, Australia, 1996.

The Painted Alphabet. A Novel Based on a Balinese Tale – Diana Darling. Periplus Editions, 2002.

Autobiographies

A House in Bali – Colin McPhee. Periplus Editions, 1947 (reprint 2002).

The Birthmark: Memoirs of a Balinese Prince – A.A.M. Djelantik. Periplus Editions, 1997.

A Little Bit One O'clock, Living with a Balinese Family – William Ingram. Ersania Books, Ubud, Bali, 1998.

Fragrant Rice: A Taste of Passion, Marriage and Food – Janet de Neefe. Consortium Books, 2004.

Colors of Bali

Bali Sketchbook – Watercolors by Graham Byfield, text by Diana Darling. Archipelago Press, 2002.

Bali: The Ultimate Island – Leonard Lueras. St Martins, 1987 (1st ed.).

Bali: The Imaginary Museum, The Photographs of Walter Spies and Beryl de Zoete – Michael Hitchcock & Lucy Norris. Oxford Univ. Press, 1996.

At Home in Bali – Made Wijaya. Abbeville Press, 2000.

Ubud is a Mood – Leonard Lueras (designer) et al. Bali Purnati Center For The Arts, Batuan, Gianyar, Bali, 2004.

Travel Guides

Maps

Periplus Bali Street Atlas – Periplus Editions, 2003.

Guidebooks

Bali Handbook – Bill Dalton. Moon Travel Handbooks, 1997 (2nd ed.).

Bali: A Traveller's Companion – Edited by Debbie Guthrie Haer et al. Archipelago Press, 2000.

Bali and Lombok – DK Eyewitness Travel Guides – Edited by Timothy Auger. Dorling Kindersley Ltd., 2001.

Bali (Periplus Adventure Guides) – Edited by Eric Oey. Periplus Editions, 2001.

Footprint Bali: Handbook with Lombok and the Eastern Islands – Liz Capaldi, Joshua Eliot, Jane Bickerseth & Jasmine Saville. McGraw Hill, 2001.

Insight Guide Bali – Scott Rutherford (Managing Editor) & Brian Bell (Editorial Director). APA Publications GmbH & Co., 2002 (repr. 16th ed.).

The Rough Guide to Bali and Lombok – Lesley Reader & Lucy Ridout. Rough Guides, 2002 (4th ed.).

Bali and Beyond: Explorations in the Anthropology of Tourism (Asian Anthropologies, 2) – Shinji Yamashita (John Eades translator). Berghahn Books, 2003 (9th ed.).

Bali (includes chapter on Lombok) – Kate Daly & James Lyon. Lonely Planet Publications, 2003 (9th ed.).

Seasports

Surfing Indonesia: A Search for the World's Most Perfect Waves – Leonard and Lorca Lueras & Michael Stachels. Periplus Editions, 2002.

Diving Bali: The Underwater Jewel of Southeast Asia – David Pickell & Wally Siagian. Periplus Editions, 2000.

Diving & Snorkeling. Bali & Lombok – Tim Rock & Susanna Hinderks. Lonely Planet Publications, 2001.

An Underwater Guide to Indonesia – R. Charles Anderson. Times editions, 2000.

Language

Indonesian

Lonely Planet Indonesian Phrasebook (with two ways dictionary) – Patrick Wilton. Lonely Planet Publications, 2001.

Indonesian in a Flash, Volume I – Zane and Junaeni Goebels & Soe Tjen Marching. Tuttle Publishing, 2003.

Bahasa Indonesia. Book One: Introduction to Indonesian Language and Culture – Yohanni Johns & Robyn Stokes. Periplus Editions, 1995.

Tuttle's Concise Indonesian Dictionary: English– Indonesian, Indonesian– English – A.I.N.Sr. Kramer & Willie Koen. Periplus Editions, 2001.

Balinese

Practical Balinese: A Communication Guide – Gunter Spitzing. Periplus Editions, 2002.

Web Sites

General Sites, Portals, Accommodation

www.bali-travelnews.com 🍃
A lot of original, interesting information. Promotes the Tri Hita Karana, the Balinese system of social and environmental certification for tourism. Check the archives section for articles since 1998.
www.balivision.com 🍃
Check out the "Bali Resources" section for an amazing collection of articles by the best scholars on Balinese culture.
www.baliblog.com 🍃
Interactive, focuses mostly on Kuta and Ubud, with a rich forum full of practical information and travellers' stories.
www.budgetbali.com 🍃
Specifically for backpackers, with a selection of budget accommodation and outdoor activities from biking to rafting and trekking.
www.baliaga.com
Check out the English language version for a selection of sites to visit in the Tour section, and the agenda for a variety of performances from Bali Boys Bands to Traditional Dances.
www.bali-portal.com
An odd maze of links, from Street Dogs to Love in Bali, Kite Flying and Retirement Visas.
www.99bali.com
Simple, clear information (including a calendar of events), some of it outdated.
www.baliforyou.com
www.baliwww.com
www.balilife.com
www.baliclick.com
www.bali-paradise.com

www.gatewaytobali.com
www.bali-hotels-resorts.com
www.tourismindonesia.com
www.indo.com
www.bali-info.de
http://bali.2link.be
http://bali.startkabel.nl

Alternative Travel and Sustainable Tourism

www.fostertravel.com 🍃
Travel writer Lee Foster tells us about "the Spice Trade of the Spirit" – why you will bring home much more than pictures from Bali.
www.strangerinparadise. com Totally unclassifiable, witty and acid, the diary of architect and writer Made Wijaya (born Michael White in Australia) takes Bali seriously, but not the flock of expats and merchants who live off "Bali-the-Paradise".
www.edvos.demon.nl 🍃
Bit and pieces. Pay Wayan (Ed Vos) shares his knowledge and interests about Bali, and more.
http://werple.net.au 🍃
An online travel guide by Wayne Reid.
www.indonesiaphoto.com 🍃
A plain, informative site with images, articles and travel info about Indonesia.
http://wwwistp.murdoch. edu.au 🍃 Institute for Sustainability and Technology Policy, Murdoch University, Western Australia. In the list of ISTP e-publications, browse Sustainable Development Case Studies for a few biting stories about the impact of tourism in Bali. Links to related readings published by Inside Indonesia magazine.

www.baliautrement.com 🍃
(French) or
www.baliauthentisch.com
(German). Tailor-made tours to Bali, organized by French people living in Bali with trained english and french-speaking local guides.
www.balispirit.com 🍃
The ultimate New Age portal to Bali – from alternative eating to yoga classes, meditation retreats and eco-cultural tours.
www.greentours.co.uk 🍃
Take a Greentours natural history holiday and the CO_2 emissions from your flight will be offset by Climate Care. A percent of the profits go to conservation projects.

Nature and Ecology

http://users.bart.nl/~edcolijn
The Indonesian Nature Conservation Database of all protected areas of Indonesia, by Ed Colijn a dedicated amateur in the Netherlands. See also sister-site:
www.pili.or.id
www.fipaweb.com
Forum for Indonesia's Protected Areas.
www.vsi.esdm.go.id
Detailed information on Indonesia's volcanoes.
www.volcano.si.edu
An outstanding catalogue on global volcanism by Smithsonian scientists; check the world section and click "Find a Volcano by Region" to get facts about Indonesian fire mountains.
www.profauna.or.id
ProFauna Indonesia struggles for the protection of wild animals and their habitats.

www.wwf.or.id
Keep your eyes on the coral reefs and support WWF Indonesia in its efforts to support Indonesia's battled environment.

www.orchidindonesia.com
An introduction to the 4,000 species of orchid native to the Indonesian archipelago.

www.bsc-eoc.org/links/links. jsp?page=1_asi_id
Avibase, the world bird database gives a full list of the 345 Bali bird species, and many Bird links to Indonesia.

www.solutions-site. org/exhibits/coral
The Coral Reef Odyssey, a gallery of photographs by Jan C. Post. A wonderful glimpse into the symbiotic relationships in the reefs of many parts of the world.

Arts, Culture, Readings, News

www.geocities.com/bali_ art_story/bali_link.htm
The story of Balinese art development, initiated by Robert Handley, American artist living in Ubud. Everything from Bali arts, paintings, sculpture to galleries and more.

www.balibeyond.com
Everything about traditional gamelan music, history, instruments, with audio samples and original shadow plays.

www.travelforum.org/bali/ culture.html

http://homepages.shu.ac. uk/~scsgcg/spies/
The work of Walter Spies who lived in Ubud from 1927 to 1942, by Geff Green.

www.alphalink.com. au/~grum/oldbalipics
A small collection of images of Bali from 1597 to the 1980s.

www.insideindonesia.org
A quality magazine with many on-line articles and book reviews.

www.murnis.com
The culture section has a large selection of original introductory articles to many aspects of Balinese culture, with a mouth-watering introduction to Balinese food.

www.latitudesmagazine. com "Travel writing that doesn't insult your intelligence" is the motto of this great Bali-based magazine. Wit tackles travel, culture and society around Indonesia with a bit of a humour twist and great insights.

www.goarchi.com/archo/ mag/mag.html
by Archipelago, "the only website entirely made of recycled electrons", fun and serious, with great frog songs.

www.balidiscovery.com/ update
The Bali Update section is published since more than 5 years. Thousands of articles are waiting for your browsing.

www.thejakartapost.com
The main English daily newspaper in Indonesia.

Food and Entertainment

www.balieats.com
Eating out in Bali. An updated guide to Bali restaurants, with extensive reviews and a user-friendly search.

www.bali-cooking.com
Learn the basics of Balinese food with Warung Bambu restaurant in NorthBali.

www.beatmag.com
The bi-monthly Bali entertainment guide, an update of the island's night life.

Language

www.seasite.niu.edu/ Indonesian
A good selection of links for beginners.

http://iteslj.org/v/in
Indonesian basic vocabulary test, with English-Indonesian quizzes.

Surfing

www.surfrider.org
www.surfrider-europe.org
Dedicated to the protection and enjoyment of the world's oceans, waves and beaches for all people.

www.baliwaves.com
Almost daily reports on Bali waves

www.indosurf.com.au

Non-Profit and Charities Portals

www.balisos.com
A portal in several languages coordinating the action of several NGOs for the recovery of Bali after the 2002 terrorist attack.

www.balirecoverygroup.com
Also a coordination committee of Balinese NGOs.

Credits

Editor: Anne Gouyon

Research, writing and editing:
Jean-Marie Bompard,
Godeliva D. Sari,
Titiek Pratiwi.

With the contributions of:
Bodrek Arsana, Tree Bernstein,
Andrea Brae, Anne Casson,
Muriel Charras, Jonathan
Copeland, Jean Couteau,
Terry Cox, Bill Dalton, Diana
Darling, Ketut Deddy, Anda
Djoehana, Leslie Dwyer,
Rodney Foster, Lisa Steer-
Guerard, Jim Jarvie, Benjamin
Kahn, John MacDougall,
François Mans, Ita Mucharam,
Dwi Rachmat Muhtaman,
Ni Wayan Murni, Michel Picard,
Edward Pollard, Degung
Santikarma, Cok Sawitri.

Art Director: Liang
Finished Art and Layout:
Kristi D. Widjaja
Cover design:
Miranthi C. Dewi

Ilustrations and Photographs: Supardi
Asmorobangun, Jean-Marie
Bompard, Dominique Clarisse,
Godeliva D. Sari, Troy Davis,
A. A. B. Dianatha Kusuma,
Dedok, Elizabeth E. Listyowati,
Alexis Goux, Gilles Guérard,
Iskandar, Djuna Ivereigh, Jim
Jarvie, Marion Lammersen,
Erdi Lazuardi, Leonard Lueras,
Lukman, Dwi Rachmat
Muhtaman, Eric Penot, Will
and Demeiza Postlethwaite,
Irawan Prasetyo, Titiek
Pratiwi, Rama Surya, Tonozuka
Dive and Dives, Murdani
Usman, Ulung Wicaksono.

Maps by PT Enrique and
Occidental Design: many
thanks to Marc Le Moullec,
Juli Aryanto, Wijono, Arnaud
Corent, Nicolas Georget.

Administration:
Rinni Moersahid and Erlina
Yuniningsih

Sponsorship Sales:
Graham Allain

Web Design and Development by
PT Menaravisi. Many thanks
to Tono Rahardja as well as
Aditama, Setiyo Gunawan,
Vicky Simatupang.

Proofreading, finalisation, printing supervision by
Equinox Publishing. Many thanks
to Mark Hanusz, as well as
John Hanusz, Suli Widodowati
and Miranthi C. Dewi.

The following features are modified versions of articles previously published in *Latitudes* Magazine:
In the Hidden Life of Bali:
What's in a name (*Latitudes*
Vol. II, Dec. 2001), Animal
Sacrifices (Vol. 24, Jan. 2003),
From Illegal to Compulsory
Cockfights (Vol. 27, April
2003), Is Sex a secret in Bali?
(Vol. 5, June 2001), Vegetarian
in Bali (Vol. 26, March 2003),
Selling Lust and Love in Bali
(Vol. 7, Aug. 2001), The
Backstage of Bali Tourism (Vol.
8, September 2001), Primitive
in Bali (Vol. 10, Nov. 2001), A
Child's Life of Labour (Vol. 13,
February 2002), Introduction
of Where to Stay Candidasa
(Vol. 28, May 2003), Subak:

The Green Democracy (Vol. 17,
June 2002).

Partner Organisations:
The Natural Guide is a project
of the Bumi Kita Foundation,
Jakarta, an organization
dedicated to the promotion
of sustainable tourism.

Board of Directors:
Anne Gouyon, Nena
Soeprapto, Gede Wibawa.

The following organizations have worked closely with the research and editing team to support the writing of *The Natural Guide*:
Bina Swadaya Tours
(www.binaswadaya.org).
Thanks to Bambang Ismawan,
Jarot Sumarwoto, DE.
Susapto, C. Istu Pinilih, and B.
Siwi Christyanto.

The Indonesian Ecotourism
Network (www.indecon.or.id).
Thanks to Ary Suhandi and
Indriani Setiawati.

Yayasan Wisnu Bali
(www.baliwww.com/wisnuen-
viroworks). Thanks to Made
Suarnatha, Yoga, and friends of
the Village Ecotourism
Network in Tenganan,
Ceningan, Pelaga, and Sibetan.

Bali Fokus (www.balifokus.or.id).
Thanks to Yuyun Ismawati.

Bhakti Wahana Bali. Thanks to
Ni Made Widiasari.

The Department of Culture
and Tourism, Republic of
Indonesia. Thanks to Myra
Gunawan, Hamdan Rivai,
Vinsensius Jemadu and Tenni
Yuniarsih.

Acknowledgements

Special thanks to those who donated illustrations and photographs: Donald Bason of The Nature Conservancy, Chris Brown of Reefseen Aquatic, Daniel Carré, Dominique Clarisse of Azimuth Travel, Troy Davis of Bali Orchid Garden, Alexis Goux, Gilles Guérard, Jim Jarvie, Dwi Rachmat Muhtaman, Eric Penot, Will and Demeiza Postlethwaite, Cokorde Gede Putra Sukawati of Puri Ubud, Made Suarnata of Wisnu Foundation, Annabel Thomas of Aqua Marine, Heinz von Holzen of Bali-Photo, Ida Bagus Kadek Yoga Atmadja, Yoshida of Jasa Tours, Bali Bird Park, Bahtera Nusantara Foundation, Karang Lestari Foundation, Sobek Adventure Rafting, Waka Experience, World Wildlife Fund

Thanks for advice, information and support: Ketut Ardani, Dwi Ariyanti at Anta Tour, Irdez Azhar, Thierry Barjonet, Marie-Sophie Boivin, David Booth, Juan Casla, Emilie Chambert, Dominique Clarisse, Carole Collignon, Indraneel Datta, Géraud Devred, Gabriel de Taffin, Ian Dutton, Ellyani, Annie Evrard, Alain Floiras, Dominique Freslon, Philippe Freund, Alexis Goux, Florian Grill, Gilles Guérard, Paul Hartman, Ulrich Hauptmeier, Jeffrey Hayward, Savitri Hanartani, Carsten Huttsche, Yuyun Ismawati, I Made Iwan Dewantama, Karin Johnson, Franck Jésus, Kashi, Landriati, Erdi Lazuardi, Cécile Leroy-Iskandar, Gaelle Le Boulicaut, Patrice Levang, David Liebhold, Anne Lothoré, Leonard Lueras, Ronan McAongusa, Ida Bagus Gede Manu Drestha, Margie, Tia and Stéphane Markovic, Robin Marinos, Jean-Luc Mathion, Reki Mayangsari, Angela Mayda, John McGlynn, Mario Negri, Emmanuelle Neyroumande, I Made Nuja, Pinky and Teguh Ostenrik, Laksmi Pamuntjak, Lucas Patriat, Jenli Poli, Hidayat Prayogo, Bramantyo Prijosusilo, A.A.G. Raka Dalem, Retno, Monika Sri Roesmijati, Arnaud Rogé, Roro, Dominique Roubert, Maximilien Rouer, Cecep Saepullah, Donatella Salvi, A.A. Ngurah Santosa, Ketut Sarjana Putra, John Quayle, Monty Sorongan, Andrew Sriro, Scott Stanley, Andrew Stevens, Ignatius Sunaryo, Diah & Ketut Suwitra, I Ketut Suwitra Yasa, Emmanuel Tarika, Rodney Taylor, Sarah Tesei, Mahmud Thohari, Cathy Tollet, Anne-Sophie and Philippe Tricaud, Norman Van't Hoff, Marthen Welly, Gary Wohlman, Ketut Yasmin, Muriel Ydo, Yos, Yuningsih, Daniel Ziv.

Thanks for support during tough moments: Fernande Gouyon, Françoise et Florian Grill, Jean-Philippe Babut et William Turpin, Marie-Pierre Mézin et Gabriel Balthazard, Nena Soeprapto, Ita Mucharam, Dominique Guiet, Hartmuth Schuller, Paul Di Rosa, Hadrien Crampette.

Thanks to the people who welcomed us in:

South Bali
Kuta Seminyak: Stéphane Juncat at Tugu; Doudou and Saïd at Kafé Warisan; Sabine Kaufmann, Putu, Made Artha, Ketut and all the staff of Umalas Stables, Suzanna Halsey, Will and Demeiza Postlethwaite, Annabel Thomas at Aqua Marine, Susanne Schaettin and Teguh at Sunrise School, Bill Quinland and Nyoman Puspani at Waka Experience, Cok Sawitri, Novi Eko Putranto at Art Vision Bali, Luh Putu Anggreni at LBH Bali, Made Kushandari at Yayasan Gelombang Udara Segar, Piping at Magic Wave, Putu Santosa at Gemini Studio, AA Gede Gunaharta and Ni Made Trisnawati, Paul Boehmer and the team of Loloan.

Sanur: Enny Catur Yudha at PPLH, Timothy Woworuntu and all staff at Tandjung Sari, Iskandar Waworuntu at Café Batujimbar, Cipto Aji Gunawan at Air Dive Academy, Avandy Djunaidi and all staff at BIDP, Arief Mahmud, I Nyoman Sarwe, I Ketut Santi Budi of MIC, Troy Davis at Bali Orchids Garden, Wayan Patut of Serangan Youth Community, Dhani Tjana at Sobek, Made Kaek at Ayung Rafting, Gilda L. Sagrado & Andisuari Dewi at Bali Travel Work, Dick Bergsma, Marc Bergeron and Juwita Nilam Sari at Sea Trek, Dwi Dharmawijaya at Sail Sensation, Jonathan at Bali Hai Diving & Adventures, Susi Andrini.

Jimbaran-Bukit: I Nyoman Dedi of Udayana Eco Lodge, Jérôme at Mu, Heinz von Holzen, Made Suadnyana, Diah Octaviana and Boyke Petersy of Bumbu Bali and Rumah Bali, Wita Wahyudi of Profauna

Ubud: Nyoman Suradnya at Nirvana Gallery Pension, Paolo at ABC Solutions/Bali Buddha, Nyoman Sarma and Mrs. Suriati at Ubud Sari Health Resort, Pak Darta at Rumah Roda, A.A. Gede Ariawan at Ary's Warung, Linda Garland, Agung Rai at ARMA, Ni Wayan Murni at Murni's Warung, David Haughton at Bukit Jati, Jonathan Copeland at Villa Kunang-Kunang, Cokorde Gede Putra Sukawati and I Gusti Putu Lendra at Puri Ubud, Ni Wayan Suarniti, Lastri, Jero Parmini, Komang Sriningsih, Ni Made Sriasih at Seniwati Gallery, Ni Wayan Lilir and I Made Westi at Herb Walks, Dewa Nyoman Batuan at Pengosekan Community of Artists, Pranoto and Kerry Pendergrast at Pranoto's Gallery, Petra at IDEP, Agung Alit at Mitra Bali Foundation, Ni Made Trisnawati and Agung, Abeth

East Bali
Klungkung: Ida Bagus Wijana, Ida Bagus Wijaya and Ida Bagus Gde Ferry at Kamasan Art Center

Padangbai-Candidasa: Tania and Lempot at Lumbung Damuh, Amanda Pummel at The Alila, Karen at The Water Garden, Terry Cox, Ukie, Ilo, Patrick and Kadek at the Gandhian Ashram, Nyoman Sadra, Nyoman

Domplong and the members of the Village Ecotourism Network in Tenganan

Amlapura-Tirtagangga: Annie and Jacques Gouyot at Villa Gangga, Nyoman Budiarsa at Warung Genta Bali

Amed-Tulamben: Hartmuth Schuller, Nyoman Sudiana and the staff of Hotel Uyah, Marie at Le Jardin, Baba Karasubali at Good Karma, Georges Cowan, Made Jati and all the staff at Eka Purnama, David J. Booth & Tri Budiono at East Bali Poverty Project

Sidemen-Mount Agung: Ida Ayu Mas Andayani at Patal Kikian, I Nyoman Kari at Lihat Sawah, I Wayan Arka, I Wayan Tegteg, I Nengah Kari, I Ketut Kari, I Nyoman Nise, I Wayan Sukre and I Ketut Gde Sumarajaya at Puri Agung Inn

Bangli: I Nengah Rame of Pura Kehen, Wayan Warta Megantara and all staff at Dinas Pariwisata Bangli, Ketut Pendog, Ketut Namarupa, Nengah Mudiara and I Wayan Longop of Bukit Demulih, Madya Adyana, Madya Astina and people of Kuning village

Gunung Batur: I Gede Suastawan at Lakeview Hotel

Nusa Lembongan-Penida: Made Lembongan at Two Thousand Café and Bungalows

North Bali
Air Sanih-Tejakula: Thomas Brandt and Gary Wohlman at Gaia-Oasis, Ni Luh at Pondok Sembiran Bungalows, Arsonetri, Ruwi Windijiarto and Dodi at Bahtera Nusantara Foundation, Nengah

Artiawan, Nengah Arsana, Nengah Dauh, Ketut Kersi, Gede Subandiadnyane in Les village

Lovina: Bagus Sudibya, Ayu Ardini, Sri, Gede Ketut Anom and Putu Darma at Puri Bagus Lovina, Burgel Schefer and Made Ariawan at Saraswati Holiday House, Jette and Kletak at Rumah Cantik, Gina Menegola, Pak Boos and Ibu Sila at Sananda Centre of Light, Glenn Knape and Per Thoftesen at The Damai, Beate Theresa Dotterweich and Nyoman Tirtawan at Warung Bambu Pemaron, Andy and Immanuel at Spice Dive, Dewa Komang Tantra at IKIP Singaraja, Putu Tastra Wijaya at BAPPEDA, Wismaya of LP3B in Pemaron

Seririt-Munduk: Dewa Made Suarsana, Claude Chouinard and Yann at Zen Lifestyle, Nyoman Bagiarta and Nyoman Sutanya at Puri Lumbung Cottages, Made Murjasa, Made Karsini, Kadek Ayu Purwani & Gede Suarsada at Mayong Bali Panorama, Putu Panca Wardana, Drs. Ketut Wirata Sindhu and family in Banyuatis

Pemuteran: The management and staff of Pondok Sari Hotel, Yos, Suyono and Herman at Yos Bali Adventure, Agung Prana, Putu Yasa and Gede Brata of Taman Sari, Chris Brown and mbak Dewi at Reefseen Aquatic, Komang Artika, Ketut Santika dan Sri Wardani at Archipelago Dive, Wibowo and Anto at Hatten Vineyard in Gerogak, Putu Syase, Ketut Sekar and Nyoman Sukanata in Pemuteran village, Narayana Deva at Karang Lestari Foundation

West Bali
Tabanan: I Ketut Siandana of Waka Experience, Agung Prana, Gede Brata and Ngurah at Puri Taman Sari, Jochen Kauffmann of Matangi Tours

Mt. Batukaru-Jatiluwih: Dehan, Franzisca Rapp and Gede at Prana Dewi Resort, I Wayan Miora, Ferry Aprillio, Gede Asmara Yasa, I Wayan Miora at Galang Kangin Inn

Bedugul-Lake Beratan: H.Moh. Ali Bick in Candikuning II, Rajeg and family in Baturiti, Drs. I Wayan Sumantera and I Wayan Mudarsa at Kebun Raya Eka Karya Bali

Antosari-Pupuan: Dominique Guiet, Wayan and all the staff at Gajah Mina, Al Purwa of Cempaka Belimbing, Ted and Lillen Kruuse-Jensen at Sanda, Norman Van't Hoff at Sarinbuana Jungle Lodge, Nyoman Jiwa

Jembrana: I Ketut Surung and I Ketut Suwentra in Suar Agung, I Gusti Ketut Wiradi of Pura Rambut Siwi, Anak Agung Ngurah Santosa, I Gusti Ayu Kadek Rai and Komang Gunawan in Negara

West Bali National Park: I Made Iwan Dewantama and Ida Bagus Gede Manu Drestha of WWF, Agus Krisna and Komang Sarira of WBNP, Ni Made Indrawati of KUB Sumber Klampok, Misnawiyanto of FKMBB

Sponsors

This first edition of *The Natural Guide to Bali* was co-funded by the

– an initiative by the European Commission to promote economic co-operation between Indonesia and the European Union. The programme supports small and innovative projects of high visibility in areas of mutual interest to Indonesia and the EU.

The Natural Guide to Bali was also co-funded by the **Cultural Section of the French Embassy in Jakarta**.

Liberté • Égalité • Fraternité
RÉPUBLIQUE FRANÇAISE
Ambassade de France en Indonésie

Disclaimer: This document has been produced with the financial assistance of the European Commission and the French Government. However, the views expressed herein are those of The Natural Guide *and can therefore in no way be taken to reflect the official opinion of the European Commission or the French Government.*

The following organisations also provided financial support for the first edition of *The Natural Guide to Bali*:

International SOS

An AEA Company

WWF Indonesia

The Body Shop

MenaraVisi
www.menaravisi.net

Language

The Languages of Bali

The indigenous idiom is Balinese (Basa Bali), spoken at home by every Balinese, and the only language understood by old people in remote areas. Like its close relative, Javanese, Balinese uses a different set of vocabulary depending on the relative social level (mostly caste and age) of people addressing each other. There are hence three versions of Balinese language. Low Balinese (lumrah) is used among friends and family or when talking to people of equal or lower level. High or refined Balinese (alus) is used among people of high caste or to indicate respect. Intermediate Balinese (madia) is the polite way of addressing a stranger or someone equal or superior. Foreigners can get away with any form, but it is safer to stick to the high ones.

The official language of the island, however, is Indonesian (Bahasa Indonesia), which is increasingly used among Balinese who want to avoid caste intricacies. Much simpler than Balinese, it enables communication in the rest of the country. Foreigners planning to spend time in Indonesia should learn the basics of this simple language, which opens the door to people's hearts. A good phrasebook is a worthwhile investment. A few words of Balinese can be added — it usually attracts the sympathy of local people — but unless you plan to spend years in the island, it is more practical to stick to Indonesian.

Another "language" is spoken in the tourist areas of Bali — a medley of broken English with a few added words in French, Italian, German, and Japanese, that is ample enough to solve most problems of everyday life. Young people all around Indonesia also love to practice their tentative English with foreigners.

Pronunciation

The pronunciation of Indonesian and Balinese is rather simple. All letters are pronounced more or less like in English. Below are the main differences worth keeping in mind as you try to learn a few words, or ask your way around. To learn more subtleties, pick up a good phrasebook, language book, or dictionary (look in our book list, p.429, or in our web sites list, p. 431).

Tips for beginners:

C is always pronounced like **ch** in **ch**oose. For example, Candidasa is pronounced "**Ch**andidasa".

K at the end of a world is barely pronounced, and indicates a "glottal stop", i.e. an abrupt ending of the word with the emphasis on the last vowel. For example, tidak (no) is pronounced "tida'."

R is softly trilled, like in Spanish.

A Few Useful Expressions

English	Indonesian	Balinese (high / low)
yes	ya	inggih or nggih / ae
no	tidak	nenten or ten / sing
already, done	sudah	sampun / suba
not yet	belum	durung / dereng
never mind	tidak apa-apa	ten kenapi / sing kenken
thanks	terima kasih	matur suksma
please, go ahead	silahkan ; mari	ngiring
excuse me	maaf ; minta maaf	nunas ampura ; ngidih pelih
welcome	selamat datang	om swastiastu
good bye	selamat tinggal (to those staying) selamat jalan (to those leaving)	om swastiastu
how are you	apa khabar	punapi kabare / kenken kabare
please, help	tolong	tulung
eat	makan	ngajeng
I'd like to eat	saya mau makan	tiang jagi ngajeng / dot ngajeng
good, well, enjoyable	bagus, baik, enak	becik / melah, luung, jaen
to like	suka, senang	seneng / demen
sweet	manis	manis
hot (as in spicy hot)	pedas	lalah
hot (as in hot temperature)	panas	kebus
how much?	berapa?	kayun malih / nagih biyin kuda?
one, two, three, four	satu, dua, tiga, empat	siki / besik, dua, telu, papat
five, six, seven eight	lima, enam, tujuh, delapan,	lima, nenem, pitu, kutus
nine, ten	sembilan, sepuluh	siya, dasa
hundred, thousand	ratus, ribu	atus, siyu
expensive	mahal	mael
cheap	murah	mudah
sleep	tidur	sirep / pules
bedroom	kamar	meten / pesarean
house	rumah	genah / umah
where is...?	di mana...?	ring dije genah...? / tongosne...?
I want to go to...	saya mau (pergi) ke...	tiang jagi ke... / tiang lakar ke...
stop here	berhenti di sini	mereren diki / setop dini
wait a moment	tunggu sebentar	jantos jebos / antosang kejeb
slowly, carefully	pelan-pelan, hati-hati	alon-alon / adeng-adeng
I'd like to pay	saya mau bayar	tiang jagi nawur / lakar mayah
I am sick	saya sakit	tiang sungkan / tiang gelem

How to address people:

Sir	Bapak (*lit. father*)	Bapa
Madam	Ibu (*lit. mother*)	Meme
young guy	mas	beli
young woman	mbak	mbok
I	saya (*polite*) / aku (*familiar*)	tiang / dewek
You	anda (*polite*) / kamu (*familiar*)	ragane / awake

Glossary

The spelling of Balinese words and names is flexible. There are variations in the use of H (sometimes present, sometimes omitted as in Tirta/Tirtha), and E (sometimes present between two consonants, sometimes omitted as in keris/kris), as well as Y vs. I, V vs. W, O vs. U, P vs. F, etc. Some personal names, like Soekarno, may still be spelled with the orthograph used during the Dutch colonial times, using OE instead of U, DJ instead of J, and TJ instead of C. We usually tried to stick to the simplest spelling or the most widely used, but don't be surprised if you find different versions.

A

adat traditional law and custom

Agama Hindu Dharma Balinese Hinduism, also called **Agama Tirta**, the Religion of the Holy Waters

agung great, big

air jeruk orange juice or tangerine juice

air minum drinking water (bottled mineral water or boiled tap water)

air panas hot water or hot springs

alang-alang or **lalang** *Imperata cylindrica;* a rough, tall grass growing on road sides and dry hilltops

alas forest

Anak Agung honourable title given to members of the princely *ksatria* caste

ani-ani traditional hand-held blade used in harvesting rice

arak a strong, clear liquor obtained by distilling *tuak*, the fermented sap of coconuts or *lontar*

Arjuna the most famous of the five heroic Pandawa brothers in the Mahabharata

ayam chicken

B

babi pig or pork; **babi guling** roast pig

bahasa language

baju shirt, dress, clothes

bakar burn or grill

bakso meat or fish balls

bale open sided pavilion used for resting or working

Bali Aga literally "mountain Balinese", the descendants of the original inhabitants of Bali, who have retained customs pre-dating the Javanese Majapahit empire

balian traditional faith healer

banjar small village or hamlet, the basic social and political unit in Bali, usually grouping 100 to 500 people

banyan large, sacred ficus tree found in many villages and temple grounds

banten ritual offerings

baris warrior dance

barong mask and costume worn by men during rituals. representing a mythical, protective beast, usually lion like, who battles the evil witch queen Rangda; worn by men during rituals

Baruna God of the sea

batik traditional process of dying clothes using wax, most *batik* textiles come from Java

Bayu God of the wind

bebek duck

belimbing star fruit (*Averrhoa carambola*); a crispy, watery, thirst-quenching fruit with a characteristic star shaped section and a yellowish colour.

bemo public minibus, may be chartered for private use

bengong laze or day dream

bensin petrol, gasoline

beras uncooked, hulled rice

bingin banyan tree

buah fruit

bukit hill

Brahma God of Creation; head of the Hindu Trinity

Brahmana the highest, priestly Balinese caste; bearing the titles Ida Bagus (men) or Ida Ayu (women)

brem mildly fermented rice brew

Bugis or **Buginese** a seafaring, muslim folk from South Sulawesi, who have populated the northern and western coasts of Bali

bumbu spice

C

candi bentar roofless, split temple gate, allegedly representing the sacred Mt Meru after Siva split it in two, and placed in Bali as the twin peaks of Mt Agung and Batur.

Cokorda or **Cok** Prince

D

dalang the *wayang* director, poet and performer who either manipulates the *wayang kulit* puppets and speaks the words, or narrates a plot for live actors

danau lake

Danghyang Nirartha a legendary Hindu priest from Majapahit, who is said to have landed in Bali in the 16th century and reformed its religion

desa village, basic official administrative unit in Indonesia

Dewa/Dewi God/Goddess

dinas official duty, government service or agency

Dewi Sri Goddess of rice and prosperity

dokar pony cart

dukun Indonesian for *balian*

durian *Durio zibethinus;* a spiky, greenish fruit the size of a coconut, with a pungent smell and a strongly flavoured soft flesh, reputed to be mildly intoxicating and stimulant.

E

endek Balinese *ikat*

G

Ganesha the fat-bellied, elephant-headed son of Siva; god of learning and prosperity

Galungan the most important religious festival in Bali, held for ten days every 210 days and ending on the Kuningan holiday

gado-gado vegetable salad with spicy peanut sauce, originally from Java

gambuh oldest form of Balinese sacral dance, typically performed with large orchestra in inner temples

gamelan Balinese percussion-type orchestras with instruments made of bronze and wood, first developed on Java

gang small lane or alley

garam salt

Garuda mythical eagle, mount of Wisnu; also a symbol of modern Indonesia and its national airline

gede large, great; sometimes given as a first name to the first born in a family

Gelgel Bali's first great dynasty, based near Klungkung from the 15th to 17th century

gili small island

goa cave

goreng fried

gringsing double *ikat* weaving from Tenganan, considered sacred and protective

gunung mountain

Gusti title given to members of the *wesia* caste, the third and lowest of the Balinese nobility

H

halal food prepared according to Muslim precepts

I

Ida Ayu/Ida Bagus title given to the female/male members of the priestly *brahmana* caste, the highest in Bali

ikan fish

ikat traditional form of textile found in Bali and Eastern Indonesia, in which the weft threads are dyed to the final pattern before being woven

J

jalan (abb. **Jl.**) road or street

jalan-jalan wander

jeruk citrus, usually refers to the tangerine, sweet in flavour with a greenish skin **jeruk Bali** sort of large grapefruit **jeruk nipis** small green lime

jukung traditional outrigger, a fishermen's sailboat

K

kabupaten district, administrative level below the Province, with strong autonomy since 2000, and headed by a *Bupati*. There are eight in Bali (plus the capital district of Denpasar), corresponding to ancient kingdoms, or Dutch regencies

kain cloth, typically unsewn and worn around the hips

kaja upstream direction, considered as heavenly

kangin east

kantor office

kauh west

kecak a seated men's dance inspired from the fight of the monkey's army in the Ramayana, with a loud chorus of men repeating the sounds "chak-chak"; often performed as the "Monkey Dance" for tourists

kecamatan administrative division below the *kabupaten* and above the village, headed by a *Camat*

kelapa coconut

kelod downstream direction, considered as impure

keris a double-edged dagger, often with a wavy blade, invested with sacral and magic powers, and part of the traditional male attire

ketan glutinous rice, a Balinese delicacy

Ketut first name given to children born fourth or eighth outside the most aristocratic castes

kopi coffee

kretek clove cigarette

ksatria princely and warrior caste, the second in rank in the aristocracy

kulkul a hollow tree-trunk drum used to call villagers or sound warnings

Kuningan ritual during which the family's deified ancestors are invited to come down from Heaven; taking place at the end of the ten day festival of

Galungan, and celebrated with yellow (*kuning*), turmeric perfumed rice

kulit skin, leather

L

lamak woven coconut leaf mat used as ritual decoration

lawar ritual dish prepared by men; mixture of greens, shredded meat and spices

legong a classical dance traditionally performed by three girls

Linga a Hindu religious symbol in the form of a phallus, symbol of Shiva as recycler of life. The yoni is the female counterpart.

lontar *Borassus flabellifer*; a palm grown mostly in the semi-arid areas of east Bali; a manuscript written on dried *lontar* leaves

losmen small, inexpensive hotel, often family-run

luhur above; of the ancestors

lulur traditional body scrub

lumbung rice granary, which form vary according to the regions, consisting of either a double-slope roofed or arch-shaped, thatched roofed structure, perched on tiles over a wooden platform.

M

Made first name given to children born second or sixth outside the aristocratic castes

Mahabharata The Hindu epic depicting the legend of the descendants of the gods, mostly centred around the battles between the five Pandawa brothers and their cousins, the Korawas. A major source of inspiration for Balinese art

malam night

Majapahit the East Javanese empire which is said to have ruled over much of Indonesia, including Bali, in the 14th and 15th century

mandi bath (taken in the river or by splashing oneself with cold water from a tub)

manggis mangosteen; fruit the size of a small apple, with a thick, dark purple skin and white segments of juicy flesh with an exquisite, sweet-sour taste

Melasti purification ceremony in which the village gods are taken to the sea or to a source of Holy Water; usually held before Nyepi

meru a multi tiered shrine with an odd number of black thatched roofs (from one to eleven), which symbolizes Mt Mahameru, the centre of the world in Hindu mythology

mie noodles

MSG Monosodium Glutamate

N

nangka jackfruit, an enormous fruit with a spiky skin and a strongly flavoured yellow flesh; often cooked and eaten as a vegetable

nasi cooked rice

nasi campur rice mixed with various condiments

ngaben cremation

NGO Non-Governmental Organization, non profit

Ngurah common title of the *Wesia* caste

nusa Island

Nyepi the Balinese New Year, in the beginning of April — a day of silence, prayer, meditation, and fasting in order to delude evil spirits into thinking

that all mankind has deserted the island so that they will also leave.

Nyoman first name given to children born third or seventh outside the most aristocratic castes

odalan anniversary festival of a temple, held every 210 days or every lunar year

ogoh-ogoh huge paper monster puppets paraded on the eve of Nyepi and later burnt, symbolizing the evil from the previous year

ojek motorcycle taxi

otonan a ceremony held six Balinese months, or 210 days, after the birth of a child, and sometimes repeated later at similar intervals.

P

padi cultivated rice

padmasana in a temple, the lotus-shaped throne reserved for the deity

pandan or **pandanus** screw pine; a stilt-rooted shrub species growing in coastal areas, which leaves are used for building, wrapping or making utensils

pande the clan of smiths, vested with magical powers as they can handle such dangerous, holy elements as fire and iron

pande besi ironsmith

pande mas goldsmith.

panggang roasted

pantai beach, coast

pariwisata tourism

pasar market

paras soft, grey volcanic sandstone, used for carving

pecalang village militia

pedanda high priest, usually of the *Brahmana* caste

pemangku temple lay priest
penjor tall bamboo poles with offerings, arched over the streets during festivals
puputan a ritualized fight to death, a sacrifice charge during combat
pulau island
puncak summit
pura temple
puri palace
purnama full moon, an occasion for ceremonies
pria man, male

R
raja king
Ramayana Indian epic depicting the battles between Rama (a reincarnation of Wisnu and symbol of Good) and the wicked king Rawana who has stolen his wife. Together with the Mahabarata, a major source of inspiration for Balinese art.
rambutan *Nephelium lappaceum;* a cousin of the lychee, with a sweet flesh and a hairy (*rambut* means hair) red skin
raya main, great

S
salak *Salacca zalacca;* a spiky palm producing a fig-shaped fruit with a brown, snake-like skin and a crispy, astringent flesh very appreciated in Indonesia.
sambal chilli sauce
sarung sarong or sheath; piece of cloth wrapped around the hip and legs
satay or **sate** small kebabs
satria see *ksatria*
sawah Irrigated rice field
sawo sapodilla (*Achras zapota*); a fruit looking like a small dark potato, with a pear and caramel taste

segara sea, ocean
seka or **sekehe** traditional organisation around an occupation, e.g. a dancers' group, a fishermen's association, etc.
Shiva the most venerated and mightiest God of the Balinese Hindu trinity, the creator and destroyer
songket a thick silver or gold-threaded cloth traditionally reserved for high castes and ceremonies
soto soup
subak a village rice growers' association, coordinating irrigation, agriculture and related rituals for rice fields sharing a common source of water
sudra or **jaba** refers to the majority of Balinese people who don't belong to the three aristocratic castes or *triwangsa*
sungai river
swastika Hindu symbol representing a cross with its branches bent at right angles; a symbol of the sun, life and prosperity in many civilizations before the Nazis defiled it

T
taksu the divine inspiration which gives power and charisma, especially to a dancer
taman garden, park
tamu visitor, guest; often refers to foreign tourists
tanjung cape, point
tari, menari dance
tegalan rainfed fields
teluk bay
telur egg
tempe fermented soy cake
tenget magical, dangerous, mysterious; a supernaturally charged place or object

tilem new moon
Tirta Holy Water
topeng mask
toya water or spring
Trisakti the Hindu Trinity: Brahma, Siva, and Wisnu
Triwangsa the three castes of the aristocracy: *Brahmana, Ksatria, Wesia*
tuak light wine or beer made from the fermented sap of coconut or *lontar* palms
tukad river

U
uma rice field

V
vihara or **wihara** monastery

W
wanita woman
wantilan large open pavilion used for public meetings, shows and cockfights
waringin banyan tree
wartel Warung Telkom, literally telecommunications shop, a privately-owned telephone service
warung small neighbourhood, multi-purpose shop; also food stall
wates boundary, limit
Wayan first name given to children born first or fifth outside the aristocracy
wayang theater show
Wesia the third, and lowest ranking, merchant or military caste of the aristocracy
wisata tourism
Wisnu preserver of the world in the Hindu Trinity
WWF World Wildlife Fund

Y
yayasan foundation
yeh water or river

Index

Index entries are divided into several categories. If the page number is in *italics*, the entry is mentioned on one of the maps in the book. If the page number is in **bold**, then the entry refers to a chapter, section, feature, or other "main" topic. If the page number is in roman, it is simply a mention in the text.

also from
EQUINOX PUBLISHING

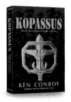